I0453895

THE GOSPEL OF
MATTHEW

Other works by Dr. Surrendra Gangadean & The Logos Foundation:

Philosophical Foundation: A Critical Analysis of Basic Beliefs

History of Philosophy: A Critical Analysis of Unresolved Disputes

Theological Foundation: A Critical Analysis of Christian Belief

Philosophical Foundation: Trivium Study Guide

The Logos Papers: To Make the Logos Known

The Westminster Confession: A Doxological Understanding

*The Westminster Shorter and Larger Catechisms:
A Doxological Understanding*

*On Natural and Revealed Theology:
Collected Essays of Surrendra Gangadean*

*The Logos Curriculum:
Grammar Catechisms: Philosophical, Theological, and
Historical Foundations*

The Contradictoriness of Sin: A Reading of Paradise Lost

Fundación Filosofica: Un Análisis Crítico de Creencias Básicas

DOXOLOGICAL REFORMED SERMON SERIES:

*The Biblical Worldview: Creation, Fall, Redemption—
Genesis 1–3: Scripture in Organic Seed Form*

The Unity of the Church: That They May Be One That the World May Believe

*The Epistle to the Hebrews: Christ Is Superior in Every Way—
Foundation to Persevere in Biblical Faith*

*The Person and Work of Christ: To Undo What Adam Did and To Do What
Adam Failed to Do—A Summary Exposition*

*The Epistle to the Romans: The Righteousness of God Revealed from
Faith to Faith—The Gospel According to St. Paul*

*The Book of Revelation: What Must Soon Take Place—
Doxological Postmillennialism*

The Natural Moral Law: The Foundation for Lasting Culture, Volumes 1–6

Biblical Foundation: In Narrative and Theological Form

The Seven Pillars of the Faith: The Theological Foundation of Scripture

PHILOSOPHICAL FOUNDATION DIALOGUE SERIES:

Introduction to Philosophy: The Basic Things Are Clear to Reason

DOXOLOGICAL REFORMED SERMON SERIES

THE GOSPEL OF
MATTHEW

The Person and Work of Christ

*The Fulfillment of Redemption
Through the One to Come*

SURRENDRA GANGADEAN

A DIVISION OF THE LOGOS FOUNDATION

Phoenix, Arizona

The Gospel of Matthew: The Person and Work of Christ—The Fulfillment of Redemption Through the One to Come

Copyright © 2004, 2025 Surrendra Gangadean

Logos Papers Press 2025
Phoenix, Arizona
logospaperspress.com
thelogosfoundation.org

All Scripture quotations, unless otherwise indicated, are taken from the Holy Bible, New International Version®, NIV®. Copyright ©1973, 1978, 1984, 2011 by Biblica, Inc.™ Used by permission of Zondervan. All rights reserved worldwide. www.zondervan.com The "NIV" and "New International Version" are trademarks registered in the United States Patent and Trademark Office by Biblica, Inc.™

Scripture quotations marked KJV are taken from the King James Version. Public Domain.

Printed in the United States of America

All rights reserved. No part of this publication may be reproduced, stored in a retrieval system, or transmitted in any form or by any means—electronic, mechanical, photocopy, recording, scanning, or otherwise—without prior written permission from the publisher, Logos Papers Press. It is illegal to copy this book, post it to a website, or distribute it by any other means without permission.

Cover design: Beth Ellen Nagle
Typesetting: Matthew P. Hicks & Brian J. Phelps

Library of Congress Cataloging-in-Publication Data pending

Gangadean, Surrendra, 1943–2022.
    The gospel of Matthew: the person and work of Christ—the fulfillment of redemption through the One to come
    Includes Index
    ISBN: 978-1-965685-00-6 (hbk.)
    ISBN: 978-1-965685-01-3 (pbk.)
    ISBN: 978-1-965685-02-0 (e-book)

1. Bible. N.T. The Gospel of Matthew 2. The Person and Work of Christ 3. Fulfillment of Redemption 4. The Fullness of the Word of God 5. Doxological Reformed I. Title

For those looking for
the city whose architect
and builder is God

CONTENTS

SERIES PREFACE

THE *DOXOLOGICAL REFORMED SERMON SERIES*[1] is a collection of
Pastor Surrendra Gangadean's sermons during his over two-decade tenure as the founder and senior pastor of Westminster Fellowship Church. During this period, he delivered over 1,000 sermons, preserved through audio recordings, handwritten outlines, and congregants' notes. These sermons now form the basis of dozens of books, offering a Doxological Reformed exposition of the Scripture, the moral law, and foundational theological doctrines.

The significance of this collection lies in its pioneering nature—in seeking to advance the kingdom of God—providing the groundwork for future hermeneutical works. Pastor Gangadean developed and applied Rational Presuppositionalism[2] to general revelation in his work *Philosophical Foundation*,[3] addressing enduring challenges of the modern and postmodern world. Similarly, he tackled central questions concerning the content and application of Scripture. Recognizing the impracticality of writing full commentaries, Pastor Gangadean utilized sermon delivery to engage with the meaning of Scripture, foundational doctrines, and moral law as they apply to all of life.

Consequently, The Logos Foundation Editorial Board has unanimously decided to present the sermon series in its original form. Minor grammatical changes aside, the content remains untouched, accurately reflecting Pastor Gangadean's ongoing thought process. We aim to prepare the way for future generations to connect directly with the mind that shaped these doctrines. This original preservation will also

---

1. Surrendra Gangadean, *The Westminster Shorter and Larger Catechisms: A Doxological Understanding* (Phoenix: Logos Papers Press, 2023), xv–xxxii.

2. Surrendra Gangadean, "Paper No. 101: Rational Presuppositionalism: Critically Examining Assumptions for Meaning," in *The Logos Papers: To Make the Logos Known* (Phoenix: Logos Papers Press, 2022), 521–526; "Paper No. 52: Common Ground (Part III)," 281–282; "Paper No. 2: Common Ground," 9–13; "Paper No. 95: Rational Presuppositional Apologetics," 503–506; "Paper No. 96: The Project of Rational Presuppositional Apologetics," in *The Logos Papers*, 507–508.

3. Surrendra Gangadean, *Philosophical Foundation: A Critical Analysis of Basic Beliefs*, Second Edition (Phoenix: Public Philosophy Press, 2022).

aid the Editorial Board in capturing the diverse contexts in which ideas were expounded. These sermons, coupled with foundational work in philosophy, theology, the humanities, and history, form the basis for forthcoming biblical commentaries. While each book is not exhaustive in itself, the series collectively reflects Pastor Gangadean's distilled wisdom throughout his body of work. As more books are published, a complete tapestry of his understanding will gradually unfold.

We regard the content of these sermons as invaluable contributions to the Next Reformation.[4] They illustrate how contextual thinking can illuminate the organic content of Scripture, reaching across every book and addressing even the most disputed passages that have troubled the Church throughout history. Through these sermons, the perspicuity of Scripture is meticulously brought into focus, shedding light on the clarity derived from general revelation, special revelation, and the cumulative insights of the Historic Christian Faith.[5] The convergence of the doxological focus, the doctrine of clarity and inexcusability, the knowledge of God as the good, and Rational Presuppositionalism collectively work to unveil the profound meaning of Scripture and encapsulate the essence of its truth.

Pastor Gangadean's preaching approach unfolds with a discernible progression. In the earlier sermons from 1993 to 2004, the emphasis rests on biblical exposition, laying a robust foundation by elucidating fundamental doctrines such as clarity and inexcusability, the divine image in man, the knowledge of God, church authority, and worship. Delivered with rapidity, these sermons were densely packed and aimed at a comprehensive exposition.

From 2005 to 2014, a pronounced shift occurred in Pastor Gangadean's sermons with a heightened focus on the need for sanctification within the context of discipleship. This period aimed to equip the congregation to grasp the interplay between foundational truths and personal application, fostering maturity. These sermons naturally evolved from the preceding foundational exposition of Scripture. After a decade of delving into the objective and subjective facets of biblical truths and

---

4. Gangadean, "Paper No. 62: The Next Reformation," in *The Logos Papers*, 335–337.

5. Surrendra Gangadean, *The Westminster Confession of Faith: A Doxological Understanding* (Phoenix: Logos Papers Press, 2023); *The Westminster Catechisms*, Surrendra Gangadean.

their integration, the imperative to address remaining sin within the congregation became increasingly apparent.

The subsequent phase of preaching, spanning 2015 to 2022, witnessed a shift towards existential hermeneutics, emphasizing the moral law, the unity of the Church, public witness, and adopting a more deliberate and rhetorical expository style. While his pace slowed, Pastor Gangadean's focus intensified on discerning how to apply truths to dismantle self-deception and self-justification among congregants and within the broader Church. The doctrine of repentance of root sin and an in-depth analysis of the doctrine of clarity and inexcusability assumed central significance.

The essence of these sermons constitutes the most profound exposition of the Word of God in its fullness to date. The expositor lived an exemplary life, building upon the cumulative insights from the three foundations, and endeavored to equip God's people with a clear understanding of Scripture amidst its myriad challenges, facilitating enduring responses.

Anticipating that this sermon series will serve as an essential source for crafting a biographical account of Pastor Gangadean's life and work, it becomes evident in these sermons how providence in his life, the challenges inherent in shepherding the flock, the practical application of doctrinal principles to the life of the Church, and a continuous response to the prevailing state of the Church and culture are interwoven. They stand as a testament to the life of a faithful servant who fought the good fight, finished the race, and kept the faith.[6]

These sermons, given initially to the congregants of Westminster Fellowship over the years, are deemed blessings that must be shared with the broader body of Christ. We consider it imperative to extend these blessings to our fellow brothers and sisters, and view it as our duty to contribute to the spiritual enrichment of the larger Christian community.

May the Lord bless the preaching and hearing of His Word, and may this compilation serve as the foundation for the contextual interpretation of Scripture for generations to come, and persist until the fulfillment

---

6. *2 Timothy 4:7–8.*

of the dominion[7] and mission[8] mandates in the earth being filled with the knowledge of the glory of the Lord as the waters cover the sea.

—THE LOGOS FOUNDATION
EDITORIAL BOARD
Phoenix, Arizona
November 2024

---

7. *Genesis 1:26–28.*
8. *Matthew 28:18–20.*

THE PERSON AND WORK OF CHRIST

A Brief Summary

T HE OLD TESTAMENT TELLS OF THE PERSON and work of the Messiah that is to come. The New Testament shows how Jesus of Nazareth fulfilled, and is fulfilling, what was written of the Messiah. The substance of the Old Testament continues in effect while the outward form is done away with (ceremonial law), or changed (civil law).

The main events of the life of Jesus are His birth (Incarnation); His baptism and temptation; His calling of His disciples; His ministry of teaching and healing; His conflict with the religious leaders (concerning the meaning of the Law and His authority); His arrest and trial; His crucifixion, death, and burial; His resurrection from the dead; and His ascension to exercise authority for the extension of His kingdom.

The reasons for the rejection of Jesus as the Messiah centered on the question of His identity as not only the son of David but as the Son of God, His interpretation of the Law in contrast to the traditions of the elders, and the nature of the kingdom He came to establish.

The main point of His teaching concerned the kingdom of God. The opening words of His ministry called for repentance because the kingdom was at hand. His parables were about the nature of the kingdom and its king. The Sermon on the Mount was about the character of the citizens of this kingdom. He taught the true meaning of the law of the kingdom. He taught entry to this kingdom was by spiritual birth. He revealed Himself to be the king of this kingdom. Lastly, He commissioned His disciples to bring all nations into this kingdom.

The prologue of John's gospel speaks of the Word of God as the One by whom all things were made. This Word that has been rejected as reason, general revelation, and Scripture becomes incarnate to restore man to the knowledge of God. Throughout the Gospels, Jesus progressively reveals Himself, through His miraculous signs and by His teaching, to be the Messiah, the Son of God, the Word incarnate, through whom alone man has eternal life, the knowledge of God.

INTRODUCTION

The Prologue to the Gospel:
The Word of God Makes God Fully Known

John 1:1–18

[1]In the beginning was the Word, and the Word was with God, and the Word was God. [2]He was with God in the beginning. [3]Through him all things were made; without him nothing was made that has been made. [4]In him was life, and that life was the light of men. [5]The light shines in the darkness, but the darkness has not understood it.

[6]There came a man who was sent from God; his name was John. [7]He came as a witness to testify concerning that light, so that through him all men might believe. [8]He himself was not the light; he came only as a witness to the light.

[9]The true light that gives light to every man was coming into the world. [10]He was in the world, and though the world was made through him, the world did not recognize him. [11]He came to that which was his own, but his own did not receive him. [12]Yet to all who received him, to those who believed in his name, he gave the right to become children of God— [13]children born not of natural descent, nor of human decision or a husband's will, but born of God.

[14]The Word became flesh and made his dwelling among us. We have seen his glory, the glory of the One and Only, who came from the Father, full of grace and truth.

[15]John testifies concerning him. He cries out, saying, "This was he of whom I said, 'He who comes after me has surpassed me because he was before me.'" [16]From the fullness of his grace we have all received one blessing after another. [17]For the law was given through Moses; grace and truth came through Jesus Christ. [18]No one has ever seen God, but God the One and Only, who is at the Father's side, has made him known.[1]

---

1. NIV 1984.

THE ACCOUNT OF CHRIST IN THE GOSPELS

EACH GOSPEL IS WRITTEN WITH A DIFFERENT audience in mind. The Gospel of Matthew is written to the Jews; it traces the ancestry of our Lord back to Abraham. The Gospel of Luke is written to the Greeks and the Gentiles; it traces the ancestry back to Adam, the father of all. The Gospel of Mark is written to the Romans, who value obedience and service. Christ is represented as the servant who straightaway does the will of the Father, and as a servant, no genealogy is given. In the Gospel of John, we are given the origin of our Lord, not in Abraham, not in Adam, but beyond that, beyond all time, to the very bosom of God. As such, John is written with a universal appeal, giving a fundamental explanation of everything as grounded in the Logos ("In the beginning was the Logos").

The main theme in the four Gospels is to provide proof that Jesus of Nazareth fulfilled, and is fulfilling, what was written of the Messiah. "But these are written that *you may believe* that Jesus is the Messiah, the Son of God, and that by believing you may have life in his name" (Jn. 20:31).[2] And again in Luke 1:3–4: "With this in mind, since I myself have carefully investigated everything from the beginning, I too decided to write an orderly account for you, most excellent Theophilus, so that *you may know* the certainty of the things you have been taught."[3]

Jesus is not simply man in His role as Messiah, but He is God: very God of very God,[4] the eternal Son of God who came down. In coming to Jesus, in coming to the Christ, we are not turning away from God, but rather, we are turning *to* God. At the beginning of the prologue to the Gospel of John, we are given teaching that brings us to see that this One that was sent and has come is *from* God and *is* God. We are told not only *who* He is, but *why* He came. Both of these points are being made for us in what we can refer to as *the prologue to the Gospel of John* in John 1:1–18; it is the explanation needed to prepare the reader to understand the content of the Gospels.[5] The prologue shows the *fullness of the Word of God*, ultimately revealed in the person and work of

---

2. Emphasis added.

3. Emphasis added.

4. *The Nicene Creed.*

5. *Isaiah 40:3.*

Jesus Christ. We will see that the word *logos* is at the very center of the redemptive work of Christ. We will go through John's prologue verse by verse, consider the meaning, and address arguments and disputes that have come up in the course of history so as to prepare the way to understand the breadth, length, depth, and height of the revelation given to us of Christ in the Gospels.

THE WORD OF GOD IS ETERNAL

In the Beginning Was the Word—Eternal with God and Is God (vv. 1–2)

As John begins his account, we should notice the presuppositional approach taken as he starts with the most basic concept of the gospel—the Word of God. "**In the beginning was the Word**" (v. 1a), that is, the Word of God; it is God's Word, and this Word was "**In the beginning.**" If we think about what is being communicated in the use of the term "**Word,**" it is the Greek term *logos*, which is translated as *word, speech, utterance*, and is often translated as *explanation* or *reason*. We can see how all of these are connected. Reason operates by forming concepts, judgments, and arguments, which are the forms of all thought. Thoughts are expressed in words; the first expression of thought is by the word. Both of these ideas—reason and the expression of one's being—are bound up in the notion of "**Word,**" the notion of idea, and the expression of the idea, which is "**the Word.**"

We cannot conceive of a time when God existed and His "**Word**" did not. The Word of God is co-eternal with God; they cannot be separated. Some have mistakenly tried to maintain that the Son of God comes after God and is not co-eternal with God.[6] This is to fail to understand the Father-Son relationship, in which the difference between the Father and the Son is not temporal but relational. The Son of God is eternally begotten of the Father, but the Father is not of the Son. Begotten is an eternal relationship; it is a timeless relationship; it is not a relationship in time, for one cannot be a father without there being a son. One is not a father before there is a son. It is a relational term and, for God the Father, it is a timeless term. The Son is introduced

---

6. Arianism in the early church and Jehovah's Witnesses currently.

here as the Word of God, and later, He will be introduced as **"the Son of God."**[7] As the Word of God, He is clearly co-eternal with the Father: God and only God is eternal, and the Word of God is eternal with God.

"The Word was with God" (v. 1). This is from the beginning, from eternity. We cannot penetrate 'before creation.' God's purpose was to reveal Himself *in* creation.[8] We can only know God insofar as the Word is brought forth.[9] When we try to speculate and go behind or beyond the Word of God coming through to us, revealing God to us in the creation, we come up with nothing, or idle speculation, or worse. For this One who is the Word of God **"was with God"** in the beginning, re-emphasizing the inherent relation between God and His Word. What is being said is that the Word of God is co-eternal with God—the Word of God **"was with God."**

"And the Word was God" (v. 1b). The Word is not only eternal in the beginning and with God, but **"the Word was God."** This introduces to us a puzzle, because we are inclined to think of this Word as a *principle* rather than a being or a *person*. We may be surprised to know that the Word is a person, but when we understand that being is a unity of diversity, that the highest being is a unity of the highest diversity, and that the highest reality in the universe is the reality of personhood, then we should expect that the highest diversity is between persons, and God, as the highest being, is a unity of persons. This unity of diversity is reflected in our being (*imago dei*)[10] and in the creation. The mystery of the Creator is being unfolded to us in this statement:

---

7. *John 1:18.*

8. Surrendra Gangadean, *The Biblical Worldview: Creation, Fall, Redemption—Genesis 1–3: Scripture in Organic Seed Form* (Phoenix: Logos Papers Press, 2024), 21–36; Gangadean, *The Westminster Confession,* 75–79; Gangadean, *Philosophical Foundation,* 144, 211–212; Surrendra Gangadean, *On Natural and Revealed Theology: Collected Essays of Surrendra Gangadean* (Phoenix: Logos Paper Press, 2023), 197.

9. Gangadean, "Paper No. 102: The Clarity of General Revelation," 527–529; "Paper No. 41: What Is Clear About God," 225–229; "Paper No. 112: Why General Revelation Is Basic in the Christian Worldview," in *The Logos Papers,* 583–585; Gangadean, *On Natural and Revealed Theology,* 213–222; Surrendra Gangadean, *The Epistle to the Hebrews: Christ Is Superior in Every Way—Foundation to Persevere in Biblical Faith* (Phoenix: Logos Papers Press, 2024), 255–271.

10. Surrendra Gangadean, *The Unity of the Church: That They May Be One That the World May Believe* (Phoenix: Logos Papers Press, 2024), 72–73, 134–136, 245–246, 275–276, 285–287.

"the Word was God." The Word of God is not an abstract principle, an activity, or an aspect of a being, but a *person*.

This is underscored in the reiteration, "**He was with God in the beginning.**" The personal pronoun "**He**" emphasizes that "**He was with God.**" It is not just the Word, but as a *person*, "**He**" was with God in the beginning—"**the Word was God.**" However else we might try to understand this, the utterance is being made clear to us that "**the Word was God,**" a *person*.[11]

The Creator: Through Him All Things Were Made (v. 3)

The second reason for saying that this One who comes to us, this Word of God, is God, is that He is the Creator of all things: "**Through him all things were made**" (v. 3a). Notice the negative reinforcement of that idea: "**Without him nothing was made that has been made**" (v. 3b). In Colossians 1:15–16, this same idea is conveyed: "The Son is the image of the invisible God, the firstborn over all creation. For in him all things were created: things in heaven and on earth, visible and invisible, whether thrones or powers or rulers or authorities; all things have been created through him and for him." He is the Creator (co-Creator), Revealer, and Heir of all things. The Son, being eternal, is not created but is present and active in the creation, manifesting the glory of the Father in all that is brought into being. Creation is revelation—all reveals the Logos.

As we read in Genesis 1, God created the world by His Word. "And God said, 'Let there be light,' and there was light" (Gen. 1:3). Again, we might mistakenly interpret *logos* as a principle or an activity or an aspect of a being, but the Scripture here says, "**the Word was God**" (v. 1b), and God created all things by His Word. We see the activity of the Holy Spirit brooding over the yet unformed waters, the vast waters that were created in the beginning. "Now the earth was formless and empty, darkness was over the surface of the deep, and *the Spirit of God was hovering over the waters*" (Gen. 1:2).[12] The Godhead, the Father,

---

11. In contrast to Gordon Clark's account of the Logos and the Word of God. Gordon H. Clark, *What Do Presbyterians Believe? The Westminster Confession Yesterday and Today* (Unicoi: The Trinity Foundation, 2001), 9–11; Gordon H. Clark, *The Johannine Logos* (Jefferson: The Trinity Foundation, 1989), 13–45.

12. Emphasis added.

the Son, and the Holy Spirit, were involved in the work of creation as they are in the work of redemption.[13]

"Through him all things were made; without him nothing was made that has been made." "For in him all things were created: things in heaven and on earth, visible and invisible, whether thrones or powers or rulers or authorities; all things have been created through him and for him" (Col. 1:16). God's dealing with His Son is "so that in everything he might have the supremacy" (Col. 1:18b). "And every tongue acknowledge that Jesus Christ is Lord, to the glory of God the Father" (Phil. 2:11). He was with God in the beginning as the Word of God, and He is God. He is unequivocally the Creator of all things without any qualification whatsoever: **"Through him all things were made."**

Summary: The Logos in Itself

The Logos is eternal; it is the Word *of* God; it is *with* God; it *is* God. The Word of God is personal—as the highest form of being (God is infinitely personal), the highest expression of His Word is a person; the Word of God (the Logos) is the Second Person of the Trinity. The Word of God is the Son of God, the brightness of His glory, the express image of His person.[14] The Logos, as the Word of God, expresses the inmost being of God—the mind of God. The Word of God in its fullness makes God fully known. God is known only by His Word and not directly, apart from His Word. The Logos is the Creator *by* whom all things were made, both visible and invisible, both matter and spirit. The Logos is the Creator of man in the image of God, in the unity of body and soul.

THE WORD OF GOD AS REASON

The Life of the Logos in Men as Light (v. 4)

Next, the connection to man is made specifically. The Logos is being sent to man, and we can understand why He is being sent. **"In him was life"**—in the Word, in the Logos, was life. That should not surprise

---

13. Gangadean, *The Westminster Confession,* 47–60; Gangadean, *The Westminster Catechisms,* 119–127.

14. *Hebrews 1:3.*

us, being God and the Creator. This is speaking about a principle in a person. **"In him was life."** And this element of the Word of God is revealed now in relation to mankind particularly. The life of the Logos comes into men as light: **"In him was life, and that life was the light of men"** (v. 4). The life of God, the Word of God, comes into all men as light. This is fairly straightforward, but we can read it and not think about it. We are drawing attention to what is being said here and its enormous implications. We must understand that life in us comes as light, but certainly not as physical light. The nature of light is *that by which we see.* Not just physically, as if it were the sun, moon, and stars, but by which we see spiritually—understand. The life of God comes into all men as that by which we understand.

At this point, drawing out the next implication is not a big step; it is just the next natural step. We ask, what is that by which we understand? It is the Logos. The life of God comes into us as reason, that by which we understand the world.[15] The animals lack reason, and they lack understanding. "Do not be like the horse or the mule, which have no understanding but must be controlled by bit and bridle or they will not come to you" (Ps. 32:9). The contrast with animals is that they do not understand. Humans understand: "For You have made him a little lower than the angels, and You have crowned him with glory and honor" (Ps. 8:5 NKJV). God puts all things under men by virtue of that elevated position because of the life that is in man.

The life of God comes into us as light. And in turn, this is the source of the life of men. We can understand that when that light is put out, we are in a condition of the darkness of spiritual death.[16] Some may want to raise the objection: Men are dead in sin, and Jesus restores us to life (by grace); therefore, Jesus is the light, not reason. But one

---

15. Gangadean, *Philosophical Foundation*, 10–15; Surrendra Gangadean, *History of Philosophy: A Critical Analysis of Unresolved Disputes* (Phoenix: Public Philosophy Press, 2022), 25–35; Gangadean, *On Natural and Revealed Theology*, 41–57; Gangadean, "Paper No. 5: Reason (The Handout)," 27–28; "Paper No. 44: Reason in Itself," 255–256; "Paper No. 48: Reason and the Word of God," 267–269; "Paper No. 57: Reason (Applied)," 315–316; "Paper No. 92: The Relevance of Reason," 485–491; "Paper No. 111: Common Christian Misconceptions About Reason," in *The Logos Papers*, 579–582.

16. Gangadean, *The Biblical Worldview*, 37–54, 197–217; Gangadean, *The Westminster Confession*, 103–110; Surrendra Gangadean, *The Contradictoriness of Sin: A Reading of Paradise Lost* (Phoenix: Logos Papers Press, 2024), 1–34; Gangadean, *The Epistle to the Hebrews*, 253–269.

cannot be dead unless they were once alive (in Adam), and one cannot be restored to life if they were never alive (before the need for redemption). If we are brought back to life in regeneration, we are brought back *from* death, understanding there was a time and condition under which we were born.[17] Non-living things do not die. When we speak of spiritual death, we are assuming a condition of life, in some sense of the term, before this death. We are brought from death back to life. There is one and only one kind of spiritual life, not two kinds: there is life and then death, and we are brought back to life.[18] Notice the life of God in us is light—understanding. When we think about this further, what the work of the Word of God is to do, we will see why this is a tight connection. The Word of God incarnate (Jesus) restores us to the life of the Word of God in us (as reason) when we were created (by that same Word of God) in the image of God.

The Life as Light Resisted but Not Overcome—Irresistible (v. 5)

This light that is in all men shines: it is there; it is present. The opposition between the light and the darkness is being introduced. It is not simply a contrast but an active *opposition*—the one is opposing the other. "**The light shines in the darkness, but the darkness has not understood it**" (v. 5), or "the darkness comprehended it not."[19] It is as if the darkness were trying to overcome the light and cannot do so. In this sense, the light is there irresistibly, inescapably, even when the darkness would do everything that it possibly can to overcome it. This is the very nature of light. And it is in man's very nature by creation—we are made in the image of God.[20] We are crowned with light and honor, and no matter what we do, we can *never* cease being the image of God. We can

---

17. *The Westminster Confession of Faith.* This is referring to the original condition of our first parents who were created spiritually alive (*WCF. 9.2*) without spiritual death (*WCF. 9.3*). "Man, in his state of innocency, had freedom, and power to will and to do that which was good and well pleasing to God; but yet, mutably, so that he might fall from it . . . Man, by his fall into a state of sin, has wholly lost all ability of will to any spiritual good accompanying salvation: so as, a natural man, being altogether averse from that good, and dead in sin, is not able, by his own strength, to convert himself, or to prepare himself thereunto."

18. Gangadean, *Philosophical Foundation*, 36–37; Gangadean, *The Westminster Confession*, 143–148; Gangadean, *The Westminster Catechisms*, 91.

19. KJV.

20. Gangadean, *The Westminster Confession*, 79–83; Gangadean, *The Westminster Catechisms*, 133–139.

never cease having the *capacity* to understand, the *desire* to understand, the *need* to understand, even when we try to avoid it. Even when we try to integrate back downward into the level of the animals, we can never eradicate the demand of being made in the image of God. It is that very attempt to do so that brings about the great destruction of man.[21] The life of the Logos *is* the light of men. It compels us to either go toward the light or further into darkness.

At this point, the opposition between the light and the darkness is not spoken of in a redemptive sense. As John continues, we will see that redemptive sense.[22] But this verse is referring to "[all] **men**" (v. 4b), and, certainly, because all men are not redeemed, it is to be taken as non-redemptive. Still, all men are given that light, and those who would try to avoid it shut their eyes to it and destroy themselves—they commit spiritual suicide.[23] This is the idea: God's Word, by whom He made all things, who reveals God in making all things, and who is *in* the creature—man—as light, is being opposed by the darkness. The attempt is made to suppress the truth of God and will go so far as to attempt to suppress the very light that is in us.[24] We will see the different senses in which the Logos makes Himself known.

Mankind attempts to suppress that very light, to *turn off* reason itself. The great death of the intellect in Zen Buddhism is the attempt to turn off reason,[25] but it cannot succeed. Nor can any other philosophical or religious claims succeed in attempting the cessation of thought as a means to enlightenment, moksha, samadhi, or nirvana. All attempts made to give up reason cannot succeed. The darkness cannot "**overcome it.**"[26] The darkness cannot resist it. We may think that the light is passive, and the darkness is pushing against it, and the light is doing nothing, but the light has a way of going out against the darkness. It is better to say that the darkness cannot *resist* it. Nothing in us can resist the way in which God has made us and the demands that are in us to

---

21. *The Contradictoriness of Sin*, Surrendra Gangadean.

22. *John 1:11–18*.

23. Gangadean, *The Biblical Worldview*, 37–54, 197–217; Gangadean, *The Westminster Confession*, 103–110; Gangadean, *The Epistle to the Hebrews*, 253–269.

24. Gangadean, "Paper No. 120: Contra Voluntarism," in *The Logos Papers*, 611–647.

25. Gangadean, *History of Philosophy*, 107–110.

26. NIV 2011.

know Him. This light is in all men; all men have this light, being made in the image of God. Again, John is speaking about this light in a more general sense, not the light of redemptive revelation.

Even in redemption, when we are brought from death to life, we are brought back to a condition we were originally in; that life is spoken of as light. The life of God in us comes to us as light. On this basis, we begin to feel and sense the darkness and the emptiness, the meaninglessness, and we see it *as* meaninglessness, not just something temporary that we might be able to get around. To paraphrase Albert Camus, the need for the absolute, being made as we are, and the absence of the absolute, the juxtaposition of those two, gives rise to the absurd, which is hell. The need for the absolute and its absence, because of resistance, give rise to the absurd.[27] **"The light shines in the darkness, but the darkness has not understood it"** (v. 5). That is why we said this is true of *all* men, not just men who are redeemed. Men who are unredeemed are in the condition of the absurdity of life, the meaninglessness of life, the emptiness of life. This is why we are saying this is not simply redemptive life; it is **"the light of** [all] **men"** (v. 4b), which is reason, that by which we understand. This is appropriately connected with the use of the term *logos*—**"In the beginning was the Word** [Logos].**"**

This is the first reason stated as to why the redemptive Word is to come in the flesh.[28] Man is in a condition of darkness and death because the light of God in man is being resisted. Even though it is resisted to a point, the light shines, and man continues to be aware of his need for meaning. By God's grace, man is not left in that condition. Jesus **"came from the Father, full of grace and truth"** (v. 14b), to redeem men from that condition.

John Testifies to That Light, the Word of God in All Men (vv. 6–7)

"There came a man who was sent from God; his name was John. He came as a witness to testify concerning that light" (vv. 6-7a). Notice the expression, **"that light."** What does that light refer to? It is referring

---

27. Albert Camus, *The Myth of Sisyphus and Other Essays* (New York: Vintage Books, 1983).
28. *John 1:14.*

to the statement in verse 5, "**The light shines in the darkness, but the darkness has not understood it.**" We are tempted to reduce John's testimony to Jesus as the Word, as the incarnate Son of God, but there is more being affirmed in John's prologue.

In the Book of Revelation, an expression is used at least four times about "the word of God and the testimony of Jesus Christ."[29] We consider that repetition not to be redundant. As we are noting, the Word of God is spoken of in several senses in the Gospel of John.[30] Here, John the Baptist is speaking about "**that light,**" so that all men may believe in Him. "**He himself was not the light; he came only as a witness to the light. The true light that gives light to every man was coming into the world**" (vv. 8–9). Whether the light "**was coming into the world,**" or whether it was given to the men who are coming into the world, *all* men are lighted by this light. Again, since all men are lighted by this light, we have to say this is a light *beyond* redemptive light. John testifies to "**that light**" and reaffirms again, "**The true light that gives light to every man.**" This light is given to all men as rational beings made in the image of God.

Summary: The Logos in Man

The life of the Logos is in all men, made in the image of God, as the light of reason; man's life is rational life, distinct from animal life. The light is that by which we see. The light in man is not a physical light but the spiritual light of reason by which we *understand* all the forms of the revelation of the Logos. We can distinguish between reason in itself, in its use, and in us.[31] It is self-evident that we think (we form concepts, judgments, and arguments); it is self-evident that there are laws of thought—identity, non-contradiction, and excluded middle, properly called "the laws of reason" or "reason in itself." Reason in man is *natural* (the same in all made in the image of God); *ontological*

---

29. *Revelation 1:2, 9, 6:9, 20:4.*

30. The Word of God (the Logos) (1) is eternal—the Son of God, (2) is in all men as reason, (3) is in creation as general revelation, (4) is in history as special revelation (Scripture), (5) is incarnate in Jesus Christ, (6) is in the Church, by the Holy Spirit, as the Historic Christian Faith, and (7) is in each believer by regeneration and sanctification. Gangadean, "Paper No. 30: The Word of God," in *The Logos Papers*, 179–180.

31. Gangadean, *Philosophical Foundation*, 10–15.

(applies to being as well as thought); *transcendental* (the laws make thought possible), and *fundamental* (to feeling and choice). Reason is the first and most immediate way the Word of God comes to man and is, therefore, the first/highest authority for man—it is the self-attesting Word of God in all men made in the image of God. Fallen man is still man—he neglects, avoids, resists, and denies reason regarding what is clear about God[32] but cannot overcome it or withstand it. The light *shines irresistibly* in the darkness of unbelief. The juxtaposition of the need for meaning and the absence of meaning gives rise to hell (spiritual death). John came as a witness to the Light, that through Him all in the darkness of sin and death might believe.

THE WORD OF GOD AS GENERAL REVELATION

He Was in the World by Creation and Providence Yet Not Recognized (v. 10)

Concerning this light that is given to all men, He also came into the world that we should see Him. **"He was in the world,"** the Logos was in the world, **"and though the world was made through him, the world did not recognize him"** (v. 10). He is in the world by creation (by virtue of the world being made by the Logos) and by the upholding of the world. Hebrews 1:2 says, "but in these last days he has spoken to us by his Son, whom he appointed heir of all things, and through whom also he made the universe." In this sense, the Word is the Creator, Upholder, Redeemer, and Heir. He, as the Son, is said to be "the radiance of God's glory and the exact representation of his being, sustaining all things by his powerful word" (Heb. 1:3). This Word is not only His incarnation; He was with God in the beginning, by which all things were made, and is revealing God's glory. And the Word is not simply to be equated with the world (just as the person is not the principle), but He is revealed *in* the world. Understanding the connection between the Word in creation and providence is necessary in order to understand how He is the very "radiance of God's glory."

---

32. *Romans 3:10–11; Psalm 14:2–3, 53:1–3;* Gangadean, *The Biblical Worldview,* 177–195, 46–52; Gangadean, "Paper No. 103: The Noetic Effect of Sin," 531–528; "Paper No. 146: The Biblical Worldview (Part VI)," in *The Logos Papers,* 741–745; Gangadean, *The Westminster Confession,* 99–110.

"He was in the world" by creation, and John Calvin certainly agrees. He says that verse 10 is not referring to the presence of Christ[33] after the Incarnation only, but *before* the Incarnation, in the world:

> This extends to every age of the world; for before Christ was manifested in the flesh, his power was everywhere displayed; and therefore those daily effects ought to correct the stupidity of men. What can be more unreasonable than to draw water from a running stream, and never to think of the fountain from which that stream flows? It follows that no proper excuse can be found for the ignorance of the world in not knowing Christ, before he was manifested in the flesh; for it arose from the indolence and wicked stupidity of those who had opportunities of seeing Him always present by his power. The whole may be summed up by saying, that never was Christ in such a manner absent from the world, but that men, aroused by his rays, ought to have raised their eyes towards him. Hence it follows, that the blame must be imputed to themselves.[34]

The Westminster Confession of Faith speaks about it this way: "Although the light of nature, and the works of creation and providence do so far manifest the goodness, wisdom, and power of God, as to leave men unexcusable . . ." (WCF. 1.1). What the Confession refers to as "the light of nature" is what is being referred to here:[35] "that life was the light of men" (v. 4b). Later on, the Confession says that "The light of nature showeth that there is a God" (WCF. 21.1), and the light of nature shows that God ought to be worshiped, and some general things regarding the forms of worship, but not the content of worship.[36] In the Confession, the light of nature is the use of reason by inference through good and necessary consequence. "The whole counsel of God concerning all things necessary for his own glory, man's salvation, faith and life, is either expressly set down in Scripture, or by good and necessary consequence may be deduced from Scripture" (WCF. 1.6).

---

33. It should be noted that in his own theological work, Pastor Gangadean took care to distinguish the preincarnate eternal Son of God (who is revealed in the creation) from the eternal Son of God made flesh in the person of Jesus Christ, in history.

34. John Calvin, *Commentary on John* (Grand Rapids: Christian Classics Ethereal Library), 19–20.

35. Gangadean, *The Westminster Confession*, 1–13.

36. Gangadean, *The Westminster Confession*, 233–244.

That expression, "by good and necessary consequence," is referring to deductions and inferences made by reason—the light of nature. The Confession affirms reason as a reality in us.

"He was in the world, and though the world was made through him, the world did not recognize him" (v. 10). The Logos in the world by creation is what is referred to as general revelation. **"He was in the world,"** but **"the world did not recognize Him."** The world should have recognized Him, even as we see in Proverbs 8 regarding wisdom. Even as the Logos was present in the world when God spoke to Job: He was in the world and should have been recognized but was not. The Word of God comes to man, not only as reason in **"[all] men,"** but as general revelation. The distinction between these two is not to be collapsed. Notice here, too, **"the world [men] did not recognize him."** First, men resisted it, **"The light shines in the darkness, but the darkness has not understood it,"** and could not succeed. Then, men did not recognize the Word that was in the world.

The search for the Logos as natural law is the basis guiding the scientific, industrial, and rational revolutions in the modern world. Law is one of the senses of the term *logos*, meaning *law, explanation, word,* and *reason*. The Logos is present *in* the world, and **"the world did not recognize him."** This is a second reason why the Word is to come to us in redemption. It is a sin on the part of man to fail to recognize the revelation that God made of Himself in the world by creating and sustaining all things by His Word.[37]

Summary: The Logos in the World

The Logos, by whom all things are made, is revealed in all things made. The revelation of the glory of God in creation and providence is full and clear.[38] The Logos is the object of study in all academic disciplines: in philosophy (epistemology, metaphysics, ethics, and aesthetics), in physics, biology, psychology, politics, history, and in literature. The Logos, though revealed in all that is studied by men, is not known by men. In man's fallen state, where sin rules or remains, no one seeks, and no one understands what is clear about God and man, and good and evil.

---

37. *Romans 1:20.*
38. *Isaiah 6:3; Romans 1:20.*

THE WORD OF GOD AS SPECIAL REVELATION

He Came to That Which Was His Own, the Covenant People— Yet He Was Not Received (v. 11)

"He came to that which was his own, but his own did not receive him" (v. 11). This is referring more explicitly now to "**his own,**" in contrast to the rest of mankind. Notice, by contrast, the prior revelation in the world, as made by Him, is available to *all* men, everywhere, and at all times. Mankind failed to recognize His clear general revelation in the world. Here, John speaks about how He came to His own people, "**but his own did not receive him.**" He was resisted (v. 5), He was not recognized (v. 10), and now He is not received (v. 11). By "**his own**"—we understand this to be the covenant people of God, and as is the case often enough, it was only a remnant that received Him. He came to His own, through history, again and again through the Prophets, and often, the Prophets were dismissed, disregarded, stoned, rejected, and then, ironically, their tombs were built to honor them. So, He came through the words of Scripture, the words of the Prophets, including Moses, in the context of redemption (assuming the prior rejections of the Word), and was not received. This is a third reason why He is to come redemptively.

Those Who Received Him by Believing in His Name Became the Children of God (vv. 12–13)

The Logos was resisted, not recognized, and not received. By way of contrast, John says, "**Yet to all who did receive him, to those who believed in his name, he gave the right to become children of God— children born not of natural descent, nor of human decision or a husband's will, but born of God**" (vv. 12-13). Those who receive the Word of God as it comes to men, and as it comes to men in Scripture, are the children of God.

Summary: The Logos in Redemptive History

The Logos came to the covenant people of God in redemptive history through the Prophets, through the Scriptures, which are now completed (the Word of God *written*). The covenant people, often sinking into apostasy, did not receive the Word of God. The Prophets were often rejected and sometimes killed. But a remnant remained faithful who, by virtue of spiritual rebirth given by God, became the covenant children of God.

THE WORD OF GOD INCARNATE IN JESUS CHRIST

The Word Became Flesh—the Messiah (v. 14)

This Word that has come to man, this Word that was with the Father from eternity in the bosom of the Father, by whom **"all things were made"** (v. 3), who reveals God in the creation and in providence, this Word that has been rejected, resisted, and not recognized, this Word comes once more to man: **"The Word became flesh and made his dwelling among us"** (v. 14a). He *tabernacled* among us, like God was in the midst of His people. He tabernacled in the flesh, in a human body. It is not the case that the infinite became finite, but the infinite took to Himself finite human nature. In Christ, two whole, perfect, and distinct natures, the Godhead and the manhood, were insepara-bly joined together in one person, without *conversion* (one nature does not change and become the other—God does not change into man or man into God), *composition* (Christ is not partly God and partly man), or *confusion* (each nature acts distinctly according to its own essence). Which person is very God, and very man, yet one Christ, the only mediator between God and man.[39]

This One who dwelt among us revealed to us the glory of God. The Word of God reveals God. John says, **"We have seen his glory, the glory of the One and Only, who came from the Father"** (v. 14). Whose father? The Father of the One and Only. The One and Only that comes from the Father is the Son of God. The King James version says, "the only begotten." He is the One who is first brought forth. The first begotten of all things, as thought is the first begotten of a being that is spirit, a rational being. In terms of the external manifestation, the word is the first expression of what is in a being. He is the first begotten, first brought forth, first manifested, *not* first created, as some have miscon-strued the connection between the Word and being brought forth. He

---

39. *WCF 8.2.*

is "the One and Only, who came from the Father," His Father. Here, we have the truth brought together: *the Word of God is the Son of God*, "the One and Only." There is no division in the Word; there are not many words. It is referred to as "the Word." The Word of God is singular, just as "the One and Only" is singular.

We can see how these two are related, the Son being the likeness of the Father, showing forth the Father. In God, the Word is a perfect manifestation of the Father, a perfect showing forth. This is why Jesus could say: "Anyone who has seen me has seen the Father. How can you say, 'Show us the Father'? Don't you believe that I am in the Father, and that the Father is in me?" (Jn. 14:9b–10a). The Word has come to do the will of the Father: "For I have come down from heaven not to do my will but to do the will of him who sent me" (Jn. 6:38). The love of the Father abides in the Son, and we are to abide in Him by doing the Father's will: "As the Father loved Me, I also have loved you; abide in My love. If you keep My commandments, you will abide in My love, just as I have kept My Father's commandments and abide in His love" (Jn. 15:9–10 NKJV).

The glory of this Word is seen in this, that He comes "**full of grace and truth**" (v. 14b). This is the grace that we desire and long for, both "**grace and truth.**" *Grace* to forgive our sins and *truth* by which God's intended purpose from the beginning is completed—His purpose to reveal Himself and to make Himself known. This One, who is the Word of God, whose purpose is to make God known, after being resisted, not recognized, and rejected, comes to forgive man and bring about the forgiveness of man and to bring man back to know God. No one else but the Word of God can undertake this. It is the Word who makes the Father known; it is the Word of God that makes God known.

John's Testimony (vv. 15–18)

John the Baptist testifies concerning Him: "**This is the one I spoke about when I said, 'He who comes after me has surpassed me because he was before me'**" (v. 15b), referring to the pre-existence of this One. "**He was before me.**" John is not only testifying to someone who is here but someone who is before him. John testifies to that light who is before him. John explains, "**From the fullness of his grace we have all received one blessing after another**" (v. 16). I wonder if it says "**one** blessing after another" because we could not contain them all at the same time. It has to be one after the other; these blessings have no end. If we name anything truly a blessing, we have it in Christ. We have to stop and think and name it in order to know and understand the blessings. This is where the joy of Christ's coming becomes evident: "But where sin abounded, grace abounded much more" (Rom. 5:20b NKJV). Even when we do not know how to recognize the blessings and count them, we can say, 'There will be another blessing.' Should we call it a 'supra-blessing?' A blessing that helps us to know our blessings—that would be a great blessing.[40] We can be assured that all blessings are ours in Christ—one blessing after another as we grow in grace and come into the fullness that is in God. All of this comes through Jesus Christ.

"For the law was given through Moses; grace and truth came through Jesus Christ" (v. 17).[41] Everything from the beginning, from the Garden, in God's eternal purpose, was to bring this about. He is the Word of God, the Son of God, who takes to Himself human nature. Jesus is the Christ, the Son of God. He comes to bring "grace and truth," to pardon our sins, to pour upon us every blessing that there is, "one blessing after another" until we are brought to the fullness of the knowledge of God. Throughout history, this will go on. The Holy Spirit whom He has sent will lead us into all truth[42] because He comes "full of grace and truth" (v. 14b). This is that blessing of all blessings. Verse 18 says, "No one has ever seen God." It is also said, "no one has seen or can see [God]" (1 Tim. 6:16b). When the Scriptures use the expression "we shall see face to face" (1 Cor. 13:12), it is not because God can be seen in some literal sense,[43] but God can be known as He is without shadow and type. Moses saw God in this way, without shadow and type.[44] God gave the shadows and types in the tabernacle, but Moses saw the very nature of God when God declared His name

---

40. The 'supra-blessing' referred to here is the Holy Spirit who will lead the Church into all truth. Gangadean, *The Westminster Confession*, xix–xxix, 349–351; Gangadean, "Paper No. 16: The Historic Christian Faith," in *The Logos Papers*, 103–114.

41. Emphasis added.

42. *John 16:13.*

43. Gangadean, *On Natural and Revealed Theology*, 9–39; Gangadean, "Paper No. 106: The Good and Heaven," 547–556; "Paper No. 116: The Knowledge of God vs. The Hope of Heaven," in *The Logos Papers*, 597–598; Gangadean, *Philosophical Foundation*, 40–41.

44. *Numbers 12:6–8.*

to him: "The LORD, the LORD, the compassionate and gracious God, slow to anger, abounding in love and faithfulness, maintaining love to thousands, and forgiving wickedness, rebellion and sin. Yet he does not leave the guilty unpunished" (Ex. 34:6–7a). The Lord is long-suffering, compassionate, merciful, yet just. Moses saw God *as He is* in His very nature. That is what it is to see God as He is. No one has ever seen God in terms of some outward manifestation. God is a spirit, and "**No one has ever seen God, but God the One and Only**" (v. 18a). There is that expression again; what a beautiful expression, "**the One and Only,**" the One and Only Word. "**The One and Only, who is at the Father's side**" (v. 18), who is with God in the beginning, the only begotten of the Father, that makes Him the Son. "**Who is at the Father's side, has made him known**" (v. 18b). Jesus says, "Now this is eternal life: that they know you, the only true God, and Jesus Christ, whom you have sent. I have brought you glory on earth by finishing the work you gave me to do." (Jn. 17:3–4). At the end of His prayer, He says: "I have made you known to them, and will continue to make you known in order that the love you have for me may be in them and that I myself may be in them" (Jn. 17:26). Jesus, the Word of God, wants us to know God, behold God, gaze steadfastly at the glory of God, be transformed into the same image from glory unto glory, and be conformed to His Son, Jesus Christ our Lord.

We have, in John's prologue, the explanation of this One who is coming, and why it is that He comes. He comes to bring us "**grace and truth,**" forgiveness and the fullness of life in the knowledge of God—blessing upon blessing, and we praise God for His unspeakable gift. Amen.

Summary: The Logos in Human Form

The Word was made flesh and dwelt among men in the person of Jesus Christ. Jesus was born of the Virgin Mary, suffered under Pontius Pilate, was crucified, dead, and buried. He rose again on the third day, ascended into heaven, and is seated at the right hand of God.[45] The Logos, resisted and rejected as reason, as general revelation, and as special (redemptive) revelation, comes once more to man and is crucified.

---

45. *The Apostles' Creed.*

He came to accomplish redemption and now rules to apply redemption. Jesus came as Messiah, full of grace and truth. It is by His life and death that this grace and truth come. He came to *undo* what Adam did (as the Lamb of God who takes away the sin of the world) and to *do* what Adam failed to do (to rule by His Spirit, exercising dominion through His people—the Church, to make God known). No man has ever seen God. God is made known only through His Word, His only begotten Son. The Son, through the fullness of grace, makes God fully known. John pointed men unequivocally to Jesus as the Messiah, who, coming after him, was before him, who was identified by the Spirit coming upon Him at His baptism, and who Himself baptizes all in Him, with the Spirit, to make God known.[46]

---

46. *Acts 1:4–8.*

The Gospel of

Matthew

2004 Sermon Series

———

1

REDEMPTIVE HISTORY AND THE BIRTH OF JESUS

The Seed of the Woman, Abraham, and David

Matthew 1:18–25

18This is how the birth of Jesus the Messiah came about: His mother Mary was pledged to be married to Joseph, but before they came together, she was found to be pregnant through the Holy Spirit. 19Because Joseph her husband was faithful to the law, and yet did not want to expose her to public disgrace, he had in mind to divorce her quietly.

20But after he had considered this, an angel of the Lord appeared to him in a dream and said, "Joseph son of David, do not be afraid to take Mary home as your wife, because what is conceived in her is from the Holy Spirit. 21She will give birth to a son, and you are to give him the name Jesus, because he will save his people from their sins."

22All this took place to fulfill what the Lord had said through the prophet: 23"The virgin will conceive and give birth to a son, and they will call him Immanuel" (which means "God with us").

24When Joseph woke up, he did what the angel of the Lord had commanded him and took Mary home as his wife. 25But he did not consummate their marriage until she gave birth to a son. And he gave him the name Jesus.

INTRODUCTION

W<small>E READ SOME OF THIS MATERIAL NOT TOO</small> long ago, so you might be wondering, 'Why so soon? Another Christmas message? Christmas has passed.' We have the definite feeling of being over the vacation; everything is behind us, and things are settling in for the year. Well, this is not a Christmas message, but it is about Christ. We want to begin the New Testament overview and plan to do the three Gospels—Matthew, Mark, and Luke—together, and devote particular attention to John by itself. This is not an unusual practice in the history of the Church to speak of these three Gospels. Each one, in a sense, deserves attention in itself; it has its own dynamic and significance. Lord willing, we hope we can address those in years to come.

The title of this message is "Redemptive History and the Birth of Jesus." We will spend a number of weeks going through the Synoptic Gospels by way of overview, and we might after that, go back to some of the Old Testament, continue in the Psalms,[1] and continue our process in that way.

GENEALOGIES AND REDEMPTIVE HISTORY

We want to draw attention to the genealogies of Jesus in Matthew as it traces back to Abraham and in Luke as it traces back to Adam. In the case of Mark, there is no genealogy. The genealogies become more precious over the years as we read the Scriptures and become saturated with what has happened in the past. Perhaps some of you are reading your Bible through again this year, as this is our pattern, our habit. We encourage everyone to read the Scriptures. You may have been reading through Genesis, reviewing some of the history, and thinking about it in a new way, in a deeper way, with more understanding.

The genealogies make us keenly aware of the time and how much time has passed. Mentioning these names brings to mind the events in their lives and all that has happened. This raises the whole question of history. Luke goes back to Adam. Matthew goes back to Abraham. We have all the time that has passed and want to review that history

---

1. Pastor Gangadean completed a sermon series on Psalms 1–100 with an average of five Psalms per-sermon. His preaching will be the basis of a sermon series book on the Psalms. The series began on September 1, 2002 and ended April 1, 2007.

in a way that helps us understand why it is put at the beginning of the Gospels. *History is redemptive*; it is set on a redemptive basis. It is set on the basis of the promise of redemption, that One will come who will bring redemption. We are aware of physical death, and we are aware, perhaps dimly and not in a very articulate way, of the reality of spiritual death.

As we look at biblical, redemptive history, we are aware of the ages that have come and gone, and we want to remember those ages. We do not want to let them go. We want to cultivate our historical consciousness. We want to not just read history and say, 'That is interesting here, and that is curious, and that has my interest,' but we want to read it with a sense of God ruling in history to accomplish His purpose. We want to get a sense of time, and of the time frame that is passing. We want to get a sense of what has happened in history so we have a sense of time in our own lives—we will pass from the scene, and we, as some put it, 'will be history.' We do not want our works to be in vain, and we do not want what we have done to be forgotten and neglected. This is an application to us.[2]

As we think about past history, we can think about our becoming part of that history, and the significance and the meaning of it, and we can live with an *ever-increasing historical consciousness*. Think about what it would be like if you forgot your own past. There is a sense in which your personal identity is lost if you do not remember things about your past. Think about the extreme case of Alzheimer's or amnesia. I remember eight years or so after my conversion, I started to discover Historic Christianity, and I described it this way a number of times: It was like an amnesia victim recovering their memory and remembering what has happened. I wanted to know highlights and be able to place persons and quickly keep that all in mind. We should study and make that our concern, certainly in Scripture and in other ways, too.

In Great Books,[3] we read *The Persian Wars*, and we were talking about Xerxes and asking which Xerxes was involved in coming to war with the Greeks. That is certainly part of what has happened in history.

---

2. Gangadean, *The Epistle to the Hebrews*, 51–65.

3 Pastor Gangadean along with a group of educators underwent a discussion group on the Great Books Series. The majority of these discussions have been preserved in audio format and they will be transcribed and made into books. These discussions express a philosophy of art consistent with the foundation as it applies to the humanities.

And we should not pass over the saints who have gone before. We should be going on to fellowship with them, and we can be encouraged in many ways in reading about them. As I read through Genesis these past several days, I read the life of Joseph, and I like to count the number of years that Joseph spent in Egypt and get a sense of how long he was there. I go back and look at the Scripture, and I want to get answers: He was 22 years away from his brothers before he made himself known to them—22 years! How do I process time and trials, and how has God worked in them? I want to get a sense of redemptive history. How long did it take for Judah to become humble to the point that he was willing to give himself in the place of Benjamin? It took 22 years for that process of sanctification to work. We get a sense of time and of God's working, which is an encouragement to us. As we come to our Lord Jesus Christ, all the more, history is marked by the promise of His coming—His coming and His accomplishing His work. History will come to an end when His work is completed. There will be no more marrying and giving in marriage[4] or buying and selling. The work of dominion will be completed. We need to get this sense of history, cultivate it, and live in this context more and more, not just in terms of the *interesting* but in terms of the *redemptive*: God's redemptive purpose in history. We need to place ourselves in that redemptive history, that we might be encouraged and have hope.

We need to place ourselves in redemptive history from its beginning, when death entered the world. This was not the way it was originally in creation. Death is a reminder to us in our hardened, self-deceptive, and self-justifying state. Death is a reminder to us of our need for redemption, that our body and soul will be torn apart, that we get old, sick, and die. We know that God is good and that He created the world good without death,[5] but that there is any history at all is an indication of redemption. That the judgment, the final judgment, did not come one minute after Adam sinned in the Garden means that history is on

---

4. *Matthew 22:30.*

5. God created the world good as it was emphasized seven times in Genesis 1, saying, "it was good" (Gen. 1:4, 10, 12, 18, 21, 25), and the last time, "it was very good" (Gen. 1:31). For a fuller explanation on the goodness of creation, see: Gangadean, *The Westminster Confession,* 75–79.

a redemptive basis. God's purpose is to have mercy and call us back.[6] We could have passed into judgment right then and there. Why did we not? God had a purpose to fulfill, and that purpose was redemption. So, to Adam was given the promise along with the curse. Remember, the curse is toil (in work), strife (in raising children because of the reality of sin; sin in the parents and in the children), and old age, sickness, and death. When the curse becomes intensified, it becomes war, famine, and plague.[7] Remember that our lifespans were shortened from what they were at the beginning, from 950+ years to 70 years.

We need to think about all the hardships that we have as we become teenagers and older teenagers and we start to work; we need to think about it in terms of the curse and God calling us back. If we do not, here is what happens: we lose the value of our suffering. It is one thing to have to suffer. It is another thing to suffer in vain and not learn. If we do not think about suffering (toil, strife, old age, sickness, and death) in biblical terms, in relation to something that God imposed to call us back, we will be wasting our suffering. That is, we ourselves will not benefit from the suffering.

The Curse and the Promise

History is put on a redemptive basis from the time the curse and the promise were pronounced. The curse and promise came together in Genesis. "And I will put enmity between you and the woman, and between your offspring and hers; he will crush your head, and you will strike his heel" (Gen. 3:15). This is the seed of the woman, enmity, and the spiritual war. God does not allow the seduction of mankind by the devil to stand. He says, "I will put enmity between you and the woman, and between your offspring and hers." This is the seed of the devil (unbelievers), the seed of the woman in Christ (believers), and the promise that the seed of the woman will crush the head of the serpent.

In this promise, we have an understanding of Christ coming in the place of Adam. In this promise, we have the confirmation of the Adamic covenant and the effects that pass to all mankind. There is a

---

6. Gangadean, *Philosophical Foundation*, 145–161; Gangadean, *On Natural and Revealed Theology*, 141–147; Gangadean, "Paper No. 7: The Problem of Evil," in *The Logos Papers*, 33–39.

7. Gangadean, *The Biblical Worldview*, 55–68, 275–294.

need for someone in the place of Adam, who cannot be under sin and death in Adam. We have the need, from the very beginning, of One who would be human, "the seed of the woman." An animal cannot bring redemption. "For since death came through a man, the resurrection of the dead comes also through a man" (1 Cor. 15:21). It must be a man; it cannot be an angel. It is not God apart from incarnation; it must be a man—the seed of the woman, not of Adam, but the seed of the woman apart from Adam.

In this very point is a whole teaching concerning the Virgin Birth: One must be born of a human being to whom the sin of Adam is not imputed through male headship, as Adam was the representative head. There is the need for One to come, as in the genealogy in the Gospel of Luke, which goes all the way back to Adam. There is a need for the fulfillment of the seed of the woman promised, who will *undo* what Adam did. That is, He must pay the penalty for Adam's sin and death that was brought into the world, and *do* what Adam failed to do. That is, exercise dominion on the earth in such a way as to fill the earth with the knowledge of God.[8] He is going to be a ruler in the creation. He is going to be king. This is why, before He leaves, He says, "Therefore go and make disciples of all nations . . . teaching them to obey everything I have commanded you" (Matt. 28:19a–20a).

The Seed of Abraham

The genealogies remind us that the promise goes all the way back to the Garden and the covenant God made with Adam,[9] and that Christ perfectly obeys. It also helps us anticipate that if Adam was tested during his probation, we should expect this One coming in the place of Adam to be tested. At the beginning of Christ's public ministry, this is exactly what happens. More than that, in Matthew's genealogy, He is traced back to Abraham. The promise will continue in Abraham: "Through your offspring all peoples on earth will be blessed" (Acts 3:25b).

This One who is to come will be the seed of Abraham, and He will be the One who represents all those who have special revelation. The seed of the woman represents all mankind who are under the covenant

---

8. *Genesis 1:26–28; Isaiah 11:1–9.*
9. Gangadean, *The Biblical Worldview,* 147–158.

of Adam. He is going to represent all those who have special revelation coming through Adam and his offspring, through Moses, those who have the law. This is why Jesus will live perfectly under the law and must obey all commands to those who were given the law. This is why we are going to read that Jesus was circumcised, His mother presented a purification offering, and He was baptized. Jesus said, "Let it be so now; it is proper for us to do this to fulfill all righteousness" (Matt. 3:15). Those who sin under the law must have One who perfectly obeys that law in their place, as well as those who sin apart from the law, that is, special revelation.

We are being taught by this what we are to expect: He will be the seed of Abraham. And going back to the seed of the woman, we think of the ages that have passed in the earth. There was the Flood and all that led up to that event. And after the Flood, was Babel and the scattering of the peoples on the face of the earth. All these had general revelation. They had some measure of special revelation that they took with them from the Flood and Babel. We can find traces of this in their history. In the Hindu and Chinese scriptures, in many places, there are references to the Flood and particulars about the Flood. They had some measure of special revelation, but they quickly forgot it, reinterpreted it, put the gods in the place of God, and gave them new names. But they had general revelation.

God was accomplishing His purpose through them; the purpose that was established in the Garden: "Be fruitful and increase in number; fill the earth and subdue it" (Gen. 1:28a). We saw even before the Flood that the line of Cain was instrumental in carrying forward the work of dominion and the importance of this work for mankind.[10] We must understand that general revelation should not be set over and against special revelation. And, the descendants of Abraham who have special revelation are not to hold that over and against those who have general revelation. Both must be upheld; both are revelations from God. Both must be given heed.

Whether Luke is speaking about the gospel going all the way back to the Garden (the seed of the woman), or Matthew is speaking about the gospel going back to Abraham and through the people of Israel, we have redemptive history. People were scattered over the face of the

---

10. *Genesis 4:17–22.*

earth—we have come to the end of that period. In our generation, we have come to a unique point in history where the nations that have been scattered over the face of the earth have come back together, and we can have the kind of contact with each other that we had at Babel before we were scattered. I do not think anyone can gainsay that. We have instantaneous communication, and we are at a dramatic moment in history. We can expect the same pressures that were at work at Babel, and have been at work throughout our history, to be at work now. We have to discern the signs of the times, read those signs, and understand what the pressure points will be. We have to understand the attempt to unify all of the earth, whether it be *under* God or *apart* from God—may it not be apart from God. If mankind attempts to unify apart from God, it will be a sheer disaster for those who are believers. It may invite another great judgment, that the unity apart from God may be restrained; God does not change.[11] We, as believers, have a special concern to be faithful in proclaiming the gospel at this time.

We have this history given to us going back to Abraham. Matthew's genealogy says: "Thus there were fourteen generations in all from Abraham to David, fourteen from David to the exile to Babylon, and fourteen from the exile to the Messiah" (Matt. 1:17). Think of what has happened: how Abraham, Isaac, and Jacob lived, how they waited on the Lord, how they struggled with their own limits, and how God upheld them, provided for them, and delivered them. He upheld them as they went down into Egypt, and God brought them out a few hundred years later. He upheld them as they came through the Exodus. Think of the richness of revelation that is given in those 40 years, the significance of it, and all the revelation that has been given since; and the people continue to turn away from God. This must be in our minds. The repeated apostasies of the days of the Judges, the kings becoming apostates, the judgment of God on the northern tribes, scattering them, and the judgment of God on the southern tribes. There was a struggle to come back from exile under Babylon and Persia, a struggle to rebuild the temple and the wall, and a struggle to endure the prophecies of Daniel regarding the Intertestamental period, particularly all the conflicts that would come. What this shows, what history shows,

---

11. Gangadean, "Paper No. 58: The Spiritual War (Church and World)," 317–322; "Paper No. 34: Globalism and Nationalism," in *The Logos Papers,* 191–193.

is our need for redemption. History shows the universality of sin, the pervasiveness of sin, the reality of the Adamic covenant, the failure of Adam and all those who are united to him by natural generation—the sin working there and our need for a Savior.

Redemptive history reveals something about the person and work of the One who is to come. When we pick up the gospel and begin reading, we will have this understanding if we are reading *with understanding*.[12] We have an additional understanding because we are 2000 years into history after Christ has come. We should read all the work of the pastor-teachers with an understanding of who this Messiah is and what He is to accomplish. We must say that the Christian Church has an often truncated version of this. We do not have a sense of the kingdom that He came to establish, of the work of dominion that He is to do, and that He is to fill everything in every way.[13] Christians have to accomplish this as they learn to take every thought captive and make it obedient to Jesus Christ.[14] We hem and haw, we hesitate, and we raise up other things in place of the person and work of Christ, and we worship Him hardly recognizing Him as He is revealed in Scripture. Some say that, 'Jesus died to save us from our sins, that He forgives us our sins; He sends the Holy Spirit to sanctify us, keep us, and then Jesus is going to come again and accomplish the work *apart* from the Church, or He will take us out of here to go to heaven.' Some people have even lost sight of the resurrection—that we will be resurrected. Instead, they believe that, 'We die, and we go to heaven, and we receive the fullness of the blessing.' Is that what God gave to mankind? Is that what it was all about from the beginning? Is that what all the suffering, pain, anguish, and heartache of this life has been about? Has it all been for naught, merely to endure through a veil of tears and get to the other side? Or is it to do the work under Christ that He is called to accomplish?

---

12. See the Introduction, "The Prologue to the Gospel: The Word of God Makes God Fully Known."

13. *Ephesians 1:22–23, 4:10.*

14. *2 Corinthians 10:4–5.*

The Seed of the Woman

Who is Christ? He is the covenant head in place of Adam, who will *undo* what Adam did and *do* what Adam failed to do. If you miss this point, you have missed a great deal of the promise that is given in the gospel. You have forgotten the purpose of God in the Garden: The seed of the woman will crush the head of the serpent.[15] You have forgotten the word given to Abraham: "In you, all the families of the earth will be blessed" (Gen. 12:3).

If we do not prepare our hearts, become educated to know history, understand what God has revealed, engage with the revelation, and raise our children in order to do so, then we have come short. Seriously, I mean *seriously*, with a double sense. We need to ask God to convict us of our sin for coming short in this way of not seeing Him and His purpose; for not engaging with His purpose and, in its place, putting up our own purpose. *This* is what the genealogies are about. We must hear the Word, understand it, and be saturated with it.

The Seed of David

Redemptive history shows mankind's need for redemption and God's purpose to bring redemption to all through Jesus Christ, the seed of the woman, the seed of Abraham, and the seed of David. The kingdom was promised to David,[16] and Christ has come not just to save us but to establish His kingdom in all the earth. He is to fill everything in every way, and we are to understand the whole principle of fullness that God established in the beginning, when He created everything, and He said again and again to fill the earth, and to fill the earth.[17] There is fullness in the creation and there is fullness in God permitting sin to work itself out in history in so many ways. There is fullness in terms of the numbers of human beings, the multifaceted dimension of creation, creating the heavens and the earth and all the hosts therein. There is great diversity, there is great fullness in God, and there is great fullness in the purpose of God in creation.[18] These are things that we must keep

---

15. *Genesis 3:15.*

16. *2 Samuel 7:12–16.*

17. *Genesis 1:28, 9:1; Isaiah 11:9; Habakkuk 2:14.*

18. Gangadean, *The Biblical Worldview,* 21–36, 91–158, 219–239.

in mind continually. These are the basics, these are the foundational principles, and we should not be 20 years old and having to get these things established in us again or treat them lightly and casually—in one ear and out the other. We are to give heed; we are not to let these things slip. We should be saturated in history—redemptive history.

Collective Failure of Mankind: The Need for a Perfect Representative

History shows our need for redemption as we see the failure of human beings again and again, and as we see what this One will accomplish. He is going to be the seed of the woman (in the place of Adam), and the seed of Abraham, falling under the Abrahamic covenant, bringing the blessings that came to Abraham to all the earth, and all that is involved in the giving of the law and the blessings that are spoken of there. He is to bring *all* of this to *all* the earth. He is to teach the law. When we come to the Sermon on the Mount, we hear Him speak about the law. We know the law is deep within our attitude as well as in our actions, so when Christ says, "For I tell you that unless your righteousness surpasses that of the Pharisees and the teachers of the law, you will certainly not enter the kingdom of heaven" (Matt. 5:20), we have to know the perfection of His obedience. "Until heaven and earth disappear, not the smallest letter, not the least stroke of a pen, will by any means disappear from the law until everything is accomplished" (Matt. 5:18). God calls us to perfect righteousness and we cannot be casual. What is it to obey with the whole heart? Why is it that it is Jesus and Jesus alone who stands in our place? Because He has been fully obedient, and none of us, even at our best, come sufficiently close to His full obedience. We see God's holiness in requiring perfect obedience that comes only through Jesus Christ.

Christ is the prophet, the priest, and the king in connection with the Old Testament offices. We can underscore these three things about Christ, our Lord. He comes in the place of Adam, He is the Anointed One, the Christ, the Promised One, the One who has the Holy Spirit, who is enabled by the Holy Spirit and through the Holy Spirit to accomplish the work that God has given Him in Adam, in the Adamic covenant. He is Lord and Savior. He is to save us from all of our sins—not seeking, not understanding, not doing what is right—and

He is Lord. We are to come to obey Him. He is to rule and establish His law on the earth. This is the One we are to expect.

We should understand it will be a fierce war, and as we begin to read, we will see that this is indeed a fierce war. We are to understand that God has made this promise, and He has made it in great detail from the very beginning. God is ruling in history, sovereignly ruling, and He will accomplish His purpose, and nothing can thwart His purpose.

I just read the account of His birth in Matthew and I want to bring out seven points connected with the birth and boyhood of Christ. We will see how God is faithful in accomplishing His decreed purpose.

THE BIRTH OF JOHN:
To Prepare the Way

The first of the seven points is the Annunciation by the angel Gabriel and the birth of John to Zechariah and Elizabeth. Twice the angels come, first to Zechariah and then to Mary. Then the angels come a third time to announce the birth of Christ to the shepherds. The ministry of angels is to those who are heirs of salvation. The glory of the angels and the power of the angels is so much greater than any human king or ruler. So much greater than Herod; so much greater than Caesar Augustus. One angel is sufficient to destroy all of mankind on the earth, and they come ministering to those who are the heirs of salvation.[19]

There is a promise that one will come before the Messiah: "A voice of one calling: 'In the wilderness prepare the way for the LORD'" (Is. 40:3a). John comes in this capacity. He is the last of the prophets. He is the greatest of the prophets, Jesus said. All the prophets pointed forward to Christ. John points *directly* to Jesus and says, "Look, the Lamb of God who takes away the sin of the world!" (Jn. 1:29). This one is to come, according to Scripture, and the Gospels begin with this one coming. "See, I will send you the prophet Elijah before that great and dreadful day of the LORD comes. He will turn the hearts of the fathers to their children, and the hearts of the children to their fathers; or else I will come and strike the land with a curse" (Mal. 4:5–6).[20]

---

19. *Hebrews 1:14.*

20. NIV 1984.

The alienation that goes on because of sin goes all the way back to the Garden: "with painful labor you will give birth to children" (Gen. 3:16). The alienation that comes between parents and children is because of sin on the part of both: "He will turn the hearts of the fathers to their children, and the hearts of the children to their fathers" (Mal. 4:6a).[21] He will turn the hearts, that the fathers may faithfully teach their children and the hearts of the children may listen and obey their parents in the Lord, as is fitting.[22] John is coming in the capacity to prepare the way.

THE VIRGIN BIRTH:
Conceived by the Holy Spirit

The second point has to do with the Annunciation to Mary by the angel Gabriel. We read of this in Matthew, and we have this record made specific in Luke. In Luke 1:19, Gabriel comes to Zechariah and in verse 26, he comes to Mary. In this, the point emphasized is that she will have a child. She does not have a husband, she has not been with any man, so how will this be? In this is emphasized the teaching that One is to come, who is to be born of the virgin, that He may be sinless, free of the taint of sin that comes from Adam. It is necessary that One who is free from sin be our Savior. If He had the taint of sin imputed and the effects of sin, He *could not* die on the cross and *could not* accomplish redemption.

The Annunciation to Mary must be understood in light of who we need as a Savior. The difficulties and troubles of Mary's heart and of Joseph's heart must be read in this context, that God is accomplishing His purpose. It is the fulfillment of the prophecy given through Isaiah. "The virgin will conceive and give birth to a son, and will call him Immanuel" (Is. 7:14b). *God with us.* In this is revealed the truth that Jesus is Savior, Jesus is God with us. This prophecy in Isaiah is another main point in the fulfillment of Scripture.

---

21. NIV 1984.

22. *Ephesians 6:1–4.*

GOD RULES IN THE AFFAIRS OF MAN:
Caesar's Decree, Bethlehem, and the Shepherds

Third, we have the account of Caesar's decree going out that all the world should be taxed.[23] Caesar is the greatest power on the earth, and his word reaches to the ends of the world, and people must obey regardless of their circumstance, regardless of their difficulty. Joseph took Mary to the town of his birth, to Bethlehem in Judah. In this circumstance, we see the high and mighty of the earth, and the lowliest, and the command structure, and the obedience, and yet how all of this is working to bring about the time and the place at which the Savior will be born, according to Scripture—in Bethlehem of Judah. It never would have happened in the ordinary circumstances that they were living in. God used the decree of Caesar to bring it about that Jesus would be born where the prophet said He would be born—spoken by the prophet so long ago.[24] He is of the line of David to receive the promise given to David. This is part of redemptive history that is being fulfilled. It is not just a very sentimental story that gives you 'Christmassy feelings.' It is not just *Silent Night, Holy Night*. It is not just *O Little Town of Bethlehem*. It is the Word of God Almighty, ruling in the affairs of men to bring about His purpose. Christ would be born of the house of David in the City of David, according to Scripture.

In connection with Christ's birth, we have the shepherds in the field and the angels making the announcement to the shepherds—the lowly ones coming to behold the glory of God with us. What would kings and emperors not give to behold this One, who is "KING OF KINGS AND LORD OF LORDS" (Rev. 19:16b)? God gave this privilege to the shepherds. It shows God's way of reversing the order of things. That is the third point. First, the birth of John, according to the Scripture. Second, the Virgin Birth, according to the Scripture. Third, God's rule in the affairs of men: Caesar's decree, the journey to Bethlehem, the angels announcing to the shepherds, and the shepherds coming to behold the Christ child.

---

23. *Luke 2:1.*
24. *Micah 5:2.*

CIRCUMCISION, PURIFICATION, AND SIMEON AND ANNA

The fourth point has to do with the presentation of Jesus at the temple. Before this, He was circumcised. In Luke, we have this account. "On the eighth day, when it was time to circumcise the child, he was named Jesus, the name the angel had given him before he was conceived. When the time came for the purification rites required by the Law of Moses, Joseph and Mary took him to Jerusalem to present him to the Lord" (Lk. 2:21–22). The time of purification is 40 days for a boy.[25] A 40-day-old child was taken from Bethlehem to Jerusalem, and He was presented in the temple for purification. Mary and Joseph were aware of the law of God. And although the Christ child was without sin, they were aware of the reality of sin coming down upon children, and the need for the purification of children. A child needs a new heart. Circumcision speaks about the Adamic covenant and its effects on all, including children. The purification speaks about sin. "Surely I was sinful at birth, sinful from the time my mother conceived me" (Ps. 51:5). The reality of sin is taken to heart, that children are not just cute, they are 'cute little sinners.' I have no doubt about this. When you ruffle, throw, catch, and squeeze them, you are squeezing a little sinner—a desperately wicked heart,[26] desperately self-centered. Do not let the cuteness throw you off.

Jesus was circumcised, and His mother presented Him in the temple. There is a whole theology of sin and sanctification bound up in the temple. Here, Simeon and Anna came. They were waiting for the salvation of the Lord. They spoke a word of praise to God in seeing the salvation and knowing what was to come. Simeon said that a sword was going to pierce Mary's heart, not literally physically, but about this son, this child that she was bearing in her arms. He said, "This child is destined to cause the falling and rising of many in Israel, and to be a sign that will be spoken against, so that the thoughts of many hearts will be revealed. And a sword will pierce your own soul too" (Lk. 2:34b–35). Mary and Joseph kept these things in their hearts.

---

25. *Leviticus 12:1–4.*
26. *Jeremiah 17:9* KJV.

THE WORSHIP OF THE MAGI AND
THE FURY OF HEROD

The fifth point has to do with the worship of the Magi. Here is another contrast. The Magi came to worship Him who is born king of the Jews: this is His office, this is His place. The Magi went to Jerusalem and apparently they stayed for some time in Bethlehem after the birth. The Magi went there and found Him and worshiped Him. Notice the spiritual war that is raging through the ages. Now it comes down through Herod. Herod had heard about this Messiah that was expected, and since he was king, Herod did not want this Messiah who was to be king to upset and overthrow him. So Herod, in cunning and deceitfulness, inquired of the Magi where this Messiah was. The wise men were warned by God and they returned to their country by some other way, and then Herod was furious.[27] He sent his men, those dark riders and horses, to kill the innocent, to kill the young, those who were two years old and younger in Bethlehem. Being warned of God in a dream, Joseph took the child and went to Egypt. The Scripture was being fulfilled both in the Slaughter of the Innocents in Bethlehem (and the vicinity), and in Jesus being taken by the Spirit to Egypt (and later brought out of Egypt). God is ruling. God is fulfilling His promise. God is in control: the time of the coming of our Lord, and the very circumstance and particular details of it—"And so was fulfilled what the Lord had said through the prophet: 'Out of Egypt I called my son'" (Matt. 2:15b).

Notice how God uses the very wrath of man to fulfill the exactness of His Word. The slaughter of Bethlehem was foretold by Jeremiah long before it happened.[28] Rachel weeping, weeping for her children. Rachel was buried just outside of this region; in a particular way she is connected with that slaughter. She is not the mother of David, but her children are there. Scripture foresaw this. It shows that God knows what is going to happen and things happen according to His decree. While human beings are sent to destroy the plan of God, it serves one purpose only—to fulfill the plan. We have to know that God is faithful and will fulfill His purpose, and we are to be obedient to Him even unto death.

---

27. *Matthew 2:16–18.*

28. *Jeremiah 31:15.*

ESCAPE TO EGYPT AND RETURN TO NAZARETH

The sixth point, after the worship of the Magi, the fury of Herod, and the Slaughter of the Innocents, is the escape to Egypt and the return to Nazareth.

> After Herod died, an angel of the Lord appeared in a dream to Joseph in Egypt and said, "Get up, take the child and his mother and go to the land of Israel, for those who were trying to take the child's life are dead." So he got up, took the child and his mother, and went to the land of Israel. But when he heard that Archelaus was reigning in Judea in place of his father Herod, he was afraid to go there. Having been warned in a dream, he withdrew to the district of Galilee, and he went and lived in a town called Nazareth. So was fulfilled what was said through the prophets that he will be called a Nazarene (Matt. 2:19–23).

THE YOUTH OF JESUS

There is one more point in the youth of Jesus. The seventh point is when He was 12 years old, He was taken up to Jerusalem by His parents for the Feast of Passover. His parents observed Passover in this way. They were devout Jews; they were believers. And Jesus went up and we have a glimpse of what it was like for Jesus to live the life of a human being, the life of a child. He was circumcised and presented in the temple, His parents had to flee here and there to protect Him, and He was brought back to Nazareth and raised by His father, Joseph. He was taken up to the festivals, and we have a glimpse of the heart and mind of our Lord Jesus Christ. When He was 12 years old, He went to the temple. He was aware of His purpose and His mission on earth. What He loves is to be involved in talking about the Word of God.

Jesus was there in the temple with the teachers of the law. They were asking Him questions, and He was answering them. "Everyone who heard him was amazed at his understanding and his answers" (Lk. 2:47). When Jesus was 12 years old, the people were amazed at His understanding and His answers; they were amazed at His faith. I want to underscore this whenever I have the option to do so—*faith and understanding go together.* They were amazed at His faith, His understanding.

"When his parents saw him, they were astonished." They are always surprised by holiness in their child. "His mother said to him, 'Son, why have you treated us like this? Your father and I have been anxiously searching for you.' 'Why were you searching for me?' he asked. 'Didn't you know I had to be in my Father's house?'" (Lk. 2:48–49). I think Mary forgot sometimes, and Jesus had to remind her. It shows what a mind that is not clouded by sin is like. "And Jesus grew in wisdom and stature, and in favor with God and man" (Lk. 2:52), and He went back and submitted to His parents.

Jesus knew the Scriptures. There are those who concoct some gospel of Thomas or Barnabas, and have Jesus learning from the yogis in India—well, praise be to God that Jesus could learn from the yogis of India and reject all of that teaching and go with the Scriptures. He did not just go with the Scriptures because he did not know other teachings. Of course he did not go to India to learn those teachings. Some ask, 'What about the 18 lost years of the life of Jesus?' Do not let anyone pull that kind of nonsense. Bring them to the attention of Scripture. Jesus knew the Scriptures, and others were amazed at His understanding. The Scriptures involved going up to Jerusalem on the Feast of Passover. Now, do you think Jesus, who knew the Scriptures, was going to understand the Passover and what it signifies, as well as circumcision? Do you think He was going to abandon all of that? Not at all. This is the beginning of the life of our Lord Jesus Christ. Let us take it to heart.

2

THE BEGINNING OF PUBLIC MINISTRY

Preparation, Baptism, and Temptation

Matthew 3:1–17, 4:1–11

3:1In those days John the Baptist came, preaching in the wilderness of Judea 2and saying, "Repent, for the kingdom of heaven has come near." 3This is he who was spoken of through the prophet Isaiah:

"A voice of one calling in the wilderness,
'Prepare the way for the Lord,
make straight paths for him.'"

4John's clothes were made of camel's hair, and he had a leather belt around his waist. His food was locusts and wild honey. 5People went out to him from Jerusalem and all Judea and the whole region of the Jordan. 6Confessing their sins, they were baptized by him in the Jordan River.

7But when he saw many of the Pharisees and Sadducees coming to where he was baptizing, he said to them: "You brood of vipers! Who warned you to flee from the coming wrath? 8Produce fruit in keeping with repentance. 9And do not think you can say to yourselves, 'We have Abraham as our father.' I tell you that out of these stones God can raise up children for Abraham. 10The ax is already at the root of the trees, and every tree that does not produce good fruit will be cut down and thrown into the fire.

11"I baptize you with water for repentance. But after me comes one who is more powerful than I, whose sandals I am not worthy to carry. He will baptize you with the Holy Spirit and fire. 12His winnowing fork is in his hand, and he will clear his threshing floor, gathering his wheat into the barn and burning up the chaff with unquenchable fire."

¹³Then Jesus came from Galilee to the Jordan to be baptized by John. ¹⁴But John tried to deter him, saying, "I need to be baptized by you, and do you come to me?"

¹⁵Jesus replied, "Let it be so now; it is proper for us to do this to fulfill all righteousness." Then John consented.

¹⁶As soon as Jesus was baptized, he went up out of the water. At that moment heaven was opened, and he saw the Spirit of God descending like a dove and alighting on him. ¹⁷And a voice from heaven said, "This is my Son, whom I love; with him I am well pleased."

^{4:1}Then Jesus was led by the Spirit into the wilderness to be tempted by the devil. ²After fasting forty days and forty nights, he was hungry. ³The tempter came to him and said, "If you are the Son of God, tell these stones to become bread."

⁴Jesus answered, "It is written: 'Man shall not live on bread alone, but on every word that comes from the mouth of God.'"

⁵Then the devil took him to the holy city and had him stand on the highest point of the temple. ⁶"If you are the Son of God," he said, "throw yourself down. For it is written:

"'He will command his angels concerning you,
    and they will lift you up in their hands,
    so that you will not strike your foot against a stone.'"

⁷Jesus answered him, "It is also written: 'Do not put the Lord your God to the test.'"

⁸Again, the devil took him to a very high mountain and showed him all the kingdoms of the world and their splendor. ⁹"All this I will give you," he said, "if you will bow down and worship me."

¹⁰Jesus said to him, "Away from me, Satan! For it is written: 'Worship the Lord your God, and serve him only.'"

¹¹Then the devil left him, and angels came and attended him.

INTRODUCTION

WE ARE CONTINUING IN OUR MESSAGE ON the Gospels of the life of our Lord. We come to the second part, the beginning of His public ministry. We will look at the events and circumstances surrounding the beginning of His ministry. There are three things on which we need to focus our attention. First of all, the *preparation* of

Jesus. What is involved in His preparation for public ministry? What is going on between ages 12 and 30? What pattern does that set for us as believers, how else is this pattern confirmed in Scripture, and what does this have to say to us as we think about what ministry God has for us and how we are to be prepared? The first part is the preparation for public ministry.

The second part has to do with the *baptism* of Jesus. We will look at John the Baptist being sent before the Lord (and the implications of this), what John said, how Jesus came and submitted to John for the sake of righteousness, and the events that occurred in connection with Jesus' baptism (the voice from heaven and its implications). We will look at His baptism in connection with a question that came up later regarding authority, and we will see how Jesus responded to this question in connection with John and the significance of His response.

Last of all, the greater part will be concerned with the *temptation* of Jesus. We want to look at what is occuring in the temptation. What is He being tempted, or tested, about? How are we to understand the temptation and how does it apply to our lives? We will look at each of these parts: preparation, baptism, and temptation.

PERSONAL PREPARATION:
Growing in Wisdom and Stature

We left off last time with Jesus at the age of 12 in the temple, talking with the teachers of the law, and asking and answering questions. They were amazed at Him. We saw what it is for the mind to develop without the hindrance of sin. If we, at 30, were where Jesus was at 12, that would be amazing. We are not. In addition to age 12, He had another 18 years, and we can be sure that there was preparation going on then. It is not right for us to say, 'Jesus was 30 when He began His public ministry; I am 30, so I will begin my public ministry.' You and I are not Jesus. Or we might respond, 'I know Jesus, and *you* are not Jesus.' It seems funny, but that thinking about beginning public ministry has been around, and sometimes men begin the pastoral ministry at age 30. Some might even begin at 25. This is not exactly in keeping with the *principle* of preparation. Think about the preparation of Moses. He was learned in all of the wisdom of the Egyptians,[1] which means he had two PhDs from Harvard and three from Stanford. He probably went to a community college, but that is okay, too.[2] Moses, though, had this kind of learning. I would not call it 'head learning,' I would call it not the right learning; the wisdom of Egypt was not the right content. It is not that he had 'head knowledge' and it had to drop down 18 inches into his heart, but there was something that was needed—both head and heart—to learn of God.[3] His preparation continued for forty years in the backside of the desert.

Now, others are going to come along and say, 'Well, Moses didn't begin his ministry till he was 80, and I'm 60, so I don't have to do anything.' No, you are not Moses. We do not want to go one way or the other. There is a principle of preparation, and we want to see what goes into the preparation. Think about Paul! Not all public ministry is of the same sort. We seek to be 'significant' and seek 'significance through greatness,' so sometimes, in pride, we go beyond the bounds. I mention some of these examples so that we can see that there is a process.

These persons, particularly, were outstanding in their mental abilities—a gift from God in this regard. Some might say, 'Calvin was writing at 26.' Yes he was, but he had accomplished much study by that time, and he was head and shoulders above others, and so were Saul of Tarsus and Augustine of Hippo. Even with being specially gifted, these persons went through significant preparation—but that, we will see, is not going to be the ultimate test. There is a very understandable, easy-going, practical test that everyone can see. This should also be for all those who come into office—pastor, elders, teachers, and deacons—they must be *proven* first. When we get to the temptation of Christ, we see He is being proven. What is revealed is this: The teaching that we have—if we really absorb it—is expressed in our lives.

It was there in Jesus' life when He was 12. "Didn't you know I had to be in my Father's house?" (Lk. 2:49b). It was seen by the way He asked questions. As for us, with minds darkened and hindered by sin, it is going to take longer, but we *must* have this preparation if we are

---

1. *Acts 7:22.*

2. This is a joke since Dr. Gangadean taught at the Junior College level for 45 years.

3. Gangadean, "Paper No. 70: Sources of Fideism," 375; "Paper No. 120: Contra Voluntarism," 613; "Paper No. 121: The Knowledge of God vs. Mysticism," in *The Logos Papers,* 649–650; Gangadean, *Unity of the Church,* 134–135, 209–210.

going to be in a place of profitable ministry. The underlying word is *profitable*. We will see when we come to John's baptism that he does appeal to fruitfulness. The way we know this is not difficult. Jesus said time and again and elsewhere, "By their fruit you will recognize them" (Matt. 7:16a). By their fruit you will know them, and fruit, in this sense, is multi-dimensional.

First of all, how are you doing in your home? How have you done with raising your children? How have you done in instructing your spouse? How have you done in service to the church in terms of serving others? This is before you come into a position of office. How have you done in terms of the ordinary things from day to day or week to week or month to month? Have you borne fruit there? Has there been fruit in your life in terms of your witness; your ability to communicate; your perseverance in prayer; understanding, crying out to God, and seeing fruit borne in your life? This is an ordinary part of bearing fruit.

What we see in this portion is a time of silence between age 12 and age 30 on the part of Jesus. We know how He had advanced up to 12, and we know from Luke that "Jesus grew in wisdom and stature, and in favor with God and man" (Lk. 2:52). After 12 years, He was quite far above where many of us are, even at a later age. He continued to grow in wisdom and stature, and He was bearing fruit.

There is a great deal of witness that we can have now—to give a witness of what God has done in our lives does not require anything special. This is why a new convert can say, 'This is what God has done for me; blessed be the name of the Lord.' There is a sense in which we have immediate access to our own lives and what God has done, and we *can* be witnesses to this and *should* be witnesses. You do not have to wait for special preparation to be a witness to what God has done. This is something that can be done daily. 'I called upon the Lord, and He saved me. I struggled with this, and the Lord helped me. I prayed for God to answer this prayer, and He helped me. God has led me to understand more in this area of doctrine.' These are ordinary ways that we can be witnessing. We should be sharing with each other. As we seek the Lord diligently, depending on the particular circumstances of our lives (it will be different in different persons), we will come to a mature understanding reflected by a mature life, which is evident to all.

It ordinarily takes time to come to maturity. That is not something that can be pushed. Just today, I told my wife that I received several calls in the last few days. These are tough things. Ten years ago, I do not think I would have been prepared to deal with them. As it is, I am making it by the grace of God—hopefully. I hope so. I hope not to make any major blunders. God has granted me opportunities in terms of the intellectual life and teaching courses in history, logic, and humanities year after year after year for 35 years, and that preparation has helped. Dealing with students has helped. But church-related matters are over-the-top. We are dealing with people in their lives in the depths and the intimacies and the concerns of their lives that you would not have imagined. You do not always deal with that in the classroom. All I am saying is that it takes a certain kind of time—not mere time, but a time where you have been immersed in the basic things and have engaged with them in practice. This is why we have such a thing as a *practicum*[4] in the Logos program as we seek to prepare men for ministry. We have this so that they would learn little by little as they can show confidence in handling matters; that they would learn about particular matters in people's lives and engage in discussing, praying, and ministering. This is the ordinary process by which someone becomes an elder and learns to counsel and minister.

This is why you hear it said often: 'They sure did not teach that one in seminary'—and they could not. In their wildest dreams, they could not have come up with some of the circuitous, convoluted, inside-out, backward things that happen with sin. They could not. They do not teach that in seminary, and they are not, I suppose, intended to. Seminaries are a rather new development in the process of training pastors. Augustine learned by spending time with Ambrose in Milan. In Hippo, he was with another elder, pastor, bishop, or teacher, and being there, he learned. This is the ordinary process of learning: on-the-job training without being in the position.

What was going on in Jesus' life between 12 and 30? He was learning obedience through the things that He suffered by listening to His mother and father. The One who made the universe, the Wisdom of God by whom all things were made,[5] was listening to Joseph and learning.

---

4. The *practicum* is a preparation for those in Logos Theological Seminary, which affords the opportunity for future leaders in the church and the academy to gain practical experience prior to entering fully into a position of authority. It entails service under experienced mentorship.

5. *Colossians 1:16.*

Joseph probably had a thing or two to teach Jesus in His humanity. But in Jesus' divinity, Joseph had everything to learn from the Lord, yet Jesus learned obedience in this way. He continued to meditate on the Scriptures. He participated in all of the festivals, continuing to go up to Jerusalem in those years, and He participated in fellowship. I suppose when He was 12 years old, it was not the last time He asked those persons in Jerusalem questions.

Can you imagine? Can you imagine that He came to the temple again and inquired again? We can infer from His saying, "Didn't you know I had to be in my Father's house?" (Lk. 2:49b), that it was not one-time only. Three times a year, they went up to Jerusalem according to the practice, and Jesus engaged. This shows that even at 12, He understood the Scriptures and engaged in discussion with others. He engaged in discussion in that He *asked* questions of others, and He *answered* their questions. There is a process in going through this kind of discussion. Perhaps He knew He did not have much to learn from them, but if we say that He "grew in wisdom and stature" (Lk. 2:52a), then yes, He probably meditated on the questions that were asked, searched the Scriptures, and spoke. There is a process of learning, but learning there was, and the learning transformed Him. This is necessary for preparation for ministry, but remember, we are to be serving and witnessing at whatever level we are now, and growing more able, and we should use the means. Jesus interacted and engaged with the teachers of the law. There is a place for teachers in our lives. I suppose you could be inclined to say, 'Well, Jesus knew it all by 12.' He did not; He "grew in wisdom and stature." He asked questions, and He answered questions. I suppose it may go both ways with the teachers of the law. There were certainly teachers of the law who were in error and lacking, but there were others who knew the Scriptures, and it probably gave them a special delight to discuss them. This was part of His preparation. He continued this practice until He was 30 years of age.

OUTWARD PREPARATION OF CIRCUMSTANCES:
The Expectation of Israel and the Voice of John

At that time, John came preaching in the wilderness. Remember, John was about six months older than Jesus. We have to look at his message.

He is calling for repentance. What does he mean by the kingdom of heaven is near? The Scripture says of John:

> In those days John the Baptist came, preaching in the wilderness of Judea and saying, "Repent, for the kingdom of heaven has come near." This is he who was spoken of through the prophet Isaiah: "A voice of one calling in the wilderness, 'Prepare the way for the Lord, make straight paths for him'" (3:2–3).

A second sense of preparation is not just that Jesus is prepared as He grows in wisdom and stature. He Himself is being prepared, but the outward circumstance for His ministry is being prepared: the whole of Israel as a nation expected the coming of the Messiah.

Before Jesus came, there was an additional, special preparation through John. The last words of the Hebrew Scriptures, Malachi 4:5–6 says, "See, I will send you the prophet Elijah before that great and dreadful day of the LORD comes. He will turn the hearts of the fathers to their children, and the hearts of the children to their fathers; or else I will come and strike the land with a curse."[6] This is the one, John, who came in the spirit and power of Elijah to prepare the people, calling them to repent. One of the places of repentance is to turn the hearts of fathers to the children—to diligently teach your children the Word of God—and the hearts of the children to the fathers—to obey your parents. This is the way in which wisdom is ordinarily transmitted. There is an accumulation of understanding, just as there should be in the Church, as we build on what has gone before through the pastor-teachers in Church councils and in Church history. We have the benefit of all of this accumulation. So there is an accumulation of understanding, and John bursts onto the scene, saying, "**Repent, for the kingdom of heaven is at hand!**" (3:2 NKJV). The kingdom of heaven is near. What they have been waiting for in a particular way in connection with the coming of the Messiah, the coming of the king into His kingdom; this is at hand, it is near, it is any moment now. We are to prepare our hearts for this One to come. The preaching of John was to this end.

---

6. NIV 1984.

Perhaps we could say there is a *triple* sense of preparation for Jesus' ministry: (1) His own preparation, (2) the preparation through the history of Israel, and (3) the preparation of the hearts of the people through John. This is the principle of preparation—getting the basic things in place so that we can move on and make progress. I suppose this is a form of presuppositionalism; when we get back to what is more basic and lay down what is more basic, that prepares the way to go on—get the basics first; get these things in place.[7]

The people were to repent, and they did come to him and repent, and when they were baptized in the river Jordan, by John, they stood and confessed their sins. **"Confessing their sins, they were baptized by him in the Jordan River"** (3:6). He spoke about particular things regarding the Word of God, the law of God, and how they were to live, and the response was repentance. Now trouble was brewing, and it appears here: **"he saw many of the Pharisees and Sadducees coming to where he was baptizing"** (3:7a). They came because there was a question about people gathering to John, and there was a question of authority: What is he doing? What is going on? Who is this one anyway? And is he the Christ? John points them out. They are the ones who should be preparing the people. John's ministry would not have been needed if they had been teaching and preparing the people. They are the ordinary teachers and the ordinary means of preparation. There is already a tension in the very existence of John. They had not been preparing the people. And they came now, and there was tension. When John saw them coming, he spoke to them very pointedly and bluntly:

> **You brood of vipers! Who warned you to flee from the coming wrath? Produce fruit in keeping with repentance. And do not think you can say to yourselves, "We have Abraham as our father." I tell you that out of these stones God can raise up children for Abraham. The ax is already at the root of the trees, and every tree that does not produce good fruit will be cut down and thrown into the fire** (3:7b–10).

What is John looking for? He is looking for fruit. There can be a 'repentance' with a lot of tears that does not produce fruit.

---

7. Gangadean, *The Epistle to the Hebrews*, 83–98, 253–369; Gangadean, "Paper No. 43: My Last Lecture," in *The Logos Papers*, 237–253.

We know persons by their fruit, the fruit in their lives, which is multifaceted. We speak from time to time about a particular kind of fruit—30-fold, 60-fold, 100-fold.[8] That is right, but it does not rule out fruitfulness in other ways, including the fruit of the Spirit and the fruit manifesting in your life. Fruit is a manifest state—you can *see* fruit. It is manifest in the way you have lived your life, the way you have interacted with other people, and the result of your interaction with other people over the years. John is looking for fruit in connection with repentance.

"Repent, for the kingdom of heaven is at hand!" (3:2 NKJV). This is not a kingdom that is going to be postponed for another 2,000 years after Jesus is crucified. The kingdom is there, and it began then. There is no dispensational teaching[9] in this verse. John continues and says, **"I baptize you with water for repentance. But after me comes one who is more powerful than I, whose sandals I am not worthy to carry"** (3:11a). John is alluding to this One who is so high above him, beyond any one human, that he is not fit to carry His sandals. John is testifying. This One is more powerful, and more glorious, and John makes the point, **"I baptize you with water . . . He will baptize you with the Holy Spirit and fire"** (3:11b)—two things. This is the preparation for the One coming: Who can give the Holy Spirit? No mortal possibly can. This One is divine. This One is none other than God. He will baptize with the Holy Spirit. The baptism of the Holy Spirit is the indication of the coming of the kingdom of God because now, the Holy Spirit comes upon us, and He enables us to be witnesses in Jerusalem and Judea and Samaria and unto the uttermost parts of the earth.[10] In this sense, the kingdom of God has *come* in the days of Jesus; it had been confined to Israel, but the kingdom of God is to come into all the earth, and all the nations are to be made disciples. Jesus is baptizing with the Holy Spirit—the Messiah, the Anointed One, who will anoint His people with the Spirit to enable them to do the work. When this One comes and does that work, it is the indication that the kingdom of heaven is near.

---

8. *Matthew 13:8.*

9. Gangadean, *The Westminster Confession,* 111–120.

10. *Acts 1:8.*

He will baptize with the Holy Spirit, but He will also baptize with fire. This is an allusion to the suffering that comes in connection with the advancement of the kingdom of God. It will not be easy. It will be through blood, tears, sword, and fire. It will be a spiritual war that is agonizing, and the enemy will fight back with everything he has. The Beast will bear its fangs and maul, haul, destroy, seduce, persecute, and give false teaching. There will be fire. Jesus comes to bring a sword,[11] and people will be divided. People who had formerly been so close together will experience death. It is seen in parents who were once thought to be loving, and there is now alienation from one's parents' home. He will baptize with fire. This is one of the marks of the kingdom coming. When the kingdom comes and advances, the enemy will resist with all they can. The lines will be more sharply drawn. **"He will baptize you with the Holy Spirit,"** and as the kingdom advances, there will be **"fire"** (3:11b), and there will be the sword. Time and again, we are going to be called upon to stand up for the truth, and in the process of standing up for the truth, we will suffer misunderstanding, opposition, resistance, resentment, and sometimes persecution—often enough there is persecution. Jesus included this in His teaching: "Blessed are those who are persecuted because of righteousness, for theirs is the kingdom of heaven" (Matt. 5:10). When John preaches in preparation for Jesus coming, he truly identifies those elements. Remember, he is to come before the Messiah—the One who is to come.

BAPTISM:
Fulfill All Righteousness to Redeem Those Under the Law

Jesus comes to John to be baptized, and He says, **"Let it be so now; it is proper for us to do this to fulfill all righteousness"** (3:15). When Jesus comes to John to be baptized, John realizes who he is standing before. **"But John tried to deter him, saying, 'I need to be baptized by you, and do you come to me?'"** (3:14). John understands that he is the one who is to be baptized by this One who is holy, and John is to confess his sin, and he says, **"and do you come to me?"** John is a faithful witness in this. He prepares the way by his life in *every* way. **"Jesus replied, 'Let it be so now; it is proper for us to do this to fulfill**

---

11. *Matthew 10:34–36.*

all righteousness,'" to obey every law that God has established for the sake of His kingdom—for the righteous and the unrighteous. Jesus was perfectly righteous, but He identified Himself with sinners to bring those that were under the law to redemption, having perfectly obeyed as they should have obeyed. So John baptized Him. Notice in verse 16, **"As soon as Jesus was baptized, he went up out of the water"** (3:16a). There was no confession of sin before baptism or after baptism because there was no sin to confess. He came up immediately out of the water, and a double confirmation of His sinlessness comes: **"At that moment heaven was opened, and he saw the Spirit of God descending like a dove and alighting on him. And a voice from heaven said, 'This is my Son, whom I love; with him I am well pleased'"** (3:16b–17). Jesus is going to remember this voice. He will appeal to it later, when He says, "And the Father who sent me has himself testified concerning me. You have never heard his voice" (Jn. 5:37). He has the approval of the Father. Here is what the Father said: **"This is my Son,"** this One is the Son of God, the eternal Son of God, co-eternal with the Father from the beginning. **"This is my Son, whom I love."**

God loved Him eternally. He declared His love to Him again. This is the One who will be sacrificed and who is to undergo a course of suffering immediately after this baptism. He will hear the voice of the Father, **"This is my Son, whom I love."** He did not say, 'You are my Son.' He said, **"This is my Son."** He is speaking to a third party. **"This is my Son, whom I love; with him I am well pleased."** This speaks of the perfection of Christ up to this point, and the full obedience in the way He has lived His life. He is reckoned, known to the Father, and acknowledged by the Father before all. The Word of God is spoken directly concerning our Lord Jesus Christ as He is baptized. This is the second part of the preparation between birth and age 30.

Now, as Christ comes, He is preceded by the ministry of John and all of the Scriptures. John is a fulfillment of the prophets by way of preparation, as are his preaching and baptism, the preparation of the people, and the identification of this One as the Messiah.[12] In John 5:33–47, we see how John's testimony is appealed to by Jesus, as well as the works of Jesus, the voice of God the Father, and the Scriptures.

---

12. *John 1:29.*

Both John's testimony and the voice of God refer to the time of Jesus' baptism.

THE TEMPTATION:
Understanding Good and Evil

We come now to the testing in the wilderness. **"Jesus was led by the Spirit into the desert to be tempted by the devil"** (4:1). Notice that He **"was led by the Spirit."** This is as it should be. This is God's will. Jesus could know this as He begins His public ministry. As Adam had to endure the test, the probation, the proving, to manifest what was there inside, Jesus had to be tested likewise. Jesus could know this, and we believe He did know this. So He is being led by the Spirit and not in some uncanny way. Jesus understands who He is, the work He is to do, and what He must go through before He can begin this work. The testing must occur to show that He is able to proceed and do the work.

While the testing begins here, all three years of His public life will be a test up to the moment when He says on the cross, "It is finished" (Jn. 19:30) and "Father, into your hands I commit my spirit" (Lk. 23:46). Testing is going on up to the time that He draws His last breath, then it is over. Jesus knows who is going to do the testing—the same one who did in the Garden. How would you like to have the devil walk into your class and say, 'Students, today we're going to have a test.' There is a cool chill that comes into the classroom and the clouds outside darken the sun when the devil walks in and says, 'You're going to have a test today.' No, it does not come that way. He comes camouflaged. He comes like a philosophy teacher walking into the class saying, 'We are going to have an oral quiz today, put away your notes and get ready.' You cannot always tell when the devil will test, but you can know that ultimately, the testing is coming from God. God uses the devil to test us. Christ is tested in the same way that Adam is tested. There are two ways before us, as are manifested in the two trees in the Garden: *life* and *death*, *good* and *evil*. Had you been pursuing what is good, the knowledge of God, had you been studying, as they say, 'Two hours outside of class for every hour in class,' you would do well.[13]

---

13. Pastor Gangadean is making references of his role as a philosophy instructor. A full description of his teaching practices will be published under "Philosophical Foundation Dialogue Series."

The testing began, and it began with Jesus being led into the desert and fasting, not eating any food for 40 days and 40 nights. Now that is interesting. How long can you go without food? How long can you go, let us say, without coffee? Could you go a day without coffee? How long could you go without a soda, or without ice cream, or things like fruitcake, you know, the ordinary pleasures? 'Oh, I'm willing to fast for 40 days and 40 nights. Just don't ask me to give up my coffee. That is a different story altogether!' No, it is not. He is led to give up the ordinary things. Notice, **"Jesus was led by the Spirit"** to do this after He heard the voice of God. Perhaps if John baptizes you, the heavens open, and you hear a voice, then you might say, 'I'm going to the wilderness to get tested, and then I can really start my public ministry. Boy, it is going to be fun. Watch out, world. Here I come.' No, we do not undertake this test ourselves. God brings it upon us, and it becomes quite clear that God brings it upon us. We know God brings it, and we have to respond accordingly. Jesus had to recognize this, and this was part of His response. After 40 days and 40 nights, He was hungry. This is way, way beyond anything close to ordinary. It is not a three-day fast; it is not a ten-day fast. It is 40 days and nights without food. He was hungry, and He was there in the wilderness.

First Temptation: The Identity of Jesus

Adam was tempted in the Garden, and sin came in. Jesus was tempted in the wilderness to *undo* what Adam did, and to *do* what Adam failed to do. The tempter comes to Jesus and appeals to Him in a way that is understandable. **"If you are the Son of God, tell these stones to become bread"** (4:3b). Notice the question—the insinuation. **"If you are the Son."** It is a question of identity. **"This is my Son, whom I love"** (3:17). What is Jesus thinking as He goes through the increasing pains of hunger and the approach of possible death? What is He thinking about the voice, the love of His Father, and the tempter who asks this question? Does Jesus understand the good? Has He been pursuing the good? Does He pursue it above all else? What is of first importance? When push comes to shove, what is of first importance? Is it the natural needs and concerns understandable by all? It is not. Jesus understands what life is.

THE BEGINNING OF PUBLIC MINISTRY

First Response: Ultimate Priority—Every Word of God Is Life

He responds, "Man does not live on bread alone" (4:4a). He responds with His understanding of life and His understanding about who He is and what He is to accomplish. It says that He is being tempted as a "man." As the Son of God, He cannot be tempted. His response shows that He is acting according to His human nature; there is no confusion with the divine, each nature is doing what it is to do. He acts according to His human nature, so He replies, "Man does not live . . ." There is no question in His mind that He is the Son of God, and there is no question that it is as a man that He faces the temptation. So He replies, "Man does not live on bread alone." In this, He is saying what life is all about. This is life under the most extreme conditions: 40 days fasting. What is the good? What is life all about? What is of ultimate value? Life is all about the Word of God. "Man does not live on bread alone, but on every word that comes from the mouth of God" (4:4). Man lives on *every word*. It is not some word, but every word—all of it. We are to understand that it is not just an immediate word, such as God having said, 'This is my Son'; this is a word that comes from the mouth of God, but what is meant is the *whole Word of God in all of life*. Life has to do with knowing God—understanding God's revelation of Himself. And the Word of God in its fullness makes God fully known. Man lives on every word. This is what life is about. If we try to bypass this and find life in some other person or persons—a lover, family, children, or friends—and bypass life as the Word of God, we will miss it. This is the way we most commonly go. We have not understood good and evil. This is not what life is. "Every word that comes from the mouth of God" (4:4b). If necessary, it may come to this: all those relationships will be forsaken for the Word of God. "Who is my mother, and who are my brothers?" (Matt. 12:48). "Whoever does the will of my Father in heaven is my brother and sister and mother" (Matt. 12:50). Man *lives* by every word that comes from the mouth of God, and by obeying it. This involves understanding what is revealed in the Word.

Jesus shows His understanding under the most distressing circumstance. He answers the question of His identity, knows His purpose, knows what is good and what is evil, and He has been pursuing the good. His mind has been engaged. We have to measure ourselves by Jesus. As we begin our public ministry, we should be asked: How well do we understand good and evil? How is it showing in our lives? What is it we have been able to do without, for the sake of what is good? What relationships have we put before the good? Have we been actually pursuing the good? Have we been busy with a lot of things that are right but are not the good? Have we been busy with a lot of duties, but duties divorced from an understanding of the good? "'Martha, Martha,' the Lord answered, 'you are worried and upset about many things . . . Mary has chosen what is better'" (Lk. 10:41–42b). What is better is to sit and learn and not be always busy baking cookies. There is a place for that, but the first place is sitting and learning by "**every word that comes from the mouth of God.**"

Second Temptation: Presuming on the Love of God

"**Then the devil took him to the holy city and had him stand on the highest point of the temple. 'If you are the Son of God,' he said, 'throw yourself down. For it is written . . .'**" (4:5–6a). When the devil comes quoting Scripture to you, watch out. It is either out of context, or he has left something out, or both. Do not think that the devil cannot quote Scripture to you. He quoted it to Eve and raised the question to her. Here, he left out "in all your ways" (Ps. 91:11b). We sang this in Psalm 91A.[14] 'Are you not going out of the way being on this high spot of the temple? What are you doing up there?' God permitted the devil to take Jesus there. Notice that it is the most dramatic place in all of Israel: the Holy City, the holy temple, the pinnacle of the temple, the holiest of all. A lot of drama is connected to this, and through excitement, one might do things presumptuously and may try to get a response from others by doing something spectacular. We have to know that we are to live by the Word of God: "**every word that comes from the mouth of God**" (4:4b). We have to understand the context of things.

Second Response: Live by the Revealed Will of God and Use Ordinary Means

"**Jesus answered him, 'It is also written: "Do not put the Lord your God to the test"'**" (4:7). We have to be careful that we do not think

---

14. *The Book of Psalms for Singing* (Pittsburgh: The Board of Education and Publication, Reformed Presbyterian Church of North America, 1998).

that we can depend on God to help us when we go beyond ordinary means and beyond the precepts of God. If we have to be in an emergency situation and find ourselves there, that is understandable, but do not think it is an act of trusting in God to presume on God's grace and go beyond the *ordinary means* that God has established. On the other hand, we are to be diligent in the use of ordinary means, but we should not trust in them; that is a common temptation. We are to trust in God who, by His grace, blesses the means He establishes. We are not to presume on the grace of God, in the name of trusting in God, rather than understand the precepts of God, the principles of life, and the ordinary means that He expects us to use. Watch out for this. There are options within the realm of precepts. The precepts tell us what we ought to do. We might do it in way A or B, but we are to be within the bounds of the precepts and the ordinary means and the principles of wisdom that govern the means. Someone who is ready for public ministry will show their understanding of this. They will understand not only what the end is, but how to achieve the end without being presumptuous.

Jesus passed this test, and He was going to endure this test again and again, even on the cross: 'Cast yourself down from the cross. Do something spectacular, and we will believe in you.'[15] Do a miracle. Show us that you are the Christ.'[16] This is to tempt the Lord; it is to presume on the grace of God. Notice that you can trust in God to uphold you in not eating the fruit (or not turning the stones into bread), but then you may trust beyond measure and presume on the grace of God. See how the one temptation connects with the other. We tend to go one way or the other. Trust too little or trust too much. The Word of God is the guide; the Word of God *understood* is the guide.

Third Temptation: The Kingdoms of This World Without the Glory of God

The third temptation comes when the devil "showed him all the kingdoms of the world and their splendor. 'All this I will give you,' he said, 'if you will bow down and worship me'" (4:8b–9). Here, the devil

---

15. *Matthew 27:42.*

16. *John 6:30.*

reveals his hand—fully. This is what the devil wants and what Jesus came into the world to get. "The kingdom of the world has become the kingdom of our Lord and of his Christ" (Rev. 11:15b),[17] but Jesus was going to get the kingdom in a particular way, in the only way that it would be lasting. Many have sold their souls to the devil for a little bit of Ireland, a little bit of New England, or a little bit of something or other in the world. This is not just one of the kingdoms of the world; this is all the kingdoms of the world and their splendor. They were to become the kingdom of God and of His Christ. But the kingdom of the world, as it is (from the devil), has the worm of rottenness at its core, and it is doomed to destruction. But He could have gotten an authority from the devil (since Adam yielded to the devil). He could have gotten this by submitting to the devil, honoring him in this submission, and worshiping and acknowledging him.

Third Response: Doxological Purpose—Glory to God Alone

Jesus knew how He was going to get the kingdom of the world, how God had ordained it, and what the Word of God said about who is to be worshiped and how. **"Jesus said to him, 'Away from me, Satan!'"** (4:10a). There is a *rebuke* to Satan in this, that he would attempt to draw near to God, this creature that was made so beautiful but is now so ugly in sin. He may still be outwardly beautiful, but inwardly there is a spiritual ugliness in that he tries to alienate any affection from God to himself, a mere *creature*. Jesus found it ugly and hideous and said, **"Away from me, Satan! For it is written: 'Worship the Lord your God, and serve him only'"** (4:10). Jesus loved His Father. He was bound to Him. It was a matter of allegiance and loyalty and truth, in truth, and He would not for a moment consider this temptation. He would get the kingdoms of this world by obeying His Father to the uttermost: by dying on the cross. He is upholding the honor of His Father—the infinite justice, holiness, mercy, and goodness of God—by dying on the cross. Jesus knew who He was and what He was here for. He knew what the good was, and He knew how to get it—not by presuming on God but by trusting in and obeying God to the utmost. Jesus showed clearly that He was ready to begin His public ministry.

---

17. NIV 1984.

3

THE SERMON ON THE MOUNT
Jesus' Teaching on Attitude, Law, and the Kingdom

PART I

Matthew 5:1–30

¹Now when Jesus saw the crowds, he went up on a mountainside and sat down. His disciples came to him, ²and he began to teach them.

He said:

³"Blessed are the poor in spirit,
    for theirs is the kingdom of heaven.
⁴Blessed are those who mourn,
    for they will be comforted.
⁵Blessed are the meek,
    for they will inherit the earth.
⁶Blessed are those who hunger and thirst for righteousness,
    for they will be filled.
⁷Blessed are the merciful,
    for they will be shown mercy.
⁸Blessed are the pure in heart,
    for they will see God.
⁹Blessed are the peacemakers,
    for they will be called children of God.
¹⁰Blessed are those who are persecuted because of righteousness,
    for theirs is the kingdom of heaven.

[11]Blessed are you when people insult you, persecute you and falsely say all kinds of evil against you because of me. [12]Rejoice and be glad, because great is your reward in heaven, for in the same way they persecuted the prophets who were before you."

[13]"You are the salt of the earth. But if the salt loses its saltiness, how can it be made salty again? It is no longer good for anything, except to be thrown out and trampled underfoot.

[14]"You are the light of the world. A town built on a hill cannot be hidden. [15]Neither do people light a lamp and put it under a bowl. Instead they put it on its stand, and it gives light to everyone in the house. [16]In the same way, let your light shine before others, that they may see your good deeds and glorify your Father in heaven.

[17]"Do not think that I have come to abolish the Law or the Prophets; I have not come to abolish them but to fulfill them. [18]For truly I tell you, until heaven and earth disappear, not the smallest letter, not the least stroke of a pen, will by any means disappear from the Law until everything is accomplished. [19]Therefore anyone who sets aside one of the least of these commands and teaches others accordingly will be called least in the kingdom of heaven, but whoever practices and teaches these commands will be called great in the kingdom of heaven. [20]For I tell you that unless your righteousness surpasses that of the Pharisees and the teachers of the law, you will certainly not enter the kingdom of heaven.

[21]"You have heard that it was said to the people long ago, 'You shall not murder, and anyone who murders will be subject to judgment.' [22]But I tell you that anyone who is angry with a brother or sister will be subject to judgment. Again, anyone who says to a brother or sister, 'Raca,' is answerable to the court. And anyone who says, 'You fool!' will be in danger of the fire of hell.

[23]"Therefore, if you are offering your gift at the altar and there remember that your brother or sister has something against you, [24]leave your gift there in front of the altar. First go and be reconciled to them; then come and offer your gift.

[25]"Settle matters quickly with your adversary who is taking you to court. Do it while you are still together on the way, or your adversary may hand you over to the judge, and the judge may hand you over to the officer, and you may be thrown into prison. [26]Truly I tell you, you will not get out until you have paid the last penny.

[27]"You have heard that it was said, 'You shall not commit adultery.' [28]But I tell you that anyone who looks at a woman lustfully has already committed adultery with her in his heart. [29]If your right eye causes you to stumble,

gouge it out and throw it away. It is better for you to lose one part of your body than for your whole body to be thrown into hell. [30]And if your right hand causes you to stumble, cut it off and throw it away. It is better for you to lose one part of your body than for your whole body to go into hell."

THE CENTRALITY OF THE KINGDOM

TODAY WE ARE LOOKING AT THE THIRD IN THE series of messages on the Gospel of Matthew. We will look at Jesus' teaching, with particular focus on *attitude, law,* and *kingdom.* Jesus taught by His word and works. He taught who He was and what He came to do. We saw earlier how He went through the temptation, which revealed His understanding of who He was and what He was to do. He preached and began His preaching with these words: "Repent, for the kingdom of heaven has come near" (Matt. 4:17b). This should be kept in mind throughout all of His preaching; this is a summary; this is the focus. It involves the call to repent of not knowing and not obeying the law of God's kingdom. The call to repent involves the reason for repenting, not only in general, but now more particularly because the kingdom of heaven is at hand. This is the kingdom that was promised from the earliest days. It is the kingdom that the Patriarchs, the Prophets, and the people waited for. It is the City of God, whose builder and maker is God, the city with foundations.[1] This kingdom is at hand. The king of the kingdom is here and the kingdom is about to go out into all the world and accomplish the purpose that God intended from the beginning—one and the same dominion mandate.[2] The kingdom is present in the Old Testament, but this is the inauguration of the king exercising His rule in full force, here and now, not simply after His resurrection.

We enter into this kingdom through repentance of our sin of not seeking and not understanding God, then we submit to God and bear fruit in doing the work of the kingdom. In connection with this, Jesus called disciples. "'Come, follow me,' Jesus said, 'and I will make you fishers of men'" (Matt. 4:19). In following Him, being with Him, learning from Him, and seeing how He worked, they were to become not just fishers—they were called away from this in the ordinary sense—but

---

1. *Hebrews 11:10.*

2. *Genesis 1:26–28.*

they were to become *fishers of men*. They were to bring others into the kingdom. In addition, Jesus healed the sick—miraculous healings—and He cast out demons. Both of these signify who He was and what He came to do. Jesus is the One who would restore man from sin, death, and the curse. He is the One who would restore man from the dominion of the devil. Man had yielded obedience to the devil's word at the beginning and had become children of the devil. Jesus will deliver man from the oppression of the devil.

The Law in the Context of the Kingdom: The Basics in Place— Objectively in Principle and Subjectively in Attitude and Practice

Jesus taught the law in the context of the kingdom. After announcing the coming of the kingdom, calling the disciples, and healing the sick in the second part of Matthew 4, we come to Matthew 5, where He is now teaching His disciples. It is to be kept in mind that He is speaking to His disciples, although there is a multitude around. Scripture says, **"His disciples came to him, and he began to teach them"** (vv. 1b–2). He is preparing them to go out into the world and live as citizens of the kingdom. Now, we want to keep the context in mind, and I want to make some comments about the context.

Again, it should be kept in mind that the law of God is set in the context of the kingdom. We are to keep in mind how His teaching is in contrast to what the people have heard from the present teachers— the religious leaders. It is in contrast to recurring antinomies,[3] where we take the law in a falsely strict sense, or we take the law in a loose sense, often in contrast to the strict sense. Both Pharisees and Sadducees were involved in this division about the law. In both cases, the self-life was present. In both cases, there was a failure to grasp the underlying *principle*. In both cases, there was a failure to see what was less basic in light of what was more basic.

Jesus is teaching the law. As we come to the particulars of this teaching, we see, first of all, that He is teaching the *attitudes* that believers

---

3. Contrary positions, both of which can be false at the same time because they share a common assumption. Examples include: capitalism and communism; this-worldly and other-worldly; all is eternal and none is eternal; skepticism and fideism; literalism and allegoricalism; virtue is the good and happiness is the good. Antinomies are a source of recurrent conflict within and between cultures.

should have—attitudes about things in particular. He is speaking about basic things, objectively basic and subjectively basic, and these things are to be in place. It is in the realm of the attitude that we see if these things are actually in place in people's lives. Jesus is concerned about the basics, and this is how He teaches. He is concerned about the basics doctrinally, and He is concerned about the basics subjectively in practice. He mixes these together in a *marvelous* way in the Beatitudes. Let us see how Jesus teaches and see the context of His teaching. Remember that because we have self-life, we, too, fall into just the same problems Jesus is concerned with—being too strict and too lax. We can think about some of the disputes that we have been having and consider how we are either too strict or we are too lax. I want to emphasize that this is relevant to us, not just the people then. We want to be sure that we hear what the Lord is saying and not fail to hear. The Lord, time and again, says, "He who has ears, let him hear" (Matt. 11:15)[4] and "Take heed therefore how ye hear" (Lk. 8:18a KJV).

We are to hear in the context that the Lord has established, not in the context of our concern that we bring apart from what He has established. "Take heed therefore how ye hear." We spoke recently about *intended* meaning and *interpreted* meaning.[5] "Take heed therefore how ye hear." Concerning personal relations, in case you do not hear well, or in case you think there is a problem, come inquiring. Come inquiring, saying, 'I understand you just said this. Is this what you meant?' Come inquiring. This is part of taking heed of how we hear and noting that we are inclined to hear from the perspective of our self-life.

THE BEATITUDES:
The Attitude of the Citizens of the Kingdom

Poor in Spirit: Creaturely Dependence

First of all, the most basic level that we could possibly come to is, **"Blessed are the poor in spirit"** (v. 3a). How is this so basic? What

---

4. NIV 1984.

5. Intended meaning is the objective truth conveyed by God in the Scriptures. Interpreted meaning is one's interpretation in light of one's assumptions. Hence the need to "Take heed therefore how ye hear" (Lk. 8:18a KJV), so that uncritically held assumptions do not distort, obscure, or deny the intended meaning.

exactly is this about? The *poor* in spirit is contrasted with the *proud* in spirit. The proud in spirit are those who feel self-sufficient. Notice the self-life—self-sufficient. In this, we can see the contrast in those who recognize their *creatureliness*, that they are created by God. As creatures, we are dependent on God. We are not self-sufficient. "**Blessed are the poor in spirit, for theirs is the kingdom of heaven**" (v. 3). Part of being poor in spirit is to realize that our hope is in God, our blessing is in God, and not in the world. It has to do with understanding that there is no good without God. Our good in God comes in the kingdom. "**Blessed are the poor in spirit.**" Do you see now from that short statement how I begin to say that Jesus has started with the basics, objectively and subjectively? If we believe the doctrine of creation with any degree of understanding, we will have this attitude in us of being poor in spirit. If this attitude is in us, we know the doctrine is there. There is no question of a gap between what is in our heads: 'I believe in God the Creator,' and what is in our lives: not having the attitude of creaturely dependence. Jesus starts with our creatureliness. Blessed are those who recognize their creatureliness with understanding. Blessed are those who have faith and understanding in this way, for theirs is the kingdom of heaven.

Mourn: Mindfulness of Sin

"**Blessed are those who mourn.**" We come short. Sin is coming short.[6] We mourn in connection with our sin. We are sinful in that we have not recognized God as Creator and depended on God and sought God as we should, and many problems come with this. We can see how the second beatitude is connected with the first and goes further: "**those who mourn.**" To mourn is to recognize that we are not only creatures but that we are *sinful* creatures. We do not recognize this theoretically merely; we understand it and see how it applies to us. This understanding is working its appropriate effects in us: we are mourning, distressed, not complacent, not taking it lightly, but grieved at our sin, and recognizing that we are *all the more* dependent on God. We are not seeking a way out quickly and easily through some form of self-love, but we seek the comfort that comes from God. The comfort that comes from

---

6. *Romans 3:23.*

His love in knowing that He forgives us, cares for us, and will bring us close to Himself. **"Blessed are those who mourn, for they will be comforted"** (v. 4).

Later, when we go on to speak about the law, we have to keep these attitudes in mind. These are the basics; this is the context. If the attitude is not in place, we cannot speak about the law. Even when we come to **"Blessed are those who are persecuted"** (v. 10a), we have to understand the attitude. Otherwise, we will misunderstand "persecuted." Nowadays, everybody feels persecuted. Everybody feels victimized. But is it for righteousness' sake? We need to understand what was spoken of earlier. We are to understand what comes later in light of what came earlier. This is how we understand—by thinking presuppositionally. When we come to the Sabbath and observe the Sabbath, we should be very careful about particulars in our lives over which we may dispute; let us be careful that we have the context in place and the basic things in place.

Meek: God-Centered Strength Versus Self-Centered Strength

"Blessed are the meek, for they will inherit the earth" (v. 5). Notice the connection between the meek and inheriting the earth. The meek can be contrasted in terms of strength. The meek are those who are strong in God. They are strong in God versus being strong in self. There are two kinds of strength: strong in self and for self, and strong in God and for God. The one views the other as being weak in terms of worldly kingdom and worldly power. Dostoevsky wrote a novel about someone who is 'Christlike,' and he was viewed as the idiot, not very strong or knowing in the ways of the world.[7] This is how the world may view us: 'Christianidiots' (one word, no hyphen). We would say that these persons are truly weak if they do not have the Lord and are not strong in God because, ultimately, human strength is weakness. No one can keep their soul alive. All go down to the dust.[8] We are strong in the Lord. Jesus said, **"Blessed are the meek, for they will inherit the earth"** (v. 5). This is quite in contrast to Ahab and Jezebel, and others who think they will inherit the earth. They may think, 'You have to have

---

7. Fyodor Dostoyevsky, *The Idiot* (Hertfordshire: Penguin, 1998).

8. *Psalm 22:29.*

some drive in this. You have to have some get up and go. You have to grab the bull by the horns (and mix your metaphors in every which way) and get it done. Just sheer, raw drive—power—to get ahead in the world.' We do not want to be like that, but we want to be strong in the Lord. I suppose one could not be strong in the self nor strong in the Lord (double-minded). In this case, there is a crack through which we fall, and we do not recover. We can be strong in the Lord or strong in self. The Lord is commending strength in Him: **"Blessed are the meek, for they will inherit the earth."**

Hunger and Thirst: Longing for Personal and Social Righteousness

"Blessed are those who hunger and thirst for righteousness" (v. 6a). Immediately after this verse, comes **"Blessed are the merciful"** (v. 7a), and we should see these as connected. Hungering and thirsting for righteousness is more than feeling the need for righteousness—that is passive. It is more active; it is *longing* for righteousness. It is not only longing, while doing nothing about it, but seeking it actively. Now, this righteousness is both personal righteousness and social righteousness. Put in those terms, it is *justice*.

In this relation, we see the next reference, **"Blessed are the merciful."** God speaks of both justice and mercy. In Matthew 23:23, Jesus spoke against the Pharisees: "You give a tenth of your spices—mint, dill and cummin. But you have neglected the more important matters of the law—justice, mercy and faithfulness." We can be very punctilious about some outward things and miss the principles and the basics. **"Blessed are those who hunger and thirst for righteousness."** They do what is right for themselves and for society—justice. They seek justice. We speak about the whole area of living and speaking the truth that justice might prevail.[9] We are called to be faithful witnesses and not bear false witness against our neighbor—not only in the court of law but in the larger society, that justice may prevail. Do we long for justice to be done for those who have no voice? Do we long for justice to be done for those who are aborted? Do we hunger and thirst for righteousness? This is one of many things. Do we seek this? Do we lift up our voices

---

9. Gangadean, *Philosophical Foundation*, 267–275.

and learn to speak the Word of God? **"Blessed are those who hunger and thirst for righteousness."**

First, we seek that our lives would be right before God, that we would do what is pleasing to God, and that we are walking in the Lord's precepts and ordinances. This is the way in which He says we should go about getting our end, to please Him for His purpose. Then, in connection with this, we seek righteousness in society. Jesus is saying that this is what the law is about; this is the attitude. It comes out not as an abstract, multi-layered discussion, but it comes out in an attitude—a heartfelt attitude of hungering and thirsting for righteousness. We may say, 'Righteousness? What righteousness? I do not see anything unrighteous going on here. I am hardly aware of it.' Well, the one who is meek sees that God's Word needs to come into all the world. We recognize the meekness that led Abraham, who was depending on God, to leave Ur of the Chaldees. Ur was doomed to failure because they did not live by the Word of God and they did not honor God. It was meekness that led Abraham to leave Ur and go where God led—to Palestine. There is righteousness involved in this. Abraham knew Ur of the Chaldees was not living by the Word of God. This is the same thing that led Moses to leave Egypt. Paul says, "What is more, I consider everything a loss compared to the surpassing greatness of knowing Christ Jesus my Lord, for whose sake I have lost all things. I consider them rubbish, that I may gain Christ" (Phil. 3:8). Righteousness comes by Jesus Christ—imputed righteousness and the righteousness that works itself out in our lives. **"Blessed are those who hunger and thirst for righteousness, for they will be filled"** (v. 6).

Merciful: Fullness of Mercy

"Blessed are the merciful, for they will be shown mercy" (v. 7). Having been shown mercy by God, we show mercy to others, and in connection with this, we will be shown mercy. Remember the parable of the unforgiving servant.[10] Having been forgiven, he did not forgive, then what was given to him was taken away. God calls us to be merciful as our Father in heaven is merciful. Blessing comes upon us in showing mercy.

---

10. *Matthew 18:21–35.*

Pure in Heart: Single-Minded Devotion to God

"Blessed are the pure in heart" (v. 8a). The psalmist says, "One thing I ask of the LORD, this only do I seek: that I may dwell in the house of the LORD all the days of my life, to gaze on the beauty of the LORD and to seek him in his temple" (Ps. 27:4). The whole earth is His temple in which His glory dwells. Psalm 29:9 says, "In his temple all cry, 'Glory!'" After speaking about all the works of God and the creation, it says that everything in His temple cries, "Glory!" This is the one thing the psalmist desires. The pure in heart are those who will one thing; they are single-minded in purpose. Purity of heart is to will one thing.[11] It is not to be double-minded. This is what we seek after. "One thing have I desired of the LORD, that will I seek after; that I may dwell in the house of the LORD all the days of my life, to behold the beauty of the LORD, and to enquire in his temple" (Ps. 27:4 KJV). When we seek God with all of our hearts, we will find Him, and "he is a rewarder of them that diligently seek him" (Heb. 11:6b KJV). Our reward is in God Himself: **"for they will see God"** (v. 8b).

Peacemakers: Be Reconciled with God and Man

"Blessed are the peacemakers" (v. 9a). With those who are outside of Christ, we seek to reconcile them and bring them back to God. We are not sons of thunder, or daughters of thunder, as the case might be. We do not say, 'Bomb them all. Let the Lord sort them out.' This is not our spirit, to derive satisfaction from getting our anger out, and this is not the way God calls us to be. We are called to love our enemies.[12] We do not seek their destruction; we seek their good. We may destroy things that they call good, but we are not seeking their destruction.

We are also called to be humble, gentle, patient, and kind in doing everything we can to maintain the unity of the Spirit in the bond of peace with fellow believers.[13] The peacemakers are at peace with their brothers—co-heirs with Christ who will inherit the kingdom. We

---

11. Søren Kierkegaard, *Purity of Heart Is to Will One Thing* (San Bernardino: Rough Draft Printing, 2013).

12. *Matthew 5:44.*

13. *Ephesians 4:3.*

seek to be reconciled. We make every effort to do so. "**Blessed are the peacemakers.**"

Persecuted: Because of True Righteousness

With these seven attitudes in mind—poor in spirit, mourning, meekness, hungering and thirsting for righteousness, merciful, pure in heart, and peacemakers—we can now go on to speak about the next. "**Blessed are those who are persecuted because of righteousness**" (v. 10a). This is not self-righteousness, and it is not halfway righteousness, which you may try to say is the whole of it, but it is persecution *because of* righteousness.

Many people today feel persecuted. 'People are saying bad things about me.' Jesus says, "**Blessed are you when people insult you, persecute you and falsely say all kinds of evil against you because of me**" (v. 11). We have these seven attitudes spoken of, and now we can go on to speak about persecution and see clearly whether we are being persecuted for righteousness' sake or whether it is something else. If we understand this, our proper attitude would not be to complain and feel hurt, which is often what we do, but we would rejoice and be glad. "**Rejoice and be glad, because great is your reward in heaven, for in the same way they persecuted the prophets who were before you**" (v. 12). Notice we are putting ourselves in the class of prophets who were speaking for God and His righteousness. They did not speak in a defensive manner, but meekly trusted God. They were persecuted, and great is their reward in heaven. What is this reward that is great in heaven? Initially, we may think that when we get to heaven we will see that reward. Instead, we might say that the reward is great in the *kingdom* of heaven. There is a reward, even now. Paul speaks of this reward, and he rejoices. He says, "I consider that our present sufferings are not worth comparing with the glory that will be revealed in us" (Rom. 8:18). If it is not revealed immediately, it is revealed eventually. In the case of Job, the glory of God was revealed. He came to see God at the end of his suffering, and he rejoiced.[14] His heart was at peace and he no longer complained. There is a reward that comes through suffering and persecution, and it is given to the faithful here, in this life. The

---

14. *Job 42:1–6.*

reward is especially in knowing God.[15] There are rewards beyond this, but certainly, there is the fundamental reward of knowing God. The Lord said to Abraham, "Do not be afraid, Abram. I am your shield, your exceedingly great reward" (Gen. 15:1 NKJV); God Himself is our reward. If we think of our reward this way—that the persecution that comes is refining us as we struggle and put away what remains of our self-life and going our own way—we see God more clearly. The pure in heart see God more clearly, and there is rejoicing. We can thank God that through the suffering, we came to see, and God did not leave us to go on not seeing Him.

SALT AND LIGHT:
Shewbread and Candelabra—Salt Versus Corruption and Light Versus Darkness

The Beatitudes are the attitude that we must have if we are going to be able to speak about the law of God. Before going on, the Lord speaks about the relation between the Church and the world. It is the world that is often said to be persecuting believers. We should keep in mind the dynamic of this relationship. Jesus said, **"You are the salt of the earth. But if the salt loses its saltiness, how can it be made salty again? It is no longer good for anything, except to be thrown out and trampled underfoot"** (v. 13). If we have the attitude of hungering and thirsting for righteousness, being merciful, being pure in heart, and being peacemakers in the world, I expect that we should see fruit and be salt. But if we do not have this attitude, if we lose our saltiness, we will lose our ability to preserve the world from moral corruption and decay. This is what happened in the days of Noah, what happened from time to time through history, and what is happening in our age. We cannot simply castigate the world for its moral decay. I believe we are seeing and agreeing that there is moral decay in the world. We may be

---

15. Gangadean, *The Westminster Catechisms,* 109–111, 321–325; Gangadean, *The Westminster Confession,* 8–90; Gangadean, *Philosophical Foundation,* 171–177, 208–211; Gangadean, *History of Philosophy,* 61–64; Gangadean, "Paper No. 6: The Good," 29–31; "Paper No. 42: The Moral Law (ML1 Expanded)," 231–235; "Paper No. 106: The Good and Heaven," 547–556; "Paper No. 115: Doxological Christianity," 595–596; "Paper No. 116: The Knowledge of God vs. The Hope of Heaven," 597–598; "Paper No. 117: Knowing and Making God Known," in *The Logos Papers,* 599–601.

inclined to say, 'Down with the world!' but we have to recognize that we are the salt of the earth. We believers are the ones, by our lives, that keep the world from going into moral decay. If the world is in decay, we should ask ourselves, 'Have we been salt in relation to the law of God?' If not, the decay of the world will penetrate the Church. We will see that it has and does. We have to look at the morality of believers, then and now, and throughout history.

"The sons of God saw that the daughters of men were beautiful, and they married any of them they chose" (Gen. 6:2). The Israelites compromised with the Canaanites. Time and again, the world has penetrated the Church, and this is very much at hand in our day. We are the salt of the earth. If we were living with this attitude and mindset, the world would not penetrate the Church. Jesus also says, **"You are the light of the world. A city on a hill cannot be hidden"** (v. 14).[16] It is not just an individual lamp. Certainly, an individual lamp is lit, and it gives light, but we are also a city on a hill. There is a corporate sense as well as a personal sense to being the light of the world. A lamp is lit to give light to everyone in the house. Light is to shine before men: **"Let your light shine before others, that they may see your good deeds and praise your Father in heaven"** (v. 16b).[17] If we do not become light to the world, the darkness of the world comes into the Church. In many segments of the Church, the world has come in. In many ways, the world has challenged us, and we have not responded effectively. The world has taken leadership of our institutions. There is an urgency to this when the Lord says that if we do not live according to His law, if we are not salt and light, we will be cast out and trampled underfoot. We will become the tail of the culture, not the head—to the point where we are persecuted if we do not go along with the prevailing law.

In my reading of what is going on in the world today, voices are being raised that would take away the freedom of the Church because the Church has spoken in a way that does not seem to the world to be rational. We have not taken their thoughts captive and shown that their position is incoherent—this reality is at hand. The possibility of not being able to stand in the pulpit and say that homosexuality is

---

16. NIV 1984.
17. NIV 1984.

wrong—this is already coming upon us.[18] The possibility that we may not be able to teach our children, at home or in any other way, and other things that are disturbing to liberal democracy—this reality is at hand. The Supreme Court is judging in this way now. 'We are not to disturb democratic sensibilities in the name of our private religion.' Religion has been private because we have not shown by our light how this is indeed the truth of the Word of God, known from clear general revelation. **"You are the salt of the earth . . . You are the light of the world"** (vv. 13a–14a). There is an *urgency.* It is not just positively taking thoughts captive; we are at the point now where we are perhaps concerned just for survival. One has to consider, repent, and be concerned. We are to restrain the world or the world will restrain us. We are to teach the world or the world will teach us. If our teaching does not take thoughts captive, we will be taken captive. We *must* start from general revelation. If we try to teach from Scripture alone when there are many other scriptures around, the world will laugh at us: 'Why should we believe *your* scripture? Why should we believe *your* God? What reason do we have for believing there is a God anyway, given all that we have discovered scientifically?' If we do not speak up, we will lose what ground we have.

FULLNESS OF THE LAW VERSUS APPEARANCE OF OBEDIENCE

The Lord goes on to speak about the law, first in general in terms of the fulfillment of the law, in verses 17–20. He speaks here about the *permanence, completeness,* and *fullness* of the law.

> **Anyone who breaks one of the least of these commandments and teaches others to do the same will be called least in the kingdom of heaven . . . For I tell you that unless your righteousness surpasses that of the Pharisees and the teachers of the law, you will certainly not enter the kingdom of heaven** (vv. 19–20).[19]

---

18. This sermon was delivered in 2004. By faith, Pastor Gangadean understood the signs of the times and where the culture was headed unless the Church repented of its divisions and lack of foundation.

19. NIV 1984.

We want to see what this tension is between the Lord and the Pharisees and how they interpret the law. The Pharisees are both too lax and too strict at the same time, but not in the same respect; otherwise, that would be both *a* and *non-a*. They are very lax regarding the principle of the law, but they are very strict regarding particular applications of the law. It is done in a way that promotes self-life.

The Lord goes on now to speak about the law in particular. The Pharisees had an appearance of righteousness. They seem to be very punctilious in the details. Remember, the Lord said, "You strain out a gnat but swallow a camel" (Matt. 23:24b). The camel is the principle; the gnat is an application. We may try to do better than the Pharisees by straining out *more* gnats. 'We strained out more gnats than the Pharisees today. Yes, sir, we are good; we are that good,' but we miss the principle. We think about how the Sabbath is observed. There are those who are lax about the Sabbath and those who are strict about the Sabbath, but we should see whether we are missing the principle of the Sabbath. There are those who are lax about murder and those who are strict about murder, but both miss the principle of murder. There are those who are lax about adultery and those who are strict about adultery, but both miss the principle of adultery, the more basic, the underlying principle. We have to be in the right state of mind in order to see the more basic. The Lord taught as no one taught before—He taught with wisdom. We have to think and search and seek to know.

Murder: Denial of Human Dignity

The Lord tells us not to be like the Pharisees. To be actually righteous we have to understand underlying principles. First, He speaks about murder: "**You have heard that it was said to the people long ago, 'You shall not murder, and anyone who murders will be subject to judgment.' But I tell you that anyone who is angry with his brother or sister will be subject to judgment**" (vv. 21–22a). Jesus is getting back to the principle of anger. And He explains more about what this principle of anger means and where it comes from. We might be very concerned about abortions but overlook the underlying principle. What is the fundamental principle? To fail to recognize the humanity of another. Jesus said, "**anyone who says to a brother or sister, 'Raca,' is answerable to the court. Anyone who says, 'You fool!' will** be in danger of the fire of hell" (v. 22b). Those two words seem to be synonymous. It has to do with calling someone a 'blockhead,' or 'empty-headed.' It is from the Greek term *moros*, from which we get our term 'moron.' You have heard these terms and other things we say about people. What is happening when we use a term like this? It is a word of contempt. There is anger that comes with using these terms. But there is an alternative to contempt: It is to see the person as made in the image of God, and therefore responsible. It is to see the person as able to respond to the revelation of God, and to be held responsible for their response. A 'blockhead' or an 'empty-headed' person or a 'moron' is incapable of responding. We may become angry instead of holding persons accountable. We are to recognize others as made in the image of God, address them as such, and speak to them in their beliefs—their culpable ignorance.

The principle of holding responsible and what it is to hold responsible is further declared: "**If you are offering your gift at the altar and there remember that your brother or sister has something against you, leave your gift there in front of the altar. First go and be reconciled to them; then come and offer your gift**" (vv. 23–24). "**Blessed are the peacemakers**" (v. 9a). We are to preserve the unity of the Spirit in the bond of peace.[20] Jesus is getting to the weightier matters, the underlying principle, the attitude we have toward our fellow human beings and brothers. The Pharisees did not get to this. Again, He says, "**Settle matters quickly**" (v. 25a) in terms of responsibility and being held accountable. We should hold people accountable and recognize ourselves as accountable, and if we do not do this and recognize this, we could be in trouble. Notice how detailed Jesus can get and still keep the principle:

> **Settle matters quickly with your adversary who is taking you to court. Do it while you are still together on the way, or your adversary may hand you over to the judge, and the judge may hand you over to the officer, and you may be thrown into prison. Truly I tell you, you will not get out until you have paid the last penny** (vv. 25–26).

---

20. *Ephesians 4:3.*

We are responsible for paying the last penny. We should deal with the question of our accountability—to hold ourselves and others accountable and responsible—and if we have a debt, we should be responsible to settle it. This is part of being made in the image of God—being responsible; holding ourselves and others accountable, and if not, we will be held accountable. Notice, you will be in prison. You might have paid off $9,999.99, and you are still in prison because on principle, it is 100%. You will be there till you pay the last penny. Jesus can be exact in His example and still keep the principle.

We are to understand the principle of responsibility and accountability. We are not to call someone 'blockhead' but treat them responsibly. We are to address them as rational beings, and if they are not being rational, we are to hold them accountable. We are not free not to hold them accountable. If someone moves to give up reason to avoid the discussion, we are not free to ignore this. We have to hold them responsible and able to respond to the reason that God has implanted in them. We are not to let this slide, but we never treat them with contempt. Treat them as responsible—*never* with contempt. Treat them as made in the image of God. This is the core, basic principle from which we speak about murder—destroying, disrespecting, and dishonoring the image of God. Jesus wants us to get to the more basic; He wants us to apply the law properly, including the disputes we may have.

Spiritual Adultery Leads to Ordinary Adultery

Jesus speaks about adultery. Now, we can speak about adultery in terms of the outward act and the legal aspect—the Pharisees did this—versus the moral aspect, which is the root. **"Anyone who looks at a woman lustfully has already committed adultery with her in his heart"** (v. 28b). This is a besetting sin. It occurred back in Genesis, probably in the Garden (this is a *probably*). Certainly, it occurred in the days of Noah when the sons of God saw the daughters of men,[21] and time and again through history. As seen in Romans 1:21–32, when we turn away from what is clear about God, we are given up to our desires, uncleanness, and sexual impurity. This is a besetting sin, particularly in youth, and today, it has become a flood. There must not be even a hint of sexual

---

21. *Genesis 6:2.*

immorality among you.[22] There is more than a hint. Pornography, which has become so easily available, has come into people's lives and taken its toll. We may come to God and ask for forgiveness, but we have opened that door, and it is hard to close.

When Jesus addresses this, **"You shall not commit adultery"** (v. 27b), He is not speaking about the outward act only, He is speaking about looking lustfully. If we entertain things like pornography, we are more than looking. It is to be treated seriously.

> **If your right eye causes you to sin, gouge it out and throw it away. It is better for you to lose one part of your body than for your whole body to be thrown into hell. And if your right hand causes you to stumble, cut it off and throw it away. It is better for you to lose one part of your body than for your whole body to go into hell** (vv. 29–30).

The Pharisees could get to the outward, but they did not address the inward principle. Notice the *dramatic* and *definitive* act that must be done: **"gouge it out and throw it away"** (v. 29). This is the occasion for sin. If your computer causes you to sin, bash it! Just throw it down from the 50th story window. Destroy it, right now. This has been a big source of sin. If having money in your pocket causes you to go and buy, do not ever carry money in your pocket. It is not just cutting off the tip of your finger a little bit; cut off your arm. It is not gradualism here; it is *radicalism*. All the occasions for sin must be treated. Is Jesus serious about 'more than the righteousness of the Pharisees?' Oh, yes. We must get to the root. We still have to go further to get to the root. James, in his letter, says, "Adulterers and adulteresses! Do you not know that friendship with the world is enmity with God?" (Jas. 4:4a NKJV).

Spiritual adultery leads to ordinary adultery. This is how it works, and this is the root principle. Adultery comes out of not being pure in heart. We may say, 'Well, can I look at a movie that has one bad scene in it?' We begin to strain at gnats and emphasize how righteous we are, but we are not giving ourselves to the fundamental. 'Should I turn off my lights and power on the Sabbath Day?' Or 'Is it okay to go to the store and buy groceries on the Sabbath Day?' Some people react one way, others react another way. Well, what is the principle? If we observe

---

22. *Ephesians 5:3.*

the principle, we will get the practice. The principle of the Sabbath from the beginning is about the work that God has given to mankind and the rest that we are to have in connection with the celebration of the completion of that work. If we do not have the Sabbath principle in mind, we will be straining at practices and going into the antinomies of too lax or too strict. It is the same with adultery and uncleanness— too lax or too strict. It is the same with murder. We miss the principle.

We need to have the basics in place in order to be able to progress appropriately. We must be sure that we have gotten the principle, and if not, we can ask ourselves, 'Have I heard what was said? Have I paid attention? Have I remembered what was said in terms of the underlying principle? Are these things in place? Do I come inquiring, or do I come accusing others and defending myself?' Jesus said, **"Unless your righteousness surpasses that of the Pharisees and the teachers of the law, you will certainly not enter the kingdom of heaven"** (v. 20), but we are not to exceed their righteousness by becoming more and more detailed and minute. We are not to make conscience our guide.[23] Conscience is a negative guide, not a positive guide. While conscience is a guide for oneself, it is not a guide for another. If we understand the principle, our conscience will be properly informed, and we can make appropriate judgments.

Jesus has called us to repent because His kingdom is at hand. He wants us to repent of our coming short of His Word, of His law, beginning by understanding it in principle, and knowing how it applies in detail. Let us pray and ask God for grace that we might indeed understand His law.

Let us pray: Father in heaven, we ask your grace and mercy to help us, to seek You first in Your kingdom and Your righteousness, trusting that You will add all things. Make us mindful, Lord, of ourselves and our self-life and our way and the many ways we come short, and grant us grace to seek You that we might know You and understand You, come in repentance before You, enter Your kingdom, and do what is pleasing in Your eyes. Forgive us, Lord, where we have come short, and continue Your grace to us as Your people. We ask in Jesus' name, Amen.

---

23. Gangadean, *The Westminster Confession*, 223–231.

4

THE SERMON ON THE MOUNT

Jesus' Teaching on Attitude, Law,
and the Kingdom

PART II

Matthew 5:31–48, 6:1–15

5:31"It has been said, 'Anyone who divorces his wife must give her a certificate of divorce.' 32But I tell you that anyone who divorces his wife, except for sexual immorality, makes her the victim of adultery, and anyone who marries a divorced woman commits adultery.

33"Again, you have heard that it was said to the people long ago, 'Do not break your oath, but fulfill to the Lord the vows you have made.' 34But I tell you, do not swear an oath at all: either by heaven, for it is God's throne; 35or by the earth, for it is his footstool; or by Jerusalem, for it is the city of the Great King. 36And do not swear by your head, for you cannot make even one hair white or black. 37All you need to say is simply 'Yes' or 'No'; anything beyond this comes from the evil one.

38"You have heard that it was said, 'Eye for eye, and tooth for tooth.' 39But I tell you, do not resist an evil person. If anyone slaps you on the right cheek, turn to them the other cheek also. 40And if anyone wants to sue you and take your shirt, hand over your coat as well. 41If anyone forces you to go one mile, go with them two miles. 42Give to the one who asks you, and do not turn away from the one who wants to borrow from you.

43"You have heard that it was said, 'Love your neighbor and hate your enemy.' 44But I tell you, love your enemies and pray for those who persecute you, 45that you may be children of your Father in heaven. He causes his sun to rise on the evil and the good, and sends rain on the righteous and the unrighteous. 46If you love those who love you, what reward will you get? Are not even the tax collectors doing that? 47And if you greet only your own people, what are you doing more than others? Do not even pagans do that? 48Be perfect, therefore, as your heavenly Father is perfect.

6:1Be careful not to practice your righteousness in front of others to be seen by them. If you do, you will have no reward from your Father in heaven.

2So when you give to the needy, do not announce it with trumpets, as the hypocrites do in the synagogues and on the streets, to be honored by others. Truly I tell you, they have received their reward in full. 3But when you give to the needy, do not let your left hand know what your right hand is doing, 4so that your giving may be in secret. Then your Father, who sees what is done in secret, will reward you.

5And when you pray, do not be like the hypocrites, for they love to pray standing in the synagogues and on the street corners to be seen by others. Truly I tell you, they have received their reward in full. 6But when you pray, go into your room, close the door and pray to your Father, who is unseen. Then your Father, who sees what is done in secret, will reward you. 7And when you pray, do not keep on babbling like pagans, for they think they will be heard because of their many words. 8Do not be like them, for your Father knows what you need before you ask him.

9This, then, is how you should pray:

Our Father in heaven,
hallowed be your name,
10your kingdom come,
your will be done,
    on earth as it is in heaven.
11Give us today our daily bread.
12And forgive us our debts,
    as we also have forgiven our debtors.
13And lead us not into temptation,
    but deliver us from the evil one.

14For if you forgive other people when they sin against you, your heavenly Father will also forgive you. 15But if you do not forgive others their sins, your Father will not forgive your sins.

REVIEW FROM LAST SERMON

TODAY, WE WANT TO CONTINUE WHERE WE left off in the last sermon, with the teachings of our Lord Jesus Christ, to see how He reveals who He is and what He will do through His word and works. We want to focus on His teaching regarding the character of the citizens of the kingdom and the law of the kingdom. We began this last time.

Overcoming Antinomies

Jesus taught in contrast to the teachers of His day, the scribes and the Pharisees. Jesus taught the law in context and overcame the antinomies of the teachers of the day: strict in some less basic details and loose in more basic principles. When we come to Matthew 23, we will see how many of the teachings given here come to completion in contrast with the teachers of His day. They have failed to seek the Lord and understand His Word, and they have instead interpreted the law in a way that is in keeping with their heart condition—centered on the self rather than on God. As a result, there has been a self-centered interpretation of the law, but there is a special twist to this. The attempt is made to *appear* to be zealous for the law, but in fact, there is a lack of zeal for what the law truly says. There is the antinomy of appearing to be too strict on the one hand and yet being very slack and loose on the other hand. We understand it this way: they were slack regarding the principle and the root understanding of the law, but they were quite strict in a few particulars, and many of these were twisted in a self-centered way. In sin, one is able to deceive oneself into thinking one is zealous and keeping the law, yet not be so. Remember, no less than Saul of Tarsus was caught in this problem.[1] We think that we are seeking to please God, and yet what we are doing is pleasing the self.

The Law in Context: Objectively in Doctrine and Subjectively in Attitude

Our Lord Jesus taught in contrast to obeying the law to please the self. He began His public ministry by calling people to repent: "Repent, for the kingdom of heaven is at hand" (Matt. 4:17 NKJV), and now

---

1. *Galatians 1:13–14; Philippians 3:6.*

He is teaching His disciples the law of the kingdom and what this kingdom is to be like. We see that Jesus is teaching in a very basic way. He is teaching about basic things *first*. He teaches basic things in two ways: objectively and subjectively. This is the marvel of how our Lord teaches. This is the marvel of the meaning of the Beatitudes. It takes *doctrine*, that we should understand, and translates it into the fabric of our lives—into real understanding—so that it comes out in *attitude*. If we have the doctrine in our attitude, we have it in our understanding.

Jesus calls us to recognize our creatureliness and our dependence on God: "Blessed are the poor in spirit" (Matt. 5:3a). He calls us to recognize our sinfulness, and to be in repentance of it: "Blessed are those who mourn" (Matt. 5:4a). We are to be strong in the Lord and for the Lord, not strong in ourselves and for ourselves: "Blessed are the meek" (Matt. 5:5a). We are to "hunger and thirst for righteousness" (Matt. 5:6). This has to do with justice, both personal righteousness and justice in society. And we are to be merciful. We see in Matthew 23:23b–24 that Jesus comes back to this: "You give a tenth of your spices—mint, dill and cummin. But you have neglected the more important matters of the law—justice, mercy and faithfulness . . . You strain out a gnat but swallow a camel." Remember, the law is not only the Decalogue.[2] It is given in general revelation to all[3] and it is given in the context of the promise of redemption to those who are redeemed, to those who have received God's mercy. "Blessed are the pure in heart, for they will see God" (Matt. 5:8). This applies to those who seek God, because they will find Him. The people who cry out to be reconciled to God are the sons of God. God is calling us to be reconciled to Him through Jesus Christ. "Blessed are those who are persecuted because of righteousness" (Matt. 5:10a). He recognizes that those who are peacemakers and those who call men to be reconciled with God will not always be received and understood. They will be resisted, rejected, and persecuted for righteousness and for the kingdom.

How are we to respond? He calls us to be salt and light on the earth. If we are not salt and light, the world will turn and persecute us. We are to be a light in the darkness by our lives, by our conduct. And we are to be salt as an influence. Both of these have their influence through

---

2. Gangadean, *The Westminster Confession*, 207–221

3. *Romans 2:14–15; Deuteronomy 30:11–14.*

a preserving effect in society. We are living in a culture where more people profess to believe in God, but it is going rapidly into moral and spiritual decay. This indicates that we, the people of God, are not being salt and light as we should. The call for moral reform and spiritual renewal is now being heard on every level. Thirty years ago I heard that, and I could pick up a few books, one or two, about this call for reformation, but now, wherever I turn, I hear this call for spiritual renewal. There is an awareness that we are in spiritual decay, and we need this reformation, and we need it urgently.

The Law in Principle and Practice

The Lord speaks about how we are to understand the law. The law is perpetual and reaches down to the depths. In contrast to those in His day, He said, "Unless your righteousness surpasses that of the Pharisees and the teachers of the law, you will certainly not enter the kingdom of heaven" (Matt. 5:20). Notice that this is parallel to, not a replacement of, but parallel to "no one can see the kingdom of God unless they are born again" (Jn. 3:3b). Some segments of the Church may just put emphasis on being 'born again.' Here, Jesus is teaching those who are already born again, which are His disciples: "Unless your righteousness surpasses that of the Pharisees and the teachers of the law, you will certainly not enter the kingdom." We might say that someone who is a true recipient of God's grace—ongoing in that grace—will come to obey. We are not *justified*, we do not enter the kingdom, by keeping the law—works righteousness—but by the perfect obedience of Christ fulfilling the law on our behalf. But as we are *sanctified*, sin is removed, and we are enabled to keep the law, growing into fullness in the kingdom.[4] This is to speak of salvation in a full sense. One cannot live in the kingdom—have eternal life—apart from the law of the kingdom.

We saw how Jesus is applying this law. The basic point we want to underscore is that of *principle and practice*. If we get the principle, we will have the practice. If we understand the basic assumption of the law—what is being taught in each law—we will see how it comes out in practice. We will see that the practice includes details. We will see that Jesus is more detailed than the Pharisees, so if we have the principle,

---

4. *WCF. 19.7.*

we will have the practice in detail. All of these get down to the minute details of applying the law. This is the marvel of it. Jesus is able to bring both principle and practice together, so there is no tension. There is a natural outflow from the principle to the practice.

The Principle of Responsibility Behind the Applications

We spoke last time about how we regard others in terms of man, the image of God, how we are to treat others as responsible for understanding, and the principle of responsibility taught in the law. This is perhaps *the* underlying principle being taught in the law after it is given in Exodus 20. Read each law in terms of being taught how to live responsibly and how sanctions are brought in so that we may learn to live responsibly. Think about that responsibility and what we ought to know, and think about the grades of responsibility in terms of the grades of knowledge accessible to a person.

Think about slavery and learning from slavery. We are responsible for living in a certain way; if we do not, we could lose certain privileges and freedoms and be brought into that condition. We are to be instructed. Think about the young man who seduces the virgin and what his responsibilities are—how that is being imposed upon him.[5] Think about the ceremonial law concerning infectious skin disease and how one is to be unclean and set apart from the community for a while. Think about learning what we should and dealing with sin as we should. We are to treat each other as made in the image of God: responsible and holding each other accountable, not treating each other with contempt. Responsibility is not the same as contempt. There is a big misunderstanding in thinking that capital punishment is treating the person with contempt—far from it. It upholds the dignity of both the person who murdered and the person who has been murdered. This is the principle of responsibility. Paul says, "If, however, I am guilty of doing anything deserving death, I do not refuse to die" (Acts 25:11a). He made his appeal to Caesar.

In the teaching concerning murder and the principle of the dignity of persons, consider how we are to be held responsible and how it applies while going to court. Settle your dispute with the adversary, lest you

---

5. *Exodus 22:16–17.*

be held responsible for the last penny: there are details connected with responsibility.[6] We are being taught responsibility in this way. Consider adultery and looking lustfully at a woman. The teaching calls us to look into the heart and to look at how we are to deal with the details. If there is an occasion that causes us to sin, we are to deal radically with it. If it is our arm, we are to cut it off and throw it from us. We are not to play around with sin. It is not just the outward act of adultery; it is the inward act. It is in the principle of not loving God with all of our heart, being adulterous with respect to the love of the world and love of the self. We are to deal with this radically. Crucify the flesh with the affections and the lusts thereof.[7] If there is a cause or occasion, we are to cut it off and throw it away from us. We do this by the Spirit.

THE LAW OF THE KINGDOM CONTINUED

Adultery and Divorce: Application of Principle in Detail

We pick up where we left off last time with divorce. This is a further application of the law concerning adultery. If we understand the principle of faithfulness, union, and becoming one flesh, we will understand the application. "It has been said, 'Anyone who divorces his wife must give her a certificate of divorce'" (5:31). Marital unfaithfulness is committing adultery with another, or otherwise forsaking the marriage bed, such that it cannot be corrected by the Church or by the State.[8] Both are involved in recognizing marriage. It is not just a church matter; it is a civil matter.

Jesus says, "But I tell you that anyone who divorces his wife, except for marital unfaithfulness, causes her to become an adulteress, and anyone who marries the divorced woman commits adultery" (5:32).[9] We do not want to be casual about this. If someone is divorced and they are not divorced on biblical grounds, we are to reckon with that. We are to inquire and not marry someone who has not been divorced on biblical grounds. If the person is the innocent party, they may remarry.

---

6. *Matthew 5:25–26.*

7. *Galatians 5:24–25.*

8. *WCF 24.6;* Gangadean, *The Westminster Confession,* 263–273.

9. NIV 1984.

If the person is not innocent and has been guilty, they need to deal with this sin before the law. The person is not free to go on in that way. We have become casual about marriage, divorce, and remarriage. We are not to be casual, according to the law. We are to be faithful even as the Lord our God is faithful.

Oaths: The Principle of Integrity and Application to Vows

Now we come to oaths. Jesus says:

> Again, you have heard that it was said to the people long ago, "Do not break your oath, but keep the oaths you have made to the Lord." But I tell you, Do not swear at all: either by heaven, for it is God's throne; or by the earth, for it is his footstool; or by Jerusalem, for it is the city of the Great King. And do not swear by your head, for you cannot make even one hair white or black. Simply let your "Yes" be "Yes," and your "No," "No"; anything beyond this comes from the evil one (5:33–37).[10]

It is because of evil in the world we have to take oaths and bind ourselves more strongly. We should let our "'Yes' be 'Yes,' and our 'No,' 'No'" (5:37a). There should be nothing more needed. When we get into situations requiring long-term commitment, where we come to depend on each other and expect certain things from each other, we make the commitment explicit, because we are prone to turn aside easily. We ask people to take vows in church membership, baptism, and marriage.[11] Sometimes, when we depend on each other regarding a common activity like building and needing funds, we take pledges. It is not exactly the same as an oath, but if we have made a pledge, we should keep it. There are many conditions under which we should take vows because of evil and because we are prone to turn aside when it gets difficult. There are times when all the feeling is gone, and all you can say is, 'I have taken the vow, and I fear the Lord.' We fear that if we break this vow, we will be called to account, because the Lord said, "the LORD will not hold him guiltless that taketh his name in vain" (Ex. 20:7b KJV). This is why Jesus said, "Do not swear at all: either by heaven, for it is

---

10. NIV 1984.

11. Gangadean, *The Westminster Confession*, 387–388.

God's throne; or by the earth, for it is his footstool; or by Jerusalem, for it is the city of the Great King. And do not swear by your head, for you cannot make even one hair white or black" (5:34b–36).

We do not have power, but we are to swear by God, who has the power to bring sanctions against us. We are to fear the Lord and keep our vows. Even when we swear to our own hurt, we are not to change. We should say what we mean and mean what we say. This comes out of the third commandment: "You shall not take the name of the Lord your God in vain, for the Lord will not hold him guiltless who takes His name in vain" (Ex. 20:7). This involves any light and thoughtless regard for that by which God makes Himself known. The Shorter Catechism Question 55 puts it this way: "The third commandment forbiddeth all profaning or abusing of anything whereby God maketh himself known." God makes Himself known through the preaching of His Word. He makes Himself known through creation. We are not to have light and thoughtless regard for these things—*anything* by which God makes Himself known.

Integrity: A Concern for Consistency

The Buddhists speak about right mindfulness and being focused. I just saw *The Last Samurai*,[12] and there is a modeling in this movie of how every act of these people was intensely devoted toward a particular end, let us say 'beauty,' in a combination of Shinto and Buddhism. Teaching right mindfulness, a focus of attention, was part of what was involved in the Samurai training. Nobutada says, "Too many mind."[13] Sometimes, when we are thinking a certain way, we just think about steps discreetly, but there is another way to think where you are fully focused on each moment in the flow, and you are in that moment. Should Christians have this "*right mindfulness*"[14] and more? Is this part of what it is to be walking in the Spirit?

---

12. John Logan, *The Last Samurai*, Directed by Edward Zwick (2003, Warner Bros.).

13. Nobutada means that Nathan's focus is distracted by people and objects in his close vicinity due to distributed areas of focus he simply terms as 'mind.'

14. Pastor Ganagdean is alluding to the eightfold path in Buddhism. This is an application of how unbelievers in common grace attain a certain excellence. Should not Christians by implication attain it even more? It is an *all the more* form of argumentation.

How does this translate into the command of the Lord to not take His name in vain in thoughtless disregard of anything by which God makes Himself known? If we understand this, we understand how it applies to casual oaths that we may make. You may swear by your head (as if that is anything to swear by), or say, 'I really mean it,' but the Lord says, **"Let your 'Yes' be 'Yes,' and your 'No,' 'No'; anything beyond this comes from the evil one."**[15] This is particularly so when we are working and interacting with one another. This is why we take a marriage vow. If you bring a child into the world, you take the baptismal vow to bring the child to church, to teach the child in a certain way,[16] taking the vow before others who can hear you, to whom you can be accountable, and to whom you can turn to for help. This teaching is given regarding oaths from the third commandment.

Mean what you say and say what you mean. Do not create an expectation that you cannot fulfill. This is one of the reasons why we are backing up and trying to clarify our expectations regarding the church building and get affirmation of understanding what our past is.[17] Not everyone knows our past, the history of Logos Theological Seminary and Westminster Fellowship. We want to be sure that we are together so there are no false expectations in the future, and so we can move together. We are to be careful even in the more casual things. Be careful when you talk to a friend, and you know you are not speaking the truth, or you may be giving a false impression. Be aware of how they are hearing and what impressions you can reasonably say to be giving. If you have given a certain impression and raise some expectations, do everything you can to meet them. Go quickly and make corrections. The failure to do this, to say you are going to do something and then not do it, is *hypocrisy*.

Hypocrisy involves self-deception and self-justification and all that accompanies these. We know that it is because of self-deception and

---

15. NIV 1984.

16. Gangadean, *The Westminster Catechisms*, 356.

17. Westminster Fellowship attempted to build a church in the early 2000s. This was a long process that did not materialize. As Pastor Gangadean and the oversight sought to advance the project, a lack of understanding among the congregants surfaced. For a fuller pastoral handling of this situation, a sermon was given under the title, "Little Foxes and Dead Flies: The Good Is the Source of Unity" (2004). It is currently in print in *The Unity of the Church*, 163–175.

self-justification that God imposed the curse in the Garden.[18] It is because of this that we get old, sick, and die. It is certainly due to sin, but the acknowledgment of sin was resisted by self-deception in covering up with leaves, and by self-justification in blaming others, and *then* God imposed the curse. We should remember the significance of this order. This is why there is so much in the Scriptures that say if you touch a dead body, you are unclean until evening.[19] It is a call to stop and think; it is a time-out. Do not go about the rest of your activities. Remember the curse and the significance of the curse. All kosher foods were involved with this, as well as various things that make us unclean. It is a call to stop and think; it is a time-out. 'You are unclean for the rest of the day. Take this to mind and learn.' If this were implemented, would it be a good learning tool? If it were put into effect, yes, it would. The Lord wants us to be mindful of these things.

The charge that the Lord is going to bring against the teachers of the law is that they are hypocrites. Again and again, He said, "Woe to you, teachers of the law and Pharisees, you hypocrites!"[20] At the beginning and at the end of His ministry in Matthew, He speaks this message, He judges by this message. The one charge He makes is that of hypocrisy. We know that this has been the charge that has been brought against the Church: 'Christians are hypocrites.' We should be genuine. We should be the real article. Johnny Cash was said to be the real thing in some measure—at least the world recognized him this way. He did not sell out for monetary purposes. He lived a life, good or bad, and this is what it was. He sang it. The world admires a certain amount of genuineness. Now, I could say there is a lot more genuineness that Johnny Cash needs to answer to in terms of the clarity of general revelation and his giving heed to that, but nevertheless, in some measure, it is there. The world does not often see that in Christians. Sometimes, it is because they misunderstand. Often enough, it is because we are not living as we should.

God wants us to be light. Our message cannot be heard unless we are living with integrity. **"Let your 'Yes' be 'Yes,' and your 'No,' 'No'"**

---

18. Gangadean, *The Biblical Worldview,* 241–294.

19. *Numbers 19:11.*

20. *Matthew 23.*

(5:37a).[21] We are to live without self-deception, without self-justification, in the presence of the curse that is upon all of us. Remember Job; he was the most righteous man. "His wife said to him, 'Are you still holding on to your integrity? Curse God and die!'" (Job 2:9). She thought he should commit suicide. He retained his integrity, and he should, but he needed more integrity. He had a higher level of integrity than those around him, and integrity scores high with God as expressed in the third commandment: "The LORD will not hold him guiltless that taketh his name in vain" (Ex. 20:7b KJV).

By listening to the message casually week to week, and making vows and not keeping them, we enable each other in our self-deception rather than being accountable to each other and letting others know our lives and how we are living. Without integrity, and without transparency and accountability, we will get nowhere. We will get where the Pharisees got under the hand of judgment. "**Let your 'Yes' be 'Yes,' and your 'No,' 'No.'**" This includes expectations that we create. When we take the church membership vow, we create an expectation that we will attend church regularly, that we will be ministering in the church, that we will read our Scriptures and pray, be accountable to one another, tithe, and witness. This was the expectation we created by taking the vow. We confessed that we are sinners and we need correction. We need to be humble before the Lord and receive correction. We do this by making ourselves known to others. It does not have to be made known to all; it does not have to be advertised, but two or three others should know what is going on in our lives. The elders should know what is going on in your life, pray, and watch for you. Perhaps I might say, of all laws, this is the bottom-line law of all the Commandments. This one, integrity, a concern for consistency.[22] If we had integrity, it would bring us to the Lord. If we had integrity, we would not live a lie, and we would not live as existentialists who say one thing and do another.[23] The Lord knows how we are to come to the truth, and He speaks the Word and wants us to be a faithful people.

---

21. NIV 1984.

22. Gangadean, *Philosophical Foundation*, 199–205; Gangadean, *The Westminster Catechisms*, 237–240.

23. Gangadean, *History of Philosophy*, 163–170.

Justice and Mercy: Love Your Neighbor as Yourself—Love Seeks the Good for the Other

Jesus' teaching concerns love, justice, and mercy. In this section from Matthew 5:38–48, all of these are involved, and they are not to be separated. "You have heard that it was said, 'Eye for eye, and tooth for tooth'" (5:38). This is the teaching. This is to be put in the context of loving your neighbor as yourself. Leviticus 19:18 says, "Do not seek revenge or bear a grudge against anyone among your people, but love your neighbor as yourself." When you love, you seek the good of the other, and that is what is being taught here. The underlying principle for these applications must be love and the good.

It is one thing for the State to apply this rule to someone who is unrepentant—and even to someone who is repentant. This is a life for a life: capital punishment.[24] But, on a personal level, in our relations with one another, we should be ready to forgive even as we have been forgiven. He says,

> If someone strikes you on the right cheek, turn to him the other also. And if someone wants to sue you and take your tunic, let him have your cloak as well. If someone forces you to go one mile, go with him two miles. Give to the one who asks you, and do not turn away from the one who wants to borrow from you (5:39b–42).[25]

In other words, if we have an understanding of what the good is and loving our neighbor as ourselves, and seeking the good for them, we would do these things. It is also true, at the same time, that if for some reason they become unaware of what they are doing, we are not to indulge them in a way that would further their mischief and misunderstanding. The purpose of acting in this way is to *further their understanding*. They are coming against you out of self-life, and you are to live your life in such a way, as a witness, that anger and retaliation is not the principle that is motivating you. The evil emperor in *Star Wars* wanted Luke to feel the anger, respond, and retaliate.[26] He wanted

---

24. Gangadean, *Philosophical Foundation*, 231–243.

25. NIV 1984.

26. George Lucas, *Return of the Jedi*, Directed by Richard Marquand (1983, 20th Century–Fox).

Luke to come against him in this way, and Luke did not. Sometimes people will come against you, and you may think, 'I'll retaliate in the same way,' but we are not to retaliate—we are to act for their good, and to show what life is truly about.

Would you cross the street to speak to your neighbor about the gospel? Would you make some sacrifice for their hearing of the truth? Would that include a tunic? Would that include taking an insult without retaliation? I do not think anyone really has recently struck anyone on the right cheek, physically. Certainly, in terms of insults, that has happened. Insults are to the soul what a physical strike is to the body. In that sense, abundantly, it has come. When the insults come, do you feel something deep within you rising up, wanting to come out and express itself? We could probably think to ourselves, 'This person does not know the truth. I am actually much worse than they are saying. If they saw me the way God sees me, I deserve a lot worse than that. I deserve to be cast out of God's presence forever. What they said is really nothing. I wish they would go after the real, deeper evil in me.' Of course, they cannot, because if they do that, they would have to go after the evil in themselves. Let us start by confessing that we are sinners, and further, let us see the other as they are before God. This requires long suffering.

"Do not turn away from the one who wants to borrow from you." What you can say is, 'I don't do loans, but I'm willing to give you the money.' The problem with making a loan is that you expect a return. Do it in the spirit of giving. Do it for their good. In some situations, I probably would think, 'No, perhaps I'm furthering this person's irresponsibility.' If that is so, I would not do it. If it is for their good, I would certainly do it—if I saw an actual need. I would inquire: 'Tell me what is happening.' Does that sound like a good reply?

The command to love your enemies is explicitly here, and again, it is for their good. An example is made in terms of God's goodness to us. He says, **"He causes his sun to rise on the evil and the good, and sends rain on the righteous and the unrighteous"** (5:45b). In other words, God knows what justice is, and God knows what mercy is, and He wants us to be like Him. The way He has loved us, forgiven us, and sought our good, so we are to seek the good of our neighbor. The way He has borne with us in mercy, so we are to bear with our neighbor. He says, **"Be perfect, therefore, as your heavenly Father is perfect"**

(5:48). Justice and mercy—these are the weightier matters of the law.[27] We should understand how to apply justice and mercy.

The application gets down to the details in how one greets others. If you greet only your brothers, what are you doing more than pagans? Do not even pagans greet each other? How about tax collectors? When was the last time you prayed for someone who works for the IRS? He says, "**If you love those who love you, what reward will you get? Are not even the tax collectors doing that?**" (5:46). We are to be a notch above the tax collectors and two notches above the pagans. "**Love your enemies and pray for those who persecute you, that you may be children of your Father in heaven**" (5:44b–45a). These are the basics of the law—justice and mercy. Remember, the law is applied freely. It is not the law only that is applied; if God did not have mercy, we would all be dead. When we come to obey the law, remember that there is redemption connected with the law. There is mercy connected with the law. We are to show this. Jesus is bringing this out. Jesus is teaching the law in its basics, objectively and subjectively. We know that it applies down to details, even in greeting people.

THE PIETY OF THE KINGDOM

Motive in Acts of Piety: Pleasing God Versus Self

Jesus speaks about the application of this law to acts of piety. They are called acts of righteousness. He speaks about giving to the needy, prayer, and fasting. Here, Jesus brings up the word *hypocrite*, especially in connection with visible manifestations of righteousness. Three times, He speaks about not being like the hypocrites.[28] They want to be seen by men; they want to be honored by men. This is the self-life. They want the praise of men. They want to please themselves by receiving praise from others rather than please God. This is the underlying spirit in all of these acts of piety. In seeking to do what is pleasing to God, we are not to make it known to others. This is being double-minded.

---

27. *Matthew 23:23.*
28. *Matthew 6:2, 5, 16.*

Giving to the Needy and Prayer: In Secret Versus Public

In giving to the needy, it comes down to the details: "**But when you give to the needy, do not let your left hand know what your right hand is doing**" (6:3). This is pretty detailed, is it not? Do not let it be known, even inadvertently. In other words, you should try to do it in a way that is not known by others. "**Do not let your left hand know what your right hand is doing, so that your giving may be in secret**" (6:3b–4a).

What we tend to do is reverse the order of things. We want our sin to be in *secret* and our acts of righteousness to be in *public*. We need to reverse the order and make our sin public and our acts of righteousness secret. Different, is it not? It is kind of radical. This is what the Lord is saying. When we get honor from men, we will not receive honor that comes from God. Our motto should be: to please God, not to please ourselves. God, who searches the heart, knows our hearts. "**But when you pray, go into your room, close the door and pray to your Father, who is unseen. Then your Father, who sees what is done in secret, will reward you**" (6:6). Here is that word again, "secret." Our personal piety must be done for only God to see. Secondly, it must be done with a proper knowledge of who God is. Do not think that by repeating and repeating and repeating, we will be heard—as if God does not know. God knows very well what we need. He knows what we need better than we do. We are to come praying and acknowledging that we are dependent on God for these things. Some use prayer wheels, some use rosaries, and some use repetition in praying. One may say the Lord's Prayer and repeat it eight times. One may think that prayer will be heard because of repetition, but the Lord teaches us that this is not the case.

The Lord's Prayer: This Is How You Should Pray

Furthermore, He teaches us how we are to pray. He teaches us the content of prayer. A whole theology is summed up in the Lord's Prayer. Our piety should be based on the system of theology taught here. If this is not our theology, then our piety will be false—zeal without knowledge. We, too, can empty this of meaning by falling into one or the other side of an antinomy—going to the right or left—missing the more basic principle.

I trust you are all familiar with the Shorter Catechism and what we are to pray for in each petition.[29] I will draw your attention to this again. We pray for the knowledge of God from "hallowed be your name" (6:9b). We pray for the kingdom of God coming, the will of God, and the law of God being done in all the earth. *Then*, we pray for our daily, particular needs. We should make it a habit of the heart not to rush in before God and say to the Lord, 'I need this, this, and this . . . and by the way, may your kingdom come, also. Because when it comes, I will have these things.' Rather we should pray: "**Hallowed be your name, your kingdom come, your will be done**" (6:9b–10), and then we pray for what we need in order to hallow His name and work for the kingdom. What we tend to do is the reverse. This is how self-life reverses the order of things. God wants us to pray with understanding and pray according to the will of God.

We are to pray: "**Forgive us our debts, as we also have forgiven our debtors**" (6:12). We are to recognize sin remaining and God's hand in cleansing us from sin. "**And lead us not into temptation, but deliver us from the evil one**" (6:13). God will test us. God will cause the thoughts of our hearts to be revealed. God searches our hearts through our trials. God knows where we are, He knows how to reach us. It is His intent, the intent of the infinitely wise and all-powerful God, to cleanse us from our self-life. He knows how to design the trial to bring self-life to the surface. Can you say amen to that? Amen. It is certainly true.

Our Lord says, "**And lead us not into temptation, but deliver us from the evil one**" (6:13). We want to be delivered from the evil that remains in us, which is self-life. We recognize our sin, and we pray to God for our sin. We are also encouraged to pray: "**Forgive us our debts, as we also have forgiven our debtors**" (6:12). Sin remains in us. We affirm this in principle. People, if you think you are going to die, death is an indication that you have sin remaining in you. The curse is to restrain us (in unbelief), recall us (conversion), and remove the sin remaining in us (sanctification). Do not ever forget this. There are many things in the Word of God that call us back to remember the significance of the curse and sanctification. We were expelled from Eden. We cannot make the curse into punishment. The punishment is borne by Christ.

---

29. Gangadean, *The Westminster Catechisms*, 97–106; Gangadean, "Paper No. 136: On Prayer," in *The Logos Papers*, 685–690.

Physical death is removed at the resurrection; spiritual death continues on. Both believers and non-believers experience physical death, and believers as much as non-believers. There is no proportionality in that, which is part of justice. We need to be *forgiven* and *cleansed* from sin. These petitions are focused in this way. This is our attitude. We recognize our self-life, and we ask God to forgive us. If we do not forgive, we know that God will not forgive us, and God will not hear our prayers.

We will leave off with the Lord's Prayer and speak about fasting next time.

5

THE SERMON ON THE MOUNT
Jesus' Teaching on Attitude, Law, and the Kingdom

PART III

Matthew 6:16–32, 7:1–6

6:16When you fast, do not look somber as the hypocrites do, for they disfigure their faces to show others they are fasting. Truly I tell you, they have received their reward in full. 17But when you fast, put oil on your head and wash your face, 18so that it will not be obvious to others that you are fasting, but only to your Father, who is unseen; and your Father, who sees what is done in secret, will reward you.

19Do not store up for yourselves treasures on earth, where moths and vermin destroy, and where thieves break in and steal. 20But store up for yourselves treasures in heaven, where moths and vermin do not destroy, and where thieves do not break in and steal. 21For where your treasure is, there your heart will be also.

22The eye is the lamp of the body. If your eyes are healthy, your whole body will be full of light. 23But if your eyes are unhealthy, your whole body will be full of darkness. If then the light within you is darkness, how great is that darkness!

24No one can serve two masters. Either you will hate the one and love the other, or you will be devoted to the one and despise the other. You cannot serve both God and money.

[25]Therefore I tell you, do not worry about your life, what you will eat or drink; or about your body, what you will wear. Is not life more than food, and the body more than clothes? [26]Look at the birds of the air; they do not sow or reap or store away in barns, and yet your heavenly Father feeds them. Are you not much more valuable than they? [27]Can any one of you by worrying add a single hour to your life?

[28]And why do you worry about clothes? See how the flowers of the field grow. They do not labor or spin. [29]Yet I tell you that not even Solomon in all his splendor was dressed like one of these. [30]If that is how God clothes the grass of the field, which is here today and tomorrow is thrown into the fire, will he not much more clothe you—you of little faith? [31]So do not worry, saying, "What shall we eat?" or "What shall we drink?" or "What shall we wear?" [32]For the pagans run after all these things, and your heavenly Father knows that you need them.

[7:1]Do not judge, or you too will be judged. [2]For in the same way you judge others, you will be judged, and with the measure you use, it will be measured to you.

[3]Why do you look at the speck of sawdust in your brother's eye and pay no attention to the plank in your own eye? [4]How can you say to your brother, "Let me take the speck out of your eye," when all the time there is a plank in your own eye? [5]You hypocrite, first take the plank out of your own eye, and then you will see clearly to remove the speck from your brother's eye.

[6]Do not give dogs what is sacred; do not throw your pearls to pigs. If you do, they may trample them under their feet, and turn and tear you to pieces.

THE BASICS FIRST:
Principle Precedes Practice

WE CONTINUE WHERE WE LEFT OFF ON THE teaching of Jesus as He teaches the basic things—the first things. This is how we should approach the Sermon on the Mount and consider its practical importance. *If* we understand the basic things, the principles, we *will* understand the practice. Jesus taught in contrast to others in His day; they often understood some elements of the practice but missed the principle. As we look at the time of Jesus, throughout Church history, today, and in our congregation, we will see that our disputes can be settled if we understand the principle and learn how to put the practice into effect. We want to avoid both antinomianism (anti-law) and legalism. Those are the two antinomies. We want to avoid being libertines

and going in whichever way we please. As I drove here, I was reminded when I saw a restaurant with a full parking lot. I thought, 'These
people do not observe the Sabbath.' There has been legalism about the
Sabbath and now there is total antinomianism regarding the Sabbath;
how evident this is in so many ways.

THE PIETY OF THE KINGDOM CONTINUED:
Pleasing God Versus Self

We want to look at the teaching of Jesus and see how He taught the
basic things, both theoretically (objectively) and at the level of attitude
(subjectively). Last time, we looked at the works of piety—giving to
the needy and prayer—and we come now to fasting.

We see that these acts are not to be done before men—to be seen
by men—but they are to be done privately before our Father. In this,
we see something about the self-life. If we do it before men to be seen
by men, we have our reward, and our reward is the praise of men. This
hinders us from receiving the true reward—the praise of God—and
the blessing of knowing Him. This is basic. Jesus said, "How can you
believe if you accept praise from one another, yet make no effort to
obtain the praise that comes from the only God?" (Jn. 5:44). This was
how He explained their inability to hear, understand, believe, and obey.
Jesus is getting to what is basic. It is the self-life—being self-centered
more than God-centered.

Fasting: A Sacrifice of Self-Denial to Seek and Obey God

When it comes to fasting, we see that it is to be pleasing to God rather
than pleasing to self. As a matter of fact, fasting is a form of self-denial.
It is clearly a form of self-denial in that you are denying yourself what is
legitimate in ordinary circumstances for a purpose, and the purpose is to
seek God. This principle may be extended into the area of obeying in a
way that involves a sacrifice, a form of self-denial. Self-denial is bound
up in the notion of fasting. Self-denial is also bound up in the idea of
sacrifice, giving up something that the self may have for God. In both
seeking God and obeying God, we must live a lifestyle of self-denial.

Some have missed the *principle* of life and have sought to extend the
practice into every area of life, thinking that the practice is the principle.

One way this has come out is that some persons have historically worn 'hairshirts.' Hairshirts are very uncomfortable, but it is a self-denial of comfort; it is a deliberate denial of comfort. It is continuous, as if this act is getting to the principle, and it is not. The way Jesus put it is, "If anyone would come after me, he must deny himself and take up his cross daily and follow me" (Lk. 9:23). Some people have said, 'Celibacy is the way to serve in the kingdom of God,' rather than learning to serve God in marriage or out of marriage. We can do acts of self-denial, enlarge it this way, and think we are getting to the principle, yet we have missed it. The principle is to deny ourselves daily and take up our cross. The principle is to walk in the Spirit and not in the flesh,[1] to learn to crucify the flesh with the affections and the lusts thereof.[2] This is both in terms of our actions and our thought life—our desires. It can get into the most intimate details of our lives as we are to learn to honor God there.

The worldly way of life is putting the self first. This is how the world is distinguished from God: those who *love self more than God*, as against Christians who *love God more than self*. It does not mean believers do not have sin in their lives, but the pattern will be that over a period of time, when push comes to shove, you have these desires, but if you think it is not pleasing to God, you will put it away. We live in this world, which puts the self first, continually.

When we fast publicly, and do our acts of self-denial publicly, we want to appear to others to be seeking God. Fasting is, first and foremost, for the purpose of seeking God. We should deny ourselves generally and be seeking, but there are times when we fast especially for the purpose of seeking God. Jesus puts it this way: *when* you fast, not *if* you fast. He took it for granted that fasting would be practiced. Some of us may fast and think, 'I'll lose some weight, this is not a bad deal.' You can go on a juice fast or whatever you want for your health reasons, and that is fine, but that is different from fasting before the Lord. Let us not mix self and God. This is the essence of fasting: not mixing *self* and *God*. If you are fasting before God and you happen to lose weight, fine, but what is the innermost thought while fasting? It should be that we are doing this *as unto the Lord*.

If we fast to be seen by others, we want to appear to others to be seeking God, but the self-life is still there, and we are involved in

---

1. *Galatians 5:16.*
2. *Galatians 5:24.*

self-deception. We want to appear as if we are seeking God and denying ourselves, but we want others to see it and notice it, which is an indication that self-life is at the center and there is self-deception there. The Lord calls us away from self-life in these practices of piety that are to be done secretly before the Lord. We have a natural desire in our self-life to receive the honor that comes one from another. We want people to think that we are 'spiritual.' Not spiritual in the contemporary sense, but spiritual in that we seek the Lord and we are holy and pious. But how we appear before men should not be a concern of ours. The concern should be how we *are* before God.

Resolving Disputes: The Need for and the Source of Unity

What is the reward? In all of these acts of piety, God will reward you. Jesus speaks of giving to the needy in Matthew 6:2–4, and He speaks of prayer in Matthew 6:6, and in verse 18, He says that God "**will reward you**" (6:18b). What is our reward? We are called to think about this. In the next passage, He speaks about treasures in heaven. He is going to accentuate this point. What is our reward? This is basic. We cannot really get into a discussion about much without acting in self-life and getting into tangles and quarrels if these basic things are not in place. We are not only to profess basic things objectively, but we are to have them in place subjectively. If we ever try to get into discussion without basic things being in place, we will wrangle. It will be an interminable discussion and result in bad feelings, acrimony, biting, and devouring because it is out of self-life.

This week, about 62 audio book CDs came into my possession, by my choice. Each CD has about 11,000 pages. I have been looking at much of Church history coming out of the Reformation and the Puritans. In God's providence, now that these have come into my possession, I had an opportunity to search into this history. I found a lot of disputes going on there. I have to watch myself closely and not be overwhelmed by the disputes. I have to remember that these disputes *need not have occurred.* If we had kept the principle, knew it, and understood it, we could have dealt with its application in practice. There were disputes about the Church and State in the Puritan period, the covenanting, the whole question of toleration, or whether all of England, Scotland, and Ireland should have a uniform religious belief. Disputes have gone on in the past because we have not held onto the principle, and disputes are going on now. Groups have cut themselves off, separated, quarreled, and have tension with other groups. The Stillwater Group engaged with the group in Moscow, Idaho—the Reconstructionists—and the Reformed Episcopalians. There is a lot of difficulty and quarreling there.

I read in the history of the Westminster Assembly about the Independents and the Presbyterians. A question came up this week about ordination, and a number of pages were devoted to that dispute: Which is the way to go? If we understood the principle, we could have known how to put it into practice in this situation. I went back and read the life of John Knox. I looked at his ordination. I read Calvin's life and looked at his ordination. If the person who raised the question about ordination had just looked at what happened in these lives, the question could have been resolved without this kind of tension. We have to know the principle so that we might put it into practice. I read disputes about the regulative principle of worship.[3] If we understood the principle and had the more basic in place, we could have had resolution. In our lives, we have had conflicts and questions about courtship: If we have the principle, we can have the practice. Husbands, wives, and headship: If we have the principle, we have the practice. Parents and children: If we have the principle, we have the practice. We have had questions about the church nursery and its size. We had to back up and think about the *principle* connected with this. We went through several discussions about the principle, and hopefully, the practice will fall into place. The point is that we do not have to get into these disputes if we have the more basic in place and understand the principles. Christianity is full of these conflicts, and it can be quite disheartening unless we remember this and know that we can resolve it.

One of the things that happens often enough is that because we do not get back to the principle, we wrangle and strain at gnats[4] with each other. We do not know how to get back to the principle and *discuss* it. Things break down quickly, groups divide, and Christianity splinters up. We should say, shame on us for not being able to continue a discussion without getting heated. We have disputes among us over politics in Christianity. We have disputes among us over Christianity and

---

3. Gangadean, "Paper No. 105: The Regulative Principle of Worship," 545–546; "Paper No. 134: Worship, the Sabbath, and the Church," 679–682; "Paper No. 135: On Worship," in *The Logos Papers*, 683–684; Gangadean, *The Westminster Confession*, 233–244.

4. *Matthew 23:24.*

the arts. Nothing is exempt. We can expect that there will be disputes everywhere. Can we discuss it? Shame on us if we cannot. We do not know how to discuss because we do not see what is more basic and what is clear. If we go through the process of thinking, we will be able to get back to assumptions, to the principles, to what is more basic, and make progress.

Christ, our Lord, wants us to be *one* as the Father and the Son are *one*.[5] Is this an ideal to shoot for? This should be very, very, very high in our priorities.[6] Therefore, be able to discuss things by getting back to the principle rather than getting hurt feelings so quickly. We are to have the attitude of seeking God in fasting: "he is a rewarder of them that diligently seek him" (Heb. 11:6b KJV). What is the reward? The reward is knowing Him.[7] If we have the attitude of wanting to know Him as He has revealed Himself, we *will* be able to get to first principles, to what is more basic. We *will* be able to resolve our disputes, and we will not be tense and have these walls between us—not here, nor in Church history, or anywhere. So this is a call, in terms of seeking God, in fasting, to learn to know Him, to get to know the principles, and to see the practice. God rewards those who diligently seek Him. "Without holiness no one will see the Lord" (Heb. 12:14b).

THE TREASURE OF THE KINGDOM

Treasures in Heaven: Eternal Life Is Knowing and Enjoying God

"Blessed are the pure in heart, for they will see God" (Matt. 5:8). How are we progressing in our knowledge of God? Let us continue and see how the Lord develops this. He says,

---

5. *John 17.*

6. Given the degree of importance that unity entails for the completion of the dominion and mission mandates, Logos Papers Press has published the second book in the *Doxological Reformed Sermon Series* on *The Unity of the Church: That They May Be One That the World May Believe* (2024).

7. Gangadean, *The Westminster Catechisms*, 109–111, 321–325; Gangadean, *The Westminster Confession*, 88–90; Gangadean, *Philosophical Foundation*, 171–177, 208–211; Gangadean, *History of Philosophy*, 61–64; Gangadean, "Paper No. 6: The Good," 29–31; "Paper No. 42: The Moral Law (ML1 Expanded)," 231–235; "Paper No. 106: The Good and Heaven," 547–556; "Paper No. 115: Doxological Christianity," 595–596; "Paper No. 116: The Knowledge of God vs. The Hope of Heaven," 597–598; "Paper No. 117: Knowing and Making God Known," in *The Logos Papers*, 599–601.

Do not store up for yourselves treasures on earth, where moths and vermin destroy, and where thieves break in and steal. But store up for yourselves treasures in heaven, where moths and vermin do not destroy, and where thieves do not break in and steal. For where your treasure is, there your heart will be also (6:19–21).

Where is your treasure? What do you treasure? I suppose *what* we treasure is more basic than *where* the treasure is. Always get back to the more basic, and we can proceed from there. What is our treasure? What is our reward? God said to Abraham, after he came back from the conquest of the kings that had captured Lot, "Fear not, Abram: I am thy shield, and thy exceeding great reward" (Gen. 15:1b KJV).

What is the treasure of the apostle Paul? He said, "What is more, I consider everything a loss compared to the surpassing greatness of knowing Christ Jesus my Lord, for whose sake I have lost all things. I consider them rubbish, that I may gain Christ" (Phil. 3:8). Christ—the One in whom there is all fullness, the One who is to fill everything in every way,[8] the One by whom all things are created,[9] who upholds all things, the One who is revealed in all things, the very Word of God. He is the Logos—a person—the Word of God. How God makes Himself known is revealed to us in His works of creation, in all of history, and in our lives. Of all the things that Paul wants to know, he wants to know this above all else, and he considers everything else rubbish. He had privilege, position, and relations, and all of this he counted as a loss for the sake of knowing Christ Jesus. We can say this theoretically. We can say this until we are blue in the face, but unless we are actually *seeking diligently*, we will not understand. It will be in vain. It will be more than that; it will be self-deceiving. The psalmist says, "One thing I ask from the LORD, this only do I seek: that I may dwell in the house of the LORD all the days of my life, to gaze on the beauty of the LORD and to seek him in his temple" (Ps 27:4). Psalm 29 says that everything in His temple cries, "Glory!"[10] In that Psalm, the temple is the whole of creation.

---

8. *Ephesians 1:23.*
9. *Colossians 1:16.*
10. *Psalm 29:9.*

Westminster Shorter Catechism Question 1 states, "Man's chief end is to glorify God, and to enjoy him forever."[11] There are two parts, and there is an order between them and a relation between them. There is not one part, there are two parts. If you think there is one part, it will not be complete. It is to glorify God—know His glory and make it known—*and* enjoy Him forever. This is the goal of our lives. This is our treasure—to know Him. This is eternal life.[12]

We know all Christians will confess this. But one way to examine it is by asking, where is the enjoyment? We tend to profess it, go through the process of obeying some rules that are 'right'—deontologically, in virtue, or with some measure of legalism—not find joy in that process, and then we add celebration. We celebrate with food and with relations, but this celebration is an attempt to find joy in our lives when we are not finding it in truly enjoying God. We will not be able to truly enjoy God, in terms of knowing His glory, unless we start where we are supposed to start—with seeing the clarity of general revelation. We will not be able to interpret life. We will reduce glorifying God to a set of rules, and this is not going to do it. Some have thought, 'If I obey God (in terms of rules) and glorify God, then I should be blessed by God. I've been obedient to God; why doesn't God bless me in this way or that way or the other?' We try to go from virtue to happiness rather than seeing that virtue is a means to the good.[13] We are to understand these rules in relation to the goal of the good. Virtue brings us to achieve the good, and out of the good, the knowledge of God, there is enjoyment—true and lasting happiness.

The philosopher, Immanuel Kant, tried to go from virtue to happiness.[14] He spoke deontologically. He said that nothing is of greater worth than a good will,[15] the good will that is moved by reason alone, and reason tells you what to do and say. The categorical imperative requires that those things that you choose to become a universal law

---

11. Gangadean, *The Westminster Catechisms*, 109–111.

12. *John 17:3.*

13. Gangadean, *Philosophical Foundation*, 172–174.

14. Gangadean, *History of Philosophy*, 151–158.

15. "Nothing can possibly be conceived in the world, or even out of it, which can be called good, without qualification, except a good will." Immanuel Kant, *Fundamental Principles of the Metaphysic of Morals* (New York: Bobbs-Merrill Company, Inc., 1949), 11.

should become the maxim of your action—the guide for all action.[16] Then philosophers later dealt with this, showing that all of these rules can conflict with each other. Why? Because they were not understood in relation to the good. Why did Kant import God into the picture and a blessing in the afterlife? He did this because he could not stand the thought of the virtuous man being unhappy. Virtue had to be rewarded, not with the good, but with happiness. Some persons, in their disposition, are inclined toward happiness, and some are inclined toward deontology. Some personality orientations are inclined to be simply 'rule-governed' and not 'goal-oriented.' Man's chief end (goal) is to glorify God—to know His glory and make it known.

Where is your treasure? Is it stored up in heaven? In what sense? In the sense that we will go to heaven, and there we will have streets of gold that will not be subject to rust, and no one can break into heaven and steal? Or is it the blessing of seeing God? You know, our bodies get older, and we become less able to enjoy certain things as we age. If my treasure were just in enjoying things of this life, in the body, I would be getting more and more depressed every day. The Scripture teaches, "Though outwardly we are wasting away, yet inwardly we are being renewed day by day" (2 Cor. 4:16b), and by the grace of God, hoping I do not have Alzheimer's, I hope to be growing in my understanding day by day, week by week, month by month, and year by year. This is my enjoyment, and this is my treasure: to be growing in my understanding of the Word of God, and of what God has done in history. As I read and study, I hope to go into my old age growing in this way. I am right there; I am right there at the beginning of old age.[17] Do you know that? I am in the youth of my old age. I have things to look forward to! It is in the realm of understanding. It is like money invested in the stock market, sort of; it compounds ordinarily over a long period of time. I am looking for *compounded understanding*. Understanding some things helps me understand more; it grows, flourishes, and gets very large. By the grace of God, I hope this will be my lot. This would be my inheritance, this would be my joy, this would be my peace, this

---

16. "Act only on those maxims which can be willed to be universal laws." Immanuel Kant, *Fundamental Principles of the Metaphysic of Morals* (New York: Bobbs-Merrill Company, Inc., 1949), 19.

17. Pastor Gangadean was in his early sixties at this time.

would be my comfort. In my old age, presently and in the years to come, this is something to look forward to.

Paul says, "Though outwardly we are wasting away, yet inwardly we are being renewed day by day." Make good investments now, people! Invest yourself in understanding now so that it may grow as you meditate, as you go in and out daily, rise up and sit down,[18] and it grows. Give yourself to study, thinking, praying, and crying out to God for faith that understands these things. Where is your treasure? Give yourself to this.

"If your eyes are healthy, your whole body will be full of light" (6:22b). If this is the goal, and we keep our eyes on it, we will see it clearly, and it will be wonderful. The light of truth will become magnified. But if we are divided and double-minded, Scripture says, "No one can serve two masters" (6:24a). We may try to do both, but really we do one rather than the other. "You cannot serve both God and money" (6:24b). We cannot serve God and self. We cannot pursue the knowledge of God and pursue the self-life. It cannot be done. Money is one of the ways to get the things we desire in our self-life. I suppose ice cream will continue to taste good for a while, but I imagine, as Solomon said, that you will not even be able to taste ice cream after a while. Is that horrible? I can tell you all the horrible things. The grinders are few[19] and so you eat baby food out of a jar—'once a man, twice a child.' But you are understanding! You are growing in your understanding! This is wonderful.

Where is your treasure? We can share with others when the treasure is in the right place, and the heart is set on it, when we are storing treasure up in the kingdom of God more and more to increase in the future. This is why when you get an education, you should get an education *for life*. Yes, you need to somehow work a job and make an income, but education should be for life. It should begin when you are young. I am talking about people ten years old and younger. They should know grammar like you would not believe. They should know the basic principles of geography and all the basic principles of history. They should be able to recite it so that when they are 12 or 13 and ready to argue with their father, they have something to argue

---

18. *Deuteronomy 6:7.*

19. *Ecclesiastes 12:3.*

with. Then, their dad can teach them dialectic, and they will be ready to dance when they are 16. *Then* they will be ready to dance, and not before this, not without this.

Invest well in your children and prepare them to rule to make God known. This is the blessing, not children *per se*, but understanding from Scripture that children who rule to make God known are the blessing.[20] Where is your treasure? The blessing is not just in the children, but that they will join with you in the work of the kingdom.[21] Once this understanding is in place, it is easy to work out the details about education, I assure you. We will not get into quarrels about, 'Do we have to learn math, and do we have to learn grammar?' You know what? You *get* to learn it! Call it a privilege—a great blessing. You will know when to use commas and how to communicate effectively, written and otherwise. It is a privilege. It is a blessing. It is a joy. There is a whole world out there to be opened up and discovered and enjoyed—the truth magnified in light of the goal. Where is your treasure? Are you going to organize your life for this? You cannot serve two masters. Did you go to college to get a degree just to get a job? If so, then you are serving mammon. Or did you go to college to get an education for life to serve God? Once you understand that the treasure is *the knowledge of God*, then it is easy to get into discussions about the clarity of general revelation, instead of having all this straining to get a little bit going, where you can see the skid marks all the way across the room because of resistance. Where is your treasure? Jesus asked, where is your heart? **"For where your treasure is, there your heart will be also"** (6:21). This is the cornerstone, the beginning of the foundation, the *existential first principle*, upon which Christ's teaching is built.[22] These are the basics that are to be in place, and when they are, we can make progress.

Do Not Worry: Seek First the Kingdom of God

Which of the Ten Commandments teaches us, 'Do not worry?' Perhaps all of them. Who among us has not been at least tempted by worry? To worry is a sin. This is a command of Christ, not some helpful suggestion.

20. Gangadean, "Paper No. 139: The Blessing of Children," in *The Logos Papers*, 701–702.
21. *Psalm 127*.
22. Gangadean, "Paper No. 4: The Cornerstone," in *The Logos Papers*, 21–25.

To worry might seem natural but only in the context of our fallenness, in which we do not trust God. It is deeply rooted in a whole way of life and reveals our worldview.

What are we worrying about? What we will eat, drink, and wear, and our job and income—our daily needs and the future. And Jesus speaks to us, "**Look at the birds of the air; they do not sow or reap or store away in barns, and yet your heavenly Father feeds them. Are you not much more valuable than they?**" (6:26). He uses an argument from general revelation. Are you, or are you not, more valuable than birds? I suppose some would say less valuable. Those of us who feel low about ourselves and less valuable than birds may say, 'God takes care of the sparrow; why doesn't He take care of me?' We have a way of twisting things. But that is obviously wrong. That may be how you *feel*. But if you had faith, you would say that God cares for us. So we should not be worrying about what we eat and drink.

People manage to twist this truth. This is, again, a principle that assumes that we have the good in place. He says, "**Is not life more important than food, and the body more than clothes?**" (6:25b). I will use our Lord Jesus' example when He was in the wilderness: "Man does not live on bread alone, but on every word that comes from the mouth of God" (Matt. 4:4b)—every word. What is your sense of the good? "**Is not life more important than food?**" Is life, eternal life, the knowledge of God, more important than this? Some people have taken this and run in one direction and become libertines. Jesus says, "**Look at the birds of the air; they do not sow or reap or store away in barns**" (6:26a). Some may say, 'So I'm going to live by faith, and God will provide.' This does not teach us that we should not sow, reap, or store away in barns. It teaches us that we should not worry, which is different. We manage to twist the truth and go the other way because we do not understand the principle.

What is the good? What is our heart set on? And what will we count as a loss for the sake of knowing Him? Are the basics in place—not just verbally, but in our hearts in terms of what we are concerned about? How many of you have come here lately worrying about not being able to show the clarity of general revelation? Now that is something to worry about. Life is more important than what we eat or drink. Some of us have managed not to worry about showing the clarity of general revelation and so we have not cried out and prayed for this understanding.

We think we can get along without it. We do not believe it is integral to growing and learning how to interpret the whole of revelation around us. We manage to be taken up with these other things rather than being taken up with what is good and trusting God for this. It is a lot easier to trust God to supply all of our needs when our needs are according to His will. Can you trust God to show you what is clear, help you see it, and then bless you in the use of means in order to see what is clear? Or do you expect to see what is clear without employing means or exercising your mind? We sow, reap, and store up; we use the means to get the physical, but do we use the means to get the spiritual?

We should be training our children and ourselves to have this kind of education, to grow in this. What is the minimum amount of education we should get? That is like asking, 'What is the minimum amount of treasure I shall have? Let's see, I don't want too much treasure now. I really don't need to know God as He has revealed Himself in the world of physics. I can afford to put that off indefinitely. Physics is for geeks. Now, music is a different story. I am there; I am down with music.' This is not how we should think. I want everything; I want it all. Let me put the question to you this way: What part of the revelation of God do you not want? Is dance something to be included? Or is *only* dance to be included? *All* is to be included. Christ is to fill everything in every way,[23] and we want it all, and we want it now, in this life, if possible, but we will get as much as we can. We will be the half pint, going into the quart, into a gallon, into a 5-gallon drum, until we come to the ocean—the knowledge of God that is like the ocean—the earth shall be full of the knowledge of the glory of the Lord as the waters cover the sea.[24] We should not settle for less; our God is great.

We should be concerned about these things and not worry about other things; we should trust God for them. What this means is that we should seek first the kingdom of God and His righteousness and trust that these other things will be added.[25] We can do this. That is the point. A lot of people are bound up in these other matters and not taking the time to seek first the kingdom of God. This conflict may come up in just taking the time for family worship. It may also come

---

23. *Ephesians 1:23.*

24. *Isaiah 11:9; Habakkuk 2:14.*

25. *Matthew 6:33* KJV.

up regarding work—how much we work and how much money we need. Some of us have to do all of this just to survive. However, even then, we still have to think about ordering our affairs in such a way that we "seek first his kingdom and his righteousness, and all these things will be given to you as well" (Matt. 6:33). This is not a message to say don't work, don't sow, don't reap, or don't store away. One can store away for the sake of the knowledge of God. I was talking with someone last night about this. It is alright to have savings that you will pass on to the next generation. It is alright to have a legacy of giving. Think about saving up a certain amount of money that can be passed on for 10, 20, 30 generations. We are not against storing up; we are against storing up *for self*. We want to invest all of our money to maximize the kingdom of God and His righteousness.

Seek *first* the kingdom of God and His righteousness. Do you see this? This is what we are after. You may have to 'brown bag it' now and save the money. I was in the locker room on campus, and one of my colleagues said, "You know, you cannot take it with you," by which he meant, 'Retire now, get your retirement money, and get going before it gets too late, you don't get to have it all.' Have you heard that kind of talk? Oh no, it does not have to be that way; it can be passed on. That is part of seeking first the kingdom of God and His righteousness. You know what? You will have a grand old time on the other side, looking down and seeing how your money is being spent for the glory of God. We do not have to indulge ourselves now; we can invest our money in the kingdom of God. We are not against saving and storing up; we are against storing up for self. We commend storing up for the kingdom of God. Amen?

THE STANDARD OF THE KINGDOM

Do Not Judge: Self-Examination Versus Self-Righteousness and Self-Justification

Jesus comes now to speak about our judging of others. "**Do not judge, or you too will be judged. For in the same way you judge others, you will be judged, and with the measure you use, it will be measured to you**" (7:1–2). This is a call to self-examination over and against self-righteousness and self-justification. Some people take this wrongly and make it absolute: 'Do not judge, do not ever utter anything that would seem to be, in the slightest way, a judgment. Do not judge, period.' This is said as if the Scripture does not speak plainly about this. We take things out of context and do not see what they mean. We will see that in this very same teaching, we are called to have discernment and judge rightly. Understanding the basic principles here is the prerequisite for judging.

Romans 2:1 says, "You, therefore, have no excuse, you who pass judgment on someone else, for at whatever point you judge the other, you are condemning yourself, because you who pass judgment do the same things." I am reminded of *Gulliver's Travels*, about being a 'yahoo.' That was so beautiful once it started to be understood. It is so concrete.[26] One of the points Swift was writing about was the cultivated Europeans; he spoke in the same breath, word beside word, about the lawyer and the pickpocket. Now, you know the pickpocket is a 'yahoo,' but if the lawyer picks your pocket legally, he is not a 'yahoo.' Do not kid yourself. He is every bit a 'yahoo.'

"For in the same way you judge others, you will be judged" (7:2a), so do not judge. We are to start with ourselves. This means we are to take the plank out of our own eye so we can see clearly to see the speck in our brother's eye.[27] This means that someone has no right, or they lose their right, to speak to us on a subject when a plank is in their eye. Let us say there is a plank of the illegitimate exercise of authority in church discipline. This has happened. Some would say that this or that is not legitimate authority. The Lord says, **"take the plank out of your own eye, and then you will see clearly to remove the speck from your brother's eye"** (7:5b). You lose your right to speak or judge on that subject. The Catholic Church loses its right to speak about authority to Protestants when the Catholics have *abused* the authority of the Word of God, and other churches have done so, as well. Do not judge; you that judge do the same thing, and you lose your right to speak.

---

26. This statement pertains to a Great Books Discussion conducted as part of a three-year training program for congregants studying the Liberal Arts. The overarching goal of this training was to eventually establish a school dedicated to providing God-centered education. The discussions conducted during this period will be published in the future with the intention of laying the groundwork for a philosophy of art and establishing interpretive principles for engaging with classical literary works.

27. *Matthew 7:3–5.*

We need to be able to say this to persons who have been using their 'officialness' and authoritarianism to speak to us about authority. Slander has been stated. Slander is the work of the devil. The word 'cult' has been thrown around. Do you understand what that word means? A group that professes to and does hold to Historic Christianity, by definition, cannot be a cult, because a cult is a departure from the historic position. There are Hindu cults that have departed from Hinduism and Christian cults that have departed from the Historic Christian Faith.[28] To call a group that holds to Historic Christianity a cult becomes slander and judging. **"For in the same way you judge others, you will be judged"** (7:2a). It is the work of the devil. Remember Psalm 15, which we memorized. The person who slanders does not dwell with God. We are not to give heed to it, and we are to confront it if need be. Some claim to know the position that we hold regarding reason and knowledge. If you were to ask them, 'What exactly is that position? Name one thing. If you are not willing to name one thing, why should you even be talking?'—you will begin to see the slander that is going on. They do not know it, and they cannot specify it. Do not judge, for by the same judgment you judge, you will be judged, and you lose your right to speak when you do not take the plank out of your eye first.

Jesus is not saying we are not to judge at all, period, because here He says, **"Do not give dogs what is sacred; do not throw your pearls to pigs"** (7:6a). It seems to me there is a judgment involved here. But we are not to judge the heart. We can judge the conduct—the outward expression; we can judge the words and the deeds. He said, "You will know them by their fruits" (Matt. 7:16a NKJV), the outward manifestation, but we are not in a position to judge the hearts of others. We can judge their actions, their words, and their fruit. We are not to judge—good or bad—in terms of the heart. Do you know there are many 'seeker-friendly' churches? There are so many churches that seek to be seeker-friendly. What does the Scripture say about seeking? No one seeks. No one understands.[29] Claiming to be seeker-friendly is *judging the heart* as if the human heart is generally seeking when the Scripture says otherwise. Left to ourselves, no one seeks. Then, they

---

28. Anthony A. Hoekema, *The Four Major Cults: Christian Science, Jehovah's Witnesses, Mormonism, Seventh–Day Adventism* (Grand Rapids: William B. Eerdmans Publishing Company, 1986).

29. *Romans 3:10–12.*

end up giving what is holy to the dogs and casting out pearls before the pigs. God tells us what the heart is, in general terms: "The heart is deceitful above all things, and desperately wicked: who can know it?" (Jer. 17:9 KJV). And this requires the curse to be upon us to the end of our days to be cleansed of sin. We can take this as the standard in general terms. God judges the heart and may reveal it to us, but we are not to judge the heart. We are to judge what is *said* and what is *done*. If someone, by their life, shows evidence that they are unfaithful and lacking in understanding, then we are not to rush to speak. We are to be wise. We may get back to what is more basic and speak there, but we are not to speak on less basic matters with them. We are not to give what is holy, what is sacred, what is special, to others, because they will turn and rend us. **"If you do, they may trample them under their feet, and then turn and tear you to pieces"** (7:6b). They will "say all kinds of evil against you because of me" (Matt. 5:11b).

If we understand the basic principles involved in judging, we can understand the application. The Lord wants us to understand, and He wants us to honor Him with our lives. One indication of the heart condition, above all else, is whether or not we are teachable. By teachable, I mean, are we willing to go through a process of discussion? Teachable does not mean that we simply 'shut up and listen.' It means that we are willing to go through a process of discussion. It does not mean a process of nitpicking argumentation, but with the basics in place, and the right attitude, we go on and search the matter out. Teachableness is manifested in being willing to engage and submit our hearts to the Word of God and be instructed based on the Word. If someone is unwilling to go through the process of discussion, there is an unteachableness. This unwillingness is an objective, outward behavior; there is no question about it. We can see the difference between more and less basic when we understand what is more basic. It does not have to be hard to apply the Word of God, just as it is not hard to know what is clear. This is Jesus' teaching. What a master He is. We can look to Him for our instruction.

6

THE SERMON ON THE MOUNT
Jesus' Teaching on Attitude, Law, and the Kingdom

PART IV

Matthew 7:7–29

⁷Ask and it will be given to you; seek and you will find; knock and the door will be opened to you. ⁸For everyone who asks receives; the one who seeks finds; and to the one who knocks, the door will be opened.

⁹Which of you, if your son asks for bread, will give him a stone? ¹⁰Or if he asks for a fish, will give him a snake? ¹¹If you, then, though you are evil, know how to give good gifts to your children, how much more will your Father in heaven give good gifts to those who ask him! ¹²So in everything, do to others what you would have them do to you, for this sums up the Law and the Prophets.

¹³Enter through the narrow gate. For wide is the gate and broad is the road that leads to destruction, and many enter through it. ¹⁴But small is the gate and narrow the road that leads to life, and only a few find it.

¹⁵Watch out for false prophets. They come to you in sheep's clothing, but inwardly they are ferocious wolves. ¹⁶By their fruit you will recognize them. Do people pick grapes from thornbushes, or figs from thistles? ¹⁷Likewise, every good tree bears good fruit, but a bad tree bears bad fruit. ¹⁸A good tree cannot bear bad fruit, and a bad tree cannot bear good fruit. ¹⁹Every tree that does not bear good fruit is cut down and thrown into the fire. ²⁰Thus, by their fruit you will recognize them.

²¹Not everyone who says to me, "Lord, Lord," will enter the kingdom of heaven, but only the one who does the will of my Father who is in heaven. ²²Many will say to me on that day, "Lord, Lord, did we not prophesy in your name and in your name drive out demons and in your name perform many miracles?" ²³Then I will tell them plainly, "I never knew you. Away from me, you evildoers!"

²⁴Therefore everyone who hears these words of mine and puts them into practice is like a wise man who built his house on the rock. ²⁵The rain came down, the streams rose, and the winds blew and beat against that house; yet it did not fall, because it had its foundation on the rock. ²⁶But everyone who hears these words of mine and does not put them into practice is like a foolish man who built his house on sand. ²⁷The rain came down, the streams rose, and the winds blew and beat against that house, and it fell with a great crash.

²⁸When Jesus had finished saying these things, the crowds were amazed at his teaching, ²⁹because he taught as one who had authority, and not as their teachers of the law.

INTRODUCTION

W E ARE CONTINUING ON THE SERMON ON the Mount and our Lord's teaching. This is what our Lord wants us to know about His kingdom and how it will come about. We see that He is teaching His disciples in a way different from the teachers of His day, and at the end of the teaching, the people notice that He teaches as one who has authority.[1] This authority manifests in the insight, clarity, and definitiveness with which He speaks. It is not the hedging and quoting of this or that opinion, but speaking directly to the law because it is clear, and He is speaking that Word.

We want to finish up this section as we look at the last four parts. Jesus encourages us to ask, seek, and knock,[2] He speaks the truth about the narrow and wide gates,[3] He speaks about the tree and the fruit—to be watching out for false prophets,[4] and then He speaks about the

---

1. *Matthew 7:29.*
2. *Matthew 7:7–12.*
3. *Matthew 7:13–14.*
4. *Matthew 7:15–23.*

wise and foolish builders.[5] Remember, we seek to avoid disobeying the law, which can occur in two ways. One is neglecting the law, which is called antinomianism. This is having a very relaxed attitude, being nonchalant, and not caring. The other seems to have a great deal of zeal for the law but is likewise missing it, because it is looking at particular details of the law, and summing up the law in some of these details—many of which are distorted because the basic principle is not in place.

We have spoken about principle and practice, and we have said that if we understand the principle, we will know the practice. The Lord wants us to know Him, and through obeying this law, we come to live in a way—individually and together—so that we come to know Him and glorify Him.

THE SUPPLY OF THE KINGDOM

Ask, Seek, and Knock: Actively Seeking Versus NARD[6]

The passage we begin with today is Matthew 7:7—ask, seek, and knock. This has been a source of a great deal of perplexity. We are greatly encouraged to ask, seek, and knock, yet we have come asking, seeking, and knocking and we have found ourselves with the door closed in our faces. Yet we are assured that God will give us the things for which we ask and seek, that He will grant that for which we are knocking, and that the door will be opened. Sometimes, we wonder what more we can do. We have been asking for so long, and we have been knocking. We may ask, 'Do we have to break down heaven's doors to get this?' The answer is no, absolutely not. Yes, there is a perplexity, and yes, we can understand the perplexity in this very passage. We are assured that those who seek will find, for those who knock the door will be opened, and everyone who asks receives. The Lord explains this, and this explanation gives us the key to understanding. He says:

> Which of you, if his son asks for bread, will give him a stone? Or if he asks for a fish, will give him a snake? If you, then, though

---

5. *Matthew 7:24–27.*

6. NARD is an acronym for neglecting, avoiding, resisting, and denying reason in the face of what is clear about God and man, and good and evil. Gangadean, *Philosophical Foundation*, 4, 317.

you are evil, know how to give good gifts to your children, how much more will your Father in heaven give good gifts to those who ask him! (vv. 9–11).

The clue to understanding our perplexity is in understanding something very close to us and, therefore, should not perplex us. That is, our fathers give us good gifts. They do, and yet *we are evil*—children and fathers alike. Even when we are evil, we still give gifts in this way, and we do not give bad things to children. We do not give a snake when they ask for fish, and we do not mock our children by giving them stones instead of bread, and yet we are evil. In those two pieces put together, we can see the answer to our perplexity and, therefore, be all the more encouraged to ask the Lord and seek and knock.

Think about some of the things we ask for. Usually, in the early stages of life, the first thing we ask for is a car. Every 15-year-old knows that the first thing you want is a car, especially a certain kind of car. Guys want a certain kind of car; sometimes girls will say, 'Any car, just a car.' Then, after that, we want a special friend. A girlfriend or a boyfriend—to go with the car, of course. We sometimes see a certain one and say, 'That's the one!' It is like Romeo; he sees Juliet and says, 'That's the one!' So we see one and have our heart set on that person and say, 'That's the one for me.' Not only do we have the car and the spouse, but of course we need a house. Then we pray for a job to support the house, car, and spouse. Very natural development, is it not? 'I need a job, Lord; please provide a job.' Then we desire children. Then we pray for all kinds of things for the children such as well-being and care. Then we want world peace and harmony to bring up our children and for everything to be great. Then, after that, we pray for something more. We need something more—and that is *meaning*. Now we have to go back and ask about the meaning of the car and the spouse and the house and all of it. We begin to say, 'You know, I did not know what I was asking for.' We ask for things without understanding. Our earthly father, if we ask for bread, does not give us a stone, and neither will our Heavenly Father.

Analogy of Human Parent-Child Relation

God knows what it is we really need, and He knows the meaning of it. He sees beyond our concerns and He sees what we really need and will give it to us. We know that even earthly fathers do not give their children everything they ask. If they did, they would not be good fathers. Hebrews 12:10 says, "Our fathers disciplined us for a little while as they thought best." Think about some Christmas present you wanted, and you did not get it one year, or another year, or a third year, and then after waiting, you got it. How precious that was! How much more appreciated it was when you were ready for it. Sometimes, it is a readiness factor. You are not supposed to get a BB gun when you are nine years old. "You'll shoot your eye out."[7] Now, when you are 13, maybe you are ready. We ask for things that seem to be good but do not know what we are asking. Sometimes, after a while, we come to say, 'You know, if we had gotten what we had asked for, that would have been a snake.' That would have been a rock, not bread. It was not the real thing.

Double-Minded, Inconsistent, and Without Means—Knowing God Without Holiness

We are double-minded. Sometimes we ask for things, and we ask for the end without the means. We ask to be godly but not to have patience. We ask to be godly but not to put away our self-life. We ask to see God but not to be holy. God cannot make a square-circle, remember? It is not possible. God cannot reveal Himself to us without holiness. That is also impossible. Without holiness, no one shall see the Lord.[8] Holiness involves devotion to God. Holiness involves things being taken away from us, stripping us, that we might see God. We know that our Heavenly Father—in contrast to our earthly fathers who disciplined us as they saw fit with their *limited view* of the good—sees what the *real* good is, and would want the good for us, and would not give us a stone in place of bread, or a serpent in place of a fish. If this is true of our earthly parents, how much more our Heavenly Father? Yet, we, as earthly parents, are often self-indulgent toward our children. We

---

7. Jean Shepherd, *A Christmas Story*, Directed by Bob Clark (1983, Warner Bros.).

8. *Hebrews 12:14.*

indulge them, and we feed their self-life. We do not give them what is truly good for them, and we give them what we believe—in *our* self-life—is good for them. Our Heavenly Father will give us what is truly good. In this example, as we think about it, we should be encouraged to know that our Heavenly Father will indeed give us what is good.

Attitude: Beatitudes, the Lord's Prayer, and Earlier Teachings

We know from the earlier passages that the Lord taught us what our attitude is to be. As we come before God with that attitude—poor in spirit, mourning, hungry and thirsting for righteousness[9]—and following the Lord's Prayer—hallowed be thy name, thy kingdom come[10]—we ask for particular things in that context. Above all else, we ask that we might know Him, that we might have life and have it more abundantly.[11] The Lord knows that sometimes we take signs and symbols of things for the reality, or appearance for reality, and He will say, 'I will not give you a stone; I will give you true bread.'

As we look at the earlier teaching in this section, we remember what we spoke about last time: treasures in heaven, not to worry, but to seek first the kingdom of God, and not to seek the praise of men.[12] We often seek to be praised by men, to feel good about ourselves, or to be honored by men. We sometimes choose the person we seek to marry based on what others may think about this person, not what God thinks about this person. 'Will others be happy for me?' We may have a vain conception of things. God does not give us what we immediately ask for but will give us what is good. We often ask in double-minded ways and in inconsistent ways, and the Lord sorts this out and gives us what is truly good as we pray according to His teaching.

Summary of the Law: Do Unto Others as You Would Have Them Do Unto You (From Incompleteness to Fullness)

Interestingly, in contrast to a lot of things that have been said before—*do not, do not, do not*—in chapter 7, He says *do*. This is bringing this

---

9. *Matthew 5:1–12.*
10. *Matthew 6:9–13.*
11. *John 10:10* KJV.
12. *Matthew 6:19–34.*

section to a close: He speaks about what we should *do*. In summary of all that has gone before, He says, **"So in everything, do to others what you would have them do to you, for this sums up the Law and the Prophets"** (v. 12). The law of God can be spelled out in great detail, but the basic principle is: Love your neighbor as yourself, even love your enemies, and do unto others as you would have others do unto you. If we think in these terms, so much can be seen clearly and easily. If we thought we were incomplete and really lacking, we would want someone to be patient with us and to bring the Word of God in a way that edifies us. If we see someone lacking, remember what we want for ourselves. Let us say this other person is intellectually lacking; as we used the term last week, they are an intellectual 'yahoo.' That means, 'totally out of it,' or an emotional klutz, or an emotional yahoo. In terms of their practical life, perhaps they are really messing it up; they do not have righteousness; they are incomplete. How would you want to be dealt with? Deal with this person that way. Bring the Word of God, by the grace of God, to them. Recognize that you are incomplete, that we are all incomplete, and we need to grow. If you have any doubts about this, read the Book of Job and respond to others, acknowledging that we all come short. Let there not be divisions, disregard of others, perhaps oppression of individuals, or putting a person aside, excluding them, but learn to love them. This is the law of God—the law of God's kingdom.

We are made in His image, and God wants us to have what it takes. He wants us to learn to love Him with our whole heart, love our neighbor as ourselves, and go through the process of wanting to learn to love. This is where we said that sometimes we ask for things in a double-minded or inconsistent way. We want to learn to love but not to be patient, and the first rule of love, because of the reality of sin in the world, is that love is patient:

> Love is patient, love is kind. It does not envy, it does not boast, it is not proud. It is not rude, it is not self-seeking, it is not easily angered, it keeps no record of wrongs. Love does not delight in evil but rejoices with the truth. It always protects, always trusts, always hopes, always perseveres. Love never fails (1 Cor. 13:4–8a).

It is part of our self-centered life to say, 'I am better than you,' rather than seeing we are pressing on toward a goal *together*. We should say, 'Lord, make me a more loving person.' We will have to go through some stripping, but we should keep asking for this. 'Lord, uphold me as I go through this process—I know not what—as you make me conform to the Lord Jesus Christ and His image.' Time and again, the Lord will say, "Follow me." It is amazing just to notice this, which is one of the reasons I read the *Call to Worship* this morning from Matthew 11:29: "Take my yoke upon you and learn from me, for I am gentle and humble in heart, and you will find rest for your souls." Jesus wants us to follow Him.

He did not just point and say, 'Go there,' He said, 'Follow me.' This is very personal, very definite. He is leading the way; He is ahead of us. "Greater love has no one than this, that he lay down his life for his friends" (Jn. 15:13). He laid down His life for us. He is washing our feet; He said, "Now that I, your Lord and Teacher, have washed your feet, you also should wash one another's feet. I have set you an example that you should do as I have done for you" (Jn. 13:14–15). Ultimately, we are praying for life—to know Him, to be loving as He is loving, to be kind, just, patient, and righteous as He is. This is what our Lord is calling us to do.

We said there is a puzzle in this section. I hope that the puzzle has come together in terms of how we are to ask. We tend to ask for ends without means; we ask for two things simultaneously that are contradictory. God will not give us what appears to be good but what really is good. There are many things that appear to us to be good, but they are not good. We may be asking for a stone and not realize it. The Lord may hold back things for some time. Amy Carmichael was a missionary to India—the young woman from England who wanted blue eyes, but she had brown. She could not understand why God did not give her blue eyes. That would not have been such a hard and bad thing. But you know, there are no blue eyes in India, and that is where the Lord called her. Her brown eyes were part of how she connected with the people of India. It took a while for her to see this, but the Lord knew what she needed. We have to sort through our desires to bring them back to what the Lord is teaching us to desire.

If I were to put it negatively, we should *never* say God does not answer our prayer, or that God has yet to answer our prayer—unless we are prepared to say what we were praying for was not good. This statement is a necessarily true statement: **"For everyone who asks receives; the one who seeks finds; and to the one who knocks, the door will be opened"** (v. 8). Would you like God to give you a lot of money? Would you like to win the lottery? Who has not thought of this? This would seem to solve so many problems. It surely would—and multiply a lot more than it solved. If the Lord does not give you the lottery, it is because He knows what is good for you. We should bless the name of the Lord. We should learn to define the good as God defines it—as knowing Him and making Him known. We might say, 'Yes, that is great, but I would also like this other thing.' Then I would suggest that we have not yet known Him, because there is a satisfaction that comes in knowing God, and it does not come in any other way. Anyone who truly has this will be satisfied. We should not say, 'God does not hear and answer our prayers.' If you do, I will argue with you about it. I will stay here after church today and argue that point with you.

THE GATE OF THE KINGDOM

Narrow and Wide Gate

In exhorting us to walk in His way, the Lord says, **"Enter through the narrow gate. For wide is the gate and broad is the road that leads to destruction, and many enter through it. But small is the gate and narrow the road that leads to life, and only a few find it"** (vv. 13–14). Remember, we are talking about life and what life is. "One thing I ask of the LORD, this only do I seek: that I may dwell in the house of the LORD all the days of my life, to gaze upon the beauty of the LORD and to seek him in his temple" (Ps. 27:4). I think, in fact, many of us may speak these words, but we do not possess the reality. Sometimes, we have to get into difficulty and call upon the Lord, and the Lord reveals Himself in the midst of our difficulty before we begin to say, 'Yes, Lord.' What we are after is *life*, and there is a small gate, and the road is narrow **"that leads to life, and only a few find it."**

Sanctification: Stripping of the Self-Life

This passage, too, has been puzzling in a number of ways. If we look at other Scripture verses, we will see that it does not have to be puzzling.

We know of the eye of the needle, which our Lord spoke about: "It is easier for a camel to go through the eye of a needle than for a rich man to enter the kingdom of God" (Matt. 19:24). The rich man has put his trust in his riches rather than in God. He thinks he has these riches in his hands and that he can control things. He trusts in himself and so he has got things under control. This is not true. Rather, we should see it is in the hand of God, and it is much better that it is in the hand of God than in mine. God knows what I need, how much I need, how to give it, and that it will work together for my good. There is a kind of difficulty in going through the eye of a needle—it involves the stripping of the self-life. The one who seeks to save his life in his own way will lose it.[13] This is the one who does not take up his cross daily and "follow me."

The 'daily' reference to taking up the cross is in Luke 9:23: "If anyone would come after me, he must deny himself and take up his cross daily and follow me." Notice this reference to "follow me." In John 21:19, Jesus says to Peter, "Follow me!" Peter is looking at Jesus, and then he gets his eyes off Jesus. Jesus almost has to take Peter by his chin and turn his head and say, 'No, follow me, look here.' Peter says, "Lord, what about him?" Jesus says, 'What about him? Follow me. Keep your eyes on me.'[14]

In Matthew 10:38, He says, "Whoever does not take up their cross and follow me is not worthy of me." Now, that taking up the cross is the small gate and the narrow way. What the cross is doing is stripping us of all of the self-life that we carry with us. All of our equipment, our defense systems, and we just lug it around; we need a Hummer to take it all with us. That is, a Hummer pulling a big trailer behind us—in case you are wondering. We have to be stripped of all this, as Job, before the Lord, was stripped. 'I am in your hands, Lord, and do with me as you please. Not my will, but your will be done.'

There are many, many forms of self-life. There is envy that we have of one another, competition, and ego; and if that goes on, we cannot enter into the fullness of the kingdom. We have to be stripped of this. Without holiness, no one shall see the Lord.[15] This is a progressing

---

13. *Matthew 16:25.*

14. *John 21:20–22.*

15. *Hebrews 12:14.*

sanctification, by the Holy Spirit, crucifying the flesh with its affections and its lusts.[16] We must crucify all the self-life and the self-image,
which is a big thing. We like to think of ourselves in a certain way and
dress accordingly. I recall how I dressed; it was not a conscious decision,
but I did dress in a certain way. I aimed to convey a certain aspect of
who I am, not necessarily with deliberate intention, but it was simply
reflecting who I am. Sometimes, we have a sense of identity, and part
of what goes with that might be a PhD from a certain institution. We
might think that will fit nicely with our self-image. So we trek off to San
Francisco or to go to Berkeley. We construct a certain life for ourselves:
A self-image, identity, the praise of men who we think are important,
and what group we want to belong to. We have to be stripped of this.
If necessary, we have to hang out with the shepherds who went to see
Jesus. They were at the bottom of society; they were the 'nobodies.'
Not that we are exalting nobodies as if they are somebodies, but they
had no repute in society. They were men made in the image of God
who were hungry for God and to whom God chose to speak and reveal
Himself, to bring them to see the babe, our Lord Jesus.

Historical Context: Luke 13:22–30

There is a way that is broad and easy, and it is what comes natural to
the self-life. The puzzle comes in if we think that few will find the narrow way and that few will come into the kingdom of God. We will see
it explained explicitly in Luke 13. Before Jesus speaks about entering
through the narrow door, He gives the context in verse 18:

> Then Jesus asked, "What is the kingdom of God like? What shall
> I compare it to? It is like a mustard seed, which a man took and
> planted in his garden. It grew and became a tree, and the birds of
> the air perched in its branches." Again he asked, "What shall I com-
> pare the kingdom of God to? It is like yeast that a woman took and
> mixed into a large amount of flour until it worked all through the
> dough" (Lk. 13:18–21).

What do these two parables teach us? The kingdom of God starts *small*,
grows irresistibly to its *fullness* and *completeness*, and affects everything.

---

16. *Galatians 5:24* KJV.

The context of this teaching is that "Jesus went through the towns and villages, teaching as he made his way to Jerusalem" (Lk. 13:22). This is His last and final trip to Jerusalem. "Someone asked him, 'Lord, are only a few people going to be saved?' He said to them, 'Make every effort to enter through the narrow door, because many, I tell you, will try to enter and will not be able to'" (Lk. 13:23–24). This passage and others are parallel to, "**Lord, Lord, did we not prophesy in your name . . .**" (v. 22). Jesus is going up to Jerusalem, He is told that Herod wants to kill Him, and He says that surely no prophet can die outside of Jerusalem.[17] We will return to this when He speaks about the false prophets and weeps over Jerusalem. Then He says,

> There will be weeping there, and gnashing of teeth, when you see Abraham, Isaac and Jacob and all the prophets in the kingdom of God, but you yourselves thrown out. People will come from east and west and north and south, and will take their places at the feast in the kingdom of God. Indeed there are those who are last who will be first, and first who will be last (Lk. 13:28–30).

The context in which this occurs in Luke tells us that the Lord expects the kingdom to start small and grow to its fullness. Many will come from the east and the west, but these (the Jews) herein to whom the kingdom belongs, in terms of covenant privilege, will not receive it. Few of the Jewish people are coming in. The people were expecting many of the Jewish people—then, at that time—to come in. They expected the kingdom to appear all at once. He says, "**and only a few find it**" (v. 14b), but that is not a permanent few. The kingdom of God will not always stay small; it is expected to grow. It was a *specific historical few*, but the principle still holds. "**Broad is the road that leads to destruction**" (v. 13b). Few there are, in this situation, that will find the narrow road. People were saying, 'We are expecting this kingdom to come all of a sudden and be big, and Lord, there are just a few people, just a rag-tag bunch of guys going up with you to Jerusalem. What is the deal here?' He says, 'Do not keep your eyes on that. *You* follow me. *You* do everything you can to enter into the kingdom. Do not be looking around you and getting assurance from what the multitude is doing.'

---

17. *Luke 13:33.*

This teaching was given in Luke in that context, and it is repeated in Matthew. This has commonly been taken out of the overall biblical context and thought to be a permanent few rather than a specific historical few. But we showed otherwise from the parables and in the statement about many coming from the east and west, from north and south, and sitting down with Abraham, Isaac, and Jacob. We are to understand the parables of the kingdom growing to its fullness and many coming. We have reason to believe that Christ will accomplish His work and the nations will be converted to Him.[18] Whether there are many or few, if we are going to enter into the kingdom of God, we must put aside our self-life. There are things that may block us from entering.

I was told about someone who used to be a member here, that when they were told to pray, they said, 'God does not answer prayer.' God did not answer that particular person's prayer the way they wanted, but God had better things for them. They think that God did not want to answer the prayer, so it established them in falsehood and failure to see what is clear and take responsibility for it. They try to explain it away and say, 'Because of all my psychological background and condition, you cannot expect me to see certain things.' But since we are expected to see what is clear, we cannot use that as an excuse.[19] We cannot continue to hold things against people rather than see that God has used that in our lives for His glory. We should not hold up our hurt that we are not letting go of, which hinders us from walking in through the narrow gate in repentance.

God cannot answer contradictory prayers. He will not answer prayers that are harmful to us, though we may think it is good. He certainly does not want to answer prayers that are self-indulgent prayers. He wants life for us: the knowledge of God. He wants holiness, without which no one shall see the Lord.[20] He wants all that goes into holiness, which involves taking up our cross daily and following Him.[21] This includes being stripped of all those things that are the source of our desires and pleasures from our old way of life, those habits, the baggage that we carry, that we tend to fall into so quickly, so easily. We cannot think

---

18. Gangadean, "Paper No. 104: Eschatology (Twelve Points)," in *The Logos Papers*, 539–544.
19. *Romans 1:18–20.*
20. *Hebrews 12:14.*
21. *Luke 9:23.*

that those things are the good and that God should allow us to continue to have that kind of pleasure. All the pleasures we want outside of the knowledge of God are not lasting, and we cannot expect God to continue to indulge us and give us that pleasure again and again. Then how will the pleasure come from knowing God? Enter through the narrow gate; ask, seek, and knock; it will be opened to you. God has what is truly good for us. It may take a while for us to see this.

THE ENEMIES OF THE KINGDOM:
False Prophets—Self-Life Seducers

Opposed to True Teaching: Outward Authority Without Integrity

Jesus warns us about false prophets. False prophets are those who operate out of the self-life and will seduce people, by the words they speak, to walk in the way of self. Jesus is anticipating the coming conflict in the spiritual war between the truth and falsehood, between His teaching and what has been going on in Jerusalem. In Luke 13:33–34, on His way up to Jerusalem, Jesus said, "for surely no prophet can die outside Jerusalem! Jerusalem, Jerusalem, you who kill the prophets and stone those sent to you." And in Matthew 23, He will pronounce judgment in seven woes on the leaders with the underlying charge of hypocrisy. Jerusalem is the city where the temple and priesthood are, and the leaders have not been leading according to the Word of God. He must challenge their false teaching if He is a true prophet. What will the false prophets do who come to us in sheep's clothing? **"Watch out for false prophets. They come to you in sheep's clothing, but inwardly they are ferocious wolves"** (v. 15).

What is it like to come in sheep's clothing? It means that one could be the high priest in Jerusalem, fail to see what is truly of God, and bring about the crucifixion of Jesus. This is an example of a wolf in sheep's clothing. It was true there, and it has always been true throughout the history of the Church. It was true when the Roman Pontiff persecuted those who held to the true faith in the Reformation. It has been true of the pope—and we are not saying this of every one, but certainly, if a high priest in Jerusalem can do it, do you think the pope cannot do it? We are to watch for wolves in sheep's clothing.

This principle extends beyond the Catholic Church to others who are leaders. Some within Presbyterianism may give up on the deity of Christ. Some bishops may seek to ordain homosexuals and oppose us fiercely if we object. There are all kinds and degrees of this, all the way down the line, present in every division in Christendom. Some lead in a branch of the church that has divided from the mainline Historic Christianity for a distinctive that is not scriptural. If you oppose that person, they will fiercely resist you—they are ferocious wolves. Now, we want to be careful in judging whether these people are believers or not, but they will fiercely oppose when their leadership position is being called into question by true teaching.

The doctrine of clarity has caused many people to become fierce in their opposition. They are quite nice otherwise, but when we press on this point, then we see the opposition begin to emerge. It is not possible for a prophet to die outside of Jerusalem. It is not possible for someone who is bringing some greater measure of the Word of God not to be opposed by those who are in positions of authority but not bringing that Word. It is not possible for that not to happen. It will happen. When you speak the truth, those in positions of authority who are not living according to the truth will oppose you, and we are warned about this. We have to make some distinction between those who are non-believers and oppose and those who are brothers and op-pose. Brothers in Christ may oppose. We are to watch out for this, and the Lord instructs us how to watch.

False Prophets Do Not Speak in the Name of God

The false prophets do not speak the truth concerning the name of God. Let us ask someone to explain what sin is, so as to speak truly about the justice of God. Let us ask someone to explain the punishment of sin and see if they are speaking according to the nature of God as infinitely just—then we begin to see their lack of understanding surface. The divi-sions in the Church exist because we do not speak in the name of God.

We want to distinguish between a false prophet *per se* and a person who is teaching falsely, or teaching in limited ways, and when pressed, digging in on that limited way, and thereby begin to teach falsely. They come in sheep's clothing. They appear to be in positions of righteous-ness and innocence. We know how fierce this can be. All the challenges that exist, all the differences in the Church, are a result of a false view of God—every last one.[22] The Arminian-Calvinist divide centers upon the sovereignty of God, the goodness of God, the power of God, and whether it is that God is the one that wholly brings us out of death and into life. The Arminian position holds to a false view of God.[23] So do the charismatics, who have a view of healing that rests on assumptions about natural evil, divine goodness, what Christ's miracles were about, and what the love of God is about in relation to natural evil and suffering. We can go down the line and point out the divisions. The Anabaptists are divided from mainline Christendom on the question of baptism applied to infants. This point goes back to the unity of the Old and the New Testaments. The Old Testament *is* the covenant of grace, and the sign of the sacraments were applied to children. Circumcision was applied to children, that *is* the covenant of grace.[24]

The law of God is given to us so that we might live according to it. It is not given to us to be justified, but that we may come into the blessing and fullness of life.[25] Antinomianism has come into the Church by a distortion of Romans 6:14: "For sin shall no longer be your master, because you are not under law, but under grace." These words are used and they are misunderstood. And so there is false teaching. The Lord said, "For I tell you that unless your righteousness surpasses that of the Pharisees and the teachers of the law, you will certainly not enter the kingdom of heaven" (Matt. 5:20). There is false prophecy, false teaching, false declaration, and not speaking in the name of God. Every division in the Church can be traced back to this. We can identify the mainline historical tradition and recognize that it has to continue its work. The Lord warns us against falsehood.

We are going to push this a bit further—do you know why? Because we are long after the Westminster Confession of Faith, which ended in 1648, and it is now 2004. It has been about 356 years since the Confession was written, and much has happened. There are many places where the Church was in leadership and it has been pushed

---

22. Gangadean, *Philosophical Foundation*, 185–198.

23. Gangadean, "Paper No. 18: Salvation by Grace," in *The Logos Papers*, 119–122.

24. Gangadean, "Paper No. 140: Argument for Paedobaptism," in *The Logos Papers*, 703–704; Gangadean, *The Westminster Confession*, 111–120, 291–305.

25. Gangadean, *The Westminster Catechisms*, 227–267; Gangadean, *The Westminster Confession*, 207–221; Gangadean, *Philosophical Foundation*, 171–284.

back. Some say, 'We do not need to take thoughts captive; this is our tradition, and we started this way.' Let us push this further and say that the grandmother who cannot prove the existence of God does not get a pass. There is confusion between *nice* and what is *good*. There are a lot of non-Christian grandmothers who are nice; it is not just Christian grandmothers. So an argument from *nice* is not the same as the argument from *good*. There is a lot of common grace of God, but we cannot use that as an argument. What has happened to the work of the Church over the past 350 years? What has happened to Harvard? What happened to Yale and Princeton? Would you say those works were burned, that they did not last, that it is not the fruit that God wanted? Why did it not last? It is not because it was bad in the beginning, but because it did not continue to engage the challenges that came to it, and so it was bested. Our Lord speaks about good fruit. A good tree cannot bear bad fruit. If someone has their eye clearly on the knowledge of God—the earth being filled with the knowledge of God—and they are consistent, leading to a certain degree of maturity, they will not produce bad fruit. We will produce fruit that will last. If His Word abides in us, and we abide in Him, we will bear fruit.[26] If not, the consequence is that our works will be burned.[27]

The question is, what expectations should we have? Think about it: there are many who have come to the Lord. Some will come before the Lord and know that they have denied the existence of God; they spoke what is false about God and were wrong. But some will come, and the Lord will say, **"I never knew you. Away from me, you evildoers!"** (v. 23b). Many people believe they sincerely serve God. Saul of Tarsus believed it, and he was not really serving God.[28] I am sure many of the mullahs[29] sincerely believe they are serving God, but they have denied salvation through Christ, they have denied the need for atonement, and they have no basis to stand before God because God's mercy does not set aside His justice; mercy satisfies justice. Then there are many who

---

26. *John 15:5–8.*

27. *1 Corinthians 3:12–15.*

28. *1 Timothy 1:13.*

29. Mullah: an educated Muslim trained in religious law and doctrine and usually holding an official post.

profess to be Christians, who think that they will certainly be saved without seeking to conform to the will of God.

> Many will say to me on that day, "Lord, Lord, did we not prophe-sy in your name and in your name drive out demons and perform many miracles?" Then I will tell them plainly, "I never knew you. Away from me, you evildoers!" (vv. 22–23).

Do you imagine that Mormons, who deny God is the Creator and say that souls are eternal, that, "As man is, God once was; as God is, man may become,"[30] are accepted before God? Do we think this is a small, tiny, little mistake, and God will just say, 'Hey, no big deal, come on in.' This is someone who sincerely believes but has not seen the op-eration of God's grace; they have not been regenerated. They will say, 'Didn't we go to Argentina to prophesy in your name and do many things? Look at all these missions we went on and all this money we have given.' Be aware of false prophets. False prophets do not speak in the name of God; a true prophet does and *must* speak in the name of God—and the name of God is according to what is clear from general revelation and what is revealed in Scripture. There can be self-decep-tion here, and the Lord will say, **"Away from me."**

THE WISDOM OF THE KINGDOM

The Wise and Foolish Builders: Understanding and Putting into Practice

The section on the wise and foolish builders[31] sums up all Jesus has said. The wise ones are those who hear the Word, understand it, and bear fruit.[32] They seek, understand, obey, put it into practice, and are unlike hypocrites who hear and do not put it into practice. Jesus said, "My mother and brothers are those who hear God's word and put it into practice" (Lk. 8:21). They are not those who just hear the Word

---

30. Anthony A. Hoekema, *The Four Major Cults: Christian Science, Jehovah's Witnesses, Mor-monism, Seventh–Day Adventism* (Grand Rapids: William B. Eerdmans Publishing Com-pany, 1986), 39.

31. *Matthew 7:24–29.*

32. *Matthew 13:22–23.*

of God. James says, "Do not merely listen to the word, and so deceive yourselves. Do what it says" (Jas. 1:22). What is this Word? If we were to sum it up, we would put it this way: "Love the Lord your God with all your heart and with all your soul and with all your mind and with all your strength . . . Love your neighbor as yourself" (Mk. 12:30–31a). We could also sum it up this way: "Man's chief end is to glorify God and to enjoy him forever" (SCQ. 1). To glorify God is to come to see His glory, to gaze on His glory, to come to know Him, and to make Him known in a life of witness.

We can ask ourselves as a test of whether we are obeying: Are we coming to know God, making God known, and enjoying Him forever? Is our joy—even though the Lord may give us many other things to enjoy—is our *real* joy in knowing God? Is this what we long for at the end of the day? If this is the case, then we are knowing and doing the Word of God. Apply this test to the enjoyment of God. Apply this test to bearing fruit. Are others coming to know God as He is? Especially in light of all the challenges that exist in the world and all the false doctrines that are the source of our division—have we been challenged by these to come back and to see God as He is, to know God and glorify Him accordingly, and to witness? Are we bearing fruit in this way? Are we overcoming the divisions based on this failure to know and acknowledge God as He is? Are we enjoying Him as He is?

The wise builders are the ones who understand the law, the principles of the law, what the treasure is, what life is, and put it into practice. They give themselves to pursuing the good and produce fruit accordingly. The foolish builders are those who hear the Word of God but do not understand it; they do not seek to deal with divisions and to bring others to learn and grow in the Lord. They are not obeying in this regard. They may even utter the words, "Man's chief end is to glorify God, and to enjoy him forever."[33] We should ask: What does that mean? We had a discussion this Friday at the Reformed Reading Group about premillennialism and its implications. If we are all going to get to heaven in the end, what is the point of seeking diligently? What is the view of the good? As against understanding that *creation is revelation*; it is *full and clear*; and we know this revelation *through the*

---

33. *The Shorter Catechism Question 1.*

work of dominion.[34] Those who have died and gone on are waiting for the work of dominion to be completed. That this work will be completed, filling the earth with the knowledge of God, is our enjoyment. This is a very different view from premillennialism.[35] We are not saying that persons who are pre-mil are not saved—not at all. There are many who may put us to shame in many ways in terms of their walk. Nevertheless, we said that this is our test. Are we bearing fruit that will last, or will it be burned in the fire?

Jesus spoke these words, and the people understood something, and they recognized He was speaking with insight and authority—those two go together. He spoke clearly and to the point. He could speak in this way: "Follow me." This is very personal. He is leading, guiding, and directing in a very personal way. Let us keep our eyes on our Lord Jesus and follow Him, who has taught us the Word of God.

---

34. Gangadean, *On Natural and Revealed Theology,* 9–32; Gangadean, *The Westminster Catechisms,* 321–325; Gangadean, *The Westminster Confession,* 1–13; Gangadean, "Paper No. 106: The Good and Heaven," 547–556; "Paper No. 117: Knowing and Making God Known," in *The Logos Papers,* 599–601.

35. Gangadean, "Paper No. 49: Eschatology (FAQ)," 271–274; "Paper No. 104: Eschatology (Twelve Points)," 539–544; "Paper No. 118: Eschatology (Seven Points)," 603–607; "Paper No. 119: Pauline Eschatology," in *The Logos Papers,* 609–610.

7

THE AUTHORITY OF JESUS
Revealed in His Word and Works

Matthew 8:1–34, 9:1–17

8:1When Jesus came down from the mountainside, large crowds followed him. 2A man with leprosy came and knelt before him and said, "Lord, if you are willing, you can make me clean."

3Jesus reached out his hand and touched the man. "I am willing," he said. "Be clean!" Immediately he was cleansed of his leprosy. 4Then Jesus said to him, "See that you don't tell anyone. But go, show yourself to the priest and offer the gift Moses commanded, as a testimony to them."

5When Jesus had entered Capernaum, a centurion came to him, asking for help. 6"Lord," he said, "my servant lies at home paralyzed, suffering terribly."

7Jesus said to him, "Shall I come and heal him?"

8The centurion replied, "Lord, I do not deserve to have you come under my roof. But just say the word, and my servant will be healed. 9For I myself am a man under authority, with soldiers under me. I tell this one, 'Go,' and he goes; and that one, 'Come,' and he comes. I say to my servant, 'Do this,' and he does it."

10When Jesus heard this, he was amazed and said to those following him, "Truly I tell you, I have not found anyone in Israel with such great faith. 11I say to you that many will come from the east and the west, and will take their places at the feast with Abraham, Isaac and Jacob in the kingdom of heaven. 12But the subjects of the kingdom will be thrown outside, into the darkness, where there will be weeping and gnashing of teeth."

13Then Jesus said to the centurion, "Go! Let it be done just as you believed it would." And his servant was healed at that moment.

14When Jesus came into Peter's house, he saw Peter's mother-in-law lying in bed with a fever. 15He touched her hand and the fever left her, and she got up and began to wait on him.

16When evening came, many who were demon-possessed were brought to him, and he drove out the spirits with a word and healed all the sick. 17This was to fulfill what was spoken through the prophet Isaiah:

"He took up our infirmities
    and bore our diseases."

18When Jesus saw the crowd around him, he gave orders to cross to the other side of the lake. 19Then a teacher of the law came to him and said, "Teacher, I will follow you wherever you go."

20Jesus replied, "Foxes have dens and birds have nests, but the Son of Man has no place to lay his head."

21Another disciple said to him, "Lord, first let me go and bury my father."

22But Jesus told him, "Follow me, and let the dead bury their own dead."

23Then he got into the boat and his disciples followed him. 24Suddenly a furious storm came up on the lake, so that the waves swept over the boat. But Jesus was sleeping. 25The disciples went and woke him, saying, "Lord, save us! We're going to drown!"

26He replied, "You of little faith, why are you so afraid?" Then he got up and rebuked the winds and the waves, and it was completely calm.

27The men were amazed and asked, "What kind of man is this? Even the winds and the waves obey him!"

28When he arrived at the other side in the region of the Gadarenes, two demon-possessed men coming from the tombs met him. They were so violent that no one could pass that way. 29"What do you want with us, Son of God?" they shouted. "Have you come here to torture us before the appointed time?"

30Some distance from them a large herd of pigs was feeding. 31The demons begged Jesus, "If you drive us out, send us into the herd of pigs."

32He said to them, "Go!" So they came out and went into the pigs, and the whole herd rushed down the steep bank into the lake and died in the water. 33Those tending the pigs ran off, went into the town and reported all this, including what had happened to the demon-possessed men. 34Then the whole town went out to meet Jesus. And when they saw him, they pleaded with him to leave their region.

9:1Jesus stepped into a boat, crossed over and came to his own town. 2Some men brought to him a paralyzed man, lying on a mat. When Jesus saw their faith, he said to the man, "Take heart, son; your sins are forgiven."

3At this, some of the teachers of the law said to themselves, "This fellow is blaspheming!"

4Knowing their thoughts, Jesus said, "Why do you entertain evil thoughts in your hearts? 5Which is easier: to say, 'Your sins are forgiven,' or to say, 'Get up and walk'? 6But I want you to know that the Son of Man has authority on earth to forgive sins." So he said to the paralyzed man, "Get up, take your mat and go home." 7Then the man got up and went home. 8When the crowd saw this, they were filled with awe; and they praised God, who had given such authority to man.

9As Jesus went on from there, he saw a man named Matthew sitting at the tax collector's booth. "Follow me," he told him, and Matthew got up and followed him.

10While Jesus was having dinner at Matthew's house, many tax collectors and sinners came and ate with him and his disciples. 11When the Pharisees saw this, they asked his disciples, "Why does your teacher eat with tax collectors and sinners?"

12On hearing this, Jesus said, "It is not the healthy who need a doctor, but the sick. 13But go and learn what this means: 'I desire mercy, not sacrifice.' For I have not come to call the righteous, but sinners."

14Then John's disciples came and asked him, "How is it that we and the Pharisees fast often, but your disciples do not fast?"

15Jesus answered, "How can the guests of the bridegroom mourn while he is with them? The time will come when the bridegroom will be taken from them; then they will fast.

16"No one sews a patch of unshrunk cloth on an old garment, for the patch will pull away from the garment, making the tear worse. 17Neither do people pour new wine into old wineskins. If they do, the skins will burst; the wine will run out and the wineskins will be ruined. No, they pour new wine into new wineskins, and both are preserved."

THE AUTHORITY TO HEAL:
Power over the Curse

IN THIS SERMON, WE WANT TO LOOK AT THE works of Jesus and His teaching. We are continuing in Matthew 8, and hopefully we will get up to the middle of Matthew 9. What comes through in this section, more than anything else, is the teaching of the Lord with respect to authority. The works are done in a way that *reveals* the authority of the Lord. We will have occasion to speak about authority more and more as we go along because we will see that Jesus comes into conflict with the religious leaders over the question of authority. This is a problem that recurs in the history of the Church. Those who have been in the Church take the Word for granted, drift away from it, and because they are in positions of authority, they may exercise authority against those who speak the Word of God.

The Man with Leprosy: Authority to Remove the Curse

As we go through this section and look at authority, we will see something about the extent of the authority of our Lord Jesus Christ and how it is exercised, anticipating that His authority is going to be questioned. The works that our Lord does reveal something of His glory. In this first section of Matthew 8:1–4, we see Jesus's authority over healing. A large crowd was present, and a man with leprosy came and knelt before Jesus and said, "**Lord, if you are willing, you can make me clean**" (8:2b). Notice the relation between *willing* and *can*. He believes that Jesus *can* make him whole. There is no question in his mind about this, and this reveals something of his faith in understanding who our Lord is. Remember, this man has leprosy and is unclean. We do not know how the Lord has been speaking to his heart, but it is enough to bring him to kneel before the Lord Jesus, bowing the knee, which is an appropriate position of a humble suppliant seeking the Lord's mercy.

He says, "**Lord, if you are willing, you can make me clean**." He recognizes his need for cleansing; obviously, there is so much upon him, and the Lord is the one who can do this if He is willing. "**Jesus reached out his hand and touched the man**" (8:3a). This is to be noted: He is touching a leper, which is the one thing you do not do. The leper is unclean; they are supposed to declare they are unclean and cover their mouths so there is no possible contamination—not only spiritually but physically. Jesus, in His compassion, reached out His hand and touched the man. Jesus said, "'**I am willing . . . Be clean!' Immediately he was cleansed of his leprosy**" (8:3b). Jesus shows His authority to heal this one who was leprous, and the specific way in which He showed it was to say, "I am willing."

He has the authority to do so. The leper believed that it was a matter of His mercy. He cannot make any demands upon mercy, but he can plead for mercy. He knew Jesus was abundantly able to do so; in addition, he knew that he in no way deserved this mercy. In standing before God as sinners, we can only come asking for God's grace, and God shows His graciousness in Christ's words, "I am willing . . . Be clean!" And it was so, immediately. The Word brought the universe into existence—"Let there be light" (Gen. 1:3)—and all things were made by the Word of God. This Word *incarnate* speaks again. Not only does He create all things, but He is able, by His Word, to restore all things to their original condition. He speaks again and says, "Be clean!" The power and compassion of God came together, and he was immediately cured. It was entirely supernatural, the working of God over and above and against ordinary means to bring this about, and it was immediate.[1]

The story does not end there, and what follows is an important part. Not only does Jesus show that He has the power and authority to heal and did heal him, but "Jesus said to him, 'See that you don't tell anyone. But go, show yourself to the priest and offer the gift Moses commanded, as a testimony to them'" (8:4). This is the second part of this event—He tells him not to tell anyone. This healing was not just a witness to the masses, it was a witness to those who were in authority. Jesus is acting according to the Word of God: "show yourself to the priest and offer the gift Moses commanded." He was concerned to uphold the law, and it was to give a testimony to the priest because the leper would tell the priest how he was cleansed. The priest had oversight over lepers, and was to pronounce a leper clean when God did the work of healing. The priest would pronounce the person clean in connection with an offering they present. The leper would present himself, and he would have to say the way in which the healing was done.

God, in Christ, has done this work. Jesus said, "I am willing" in the position of God. He is God, God the Son, who says, "I am willing." The man is to go and show himself to the priest and offer the gift Moses commanded as a testimony to the priests. Jesus is revealing the legitimacy of His authority to those who are in authority—to the

---

1. Gangadean, *The Westminster Confession*, 85–97.

priests. Later on, they will not hear the Word and will be opposed to Christ and will consent, from the high priest on down, to condemning Him. All that our Lord has done is going to be a witness against them on that great day.

The Faith of the Centurion: Authority Exercised in Compassion

Next, we have the account of the centurion's faith, which likewise concerns authority. Jesus came to Capernaum, and the centurion came to Him and said, **"my servant lies at home paralyzed, suffering terribly"** (8:6b). There is an element of compassion displayed in God's work. The centurion comes on behalf of his servant. He is concerned for his servant. How much more is God concerned for His servants? Notice he says that his servant is **"paralyzed, suffering terribly."** In some paralysis, you may feel nothing. In this case, it was a paralysis that caused terrible suffering. All he said was, **"Lord . . . my servant lies at home paralyzed, suffering terribly."** He does not add anything more, and we see there is a reason he did not add anything more; it is not incidental that he stopped there. He presented his case before the Lord and left it there. Jesus responds, **"I will go and heal him"** (8:7). Again, the majesty of our Lord is seen in His exercise of authority to heal: **"I will go and heal him."** And we see the compassion of our Lord, but this is a compassion that is directed toward the glory of God, *always* toward the glory of God and the advancement of His kingdom.

Some have argued for miracles and healings in a generalized way from compassion. 'Since God is compassionate, should we be seeing healings today?' Jesus did not heal everyone in His day. Many came to be healed. In some cases He healed them, and in others, He passed by. It was a witness; He was doing the work according to the Scriptures, that He would heal the people. As we go through this, we will see He *forgives* sin and *heals* the sick. He takes away the guilt of moral evil and delivers from the power of natural evil. But natural evil has a place for us in God's providence.

"Jesus said to him, 'I will go and heal him'" (8:7). The centurion reveals his position in terms of not deserving anything, even as the leper said, **"if you are willing, you can make me clean"** (8:2b). We are to cast ourselves upon the mercy of God. We come humbly, trusting and obedient, and leave it in His hands. **"The centurion replied, 'Lord, I**

THE AUTHORITY OF JESUS

do not deserve to have you come under my roof'" (8:8a). The centurion is a Gentile. It is important to note that he is in the Roman army and has about 100 soldiers under him. He has some prominence, he has a servant, and he is concerned about his servant. Here is this military man in some position of authority; he is concerned for his servant and comes to the Lord. But he comes recognizing that he does not deserve to have the Lord come into his house. Remember, Jesus touched a leper. Jesus is not supposed to go, according to the law, into the house of a Gentile. The Jews are not to become unclean, and yet Jesus said, as he said with the leper when He touched him, "**I will go and heal him.**" The question of clean and unclean aside, the centurion is quite aware that he is not deserving: "**I do not deserve to have you come under my roof.**"

The centurion has an awareness of the law, and he knows, nevertheless, that it is sufficient for the Lord to speak a word. He said, "**For I myself am a man under authority, with soldiers under me. I tell this one, 'Go,' and he goes; and that one, 'Come,' and he comes. I say to my servant, 'Do this,' and he does it**" (8:9). He recognizes in our Lord Jesus one who is in a position of authority even greater than he, and therefore all the more able to say, 'Go,' and this one will go. As a matter of fact, at the end of this chapter, we will see that is exactly what our Lord does. He said one word to the demon, "**Go!**"[2] and the demon left.

The centurion recognizes authority in general and recognizes all the more the authority of Jesus as the one to whom he comes for healing. Our Lord is wise. Our Lord knows so much, and yet these words are recorded here in Scripture: "**When Jesus heard this, he was astonished**" (8:10a). The astonishment of Jesus is that this man would say such a thing. Why would Jesus be astonished? What does it take to astonish the Lord Jesus Christ? It takes *faith—understanding.* He marvels at it. He was astonished, and He said: "**I tell you the truth, I have not found anyone in Israel with such great faith**" (8:10b).

The Lord is not speaking rhetorically or casually. He is speaking exactly: no one in Israel has such great faith. This man understood the nature of authority and who was here to exercise authority, and he acted upon his understanding, which caused our Lord Jesus to marvel. May it be the case that the Lord might marvel at our faith rather than, as He

---

2. *Matthew 8:32.*

says to His disciples later in this chapter, **"You of little faith"** (8:26a). There are interesting contrasts and combinations within this chapter. Notice the whole question of authority and the contest to come with those who are in positions of leadership.

> **I say to you that many will come from the east and the west, and will take their places at the feast with Abraham, Isaac and Jacob in the kingdom of heaven. But the subjects of the kingdom will be thrown outside, into the darkness, where there will be weeping and gnashing of teeth (8:11–12).**

The covenant people, the subjects of the kingdom, those who had the covenant privileges and blessings and took them for granted, did not pay attention to them, emptied them of meaning, presumed and saw things only externally, and did not understand.

This is a warning to *all* who are in the Church, who have been brought up in the Church, who did not come as a Gentile from outside into the Church. For those who have children born and raised in the covenant, this is a warning that we should not take it for granted. It is easy to take it for granted when raised around it all your life. And it is those who do so who are set aside. The just shall live by faith[3] and without faith, it is impossible to please God.[4] God is not a respecter of persons; He is sovereign and He worked in the centurion's heart to bring about his faith.

The Lord may leave those who have been brought up in the Church, in the covenant community, whether it is Israel long ago or the Church today (the covenant people today). He may leave those who take it for granted. None of this applies to the centurion. Yet, it could be the case that the children of the centurion, brought up in the faith, may come to take it for granted. We have to be careful about this. **"But the subjects of the kingdom will be thrown outside, into the darkness."** They will not be included. We may be in positions of privilege, sometimes positions of authority, and not understand the authority of God. **"Then Jesus said to the centurion, 'Go! It will be done just as you believed it would.' And his servant was healed at that moment"** (8:13). Jesus has the authority to heal with a word. Notice the contrast

---

3. *Romans 1:17; Galatians 3:11; Hebrews 10:38* KJV.

4. *Hebrews 11:6.*

between those who recognize His authority and those who do not, and the judgment that will come. This conflict will come to a head as we proceed through the Gospel.

Healing Many: Peter's Mother-in-Law, Demon-Possessed, and All the Sick

Next, we have the account of Jesus healing many. Peter's mother-in-law was lying in bed with a fever. One would infer from this that Peter was married. You just cannot have a mother-in-law without being married. Some would like to be married without a mother-in-law, but it does not happen that way. Roman Catholicism teaches against the marriage of the clergy, yet, the claimed head of the Roman Catholic Church—Peter—is married, and his mother-in-law was in bed with a fever. Jesus touched her hand, and the fever left her. "**When Jesus came into Peter's house, he saw Peter's mother-in-law lying in bed with a fever. He touched her hand and the fever left her, and she got up and began to wait on him**" (8:14–15). It says in Luke 4, "So he bent over her and rebuked the fever, and it left her" (Lk. 4:39a). He *rebuked* the fever, and it went away. Jesus also rebuked the wind,[5] so it does not have to be personal, but with a word of rebuke, it departed.

Again, Jesus exercises His authority: "**When evening came, many who were demon-possessed were brought to him, and he drove out the spirits with a word and healed all the sick**" (8:16). There is such a thing as demon possession. Those who have flagrantly disregarded the Word of God and exposed themselves to evil spirits by coming in contact with them in ways forbidden may be possessed today. A spirit can lead us astray, so we need to come back, repent, and ask God's forgiveness and His cleansing to be delivered from this. He drives out the demons by the Word of God, and we see that He is able to heal all the sick that were brought to Him. They kept coming to wherever He was, probably including Peter's house.

The significance of His authority is underscored much more when Scripture says, "**This was to fulfill what was spoken through the prophet Isaiah: 'He took up our infirmities and carried our diseases'**" (8:17). He took it upon Himself, on the cross, and bore it away. Therefore, He

---

5. *Luke 8:22–25; Matthew 8:23–27; Mark 4:36–41.*

has the authority to heal. He has the authority and the power to heal. In anticipation of this work being accomplished retroactively for all who have been healed based on the finished work of Christ, **"He took up our infirmities and carried our diseases."** Christ not only takes away our sin, but all that comes with our sin to call us back from sin. He has authority according to the Scriptures, and He is acting consistently with this by healing. If He did not heal, this would be inconsistent with Scripture, and questions about His authority could be raised. Not each and every one is healed. But the purpose of healing is to show that the One whom God sends speaks in the name of God and has signs and miracles accompanying His Word to show that God is with Him. In John 5, Jesus is going to say that the works that He does bear witness that He is sent by God. This became an issue with those in authority, and He provided a fourfold witness in the works that He did, which confirmed His authority.[6]

THE COST OF FOLLOWING JESUS:
Render Honor to Legitimate Authority

Now there is a teaching concerning those who would come to Him. It is not immediately apparent how this is connected with authority; perhaps it will become clearer to me. Maybe some of you may see it, but I do not want to force the Scriptures. It is speaking about the cost of following the Lord. **"When Jesus saw the crowd around him, he gave orders to cross to the other side of the lake. Then a teacher of the law came to him and said, 'Teacher, I will follow you wherever you go'"** (8:18–19). It is interesting to note that he was a teacher of the law. **"Jesus replied, 'Foxes have dens and birds have nests, but the Son of Man has no place to lay his head'"** (8:20). I suppose you might note here that there was a certain privilege and support from Israel that the teachers of the law had at that time, but Jesus, to whom this privilege truly belonged, had none of that support. He wanted this man, this teacher of the law, to count the cost.

There are times in the kingdom of God when it may be that those in positions of authority are not recognized or supported. **"Foxes have**

---

6. *John 5:31–47.* The fourfold witness includes John the Baptist, the works of Jesus, God the Father, and the Scriptures.

dens and birds have nests, but the Son of Man has no place to lay his head." How destitute can you be? Last night, I heard the coyotes yelping and howling. We have many coyotes about 300 yards or less from my home, right down in the wash. They have a place to rest their heads; they have holes. This morning, I saw the doves coming, and one was making a nest in the cup under a light fixture that had fallen down. We sat there and looked up at that bird—it had beautiful blue markings around its eyes. They have nests, and in the evening, you see the birds flying back; they are going to make their nests somewhere. Jesus did not even have that—the One in authority. He is warning this teacher of the law not to expect much at this point—expect little. Why? For one and only one reason: because His authority is not being recognized and supported. I suppose this is where we might bring in this point on authority. They should have been supporting the Lord in every way, including financially, and they were not. They found fault when His disciples went into the grain field and picked some heads of grain.[7] They should have come out with grain to feed and support Him. Here, the high priest had a palace, and Jesus had no place to rest His head. There is a reversal of conditions when true authority is not recognized.

Then another comes to him, and I can see now how this connects with authority. **"Another disciple said to him, 'Lord, first let me go and bury my father.' But Jesus told him, 'Follow me, and let the dead bury their own dead'"** (8:21–22). The element of authority is here, I suppose, in that the disciple feels he has to honor his father and his mother. Part of this is caring for his father; if his father dies, **"Lord, first let me go and bury my father."** That is not to stand in the place of following the Lord Jesus. He calls us to seek first His kingdom and His righteousness.[8] If our relatives are unbelieving, there may be times when we cannot make them the uppermost concern when it comes to following Christ. In this case, this person was making it his uppermost concern, and he was a disciple. 'Let me finish my obligation to the one in authority, honor my father and mother, and then I will follow you.' **"But Jesus told him, 'Follow me, and let the dead bury their own dead'"** (8:22). There are ways in which these things can be taken care of and provided for without being casual and saying, 'I have no

---

7. *Matthew 12:1.*

8. *Matthew 6:33.*

obligation to you.' This is not the case; they can and should be provided for. But there is an urgency about the work of the kingdom of God that requires us to give ourselves to it, and to acknowledge legitimate authority.

REBUKING THE WIND AND THE WAVES:
Authority over the Elements

Next, we see Jesus' authority over the elements: the wind and the waves. **"Then he got into the boat and his disciples followed him. Suddenly a furious storm came up on the lake, so that the waves swept over the boat. But Jesus was sleeping"** (8:23–24). What a sight that must have been. Amid this boat tossed back and forth, Jesus' humanity is so present. He must have been tired. I do not think He was just faking with one eye peeked open to see what these guys would do. He was asleep in the midst of the storm, committing Himself to the hand of His Father, knowing that as need arises, God will raise Him up. It would be nice to be able to go to sleep like that at times, in the midst of it all, would it not? Jesus had left things in good hands. He knew the limits of people; when they got in real trouble, they would cry out. 'In the meantime, you guys, disciples, manage the affairs, take care of it.' Sure, they managed, alright. **"The disciples went and woke him, saying, 'Lord, save us! We're going to drown!'"** (8:25). Jesus was unimpressed. He was impressed by the faith of the centurion, but His own disciples, who have seen all the healings, are not getting it. And He reproves them!

First, He reproves the disciples, then rebukes the waves, and probably returns to bed—I would not be surprised. **"You of little faith, why are you so afraid?"** (8:26a). I suppose His concern is their fear. The Lord is with us. "Even though I walk through the valley of the shadow of death, I will fear no evil, for you are with me" (Ps. 23:4a). Recognizing who is with them and recognizing that this One who is with them has this kind of power and control and will certainly not go down with the ship, they should not fear. This is one captain who will not go down with the ship because He will not let the ship go down. Did they recognize this? The centurion recognized His lordship, and the disciples were closer than the centurion. **"Then he got up and rebuked the winds and the waves, and it was completely calm. The men were** amazed and asked, 'What kind of man is this? Even the winds and the waves obey him!'" (8:26b–27). Jesus had authority over the elements. He is the One who created all things. He is God, the Son incarnate, by whom all things were made. He certainly knows how to still the waves. He parted the waters; He brought the plagues in on Pharaoh; He is in control. Even when He is asleep, He is in total control. "**Lord, save us! We're going to drown!**" No, the Lord knows altogether. We have to call upon Him without fear: 'Lord, what would you have us do about the waves? Should we do anything? Or should we lie down beside you and sleep?'

This would be a good way to go, you know—with Jesus. I remember getting over the problem of predestination by thinking: 'If Jesus is the Lamb of God, slain from the foundation of the world, and if that makes him an automaton, I'm willing to be an automaton.' That settled that question for me. If Jesus goes down by the waves, you go down by the waves, too. If Jesus is an automaton, you will be an automaton, too. It is that simple; it is not rocket science. Who will deny that He is the Lamb of God, slain from the foundation of the world[9] according to the sovereign purpose of God?

DELIVERING TWO DEMON-POSSESSED MEN:
Authority over Demons and Judgment on the Unclean

Now we have the account of two demon-possessed men. Again, we have a struggle about who Jesus is, His authority, and the response and limits of others to His authority. Jesus now shows His authority over the demons.

> When he arrived at the other side in the region of the Gadarenes, two demon-possessed men coming from the tombs met him. They were so violent that no one could pass that way. "What do you want with us, Son of God?" they shouted. "Have you come here to torture us before the appointed time?" (8:28–29).

What does this say about authority? They recognize Him, and they recognize that the outcome of their ways is to be tortured. This is not to

---

9. *Revelation 13:8.*

say they recognize everything that there is to recognize about Jesus. You can recognize some things and not recognize everything. For example, the devil did not think Job would keep his integrity.[10] There are things the demons do not know, but there are some things they do know.

The recognition of His authority and His presence stirred them up. They saw what was coming: **"The demons begged Jesus, 'If you drive us out, send us into the herd of pigs'"** (8:31). For some reason, they wanted to be sent into living beings. It will require more study to understand why. But they begged to be sent into the herd of pigs. Demons are created by the Lord; they are created angels. They rebelled against Him and came into a fallen state. **"He said to them, 'Go!'"** (8:32a). There is that word of command again; earlier, he had said, **"Go!"**

> **So they came out and went into the pigs, and the whole herd rushed down the steep bank into the lake and died in the water. Those tending the pigs ran off, went into the town and reported all this, including what had happened to the demon-possessed men. Then the whole town went out to meet Jesus. And when they saw him, they pleaded with him to leave their region** (8:32b–34).

Jesus accomplished a number of things here, not only revealing His power over the demons but also bringing judgment on those who were keeping these pigs. The Israelites were not to keep pigs; it violates the law of God. A judgment came upon them when the demons went out into the pigs, and they ran down and perished in the lake.

Instead of recognizing Jesus' authority and power and being thankful for it, they tried to find a way out. They did not want Jesus to interfere with their situation. They failed to see; they failed to appreciate what was there. They begged Him, they pleaded with Him, to leave that region. They did not consider the demon-possessed men, their deliverance, and the power of God, which is proof that the kingdom of God has come. They wanted their pigs. They preferred their pigs over the kingdom and the blessings of the kingdom. What is so great about pigs that they would want them over the kingdom? This is what it amounts to: "If I drive out demons by the finger of God, then the kingdom of God has come upon you" (Lk. 11:20). **"They pleaded with him to leave their region"** (8:34b). It shows something about what our Lord said, "Do

---

10. *Job 2:1–13.*

not give dogs what is sacred; do not throw your pearls to pigs" (Matt. 7:6a). These persons were without faith—unclean and unholy.

They manifest their condition when "they pleaded with him to leave their region." Christ performed a great deliverance, their finances were affected, and their pigs were all they could think about. Our minds can be so closed. I am trying to think about it. What is there about pigs that sent the Israelites off in this direction, which they could not get from lambs? Other forms of meat were permitted to them. There is no justification.

HEALING THE PARALYTIC MAN:
Authority to Forgive Sins and Opposition to the Word of God

At the beginning of Matthew 9, Jesus now comes to his own town— Nazareth. And in this account, Jesus says: "But I want you to know that the Son of Man has authority on earth to forgive sins" (9:6a). And in verse 8, "When the crowd saw this, they were filled with awe; and they praised God, who had given such authority to man." His authority is seen in relation to forgiving sins and removing sickness. He said, "Which is easier: to say, 'Your sins are forgiven,' or to say, 'Get up and walk'?" (9:5). The question is made explicit by our Lord. "But I want you to know that the Son of Man has authority on earth to forgive sins" and therefore to remove those things which accompany sin. We know this goes back to the beginning. The curse was put upon mankind as a call back to repentance from sin. The authority of our Lord Jesus Christ is again revealed.

"At this, some of the teachers of the law said to themselves, 'This fellow is blaspheming!'" (9:3). Notice how the conflict is gradually rising. It is like the pot of water is on the fire, and the temperature is rising, and the conflict will rise all the way up to Matthew 22 and 23. It will get sharper and sharper. I want us to notice a dynamic about this. Jesus will pronounce judgment on those in positions of authority because of this persistent resistance to the Word of God. This is the same resistance that came in the Garden in response to the authority of the Word of God. It was there from the beginning. This resistance can go far, and men can become even as demons. Rational beings without bodies—spirits—became evil, they became demons, because they persisted in their rebellion against God. That should be a warning to us that we can progress to a depth of evil the way demons have. It is the same principle of evil at work, and it comes when we fail to recognize the authority of God.

God's authority is not just an authority based on power; this is an authority based on truth and insight. It is an authority supported by reason. There is nothing that stands against the authority of God. God Himself, who could exercise power by might, said: "Come now, let us reason together, saith the LORD: though your sins be as scarlet, they shall be as white as snow; though they be red like crimson, they shall be like wool" (Is. 1:18 KJV). This is how God exercises His authority. He sent the prophets, again and again, to call men back. He sent warning upon warning upon warning. He sent warnings to Pharaoh. God does not exercise His authority through sheer might to overpower, but He exercises it according to His Word.

"FOLLOW ME":
Authority to Call Disciples and Sinners

Jesus calls Matthew—a tax collector. These are not the people you want to hang around with. Matthew was double trouble. He was a tax collector, and he was collecting for the Romans. He was politically on the wrong side of the fence. **"As Jesus went on from there, he saw a man named Matthew sitting at the tax collector's booth. 'Follow me,' he told him, and Matthew got up and followed him"** (9:9). Jesus says to him—because Jesus knows our hearts and sees where we are—"Follow me." Notice the authority of the Lord: **"Follow me."** We cannot say this. We can say, "Follow my example, as I follow the example of Christ" (1 Cor. 11:1), but we cannot say simply, "Follow me." If we ever do say, "Follow me," it is to be understood "as I follow the Lord" or "insofar as I follow the Lord" and nothing more. Jesus could say to Matthew, simpliciter, **"Follow me."**

> While Jesus was having dinner at Matthew's house, many tax collectors and sinners came and ate with him and his disciples. When the Pharisees saw this, they asked his disciples, "Why does your teacher eat with tax collectors and sinners?" On hearing this, Jesus said, "It is not the healthy who need a doctor, but the sick" (9:10–12).

We need to understand this as spoken phenomenologically in terms of how things *appear*, and not actuality. **"It is not the healthy who need a doctor, but the sick."** It is literally true that the healthy do not need a doctor, but in this case, since the Pharisees think they are well, they do not need a doctor.

Does the doctor have the authority to discern? Yes, he does, and he discerns right, and he can only minister to those who come to acknowledge their condition. With Christ, they acknowledge their sin, and He restores them. This is also why He sends away empty those who are filled.[11] **"But go and learn what this means: 'I desire mercy, not sacrifice.' For I have not come to call the righteous, but sinners"** (9:13). He exercises His authority in wisdom and grace, in a way that brings honor and glory to God.

A QUESTION OF AUTHORITY:
New Wine into Old Wineskins

Last of all, we come to this passage regarding fasting. **"Then John's disciples came and asked him, 'How is it that we and the Pharisees fast often, but your disciples do not fast?' Jesus answered, 'How can the guests of the bridegroom mourn while he is with them? The time will come when the bridegroom will be taken from them; then they will fast'"** (9:14–15). To recognize who is here—the bridegroom to whom the bride belongs—is to recognize that now is not the time for mourning. Do you mourn on your wedding day or during your honeymoon when you are with the bridegroom? Do you mourn and fast, or do you recognize who you are with and rejoice, as it should be? It is that straightforward. The bride belongs to the bridegroom. Apparently, John's disciples did not understand, so they came to Christ to ask. Jesus goes from there to further elaborate on who He is and what He is bringing:

> No one sews a patch of unshrunk cloth on an old garment, for the patch will pull away from the garment, making the tear worse. Neither do men pour new wine into old wineskins. If they do, the skins will burst; the wine will run out and the wineskins will

---

11. *Luke 1:53.*

be ruined. No, they pour new wine into new wineskins, and both are preserved (9:16–17).

Something new is happening in our Lord's ministry that is different from the old—He is bringing a new covenant. He cannot simply do things in the old way. He cannot patch up that old system which is ready to pass away. Furthermore, it is not just old and ready to pass away at its best, but is now corrupt to the point of opposing Him, resisting Him, denying Him, and crucifying Him. How do you get along with others? How do we get along with those whose lives have been stretched and fashioned in an old pattern, who have aged and become accustomed to their ways? Do you 'fit in' the new truth God gives us? Do you fit it into that old system? Will the old system accommodate it? God opened the Church's eyes to the truth of the gospel when it had turned away from it prior to the days of the Reformation. You cannot put new wine into old wineskins, but this is also true in other cases. People may work out their epistemology, their view of how it is that we know what is clear, and they develop it and live according to it. And if you try to question it, what happens? There comes immediately a question of authority.[12] They will respond, 'We have been doing it in this way, and if you can fit into our system, well and good, but if you challenge the system, things will fall apart.'

Jesus is teaching that you cannot put new wine into old wineskins. It has to be built on a firm foundation. The authority has to be well laid at the basic level. If you start off and go off track somewhere, if necessary, you must go back to the ground and rebuild. If the foundation needs to be laid deeper, you must come back and deal with it.

Building a foundation under a house is difficult once the house is built. *Do not try it.* It is hard to put new wine into old wineskins. Wineskins have this natural way of expanding, stretching, and growing. If something is already stretched under the old limits, and you add new wine, and fermentation occurs, it begins to stretch more; you can only stretch so far. There is a question of authority in this teaching about new and old wine.

Our Lord's authority is seen in this section of the Scriptures. It comes out in many places explicitly, and in other cases, clearly implicitly. Much is being taught about authority, and we need to heed this so that we may be instructed and blessed by the Lord. Amen.

---

12. Gangadean, "Paper No. 64: Aaron's Rod," in *The Logos Papers*, 341–352.

8

THE LORD OF THE HARVEST

*Jesus Comes to Destroy the
Works of the Devil*

Matthew 9:18–38, 10:1–42

9:18While he was saying this, a synagogue leader came and knelt before him and said, "My daughter has just died. But come and put your hand on her, and she will live." 19Jesus got up and went with him, and so did his disciples.

20Just then a woman who had been subject to bleeding for twelve years came up behind him and touched the edge of his cloak. 21She said to herself, "If I only touch his cloak, I will be healed."

22Jesus turned and saw her. "Take heart, daughter," he said, "your faith has healed you." And the woman was healed at that moment.

23When Jesus entered the synagogue leader's house and saw the noisy crowd and people playing pipes, 24he said, "Go away. The girl is not dead but asleep." But they laughed at him. 25After the crowd had been put outside, he went in and took the girl by the hand, and she got up. 26News of this spread through all that region.

27As Jesus went on from there, two blind men followed him, calling out, "Have mercy on us, Son of David!"

28When he had gone indoors, the blind men came to him, and he asked them, "Do you believe that I am able to do this?"

"Yes, Lord," they replied.

29Then he touched their eyes and said, "According to your faith let it be done to you"; 30and their sight was restored. Jesus warned them sternly,

"See that no one knows about this." [31]But they went out and spread the news about him all over that region.

[32]While they were going out, a man who was demon-possessed and could not talk was brought to Jesus. [33]And when the demon was driven out, the man who had been mute spoke. The crowd was amazed and said, "Nothing like this has ever been seen in Israel."

[34]But the Pharisees said, "It is by the prince of demons that he drives out demons."

[35]Jesus went through all the towns and villages, teaching in their synagogues, proclaiming the good news of the kingdom and healing every disease and sickness. [36]When he saw the crowds, he had compassion on them, because they were harassed and helpless, like sheep without a shepherd. [37]Then he said to his disciples, "The harvest is plentiful but the workers are few. [38]Ask the Lord of the harvest, therefore, to send out workers into his harvest field."

[10:1]Jesus called his twelve disciples to him and gave them authority to drive out impure spirits and to heal every disease and sickness.

[2]These are the names of the twelve apostles: first, Simon (who is called Peter) and his brother Andrew; James son of Zebedee, and his brother John; [3]Philip and Bartholomew; Thomas and Matthew the tax collector; James son of Alphaeus, and Thaddaeus; [4]Simon the Zealot and Judas Iscariot, who betrayed him.

[5]These twelve Jesus sent out with the following instructions: "Do not go among the Gentiles or enter any town of the Samaritans. [6]Go rather to the lost sheep of Israel. [7]As you go, proclaim this message: 'The kingdom of heaven has come near.' [8]Heal the sick, raise the dead, cleanse those who have leprosy, drive out demons. Freely you have received; freely give.

[9]"Do not get any gold or silver or copper to take with you in your belts— 10 no bag for the journey or extra shirt or sandals or a staff, for the worker is worth his keep. [11]Whatever town or village you enter, search there for some worthy person and stay at their house until you leave. [12]As you enter the home, give it your greeting. [13]If the home is deserving, let your peace rest on it; if it is not, let your peace return to you. [14]If anyone will not welcome you or listen to your words, leave that home or town and shake the dust off your feet. [15]Truly I tell you, it will be more bearable for Sodom and Gomorrah on the day of judgment than for that town.

[16]"I am sending you out like sheep among wolves. Therefore be as shrewd as snakes and as innocent as doves. [17]Be on your guard; you will be handed over to the local councils and be flogged in the synagogues. [18]On my

account you will be brought before governors and kings as witnesses to them and to the Gentiles. ¹⁹But when they arrest you, do not worry about what to say or how to say it. At that time you will be given what to say, ²⁰for it will not be you speaking, but the Spirit of your Father speaking through you.

²¹"Brother will betray brother to death, and a father his child; children will rebel against their parents and have them put to death. ²²You will be hated by everyone because of me, but the one who stands firm to the end will be saved. ²³When you are persecuted in one place, flee to another. Truly I tell you, you will not finish going through the towns of Israel before the Son of Man comes.

²⁴"The student is not above the teacher, nor a servant above his master. ²⁵It is enough for students to be like their teachers, and servants like their masters. If the head of the house has been called Beelzebul, how much more the members of his household!

²⁶"So do not be afraid of them, for there is nothing concealed that will not be disclosed, or hidden that will not be made known. ²⁷What I tell you in the dark, speak in the daylight; what is whispered in your ear, proclaim from the roofs. ²⁸Do not be afraid of those who kill the body but cannot kill the soul. Rather, be afraid of the One who can destroy both soul and body in hell. ²⁹Are not two sparrows sold for a penny? Yet not one of them will fall to the ground outside your Father's care. ³⁰And even the very hairs of your head are all numbered. ³¹So don't be afraid; you are worth more than many sparrows.

³²"Whoever acknowledges me before others, I will also acknowledge before my Father in heaven. ³³But whoever disowns me before others, I will disown before my Father in heaven.

³⁴"Do not suppose that I have come to bring peace to the earth. I did not come to bring peace, but a sword. ³⁵For I have come to turn

"'a man against his father,
  a daughter against her mother,
a daughter-in-law against her mother-in-law—
³⁶ a man's enemies will be the members of his own household.'

³⁷"Anyone who loves their father or mother more than me is not worthy of me; anyone who loves their son or daughter more than me is not worthy of me. ³⁸Whoever does not take up their cross and follow me is not worthy of me. ³⁹Whoever finds their life will lose it, and whoever loses their life for my sake will find it.

[40]"Anyone who welcomes you welcomes me, and anyone who welcomes me welcomes the one who sent me. [41]Whoever welcomes a prophet as a prophet will receive a prophet's reward, and whoever welcomes a righteous person as a righteous person will receive a righteous person's reward. [42]And if anyone gives even a cup of cold water to one of these little ones who is my disciple, truly I tell you, that person will certainly not lose their reward."

INTRODUCTION:
The Lord of the Harvest Versus the Lord of Destruction

TODAY, WE WANT TO LOOK AT MATTHEW 9:18 through the end of chapter 10. There is a connecting feature throughout. I called this section *The Lord of the Harvest* for obvious reasons from the passage that we read. We are to **"Ask the Lord of the harvest, therefore, to send out workers into his harvest field"** (9:38). We see Jesus doing this; He is seeing the need, calling for prayer, then calling and instructing His disciples. We are going to look at four aspects of His instruction. We will see the religious leaders' response to Jesus, and we have been noting that as He does miracles, we see a growing contest with the religious leaders. We might put it this way: they are the establishment.

The word *establishment* has a negative connotation, and it is intended to have one. The establishment consists of those who are in positions of authority but are not acting with authority in the sense of having insight into the Word. Jesus saw that the people were harassed and helpless, and this was not God's plan. The leaders should have been shepherds for the people, and they were not. They were not doing what God had called them to do; rather, they were doing what they were not supposed to do. They were opposing Jesus in a most vehement way, in a very deadly way. When we come to Matthew 12, we will see Jesus' specific response to their opposition.

Let us contrast those in positions of authority with Jesus calling upon the Lord of the Harvest. He is going to explain why it is false that He would be casting out demons by the prince of demons, Beelzebul, which means Lord of the Flies. It comes from *Beel*, which means *husband, lord, master,* and *Zebub,* either *dung* or *flies*. There is a close connection between the two. We know the book *Lord of the Flies* by

William Golding[1] and what our hearts turn to without the grace of God; what our natural condition is. There is a contrast throughout this section between the Lord of the Harvest and the fruitfulness that is to come in, and the lord of dung, the flies, who is Satan. There is the lord of destruction, or the dark lord, versus the Lord of Glory, the Lord of Light, the Lord of Life—the Lord of the Harvest.

THE WORK OF JESUS:
Destroy the Works of Satan, Undo Sin, and Exercise Dominion

We are looking at the words and the works of our Lord Jesus Christ. We gave considerable attention to the words of our Lord as we went through the Sermon on the Mount. Now we are looking at the works of our Lord and how they reveal who He is, what He is to do, the opposition, and the dynamic of this revelation as people encounter it. The Word is *life unto life* to those who believe and *death unto death* to those who do not believe.[2]

What is the work of Jesus? The work of Jesus, according to the apostle John, is that He might destroy the works of the devil. 1 John 3:8 says, "The reason the Son of God appeared was to destroy the devil's work." Paul describes it as follows: "For he must reign until he has put all his enemies under his feet. The last enemy to be destroyed is death" (1 Cor. 15:25–26). That is, physical death, which was brought in through the temptation of Satan and God's pronouncement of the curse on sin to call man back from sin. The Lord is dealing with the curse in this chapter as He heals people under the destroyer's power. Think of the condition of our lives and the waste of time, energy, and effort as we see the effects of the destroyer's work through sin. We know that God imposed the curse, but it was because of sin, to call us back from sin. We saw the intimate connection between the forgiveness of sins and deliverance from the curse.[3] Our Lord Jesus can remove the curse because He has the power to remove sin, and this ability comes from His willingness to bear the penalty for sin personally.

---

1. William Golding, *Lord of the Flies* (United Kingdom: Faber and Faber, 1954).

2. *2 Corinthians 2:12–17; Isaiah 55:10–11.*

3. *Matthew 9:1–8.*

As we read last time in Matthew 8:17, "This was to fulfill what was spoken through the prophet Isaiah: 'He took up our infirmities and bore our diseases,'" and in Isaiah 53:5, "By His stripes we are healed."[4] We should say this to ourselves again and again—even as a chorus in Handel's Messiah repeats: "And by His stripes, we are healed." Jesus, the Son of God incarnate, is manifest to destroy the works of the devil. God uses secondary causes. The devil worked by tempting Adam and leading Adam astray through *Adam's own sin*. Adam's own not seeking and not understanding were revealed when he was tested; he turned aside and then covered it up. The self-deception is seen in the coats of leaves, and the self-justification is seen in blaming the other. And so God brought the curse.[5]

Our Lord Jesus Christ came to *undo* what Adam did, which does not override the responsibility of Satan, Adam, or us. The fact that there are secondary causes does not override the primary cause; it does not mean that Satan is not responsible, Adam is not responsible, or that we ourselves are not responsible. God has established many levels of responsibility. It is like concentric circles protecting what is right, and sin will destroy them all and wipe them out. Psalm 2:3 says, "Let us break their bands asunder, and cast away their cords from us."[6] We cannot stand to be in the presence of God in our sin. We do not want God near us, so we remove everything that reminds us of God. Now we will see the world's hatred for the One who is the Word incarnate, who lives that out, and who reminds us of our sin and exposes us. He reminds us as Adam was reminded when God was present in the Garden; he feared, hid, and lied.

Jesus came to *undo* our desperate condition of sin and death and to *do* what Adam failed to do: to exercise dominion, rule, and have mastery over all things in the creation to reveal God's glory—to fill the earth with the knowledge of God.[7] Jesus came to destroy the destroyer and to end his works. This is what hell signifies: destruction. Hell, death, and Hades are cast into the lake of fire and destroyed.[8] Lives that are

---

4. NKJV.

5. Gangadean, *The Biblical Worldview*, 241–294.

6. KJV.

7. *Isaiah 11:9; Habakkuk 2:14.*

8. *Revelation 20:14.*

wasted because of sin are self-destructive, and all the efforts come to naught. Look at the world around us. In *The Bonfire of the Vanities*,[9] Tom Wolfe writes about the blaze going up around us in terms of the vanity of this world. As God imposes the curse and disciplines us, the things we hold dear are taken away. This happens so that every Lord's Day, we may approach Him, putting aside all our endeavors and acknowledging what is truly worthy—coming to worship and finding rest in Him. We do not often do this unless we are stripped of things we would hold on to. Every one of us, through the week, encounters and faces this stripping process. We have to ask ourselves: Why are we alive? Why do we go through the effort? Why do we endure? Because there is something worthwhile. The sufferings work to bring us to holiness, without which no one shall see the Lord.[10] Jesus came to destroy the works of the devil.

The Dead Girl and the Sick Woman

In Matthew 9:18–34, we encounter the dead girl, the sick woman, the blind, and the mute. Jesus manifests His compassion and His rule in the world by healing. Examining these aspects is crucial, as it forms the basis upon which He will dispatch His disciples for preaching with warnings. To understand how our Lord sends His disciples and wants them to grasp the significance of their work, it is essential to comprehend His actions. **"While he was saying this, a ruler came and knelt before him and said, 'My daughter has just died'"** (9:18a). Those who possess great power cannot withhold their souls from death.[11] Redemption of the soul is precious, and this ruler, with all of his power, was powerless before death, and so he came to Jesus and said, **"My daughter has just died."** Think of the effort that he has put into the work of raising his daughter. The care, affection, and tenderness—how frequently he held his daughter close to his heart, expressing his love. She is now gone— struck down. What he cherished so deeply has been snatched away. We would readily part with our wealth to have our children by our side. The pain of this strikes deep into the heart. **"My daughter has just**

---

9. Tom Wolfe, *The Bonfire of the Vanities* (New York: Farrar, Straus Giroux, 1987).

10. *Hebrews 12:14.*

11. *Psalm 22:29.*

died. **But come and put your hand on her, and she will live"** (9:18b). And Jesus responded. This ruler humbled himself and came bowing before Jesus, seeing that He is the One who is the true Ruler and Lord; He could touch her with His hand and bring life, whereas as a ruler himself, he could not. This ruler recognized the true Ruler and came to Him. Jesus recognized his faith and responded and went with him.

On His way, **"a woman who had been subject to bleeding for twelve years came up behind him and touched the edge of his cloak. She said to herself, 'If I only touch his cloak, I will be healed'"** (9:20–21). One has to see the boldness, the radicalness of her act, the circumstance, and the comparison. Here was a daughter, 12 years old, and here is a woman who for 12 years has had an issue of bleeding. She is unclean. She is not to be among others. She is in the crowd, and others are touching her, and she does a daring thing: She reaches her hand to touch this Holy One, which is the last thing she should do, being unclean. Yet, she recognizes the truth that His holiness will come to her, and that her defilement will not defile Him—she recognizes this. She reached out her hand and touched the edge of His cloak. She knew that only the minimum was required. Just the edge of His cloak—not His shoulder, not His hand, just the edge of the cloak, and this would have been enough. She saw this.

Jesus saw her and spoke to her. He spoke to her words of compassion and tenderness. He said to her, **"Take heart, daughter."** Jesus calls her daughter. She may be His age, but she is a daughter of the King. She is a daughter of the faith. **"'Take heart, daughter,' he said, 'your faith has healed you'"** (9:22a). Despite everything, she possessed the insight to reach out and touch His garment. Jesus *marveled* at the faith of the centurion: "I tell you the truth, I have not found anyone in Israel with such great faith" (Matt. 8:10b). Jesus is pleased by faith. Without faith, it is impossible to please Him.[12] This faith has certainty regarding what is unseen, because it is based on understanding and not on sight.[13] To have faith is to understand the nature of things. God wants us to seek Him, understand Him, and do what is right. **"'Take heart, daughter,' he said, 'your faith has healed you.'"** In all this, God is working so that we might seek Him, know Him, understand Him,

---

12. *Hebrews 11:6.*
13. Gangadean, *The Biblical Worldview*, 3–20.

and have faith; then the healing comes as it pleases Him, unless God is so pleased to further glorify Himself by our continuing to bear it. There are times when we continue bearing it. The apostle Paul was beaten much, suffered much, and thrice he pleaded with the Lord to deliver him from the messenger of Satan that was to buffet him. The Lord said, "My grace is sufficient for you, for my power is made perfect in weakness" (2 Cor. 12:9a). Paul rejoiced in his suffering. What was the benefit? He came to know the Lord. He had revelations that were surpassing, which he could not speak of.[14] This was the comfort of his heart. He would have this revelation and not be conceited, so he was beaten down.[15] What does this say about the condition of our hearts? To be autonomous is to say it is of ourselves and not to honor God, who is the giver of life.

When Jesus entered the synagogue leader's house and saw the noisy crowd and people playing pipes, he said, "Go away. The girl is not dead but asleep." But they laughed at him. After the crowd had been put outside, he went in and took the girl by the hand, and she got up. News of this spread through all that region (9:23–26).

Notice the words, "News of this spread through all that region." He had brought back this young girl from death, the daughter of this ruler, who was known to many. They had come there to mourn her death, and then they saw the girl alive. God purposed it this way, that the glory of God might be revealed, even as it was in the case of the man who was born blind.[16] Our lives are ripped apart, and those things that are precious to us are taken away—this is so the glory of God may be revealed. Paul's heart was content with this, and so are the hearts of all the saints in all the ages as they come to see the Lord. Let our hearts be content as we face trials of many kinds, knowing that God is working to bring us to seek Him, and to have holiness by which we seek Him, by which we come to understand, which is pleasing to God.

---

14. *2 Corinthians 12:4.*
15. *2 Corinthians 12:5–10.*
16. *John 9:1–12.*

The Blind and the Mute

"As Jesus went on from there, two blind men followed him, calling out, 'Have mercy on us, Son of David!' When he had gone indoors, the blind men came to him, and he asked them, 'Do you believe that I am able to do this?' 'Yes, Lord,' they replied" (9:27–28). Think about the waste, the destruction, and the work of the destroyer. Think about the woman who for 12 years was bleeding, and her life was so constrained, so restricted. Think of these two blind men. Visualize the blind men making their way into the house where Jesus was. It was not their usual path. Think about their pressing in to come near to Jesus. Think about how their lives are affected, how much loss there is in their lives, and how much pain and distress is caused by blindness. Think of how it affected their relationships with others. Let not our sufferings slip from us—the sufferings so abundantly present here in the Scriptures to which our Lord Jesus responds. Let us take time to look at it. **"He asked them, 'Do you believe that I am able to do this?' 'Yes, Lord,' they replied. Then he touched their eyes and said, 'According to your faith let it be done to you'"** (9:28b–29). They believed that Jesus is the Christ, the Son of God, the One who was able to do this; no one else is able. They called Him Lord. He is the Lord of Glory, He is the Lord of Life, He is the Lord of the Harvest who is bringing in the harvest, bringing men to God, revealing God to men. He is doing the work for which God sent Him—the Word of God incarnate, who makes God known. **"Jesus warned them sternly, 'See that no one knows about this.' But they went out and spread the news about him all over that region"** (9:30b–31).

"While they were going out, a man who was demon-possessed and could not talk was brought to Jesus" (9:32). Try going silent for a day. If that is too hard, try it for an hour. Imagine the constraints not being able to speak would place on your life as you are with others with whom you cannot communicate. You do not understand; you are as good as dumb. So much of our lives flow through communication, back and forth, interaction, and dialogue. If you cannot speak, you cannot dialogue; someone can speak to you, but you cannot dialogue. It is a great loss, great suffering, and a great waste. **"And when the demon was driven out, the man who had been mute spoke. The crowd was amazed and said, 'Nothing like this has ever been seen in**

THE LORD OF THE HARVEST

Israel'" (9:33). Jesus drove out the demon from the man—notice it was *driven out*. **"The crowd was amazed and said, 'Nothing like this has ever been seen in Israel.'"** Again, the news spread from there. His deeds serve as evidence that He is sent by God. He speaks in God's name, performs these works, and is unmistakably sent by God. Nicodemus said, "For no one could perform the signs you are doing if God were not with him" (Jn. 3:2b). This is exactly right. This is the power of the Holy Spirit working evidently and clearly. Not only is it clear from general revelation, but it is clear from actual historical revelation, on the scene, that Jesus is the Son of God—approved by God.

And yet, those who are in authority, who are not doing what they *should* do and starting to do what they *should not* do, attributed the work of the Holy Spirit to Satan. **"But the Pharisees said, 'It is by the prince of demons that he drives out demons'"** (9:34). More antithetical than this, you cannot get! What a reversal of good and evil. We shall see later on that this sin will not be pardoned in this age or the age to come. Take this to heart. Do not call evil good or good evil. Do not call evil those who are doers of good. This is what the Pharisees did. It is the very nature of evil to reverse the order of things, the order established by God.[17] Evil can only try to reverse; it cannot do anything positive. We find this reversal here in the Pharisee's accusation. Jesus is going to speak about this when He warns His disciples in sending them forth. In Matthew 12, Jesus will use logic in the most natural, easy, straightforward, piercing way to totally wipe this out as a possible interpretation of what He has done.

Jesus Came to Bring in the Harvest—the Fullness of Life

Continuing His mission in the villages, Jesus preached about the kingdom. He proclaimed the good news that the kingdom was imminent and approaching. Of the outcomes of the kingdom are the forgiveness of sins, purification from sin, holiness, restoration, and the removal of the curse. He does this until the work is finally completed, when He ascends into heaven and rules until all of His enemies are subdued, and the last enemy that remains is death itself, which will be removed by His personal, bodily, visible Second Coming from heaven in glory,

---

17. Gangadean, *The Westminster Confession*, 369–376.

raising the dead, and finally, overcoming death.[18] This is the work of the kingdom: to bring wholeness, and to bring life where there is death. To bring life where there is death physically, and to bring life where there is death spiritually. Both are connected. There is a corporate aspect of this work, and when the work is done corporately, the curse will be fully and finally removed with the Second Coming.

"**When he saw the crowds, he had compassion on them, because they were harassed and helpless, like sheep without a shepherd**" (9:36). Jesus saw this and He had compassion on them. God had given them shepherds in the priests, the priesthood, the religious leaders, and the teachers, who should have taught the people. They were not doing their work, and so the people were left on their own. There was to be discipline brought into people's lives, and teaching the Word by discipline, so that they might learn the Word of God, but that was not being done. The devil oppressed them by illnesses, harassed them, and they were helpless because they did not have those who would teach them the Word of Life. The whole institution of the priesthood that God had established in Exodus and Leviticus was for the people to be sanctified and taught the way of holiness. It had become corrupted by the leaders who had lost their vision of God. Our Lord does not say that this is too much and cannot be done; instead, He said, "pray." We should not have to reach our limits, we should know our limits. Our limits are really zero. "I can do all this through him who gives me strength" (Phil. 4:13), but without Him, I can do nothing. This is our limit, exactly our limit, as *a priori* truth. You do not have to wonder, 'Is it probably close to zero?' It is necessarily zero. So we should be in prayer to God.

Our Lord shows us the way: "**He said to his disciples, 'The harvest is plentiful but the workers are few'**" (9:37). I do not think we should say, 'You know, the pickins' are few. I've been out fishing, and I just can't seem to catch any fish. There are just no fish out there today.' This does not seem to be consistent with what our Lord is saying: "**The harvest is plentiful.**" When He was in Samaria, He said to His disciples, "I tell you, open your eyes and look at the fields! They are ripe for harvest" (Jn. 4:35b). Are we saying, 'What harvest? I don't see any harvest; what are you talking about?' Blind we are; dumb we are; paralyzed we are.

---

18. *1 Corinthians 15:20–28.*

We need the healing of God so that we might see, act, and work in the kingdom of God. Would the disciples have spoken to the woman at the well? No, and here is our Lord; Jesus saw an opportunity to advance the kingdom of God, and He spoke.

Do we know how to speak to those who are rulers and in authority in whatever place we are? Have we prepared our hearts? Have we been seeking the Lord? Are we able to demolish arguments and every pretension that raises itself up against the knowledge of God? The harvest is plentiful. Let us pray that God will send workers into His harvest. **"Ask the Lord of the harvest, therefore, to send out workers into his harvest field"** (9:38). It is not a good picture to go out on the job site and see people standing around, not working, but it is common. God wants workers! He does not just want *zealous* workers; He wants *skilled* workers. Bring your tools and come with an attitude ready to work. God wants workers, and we are to pray that God will send workers into the harvest. The workers are few. There are many believers but few workers. There are many converts but few disciples. Panic not, but pray. **"Ask the Lord of the harvest, therefore"**—I want to underscore *therefore*. It is there for a reason. We should infer that this is what we should do; obviously, it is what we should do. **"Ask,"** obviously, **"to send out workers into his harvest field."** I know we may rely on the doctrine of the sovereignty of God and we may say, 'Well, the elect will come one way or the other,' and we may let it go at this. 'Worker or no worker, it will come.' Do not even give yourself an opportunity to think this. This is the truth but not the half of it. No one who is elect will be lost; we are sure of that. But our responsibility is to speak the Word. God is able to raise up from these stones children of Abraham,[19] but He wants workers. He wants human beings who will go out and do the work, and it begins with prayer: **"Pray ye therefore the Lord of the harvest"** (9:38a KJV). What a word. I love that word: the Lord of the Harvest. He who is the Lord of Hosts is the Lord of the Harvest. He is the Lord of Hosts not only by creation but by redemption. He will bring this host in as the One who sends out workers into the harvest.

---

19. *Matthew 3:9.*

THE CALL AND PREPARATION OF THE TWELVE

In Matthew 10, Jesus calls His disciples to Him, the 12 are named, and they are sent out.

> Jesus called his twelve disciples to him and gave them authority to drive out impure spirits and to heal every disease and sickness. These are the names of the twelve apostles: first, Simon (who is called Peter) and his brother Andrew; James son of Zebedee, and his brother John; Philip and Bartholomew; Thomas and Matthew the tax collector; James son of Alphaeus, and Thaddaeus; Simon the Zealot and Judas Iscariot, who betrayed him (10:1–4).

They are named and sent out in pairs, and He gave them instructions. The instructions have four parts: (1) What to do, (2) How to do it, (3) What to expect, and (4) What our attitude should be. If we know what to expect but do not have the right attitude, this will not be good. There is an attitude that goes with expectation. Let us keep this equation balanced. Know what to expect; do not be naive. Let us be *innocent* as doves but not *silly* as doves. In understanding, be grown-ups, be men.[20] Let us not be naive as we go out. Jesus gives the first instruction of what we are to do: "**These twelve, Jesus sent out with the following instructions: 'Do not go among the Gentiles or enter any town of the Samaritans. Go rather to the lost sheep of Israel'**" (10:5–6). There will come a time when He will send them to the Gentiles, but they will first go to the Jews. What they are to do is "**proclaim this message: 'The kingdom of heaven has come near'**" (10:7b), as Jesus has been proclaiming. That does not mean just uttering the words, "**the kingdom of heaven has come near.**" It is not bumper sticker evangelism or t-shirt evangelism. But *with understanding*, explain the meaning of "**the kingdom of heaven has come near,**" in terms of all that God has promised, that the Promised One is here now, where the message is to go, and the work that has been and is to be accomplished. Today, we are still to preach that the kingdom of heaven is near wherever we go. It is expanding; it is coming near to us in the message of the gospel; the kingdom of heaven is near—repent and enter in. Join in, get behind us, push, or be crushed on the opposite side. Repent.

---

20. *1 Corinthians 14:20.*

What to Do: Be Life-Bearers—Heal and Preach to Israel

The disciples are to "Heal the sick, raise the dead, cleanse those who have leprosy, drive out demons" (10:8a). Extraordinary healing is not permanent, but it is necessary for the initiation of the Church. The work of healing and cleansing may go on by *ordinary* means. The Christian community has often been noted for doing works of mercy in medicine and education. We should abound in these works. It was done extraordinarily at first to confirm the message preached, but this should be the ordinary process of advancing the kingdom of God. To *educate* is to speak to the death in the soul. To *heal* is to speak to the death in our bodies. We should be *life-bearers*. What a calling we have. This is the message of the kingdom—the kingdom of heaven is near. We are not to charge: "**Freely you have received; freely give. Do not take along any gold or silver or copper in your belts—no bag for the journey or extra shirt or sandals or a staff, for the worker is worth his keep**" (10:8b–10). They go out among believers; believers should be the first to support them. We cannot generalize this for all times and places. Please notice that they first went out to the house of Israel. They, too, need to be taught and to hear that "**the kingdom of heaven has come near.**" Jesus says to take "**no bag for the journey or extra shirt or sandals or a staff, for the worker is worth his keep.**" Those who had this teaching should be among the first to support others who preach the Word of God to them. This is what they are to do, beginning with doing it freely.

> Whatever town or village you enter, search there for some worthy person and stay at their house until you leave. As you enter the home, give it your greeting. If the home is deserving, let your peace rest on it; if it is not, let your peace return to you. If anyone will not welcome you or listen to your words, leave that home or town and shake the dust off your feet (10:11–14).

We are not to force ourselves in. If they do not welcome you or listen, leave. We are not to beat down the door but to proclaim the Word. But they should know that the kingdom of heaven is near, and that they have turned away from it. They had greater privilege than Sodom and Gomorrah. "**Truly I tell you, it will be more bearable for Sodom and Gomorrah on the day of judgment than for that town**" (10:15).

The heinousness of sin is proportionate to the amount of light we have had and have rejected. This is why blasphemy against the work of the Holy Spirit is so immediate, poignant, clear, and powerful; when the Spirit is rejected, it is the ultimate light that is rejected—particularly as one persists in this and hardens oneself in it. Persistent rejection of the testimony of God through the work of the Holy Spirit is the unpardonable sin. Sodom and Gomorrah, we think, did heinous things, but self-righteousness and turning from the light is the sin that God sees. Let us keep in focus that it was not Sodom and Gomorrah's sin that brought destruction upon the human race. There is no such outward sin. The *only* sin Adam committed was not seeking, not understanding, and not doing what is right. The eating of the forbidden fruit was outwardly expressing what went on inwardly—this is sin. This is the root of all sin—not the outward fruit that becomes hideous and perverse.

How to Do It: Gently and Wisely

Jesus tells the disciples how to conduct themselves with an understanding of judgment. We have to realize the seriousness of what is happening. When we speak a word to someone, hopefully, we are speaking it truthfully, clearly, fully, with understanding, and when the word is rejected, we need to understand what a serious thing this is. We are *life unto life* to those who believe and *death unto death* to those who do not believe.[21] Then, He tells them what to expect: "**I am sending you out like sheep among wolves. Therefore be as shrewd as snakes and as innocent as doves**" (10:16). Now, who in their right mind would do this? There are wolves, and He will just open the sheep pen and let them go out among the wolves? It is figurative—it is *like* sheep among wolves. To say it is figurative does not minimize the reality of it. It is real—very real. The spiritual reality is more real than the physical reality. The spiritual is the reality: "**like sheep among wolves.**" He says, "**Therefore be as shrewd as snakes.**" We must be like a snake and be a dove at the same time. In terms of awareness of the harm that can be inflicted, the reality of evil in the world, how it manifests itself, and what we are going up against, we have to know this, and not be naive. Be *innocent* like a dove, do not be *naive* like a dove. In Scripture, this

---

21. *2 Corinthians 2:16* KJV.

concept is present. Be on your guard against men. These sheep going out among the wolves are to be like snakes. If you press the metaphor, include this, and be on your guard. Do not press the metaphor beyond its appropriate bounds; see it in context.

What to Expect: Opposition and Persecution

What will happen? "Be on your guard; you will be handed over to the local councils and be flogged in the synagogues" (10:17). You might put it this way: they will flog you in their churches. In the churches is the chief place where you will be flogged. They are in positions of authority but have lost sight of what they should do and what it means to glorify God and enjoy Him forever. They will oppose you, and in the name of God, they will persecute you.[22] And so they will flog you in their synagogues—in their churches. Why? Because they are the rulers, and when you challenge the authority of those in positions of power, they are very jealous to guard it—its honor, privilege, and prestige. Or, to simplify it—money and glory. People do not give this up very easily. The self-life does a great deal to get there; when it is there, it will not tolerate any shadow cast on the position of ruler or teacher. There is ego, pride, and the concern that we might lose out on our privileges. This is where the viciousness of the counter-attack comes in; they will be "flogged in the synagogues."

"On my account you will be brought before governors and kings as witnesses to them and to the Gentiles" (10:18). They will be arrested, and part of what they are to expect is this: they will go before rulers. Remember, we sang, "All kings of earth shall thanks accord when they have heard Thy words, O LORD"[23] Let us be sure that we are speaking the Word. It does not mean this will happen in each and every case, but generally, this is what will happen. We have to ask whether the rulers are hearing. We know of individual cases, as when Paul spoke, some of the rulers heard and some did not. We have to see the context. Let us say the Church had its act together—what a wild thought; you have to really stretch your imagination for this—and then someone is speaking the Word concerning clarity. The rulers hear this Word. Now,

---

22. *John 16:2–3.*
23. *Psalm 138:4, 138A, The Book of Psalms for Singing.*

what will the rulers do? They would affirm: 'There is no God like your God. Indeed, if He can bring people to get along, and this group of people get along, behold, see how they love one another. They can deal with sins and offenses and forgive, receive, and encourage one another. Behold how they love one another.' Do you think a ruler would heed this? Rulers are very aware of divisions in their realm. So when they see unity, they are highly impressed. "When they have heard Thy words, O LORD." But in the beginning, it is usually not so, because the body of witness is not there. We have to build, sometimes suffering persecution.

We are to expect the Spirit of our Father to be speaking through us. **"But when they arrest you, do not worry about what to say or how to say it. At that time you will be given what to say, for it will not be you speaking, but the Spirit of your Father speaking through you"** (10:19–20). This is in the Church, among rulers, and in your family: **"Brother will betray brother to death, and a father his child; children will rebel against their parents and have them put to death"** (10:21). I imagine some parents will want their children put to death, and to cast them out, because they become believers. Some people have experienced this. **"You will be hated by everyone because of me"** (10:22a). The Word, who reveals our true condition, is hated. Men hate the light, and they hate the Word that brings the light, **"but the one who stands firm to the end will be saved"** (10:22b). Do not miss this. This is what we are to expect. If they persecute you in one place, do not just stand around and say, 'Hit me again. Hit me again.' Do not see how much you can take before you fall. Flee! **"When you are persecuted in one place, flee to another"** (10:23a). This is the Word: **"flee to another."** And, **"If anyone will not welcome you or listen to your words, leave that home or town and shake the dust off your feet"** (10:14). They are in the Lord's hands. God will deal with them.

"Truly I tell you, you will not finish going through the towns of Israel before the Son of Man comes" (10:23b). This is not the glorious Second Coming. This is the coming in A.D. 70 in judgment, when He judges the nations. What are we to expect further? **"The student is not above the teacher, nor a servant above his master"** (10:24). He refers to what happened earlier when He was told by the Pharisees, "It is by the prince of demons that he drives out demons" (Matt. 9:34). **"It is enough for the student to be like their teacher, and servants like**

his masters. If the head of the house has been called Beelzebul, how much more the members of his household!" (10:25).

What Attitude to Have: Do Not Fear and Pick Up the Cross

Our attitude should be to have no fear:

> So do not be afraid of them. There is nothing concealed that will not be disclosed, or hidden that will not be made known. What I tell you in the dark, speak in the daylight; what is whispered in your ear, proclaim from the roofs. Do not be afraid of those who kill the body but cannot kill the soul. Rather, be afraid of the One who can destroy both soul and body in hell. Are not two sparrows sold for a penny? Yet not one of them will fall to the ground outside your Father's care. And even the very hairs of your head are all numbered. So don't be afraid; you are worth more than many sparrows (10:26–31).

God is concerned about your bones, about your hair, about every last thing that happens to you, because He is the infinite God who is *infinitely personal*. A thousand billion times more personal than you or I could be. We do not number our hairs, but "**the very hairs of your head are all numbered.**" This is personal, and it takes a lot to get into our minds that God *really* loves us. He really cares for us.

Our attitude should not be to disown Him but to acknowledge Him. "**Whoever acknowledges me before others, I will also acknowledge before my Father in heaven. But whoever disowns me before others, I will disown before my Father in heaven**" (10:32–33). This should be our attitude about our own family—He returns to this—He has come to bring the sword. He has come to turn a man against his father. Because of the truth of the Word of God, one will be turned against the other. He says He has come to do this; He has come to do the work of destroying the devil.

> Do not suppose that I have come to bring peace to the earth. I did not come to bring peace, but a sword. For I have come to turn "a man against his father, a daughter against her mother, a daughter-in-law against her mother-in-law—a man's enemies will be the members of his own household" (10:34–36).

He has come to oppose falsehood wherever it is, including in families and among loved ones. He has come to turn a daughter against her mother, which is supposed to be a very special bond. Some of you have experienced this. What are you going to do? Are you going to compromise, or are you going to acknowledge Him before men? **"A man's enemies will be the members of his own household"** (10:36).

I should say that some of what is given in Matthew is not what you would call a historical narrative or empirical data just being poured out; it is an interpretation to make a point. Many of you have been struggling with how to deal with apparent discrepancies in accounts. Things that seem to be out of sequence are put together. There is no distortion of historical fact. We have to know that some things are not given as a matter of historical fact but put together to make a point. Let us distinguish this when we come to the Word of God.

Jesus warns us where we might compromise—loving our father or mother more than Him. **"Anyone who loves his father or mother more than me is not worthy of me; anyone who loves their son or daughter more than me is not worthy of me"** (10:37). Loving your son or your daughter—and Oh! how much we love our sons and daughters—we love them dearly. Remember the ruler coming to Jesus for his daughter. But we cannot love them more than God. We cannot love ourselves more than God: **"Whoever does not take up their cross and follow me is not worthy of me"** (10:38). If you think you are going to gain your life in some other way, you will not—you will end up losing it. This should be our attitude.

There is a reward for those who are faithful:

> **Whoever finds their life will lose it, and whoever loses their life for my sake will find it. Anyone who welcomes you welcomes me, and anyone who welcomes me welcomes the one who sent me. Whoever welcomes a prophet as a prophet will receive a prophet's reward, and whoever receives a righteous person as a righteous person will receive a righteous person's reward** (10:39–41).

The prophets are the ones who are particularly harmed. The prophetic ministry is the one that confronts more so than the priestly. The priestly will confront in a certain way, in a certain context within the community. But the prophet goes out there, and they are the ones who are most harmed. If you receive a righteous man, you receive this reward. "**And if anyone gives even a cup of cold water to one of these little ones who is my disciple, truly I tell you, that person will certainly not lose their reward**" (10:42). The Lord Jesus sent the disciples with these instructions. They went and preached in the towns, and the Word spread more in a remarkable way. Next, we will pick up with the advancement of the work of the kingdom through Christ and His disciples.

9

THE KINGDOM ADVANCES
The Compelling Revelation of the Kingdom Coming

Matthew 11–12

[11:1]After Jesus had finished instructing his twelve disciples, he went on from there to teach and preach in the towns of Galilee.

[2]When John, who was in prison, heard about the deeds of the Messiah, he sent his disciples [3]to ask him, "Are you the one who is to come, or should we expect someone else?"

[4]Jesus replied, "Go back and report to John what you hear and see: [5]The blind receive sight, the lame walk, those who have leprosy are cleansed, the deaf hear, the dead are raised, and the good news is proclaimed to the poor. [6]Blessed is anyone who does not stumble on account of me."

[7]As John's disciples were leaving, Jesus began to speak to the crowd about John: "What did you go out into the wilderness to see? A reed swayed by the wind? [8]If not, what did you go out to see? A man dressed in fine clothes? No, those who wear fine clothes are in kings' palaces. [9]Then what did you go out to see? A prophet? Yes, I tell you, and more than a prophet. [10]This is the one about whom it is written:

"'I will send my messenger ahead of you,
who will prepare your way before you.'

[11]Truly I tell you, among those born of women there has not risen anyone greater than John the Baptist; yet whoever is least in the kingdom of heaven is greater than he. [12]From the days of John the Baptist until now, the kingdom of heaven has been subjected to violence, and violent people have been raiding it. [13]For all the Prophets and the Law prophesied

until John. [14]And if you are willing to accept it, he is the Elijah who was to come. [15]Whoever has ears, let them hear.

[16]"To what can I compare this generation? They are like children sitting in the marketplaces and calling out to others:

[17]"'We played the pipe for you,
  and you did not dance;
we sang a dirge,
  and you did not mourn.'

[18]For John came neither eating nor drinking, and they say, 'He has a demon.' [19]The Son of Man came eating and drinking, and they say, 'Here is a glutton and a drunkard, a friend of tax collectors and sinners.' But wisdom is proved right by her deeds."

[20]Then Jesus began to denounce the towns in which most of his miracles had been performed, because they did not repent. [21]"Woe to you, Chorazin! Woe to you, Bethsaida! For if the miracles that were performed in you had been performed in Tyre and Sidon, they would have repented long ago in sackcloth and ashes. [22]But I tell you, it will be more bearable for Tyre and Sidon on the day of judgment than for you. [23]And you, Capernaum, will you be lifted to the heavens? No, you will go down to Hades. For if the miracles that were performed in you had been performed in Sodom, it would have remained to this day. [24]But I tell you that it will be more bearable for Sodom on the day of judgment than for you."

[25]At that time Jesus said, "I praise you, Father, Lord of heaven and earth, because you have hidden these things from the wise and learned, and revealed them to little children. [26]Yes, Father, for this is what you were pleased to do.

[27]"All things have been committed to me by my Father. No one knows the Son except the Father, and no one knows the Father except the Son and those to whom the Son chooses to reveal him.

[28]"Come to me, all you who are weary and burdened, and I will give you rest. [29]Take my yoke upon you and learn from me, for I am gentle and humble in heart, and you will find rest for your souls. [30]For my yoke is easy and my burden is light."

[12:1]At that time Jesus went through the grainfields on the Sabbath. His disciples were hungry and began to pick some heads of grain and eat them. [2]When the Pharisees saw this, they said to him, "Look! Your disciples are doing what is unlawful on the Sabbath."

[3]He answered, "Haven't you read what David did when he and his companions were hungry? [4]He entered the house of God, and he and his

companions ate the consecrated bread—which was not lawful for them to do, but only for the priests. ⁵Or haven't you read in the Law that the priests on Sabbath duty in the temple desecrate the Sabbath and yet are innocent? ⁶I tell you that something greater than the temple is here. ⁷If you had known what these words mean, 'I desire mercy, not sacrifice,' you would not have condemned the innocent. ⁸For the Son of Man is Lord of the Sabbath."

⁹Going on from that place, he went into their synagogue, ¹⁰and a man with a shriveled hand was there. Looking for a reason to bring charges against Jesus, they asked him, "Is it lawful to heal on the Sabbath?"

¹¹He said to them, "If any of you has a sheep and it falls into a pit on the Sabbath, will you not take hold of it and lift it out? ¹²How much more valuable is a person than a sheep! Therefore it is lawful to do good on the Sabbath."

¹³Then he said to the man, "Stretch out your hand." So he stretched it out and it was completely restored, just as sound as the other. ¹⁴But the Pharisees went out and plotted how they might kill Jesus.

¹⁵Aware of this, Jesus withdrew from that place. A large crowd followed him, and he healed all who were ill. ¹⁶He warned them not to tell others about him. ¹⁷This was to fulfill what was spoken through the prophet Isaiah:

¹⁸"Here is my servant whom I have chosen,
    the one I love, in whom I delight;
I will put my Spirit on him,
    and he will proclaim justice to the nations.
¹⁹He will not quarrel or cry out;
    no one will hear his voice in the streets.
²⁰A bruised reed he will not break,
    and a smoldering wick he will not snuff out,
till he has brought justice through to victory.
²¹   In his name the nations will put their hope."

²²Then they brought him a demon-possessed man who was blind and mute, and Jesus healed him, so that he could both talk and see. ²³All the people were astonished and said, "Could this be the Son of David?"

²⁴But when the Pharisees heard this, they said, "It is only by Beelzebul, the prince of demons, that this fellow drives out demons."

²⁵Jesus knew their thoughts and said to them, "Every kingdom divided against itself will be ruined, and every city or household divided against itself will not stand. ²⁶If Satan drives out Satan, he is divided against himself. How then can his kingdom stand? ²⁷And if I drive out demons by

Beelzebul, by whom do your people drive them out? So then, they will be your judges. ²⁸But if it is by the Spirit of God that I drive out demons, then the kingdom of God has come upon you.

²⁹"Or again, how can anyone enter a strong man's house and carry off his possessions unless he first ties up the strong man? Then he can plunder his house.

³⁰"Whoever is not with me is against me, and whoever does not gather with me scatters. ³¹And so I tell you, every kind of sin and slander can be forgiven, but blasphemy against the Spirit will not be forgiven. ³²Anyone who speaks a word against the Son of Man will be forgiven, but anyone who speaks against the Holy Spirit will not be forgiven, either in this age or in the age to come.

³³"Make a tree good and its fruit will be good, or make a tree bad and its fruit will be bad, for a tree is recognized by its fruit. ³⁴You brood of vipers, how can you who are evil say anything good? For the mouth speaks what the heart is full of. ³⁵A good man brings good things out of the good stored up in him, and an evil man brings evil things out of the evil stored up in him. ³⁶But I tell you that everyone will have to give account on the day of judgment for every empty word they have spoken. ³⁷For by your words you will be acquitted, and by your words you will be condemned."

³⁸Then some of the Pharisees and teachers of the law said to him, "Teacher, we want to see a sign from you."

³⁹He answered, "A wicked and adulterous generation asks for a sign! But none will be given it except the sign of the prophet Jonah. ⁴⁰For as Jonah was three days and three nights in the belly of a huge fish, so the Son of Man will be three days and three nights in the heart of the earth. ⁴¹The men of Nineveh will stand up at the judgment with this generation and condemn it; for they repented at the preaching of Jonah, and now something greater than Jonah is here. ⁴²The Queen of the South will rise at the judgment with this generation and condemn it; for she came from the ends of the earth to listen to Solomon's wisdom, and now something greater than Solomon is here.

⁴³"When an impure spirit comes out of a person, it goes through arid places seeking rest and does not find it. ⁴⁴Then it says, 'I will return to the house I left.' When it arrives, it finds the house unoccupied, swept clean and put in order. ⁴⁵Then it goes and takes with it seven other spirits more wicked than itself, and they go in and live there. And the final condition of that person is worse than the first. That is how it will be with this wicked generation."

⁴⁶While Jesus was still talking to the crowd, his mother and brothers stood outside, wanting to speak to him. ⁴⁷Someone told him, "Your mother and brothers are standing outside, wanting to speak to you."

⁴⁸He replied to him, "Who is my mother, and who are my brothers?" ⁴⁹Pointing to his disciples, he said, "Here are my mother and my brothers. ⁵⁰For whoever does the will of my Father in heaven is my brother and sister and mother."

INTRODUCTION

W E COME TO MATTHEW 11 AND 12, and we will see the continuing message of our Lord in connection with the kingdom of God coming. We are speaking about the kingdom of God advancing. We want to keep this as our central idea as we go through because Jesus began His preaching, "Repent, for the kingdom of heaven has come near" (Matt. 4:17b). He called the disciples for the work of advancing His kingdom. He spoke about the character of the citizens of the kingdom and the law of the kingdom. We see how our Lord is doing the work of the kingdom.

JOHN IN PRISON, HIS EXPECTATION, AND JESUS' MINISTRY

John the Baptist is in prison, and that has raised a question in his mind. He was expecting Christ, as Messiah, to begin His work, and along with many others (including Jesus' disciples), he was expecting this kingdom to come with manifestation of great power and that the servants of the Lord would *not* be in prison. It is a striking problem for John. "**When John, who was in prison, heard about the deeds of the Messiah, he sent his disciples to ask him, 'Are you the one who is to come, or should we expect someone else?'**" (11:2–3). John's faith is being severely tested. John was the one who pointed out, "Look, the Lamb of God, who takes away the sin of the world!" (Jn. 1:29). It was very clear and definite, yet now, he is left with a question under the circumstances of being thrown into prison.

We see a similar question in Peter's mind and heart. Jesus said He was to die, and Peter could not receive this; he could not process it. To this day, the Jews are not able to affirm that the Messiah *must suffer*; this is a significant point. He is a glorious king, and all the truths about His glorious reign are real, but He is also the One who is to suffer and to take away sin.[1] There will not be a glorious rule without His suffering.

Our Lord instructed His disciples about the nature of the kingdom *after* He was risen. And immediately after this section, in Matthew 13, He will instruct His disciples concerning the kingdom they are to expect. Much has to do with our expectation, our hope, and how we work for it. The disciples come to ask, **"Are you the one who is to come, or should we expect someone else?"** (11:3). If John's faith can be shaken, what about our own faith? If John has some misunderstanding mixed in with his understanding, what about our own understanding? We should be cautioned by this and be careful, watchful, and search for our own shortcomings. **"Jesus replied, 'Go back and report to John what you hear and see.'"** Jesus points to the evidence of the kingdom coming. This will also be used against those who reject Him; He points to His works. **"Jesus replied, 'Go back and report to John what you hear and see: The blind receive sight, the lame walk, those who have leprosy are cleansed, the deaf hear, the dead are raised, and the good news is proclaimed to the poor"** (11:4–5). The works of the kingdom include removing the curse, and with it, the cause of the curse. He is *undoing* what Adam did. He also says, **"and the good news is proclaimed to the poor."** The work of the kingdom is *doing* what Adam failed to do: He is proclaiming the Word of God in all of life to all persons—to all those who want to hear.

If we had this understanding from Genesis, it would have been easier to see what our Lord is doing and to respond.[2] If we had understood from the beginning of Genesis that God permitted evil for a purpose and that it would be worked out in a certain way, we would be more prepared.[3] Even when we have heard this said, even when we have heard it a number of times, we are inclined to let it slip. Our hearts intuitively want to go back, immediately and quickly, to the Edenic condition. We have said that there is a spiritual war that is age-long

1. *Luke 24:25–27.*

2. *The Biblical Worldview*, Surrendra Gangadean.

3. Gangadean, *Philosophical Foundation*, 145–161; Gangadean, *On Natural and Revealed Theology*, 141–147; Gangadean, "Paper No. 7: The Problem of Evil," in *The Logos Papers*, 33–39; Gangadean, *The Biblical Worldview*, 37–54, 219–239.

and agonizing.[4] We know this, yet we do not *apply* it in our particular circumstances. We know that we have sin in us, yet we are surprised at the fiery trials that try us. As our Lord said to Peter, we need to "watch and pray so that you will not fall into temptation" (Matt. 26:41a). Be alert, be thoughtful, and do not be casual.

Jesus' Commendation of John

As John's disciples are leaving with this message, Jesus spoke of John to the people. He commends John and testifies concerning John. John had testified concerning Jesus, and Jesus now testifies concerning John.[5] The people had probably seen John's disciples come, they had probably heard them asking the question, and perhaps they are now wondering. Remember, this was one of four testimonies that Jesus had: (1) John's testimony, (2) the works He did, (3) the Father's voice, and (4) the Scriptures. In John 5, Jesus spoke about how He is not just bearing witness to Himself; others are bearing witness. John's testimony seems to be shaken, and for many, this was very dramatic, so Jesus testifies concerning John.

John is shaken at this point. He is in prison, and he is not processing this well. This needs to be put in perspective. So, **"As John's disciples were leaving, Jesus began to speak to the crowd about John: 'What did you go out into the wilderness to see? A reed swayed by the wind?'"** (11:7). Did they go out to see someone who is being moved as the wind moves the reed, someone who is emotional, and full of zeal? **"If not, what did you go out to see? A man dressed in fine clothes? No, those who wear fine clothes are in kings' palaces"** (11:8). No, this is not John. **"Then what did you go out to see? A prophet? Yes, I tell you, and more than a prophet"** (11:9). Again, what did you go out to see? Jesus asks three questions. He is intensifying the questions and preparing the people. Did they go out to see a prophet? Yes, that is what he is. John is a prophet, and he is the true prophet, even though he is shaken at this time. Jesus speaks about this prophet in terms of the Scripture: **"This is the one about whom it is written: 'I will send**

---

4. Gangadean, "Paper No. 8: Belief and Unbelief," 41–42; "Paper No. 58: The Spiritual War (Church and World)," 317–322; "Paper No. 60: The Spiritual War (Part II)," 329–330; "Paper No. 109: The Spiritual War (Dimensions)," in *The Logos Papers*, 573–575.

5. *Matthew 11:7–19.*

my messenger ahead of you, who will prepare your way before you'"
(11:10). This is spoken of in Malachi 3:1, the last book of the Old Testament. Malachi spoke about Christ's coming and what would happen
before Christ comes: "I will send my messenger ahead of you." John
is the messenger ahead of the Messiah to come "who will prepare your
way before you." Isaiah says, "A voice of one calling: 'In the wilderness prepare the way for the LORD'" (Is. 40:3a). This was spoken of
John in Luke 3:4: "A voice of one calling in the wilderness, 'Prepare
the way for the Lord, make straight paths for him.'" Jesus says John is
a prophet—that is his true identity—he is not these other things that
you might think. This is according to Scripture.

Jesus says of John, **"Truly I tell you, among those born of women
there has not risen anyone greater than John the Baptist"** (11:11a).
Among those born of women, there is none greater. This is a peculiar
statement, that John the Baptist is the greatest. What about Moses?
What about Abraham and David? In what sense is John the greatest? He
is the greatest in the sense of the work of a prophet and the prophet's
place in the kingdom of God, speaking and pointing to Christ—John
pointed *directly* at Christ.[6] We should not think he is just some figure
appearing for a while and then going away. He has accomplished the
work of God according to His Word.

Jesus says, **"Yet whoever is least in the kingdom of heaven is greater than he"** (11:11b). At this point, we have to understand the terms
great and *least* in relation to the presence and privileges of the kingdom.
Though John is the greatest among those born *before* the kingdom, the
one *in* the kingdom is greater than John. Jesus says, **"Whoever is least
in the kingdom of heaven is greater than he."** In what respect is this
one greater? The least in the kingdom is greater in terms of the privileges of the kingdom. So great is the kingdom, that the bottom of the
kingdom—in terms of the new privileges that are coming with Christ
bringing the kingdom—is greater than the height before the kingdom
came. Remember, Jesus is coming and preaching the kingdom, "Repent, for the kingdom of heaven has come near" (Matt. 4:17b). John
was a harbinger of the kingdom.

---

6. *John 1:29.*

THE STATUS OF THE KINGDOM AND
HOW IT IS ATTAINED—FORCEFULNESS

"From the days of John the Baptist until now, the kingdom of heaven has been forcefully advancing, and forceful men lay hold of it" (11:12). We see the centrality of the kingdom since the days of John. John came preaching, "Repent, for the kingdom of heaven has come near" (Matt. 3:2). Jesus began with this same message. Notice how the concept of *the kingdom* keeps coming back to the center of His message and becomes the measure of things. In the NKJV, He says, "**And from the days of John the Baptist until now the kingdom of heaven suffers violence, and the violent take it by force**" (11:12). The NIV says "forceful men."[7] The idea is that the conflict has intensified with the coming of the kingdom; it is greater than before. The conflict is age-long, but now the kingdom is present and growing and breaking down the barriers erected by Satan. This kingdom is forceful and the force is being felt all around.

One of the reasons John is in prison is because he is preaching the Word and preaching against Herod having his brother's wife. John preached this word to Herod in the context of repentance, saying that Herod was to submit himself to the kingdom of God. This, of course, offends Herod, and Herod has John put in prison. John then dies what seems to be a most ignominious death. A girl danced and pleased the king. She and her mother (Herod's wife) contrived to have John beheaded and his head brought in. Yet for the one who has eyes to see and ears to hear, one can see that John is a faithful witness, which is not meaningless or trivial. We would not expect a prophet to go out this way; we would expect the prophet John to go out in chariots of fire that come down and sweep him up to heaven.[8] That is the way to go—one would think. We would not expect him to be beheaded and his head presented on a platter to satisfy some man's lust and some woman's ambition. "**The kingdom of heaven has been forcefully advancing**" (11:12b), and pressure is growing on the forces of darkness as this witness continues.

---

7. NIV 1984.
8. *2 Kings 2*.

The kingdom is *pressing out*—this is going to be a very significant part of the context of what follows—but those who enter the kingdom enter it by virtue of *pressing in*. To come into the kingdom we cannot be casual; we must exert a kind of pressure. Take up your cross daily, sell everything you have, and forget everything else, that you might possess it. The kingdom will not be had by those who do not seek diligently.[9] The kingdom will not be had by someone who does not submit himself to be a disciple. This is how we are to expect the kingdom to come; there will be pressure and tension because of the reality of sin. One must act against sin in the world as the kingdom presses out, and one must act against sin in oneself—forcefully ridding oneself of sin and crucifying it—in order to enter the kingdom. All of this Jesus is saying in connection with John and how people might hear John's testimony, especially in light of the kingdom that John prophesied. **"For all the Prophets and the Law prophesied until John"** (11:13). This is the sense in which John is the greatest in the kingdom. All the prophets were pointing *forward* to Jesus' coming. John had the privilege of pointing to Jesus *directly*. This privilege puts him so close to the kingdom of God, yet he was still under the old covenant. Because of this, he was the greatest of those born of women, and yet still less than the least in the kingdom. The new privileges that are coming are greater than those of John. The privilege of access to the presence of God was not through the temple, but through the Holy Spirit that was poured out and working in the heart.

THE REJECTION OF THE KINGDOM

Having Ears to Hear Versus Being Casual

Jesus goes further and says, **"And if you are willing to accept it, he is the Elijah who was to come"** (11:14). He says, **"He who has ears to hear, let him hear!"** (11:15 NKJV). This is an interesting phrase. The phrase implies that we *should* have ears to hear. Those who do—those who are seeking, who have this attitude of pressing in and exerting energy to understand—are the ones who will hear and understand, and they are the ones who possess the kingdom. You must seek. You

---

9. *Hebrews 11:6.*

must diligently seek; it cannot be casual. Only in this context of diligently seeking will our faith grow. Left to ourselves, "There is no one righteous, not even one; there is no one who understands, no one who seeks God" (Rom. 3:10–11).

Jesus now compares this generation to those like children in the marketplace. **"To what can I compare this generation? They are like children sitting in the marketplaces and calling out to others: 'We played the pipe for you, and you did not dance; we sang a dirge and you did not mourn'"** (11:16–17). If we come to them in one way, they explain us away; if we come in another way, they explain us away.

> **For John came neither eating nor drinking, and they say, "He has a demon." The Son of Man came eating and drinking, and they say, "Here is a glutton and a drunkard, a friend of tax collectors and sinners." But wisdom is proved right by her deeds** (11:18–19).

People very casually explain away things that would confront them and call them to repentance. This is the condition in which we find the kingdom advancing. This is the condition of the kingdom itself, the condition of the hearts of the people, the reality of sin, and the royal battle that is going on. We are not to be put off, we are not to be offended, and we are not to be surprised by these sorts of circumstances. John is in prison, and he would ask, **"Are you the one who is to come, or should we expect someone else?"** (11:3). Have you had your faith shaken? Have you wondered whether God is with you, whether God loves you, whether this is the way we should go? I dare say that many of us have had that experience and will have that experience. Remember these words, the way our Lord spoke to John in relation to the kingdom.

Woe on Unrepentant Cities with Greater Light

Jesus pronounces judgment on those who had these works done among them—the same works that He reported to John's disciples, especially in the cities of Bethsaida and Chorazin and the cities around the Sea of Galilee. These works were done in these places and they did not repent and believe. **"Then Jesus began to denounce the towns in which most of his miracles had been performed, because they did not repent. 'Woe to you, Chorazin! Woe to you, Bethsaida!'"** (11:20–21a). They should have seen these miracles and come to the Lord. Our Lord said,

"Even though you do not believe me, believe the works" (Jn. 10:38a). It is *very clear* that God has sent Jesus. Jesus compares these cities with Tyre and Sidon: "**For if the miracles that were performed in you had been performed in Tyre and Sidon, they would have repented long ago in sackcloth and ashes**" (11:21b). Please keep this in mind: Greater revelation brings greater responsibility.

> **But I tell you, it will be more bearable for Tyre and Sidon on the day of judgment than for you. And you, Capernaum, will you be lifted up to the heavens? No, you will go down to the Hades. For if the miracles that were performed in you had been performed in Sodom, it would have remained to this day. But I tell you that it will be more bearable for Sodom on the day of judgment than for you** (11:22–24).

It will be more tolerable for Sodom and Gomorrah on the Day of Judgment than for these cities because Sodom and Gomorrah rejected the light that they had, and judgment came upon them. As certain as we see from Scripture, Capernaum may not have engaged in some of the depraved behavior of Sodom and Gomorrah, but they rejected greater light, and for that reason, they came under greater judgment. We are always judged according to the light that we have and our manifest deeds, especially as they manifest in our words. "**It will be more bearable for Sodom on the day of judgment than for you.**" The kingdom is here, and the works are being done. These are mighty works, and they are not to be taken casually. We are to give diligent heed; we are to consider carefully and not be casual about it, that we may hear, understand, believe, and obey.

Praise to God in His Sovereign Rule: Hidden from the Wise and Revealed to Little Children

In the context of the question from John, the people there with Him hearing this, and the cities of Bethsaida, Chorazin, and Capernaum, our Lord responds to the rejection of His Word. He sees the sovereignty of God. "**At that time Jesus said, 'I praise you, Father, Lord of heaven and earth, because you have hidden these things from the wise and learned, and revealed them to little children'**" (11:25). The way of God, in general, is to reveal the truth unto little children and to hide it from those who claim to understand but do not. "**Yes, Father, for this is what you were pleased to do**" (11:26). In this, God's name is honored, and human pride is humbled. This is the way of God. 1 Corinthians 1:26–29 says,

> Brothers, think of what you were when you were called. Not many of you were wise by human standards; not many were influential; not many were of noble birth. But God chose the foolish things of the world to shame the wise; God chose the weak things of the world to shame the strong. God chose the lowly things of this world and the despised things—and the things that are not—to nullify the things that are, so that no one may boast before him.

Blessed are the poor in spirit; blessed are those who mourn.[10] The sacrifices of God are a broken spirit; a broken and contrite heart, O God, you will not despise.[11] Jesus praises God for this: "**I praise you, Father**" (11:25a). God reveals this to little children and not to the wise in their own eyes. This is done sovereignly by God. He also recognizes His own involvement in this sovereignty. "**All things have been committed to me by my Father. No one knows the Son except the Father, and no one knows the Father except the Son and those to whom the Son chooses to reveal him**" (11:27).

Sovereignty and an Invitation to All: Rest for the Weary and Burdened in Christ

In the face of the rejection of God, the sovereignty of God and the way of God are affirmed. Sovereignty does not work in ways that fail to manifest the glory of God. Rather, it works in ways that make His glory *more* manifest—in humbling the pride of men. We, too, should appeal to the sovereignty of God, hoping that we have been faithful, and giving a faithful witness even when it is not received. We are to notice the way of God, praise God for this, and take comfort in His way. Notice that when our Lord Jesus speaks about the sovereignty of God—"**those to whom the Son chooses to reveal him**"—He at the same time makes an invitation that is open to all. People have had questions

---

10. *Matthew 5:3–4.*
11. *Psalm 51:17.*

about the sovereignty of God and the genuineness of this open invitation. Here is this invitation: **"Come to me, all you who are weary and burdened, and I will give you rest"** (11:28). There is no limitation in the invitation, though the words immediately proceeding speak about the sovereignty of God, the praise of God, and the way of God. These are the basics that are in place in our Lord's mind that enable Him to continue to praise God, persevere, and rejoice. **"Come to me, all you who are weary and burdened, and I will give you rest. Take my yoke upon you and learn from me, for I am gentle and humble in heart, and you will find rest for your souls"** (11:28–29).

The Son chooses to reveal, but He calls men to take His yoke upon them, to learn of Him, that He is humble and gentle. How our hearts long to have that same humility and gentleness and not to carry the burden of pride and arrogance. As you come to Him, **"you will find rest for your souls."** We are troubled by many things, but as we come to our Lord and submit to His ways, we will find rest in Him. **"For my yoke is easy and my burden is light"** (11:30). The call is, in every way, inviting. **"Come to me, all you who are weary and burdened, and I will give you rest. Take my yoke upon you and learn from me, for I am gentle and humble in heart, and you will find rest for your souls."** He is not asking us to pick up some impossible burden. It is our yoke, our own yoke, that is heavy. It is made of the things we put upon ourselves in our own self-life. His call is to put those things aside and come to Him. We have to exert a certain amount of forcefulness in order to put aside our own way—to say no to it, and to crucify it—but in reality, it is a way of life, and it is the easy way. It is the gentle and humble way, as our Lord Jesus is gentle and humble in heart. This is a heart condition that finds rest in God. May God grant us grace to take His yoke upon us.

THE LORD OF THE SABBATH:
Bringing Rest from the Burden of Sin

The conflict continues in Matthew 12. The disciples walk through the grainfields and eat the heads of grain on the Sabbath.

> **At that time Jesus went through the grainfields on the Sabbath. His disciples were hungry and began to pick some heads of grain**

and eat them. When the Pharisees saw this, they said to him, "Look! Your disciples are doing what is unlawful on the Sabbath." He answered, "Haven't you read what David did when he and his companions were hungry? He entered the house of God, and he and his companions ate the consecrated bread—which was not lawful for them to do, but only for the priests" (12:1–4).

Circumstance and Objection

The Pharisees are concerned about lawfulness, and Jesus answers them in terms of lawfulness. Under the condition of hunger, David went into the house of God and ate the consecrated bread. He calls them to put this in context and understand it properly. The priests also desecrate the Sabbath: "Or haven't you read in the Law that the priests on the Sabbath duty in the temple desecrate the Sabbath and yet are innocent?" (12:5). They are innocent in the work that they must do. There is a certain kind of work that is done on the Sabbath. For example, preaching is a kind of work. It is a real work, but it is appropriate, because of the reality of sin and the need to do this work on the Sabbath Day. Jesus speaks about the Sabbath, and both concerns are about the house of God. Jesus said, "I tell you that one greater than the temple is here" (12:6).[12] Notice how He is focusing on the temple: David going to the temple, the priest of the temple, and One greater than the temple is here. He is calling them to understand what the temple is all about—the things that are consecrated and connected with the temple—and to truly understand what the Sabbath rest is about. The temple is to restore us to that rest because of our sin. He had just said, "Take my yoke upon you and learn from me, for I am gentle and humble in heart, and you will find rest for your souls" (11:29). Then He speaks about the Sabbath, and then He speaks about the temple as that which symbolizes the way to rest in God. He is greater than the temple because He is the fulfillment of what the temple speaks about.

In the temple, the sacrifices were given. The Pharisees had not understood this, and they were looking at the law apart from the sacrifice and what it signifies. Jesus said, "If you had known what these words mean, 'I desire mercy, not sacrifice,' you would not have condemned the innocent" (12:7). They may go to the temple, offer the sacrifice, miss

---

12. NIV 1984.

the principle of God's mercy revealed in this, and not do the works of mercy on the Sabbath day. They should have brought our Lord Jesus in and provided for Him and His disciples. "Do not muzzle an ox while it is treading out the grain" (Deut. 25:4). He is doing this work, and yet they are not providing for Him, not supplying this need, which would have been the right, kind, and merciful thing to do, rather than finding fault. If they had understood what the temple was about, that He was the fulfillment of it, and that He desires mercy, not the outward sacrifice without the spirit of mercy, they would not have condemned the innocent. **"For the Son of Man is Lord of the Sabbath"** (12:8). I like this—the Lord of the Sabbath. Did He not just say, **"and you will find rest for your souls"**? This is what redemption is about—to restore us to rest in God. He is the fulfillment of the temple, and He is the Lord of the Sabbath. He says, **"Come to me, all you who are weary and burdened, and I will give you rest. Take my yoke upon you and learn from me, for I am gentle and humble in heart, and you will find rest for your souls"** (11:28–29).

Healing on the Sabbath: Is It Lawful?

Jesus goes on from there and heals the man with the shriveled hand. **"Going on from that place, he went into their synagogue, and a man with a shriveled hand was there. Looking for a reason to bring charges against Jesus, they asked him, 'Is it lawful to heal on the Sabbath?'"** (12:9–10). They are looking for a reason to accuse Him. The assumption in their mind is that it is not lawful. Jesus instructs them. **"He said to them, 'If any of you has a sheep and it falls into a pit on the Sabbath, will you not take hold of it and lift it out? How much more valuable is a man than a sheep! Therefore it is lawful to do good on the Sabbath'"** (12:11–12). How clear it is; how obvious it is, once it is pointed out. We can miss it; we can strain at gnats and swallow camels.[13] We do not get the basic principle, so we ask, 'Can I go this far? Can I do this much?' We do not have the basics in place. If the principle is understood, the application and practice will be clear, but the principle is not understood. **"Then he said to the man, 'Stretch out your hand.' So he stretched it out and it was completely restored, just**

---

13. Gangadean, "Paper No. 64: Aaron's Rod," in *The Logos Papers*, 341–352.

as sound as the other" (12:13). In the presence of all these leaders, it becomes manifest that they do not understand the Sabbath, and yet they are in positions of authority. Jesus is challenging them by His act of obedience to God, which sets them off. Their position—presumed position—is called into question. "But the Pharisees went out and plotted how they might kill Jesus" (12:14). They plot how they might kill Him. They do not see the obvious in front of their eyes. Bethsaida and Chorazin had this witness, too; they did not give heed.

GOD'S CHOSEN SERVANT:
The Hope of the Nations

We see the Lord's response in detail and the connection to the words of the prophecy fulfilled:

> Aware of this, Jesus withdrew from that place. A large crowd followed him, and he healed all who were ill. He warned them not to tell others about him. This was to fulfill what was spoken through the prophet Isaiah: "Here is my servant whom I have chosen, the one I love, in whom I delight; I will put my Spirit on him, and he will proclaim justice to the nations. He will not quarrel or cry out; no one will hear his voice in the streets. A bruised reed he will not break, and a smoldering wick he will not snuff out, till he has brought justice through to victory. In his name the nations will put their hope" (12:15–21).

This is the character of Jesus: "He will not quarrel or cry out; no one will hear his voice in the streets." He is not going to force Himself upon others. If someone does not hear, He will go on. Notice His gentleness: "A bruised reed he will not break, and a smoldering wick he will not snuff out." He will continue to do the work of God "till he has brought justice through to victory," and the result is that the Gentiles will hear and put their hope in Him: "In his name the nations will put their hope." The Jews, who have had the covenant privileges, have taken it for granted, misunderstood it, and missed the meaning of it, because they were around it without paying attention and they did not hear. All those who have been brought up around the holy things of God had it presented to them, and they have not paid attention or given heed—something is going on in them, and they are losing their ability to hear. This victory is going to go forth and the *Gentiles* will put their hope in Him—all the nations of the earth. Those outside the Church are the Gentiles. Those outside the covenant are the Gentiles. Those who did not have the covenant privileges are the Gentiles.

THE WORD OF GOD IS COMPELLING:
Life unto Life, Death unto Death

Jesus continues His work according to the Scripture. Remember the ultimate testimony to Jesus is that His works according to the Scripture are being fulfilled. Jesus continues to heal, and now He brings healing to a man who is blind and mute. **"Then they brought him a demon-possessed man who was blind and mute, and Jesus healed him, so that he could both talk and see"** (12:22). What a combination—he cannot see, hear, or communicate. He is desperate, demon-possessed, and afflicted by the devil—the destroyer. Jesus came to destroy the works of the devil. Jesus healed the man, and **"all the people were astonished and said, 'Could this be the Son of David?'"** (12:23). The leaders hear that the attention is going to someone else, who is *the* leader, and they are put off. This drives them deeper into the darkness: **"But when the Pharisees heard this, they said, 'It is only by Beelzebul, the prince of demons, that this fellow drives out demons'"** (12:24). He has done an obvious work of God. Yet, it is being gainsaid and resisted. The conflict escalates by charging Christ with casting out demons by Beelzebul. Notice that before, they opposed Jesus for healing on the Sabbath but had not spoken against *Him*. Now, they go further in their opposition by accusing Christ. Please note the words spoken by the Pharisees, because Jesus is going to draw attention to them by saying: **"For by your words you will be acquitted, and by your words you will be condemned"** (12:37). Notice the significance of the words spoken in the heart, and the words revealing the thoughts of the heart.

Silencing the Opposition

Jesus responds to this obvious falsehood:

Jesus knew their thoughts and said to them, "Every kingdom divided against itself will be ruined, and every city or household divided
against itself will not stand. If Satan drives out Satan, he is divided
against himself. How then can his kingdom stand?" (12:25–26).

It is clear that their accusation is not true. Jesus appeals to a kingdom
divided, a city divided, and a household divided, which cannot stand.
How can Satan's kingdom stand? Satan does not cast out Satan, as he
would be divided against himself; he cannot stand. It is obviously rotten logic that is being used here. It is carelessly spoken because of the
self-life—they want to hold on to their position.

This is the first part of His response. The second part is: How do
your people cast him out? "And if I drive out demons by Beelzebul,
by whom do your people drive them out? So then, they will be your
judges" (12:27). It is impossible for demons to be cast out by Satan,
others cast them out, so how do they think Jesus is casting them out? It
is very obvious that the Spirit of God is doing this, which is connected
with the words that He spoke and with whom He claims to be. The
power of God is with Him, what He is saying is the truth, God has
sent Him, and God is with Him. "But if it is by the Spirit of God that
I drive out demons, then the kingdom of God has come upon you"
(12:28). Therefore, the kingdom of heaven is among them. Notice this
focus on the kingdom of heaven. They should repent and enter the
kingdom, but they do not.

Furthermore, to drive out demons, particularly the way in which
Jesus is driving them out, means that One stronger than Satan is here,
who can bind Satan and rob him. "Or again, how can anyone enter
a strong man's house and carry off his possessions unless he first ties
up the strong man? Then he can plunder his house" (12:29). Satan is
holding this blind and mute man in bondage, and Jesus releases him.
This shows the power of God present in the Lord Jesus.

Jesus answers their question clearly by three examples—the kingdom, the city, and the household—and then He asks them a question:
"By whom do your people drive them out?" Therefore, the conclusion is that the kingdom of heaven is among you, and One greater and
stronger than Satan is here. Five points are made in this short compass,

including the consequences to follow.[14] Notice how Jesus is giving reasons to respond to their unbelief.

Consequences of Opposition to the Work of God

Jesus begins to speak about the consequences of their position. "**Whoever is not with me is against me**" (12:30). In this context, they are not building with Him, and they are against Him—trying to trap Him in every way. A second consequence is that "**whoever does not gather with me scatters.**" They are trying to destroy His work of gathering by interrupting and trying to draw people away. And what they have done now is to attribute the work of God—the work of the Holy Spirit—to an evil spirit, which is blasphemy. It is blasphemy against the Holy Spirit. "**And so I tell you, every kind of sin and slander can be forgiven, but blasphemy against the Spirit will not be forgiven**" (12:31). It will not be forgiven because it is the Holy Spirit who takes the words of the Son of Man and brings them and applies them to the hearts and minds of men. "**Anyone who speaks a word against the Son of Man will be forgiven, but anyone who speaks against the Holy Spirit will not be forgiven, either in this age or in the age to come**" (12:32). In the process of opposing His authority, they have now come to oppose the work of the Holy Spirit in the heart of man, especially in illuminating the mind of man to reveal the obvious and make things clear. When this work of the Spirit is resisted, and they have to go so far as to speak evil against the Holy Spirit in order to get away from it, the line has been crossed. They have crossed the line when they go so far in their denial. And this will not be forgiven, in this age or in the age to come.

A persistent rejection of that which is clear, made so by the working of the Holy Spirit inwardly in our minds, can only be carried out by denying a fundamental reality. It is fundamental logic that a kingdom divided against itself cannot stand; this is obvious—it is maximally clear. Blasphemy against the Holy Spirit will not be forgiven when one goes so far in denying the truth and the light that is given. We should not truncate the meaning of this sin but rather understand that ultimately,

---

14. These five points are taken from the handwritten outline: (1) Every kingdom (city or family) divided will be ruined. (2) By whom do you people drive them out? Therefore, the kingdom of God has come upon you. (3) Strong man argument. (4) If not with me, then against me. (5) Sin against the Holy Spirit will not be forgiven (denying the obvious).

all the sins that will not be forgiven in this age or the age to come are against the Holy Spirit. Do you see this? Do you understand this? If a person is not forgiven, it is because they have resisted or rejected the work of the Holy Spirit in their lives. Perhaps you might say there is a work of the Holy Spirit upholding men in the general revelation point that Jesus makes: A kingdom divided against itself cannot stand.

An Explanation and Warning About Their Rejection

Jesus gives an explanation of the Pharisees' rejection of the work of the Holy Spirit: **"Make a tree good and its fruit will be good, or make a tree bad and its fruit will be bad, for a tree is recognized by its fruit"** (12:33). The charge against Christ is not only rotten logic; this is rotten fruit, this is bad fruit, it is coming from a rotten heart, a rotten mind, an evil mind, a mind that is self-centered and opposed to God and will not bow before God. It is a mind that is satanic, because that is the principle of Satan. They are hearing the word of Satan, and they are children of the devil. This is why He describes them this way: **"You brood of vipers, how can you who are evil say anything good? For the mouth speaks what the heart is full of"** (12:34). In the previous confrontation, they did not say anything, they just went out and plotted. Now, when the people are saying, **"Could this be the Son of David?"** (11:23b), in order to block the people from going to Him, they say He is casting out demons by Satan. Jesus says, **"For the mouth speaks what the heart is full of."** Those thoughts come out of a rotten heart, an evil heart, a satanic heart. We have heard much about the words of our mouths and how they reveal what is in us, and Jesus brings attention to this.

> A good man brings good things out of the good stored up in him, and the evil man brings evil things out of the evil stored up in him. But I tell you that everyone will have to give account on the day of judgment for every empty word they have spoken (12:35–36).

Perhaps they did not use care; perhaps they are just speaking hastily out of opposition. Even if it is careless, one must give an account **"on the day of judgment for every empty word they have spoken. For by your words you will be acquitted, and by your words you will be condemned"** (12:36b–37). The words reveal what is in the heart. This is part of the manifestation. The words Jesus has spoken will judge them, and their own words will judge them.

A Rebuke of Self-Deception and Self-Righteousness: Deeper into Darkness

"Then some of the Pharisees and teachers of the law said to him, 'Teacher, we want to see a sign from you.' He answered, 'A wicked and adulterous generation asks for a sign!'" (12:38–39a). They did not understand. Notice it is because of their failure to understand— their lack of faith—that they are asking for some visible manifestation. It *seems* that they are interested in proof, but they have had abundant proof all around them, they had not paid attention to it or understood, and now they are asking for more. They say to themselves, 'We are seek- ing—show us a sign!' Jesus rebukes them: **"A wicked and adulterous generation asks for a sign! But none will be given it except the sign of the prophet Jonah"** (12:39). Jesus knows they are wicked and how far they have gone—they are going to kill Him and He will be resurrected, the sign of the One approved of God. Again, there is the principle of more light connected with greater judgment. This generation had more light and did not respond. The Assyrians repented at the preaching of Jonah in Nineveh. The Queen of Sheba came from the south to hear Solomon's wisdom, and One greater than Solomon is here.

> For as Jonah was three days and three nights in the belly of a huge fish, so the Son of Man will be three days and three nights in the heart of the earth. The men of Nineveh will stand up at the judg- ment with this generation and condemn it; for they repented at the preaching of Jonah, and now something greater than Jonah is here. The Queen of the South will rise at the judgment with this generation and condemn it; for she came from the ends of the earth to listen to Solomon's wisdom, and now something greater than Solomon is here (12:40–42).

Notice that Jesus emphasizes these terms: *greater* than Satan, a *strong* man, *greater* than the temple, the *fulfillment* of the temple, and John being the *greatest* man because he points toward Christ and His kingdom. It always comes back to the *greatness* of our Lord Jesus Christ and who He is. Now, One greater than Jonah and Solomon is here, One full of grace and truth. As He said for Bethsaida and Chorazin,[15] the judgment will be more tolerable for these nations than for the Pharisees because the Pharisees had greater light and rejected it. Christ says, "Blessed are you when people insult you, persecute you and falsely say all kinds of evil against you because of me" (Matt. 5:11). They spoke careless words, but they will still have to give an account on the Day of Judgment. Do not partake in their careless words. Be on your guard against careless words, and be on your guard concerning what is in your heart.

Jesus speaks about the real condition of the people:

> **When an evil spirit comes out of a person, it goes through arid places seeking rest and does not find it. Then it says, "I will return to the house I left." When it arrives, it finds the house unoccupied, swept clean and put in order. Then it goes and takes with it seven other spirits more wicked than itself, and they go in and live there. And the final condition of that person is worse than the first. That is how it will be with this wicked generation (12:43–45).**

Jesus says that cleaning up by outward reform, without coming to Him and acknowledging Him, only invites other spirits more evil than the original to come in. Sometimes outward religious reform, without the true Spirit of God in Christ, can bring us into a worse condition than before. The condition of this generation is outwardly righteous, out-wardly moral, but they resist God. They are not like the prostitutes and tax collectors who humble themselves before God. **"The final condition of that person is worse than the first"** (12:45). They become twice the child of hell.[16] He is going to explicitly make this point later on when He pronounces "Woe" on the religious leaders.[17]

JESUS' MOTHER AND BROTHERS:
Those Who Seek First the Kingdom

We come to the last section in this passage: **"While Jesus was still talking to the crowd, his mother and brothers stood outside, wanting**

---

15. *Matthew 11:20–24.*

16. *Matthew 23:15.*

17. *Matthew 23.*

to speak to him. Someone told him, 'Your mother and brothers are standing outside, wanting to speak to you'" (12:46–47). For our Lord, everything is subordinated to the Word of God and the kingdom of God. "He replied to him, 'Who is my mother, and who are my brothers?' Pointing to his disciples, he said, 'Here are my mother and my brothers. For whoever does the will of my Father in heaven is my brother and sister and mother'" (12:48–50). It all comes back to His Father, the will of His Father, and the will of God being done on earth—His kingdom. Anyone who does the will of His Father is His "brother and sister and mother." These are the words of our Lord. It seems, at this time, His mother and brothers are not where they ought to be in understanding. People might think that family relationships bind in a particular way, but here, Jesus points to His disciples and says, "Here are my mother and my brothers. For whoever does the will of my Father in heaven is my brother and sister and mother." We are in a new reality in the kingdom of God. The kingdom is based on God as our Father and on our obedience to Him. Our Lord, who is meek and humble in heart, calls us to come to Him, to imitate Him, to follow Him, to take His yoke and learn of Him. May God grant us the grace to do so.

———

10

THE PARABLES OF THE KINGDOM

He Who Has Ears to Hear,
Let Him Hear

Matthew 13

¹That same day Jesus went out of the house and sat by the lake. ²Such large crowds gathered around him that he got into a boat and sat in it, while all the people stood on the shore. ³Then he told them many things in parables, saying: "A farmer went out to sow his seed. ⁴As he was scattering the seed, some fell along the path, and the birds came and ate it up. ⁵Some fell on rocky places, where it did not have much soil. It sprang up quickly, because the soil was shallow. ⁶But when the sun came up, the plants were scorched, and they withered because they had no root. ⁷Other seed fell among thorns, which grew up and choked the plants. ⁸Still other seed fell on good soil, where it produced a crop—a hundred, sixty or thirty times what was sown. ⁹Whoever has ears, let them hear."

¹⁰The disciples came to him and asked, "Why do you speak to the people in parables?"

¹¹He replied, "Because the knowledge of the secrets of the kingdom of heaven has been given to you, but not to them. ¹²Whoever has will be given more, and they will have an abundance. Whoever does not have, even what they have will be taken from them. ¹³This is why I speak to them in parables:

"Though seeing, they do not see;
    though hearing, they do not hear or understand.

¹⁴In them is fulfilled the prophecy of Isaiah:

"'You will be ever hearing but never understanding;

you will be ever seeing but never perceiving.
¹⁵For this people's heart has become calloused;
    they hardly hear with their ears,
    and they have closed their eyes.
Otherwise they might see with their eyes,
    hear with their ears,
    understand with their hearts
and turn, and I would heal them.'

¹⁶But blessed are your eyes because they see, and your ears because they hear. ¹⁷For truly I tell you, many prophets and righteous people longed to see what you see but did not see it, and to hear what you hear but did not hear it.

¹⁸"Listen then to what the parable of the sower means: ¹⁹When anyone hears the message about the kingdom and does not understand it, the evil one comes and snatches away what was sown in their heart. This is the seed sown along the path. ²⁰The seed falling on rocky ground refers to someone who hears the word and at once receives it with joy. ²¹But since they have no root, they last only a short time. When trouble or persecution comes because of the word, they quickly fall away. ²²The seed falling among the thorns refers to someone who hears the word, but the worries of this life and the deceitfulness of wealth choke the word, making it unfruitful. ²³But the seed falling on good soil refers to someone who hears the word and understands it. This is the one who produces a crop, yielding a hundred, sixty or thirty times what was sown."

²⁴Jesus told them another parable: "The kingdom of heaven is like a man who sowed good seed in his field. ²⁵But while everyone was sleeping, his enemy came and sowed weeds among the wheat, and went away. ²⁶When the wheat sprouted and formed heads, then the weeds also appeared.

²⁷"The owner's servants came to him and said, 'Sir, didn't you sow good seed in your field? Where then did the weeds come from?'

²⁸"'An enemy did this,' he replied.

"The servants asked him, 'Do you want us to go and pull them up?'

²⁹"'No,' he answered, 'because while you are pulling the weeds, you may uproot the wheat with them. ³⁰Let both grow together until the harvest. At that time I will tell the harvesters: First collect the weeds and tie them in bundles to be burned; then gather the wheat and bring it into my barn.'"

³¹He told them another parable: "The kingdom of heaven is like a mustard seed, which a man took and planted in his field. ³²Though it is the

smallest of all seeds, yet when it grows, it is the largest of garden plants and becomes a tree, so that the birds come and perch in its branches."

33He told them still another parable: "The kingdom of heaven is like yeast that a woman took and mixed into about sixty pounds of flour until it worked all through the dough."

34Jesus spoke all these things to the crowd in parables; he did not say anything to them without using a parable. 35So was fulfilled what was spoken through the prophet:

"I will open my mouth in parables,
   I will utter things hidden since the creation of the world."

36Then he left the crowd and went into the house. His disciples came to him and said, "Explain to us the parable of the weeds in the field."

37He answered, "The one who sowed the good seed is the Son of Man. 38The field is the world, and the good seed stands for the people of the kingdom. The weeds are the people of the evil one, 39and the enemy who sows them is the devil. The harvest is the end of the age, and the harvesters are angels.

40"As the weeds are pulled up and burned in the fire, so it will be at the end of the age. 41The Son of Man will send out his angels, and they will weed out of his kingdom everything that causes sin and all who do evil. 42They will throw them into the blazing furnace, where there will be weeping and gnashing of teeth. 43Then the righteous will shine like the sun in the kingdom of their Father. Whoever has ears, let them hear.

44"The kingdom of heaven is like treasure hidden in a field. When a man found it, he hid it again, and then in his joy went and sold all he had and bought that field.

45"Again, the kingdom of heaven is like a merchant looking for fine pearls. 46When he found one of great value, he went away and sold everything he had and bought it.

47"Once again, the kingdom of heaven is like a net that was let down into the lake and caught all kinds of fish. 48When it was full, the fishermen pulled it up on the shore. Then they sat down and collected the good fish in baskets, but threw the bad away. 49This is how it will be at the end of the age. The angels will come and separate the wicked from the righteous 50and throw them into the blazing furnace, where there will be weeping and gnashing of teeth.

51"Have you understood all these things?" Jesus asked.

"Yes," they replied.

[52]He said to them, "Therefore every teacher of the law who has become a disciple in the kingdom of heaven is like the owner of a house who brings out of his storeroom new treasures as well as old."

[53]When Jesus had finished these parables, he moved on from there. [54]Coming to his hometown, he began teaching the people in their synagogue, and they were amazed. "Where did this man get this wisdom and these miraculous powers?" they asked. [55]"Isn't this the carpenter's son? Isn't his mother's name Mary, and aren't his brothers James, Joseph, Simon and Judas? [56]Aren't all his sisters with us? Where then did this man get all these things?" [57]And they took offense at him.

But Jesus said to them, "A prophet is not without honor except in his own town and in his own home."

[58]And he did not do many miracles there because of their lack of faith.

PARABLES AND UNDERSTANDING

TODAY, WE COME TO OUR LORD'S TEACHINGS on the parables. Matthew 13 has several parables, some of which go together in pairs. As we approach this chapter, one of the questions we ask is: Why does our Lord speak to the people in parables? The explanation is given at the beginning of this section. After Jesus had spoken the parable, "**The disciples came to him and asked, 'Why do you speak to the people in parables?'**" (v. 10). Please note the way the Lord ended His teaching on this parable: "**He who has ears to hear, let him hear!**" (v. 9 NKJV). This is an expression that occurs again and again. It reckons with the fact that parables will not be understood unless we have an ear to hear—unless there is some prior work of the Holy Spirit and understanding is in place.[1] We might put it this way: Unless the presuppositions are in place, we will not hear the things that are taught. This explanation is in keeping with the truth that the *less basic* is understood in light of the *more basic*. If we have ears to hear what is more basic, we can understand the less basic things.[2]

1. Gangadean, *The Westminster Confession*, 143–206; Gangadean, *The Westminster Catechisms*, 191–207.

2. Gangadean, *Philosophical Foundation*, 19–23; Gangadean, "Paper No. 101: Rational Presuppositionalism," 521–526; "Paper No. 52: Common Ground (Part III)," in *The Logos Papers*, 281–282; Gangadean, *On Natural and Revealed Theology*, 59–66.

This teaching also emphasizes the call for understanding. On the one hand, teaching in parables helps people to see that they do not understand as they puzzle over it. In a way, this is a protection of the truth of God, and it is a protection of people from being overexposed to the truth of God when a more basic truth is not in place. The parables were spoken, and the explanation for speaking in parables emphasizes faith, or understanding. I want to look at the connection between the parables and understanding.

THE PARABLE OF THE SOWER:
The Need for Understanding

Jesus begins with this parable:

> A farmer went out to sow his seed. As he was scattering the seed, some fell along the path, and the birds came and ate it up. Some fell on rocky places, where it did not have much soil. It sprang up quickly, because the soil was shallow. But when the sun came up, the plants were scorched, and they withered because they had no root. Other seed fell among thorns, which grew up and choked the plants. Still other seed fell on good soil, where it produced a crop—a hundred, sixty or thirty times what was sown. Whoever has ears, let them hear (vv. 3b–9).

The entire first parable underscores the relationship between parables and understanding, and there are several places in which this is brought out very explicitly. At the end of the parable of the sower, Jesus says, **"He who has ears to hear, let him hear!"** (v. 9 NKJV). Then He says, **"Whoever has will be given more, and they will have an abundance"** (v. 12a). This assumes that we have something already, and on the basis of what we have, we get more. It refers to foundational truth; if the basics are in place, we can understand more. **"Whoever has will be given more, and they will have an abundance. Whoever does not have, even what he has will be taken from them"** (v. 12). In addition, He says, **"The knowledge of the secrets of the kingdom of heaven has been given to you"** (v. 11). In that respect, **"the knowledge of the secrets"** (v. 11a) has to do with the understanding of that secret. Immediately after, He says, **"This is why I speak to them in parables: 'Though seeing, they** do not see; though hearing, they do not hear or understand'" (v. 13). The concern about understanding is foremost in the parables. If we understand more basic things, we will understand "the knowledge of the secrets." Our Lord said about those who hear Him, "If you believed Moses, you would believe me, for he wrote about me. But since you do not believe what he wrote, how are you going to believe what I say?" (Jn. 5:46–47). Moses, in this case, was the more basic revelation.

What will happen is that people will wrestle with the parable that is given, misinterpret or misunderstand it, and lose even more of what they did have. "Whoever does not have, even what they have will be taken from them." The Word of God comes to us as *life unto life* and *death unto death*.[3] We should say this: There are many within Christianity, the history of the Christian Church, and in the present day, who struggle with understanding these parables. They perhaps struggle even with the idea of faith as understanding,[4] and yet the Word here emphasizes this. "He who has ears to hear, let him hear!" and "Whoever has will be given more, and they will have an abundance," and "Though seeing, they do not see; though hearing, they do not hear or understand." They can see what is being done but not understand. They can hear what is being said but not understand. This calls for faith.[5] "He who has ears to hear, let him hear!"

Let us further open up the word of the prophecy in Isaiah that is spoken: "You will be ever hearing but never understanding; You will be ever seeing, but never perceiving" (v. 14). How strong are these words? *Ever seeing.* The truth of God will be there again and again and again, perhaps all through one's life, and one can miss it, misunderstand it, and not understand it. We have to be careful that we have the basics in place so that we do not miss obvious truths. We have to have a heart that is willing to be teachable, a heart that is willing to back up and examine our assumptions. We should not be so invested or fearful about our way of life and beliefs that we do not look at these

3. *Isaiah 55:10–11*; *2 Corinthians 2:15–17.*

4. Gangadean, *Philosophical Foundation*, 32–45, 121–127; Gangadean, *History of Philosophy*, 3–12, 163–167; Gangadean, "Paper No. 21: Faith and Reason in Christianity," 135–138; "Paper No. 28: Prepare the Way of the Lord," 171–173; "Paper No. 98: Faith and the Word of God," 511–514; "Paper No. 128: Abraham's Faith," 665–666; "Paper No. 129: Faith and Reason in the Life of Abraham" in *The Logos Papers*, 667–669.

5. Gangadean, *The Biblical Worldview*, 3–20.

assumptions. We must examine the beliefs we hold most strongly, especially those that differ from Historic Christianity. We might think the Church historically has 'gone off.' We have to be careful about this and back up and examine it.[6] The hearts of the people are described as calloused. **"For this people's heart has become calloused"** (v. 15a). At the end of this chapter, we are going to see particular cases of callousness. **"A prophet is not without honor except in his own town and in his own home"** (v. 57). We will have to apply this principle to explain how these persons were hearing, but they were not understanding. Their hearts have become calloused: **"They hardly hear with their ears, and they have closed their eyes"** (15a).

There is an objective responsibility on the part of those who do not hear. If we had been seeking, we would have understood.[7] We have not been seeking and we have closed our eyes. Isaiah said, **"Otherwise they might see with their eyes, hear with their ears, understand with their hearts and turn, and I would heal them"** (v. 15b). Notice how many times He speaks about understanding. Three times, *understanding* is emphasized. He says: they do not *see*, they do not *hear*—they do not perceive—and they do not *understand* because their hearts are calloused. Jesus is explaining why He speaks to the people in parables. If they have, they can get more; if they do not have, it will become evident. The commendation of Jesus is, **"But blessed are your eyes because they see, and your ears because they hear"** (v. 16). There is a blessing that comes with seeing and understanding. Why, particularly? **"For I tell you the truth, many prophets and righteous men longed to see what you see but did not see it, and to hear what you hear but did not hear it"** (v. 17).[8]

Jesus says in verse 52, **"Therefore every teacher of the law who has become a disciple in the kingdom of heaven is like the owner of a house who brings out of his storeroom new treasures as well as old."** He brings out treasures both new and old. The prophets in the Old Testament had some of this revelation, but there was a new revelation, a greater fullness, given in the New. The Word has unfolded, which will

---

6. Gangadean, *The Westminster Confession*, xix–xxix, 349–351.

7. Gangadean, *Philosophical Foundation*, 3–5, 287–292; Gangadean, *The Westminster Confession*, 1–13; Gangadean, "Paper No. 53: Common Ground (Part IV)," in *The Logos Papers*, 283–286.

8. 1984 NIV.

be important as we interpret these parables. As we interpret parables, we know things have been revealed before and we must keep them in mind. We know there is more basic revelation and there are assumptions. If we do not keep the more basic things in mind, we will not understand these parables; we will miss their meaning. We have to say this because the Church is divided,[9] and therefore, at least some are missing this.

The Meaning of the Parable: Understanding and Fruit

Jesus then explains the parable:

> Listen then to what the parable of the sower means: When anyone hears the message about the kingdom and does not understand it, the evil one comes and snatches away what was sown in their heart. This is the seed sown along the path (vv. 18–19).

When we hear and do not understand, we do not retain it; it is taken away. It has no fruit. There is no profit to the person, and it probably shows a calloused heart. They are not seeking or understanding, and so they lose what they have. "As he was scattering the seed, some fell along the path, and the birds came and ate it up" (v. 4). This is the devil! "The evil one comes and snatches away what was sown in their heart" (v. 19). This is what happens when the Word is spoken and it is heard but not understood. What are we to focus on in this parable? We are to focus on the need for understanding.

The second group is described as the seed that fell on rocky places.

> The seed falling on rocky ground refers to someone who hears the word and at once receives it with joy. But since they have no root, they last only a short time. When trouble or persecution comes because of the word, they quickly fall away (vv. 20–21).

These are persons who undergo outward trials of faith, such as persecution and circumstantial troubles. Notice how these persons are described: "they have no root"—the foundation is not in place. He hears the Word and responds joyfully for a while but without much understanding and with misunderstanding. He thinks the Christian

---

9. *The Unity of the Church*, Surrendra Gangadean.

life is going to be a certain kind of life. There is joy at the beginning. The immediate impression of the work of the kingdom is joyful, but he does not understand what one has to go through to retain and grow in that joy. When troubles come and the joy is gone, and it is not 'fun' anymore, these people wither and fall away. We know that many have made outward professions of faith, but within a few weeks or months, they are not there. This is describing another real category of people. So, in the first group are those who never even respond—the seed that fell along the pathway, and the birds came and ate it up. It is as if they never heard it and did not consider it as the truth. **"Whoever does not have, even what they have will be taken from them"** (v. 12b). So, the last condition of that person is worse than it was before. They lost whatever understanding they had because of this calloused and casual attention to the Word. If there is not seeking, there is not going to be understanding. The second group are those who hear without foundational understanding—they have no root—a shallow understanding. It lasts a short while, and they turn aside. Again, the parable emphasizes the need for understanding. There are those who have no understanding and those who have shallow understanding.

There is a third group of people who hear about the kingdom: **"The seed falling among the thorns refers to someone who hears the word, but the worries of this life and the deceitfulness of wealth choke the word, making it unfruitful"** (v. 22). There is a certain amount of double-mindedness here. We know how we can struggle with worries, the deceitfulness of riches, and the promise that does not and cannot deliver. We do not have the faith to see through this. We go along month after month, year after year, and never seem to come to the point where we are bearing fruit. They did not fall away; they remained, and they may have been in the Church most of their lives, all of their professing life, yet were not fruitful. "In fact, though by this time you ought to be teachers, you need someone to teach you the elementary truths of God's word all over again. You need milk, not solid food!" (Heb. 5:12).[10] There was not a certain kind of discipline of picking up the cross daily, a certain humility of heart to receive correction or to accept the affliction of one's soul before God as a cleansing process. This was not there.

---

10. *The Epistle to the Hebrews*, Surrendra Gangadean.

They wanted a certain amount of comfort, peace, and satisfaction in life, and they are unfruitful. They do not gain what they are seeking.

The last group are those who hear the Word and understand it. **"But the seed falling on good soil refers to someone who hears the word and understands it. This is the one who produces a crop, yielding a hundred, sixty or thirty times what was sown"** (v. 23). There are all kinds of degrees of understanding—from zero, to shallow, to some more (but choked with other things), and then there are those who hear and understand. This is the second reason why we say the parables are being taught. The content of this parable focuses on faith/understanding, and it says that fruitfulness is according to faith/understanding. There seems to be a disconnect between faith and understanding in many sections of Christianity. There may be a lot of enthusiasm and they may keep that enthusiasm going in ways that are not always spiritually honoring to God, but the fruit is not there. **"This is the one who produces a crop, yielding a hundred, sixty or thirty times what was sown"** (v. 23b). The Word is multiplied. We assume it is multiplied not in some abstract way, but in the lives of others, it is reproducing, and the number is 30, 60, and 100. We cannot say, 'We are different kinds of persons that bear different kinds of fruit.' The emphasis here seems to be on the quantity: 100, 60, or 30. Thirty is great, 60 is better, 100 is wonderful, and maybe even more. It is not unusual to think that we should be bearing fruit, and as we understand, by the grace of God, we will.

This is how we are to think about the kingdom and the Word of God that we preach. There will be different conditions of hearers at any given time, and people will respond accordingly. We should be prepared for the variety of responses in the kingdom. We should be watchful for ourselves, that our hearts are humbled before God, that we are seeking God, given to understanding, correction, and appropriate discussion, that we might grow, and that the basics might be in place—that we might produce fruit that is honoring to God. "This is to my Father's glory, that you bear much fruit" (Jn. 15:8a)—fruit that will *last*.[11] We should understand the dealings of God with us—He prunes the vine; He lifts it and cuts it back. We should understand that He disciplines us in our lives and takes away certain things, that we might be more fruitful. "This is to my Father's glory, that you bear much fruit."

---

11. *John 15:16.*

So we are to have faith in the sense of understanding, as we understand the Word, and we can examine ourselves to see whether this understanding is true. If we understand the Word—and not apart from it, nothing less will do—by God's grace, we will be fruitful. We cannot say theoretically, 'Well, I understand.' If so, where is the fruit? This option is not left open for us in this parable. If there is faith, there will be fruit. We can examine our understanding, and if there is no fruit, you can cry out to God and say, 'Lord, teach me that I might understand.' The Lord will teach us, but it will involve trials of our faith, testing of our faith, so that which is not *true* understanding might be revealed for what it is. We will have to struggle to come into understanding. It can be painful and fiery, but what we will get is the glory that will be revealed by multiplying this in the understanding of others—it is certainly worth it. Mothers and fathers who have children—mothers particularly—go through the pain of childbirth, and when their child is born, they rejoice—so it is spiritually. We go through trials in our lives, and then God blesses and grants us fruit. And we rejoice that it has borne fruit. We can see the fruit. It is a great joy.

THE PARABLE OF THE WEEDS EXPLAINED:
Admixture in the Church Until the End

The first parable emphasizes understanding, and the explanation of why He speaks in parables also emphasizes understanding. Jesus tells them another parable:

> The kingdom of heaven is like a man who sowed good seed in his field. But while everyone was sleeping, his enemy came and sowed weeds among the wheat, and went away. When the wheat sprouted and formed heads, then the weeds also appeared. The owner's servants came to him and said, "Sir, didn't you sow good seed in your field? Where then did the weeds come from?" "An enemy did this," he replied. The servants asked him, "Do you want us to go and pull them up?" "No," he answered, "because while you are pulling the weeds, you may root up the wheat with them. Let both grow together until the harvest. At that time I will tell the harvesters: First collect the weeds and tie them in bundles to be burned; then gather the wheat and bring it into my barn" (vv. 24–30).

I am thinking of ways we might misunderstand the parables so as to avoid those misunderstandings. I do not know that there is much controversy about the parable of the sower, except to say this: Even when we speak that parable, which makes a connection between understanding and fruitfulness, *that point* is not retained. In many parts of the Christian Church, the focus on understanding and fruitfulness is not maintained. Since this is the most significant and central point of that parable, something very important is being missed when it is not retained. I invite you to stay after the service and raise questions, and if you think otherwise, we can begin the process of wrestling with it and trying to understand.

The parable of the weeds has been understood in different ways, and the following parables have also been set against things that are misunderstood from elsewhere in Scripture. Jesus explains the meaning of the parable of the weeds in verses 37–39:

> He answered, "The one who sowed the good seed is the Son of Man. The field is the world, and the good seed stands for the people of the kingdom. The weeds are the people of the evil one, and the enemy who sows them is the devil. The harvest is the end of the age, and the harvesters are angels."

Let us see what we can draw from this. The sower of the good seed is the Son of Man; therefore, the sower of the bad seed is the devil. The good seeds are the sons of the kingdom, and the weeds are the sons of the evil one. What this says is that there is going to be, in the kingdom—notice I said *in the kingdom*, not in the world—both those who do believe and those who do not but who may *appear* to believe. Those who do not believe are known at the time of bringing forth fruit when the heads of grain appear.

The weeds were sewn while everyone was sleeping. I do not know if I should press this at all, but it is suggestive that we have to be watchful that this does not come about. It is almost taken for granted that we are not going to be that watchful, and it is going to happen. The shepherd of the sheep is especially to be watchful, especially those who are in oversight and overseeing. When the wheat formed, then the weeds also appeared. Notice this: it became known when it started to bring forth fruit. Outwardly, they appear to be the same. Verse 26 says, **"When**

the wheat sprouted and formed heads, then the weeds also appeared."
Do we mean all of a sudden the weeds sprung up? No, rather, we are
saying that the weeds were growing side by side with the wheat, but
they had the *outward appearance* of being wheat to the casual observer
(the one not looking carefully). When the heads of wheat were formed,
then the difference between the two could be seen. The harvesters said,
'How do we deal with this? Do we go and pull the weeds up?' But the
owner said, 'No, let them both grow until the harvest, and then collect
the weeds to be burned.' Even the weeds will be useful. I do not want
to press this too far, but all things serve God's purpose. Cain served
the purpose of God in His work of dominion,[12] though Cain did not
and will not enjoy it forever.

We first collect the weeds and then gather the wheat. You can understand this: we do not cause a disturbance that will harm the wheat
because of the close proximity of the two; if you pull one up, you will
uproot the other. But when the harvest is ready, and you do not have to
worry about the root of the plant, or you are just gathering the wheat
seed at harvest, you can pull out the weeds. It will not affect the harvest
itself; the plant will die at that point anyway. Understand the timing of
this and why He says not to pull up the weeds yet. I have been thinking
about this for a while and may come up with a more appropriate term,
but this parable has been used to support *non-victorious amillennialism*. I do not want to say pessimistic amillennialism because some will
say that is not quite right, but at least it is *not victorious*. In this view,
good and evil grow side by side to the end of the age, and good does
not overcome evil. This is *not* what Scripture is saying.

The difference is between non-believers in the Church and non-believers in the world. Notice, the field is the world, the Church is worldwide, and the weeds are sown among the wheat. The wheat is not sown
among the weeds; it is a different dynamic. It is in the Church where
the weeds are planted, and they outwardly look like wheat. So, this
parable cannot be used to support a side-by-side growth of the kingdom of God and the kingdom of darkness to the end of the age. It
refers to non-believers who appear to be believers, or who profess to
be believers, and may continue with believers until the end of the age.
The weeds are not non-believers in general. The parable is not to be

---

12. *Genesis 4.*

used to support this, though I have heard men in Reformed churches, whom you know as well as I, who have used this parable to dismiss the idea of the victory of the kingdom and just set it aside.[13] If they had known earlier things about what the good is, the knowledge of God filling the earth, and it is through dominion—if they understood the promise to Abraham and the promise in the Garden of Eden before the expulsion—things new and old—they could have heard this parable and not allowed this surface reading to lead astray.

This misunderstanding reinforces the view that we do not have to come to a common agreement on the good as the knowledge of God through the work of dominion.[14] This is a block—a hindrance. Some persons are writing on the subject today and speaking about and against what is called *triumphalism*. As soon as people hear about postmillennialism, they think, 'Theonomy, Bahnsen, crazy people. Forget it!' There are many kinds of postmillennialism.[15] They all say that the kingdom of God will grow and advance and overcome the kingdom of darkness in *this life*. Exactly what some of the particulars of these views are needs to be identified and contextualized.

If the field is the world, and the Church is planted in the world, as expected through the Great Commission, then the ones remaining at the end, to be removed, are those in the kingdom (in the Church), outwardly professing but not truly believers. This explanation is consistent with the world coming to believe, and that those who remain are the weeds among the wheat. Those remaining are outwardly professing but not truly believers, because they are the ones that are gathered to be burned. These are not unbelievers in general. So, we can expect that there will be this admixture within the Church. There is this admixture to which the Word of God comes in terms of different levels of understanding and, therefore, an admixture of fruit. There will be an admixture within the kingdom in terms of outward appearance,

13. Gangadean, *On Natural and Revealed Theology*, 229–238.

14. Gangadean, *The Westminster Catechisms*, 321–325; Gangadean, *On Natural and Revealed Theology*, 9–32; Gangadean, "Paper No. 106: The Good and Heaven," 547–556; "Paper No. 117: Knowing and Making God Known," in *The Logos Papers*, 599–601; *The Unity of the Church*, Surrendra Gangadean.

15. The three waves of postmillennialism will be explained in the introduction to *The Book of Revelation: What Must Soon Take Place—Doxological Postmillennialism* (Phoenix: Logos Papers Press, 2025).

but it still comes to be known by the fruit. The separation comes in connection with harvesting the fruit.

THE PARABLES OF THE MUSTARD SEED AND THE YEAST:
The Kingdom Is Here, Begins Small, and Grows Gradually to Fullness

We come to the parable of the mustard seed and the yeast, and these two are a pair—just as the parable of the hidden treasure and the pearl seem to go together. This leads one to wonder whether the parable of the sower and the parable of the weeds form a pair and interpenetrate each other, play off each other, and deepen the understanding. I am not ready to say this, but I am mentioning it as a possibility. "He told them another parable: 'The kingdom of heaven is like a mustard seed, which a man took and planted in his field.'" Notice what is emphasized about this: "Though it is the smallest of all seeds, yet when it grows, it is the largest of garden plants and becomes a tree, so that the birds of the air come and perch in its branches" (vv. 31–32). It is so simple. Jesus is teaching about something that is so basic, and yet there is much difference within Christianity about this today. At this point, we can address both premillennialism and amillennialism. Think about the understanding here.

Just before we do that, let us look at the other parable. "He told them still another parable: 'The kingdom of heaven is like yeast that a woman took and mixed into about sixty pounds of flour until it worked all through the dough'" (v. 33). Notice it is a little amount: "A little yeast works through the whole batch of dough" (Gal. 5:9), and it is "mixed into about sixty pounds of flour until it worked all through the dough."

What are we being taught here? The kingdom begins small, like a tiny seed or just a little bit of yeast—it starts *small*. That is one point. This means the kingdom of God is *here*. Which is to say the kingdom of God is not going to come at some future time in the Second Coming. The kingdom of God is here.

The second point is that the kingdom is *growing*. The mustard seed grows, and the yeast grows and increases. Notice that it is a *manifest* cumulative, not just a cumulative invisible, through history. You can see the mustard seed grow into the tree year after year through the centuries. In this respect, the kingdom of God is here and not merely in the future. Some have tried to say that it comes in the future, and others have tried to say this is a church age, not a kingdom age. That is not being taught here.

The kingdom of God is here: it grows and grows. There are some implications to saying that it grows. It does not come in suddenly, but rather it grows gradually. The disciples expected it suddenly.[16] Many premillennial teachings expect it to come suddenly with the Second Coming of Christ. But it is here, it begins small, and it is growing gradually. The third point is that it will grow to its *fullness*. If it is going to grow to its fullness, the implication is that good and evil will not exist side-by-side. The reason is that the kingdom of God and the kingdom of darkness are mutually exclusive. Every inch gained by the kingdom of God is lost by the kingdom of darkness. The kingdom of God is taking over that realm and those persons. They are mutually exclusive.[17] There is no third realm. The kingdom of God starts small; the rest of it is darkness. The kingdom of God is growing, and it is going to displace the darkness. And in doing so, God removes evil gradually, in order to deepen the revelation of His glory.[18] So, the kingdom of God is growing to its fullness like the yeast that works all through the dough, irresistibly affecting and working through everything, and it will leaven to fullness and exclude the other kingdom. If that is true, then we do not have a side-by-side development of the kingdom of God and the kingdom of darkness to the end of the age.

This is a very simple truth—very basic. Yet, there are interpretations that are different from this. We have to back up and ask if the basics are being taught here. Is the kingdom here? Is it growing? Will it grow to its fullness? And are the kingdom of God and the kingdom of darkness mutually exclusive? Now, someone might ask, 'Does that mean each and every one is saved?' Clearly it does not. The earlier parable says there are persons who could 'get on the bandwagon.' They go along with it and are not saved. They outwardly appear as believers,

16. *Acts 1:6–8.*

17. Gangadean, *The Westminster Catechisms*, 101–102.

18. Gangadean, *Philosophical Foundation*, 145–161; Gangadean, *On Natural and Revealed Theology*, 141–147; Gangadean, *The Biblical Worldview*, 219–239; Gangadean, "Paper No. 7: The Problem of Evil," in *The Logos Papers*, 33–39.

but we are not always able to say. We know that after the devil is loose for a short while, in the Book of Revelation, he gathers the people for the war against the kingdom of God.[19] Every child born on earth is born in the kingdom of darkness. Until they are received by baptism, they do not have the outward sign of being in the kingdom of God.[20] Baptism is an outward sign of the covenant of grace; it is not the reality. Until Christ's accomplished work is applied to a person's heart in regeneration, we have a host of unbelievers in the world, and they can easily outnumber the believers. God will bring his kingdom about. God will have all the glory. This is not the point of this parable. Yet, it is an implication that some of you may be concerned about.

THE PARABLES OF THE HIDDEN
TREASURE AND THE PEARL:
Sacrifice Everything to Possess the Kingdom

We come to the parables of the hidden treasure and the pearl. "**The kingdom of heaven is like treasure hidden in a field. When a man found it, he hid it again, and then in his joy went and sold all he had and bought that field**" (v. 44). We may think that the owner of the field did not know about the treasure. That is not the point. The point is that the kingdom of God is like *treasure* hidden in a field. This speaks about how valuable, great, and wonderful the kingdom of God is in itself. And when it is seen, the person goes and sells everything they have to possess it. It shows something about how the kingdom of God is possessed—"and the violent take it by force" (Matt. 11:12b KJV). You have to press in hard. This point is reiterated when the merchant was looking for pearls: "**Again, the kingdom of heaven is like a merchant looking for fine pearls. When he found one of great value, he went away and sold everything he had and bought it**" (vv. 45–46). We are not saying literally that the kingdom of God is to be bought with money; that would be taking the parable out of context. But it is about giving everything you have to possess it.

---

19. *Revelation 20:7–9.*
20. Gangadean, *The Westminster Confession*, 291–305; Gangadean, *The Westminster Catechisms*, 281–286.

The Scripture says in Proverbs 23:23, "Buy the truth and do not sell it; get wisdom, discipline and understanding." Do not compromise; do not let it go. This is how the kingdom of God will be possessed by those who value it and give everything they have for it. The kingdom of God will not be possessed by those who 'dally'—by those who are casual and relaxed. It is not going to be possessed by the 'up-tight' either, but there is a difference in those who are pressing in on the kingdom to possess it. You sell everything because you have to possess it, and there is joy in this. You do not feel it is a sacrifice. You feel you are getting *more* than you are giving up; it is worth it. What else would you spend your money on? What better way to spend your money than on things that produce fruit? It is lasting fruit. It is called *kingdom investment*. Literally, you put your money where it will produce the most fruit. If God blesses you with money—and there is absolutely nothing wrong with money—this is how you should use it as an investment. I can have money and save it, not to hoard it, but to use it and invest it for the kingdom of God. If it has to be invested for the generations to come, what is the wisest way to do it? We have to consider time and investment. Money is for the kingdom. You spend to increase the glory of God on the earth. We have no trouble with money itself, but we have trouble with hoarding money, consuming it on our lust, and not spending it for the kingdom. Those who spend their money for the kingdom see the fruit, what a joy it is, what a blessing, what a privilege it is. This is the truth of the kingdom and how the kingdom will be possessed.

THE PARABLE OF THE NET:
Admixture and Separation of Good from Bad

The parable of the net serves to illustrate the mixed condition of believers and unbelievers that will exist within the kingdom until the end of the age.

> Once again, the kingdom of heaven is like a net that was let down into the lake and caught all kinds of fish. When it was full, the fishermen pulled it up on the shore. Then they sat down and collected the good fish in baskets, but threw the bad away. This is how it will be at the end of the age. The angels will come and

separate the wicked from the righteous and throw them into the blazing furnace, where there will be weeping and gnashing of teeth (vv. 47–50).

There is an admixture and a process. In the end, the good are kept and the bad are thrown out in judgment, where there will be weeping and gnashing of teeth. In the Church, preparation and discipline is a protection against unbelievers being mixed in with believers.

HAVE YOU UNDERSTOOD THESE THINGS?
Teaching Things New and Old—The Unity of the Truth

"'Have you understood all these things?' Jesus asked" (v. 51a). Notice, again, the emphasis on understanding. What do they say, as good students? "'Yes,' they replied" (v. 51b). 'We understand. We hope so.' We like to think we understand. "He said to them, 'Therefore every teacher of the law who has become a disciple in the kingdom of heaven is like the owner of a house who brings out of his storeroom new treasures as well as old'" (v. 52). As we sing Psalm 78,[21] think about the power of the things of old that have been taught to our children. This is of old; this is not new. This is in Genesis 3.[22] This is all through the Scriptures, the truth of God present from the beginning in organic seed form to which more is added and unfolded—the new builds on the old. This is how the truths of the kingdom of God are known. If we understand what is prior, we will understand what is to come. But notice, many do not understand, and among those who do not understand may be those who have been around you and know something about your outward life but not your inward life. Some individuals *should have* understood the truth but failed to do so, leading to offense when confronted with the reality of their lack of understanding.

---

21. *78A, The Book of Psalms for Singing.*
22. Gangadean, *On Natural and Revealed Theology,* 195–212; *The Biblical Worldview,* Surrendra Gangadean.

A PROPHET WITHOUT HONOR:
Seeing the Outward but Not the Inward Reality

When Jesus had finished these parables, he moved on from there. Coming to his hometown, he began teaching the people in their synagogue, and they were amazed. "Where did this man get this wisdom and these miraculous powers?" they asked. "Isn't this the carpenter's son? Isn't his mother's name Mary, and aren't his brothers James, Joseph, Simon and Judas? Aren't all his sisters with us? Where then did this man get all these things?" (vv. 53–56).

Jesus learned these things from the Scriptures and by praying, which is the same place from which you and I should get them. You can see the problem. If someone from your very midst can show by their lives proper understanding, people are going to take offense with it unless they are willing to be corrected, instructed, taught, and humbled. This is exactly what it says: **"They took offense at him"** (v. 57a). This is because their lack of understanding is manifest. They saw the outward but not the inward reality. They did not have understanding. Again, this emphasizes the problem of understanding. **"But Jesus said to them, 'A prophet is not without honor except in his own town and in his own home'"** (v. 57b). He is without honor in that He is not paid attention to, and His teachings are not listened to. People feel they know you, and they do not want to say they do not know the things that they should. They think they already know you, so they take offense and do not hear. What they do have is taken from them, and the latter condition is worse than the first, because they have rejected a greater light.

Our Lord teaches us about the kingdom. If we get the things that are more basic in place, we will receive an increase in what is to come. We are to give ourselves to understanding. We are to humble our hearts and be willing to engage in discussion. We can and should have questions; they should be legitimate. If you have heard otherwise, please do raise questions. Do not let it go; do not let it slip. Get involved in discussion; do not hesitate. Say to others, 'We need to sort this out and discuss it.' If there are differences in understanding, let us press on together for understanding through a process of discussion. Yes, we can and will stumble in this, and because we have sin, we take offense, but this is the treasure that is so great. I want the treasure of the kingdom; I do not want to come short of it; I want it all. I will do what it takes to get it. Amen.

11

FAITH—TRIED AND REVEALED

Without Holiness, No One Will See the Lord

Matthew 14

¹At that time Herod the tetrarch heard the reports about Jesus, ²and he said to his attendants, "This is John the Baptist; he has risen from the dead! That is why miraculous powers are at work in him."

³Now Herod had arrested John and bound him and put him in prison because of Herodias, his brother Philip's wife, ⁴for John had been saying to him: "It is not lawful for you to have her." ⁵Herod wanted to kill John, but he was afraid of the people, because they considered John a prophet.

⁶On Herod's birthday the daughter of Herodias danced for the guests and pleased Herod so much ⁷that he promised with an oath to give her whatever she asked. ⁸Prompted by her mother, she said, "Give me here on a platter the head of John the Baptist." ⁹The king was distressed, but because of his oaths and his dinner guests, he ordered that her request be granted ¹⁰and had John beheaded in the prison. ¹¹His head was brought in on a platter and given to the girl, who carried it to her mother. ¹²John's disciples came and took his body and buried it. Then they went and told Jesus.

¹³When Jesus heard what had happened, he withdrew by boat privately to a solitary place. Hearing of this, the crowds followed him on foot from the towns. ¹⁴When Jesus landed and saw a large crowd, he had compassion on them and healed their sick.

¹⁵As evening approached, the disciples came to him and said, "This is a remote place, and it's already getting late. Send the crowds away, so they can go to the villages and buy themselves some food."

¹⁶Jesus replied, "They do not need to go away. You give them something to eat."

¹⁷"We have here only five loaves of bread and two fish," they answered.

¹⁸"Bring them here to me," he said. ¹⁹And he directed the people to sit down on the grass. Taking the five loaves and the two fish and looking up to heaven, he gave thanks and broke the loaves. Then he gave them to the disciples, and the disciples gave them to the people. ²⁰They all ate and were satisfied, and the disciples picked up twelve basketfuls of broken pieces that were left over. ²¹The number of those who ate was about five thousand men, besides women and children.

²²Immediately Jesus made the disciples get into the boat and go on ahead of him to the other side, while he dismissed the crowd. ²³After he had dismissed them, he went up on a mountainside by himself to pray. Later that night, he was there alone, ²⁴and the boat was already a considerable distance from land, buffeted by the waves because the wind was against it.

²⁵Shortly before dawn Jesus went out to them, walking on the lake. ²⁶When the disciples saw him walking on the lake, they were terrified. "It's a ghost," they said, and cried out in fear.

²⁷But Jesus immediately said to them: "Take courage! It is I. Don't be afraid."

²⁸"Lord, if it's you," Peter replied, "tell me to come to you on the water."

²⁹"Come," he said.

Then Peter got down out of the boat, walked on the water and came toward Jesus. ³⁰But when he saw the wind, he was afraid and, beginning to sink, cried out, "Lord, save me!"

³¹Immediately Jesus reached out his hand and caught him. "You of little faith," he said, "why did you doubt?"

³²And when they climbed into the boat, the wind died down. ³³Then those who were in the boat worshiped him, saying, "Truly you are the Son of God."

³⁴When they had crossed over, they landed at Gennesaret. ³⁵And when the men of that place recognized Jesus, they sent word to all the surrounding country. People brought all their sick to him ³⁶and begged him to let the sick just touch the edge of his cloak, and all who touched it were healed.

INTRODUCTION

W E ARE GOING TO LOOK AT HOW OUR FAITH is tried and revealed. Previously, we discussed the parables, which spoke about faith and understanding, how we are called to understand, and—by having understanding—we are to be fruitful. We will now look at how our faith is tried and apply this teaching to ourselves because, daily, our faith is tried, and hopefully, we will be strengthened and comforted by the Word of God and learn to trust in Him.

THE FAITH OF JOHN THE BAPTIST:
Even unto Death

First is the account of John the Baptist, who is beheaded in what seems to be a most ignominious way. We may struggle, and we may wonder about this. Events happen to us so contrary to our expectations. John was expecting the kingdom of God to come through Christ and come in a certain way, and he sent his disciples to ask, "Are you the one who was to come, or should we expect someone else?" (Matt. 11:3). He was in prison, and it seems so contrary to what should be. In trials like this, faith enters the picture. By faith, we are to see beyond that which *seems* so contrary, to the *reality* of things—we are to have true understanding. Daily, we are called upon to struggle in this way.

The Ministry of the Prophet: Calling to Repentance (Elijah)

The ministry of the prophet is to call men to repentance. John served faithfully in this way, and part of his faithfulness was that he did not hesitate to call the rulers to repentance. He called men to repent, whether it was the political rulers, religious rulers, or the people. This call to repent from sin, as carried out by the prophet, is difficult and dangerous, which is why the prophets are often killed. We do not hear about the priests being killed. It is a peculiar work that the prophet has—to speak on behalf of God to men, not on behalf of men to God, as the priests do when they intercede. The prophet has a different ministry, and John carried out his work faithfully.

> Now Herod had arrested John and bound him and put him in prison because of Herodias, his brother Philip's wife, for John had been saying to him: "It is not lawful for you to have her." Herod wanted to kill John, but he was afraid of the people, because they considered him a prophet (vv. 3–5).

In calling the ruler, Herod, to repentance, John incurred the wrath of Herodias, whom Herod had married. Herodias was his brother Philip's wife. She had a child, and it was not called for, according to the law, that he should marry her. If the wife was childless, that may be a different case, but that was not so. John spoke the Word consistently with his message. He is not to avoid the difficult case and let people be led astray by a false example.

Herod had heard of Jesus, and the account begins in this way: "At that time Herod the tetrarch heard the reports about Jesus, and he said to his attendants, 'This is John the Baptist; he has risen from the dead! That is why miraculous powers are at work in him'" (vv. 1–2). Herod had heard the reports about Jesus, the mighty works being done, and his conscience struck him, and he said, "This is John the Baptist; he has risen from the dead!" (v. 2a). We see something about the superstitious nature of Herod and it is going to be manifest again. It is not the case that John rises from the dead as Jesus does. It is factually and conceptually wrong.

Noble or Ignoble Death? An Entire Life of Faith Manifested

An account is given about why Herod is in this state: "On Herod's birthday the daughter of Herodias danced for the guests and pleased Herod so much that he promised with an oath to give her whatever she asked" (vv. 6–7). It is in keeping with Herod's character that this would happen; he speaks rashly when his feelings move him and does not consider what he is saying. The daughter of Herodias' dance was probably quite seductive and suggestive, and it pleased Herod. It satisfied his lust both for the mother and for the daughter, and "he promised with an oath to give her whatever she asked." Then, "prompted by her mother," who had a grudge against John for calling them to repentance, "she said, 'Give me here on a platter the head of John the Baptist'" (v. 8).

It is quite ignominious, this petty lust on the part of human beings and the traps into which they fall, and John is going to be killed
because of this girl dancing seductively and Herod making this vow.
Yet, it was precisely because John confronted Herod on his lust earlier
and said, "It is not lawful for you to have her" (v. 4b), that this has
come to a head. He dies because of his faithful witness and he does
not shrink back from it. John's faith is manifest in his entire life and
the manner and peculiar circumstances of his death. This conflict is
not something on the side that just happened; it is integral to John's
whole life of calling men to repentance, not shrinking, calling the king
to repentance, being faithful, incurring wrath, and being put in prison.
Under this additional circumstance, given the king's lust and his rash
oath, John is executed.

"The king was distressed, but because of his oaths and his dinner
guests, he ordered that her request be granted and had John beheaded
in the prison" (vv. 9–10). Herod was distressed; he did not want to do
this. He had feared John because the people considered him a prophet, and he should not have murdered him. An oath can only bind us
to do what is lawful; it cannot bind us to do what is unlawful. Herod
has several misconceptions about things and has a kind of false piety:
He is going to keep his oath, whatever it costs. Yet this is precisely the
time when he should not have made this oath, and he certainly should
not have kept it.

We are reminded of John coming in the spirit and power of Elijah,[1]
and we remember when Elijah was on earth, he testified against Ahab
and Jezebel. Herodias seems to be like Jezebel in the way she instigates
and presses to get her way. Remember Ahab wanted to get Naboth's
vineyard, and remember the way Jezebel secured it for him. It is something gruesome. You may think that these things do not go together,
this dancing and lust and Jezebel's securing the vineyard. But the same
lack of self-control present in lust is also present in violence. We go to
the point of violence to secure what we have, and these are the twin
characteristics of the human condition apart from God that we progress
more and more deeply into. Corruption and violence from the days of
Noah continue down to our day. We see this as the prophets are called
to speak the Word of God, and they are often under the power of the

---

1. *Luke 1:17.*

Beast. Because Herod had the power to kill, he exercised this power in his self-interest at the instigation of Herodias. John is killed in a way that is consistent with his whole life. "His head was brought in on a platter and given to the girl, who carried it to her mother. John's disciples came and took his body and buried it. Then they went and told Jesus" (vv. 11–12). John spoke against the rulers, the Pharisees, the Sadducees, and the leaders, and if they had the power, they would have killed him. Herod did exercise that power. The question remains whether he should have lawfully done so, being under Roman rule. This is an additional question, but he had the power as king to act in this way.

Our eyes of faith and understanding see that God calls us to be faithful even unto death. John the Baptist was faithful, though the way his death came about may seem so casual and indifferent. Much of our suffering stems from the apparent casualness and incidental quality of the suffering. How does this suffering connect with anything else in our lives? But if we have understanding, we can see how it came about very precisely. We are not to think that it is something meaningless, casual, or a matter of indifference, but we are to see God at work in suffering. Seeing God at work, knowing that God is being honored, we are to show our love for God. God does not abandon us, but calls us to be faithful even unto death. The meaningless, incidental sorts of suffering throw us most for a loop. We cannot understand it, it does not seem to fit, and is just something weird. The weirdness of things that seem to be meaningless and out there by themselves, throws us for a loop. We are to have faith/understanding, see God working, honor God with our lives, and thank God for upholding us.

Feeding the Five Thousand: An Exercise of God's Power, Wisdom, and Love

Jesus continues His teaching and preaching, and the people come to Him. "He withdrew by boat privately to a solitary place. Hearing of this, the crowds followed him on foot from the towns. When Jesus landed and saw a large crowd, he had compassion on them and healed their sick" (vv. 13b–14).

He had compassion on them and healed them. Then,

As evening approached, the disciples came to him and said, "This is a remote place, and it's already getting late. Send the crowds away, so they can go to the villages and buy themselves some food." Jesus replied, "They do not need to go away. You give them something to eat" (vv. 15–16).

He Himself knew what He would do. He was testing the disciples' faith.

"We have here only five loaves of bread and two fish," they answered. "Bring them here to me," he said. And he directed the people to sit down on the grass. Taking the five loaves and the two fish and looking up to heaven, he gave thanks and broke the loaves. Then he gave them to the disciples, and the disciples gave them to the people. They all ate and were satisfied, and the disciples picked up twelve basketfuls of broken pieces that were left over. The number of those who ate was about five thousand men, besides women and children (vv. 17–21).

This miracle makes it quite clear that the loaves were multiplied and increased, and it was a miracle of God. Five thousand men, besides women and children, ate. One could imagine that up to 10,000 people were there. It could be that many because women and children were there, too, and Jesus fed them all. This miracle says something about Jesus' care and concern about God's working, our trust in God, and how we should respond.

God's Care and Ample Provision

We often ask, does God know? Does God care? This miracle tells us that He does know and He does care. He is able to exercise His power to provide. There is no shortness in the hand of God to provide. He is able to multiply the loaves and the fish. We are reminded of how He provided bread for the people as they came out of Egypt, He provided bread from heaven (manna), and He gave them water in the desert from the rock. God's hand is not shortened, so when we come into our situation, we know God can easily exercise His power to bring change in our circumstance and to deliver us. He knows and cares. If He chooses not to deliver us, it does not mean He does not know or care. It means that He is working out His purpose in our lives.[2] We are to learn to submit to Him and trust in Him. The extent of His power and that He knows, cares, and provides is clearly revealed to us in this miracle. We are not to fret, we are not to complain, we are not to be discouraged in our hardships, but we are to trust in God and obey Him, even if it means that we suffer and we suffer unto death. The Scripture does speak about having faith even unto death. If we are to glorify God in our death as John the Baptist did—and the glory is to God and not something incidental—having the glory of God in mind, we are to live the same.

The people had seen this miracle. All miracles are an exercise of God's great power, as well as His wisdom and His love. I do not know if we can say one miracle is greater than another. Some miracles may be more evident in a way, or of a different kind. The healing may come invisibly, inwardly, but the loaves are multiplied outwardly. In both miracles, God exercises His power. We must not forget this; we must meditate on it, especially in times of trouble.

Learning Holiness Through Trials to See the Lord

We might say this: when we get into trouble, we sometimes question what we are to learn in the situation; we are perplexed and do not know what we need to learn. What are we to learn? Holiness. That is what we are to learn: holiness. As I was coming in, I was thinking about others who are suffering, and there seems to be a great disconnect between our theology and the nitty-gritty, daily struggle. I remember thinking quite consciously that there is a gap there. This past week, I have been working on "the ugly broad ditch"[3] that there is between general revelation and special revelation. We have worked on that issue this week in our class, and we progressed in filling in that ditch with 10 steps: the necessity for special revelation, then its content, origin, existence, transmission, completion, translation, clarity, sufficiency, and interpretation.[4] We filled in the ditch in the places where people have objected

---

2. Gangadean, *The Westminster Confession*, 192–195.

3. James C. Livingston, *Modern Christian Thought: The Enlightenment and the Nineteenth Century* (Upper Saddle River: Prentice Hall, 1997), 31–35.

4. Gangadean, "Paper No. 11: From General Revelation to Special Revelation," in *The Logos Papers*, 69–73.

and raised questions. I thought that I would also like to fill in the gap between this theoretical knowledge and our ordinary experience of our trials. There does seem to be a gap, a disconnect there.[5]

After discussing it and dwelling on it, it became clear that what we are to learn is holiness—nothing more, nothing less. Do not try to figure out the specifics of the trial; it cannot be figured out. I say this with some confidence. It seems to counter everything; it is to puzzle you, perplex you, and reduce you to despair—all your efforts to despair. But you must learn holiness, which is submission to God in the trial, and trust in God. Our self-will is being negated. We do this, that, and the other, wanting to get the job done, but the wind blows, and it spoils all the work that we have done. The essence of it is something that Job expressed: "Though he slay me, yet will I trust in him" (Job 13:15a KJV). We are all to learn from our trials. We are scourged by God, beaten, and brutalized in so many ways, but God is receiving us as His children, and He is cleansing us from sin.[6] Jesus says, "yet not my will, but yours be done" (Lk. 22:42b). When our will is frustrated again and again and again, and we submit and say, "yet not my will, but yours be done," and endure through the trial, this is devotion to God. This is holiness. When we have manifested this in our lives, it is then that God is pleased to reveal Himself to us. The Scripture says, "without holiness no one will see the Lord" (Heb. 12:14b). It is at this point that the nitty-gritty of our trials is connected to the grand scheme of what we are looking for: to glorify God, to enjoy Him forever, and to see the earth filled with the knowledge of God. This was the connection.

In our trials of faith, when we are perplexed and do not know which way to turn, when all of our natural desires are frustrated, we submit to God, trust in Him, and know that He has not abandoned us and He is with us. We will see this in the account of Jesus walking on the water. He is with us, and we are to have a heart for Him. We are to love Him, be near to Him, know that He is near to us, and know that nothing will separate us from the love of God through Christ Jesus our Lord,[7] no matter how puzzling it is in terms of our particular desires and expectations. We are to learn holiness, without which no one shall

---

5. Gangadean, *The Unity of the Church*, 197–215; *1 Corinthians 3:1–15*.

6. *Hebrews 12:4–10.*

7. *Romans 8:35–39.*

see the Lord. What was the outcome of Job's life? "My ears had heard of you but now my eyes have seen you. Therefore I despise myself and repent in dust and ashes" (Job 42:5–6). "I consider that our present sufferings are not worth comparing with the glory that will be revealed in us" (Rom. 8:18).

I do not mean to say this otherwise, but in this context I will say it: Men seem particularly to have their minds set on the goal. When we get into a situation, we want to get the job done; that is it, everything out of our way. Anything that frustrates getting that job done is a peculiar hardship. God, however, is working on our relationship to Him, not the job. In this context, there is a sense, men, in which you must think like a woman. You have to think in terms of the relationship. This may be hard, but the Lord is working on the relationship. Those who are particularly goal-oriented seem to have the hardest time with this way of thinking. The desires get frustrated and yet God is working in this— in the very frustration of the desires. I took off my shoe three times to get a little something out of it. Once is bad, twice is horrible, and three times is total perplexity! Why am I wasting time and effort taking off my shoe to get a little something out of it? It may mean nothing to you, but to me, it is my time and effort. There is no wisdom in it. It is a waste of time! So, God tries us in little things and in big things. But, "God is faithful; he will not let you be tempted beyond what you can bear" (1 Cor. 10:13). He will bring us out of the trial.

God provides for us, and He is abundantly able to provide in any circumstance. In the thing closest to our heart and most frustrating, where we are living much of the time—this is where we need to know that God is living with us. It is not pleasant but grievous; it *is* grievous. You have to be ready for grief. No amount of intellectualizing will eliminate the grief; it is grief that is to be borne before God. When Job's children were killed, it was grief; there is no way around it. We cannot explain it away or minimize it. It is real grief, and you bear it, persevere in it, endure it, and endure it even to the point of death,[8] knowing that God is abundantly able to deliver. We are to know that it is not incidental and that God is glorified through this. There are no *incidental truths* in the infinite wisdom of God. God works all together for good, and knows what He is doing. If He counts the very

---

8. *Matthew 26:38.*

hairs of our heads, then He knows what we are doing. How many of us have not had trials of the sort that perplex us to the *nth* degree? If we say theoretically, 'God is with us,' we are to gird up the loins of our minds[9] and be prepared for learning holiness, which is to say 'no' to my will. It is not my will to take my shoe off the third time; this is not my will. Say 'no' to my will, submit to God, trust Him, and say, 'My self-life, my self-will, is being denied.' This is part of being holy, in the providence of God and in devotion to God. Afterward, it yields the peaceable fruits of righteousness.[10] There is a glory that is revealed. God does not show Himself to us apart from holiness. We have to be seeking God. This account of the miracle of feeding the multitude shows God's ability to provide.

WALKING ON THE WATER:
Nothing Can Separate Us from the Love of God

Immediately Jesus made the disciples get into the boat and go on ahead of him to the other side, while he dismissed the crowd. After he had dismissed them, he went up on a mountainside by himself to pray. When evening came, he was there alone, but the boat was already a considerable distance from land, buffeted by the waves because the wind was against it (vv. 22–24).

Context: After the Miracle, Expectation, and Time of Prayer

It was getting to be evening. He had fed the people, he sent them away, and he went up to the mountain to pray. There are reasons why He would send the people away, but remember, they did not really go away. They returned looking for Him and wanted to make Him king, but they sought food that perished. He was on the mountain in prayer. Our Lord was praying in the context of the miracle of the loaves and fish, and He went to His disciples.

---

9. *1 Peter 1:13.*
10. *Hebrews 12:11.*

An Anatomy of a Trial: Recognizing the Pattern to Trials

The disciples were far from land, maybe a few miles, and He came to them. They were to cross the lake, but the boat was **"buffeted by the waves because the wind was against it."** Here are the circumstances: you are going somewhere, and the wind is against you.

Sometimes, the wind is against you, but when you are rowing in a boat across the lake, it is late at night, and the wind is against you, it is just so much harder. These are the circumstances in which the trials begin, but we are to persevere. 'Okay, well, sometimes the wind does blow against you.' But now, in the middle of the night, you see a figure approaching you, and the only thing you can think of, the only explanation in the world that makes any sense is, 'It's a ghost!' **"Shortly before dawn Jesus went out to them, walking on the lake. When the disciples saw him walking on the lake, they were terrified. 'It's a ghost,' they said, and cried out in fear"** (vv. 25–26). This figure is coming towards them on the water. Why would a ghost come towards them on the water? What is going on in their minds? How can they explain it? The ghost is coming after them. There are 11 or 12 men in the boat, but this is no match for a ghost on the water, or a ghost under any circumstance! How do you deal with a ghost? It creates a special fear because there is intentionality in it.

There is a numinous element; Rudolf Otto speaks about this element: a special fear. If there is a tiger in the room next door, that is one thing; but if there is a ghost or a spirit in the room, that is fear. Rudolf Otto likened this kind of fear to a fear of the holy—a trembling in the face of that which is other, different, a peculiar kind of otherness—holiness is the essence of religion. Otto thought so, in any case. These men were terrified, and they cried out. So in this hardship that you are enduring, it gets particularly acute, and you come to the point of crying out. I was thinking about writing up an anatomy of a trial.[11] I think I need to do more work on it, but there is a set of features that a trial has; it builds on the ordinary circumstances and the extraordinary circumstances—a call back that was unexpected, a hardship—and then it comes to the

---

11. Pastor Gangadean's handwritten sermon notes provide a detailing of his thoughts on the anatomy of a trial: (1) Ordinary and extraordinary circumstances. (2) Unexpected hardship. (3) Acute: fear, expectation, and the cry out. (4) The Peter Principle: double-mindedness, little faith, perplexed. (5) The revelation: not abandoned, not separated from the love of God, God is near.

point where things become quite acute, it peaks, and at that point, you cry out. Can you notice that particular point in the trial?

Normally, we are so involved in the hardship, just doing all we can to get it done, and we do not self-consciously reflect. We need to be able to back up and say, 'Hmm, this is a trial; there is a pattern to trials. It might become acute; I should be watching, praying, remembering, and trusting in God.' Perhaps we will become more familiar with trials over time. I trust we will get this more clearly focused by God's grace. I will need to do a lot more analysis of the trials in the Scriptures and the lives of biblical characters to see how it works out. But usually, the trials work until they get acute and you reach your breaking point. It *must* reach the breaking point. It is like weight lifting, and that last repetition, you go until you cannot do it anymore, your hands come down, and you ask for the weights to be taken from you. So you reach your limits, break, and cannot go on.

The Word Comes at Our Breaking Point: "Take Courage! It Is I. Don't Be Afraid."

"But Jesus immediately said to them: 'Take courage! It is I. Don't be afraid'" (v. 27). We need to meditate on this *courage* and how it becomes *discouraged*. We do not have the heart to go further; we are ready to give up and do not have the mindset to persevere and endure. We get to the point where we break down and say, 'I cannot go any further.' And immediately, the Word comes: "Take courage!" Be strong, continue, persevere, endure. We are trusting in God for the next step, for the next breath. Persevere. Jesus says, "Take courage! It is I. Don't be afraid." When we reach our breaking point and cry out, terrified, the Lord comes to us and says, "Take courage! It is I. Don't be afraid." He identifies Himself and tells them, "Don't be afraid." In contrast to the breaking point in fear, when it reaches the panic point, that is when He comes. In a trial, we should be aware of when the pressure builds. Sometimes it builds slowly, sometimes it is over weeks, and then all of a sudden, a number of things come together. As they say, it is 'the straw that breaks the camel's back.' This is the proverbial statement. It breaks. At that point, the Word of the Lord comes to us: "Take courage! It is I. Don't be afraid."

The Peter Principle: Fix Your Eyes on Jesus Versus Self

What comes next with Peter illustrates something we can call the *Peter Principle*. This is a small episode within a larger episode. The small episode highlights, summarizes, and condenses the larger episode to show what is happening. Let us look at this episode. Peter is encouraged by Jesus' words: "'Lord, if it's you,' Peter replied, 'tell me to come to you on the water'" (v. 28). What was going through his mind? He has this boldness, perhaps thinking, 'This is great, let's go, we are there!' So he speaks this way, and the Lord says, "Come" (v. 29). You wonder what is going through the Lord's mind when He says to Peter, "Come." I think He knows exactly what is going to happen. He knows Peter. Peter is going to do this. I am not saying that the Lord is going to make Peter an object lesson for the other disciples. Many of us feel like object lessons sometimes. 'Hey everybody, look at me; this is how you are not supposed to be. I'm here to prove a point that God wants to make to you.' Many of us feel this way, but I think the Lord is teaching both Peter and the other disciples.

"Then Peter got down out of the boat, walked on the water and came toward Jesus" (v. 30a). What is happening in all of this is that he sees Jesus, he is strengthened, he is encouraged—as he should be—and he feels he can do anything since God is with him. Peter can even walk on water if the Lord says so and he is willing to do it. He says to Jesus, 'If it is you, Lord, bid me come to you.' If you are going to walk on water, He is the One you want to walk to, right? You do not want to walk to some buddy or friend. You are walking to Jesus. He is the only one that will get me out of the boat! If Jesus is standing there, I am walking to Jesus. But what happens? Here is the *Peter Principle*: He gets his eyes off of Jesus. "But when he saw the wind, he was afraid and, beginning to sink, cried out, 'Lord, save me!'" (v. 30b). The trouble begins. We begin to sink when our eyes are off the Lord at any time in our trials. Does Peter illustrate that principle here? Yes, when he saw the wind. Actually, literally, you do not see the wind; you see the effects of the wind, you hear its effects, and feel it. Clearly, he took his eyes off of Jesus—who spoke to him and bid him come—and onto the natural. He took his eyes away from God and onto self and his own resources. Whenever we have our eyes on ourselves and our own resources, that is when we sink, invariably.

Without Holiness, No One Will See the Lord

How can we fix our eyes on Jesus? How can we rivet our eyes there and not take them off of Him? We are not to presume and do more than we ought, and we are not to fear and become discouraged and do less than we ought. This is what our faith is. It is to look to God and have our eyes on who God is, His purposes, and how He works. What is the good that He has for us? It is holiness: "without holiness no one will see the Lord" (Heb. 12:14b). He wants to bring us through holiness to prepare us to have a heart that is disposed toward Him in this way. Job says, "Though he slay me, yet will I trust in him" (Job 13:15a KJV). He wants us to have a heart for Him that He might reveal Himself to us. He cannot reveal Himself in any other way. Those who seek Him, find Him. They must seek Him diligently. In holiness, we will be devoted to Him above all else, seeking Him, which is the condition by which we find Him. This is a necessary truth: "without holiness no one will see the Lord." What He wants to reveal to us is that He loves us, He cares for us, He is abundantly able to provide for us, we do not have to live in fear, we can lean on Him. He is with us, His Word is in us, and we are with Him. We love Him, our hearts are toward Him, He loves us, and His heart is toward us, and that is all. Nothing more, nothing less. Paul says,

> Who shall separate us from the love of Christ? Shall trouble or hardship or persecution or famine or nakedness or danger or sword? . . . For I am convinced that neither death nor life, neither angels nor demons, neither the present nor the future, nor any powers, neither height nor depth, nor anything else in all creation, will be able to separate us from the love of God that is in Christ Jesus our Lord (Rom. 8:35, 38–39).

It is in this context that he says, "And we know that in all things God works for the good of those who love him, who have been called according to his purpose" (Rom. 8:28). All the things that are so averse to our most intimate and personal desires are working together for good because what we desire above all else is to know Him. When this knowledge of Him comes to us, our hearts are satisfied.

"Immediately Jesus reached out his hand and caught him. 'You of little faith,' he said, 'why did you doubt?'" (v. 31). You of *little* faith.

In the next chapter, Jesus will commend the Canaanite woman for her *great* faith. He is going to rebuke His disciples about being so dull in the next chapter after He explains to them about being clean and un-clean. Jesus caught Peter and reproved him in this statement: **"You of little faith . . . why did you doubt?"** What does the Lord want us to have? He wants us to have faith in Him, knowing who He is and how He works. We can discern God's workings by looking at the Scripture, the meaning of things, and how He has provided in the past, in history, and in our own past. We are to know that He is with us and will pro-vide for us. The question remains, **"why did you doubt?"** How do we explain this to the Lord? 'Well, Lord, here is why I doubted. I have four reasons why I doubted. I was sinking in the water . . .' God says, 'Why did you get your eyes off me? I know you were sinking in the water. I know it is the tendency of objects on water to sink.' 'Well, I got out of the boat a little hastily.' 'No, you did ask before you came, and I did say come.' So, what are the troubles that are before us today? Some of you have shared your prayer requests. I heard the pain and the aching in some of your hearts and lives. Now, the Lord says, **"Take courage! It is I. Don't be afraid"** (v. 27b). He knows us, He can provide for us, and He knows what He is doing. Do not be afraid. Trust God, no matter how long it is or what it takes. Nothing separates us from His love. He is working holiness in our lives so that He may reveal Himself to us more fully. This revelation will come after the trial has done its work—after we have learned to come to a new level of submission to Him, looking to Him and leaning on Him.

"And when they climbed into the boat, the wind died down" (v. 32). Jesus climbed into the boat, and Peter with Him. Oh, Peter was shaken. The wind died down, that wind that was contrary to them. It was a wind sent by God for His purpose, that He might reveal His glory. At another time, He *rebuked* the wind. He climbed into the boat, and the wind died down. At another time, He was in the boat sleeping, and the wind was coming. We cannot figure out all the ways in which it works, but we know the general principle—the Lord is in control. We cannot say, 'Well, if Jesus is in the boat, there will be no wind, right?' No. When He got in this time, there was no wind, but at another time, there was wind. We must trust. You cannot figure out the trials and try to analyze them. Maybe you can do an anatomy of the fundamental structure of the trial, but for those of us who love to figure things out—you cannot figure it out. I suppose all of us try to figure it out. But it is a perplexity, and the more you try to figure it out, the more you are perplexed. You have to trust in Him—in His love and in His wisdom.

Worship: The Response to New Understanding

So Jesus got into the boat, and the response of all, including Peter, was to worship Him. "**Then those who were in the boat worshiped him, saying, 'Truly you are the Son of God'**" (v. 33). This is to be our response in our trials and as we come through the trials. It is to see Him in a new light; we see Him in a greater way. We see the majesty of His rule. We see that He comes into the boat, and everything is fine. This is after hours of rowing. It was quite some time; they should have been there in one hour, but they were rowing for hours and still were not there. The Lord reveals Himself to us, and we worship Him. This should be our response coming out of every trial. This is the closing line of every trial: "**Truly you are the Son of God.**" Truly, You love us. Truly, nothing can separate us from You. Truly, we love You, and trust You, and obey You. Amen.

12

THE CLEAN AND THE UNCLEAN

True Holiness Is by Knowing the Truth

Matthew 15

[1]Then some Pharisees and teachers of the law came to Jesus from Jerusalem and asked, [2]"Why do your disciples break the tradition of the elders? They don't wash their hands before they eat!"

[3]Jesus replied, "And why do you break the command of God for the sake of your tradition? [4]For God said, 'Honor your father and mother' and 'Anyone who curses their father or mother is to be put to death.' [5]But you say that if anyone declares that what might have been used to help their father or mother is 'devoted to God,' [6]they are not to 'honor their father or mother' with it. Thus you nullify the word of God for the sake of your tradition. [7]You hypocrites! Isaiah was right when he prophesied about you:

[8]"'These people honor me with their lips,
    but their hearts are far from me.
[9]They worship me in vain;
    their teachings are merely human rules.'"

[10]Jesus called the crowd to him and said, "Listen and understand. [11]What goes into someone's mouth does not defile them, but what comes out of their mouth, that is what defiles them."

[12]Then the disciples came to him and asked, "Do you know that the Pharisees were offended when they heard this?"

[13]He replied, "Every plant that my heavenly Father has not planted will be pulled up by the roots. [14]Leave them; they are blind guides. If the blind lead the blind, both will fall into a pit."

[15]Peter said, "Explain the parable to us."

[16]"Are you still so dull?" Jesus asked them. [17]"Don't you see that whatever enters the mouth goes into the stomach and then out of the body? [18]But the things that come out of a person's mouth come from the heart, and these defile them. [19]For out of the heart come evil thoughts—murder, adultery, sexual immorality, theft, false testimony, slander. [20]These are what defile a person; but eating with unwashed hands does not defile them."

[21]Leaving that place, Jesus withdrew to the region of Tyre and Sidon. [22]A Canaanite woman from that vicinity came to him, crying out, "Lord, Son of David, have mercy on me! My daughter is demon-possessed and suffering terribly."

[23]Jesus did not answer a word. So his disciples came to him and urged him, "Send her away, for she keeps crying out after us."

[24]He answered, "I was sent only to the lost sheep of Israel."

[25]The woman came and knelt before him. "Lord, help me!" she said.

[26]He replied, "It is not right to take the children's bread and toss it to the dogs."

[27]"Yes it is, Lord," she said. "Even the dogs eat the crumbs that fall from their master's table."

[28]Then Jesus said to her, "Woman, you have great faith! Your request is granted." And her daughter was healed at that moment.

[29]Jesus left there and went along the Sea of Galilee. Then he went up on a mountainside and sat down. [30]Great crowds came to him, bringing the lame, the blind, the crippled, the mute and many others, and laid them at his feet; and he healed them. [31]The people were amazed when they saw the mute speaking, the crippled made well, the lame walking and the blind seeing. And they praised the God of Israel.

[32]Jesus called his disciples to him and said, "I have compassion for these people; they have already been with me three days and have nothing to eat. I do not want to send them away hungry, or they may collapse on the way."

[33]His disciples answered, "Where could we get enough bread in this remote place to feed such a crowd?"

[34]"How many loaves do you have?" Jesus asked.

"Seven," they replied, "and a few small fish."

[35]He told the crowd to sit down on the ground. [36]Then he took the seven loaves and the fish, and when he had given thanks, he broke them and gave them to the disciples, and they in turn to the people. [37]They all ate and were satisfied. Afterward the disciples picked up seven basketfuls of

broken pieces that were left over. [38]The number of those who ate was four thousand men, besides women and children. [39]After Jesus had sent the crowd away, he got into the boat and went to the vicinity of Magadan.

TRADITION SETTING ASIDE THE LAW:
Emptying the Law of Meaning

Unwashed Hands: Outward and Inward Cleanness

MATTHEW 15 CONCERNS THE *clean* and *unclean*, and it is connected with the nature and purpose of trials, which is to learn holiness. Clean and unclean has to do with holiness. There is continuity with the passage from the last sermon. This comes up explicitly here in that the teachers of the law came and raised a question to Jesus. **"Then some Pharisees and teachers of the law came to Jesus from Jerusalem and asked, 'Why do your disciples break the tradition of the elders?'"** (vv. 1–2a). Interestingly, the question is put in this way with these words—not just the law of God but also the tradition of the elders. By this time in history, the Jews had developed the notion of tradition. We know that in history, focus on tradition came to be of great significance. They said, specifically, **"They don't wash their hands before they eat!"** (v. 2b). We can see the concern for following rules, regulations, and doing what is right and wise; it certainly has an *appearance* of wisdom. But Jesus saw through this pretension. This teaching has been passed down in the tradition, and although it is not taught in the Scripture, it may be an extrapolation from Scripture, applied in this way to washing their hands before they eat. What Jesus was concerned with was the appeal to tradition and the relation between tradition and the law.

Tradition, in this case, was not just the spelling out of the law further through extrapolation but something done under the pressure of our sinful hearts to set aside the law. It is not tradition unfolding the meaning of the law but tradition setting aside the law. This would become a significant problem. Remember how the law was not properly interpreted, and Jesus warned His disciples about this: "For I tell you that unless your righteousness surpasses that of the Pharisees and the teachers of the law, you will certainly not enter the kingdom of heaven"

(Matt. 5:20), and we are not to break the least of these Commandments.[1] Jesus is not minimizing the law; He is affirming the compre-
hensiveness of the law just as He spoke about in Matthew 5–7 in the
Sermon on the Mount.

"**Jesus replied, 'And why do you break the command of God for the
sake of your tradition?'**" (v. 3). What the Pharisees said to Jesus was a
direct challenge—that He was not keeping the law. It was bold. It was
an attempt to set aside His authority, diminish it, and undermine it.
Jesus, I believe, is not concerned so much with the defense of His own
authority, but with the authority of the Word of God and honoring
that authority. Particularly, these persons in the position to teach the
law of God are not doing so but are doing just the opposite—this is
the nature of sin. This is what we can expect and perhaps should expect. Without becoming cynical, we should be alert to the reversal—
in sin, the very ones who are supposed to teach the law and uphold
it are the ones who are undermining it, but they are undermining it
in the name of appearing to keep it. There are several layers of things
contrary to expectation.

Honor Father and Mother: The Sanctity of the Law Embodied in a Whole Way of Life

Jesus must bring the Word to correct the misapplication of the law by
tradition. He applies it, particularly, regarding the teaching of honoring your father and mother. Interestingly, He draws attention to this
command. "**For God said, 'Honor your father and mother'**" (v. 4a).
It is the first commandment with a promise. It is through the parents
that the child is taught, and the child is to be taught the Word of God.
A whole way of life is bound up in the command, "**Honor your father
and mother.**" Notice that both the father and mother are in authority over the child, even though Scripture teaches there is a particular
headship of the father in the family. But here, "**God said, 'Honor your
father and mother' and 'Anyone who curses their father or mother
is to be put to death'**" (v. 4). There were sanctions, and this law was
so important because so much rests on it. The whole communication

---

1. *Matthew 5:19.*

of the way of life rests on parents teaching their children the Word of God. This command is to be kept and is expected to be kept.

There is a way in which it is protected so it is kept. There is a sense in which anyone who fails to honor their father and mother or fails to receive the teaching of father and mother is removed from the Church. They are removed from the Church under the Old Testament by death. They are removed from the Church in the New Testament by excommunication. Anyone who fails to heed this very basic ordinance (honoring father and mother) by which God's commands are taught and put into practice should be removed from the community of believers to preserve the way of life. We can see this manifestation most clearly when someone curses his father or mother. There is no option: they must be put to death,[2] or they must be excommunicated. Discipline *must* be brought in to uphold and protect the sanctity of the law of God and the way of life. Otherwise, everything falls into disrepute, disarray, chaos, and the whole culture tumbles. We can look at our own lives individually and in relation to our parents and think about how we have responded. We can think about our children and how we teach them; there is much to reflect on here. If this command had been upheld, the purity and strength of the Church would have been preserved by separating from the community those who did not heed what they had been taught. One might ask, 'What about when the child grows up and seems to be okay, and then later on, they depart?' We do have a promise: "Train a child in the way he should go, and when he is old he will not turn from it" (Prov. 22:6).

What God intends in this commandment is for the way of life to be taught from one generation to the next. He intends for children to receive the teaching and training, grow up in it, enjoy it, appreciate their parents, be bonded to their parents in this common vision of life, and have all the joys and pleasures of fellowship. If the parents are faithful and the child rebels when he is an adult, the child is to be removed (excommunicated). If the children do not live according to the Word of God while living in their parents' house and are past the age of accountability, they must be dealt with by excommunication.

One of the things that will happen as a result of this commandment is that there will be a natural care of the parents for the children to

---

2. *Leviticus 20:9; Exodus 21:15.*

pass on their way of life. The parents will lay up in store for the children what to pass on. But it is also the case that children will love and appreciate their parents who have taught them this way, with whom they are bonded in fellowship, and with whom they can share their deepest concerns because they share a common vision of the good. In this love, they will care for their parents. This way of life that God has intended to be transmitted from generation to generation will be passed on. The blessing will come upon the succeeding generations and spread throughout the earth.

Hypocrisy: Self-Deception and Self-Justification

If the parents were in need of monetary support, the teachers of the law found a way to annul the children's responsibility in a way that would benefit *their* interest. **"But you say that if anyone declares that what might have been used to help their father or mother is, 'devoted to God,' they are not to 'honor their father or mother' with it"** (vv. 5–6a). In other words, if a person makes a promise to God of a certain amount of money, they are not required to help their parents with that money. The assumption here is that tithing would be in place. Over and beyond the tithe, before you commit to giving a gift to the church, you are to be concerned that your parents are provided for. The Pharisees, who were concerned about the things of man, not this way of life and the knowledge of God, found a way to increase the funds which would serve their interest. They *nullified* the Commandments by their rules, regulations, and traditions. The human heart is very subtle; it finds ways to do its own will. Once it turns away from God and the teaching that was implanted over the years by the parents, it finds ways to justify other things. There will be a society of mutual justification between those who have turned away and the religious leaders who benefit. This is because they have not been overseeing the process to be sure that the teaching and discipline have been maintained, both while a child is growing up and as an adult in the community. Instead, they have raised up their tradition; they hold this intact, but the tradition has been an interpretation that essentially has gutted the meaning of the law and emptied it of its significance. If we understood how this law was intended for life and had delighted in it, this would not be occurring. When we take our eyes off of life as God has defined it—life indeed—we put something else in the place of it, creaturely things and what money can buy, and so begin to maneuver to benefit in this way. We nullify the commands of God by our interpretation, by our own imagination.

"Thus you nullify the word of God for the sake of your tradition" (v. 6b). It is not just these persons mentioned in Matthew who have done it, but there is an 'across-the-board' teaching in Romans 2 of those who have the law and have been brought up in biblical teaching: "You who preach against stealing, do you steal?" (Rom. 2:21b). They speak about keeping the Sabbath and are very concerned about keeping the Sabbath in an outward, legalistic way, and miss the real meaning of the Sabbath—the work of dominion, the goal of the knowledge of God, the completion of the work,[3] and the rest that is to come. We, as human beings, have it in us to set up our limited understanding coupled with a misunderstanding of the law in such a way as to empty and set aside the commands of God by our understanding, which we then pass on.

The Scripture teaches us about clean and unclean, holiness and un-holiness, devotion to God and not being devoted to God, and emptying the commands of meaning and giving an appearance without the reality. This has to do with a lack of understanding and a lack of faith, since faith is synonymous with understanding in a particular sense—not in the sense of trusting in God but understanding His Word and His way. We focus on things *outward and visible*; we have a concern for being clean in an outward way; we are concerned about the washing of our hands, the washing of pots, et cetera, and we are not concerned about the *inward and invisible*—true holiness, true cleanness, true devotion to God which comes out of faith/understanding. There is an unholiness on the part of the Pharisees in seeing the outward only, not the inward reality of holiness that comes with understanding. As a result, they are not truly devoted to what is good; instead, they are devoted to what is not good. In this case, they were devoted to money and this affected how they interpreted the law. Jesus brings correction here, just as He spoke in the Sermon on the Mount concerning what it is to obey the

---

3. Gangadean, *Philosophical Foundation*, 171–177, 208–211; Gangadean, *The Westminster Cat-echisms*, 109–111, 321–325; Gangadean, *On Natural and Revealed Theology*, 33–39, 127–139; Gangadean, *History of Philosophy*, 61–64; Gangadean, "Paper No. 15: Hermeneutics," 91–101; "Paper No. 16: The Historic Christian Faith," 103–114; "Paper No. 17: The Five Solas," in *The Logos Papers*, 115–118.

Commandments: not to murder, not to commit adultery, not to swear falsely. What He is saying here is consistent with what He taught before regarding the true meaning of the command.

The Effect of Hypocrisy in Worship: Hearts Far from God

This unholiness comes out in their worship. **"You hypocrites! Isaiah was right when he prophesied about you: 'These people honor me with their lips, but their hearts are far from me. They worship me in vain; their teachings are merely human rules'"** (vv. 7–9). Notice the self-deception that is involved in this. We think we are near, we think we are clean, we think we are holy, but we are not, yet we can and should know. We should not have set aside the command of God in such an egregious way. He says, **"You hypocrites!"** When we hear the word hypocrite, we should understand that self-deception and self-justification are involved, as they were in the Garden after Adam's sin, in the way he covered his nakedness and justified himself. There is this lack of understanding, lack of faith, and looking at the outward reality, taking appearances for reality, taking the appearance of holiness for holiness, taking the outward cleanness for the inward cleanness, and being satisfied with this. So, we can draw near to God with our mouths but our hearts are far from God. We may have a form of godliness but deny the power of it.[4] The worship of God, in this sense, is in vain, because the rules are rules taught by men. It is not worship in spirit and in truth;[5] it is not with understanding. We have to be careful. We have to be on our guard. We may think that we are worshiping the Lord, but we have not been taught, we have not been seeking, we do not understand, and we are doing something outward in place of the true reality.[6] We have to be on our guard against this. We cannot presume that other folks may be caught in it, but we will not be caught in it. We have to be concerned about true holiness which is devotion to God and knowing God.

---

4. *2 Timothy 3:5.*

5. *John 4:23–24.*

6. Gangadean, "Paper No. 105: The Regulative Principle of Worship," 545–546; "Paper No. 134: Worship, the Sabbath, and the Church," 679–682; "Paper No. 135: On Worship," in *The Logos Papers*, 683–684; Gangadean, *The Westminster Confession*, 233–244.

The Purpose of Trials: To Learn Holiness

One of the ways to see our holiness is to see how we respond during trials. Remember, the purpose of trials is to learn holiness. God chastens us so that we might be partakers of His holiness, without which no one shall see the Lord.[7] Notice that the goal of holiness is seeing the Lord. The idea of submission is not *my* will, but *your* will be done. If we want to see how we are doing in holiness, whether we are truly devoted to God, look at how we are responding under trial. Are we submitting? Are we quieting our hearts? Are we discouraged? Are we blowing up? Are we breaking down? Are we looking to God? Are we hoping in God? Are we trusting in God even as Job did? We may speak about Job's trial as a maximal trial, but it is held up for our example. Remember the perseverance of Job and God's goodness—God's purpose was served.[8] The Lord Jesus counters this presumptuous attempt to be corrected by blind teachers. He points out the truth. In their response, we see Jesus is not being heard, given the condition of their hearts.

Listen and Understand: Into the Mouth Versus Out of the Mouth

"Jesus called the crowd to him and said, 'Listen and understand'" (v. 10). If we are devoted to God and seek God, we will have this understanding. Listen and understand. "What goes into someone's mouth does not defile them, but what comes out of their mouth, that is what defiles them" (v. 11). It is not what goes into the mouth, but what comes out of the mouth. It is not the food we eat that goes into our mouth that makes us unclean, or eating with unwashed hands, but what comes out of our mouth. The question is, what comes out of our mouths? Words come out of our mouths. Words are the primary things that come out of our mouths. Our words *reveal* our uncleanness, since our heart is corrupted from birth. This is why children are baptized—not that baptism takes away sin, but baptism is a *sign* that sin needs to be taken away, the sinful heart needs to be taken away.[9] A child has been born, and eight days later, we say, 'He needs to be born again.' It

---

7. *Hebrews 12:14.*

8. *James 5:11.*

9. Gangadean, *The Westminster Confession*, 299–305; Gangadean, "Paper No. 140: Argument for Paedobaptism," in *The Logos Papers*, 703–704.

THE GOSPEL OF MATTHEW

should be this way; those two—born and reborn—are intended to be juxtaposed. The child is born and he needs to be reborn, especially in this most innocent state. It is not that the words make us unclean, but they reveal the uncleanness in our hearts.

Offense at Correction and Christ's Response: Peace and Comfort in God's Sovereignty

"Then the disciples came to him and asked, 'Do you know that the Pharisees were offended when they heard this?'" (v. 12). Notice that the Pharisees did not receive this correction; rather, they took offense. What is Jesus' response when the teaching is not heard? Assuming that the teaching was given, Jesus finds His peace and comfort in knowing God is sovereign. "He replied, 'Every plant that my heavenly Father has not planted will be pulled up by the roots'" (v. 13). God is the one who plants, and what He plants will remain. If it is not planted by Him, it is not the work of God. If God has not begun this work, this is not the child of God, and the person is resisting the Word of God as far as their responsibility is concerned. They are not seeking and not understanding. They are resisting the teaching, going on their way, taking offense when correction comes, and presuming to teach the One by whom they are to be taught. There is a high degree of presumption here, and offense is taken. Jesus just looks at this, sees God's sovereignty, and submits to it. He does say, "how often I have longed to gather your children together . . . and you were not willing" (Lk. 13:34), but he submits to God's will. Remember earlier when the secrets of the kingdom were revealed to some and not to others? Jesus rejoiced and thanked God: "I praise you, Father, Lord of heaven and earth, because you have hidden these things from the wise and learned, and revealed them to little children. Yes, Father, for this is what you were pleased to do" (Matt. 11:25–26).

There is comfort and strength in looking to God's sovereign will, just as we must look to His sovereign will in our trials. Remember, in the third petition, "*Thy will be done on earth as it is in heaven*, we pray, that God, by his grace, would make us able and willing to know, obey, and submit to his will in all things, as the angels do in heaven."[10] We

---

10. Gangadean, *The Westminster Catechisms*, 102.

THE CLEAN AND THE UNCLEAN   227

are to do His revealed will and to submit to His sovereign, providential will in the events that come to pass. This is trusting in God, having patience, and persevering without murmuring and complaining. We are not saying we are stones, and we feel no pain. We do feel pain; we are grieved, but we learn to submit. Even as Job said, "Though he slay me, yet will I trust in him" (Job. 13:15 KJV). We are not to yield to discouragement and cynicism; we are not to allow the root of bitterness to spring up,[11] but we are to know that God is working this together for good. 'God intends it for my good, and I can be at peace.' I think God wants us to be cheerful—not to be weighed down—knowing that these things work together for good. This is part of being devoted to God and knowing that God is sovereign. Even when we struggle for a long time with particular situations, we keep affirming that God is sovereign and that He is working these things together for the good of those who love Him, and we find peace in this truth.

Jesus describes the Pharisees as blind guides. "**Leave them; they are blind guides. If the blind lead the blind, both will fall into a pit**" (v. 14). The presumption is in coming to teach the Lord and correct the Lord and not being open to correction. And now the Word of the Lord says, "**They are blind guides. If the blind lead the blind, both will fall into a pit.**" We should not presume that this does not happen. Many who do not know the Lord are in positions of teaching. Many who do not understand the Scriptures, many who do not understand the basics, the foundations of Scripture, are teaching and being followed, and will lead others into the pit.

Jesus Explains the Parable: Are You Still So Dull?

The disciples ask for the parable to be explained, and Jesus reproves them. "**Peter said, 'Explain the parable to us.' 'Are you still so dull?' Jesus asked them'**" (vv. 15–16). They lack faith. Remember, we should perhaps back up and put this in the perspective that we are being sanctified, we are made holy through knowing the truth, and that knowing involves an understanding. It is not apart from knowing and understanding that we are sanctified, cleansed, and made holy. We need to be sanctified because we lack understanding. There is unbelief and sin

---

11. *Hebrews 12:15.*

in us, we trust in idols, and we do not heed correction and teaching by parents—assuming that this teaching is done in the Lord.

I know that because of a broken situation, many parents are unbelievers. The children may come to believe and there is a whole reversal and breakdown of the process. I am aware of this. But when we persist in this sin, it brings death. There is a word, a phrase that is very intense, that the Scripture uses; it speaks about "the abomination that causes desolation" (Matt. 24:15). Lives have become desolate because of walking sinfully, not in the way of truth but the way of death that has been perpetuated over the years. Whole communities of people have come under what could be described as *sin and death*. When it comes to a mature stage, this can be described as the *abomination that causes desolation*. You can see this in individual lives, in communities, and various places on earth. Remember how the land of Israel was left desolate? Why? Because of sin and the judgment of God that came upon that place. Some places are spoken of as God-forsaken places, desolate, with no sense of life—just death and more death. We are brought out of that by regeneration, conversion, repentance and faith, trusting in God for salvation, and being sanctified through the truth.[12]

The disciples reveal this need for being sanctified and cleansed. They did not understand. Jesus reproves them, **"Are you still so dull?"** (v. 16a). **"Don't you see . . . ?"** (v. 17a). Notice the line of thinking that the Lord is using. How should they see? They should see from a principle of general revelation.

> Don't you see that whatever enters the mouth goes into the stomach and then out of the body? But the things that come out of a person's mouth come from the heart, and these defile them. For out of the heart come evil thoughts—murder, adultery, sexual immorality, theft, false testimony, slander. These are what defile a person; but eating with unwashed hands does not defile them (vv. 17–20).

These are what make a man unclean, unholy, and not devoted to God. These things reveal a lack of holiness. Why do we have murder and anger and all that goes with it? Because we are not getting what we

---

12. Gangadean, *The Westminster Confession*, 143–206; Gangadean, *The Westminster Catechisms*, 191–207.

want. It is not the attitude of submission to God in His chastening. We hear talk about people who are angry. Teenagers who grow up angry go into adult life angry, thinking they have been put upon and they have been the victims. They blame others and they justify themselves. Sometimes, this anger flashes out in murder, or they may try to find satisfaction in adultery—unholiness, lack of devotion to God, and attempting to find satisfaction and joy, and that leads to these other things. Jesus explains what clean and unclean means in terms of holy and unholy. He applies it very relevantly, explaining to His disciples that they should have seen this. They are not making the connection; they are not understanding and, therefore, not being sanctified through knowing the truth.

CONTRAST—THE FAITH OF
THE CANAANITE WOMAN:
The Unclean Purified by Faith

This next passage is included to help us understand clean and unclean further—the faith of the Canaanite woman. By contrast, she is clean and the religious teachers are not. The contrast could not be greater.

> Leaving that place, Jesus withdrew to the region of Tyre and Sidon. A Canaanite woman from that vicinity came to him, crying out, "Lord, Son of David, have mercy on me! My daughter is demon-possed and suffering terribly." Jesus did not answer a word. So his disciples came to him and urged him, "Send her away, for she keeps crying out after us." He answered, "I was sent only to the lost sheep of Israel." The woman came and knelt before him. "Lord, help me!" she said (vv. 21–25).

The second time she said, "**Lord, help me!**" She did not say "Son of David"—this phrase has a particular application to the Israelites. "**He replied, 'It is not right to take the children's bread and toss it to the dogs'**" (v. 26). You might say that to speak in this way, Jesus is not being sensitive and politically correct. Yet, He is speaking very accurately and very pointedly, and He is, in a sense, probing her faith, her understanding, her devotion, her holiness. "**It is not right to take the children's bread and toss it to the dogs.**" Please keep this in mind.

Let us talk about the bread because this is coming up in the next passage. What is the children's bread? What are we to pray for? "Give us this day our daily bread" (Matt. 6:11 NKJV). Here, the healing and deliverance from the curse is considered part of the children's bread. In speaking about bread, Jesus also says, "Man shall not live on bread alone" (Matt. 4:4). Bread is not primary; it is needed, but it is not the most basic. "'Yes it is, Lord,' she said. 'Even the dogs eat the crumbs that fall from their masters' table.' Then Jesus said to her, 'Woman, you have great faith! Your request is granted.' And her daughter was healed at that moment" (vv. 27–28).

In Acts 10, Peter had a vision of the gospel going to the Canaanites. Three times, all kinds of creeping creatures in a sheet were let down. Three times, it was told to Peter, "'Get up, Peter. Kill and eat.' 'Surely not, Lord!' Peter replied. 'I have never eaten anything impure or unclean'" (Acts 10:13b–14). Notice the reference to *unclean*, and the discussion with Jesus earlier about clean and unclean. The response to the Pharisees about unwashed hands and the faith of the Canaanite woman are being put together side by side in the gospel to make a point clearer. The Lord said, "Do not call anything impure that God has made clean" (Acts 10:15b). Then, in Acts 15:9, when Peter gives an account of the gospel going out to the Gentiles, he said God has "purified their hearts by faith" and given them the Holy Spirit. Notice the emphasis on purity, being purified, and being cleansed by faith. This Canaanite woman had faith, whereas those in the tradition, who were locked into it and had it merely outwardly, thought they understood, and did not understand—they lacked faith. They failed to see what true holiness is. I think the passages concerning the unwashed hands and the Canaanite woman are put together and should be read as a contrast that heightens the meaning of what it is to be clean—that our hearts are cleansed by faith.

"Woman, you have great faith! Your request is granted." This statement by Jesus reveals that she understood the difference between the Jews and the Gentiles: that the Gentiles were like dogs in the sense of being unfaithful. I am not sure how this connects, because dogs are supposed to be very faithful creatures. I am not sure how to comment on that, but the Canaanites were unfaithful, and dogs are connected. The Gentiles were seen as unfaithful and like dogs. This one who is supposed to be unfaithful reveals great faith—what many who had been brought up in the tradition did not have. Jesus recognizes this is one who has been planted by God, one in whose heart God has worked, one who has been taught by God, one in whom the Spirit of God has worked to bring her to this point—to understand. This woman has no presumption in casting herself on the mercy of God, compared with the presumption of the Pharisees that comes out of their failure to understand. Even as the Lord said, "Father, forgive them; for they know not what they do" (Lk. 23:34a KJV)—it is sinful ignorance. This woman had faith. She understood who He is and the extent of His rule. She acknowledged this and said, **"Even the dogs eat the crumbs that fall from their masters' table."** Even a little bit will do. How true is this? You do not take the child's food and throw it to the dogs, but dogs do come around when you sit at the table, and are ready to get any crumb that falls. Isn't that true? Isn't that the way dogs are? They lick it up, and she is willing to humble herself and take this position. Even a crumb will do; it would be sufficient; the least favor would be enough. It shows her understanding, her faith, and the Lord commends her. It shows that God has cleansed her heart by faith. She understood what holiness is, what devotion is, and others who should have understood, did not.

THE CHILDREN'S BREAD:
Meeting the Needs of His People

Next, we have the account of the feeding of the 4,000. There is a parallel passage here before Jesus fed the 4,000; He healed them: the lame, the blind, the crippled, the mute, and many others.

> Great crowds came to him, bringing the lame, the blind, the crippled, the mute and many others, and laid them at his feet; and he healed them. The people were amazed when they saw the mute speaking, the crippled made well, the lame walking and the blind seeing. And they praised the God of Israel (vv. 30–31).

What had He just said? He said that healing is the children's bread. The Israelites are getting their daily needs met. "Give us this day our daily bread."[13] Our daily bread is our daily needs. Our daily bread concerns

---

13. *Matthew 6:11* KJV.

dealing with the curse—not just literally food on the table. Without food, starvation leads to death, but sickness can also lead to death. Daily bread concerns all those things that we need in a temporal way: "Give us this day our daily bread." So Jesus heals them. In a parallel passage, He not only heals them, but He gives them literal bread—He feeds them. He multiplies the loaves and the fish, feeds them, and then sends them away.

DEMAND FOR A SIGN/PROOF FROM THE LEADERS:
Failing to Understand General Revelation

In connection with this, the Pharisees come to Jesus and ask Him for a sign from heaven. "The Pharisees and Sadducees came to Jesus and tested him by asking him to show them a sign from heaven" (Matt. 16:1). We might ask ourselves: 'What is it that Jesus just did? Is that not a sign from heaven? Why are they asking for a sign?' If there were 4,000 who saw the miracle, and many gave their testimony and shared their healing, then why are they asking for a sign? How many healings and miraculous signs does it take to accomplish His purpose? I want to put this into a little more context. What is it to ask for a sign? Do *we* ask for signs? The theme of *bread* is still going to continue because Jesus, after He speaks to the Pharisees, is going to tell the disciples, "Be on your guard against the yeast of the Pharisees and Sadducees" (Matt. 16:6b). I want to at least introduce this idea, but we will not have time to develop it completely now. The demand for a sign by the Jews is a demand for proof so that they can be in a position of authority. They want to be in the position to attest to whether what they witness passes their scrutiny.

This weekend, we were at a conference where there was great concern given to proof. There was a concern for scientific proof that the order in the universe did not happen by chance (combined with law), but this happened by intelligent design. All kinds of responses were being given by way of coming up with proof. The Scripture says, "Be on your guard against the yeast of the Pharisees and Sadducees" (Matt. 16:6b). We have to raise the question: Are *we* being caught up in this request for *proof* in an inappropriate way? We should understand how signs work. Signs of special revelation were never intended to work by themselves apart from teaching and general revelation. It is not only that the person does a sign, but what he is saying must be according to the Word of God, which is known from general revelation. Many things should already be settled when one comes to ask for a sign. But often, those who have not seen and understood what is clear from general revelation get caught up in asking for proof in this way. Those who do not want to (and are not ready to) address the concern about seeing what is clear from general revelation are attempting to give a sign. This approach to proof becomes a problem, and it shows a lack of understanding.

There is a lack of understanding because we have not been seeking God. Sin is described as not seeking, not understanding, and not doing what is right.[14] In not seeking, there is a lack of holiness, and there is uncleanness. Jesus describes those asking for a sign as a wicked and adulterous generation: "A wicked and adulterous generation looks for a sign" (Matt. 16:4a). We can open this up more, and we will go back soon and speak about the reference in Matthew 12 where Jesus spoke about the sign of Jonah and what it meant.

We are being called in these passages that go together to be concerned about clean and unclean; to be concerned about holy and unholy; to be concerned with being devoted to the Lord and seeking the Lord. We may say, "without faith it is impossible to please God, because anyone who comes to him must believe that he exists and that he rewards those who earnestly seek him" (Heb. 11:6). Holiness involves seeking God. It is different from understanding and faith. It is seeking God. But if we do seek, we will see and understand. Without holiness, no one shall see the Lord. The Lord calls us away from sin, He calls us to holiness, He calls us to seek Him, to understand Him, to serve Him, to rejoice in Him, and to praise Him.

---

14. *Romans 3:10–11; Psalm 14:2–3, 53:1–3.*

13

THE YEAST OF THE PHARISEES

Beware of Hidden Assumptions in Ourselves and Others

Matthew 16

[1]The Pharisees and Sadducees came to Jesus and tested him by asking him to show them a sign from heaven.

[2]He replied, "When evening comes, you say, 'It will be fair weather, for the sky is red,' [3]and in the morning, 'Today it will be stormy, for the sky is red and overcast.' You know how to interpret the appearance of the sky, but you cannot interpret the signs of the times. [4]A wicked and adulterous generation looks for a sign, but none will be given it except the sign of Jonah." Jesus then left them and went away.

[5]When they went across the lake, the disciples forgot to take bread. [6]"Be careful," Jesus said to them. "Be on your guard against the yeast of the Pharisees and Sadducees."

[7]They discussed this among themselves and said, "It is because we didn't bring any bread."

[8]Aware of their discussion, Jesus asked, "You of little faith, why are you talking among yourselves about having no bread? [9]Do you still not understand? Don't you remember the five loaves for the five thousand, and how many basketfuls you gathered? [10]Or the seven loaves for the four thousand, and how many basketfuls you gathered? [11]How is it you don't understand that I was not talking to you about bread? But be on your guard against the yeast of the Pharisees and Sadducees." [12]Then they understood that he was not telling them to guard against the yeast used in bread, but against the teaching of the Pharisees and Sadducees.

13When Jesus came to the region of Caesarea Philippi, he asked his disciples, "Who do people say the Son of Man is?"

14They replied, "Some say John the Baptist; others say Elijah; and still others, Jeremiah or one of the prophets."

15"But what about you?" he asked. "Who do you say I am?"

16Simon Peter answered, "You are the Messiah, the Son of the living God."

17Jesus replied, "Blessed are you, Simon son of Jonah, for this was not revealed to you by flesh and blood, but by my Father in heaven. 18And I tell you that you are Peter, and on this rock I will build my church, and the gates of Hades will not overcome it. 19I will give you the keys of the kingdom of heaven; whatever you bind on earth will be bound in heaven, and whatever you loose on earth will be loosed in heaven." 20Then he ordered his disciples not to tell anyone that he was the Messiah.

21From that time on Jesus began to explain to his disciples that he must go to Jerusalem and suffer many things at the hands of the elders, the chief priests and the teachers of the law, and that he must be killed and on the third day be raised to life.

22Peter took him aside and began to rebuke him. "Never, Lord!" he said. "This shall never happen to you!"

23Jesus turned and said to Peter, "Get behind me, Satan! You are a stumbling block to me; you do not have in mind the concerns of God, but merely human concerns."

24Then Jesus said to his disciples, "Whoever wants to be my disciple must deny themselves and take up their cross and follow me. 25For whoever wants to save their life will lose it, but whoever loses their life for me will find it. 26What good will it be for someone to gain the whole world, yet forfeit their soul? Or what can anyone give in exchange for their soul? 27For the Son of Man is going to come in his Father's glory with his angels, and then he will reward each person according to what they have done.

28"Truly I tell you, some who are standing here will not taste death before they see the Son of Man coming in his kingdom."

REVIEW OF MATTHEW 14–15

BEFORE I PROCEED, I WOULD LIKE TO DO A review of Matthew 14 and 15, which come after the parables of our Lord concerning the kingdom of God. In chapter 14, we saw John the Baptist's death, the 5,000 fed, and Jesus walking on the water. Through all of this, we brought out the idea of trials of faith, the anatomy of a trial, and that the purpose of the trial is to partake of holiness, without which no one will see the Lord.[1] The daily trials of our faith are so that we might come to holiness and see the Lord.

I realized that I was trying to express three things in the prior message. First, we explained holiness in terms of clean and unclean regarding the Pharisees and the faith of the Canaanite woman, and how that contrast heightened the meaning of the teaching. The Canaanite woman is considered unholy, like the dog, yet she has faith; her heart was cleansed. We are seeing the nature of faith, which includes cleansing and holiness. Second, we explained the nature of holiness and the relationship between knowledge, holiness, and righteousness. We are trying to bring this message out of the passage we are reading. Third, we tried to relate those two elements to you. Three things were brought out all at once, and sometimes it is hard to chew gum and walk simultaneously. We have to keep going back and trying to get it better and improve upon the work previously done.

The Relationship Between Knowledge, Holiness, and Righteousness

A brief word on the relationship between knowledge, holiness, and righteousness. It is a complex relationship. It is grounded in the tri-unity of our personality, and there is an interaction between the three. Even though, as in the Godhead, there is an order between Father, Son, and Holy Spirit, there is likewise interaction, which is very dynamic. We can put it this way: holiness leads us to knowledge; seeking leads us to understanding. Holiness is connected to the devotion by which we seek. We speak about no one seeking (holiness), understanding (knowledge), or doing what is right (righteousness).[2] The three aspects of our triune personality are present (knowledge-holiness-righteousness). Likewise, knowledge leads to holiness: "Sanctify them"—make them holy—"by the truth; your word is truth" (Jn. 17:17). And knowledge and holiness lead to righteousness: "Then you will know the truth, and the truth will set you free" (Jn. 8:32). Again, holiness leads to knowledge: If we

---

1. *Hebrews 12:14.*
2. *Romans 3:10–12.*

seek, we will understand, and "without holiness no one will see the Lord" (Heb. 12:14b). Also, righteousness leads to holiness: In trials, we become partakers of His holiness after we suffer, submit, and do what is right before God.

> Consider it pure joy, my brothers, whenever you face trials of many kinds, because you know that the testing of your faith develops perseverance. Perseverance must finish its work so that you may be mature and complete, not lacking anything (Jas. 1:2–4).

It is also true that righteousness leads to knowledge. "I consider that our present sufferings are not worth comparing with the glory that will be revealed in us" (Rom. 8:18). I wanted to clarify this to increase our understanding of the relationship between knowledge, holiness, and righteousness.

Listen and Understand Versus the Blind Leading the Blind

Continuing with the review from the last sermon, we spoke about clean and unclean, holy and unholy, the lack of understanding on the part of the Pharisees about what true holiness is, and their concern with the *outward*—being concerned with not washing hands before eating rather than the *inward* spiritual reality. This has to do with the need to understand the relation between the sign and reality—the visible reveals the invisible. By faith, we understand that which is not seen.[3] Certainly, the future hope is not seen, and the act of God as Creator is not seen, but we see it through its effects. Faith has to do with grasping the invisible from the visible, and we can focus on the visible (the washing of hands), and not see the truth of the invisible behind it. This is a lack of faith, a lack of understanding, and, with this, a lack of holiness. There was a misunderstanding of holiness regarding cleanness because there was a lack of holiness—devotion—on the part of the Pharisees. Their lack of understanding was made explicit. It is particularly difficult for those in leadership positions to be confronted with their lack of insight—they came trying to correct Jesus, they did not come to be

---

3. *Hebrews 11:3;* Gangadean, *The Epistle to the Hebrews,* 167–183, 185–201; Gangadean, *The Biblical Worldview,* 3–20.

corrected. It is most difficult for those who, in a religious context, are leading without understanding.

The Pharisees did not have understanding, yet they were trying to lead and, in a sense, teach Jesus. When they come again to try to test Jesus, we see their failure to see their true condition. "These people honor me with their lips, but their hearts are far from me" (Matt. 15:8). They teach rules taught by men. This lack of holiness, devotion, and understanding leads to *changing* the teaching of God, particularly the way God has intended for it to be taught through the parents.

> Jesus replied, "And why do you break the command of God for the sake of your tradition? For God said, 'Honor your father and mother' and 'Anyone who curses their father or mother is to be put to death.' But you say that if anyone declares that what might have been used to help their father or mother is 'devoted to God,' they are not to 'honor their father or mother' with it. Thus you nullify the word of God for the sake of your tradition" (Matt. 15:3–6).

A distinction exists between tradition and the law of God, with the latter being disregarded in favor of the former. Among the various laws being ignored, the Lord specifically highlighted the commandment: "Honor your father and your mother" (Ex. 20:12a), emphasizing the importance of teaching, legitimate authority, and the structure and care that God has for the role of parents. This commandment was set aside due to their adherence to tradition. Lack of righteousness comes with a lack of holiness and lack of understanding.

The crowds were called to listen and to understand: "Jesus called the crowd to him and said, 'Listen and understand'" (Matt. 15:10). Contrast listening and understanding with the religious leaders who are blind and are leading the blind. "Leave them; they are blind guides. If the blind lead the blind, both will fall into a pit" (Matt. 15:14). The leaders did not understand. Again, in typical fashion, Jesus had to correct the disciples when they asked Him to explain; He said, "Are you still so dull?" (Matt. 15:16). Notice the focus on faith and understanding and what it reveals about not seeking and not understanding. Remember these three groups: the crowds, the religious leaders, and the disciples. All three of these are addressed in Matthew 15, and all three are addressed again in Matthew 16. We would do well to keep this in mind as we read the Scripture and see how He is addressing them in the area of their understanding—all three of them. Jesus wants us to have faith, and faith *is* understanding—*by* faith we understand.[4] I know the popular view is to say faith is *without* understanding (fideism), but according to the Scripture, there must be understanding, and without understanding, it is empty of meaning. By way of contrast, the Canaanite woman understood, had faith, and received the blessing as she came to Jesus and called upon Him for the wellbeing of her daughter.

THE THEME OF BREAD CONTINUES

We will see that the theme of bread is continuing. Remember, Jesus first healed the people and multiplied the loaves to feed 5,000 in Matthew 14 and to feed 4,000 in Matthew 15. He said to the Canaanite woman, "It is not right to take the children's bread and toss it to the dogs" (Matt. 15:26). The bread spoken of there was particularly in connection with the needs that they had for healing and the provision of God in daily sustenance. We pray for this when we pray, "Give us this day our daily bread."[5] We pray for our needs, particularly under the condition of the curse.[6] We pray for healing and food, or provision, which is our daily bread. This theme continues. He warns the disciples about the yeast of the Pharisees, and they took it to mean physical bread, which shows that they did not understand.

> When they went across the lake, the disciples forgot to take bread. "Be careful," Jesus said to them. "Be on your guard against the yeast of the Pharisees and Sadducees." They discussed this among themselves and said, "It is because we didn't bring any bread" (vv. 5–7).

There is a contrast between the religious teachers, who do not understand, and the believers, who understand a little. The disciples are not blind; they are just dull. There is a contrast. The Canaanite woman shows a real instance of faith. The faith of the three groups is displayed.

---

4. *Hebrews 11:3*; Gangadean, *Philosophical Foundation*, 32–45; Gangadean, *History of Philosophy*, 3–12.

5. *Matthew 6:11* KJV.

6. Gangadean, *The Biblical Worldview*, 55–68, 275–294.

DEMAND FOR PROOF OF JESUS' AUTHORITY

Asking for a Sign from Heaven Versus Past and Present Signs

The Pharisees desire a sign. "The Pharisees and Sadducees came to Jesus and tested him by asking him to show them a sign from heaven" (v. 1). We have to understand what this is in a larger, broader context. The Pharisees wanted proof that Jesus was sent by God. This is what the sign represents: confirmation that this one has power from God. Remember, Nicodemus said, "Rabbi, we know you are a teacher who has come from God. For no one could perform the signs you are doing if God were not with him" (Jn. 3:2). This is the purpose of signs. The Pharisees want proof that God sent Him and that He is legitimately in authority—it *appears* that they want to know that He has this authority from God. But this is the farthest thing from their minds. They, in their hearts, assume that they are in positions of authority, and Jesus is not in agreement with them, so they already believe that He has not been sent by God. Thus, their question comes as a challenge.

We need to see that they are asking for a sign amid a particular circumstance. Jesus had just fed the multitudes and had been healing many. What are these, if they are not signs? Jesus said, "But if I do them, even though you do not believe me, believe the works" (Jn. 10:38a). They had signs right and left, and when He gave them the sign, they explained it away. Jesus is healing on the Sabbath and they say, 'No, He is not from God.' Jesus is casting out demons and they say, 'No, this is by Beelzebul.' And these same men are now coming and asking for a sign. They were not paying attention to the signs given. One does not need to ask for a sign; if God sends someone, God gives them the sign. They do not have to wait and ask for a sign; Jesus came and gave them the sign. So it has been with the prophets of old; they did signs abundantly.

Failing to Understand General Revelation: The Visible Reveals the Invisible

They are asking for a sign with a lot of things not in place. Not only are more immediate, special revelation signs being given, but there is also a general revelation understanding of the nature of holiness. But they were caught up in the idea of washing outwardly and not seeing the inward reality. It is a general revelation principle that the outward is a sign and expression of the inward. They and we should understand this. There are layers upon layers of unbelief because of not seeking (no holiness) and not understanding. This unbelief is being manifested in asking for a sign. When we come near to our Lord Jesus Christ, or when He comes near to us, our heart condition is made manifest. We come to see ourselves. But He did not come to condemn us; He came to save us. He came to reveal what is in our hearts so that we might repent and turn to Him and love Him with our whole heart.

There was self-deception in the religious leaders in that they were not seeking; they did not understand what had already been given. Remember, sin is not seeking, but it is more than not seeking. The curse is on the world from the days of Adam because he was not only not seeking, but he was in self-deception and self-justification (blaming God for the woman He put there with him), and then God brought the curse.[7] The curse is still with us, and we find these elements are still here and we can see it in this question of the Pharisees. They *think* they want proof, and they want *others* to think they want proof. It is not true; they do not want proof. The Pharisees are in self-deception about their not seeking and not understanding of what they are doing. They are not seeking. They *appear* to be seeking; they may think they are seeking, and they want Jesus and others to think they are seeking, but they are not, which is to be in self-deception.

The Pharisees come to discredit His authority, not to acknowledge His authority. They come to discredit His authority over the people and assert that they are the ones in authority. They do not see all the correction that the Lord is bringing, and they do not see all that they are resisting in their self-justification. They think that they do not have to submit to His authority if He does not give them a sign, on their terms, while Jesus is giving signs right and left. They asked for the sign in order to justify themselves in their own minds and before others. So, there is not seeking, there is self-deception, and there is self-justification. You do not have to dig very far to see this. Pay attention, know that not seeking plus self-deception and self-justification are in all human beings universally, and ask yourself if it is in you, too. If we ask this question as we come to this passage, we will begin to see.

---

7. Gangadean, *The Biblical Worldview*, 147–294.

EXPOSING THEIR UNBELIEF:
An Example and Rebuke with Explanation

Jesus replied to their request for a sign by giving them an example. Jesus is so patient and wise, and He knows how to teach. He begins very concretely: "**When evening comes, you say, 'It will be fair weather, for the sky is red,' and in the morning, 'Today it will be stormy, for the sky is red and overcast'**" (vv. 2–3a). This is a clear, straightforward example. There are no questions about this. There is common ground, and there is agreement. He says, "**You know how to interpret the appearance of the sky**" (v. 3). Notice the word *interpret*—interpret the appearance of the sky; they know how to interpret what appears. What appears does need to be interpreted. What is the color of the wall? It *appears* to be white. Interpretation is required to get from appearance to reality, even with something like the color of the wall. Interpretation is required all the more so with signs. In other words, they see the redness of the sky, and they think, because of background knowledge from general revelation, that there will be fair weather. And at another time of day, the red sky means it is going to be stormy. Jesus says, "**You know how to interpret the appearance of the sky**," and then adds, "**but you cannot interpret the signs of the times**" (v. 3b). They cannot interpret the moral condition of the people.

Led Astray by Their Love of the World

Isaiah said, "The whole head is sick . . . From the sole of the foot even unto the head there is no soundness in it; but wounds, and bruises, and putrifying sores" (Is. 1:5–6a KJV). Isaiah is speaking of the condition of the people in terms of social disorders and difficulties in society, and the corruption and decay that exists in society. This moral condition is the sign of the times. This should tell us something about the state of the culture and the failure of leadership to witness in teaching the people. Jesus explicitly says to them, "**A wicked and adulterous generation looks for a sign**" (v. 4a). This is the condition of the times. We are not seeing the nature of sin and the nature of wickedness. As a matter of fact, those who are *leading* in the churches are not seeing this. The Pharisees and the Sadducees are not seeing the wickedness and the adultery in the generation. Because, as leaders, their hearts are turned away from God and toward money. They are in the condition of spiritual adultery, loving the world more than loving God, so they cannot see it. They do not know how to interpret the signs of the times, and all that Scripture says concerning the One to come and the nature of the One to come. Jesus will say that one greater than Jonah is here, and they are not seeing it: "'but none will be given it except the sign of Jonah.' Jesus then left them and went away" (v. 4b).

Interestingly, regarding this question about the signs of the times, the Scripture speaks about the person and work of the Messiah to come and of the people's rejection of His coming.[8] We will see how the disciples go so far in their thinking, and then they come short. Jesus is raising their and our awareness. He said, "Be on your guard against the yeast of the Pharisees and Sadducees" (v. 6b). By warning them, He is warning us—we, the disciples. We come short and must be on our guard. We have been taken up by the yeast of the Pharisees and Sadducees, and sin remains in us as it was in them. Things that unbelievers do will appeal to us because it appeals to sin in us, and we will follow in their ways.

Led Astray by Not Seeking, Self-Deception, and Self-Justification—Third-Degree Sin

Jesus gave the example of interpreting the signs of the sky and applied it: "You cannot interpret the signs of the times" (v. 3b). Signs require interpretation in terms of what has been told from the Scripture. Jesus said, "If you believed Moses, you would believe me, for he wrote about me" (Jn. 5:46). If they believed Daniel, or the prophets who had come and called the people to repentance, they would know who Jesus was. If they believed John, who came and called the people to repent and showed the need for repentance, they would know who Jesus was. If they believed that the Messiah would come, if they knew who He is and what He would do, they would know who Jesus was. One greater than Jonah had come. They asked for a sign while signs were all around them, and they did not know how to interpret these signs, so why should Jesus then give them more signs? There are signs from general revelation, the signs of the times—not in Scripture, but

---

8. *Isaiah 53.*

in the times—in the circumstances around them, and they do not know how to interpret them.

They get the physical and the visible, but when it comes to understanding the moral and spiritual, there is a lack of understanding of the invisible. They do not know how to interpret the signs of the times—in a spiritual sense—and yet, they ask for another sign. This is not reasonable, yet this is precisely what people do all the time. They do not notice what is more basic, and they do not notice what is already given, but they want more. This is in our hearts. The third-degree level sin is in our hearts—not seeking, self-deception, and self-justification. People may say, 'If God would do a miracle, I would believe.' Jesus said, "If they do not listen to Moses and the Prophets, they will not be convinced even if someone rises from the dead" (Lk. 16:31). Since they did not believe Moses, they will not believe these signs, and without what is prior, they cannot interpret—they will misinterpret. The leaders, who try to explain away Jesus' miracles, will affect the people and the people will follow them.

Jesus not only responded first with an example and explanation, **"you cannot interpret the signs of the times"** (v. 3b), which was relevant since they were seeking a sign, but now He rebukes them with an explanation. **"A wicked and adulterous generation looks for a sign"** (v. 4a). They are unbelieving in their wickedness. They are not seeing what is already given and not seeing what is clearly given. Then Jesus pronounces a judgment sign upon them. It is a rebuke when He says they are **"wicked and adulterous."** Because of their wickedness and adultery, they are the ones who are ever seeing and never understanding.[9] They are the ones who keep asking for more.

The Sign of Jonah: A Sign of Authority, Judgment, and the Need for Repentance

Jesus gives them the sign of Jonah. **"'None will be given it except the sign of Jonah.' Jesus then left them and went away"** (v. 4b). There are three points connected with the sign of Jonah. First, Jonah was in the belly of a great fish for three days and nights and then came out; it was a sign of death and life from death—resurrection. We know that

---

9. *Isaiah 6:9.*

resurrection is the sign of the one that God has chosen. God caused the rod of Aaron to bud, blossom, and produce almonds—resurrection.[10] Aaron's rod was a dead stick coming to life. When there was a question of who was in authority and who God had appointed to rule, resurrection life was given for Aaron, and so it will be of Jesus, too. The One who is raised from the dead is the One that God will raise up, who will sit at His right hand, and be given the authority to rule. So, it is relevant to be speaking about Jonah in this way, but it is more.

Second, it is a judgment sign, because this wicked and adulterous generation will kill Jesus. And He will be raised from the dead, and it will be a judgment on them, on their wickedness, because they killed Him. But they will have difficulty receiving that sign because, having killed Him, they cannot bring themselves to acknowledge the dreadful thing that they have done, and they will suppress it in unbelief. Yet the sign will be there.

Third, Jonah is a sign to them in a larger sense. After Jonah came out of the fish, he went to the Gentiles and preached to them. The Assyrians were the worst nation on the face of the earth, the most ruthless, cruel people—and they repented. So, too, Jesus, being raised from the dead, will send the Holy Spirit to lead the Church and preach to the Gentiles, and they will hear. That, likewise, is part of the sign of Jonah. They should see this, and they should turn in repentance at the sign of Jonah. How marvelous our Lord is. In His wisdom, He can answer them in particular ways, draw out and put His finger right on the heart of the unbelief—and the appropriateness of the way in which He does so. Also, as Lord, He speaks the Word, which should humble their hearts and at the same time bring them to repentance. He gives them the sign of Jonah.

WARNING THE DISCIPLES:
Beware of the Yeast of the Pharisees and Sadducees

As they went on, Jesus gave a warning to His disciples. "**Be careful . . . Be on your guard.**" This is a double statement—He says it twice. "**Be on your guard against the yeast of the Pharisees and Sadducees**" (v. 6b). They did not know, and they did not understand. Jesus heard

---

10. *Numbers 17.*

their discussion: "They discussed this among themselves and said, 'It is because we didn't bring any bread'" (v. 7). So Jesus will explain it to them. "Aware of their discussion, Jesus asked, 'You of little faith, why are you talking among yourselves about having no bread?'" (v. 8). There are a number of reasons why we should be on guard against the yeast of the Pharisees and the Sadducees, and we will see how He reproves and exhorts His disciples.

Be On Guard Against Worldview Assumptions in Culture

First of all, the Pharisees and Sadducees are teachers; they are in positions of teaching and in positions of influence. There are teachers in our society, and they are in positions of influence. Their influence comes through the media—what is approved and what gets recognized—and through pop culture, university culture, academic culture, law, and business. We can be influenced because there is an instinctive sense to go along with the teaching. Being around the influence, we are shaped by it. There is a *worldview* that is operating in this teaching. You have to be on your guard against the influence of the worldview. You should be on your guard against the assumptions used by the teachers in your day—particularly the religious teachers, but not exclusively. Be on your guard against their teaching, particularly the hidden things, at the level of *assumption*. The assumption is much more potent and powerful because it is not explicit. It is much more dangerous because it is hidden, and we do not notice it. Be on your guard against their teaching and their assumptions. Watch for it.

Be On Guard Against Worldview Assumptions in the Church

There is all kinds of teaching going on around us, and we have to be aware of the teaching. We need to be on guard against religious teachers, particularly religious teachers who do not have faith and understanding. As it was in Jesus' day, it has been in the history of the Church. This was the Church then, and the Church is not exempt from sin. In the spiritual war, sin can get control of the leadership of the Church and turn it aside. Be on your guard against the religious teachers—the Pharisees and Sadducees. Be on your guard against the assumptions from which they are working. Be on your guard against these teachers who are in *authority* but do not have *insight*. It is all the more dangerous because we are not talking about general teaching; we are talking about scriptural teaching and how this will be misunderstood.

Be On Guard Against Seeking Proof in a Worldly Way

Religious life is often reduced to rituals and practices, having a *form* of godliness, but denying the truth of God.[11] It can be very appealing and beautiful. All nations have their religious teachers who do not understand; they have their beautiful rituals, customs, traditions, and great big swelling words, but they lack the truth of God and the power of the truth. Be on your guard against the religious teachers; be on your guard against the assumptions from which they are operating; be on your guard against focusing on the outward and not thinking about the true, inward meaning of things. Most specifically addressed here, be on your guard about seeking *proof*, as many have, without prior assumptions and understanding in place—seeking proof in a worldly sense. For example, the evidentialists pour evidence upon evidence upon evidence, not seeing that the evidence has to be interpreted, and not noticing the assumptions in light of which evidence is to be interpreted. They do not see that without those assumptions in place, the evidence becomes of no effect. As they see that their 'proofs' become of no effect, they turn to fideism: 'It is a matter of faith, not proof.' **"Be on your guard against the yeast of the Pharisees and Sadducees"** (v. 6b). Be on your guard against either buying into their assumptions, or reacting against it—we can go wrong both ways. Be on your guard against both. Be on your guard when thinking about seeking proof and how we approach proof. We are not to say there is no proof, nor turn to proof in an improper way, but we are to think about the presupposition by which we pursue proof: the worldview assumptions and our understanding of good and evil. Think about the clarity of general revelation and what is already stated in Genesis and in the rest of Scripture. Think about *the less basic in light of the more basic.* Think about whether the person who is speaking to you has these things in place. Be on your guard; be careful about this, especially when it comes to questions of proof and authority.

---

11. *2 Timothy 3:5.*

Be on Guard Against the Fallen Human Heart

Do not assume that people are seeking. Do not assume that integrity is in place. Do not assume the *subjective* is in place: integrity and seeking. Remember the reality of the curse; it is a call back from moral evil—our failure to seek, understand, and do what is right. Remember the reality of the curse—the self-deception that is there. Remember the reality of the curse—the self-justification that is there. We see this in this passage. Do not assume that the more basic is in place at the *objective* level, in terms of understanding what commitment to *reason* means, a concern for *meaning*, and having *basic things* in place—do not assume those things. Be careful; be on your guard. We should not only not assume these things, but we should assume otherwise. We should positively assume otherwise—assume the reality of the curse and of the promise, the meaning of the curse, and its presence. This is something very hard for us to do. We do not want to think the worst, but this is how we get away from thinking the worst: we have hope in understanding the meaning of the curse—toil, strife, and old age, sickness, and death. This is in Genesis 3, which is imposed by God to call us back. We are to think about the curse, and we are to see the hope of God. We are to see that it is a call back—it is mercy, not punishment—and it comes with a promise. We are to declare the promise. Remember that we ourselves have been saved by the grace of God and others can likewise be saved. That is what we are to assume. That is how we avoid becoming negative and cynical. We can, in meekness, instruct those who oppose the truth of God in the hope that God will grant them repentance and salvation.

We are to assume the curse, its meaning, and the promise as we go into any witness situation. Have the belt of truth around you.[12] Have truth, like a belt, around you—the basic things. Think about what it means to be a sinner and whether the reality of sin is being acknowledged going into any discussion and conversation. People come into the church and take vows saying that they are a sinner. We must understand what sin is. We must understand sin at the root level, not just at the fruit level, because the fruit you might pick off, but the root remains and will produce more fruit. We want to get at the root. Matthew 3:10 says, "The ax is already at the root of the trees, and every tree that does

---

12. *Ephesians 6:14.*

not produce good fruit will be cut down and thrown into the fire." We must deal with root sin.

The Disciples' Response: The Literal and Visible

Jesus speaks to His disciples: "**You of little faith, why are you talking among yourselves about having no bread?**" (v. 8). Notice He says, "**You of little faith.**" Last time, Jesus asked them, "Are you still so dull?" (Matt. 15:16), and now He corrects them for their little understanding.

> You of little faith, why are you talking among yourselves about having no bread? Do you still not understand? Don't you remember the five loaves for the five thousand, and how many basketfuls you gathered? Or the seven loaves for the four thousand, and how many basketfuls you gathered? (vv. 8–10).

Jesus is not speaking about the bread. The disciples were thinking in the same way that the Pharisees were thinking; they were thinking about *literal* yeast and *literal* bread. And Jesus is saying not to be worried about bread; it is not bread that He is talking about. They make the same error. They have the same outward, physical understanding without understanding the spiritual significance. They are hearing the words without understanding the *meaning*. He does not tell them what He means. "**How is it you don't understand that I was not talking to you about bread? But be on your guard against the yeast of the Pharisees and Sadducees**" (v. 11). Then they understood. "**Then they understood that he was not telling them to guard against the yeast used in bread, but against the teaching of the Pharisees and Sadducees**" (v. 12). Notice the connection between understanding and faith and the relation between the visible and the invisible. So, we see the contrast between the Pharisees and the disciples.

THE DISCIPLES' FAITH IS TESTED:
"Who Do You Say I Am?"

We come to another question about the disciples. The religious leaders were asking for a sign to prove who Jesus was, and now Jesus is going to talk to His disciples about who He is. They come to Caesarea Philippi, and He asks about the people.

When Jesus came to the region of Caesarea Philippi, he asked his disciples, "Who do people say the Son of Man is?" They replied, "Some say John the Baptist; others say Elijah; and still others, Jeremiah or one of the prophets" (vv. 13–14).

This answer is so wrong. The Scripture is not speaking about reincarnation. When the Scripture does speak about Elijah, it is said, "the spirit and power of Elijah" (Lk. 1:17a), not Elijah reincarnated. The spirit and power of Elijah is the purpose and continuity of the prophetic ministry of calling the people back to repentance. John the Baptist is Elijah that was to come, understood spiritually. The people said Jesus was literally Elijah come back, or literally John the Baptist—remember Herod thought this.[13] They do not understand the significance of the words that were spoken. "'But what about you?' he asked. 'Who do you say I am?'" (v. 15). This question is put to the disciples to answer—versus what others say and what the Pharisees say. "Simon Peter answered, 'You are the Messiah, the Son of the living God'" (v. 16). There are several levels of this understanding; there are three parts. The first question is, "Who do you say I am?" Personally, who do they say Jesus is? Peter says, "You are the Christ."[14]

The second question is, 'Who is the Christ?' The answer is, "the Son of the living God." So, there are two parts to the original question: Jesus is the Christ and who the Christ is. John says, "these are written that you may believe that Jesus is the Messiah, the Son of God" (Jn. 20:31a). It is one thing to identify the person. It is another to speak of the Christ in terms of His origin. He is the son of David and the Son of God. This is quite a confession: "You are the Messiah, the Son of the living God." The confession is that God has a Son, and the Son is equal with the Father and is to be worshiped with the Father. That is a big statement, that Jesus is the Son of God. Jesus, before them in human form, is the Son of Man and is the Son of God, and in the office of the Christ. That is the second level of the answer to the question.

There is a third level that is equally relevant—perhaps more relevant—prior to, and more basic than the first two. That is: What is the Christ to do? What is the office of the Christ? The disciples should

---

13. *Matthew 14:1–2.*
14. NIV 1984.

understand the office of the Christ in terms of the promise given from the very beginning—the seed of the woman.[15] They should remember Adam's representation and that Christ comes in the place of Adam to *undo* what Adam did and to *do* what Adam failed to do, as well as all the promises that have been unfolding. You might affirm these things, but you may still ask, 'Would the disciples have seen it?' Ask yourself, should you have seen what the Messiah is to do? Should you know it is according to the promise, according to the Scripture? Christ did not bring this question of the Christ without sufficient reason. God has given a whole context and preparation in the Old Testament. What is prior needs to be in place. We are to understand what the Christ is going to do as the Son of Man, why He would come incarnate, and the redemptive purpose that there is to undo evil and to die for sin. He is to bring redemption, and we are to understand this in connection with the coats of skin that were given to Adam to wear. We are to understand through all the sacrifices, through the Day of Atonement, and through the Passover that through the death of another, our sins are covered. We are to understand that this One will come who will bring redemption and we are to make the connection between the animal sacrifice and Christ—that He is the Lamb of God who takes away the sin of the world, as John the Baptist explicitly said.[16] We should be thinking about all of these things when we think about the Christ. They were not thinking about these things. We will see how it was not the case.

Peter Commended: Jesus Affirms Peter's Confession

"Jesus replied, 'Blessed are you, Simon son of Jonah, for this was not revealed to you by flesh and blood, but by my Father in heaven'" (v. 17). All who are taught of God come to Christ. He says, "And I tell you that you are Peter, and on this rock I will build my church, and the gates of Hades will not overcome it" (v. 18). There is authority given in connection with this confession. "I will give you the keys of the kingdom of heaven; whatever you bind on earth will be bound in heaven, and whatever you loose on earth will be loosed in heaven" (v. 19).

---

15. *Genesis 3:15.*
16. *John 1:29.*

Are we to understand this literally or contextually? Is it Peter who is the one on whom the Church is built, or is it Christ, whom Peter has just confessed? Peter himself says in 1 Peter 2:4–5, "As you come to him, the living Stone—rejected by humans but chosen by God and precious to him—you also, like living stones, are being built into a spiritual house to be a holy priesthood, offering spiritual sacrifices acceptable to God through Jesus Christ." The first question that should be asked is: Is the Church to be built upon Jesus or upon an apostle? The second question is: Is it only one apostle or is it all of the apostles who have this authority? You should not have to ask the second question if you answered the first correctly, but in the history of the Church, the first question is not understood. The third question is: If it is one apostle, is it one apostle at that time only, or is it one apostle continuing, as if the apostolic office is continued? We know that this is a big dividing point in the history of Christianity concerning Peter as the apostle holding an office that has continued through the centuries.

We believe what is being spoken is that Christ is the chief cornerstone, as the Scripture says here and elsewhere. It is upon Him that the Church is built, not upon man. If it is built upon Peter, what a sorry shape the Church would be in, because Jesus has to rebuke Peter. Even when he had some measure of truth, Jesus had to rebuke him. However, none of those questions should arise if we understand that Jesus is the cornerstone.

Peter Rebuked: The Messiah Must Die for Sin

Jesus immediately begins to tell them that He is going to die.

> From that time on Jesus began to explain to his disciples that he must go to Jerusalem and suffer many things at the hands of the elders, the chief priests and the teachers of the law, and that he must be killed and on the third day be raised to life (v. 21).

He had just had His exchange with the Pharisees and Sadducees and spoke about the sign of Jonah. And Peter had just confessed that Jesus is the Christ. Does Peter understand that Jesus must die for sin? Does he understand that Jesus is the Lamb of God? Does he understand the office of the Christ that he has just confessed? Does he understand that Christ is to *undo* what Adam did, and He is to *do* what Adam failed to do? Christ is to rule where Adam failed to rule, and He is to exercise dominion as God commanded Adam to rule in the earth.[17] Do they understand that He must *undo* what Adam did and that He *must* die? Later, after His resurrection, Jesus will say, "How foolish you are, and how slow to believe all that the prophets have spoken! Did not the Messiah have to suffer these things and then enter his glory?" (Luke 24:25–26). They did not understand, and this showed their lack of faith.

"Peter took him aside and began to rebuke him. 'Never, Lord!' he said. 'This shall never happen to you!'" (v. 22). There is presumption in Peter to correct the Lord. Peter meant it in a nice way. Usually, that is the way we fall flat on our faces. We mean it in a nice way. **"'Never, Lord!' he said." "This shall never happen to you!"** 'You will never die!' Those are the *exact* words of Satan. And Jesus responded before all: **"Jesus turned and said to Peter, 'Get behind me, Satan! You are a stumbling block to me; you do not have in mind the concerns of God, but merely human concerns'"** (v. 23). That is what Satan wants. He wants Christ never to die and never to undo the sin of Adam. That is Satan speaking; that is Satan's purpose, yet Satan has no control. And the very thing that he released in the heart of Judas Iscariot brings about his own defeat. Satan is one who sins; Satan is a sinner. I do not think I have ever heard it said that Satan is a sinner, but he is. The father of sinners resists. Jesus says, **"you do not have in mind the concerns of God."** Peter does not have in mind that God will be justified and will justify those who put their trust in Him. He does not have in mind that God is righteous and bestows righteousness through the vicarious atonement of Christ, through the imputed righteousness of Christ. Just as the imputed unrighteousness of Adam comes down to all of us and we have guilt in Adam, so the imputed righteousness of Christ will come down to all who are in Him. He will *undo* what Adam did; He will remove the imputed unrighteousness of Adam. He will impute righteousness to believers—Christ will die to remove unrighteousness and live righteously to bring it about. Peter did not understand. Peter's faith came short. Though he had real faith because it was revealed to him of God, his faith came short. We are to beware. **"Be on your guard against the yeast of the Pharisees and Sadducees"** (v. 6b). Even

---

17. *Genesis 1:28.*

when we do have genuine faith, we are not to be so presumptuous in thinking we understand when we do not.

The Sin of Autonomy: The Need to Follow the Way of the Cross

There are many ways we can be cautious against coming short, and Jesus warns His disciples concerning this. What is behind the sin of the Pharisees is autonomy—the desire to live independently of God. **"Then Jesus said to his disciples, 'Whoever wants to be my disciple must deny themselves and take up their cross and follow me'"** (v. 24). He must take up his cross. He is to have in mind not the things of men, not the self-life, but the things of God, as Jesus would be obedient to God even unto death. There is a preciousness in the gain of life. **"What good will it be for someone to gain the whole world, yet forfeits their soul? Or what can anyone give in exchange for their soul?"** (v. 26). To seek to gain the world is worldliness; we do not see anything beyond the world. We do not see the glory of God and make that our possession and our treasure. There will be glory manifest abundantly. There is glory already manifested and He anticipates that there is a need to be encouraged in this. Jesus says,

> For the Son of Man is going to come in his Father's glory with his angels, and then he will reward each person according to what they have done. Truly I tell you, some who are standing here will not taste death before they see the Son of Man coming in his kingdom (vv. 27–28).

In the next chapter, we have the account of the Transfiguration. Jesus prepares His disciples for His approaching death. We are to remember the truth of the need for His death. We are inclined to forget this truth, to go our own way, and to be affected, whether we will or not, by the yeast of the Pharisees—the yeast of sin and unbelief.

14

TRANSFIGURED AND TRANSFORMED

The True Exodus from the Kingdom of Darkness

Matthew 17

¹After six days Jesus took with him Peter, James and John the brother of James, and led them up a high mountain by themselves. ²There he was transfigured before them. His face shone like the sun, and his clothes became as white as the light. ³Just then there appeared before them Moses and Elijah, talking with Jesus.

⁴Peter said to Jesus, "Lord, it is good for us to be here. If you wish, I will put up three shelters—one for you, one for Moses and one for Elijah."

⁵While he was still speaking, a bright cloud covered them, and a voice from the cloud said, "This is my Son, whom I love; with him I am well pleased. Listen to him!"

⁶When the disciples heard this, they fell facedown to the ground, terrified. ⁷But Jesus came and touched them. "Get up," he said. "Don't be afraid." ⁸When they looked up, they saw no one except Jesus.

⁹As they were coming down the mountain, Jesus instructed them, "Don't tell anyone what you have seen, until the Son of Man has been raised from the dead."

¹⁰The disciples asked him, "Why then do the teachers of the law say that Elijah must come first?"

¹¹Jesus replied, "To be sure, Elijah comes and will restore all things. ¹²But I tell you, Elijah has already come, and they did not recognize him, but have done to him everything they wished. In the same way the Son of Man is going to suffer at their hands." ¹³Then the disciples understood that he was talking to them about John the Baptist.

¹⁴When they came to the crowd, a man approached Jesus and knelt before him. ¹⁵"Lord, have mercy on my son," he said. "He has seizures and is suffering greatly. He often falls into the fire or into the water. ¹⁶I brought him to your disciples, but they could not heal him."

¹⁷"You unbelieving and perverse generation," Jesus replied, "how long shall I stay with you? How long shall I put up with you? Bring the boy here to me." ¹⁸Jesus rebuked the demon, and it came out of the boy, and he was healed at that moment.

¹⁹Then the disciples came to Jesus in private and asked, "Why couldn't we drive it out?"

²⁰He replied, "Because you have so little faith. Truly I tell you, if you have faith as small as a mustard seed, you can say to this mountain, 'Move from here to there,' and it will move. Nothing will be impossible for you."

²²When they came together in Galilee, he said to them, "The Son of Man is going to be delivered into the hands of men. ²³They will kill him, and on the third day he will be raised to life." And the disciples were filled with grief.

²⁴After Jesus and his disciples arrived in Capernaum, the collectors of the two-drachma temple tax came to Peter and asked, "Doesn't your teacher pay the temple tax?"

²⁵"Yes, he does," he replied.

When Peter came into the house, Jesus was the first to speak. "What do you think, Simon?" he asked. "From whom do the kings of the earth collect duty and taxes—from their own children or from others?"

²⁶"From others," Peter answered.

"Then the children are exempt," Jesus said to him. ²⁷"But so that we may not cause offense, go to the lake and throw out your line. Take the first fish you catch; open its mouth and you will find a four-drachma coin. Take it and give it to them for my tax and yours."

THE TRANSFIGURATION:
Confession, Confusion, and Reaffirmation

Context: Christ Must Suffer and Then Enter into His Glory

TODAY, WE WANT TO LOOK AT THE ACCOUNT in the Gospel of Matthew of the Transfiguration of our Lord Jesus Christ in the presence of His disciples. As we look at the immediate context of this, we see that Jesus had been with His disciples in Caesarea. There, He asked them, "Who do you say I am?" (Matt. 16:15b). Peter confessed that Jesus was the Christ, but immediately after Jesus told them that He must die, Peter resisted. His thinking, his understanding/faith as such, was weak, and he did not understand that Christ must suffer and then enter into His glory.[1] When Peter corrected Jesus, "'Never, Lord!' he said. 'This shall never happen to you!'" (Matt. 16:22b), Jesus rebuked and instructed him in the need to follow the way of the cross, to humble himself before God, and become obedient even unto death, the death of the cross. Having said that, He confirms to Peter and to the other disciples the reality of His glory as the Son of God, the Messiah, that both glory and suffering are true.[2] This revelation/confirmation continues through this chapter of the Transfiguration, and we want to look at both how He must suffer and that He will be the glorious ruler.

The Transfiguration account is given here, and we want to pay attention to it because our minds can become dull, sleepy, and groggy in the midst of this revelation. In the accounts concerning the Transfiguration in the other Gospels of Mark and Luke (it is not recorded in the Gospel of John), there are references made to the disciples being *sleepy* in the midst of this stupendous revelation. This is not the only place in which this description of Christ is given, and we should understand it in the context of what is revealed elsewhere.[3] Christ is the Word of God, the Son of God, eternal with God from the beginning, the Creator of all things, the Upholder of all things, the Redeemer of all things, and the Heir of all things. He is none other than the Lord God, who took to Himself human nature and dwelt among us. We sometimes see Jesus in His humanity and think of his humanity only.

---

1. *Luke 24:25–26.*

2. *Matthew 16:24–28.*

3. *Revelation 1; John 1; Philippians 2; Hebrews 1; 2 Peter 1:16–18.*

Sometimes, even when we think of His divinity, we do not recognize the stupendous glory that is there. We do not recognize that the glory of the Word of God incarnate, the glory of the Creator of the universe, was hidden and was set aside. That is, the manifestation of it was set aside as is spoken of in Philippians 2: He emptied himself and took on the form of a man.[4] He was *fully* God; He did not set that aside, but the outward manifestation of that glory was set aside for a while.

Jesus' Divinity Shines Through His Humanity

In the Book of Revelation, we see this glory again given and that is one of the reasons I read the *Call to Worship* from this passage. Similar features of the Transfiguration occur in the Book of Revelation.

> I turned around to see the voice that was speaking to me. And when I turned I saw seven golden lampstands, and among the lampstands was someone like a son of man, dressed in a robe reaching down to his feet and with a golden sash around his chest. The hair on his head was white like wool, as white as snow, and his eyes were like blazing fire. His feet were like bronze glowing in a furnace, and his voice was like the sound of rushing waters. In his right hand he held seven stars, and coming out of his mouth was a sharp, double-edged sword. His face was like the sun shining in all its brilliance (Rev. 1:12–16).

When we take into account what is described here in Matthew 17, "**There he was transfigured before them. His face shone like the sun, and his clothes became as white as the light**" (v. 2), we see that this was not some vision or manifestation merely in the mind, this was in reality before the disciples. What is happening here is His *deity* is shining through His *humanity*. It is His deity *present* in His humanity, manifesting itself, that brings it to be that "**His face shone like the sun, and his clothes became as white as the light**" (v. 2b). His face and His clothes transfigured before them with the manifestation of the glory which He had with the Father from the beginning. These two accounts are to be read together. It becomes, literally, His face shining like the sun. Who can behold that glory? This is "the glory of the one

---

4. *Philippians 2:7.*

and only Son, who came from the Father, full of grace and truth" (Jn. 1:14b), bringing redemption and bringing us to know God. Paul says, "Even though we have known Christ according to the flesh, yet now we know Him thus no longer" (2 Cor. 5:16b NKJV).

Kenosis: Jesus Empties Himself of His Divine Prerogatives

When we think about our Lord Jesus Christ, it is quite appropriate for us to think about Him as He is revealed among the seven lampstands. That is how He manifests Himself, and that is how He wants to be known. Yes, we know Him in His humanity, but we see that glory of the One and Only Son shining through. It is because of this glory that "being found in appearance as a man, he humbled himself and became obedient to death—even death on a cross! Therefore God exalted him to the highest place" (Phil. 2:8–9a). It is precisely because He did not grasp for divinity—though He was equal to God—but laid it aside and humbled Himself, that God exalted Him. That is the spirit of God; that is the spirit that God wants us to have. We are not to be grasping, but to be humble before Him. When we have that spirit in us, it is then that God can raise us to a position of rule. Philippians 2 continues,

> Therefore God exalted him to the highest place and gave him the name that is above every name, that at the name of Jesus every knee should bow, in heaven and on earth and under the earth, and every tongue confess that Jesus Christ is Lord, to the glory of God the Father (Phil 2:9–11).

How utterly different from Satan, who would reach and grasp for more. The truth is that the One who is the highest in the universe is the One who is willing to become the very lowest, to come to humiliation, the degradation that there is on the cross. That is the spirit of one who is to rule legitimately before God, not the slightest iota of pride and exaltation. It is for this very reason that we sing the praises of God. We know in the depth of our being that that is reality, that is truth, because He has that in and of Himself; there is no boasting. The infinite goodness, wisdom, power, justice, and love of God is revealed in this way of self-emptying and serving, the very opposite of self-life. Jesus said to His disciples, "For whoever wants to save their life will lose it, but whoever loses their life for me will find it" (Matt. 16:25). There is a connection: He must first suffer and then enter His glory. Had He not suffered, He could not have entered into His glory. He tells His disciples that He must go up to Jerusalem and there He is going to die, but there is a suffering to follow. He said, "Truly I tell you, some who are standing here will not taste death before they see the Son of Man coming in his kingdom" (Matt. 16:28).

The True Exodus: Preparing to Endure the Wrath of God

"After six days Jesus took with him Peter, James and John the brother of James, and led them up a high mountain by themselves" (v. 1). He led them up a mountain and left the other disciples behind. Luke says that while He was praying, they were sleepy. "There he was transfigured before them. His face shone like the sun, and his clothes became as white as the light" (v. 2). Notice the particulars of this event: "Just then there appeared before them Moses and Elijah, talking with Jesus" (v. 3). They were talking with Jesus about what He was about to accomplish in Jerusalem, the exodus that He was to accomplish. Just as Moses had accomplished that Exodus from Egypt, so now Jesus will accomplish the true exodus from the kingdom of darkness by enduring the wrath of God, by being buried and raised from the dead: "who is the faithful witness, the firstborn from the dead" (Rev. 1:5) and the firstfruits of them that have fallen asleep.[5] Jesus was to accomplish the ultimate, the true exodus. The people came out of Egypt, but many perished in the wilderness because of sin. Jesus will bring us out of the kingdom of darkness and bring us into the kingdom of light. That is what Moses and Elijah were looking forward to. They appeared before Jesus, and of all things they were talking about, this one thing they were engaged in—what He was about to accomplish through His death on the cross. That was the focal point. In the midst of the Transfiguration, they spoke about the exodus He was about to accomplish through His death on the cross. Those who have gone before, those who have been sanctified, understand the way of God, understand God's righteousness and holiness, and understand what must be done to achieve true redemption and everlasting life. So these men, glorious, prominent in their work and service in God, those who stood for God, knew that all

---

5. *1 Corinthians 15:20.*

of what they stood for and all of what they accomplished, they accomplished because of what Jesus is about to accomplish; that He is the One who would accomplish redemption. This is what they spoke about.

Peter's Words and God's Word: The Need to Be Transformed

Peter was not listening. Peter should have been listening to their conversation eagerly, thinking and trying to understand what was happening. As Moses and Elijah were about to leave, Peter saw the outward manifestation, the glory, the circumstance, and seeing, of all persons, the ones from their past history. Think of it: Jesus, of course, but then Moses and Elijah! Who else would you want there? The most dramatic figures are there with Jesus. This was it! This was the kingdom that they were looking for—where all that glory came into consummation in our Lord Jesus, and here He is before us, shining bright as the light. This is what Peter had in mind; it blew his mind away, but it was the glory that he was looking for. Peter, not listening, said to Jesus, "**Lord, it is good for us to be here. If you wish, I will put up three shelters— one for you, one for Moses and one for Elijah**" (v. 4). Just think of it—shelters! How long will the shelter be needed? How long did Peter think they would be here? He was not thinking. He just wanted to be there; he wanted this to last forever. How often have we had those times of transfiguration? We have been with Him on the mountain; He has met with us and been on that mountain when He has come close to us. We want to be there, and we want to stay there forever. We want it to always be like this. No, we do not know what we are talking about; we have not a clue. We are just reaching out somewhat instinctively to hold on to this to say, 'Oh, that it might always be this way, Lord. This is heaven. This is what we want.' But there was a world standing in need of redemption. There was a way of the cross that must be followed if that redemption was to be accomplished. We must go through suffering to enter into glory.[6] There is a reality of sin and death, and that must be dealt with; it cannot be bypassed, it cannot be minimized, it cannot be gotten around. The penalty of sin must be paid. The righteousness and holiness of God must be satisfied; they cannot be set aside.[7] The

---

6. *Acts 14:22; Revelation 21:21.*

7. Gangadean, *Philosophical Foundation*, 191–192; Gangadean, *The Westminster Confession*, 21–27, 37–41, 67–69, 129–130, 236–238; Gangadean, "Paper No. 91: Christianity and

way of the cross is marked out for our Lord Jesus Christ, and Moses and Elijah understood this. But the disciples who had been with Jesus were missing it, missing this part, missing this piece. Peter speaks as we often ourselves speak, 'This is it, I want to be here forever. Let's put up some tabernacles for you, and Moses, and Elijah, that is it. I want to be here with you forever.'

Scripture says quite explicitly, **"While he was still speaking . . ."** It is not nice to interrupt someone when they are speaking, but this is God interrupting. And God had been speaking to them—Jesus had brought them up to speak to them, and they should have been hearing. God is saying, in effect, 'Peter, shut up. This is my Son, in whom I am well pleased. Listen to Him. You had not been listening earlier; He rebuked you earlier. Now, He is speaking about the exodus that He is about to accomplish, and you are still not listening. Peter, listen.' **"While he was still speaking, a bright cloud covered them, and a voice from the cloud said, 'This is my Son, whom I love; with him I am well pleased. Listen to him!'"** (v. 5). This was addressed to Peter, who was speaking, as well as to the others, because he is the one going on talking, not knowing what he is saying. He is just speaking intuitively, speaking instinctively, just speaking what naturally comes to him, what is in his heart. Of course, we do that, but we need to have our hearts cleansed, and we need to be transformed by renewing our minds, and we would be if we were paying attention.

The Word of God came to Peter: **"Listen to him!"** When they heard that voice, when a cloud enveloped them all and the voice spoke, **"'Listen to him' . . . they fell facedown to the ground, terrified"** (v. 6b). Then as the cloud lifted, **"Jesus came and touched them. 'Get up,' he said. 'Don't be afraid'"** (v. 7). He is always concerned about the needs of His disciples. Especially when we are in fear, when there is a revelation, a correction that comes to us, and we begin to lose it, Jesus is always there to say, 'Don't be afraid. It is I, peace be with you.' He instructs them and comforts them. There is a glory that is surrounding us continually. Because our eyes are not open to it, it does not mean it is not there. It is a host, a heavenly host, that is encamped about those who fear the Lord—even as Elisha prayed that the eyes of his servant would be opened. He said that there are more who are with us than are

---

Islam," in *The Logos Papers*, 479–484.

with them; as the armed forces came up to take Elisha, the eyes of the servant were opened. He saw the chariots of fire surrounding Elisha.[8] We do not have to see this. But we must know that the angel of the Lord encamps around those who fear him,[9] that God is ever present with us, and that God is with us even as we walk through the valley of the shadow of death.[10] We have to know that, and we have to have it settled in our hearts. We have to go over that again, and again, and again, and not lose sight of it, and cultivate that awareness as part of our watchfulness, our mindfulness, and not think that because it is not an outward manifestation, God is not with us. We have to search out those Scriptures and bring them to mind and speak them to ourselves, knowing that He is with us and that we might take comfort in the Lord and be encouraged in Him. In the midst of our trials, God has not forsaken us; God is with us. We have to know that He has ordained that trial and He is bringing us through that trial one step at a time. We are in the hands of the Refiner, and He will purify us, so that we may offer praise and righteousness to God. "And he shall sit as a refiner and purifier of silver: and he shall purify the sons of Levi, and purge them as gold and silver, that they may offer unto the Lord an offering in righteousness" (Mal. 3:3 KJV).

The Restraint: Understand His Glory in Light of His Humility

"As they were coming down the mountain, Jesus instructed them, 'Don't tell anyone what you have seen, until the Son of Man has been raised from the dead'" (v. 9). Again, He speaks to them in the midst of the revelation. Before, during, and after this manifestation of His glory, He is speaking to them about the Son of Man dying—this is what they are to keep in mind. In light of His dying and the purpose of His dying, they are to understand the glory—the glory of holiness and righteousness. Otherwise, it is a kind of bombastic glory; it is not the glory of the One who emptied Himself and became obedient unto death; it is not the glory of the One who is totally selfless in love. The

---

8. *2 Kings 6:16–17.*
9. *Psalm 34:7.*
10. *Psalm 23:4.*

One who has all majesty and glory is not holding on to the glory. He is revealing that glory in His love and His emptying of Himself in love.

Jesus Will Suffer as John the Baptist: The Spiritual War Is Raging

The question of Elijah is on their minds. They have just seen Elijah, and they are coming down the mountain. You can see how this question would naturally occur.

> The disciples asked him, "Why then do the teachers of the law say that Elijah must come first?" Jesus replied, "To be sure, Elijah comes and will restore all things. But I tell you, Elijah has already come, and they did not recognize him, but have done to him everything they wished. In the same way the Son of Man is going to suffer at their hands" (vv. 10–12).

Elijah has come—John the Baptist—and caused the condition of those in authority to be revealed. It is caused to be revealed by John's death, as he has been a faithful witness, not being received and being opposed. Those in authority are the same persons who will resist Jesus. This, too, becomes a witness to what will happen. There is a war, a spiritual war, that is raging. But we may not see it, and this is another thing we must continually cultivate in our minds—the reality of the spiritual war, and not be lulled into saying, 'Things just go on the way they have' and not see it. There is a battle that is raging around us. One of the ways it rages is in an attempt to numb us. In contrast to being alert, watchful, and making use of every opportunity and pressing on, there is an attempt to lull us into complacency, lull us into quiescence, and just smooth everything along, so we do not notice what is going on. That is part of the war, the numbing of the people of God. We have to watch ourselves—a battle is raging, and we can be said to sleep through it. We say, 'What battle?' All of our concerns are about things that pertain to our immediate needs, and we are caught up in those and do not see beyond our immediate concerns.

THE BOY HEALED OF EPILEPSY:
Strong Versus Weak Faith

When they came to the crowd, a man approached Jesus and knelt before him. "Lord, have mercy on my son," he said. "He has seizures and is suffering greatly. He often falls into the fire or into the water. I brought him to your disciples, but they could not heal him." "You unbelieving and perverse generation," Jesus replied, "how long shall I stay with you? How long shall I put up with you? Bring the boy here to me." Jesus rebuked the demon, and it came out of the boy, and he was healed from that moment (vv. 14–18).

This revelation says something about the people, the disciples, the unbelief, and the failure to see the deliverance in connection with that unbelief. Perhaps it was a mixture of the unbelief of the people and the weakness of the disciples' faith, in contrast to the unbelief of the people and the strength of Jesus' faith—He can rebuke the evil spirit. There are times when the unbelief is so great that Christ abstained from doing many miracles.[11] God would not permit it. There is perhaps an equation to consider in terms of the faith of the One who would bring deliverance and those who are seeking that deliverance.

"Then the disciples came to Jesus in private and asked, 'Why couldn't we drive it out?' He replied, 'Because you have so little faith'" (vv. 19–20a). So there is unbelief, and there is little faith. Remember, we spoke about the contrast that goes on. There is unbelief in terms of this wicked and adulterous generation. He says, **"You unbelieving and perverse generation"** (v 17a). **"Because you have so little faith. Truly I tell you, if you have faith as small as a mustard seed, you can say to this mountain, 'Move from here to there' and it will move. Nothing will be impossible for you"** (v. 20). We have heard that expression, 'faith as a mustard seed'—a little bit of genuine faith. A little bit of faith can go a very long way. If we are not moving at all, it must mean we have exceedingly little faith. This is a reproof to us, and it is not something so hard to understand given what had just been revealed about Peter— what Peter had said before and during the Transfiguration. Peter was just not understanding. There is little understanding of the true nature of the glory of God and what was required in connection with holiness,

---

11. *Matthew 13:58.*

righteousness, and the necessity for Christ to die. Peter was not getting it. So those on the mountain showed their lack of faith, and those below showed their lack of faith, and Jesus reproved His disciples. Notice that even though they lack faith, Jesus does not give up; He does not abandon them. He continues to work with them and speak to them, knowing how it will come about and how they will grow. I suppose if anyone had reason to give up, it was His disciples. It is one thing, after one semester, for college students to get a D; it is another thing after three years, six semesters, including summer school, and they are still getting a D. What do you do now? When is it time to flunk them and go on and start with a new batch of students? Can you imagine that? Jesus does not give up, and we are not to give up. As we grow in grace and faith, we are not to give up, we are not to be foolish, we are not to be, in some sentimental way, holding on to false expectations, but in a realistic way, understand the true situation that we are facing and understand the ways of God. We are not to give up.

Again, He tells them, in connection with this idea of little faith:

When they came together in Galilee, he said to them, "The Son of Man is going to be delivered into the hands of men. They will kill him, and on the third day he will be raised to life." And the disciples were filled with grief (vv. 22–23).

It starts to sink in for the disciples. Jesus told them several times; this is about the fifth time; the third time for some of them. You can see it is starting to get into their minds now—the suffering. It is starting to take hold, so they become filled with grief. They are not resisting it, but they look at it as if that is going to be the end. They are not seeing the glory. Some have seen it, and they should be able to hold on to it and should be able to give some leadership among the others during that time—Peter, James, and John.

THE TEMPLE TAX:
Sons Are Exempt—A Question of Identity

All of this concerned the question: Who is Christ? We should understand this development in terms of the question, the answer given, the

suffering to come, and the glory to be revealed. That question continues now with others.

> After Jesus and his disciples arrived in Capernaum, the collectors
> of the two-drachma tax came to Peter and asked, "Doesn't your
> teacher pay the temple tax?" "Yes, he does," he replied. When
> Peter came into the house, Jesus was the first to speak. "What do
> you think, Simon?" he asked. "From whom do the kings of the
> earth collect duty and taxes—from their own children or from
> others?" (vv. 24–25).

Again, Jesus is pressing Peter to understand who He is. From whom
do they collect taxes? The *temple* tax—His Father's house! The temple
belongs to His Father and His Father is king; He said, "How dare you
turn my Father's house into a market!" (Jn. 2:16b). He is the Son of
the Father who dwells in that temple. 'So from whom do they collect
the temple tax, Peter? Do you understand the temple? Do you understand who dwells there? Do you know who I am, Peter? From whom
do they collect the temple tax?' Jesus used this instance as an instru-
ment of teaching Peter again. He gave him a true/false question. Jesus
is sometimes really easy on us. He says, "from their own children or
from others?" (v. 25b). 'True or false? From their own sons or others?'
Peter got it right: "'From others,' Peter answered" (v. 26). It does not
make sense to collect taxes from your own sons. "'Then the children
are exempt,' Jesus said to him." Some may think, 'So we don't have to
pay taxes!' Some have taken that and run with it. Jesus did not go there.
"'Then the children are exempt,' Jesus said to him. 'But so that we may
not cause offense, go to the lake and throw out your line'" (v. 27a).
Here it is, His glory is being revealed again as it was revealed when His
face shone, when His clothes were as white as light. His glory is being
revealed here in a seemingly mundane way, but nevertheless, it is His
glory. Look at it! "But so that we may not cause offense,"—He is careful to be righteous in every way—"go to the lake and throw out your
line. Take the first fish you catch; open its mouth and you will find a
four-drachma coin. Take it and give it to them for my tax and yours"
(v. 27). Oh, how much is said there. Who could think that? Throw out
your line and catch a fish. When was the last time you caught a fish and
it had a coin in its mouth? Just the very first one you catch. This is the

glory of His knowledge being revealed in this way. It is not with light but with circumstance, and it is awesome! I want you to be awestruck that this One is able to speak in this way, and it will be. The Word of God, by whom all things were made—He spoke, and it was done. This is the One who is saying now, "Go." How long was that coin in that fish? How long was that fish around? Did the fish find the coin and try to swallow it when it got caught, and was it a happy coincidence? We are not told that, are we? I suppose, to speculate, I am inclined to think that it was a special creation, like multiplying the loaves. He spoke that coin into existence. I suppose the fish could have seen a four-drachma coin and swallowed it. But how often do fish do that? Pay attention. The One who spoke the world into existence is the One who brought that about and revealed it to Peter, showing how much he cared for Peter and how much Peter was bonded to Him. It was a four-drachma coin, only one coin, so Peter could not miss it. Jesus said, "**Take it and give it to them for my tax and yours**" (v. 27b). 'Peter, you are one of the sons, you are exempt, you are part of a kingdom, and you are exempt.' Jesus was bonded to him, and Peter was bonded to Jesus in this way. If you do not take it that way, if you think Peter had to pay taxes in any case, I am not sure that is the way we should go. Peter is a son; he does not have to pay. Jesus reveals His glory, He continues to reveal His glory, and the disciples put their faith in Him. We need to pay attention to these things. We are not to read too much into them, but not just be mindless about them, either. Do not take the name of God in vain—mindlessly, thoughtlessly hearing it—but think about it. "**Take it and give it to them for my tax and yours.**" 'Peter, you and I, we are in this together. I am with you, and you are with me.' One tax payment—they filed a joint tax return, if you will. It is not a usual arrangement, but Jesus is with Peter. 'I am with you, Peter. We will take care of this.'

To summarize, we have seen the Transfiguration in Matthew 17 and what it signifies. Jesus humbled Himself, took on the form of man, and became of no reputation. He emptied himself of the glory. This is why He is going to be highly exalted to glory: "Wherefore God also hath highly exalted him" (Phi. 2:9a KJV). This reveals a fundamental reality, the core of ultimate reality: the goodness of God and the nature of God. How many have so blasphemously spoken about God being 'on some ego trip.' Nothing is as contrary to that; that is a falsehood far removed from God. If you want to know what God is like, look at our Lord Jesus as He emptied Himself.

KINGDOM ETHICS

Who Is the Greatest? Faith, Motives, and the Kingdom in the Shadow of the Cross

In Matthew 18, the disciples are still caught in the ways of the world. They argue among themselves about who is the greatest in the kingdom of heaven. "At that time the disciples came to Jesus and asked, 'Who, then, is the greatest in the kingdom of heaven?'" (Matt. 18:1). Now, wouldn't you like to know what possible answers they were considering? Who is the greatest? Have you ever wondered about that yourself? Among those here, who is the greatest in the kingdom? This is not something we like to wonder out loud, but it is in our hearts, and we think it because we are worldly, we have sin in us, and we think in this way. Even when we say, 'No, no, no, we do not think that way'—if we do not watch it, we will find it creeping up on us and getting us. Who is the greatest in the kingdom? What a discussion to have after Jesus told them He will go up to Jerusalem and die. We can understand why He said, **"Because you have so little faith. Truly I tell you, if you have faith as small as a mustard seed . . ."** (v. 20a). That is a reproof to all of us, isn't it? We may say, 'When am I going to learn? What is the matter?' We have a serious case of sin, and we need to be transformed by renewing our minds.[12] Line upon line, precept upon precept,[13] it will come.

Humble Like a Child

He called a little child to him and placed the child among them. And he said: "Truly I tell you, unless you change and become like little children, you will never enter the kingdom of heaven. Therefore, whoever takes the lowly position of this child is the greatest in the kingdom of heaven" (Matt. 18:2–4).

---

12. *Romans 12:2.*
13. *Isaiah 28:10–13* KJV.

This is the theme of humbling. Do not be taken up with yourself. He called a little child and put him in their midst—someone who is self-less. There is a kind of selflessness in a child—unconsciousness, not being taken up with self. I suppose that is the quality we learn from little children. He says, "become like little children," that have no sense of self, not taken up with self, and also, not too worried about things, knowing that there is someone who is going to be there to take care of them. Jesus brings a little child and says, "whoever welcomes one such child in my name welcomes me" (Matt. 18:5). This is how we are to be before God. Is that right? Does that make sense? We are grown-up parents and adults, but you know what? In relation to God, our Heavenly Father, we are like little children; this is what we should realize and how we should act in the kingdom. We call upon God as *Abba Father*.

The Seriousness of Sin

Jesus then warns against those who cause one of the little ones to stumble, to sin, and He speaks about the seriousness of this.

> If anyone causes one of these little ones—those who believe in me—to stumble, it would be better for them to have a large mill-stone hung around their neck and to be drowned in the depths of the sea. Woe to the world because of the things that cause people to stumble! Such things must come, but woe to the person through whom they come! (Matt. 18:6–7).

And He further warns, "If your hand or your foot causes you to stumble, cut it off and throw it away" (Matt. 18:8a); that is the seriousness of sin. Worldliness reinforces and encourages us in the sin of pride. The world taunts us to maintain that posture of pride and keeps us away from obedience in suffering and submission to God. The world has sin in that way, and we are not to go that way. Though someone very close to us and dear to us may call us toward the way of the world, we are not to go that way. It may be something as dear to us as our eyes; we may have to go into life maimed in terms of *relationships* that may cause us to sin, that may entice us to sin.

> It is better for you to enter life maimed or crippled than to have two hands or two feet and be thrown into eternal fire. And if your

eye causes you to stumble, gouge it out and throw it away. It is better for you to enter life with one eye than to have two eyes and be
thrown into the fire of hell (Matt. 18:8b–9).

We are to put that away from us and recognize that God's angels can
and do care for, watch over, and protect us so we can trust the Lord
and not go in the way of sin and self-love to get our own way.

The Parable of the Lost Sheep: Recovering One from Sin

Then Jesus gives the parable of the lost sheep, still thinking about the
little ones, because He answers, "In the same way your Father in heaven
is not willing that any of these little ones should perish" (Matt. 18:14).
This passage is also connected with His answer to who is the greatest
and His call to be like a little child. "What do you think? If a man
owns a hundred sheep, and one of them wanders away, will he not leave
the ninety-nine on the hills and go to look for the one that wandered
off?" (Matt. 18:12). He leaves the ninety-nine other sheep and goes off
looking for that little one that has wandered off because of sin. "And
if he finds it, truly I tell you, he is happier about that one sheep than
about the ninety-nine that did not wander off" (Matt. 18:13). Sometimes sin may come in and cause one to wander off to the ways of the
world, and we have to go out and look for this sheep.

Dealing with Offenses in the Body of Christ

I want you to notice, it is in this context that He speaks of this verse
that we have often quoted in Matthew 18.[14] Part of going out and looking for the little one is dealing with any sin that may cause offense. It
is in this context that the Matthew 18 passage occurs and I think it is
appropriate we look at it in this way. "If your brother or sister sins, go
and point out their fault, just between the two of you" (Matt. 18:15a).
There can be a lot of distance put between us by sin, one can wander
off because of sin. Our sin may cause a little one to stumble and wander off. We are to be careful that we do not have that sin. We are to
deal with it; we are to take sin seriously; we are not to allow our sin

---

14. A fuller exposition on the application of Matthew 18, can be found in Gangadean, *The
Westminster Confession*, 391–395.

to cause a brother or sister in Christ to stumble and fall. We are to be careful about this, and the warning comes to us. "If anyone causes one of these little ones—those who believe in me—to stumble, it would be better for them to have a large millstone hung around their neck and to be drowned in the depths of the sea" (Matt. 18:6). This is what should be if our sin causes another believer to stumble. It teaches us about sin's seriousness and how we must deal with it.

But now, if there is sin in someone, you go to them. If they do not deal with it, then take another with you. If they do not listen to the two, tell it to the church. If they refuse to listen *even* to the church, treat them as you would a pagan or a tax collector.

> If your brother or sister sins, go and point out their fault, just be-tween the two of you. If they listen to you, you have won them over. But if they will not listen, take one or two others along, so that 'every matter may be established by the testimony of two or three witnesses.' If they still refuse to listen, tell it to the church; and if they refuse to listen even to the church, treat them as you would a pagan or a tax collector (Matt. 18:15–17).

There is a process by which we can say that it is not a little one who is wandering off now; it is someone who has gone off in sin and is no longer to be regarded as such if they will not listen to the church.

Please notice this: "Truly I tell you, whatever you bind on earth will be bound in heaven, and whatever you loose on earth will be loosed in heaven" (Matt. 18:18). This is the same word that was spoken to Peter[15] and is now spoken in connection with church discipline. Fur-thermore, he says, "Again, truly I tell you that if two of you on earth agree about anything they ask for, it will be done for them by my Father in heaven. For where two or three gather in my name, there am I with them" (Matt. 18:19–20)—if we come together in His name. Notice how the disciplinary process, oversight, and accountability work if we are walking in the Lord and agreeing. If it is the case that someone is not repenting, they are to be treated accordingly. Discipline is to be done by the oversight of the church. We can discern between those who are little ones wandering off because of the sin of someone else

---

15. *Matthew 16:19.*

and those who are in sin—dug in—and will not come back, and must be brought under discipline.

Now, it is this which leads to the question, "Lord, how many times shall I forgive my brother or sister who sins against me? Up to seven times?" (Matt. 18:21). Jesus reminds them, "I tell you, not seven times, but seventy-seven times" (Matt. 18:22). One would be good; two would be great; three would be stupendous; four would be beyond superlative. Some of you in marriages have to reckon with this statement. There is a 'little one' beside you in marriage, another believer in Christ; we are not to cause that one to stumble. It is after this, in chapter 19, that He speaks about divorce. The reaction then is that it is not good for a man to marry. The Lord brings it home very closely. Sin is present in all of our relationships; we are to deal with it appropriately and not cause someone to stumble. There, He gives the parable about the unforgiving servant. We will not have the time to do that today, but God willing, we will pick up with that next time. There is a connection between sinning and self-will, and humility and obedience, and being like a child. We want to keep those connections before us as we go further.

15

KINGDOM ETHICS

The Greatest in the Kingdom—
Blessed Are the Poor in Spirit

Matthew 18:1–14

¹At that time the disciples came to Jesus and asked, "Who, then, is the greatest in the kingdom of heaven?"

²He called a little child to him, and placed the child among them. ³And he said: "Truly I tell you, unless you change and become like little children, you will never enter the kingdom of heaven. ⁴Therefore, whoever takes the lowly position of this child is the greatest in the kingdom of heaven. ⁵And whoever welcomes one such child in my name welcomes me.

⁶"If anyone causes one of these little ones—those who believe in me—to stumble, it would be better for them to have a large millstone hung around their neck and to be drowned in the depths of the sea. ⁷Woe to the world because of the things that cause people to stumble! Such things must come, but woe to the person through whom they come! ⁸If your hand or your foot causes you to stumble, cut it off and throw it away. It is better for you to enter life maimed or crippled than to have two hands or two feet and be thrown into eternal fire. ⁹And if your eye causes you to stumble, gouge it out and throw it away. It is better for you to enter life with one eye than to have two eyes and be thrown into the fire of hell.

¹⁰"See that you do not despise one of these little ones. For I tell you that their angels in heaven always see the face of my Father in heaven.

¹²"What do you think? If a man owns a hundred sheep, and one of them wanders away, will he not leave the ninety-nine on the hills and go to look for the one that wandered off? ¹³And if he finds it, truly I tell you,

he is happier about that one sheep than about the ninety-nine that did not wander off. [14]In the same way your Father in heaven is not willing that any of these little ones should perish."

CONTEXT:
Jesus' Transfiguration and the Cross

TODAY, WE WANT TO LOOK AT THE TEACHING of Christ, which we began last time, concerning 'Who is the greatest in the kingdom of heaven?' That the question would be asked at all is indicative of a problem on the part of the disciples—a problem that has been present and recurring. It is a problem of seeking glory and not recognizing the reality and the necessity for suffering in service in the kingdom of God. In chapter 16, our Lord Jesus had asked the question, "Who do you say I am?" Peter said, "You are the Christ, the Son of the living God." Jesus told them that He must die, and Peter resisted and rejected it. "Never, Lord!" he said. "This shall never happen to you!" Jesus rebuked Peter, corrected him, and warned him about this.[1] Peter was looking for glory. In chapter 17, on the Mount of Transfiguration, Jesus revealed and manifested His glory; His divinity shone through His manhood:[2] His face was bright as the sun, and His clothes were shining as the light. Peter wanted to hold on to glory and said, "I will put up three shelters—one for you, one for Moses, and one for Elijah."[3] Peter did not see; he did not understand the way of God and the way of the Lord Jesus Christ. He resisted that position.

---

1. *Matthew 16:13–28*.

2. In reference to *WCF 8.2:* ". . . So that two whole, perfect, and distinct natures, the Godhead and the manhood, were inseparably joined together in one person, without conversion, composition, or confusion . . . ."

3. *Matthew 17:1–13*.

LEVELS AND DEPTH OF UNBELIEF, PRIDE, AND SELF-LIFE

Who Is the Greatest? An Object Lesson of the Need for Change from Pride to Humility

The question of 'Who is the greatest?' comes up here, and this time, all the disciples seem to be involved in the question. They were expecting the kingdom, and rewards in that kingdom, as well as positions, privileges, and honors—as have often been sought after in the history of the Church. They were quarreling, disputing, and discussing among themselves who was the greatest in the kingdom of God. We are left to think about the motivation behind that question. Behind the question was a certain amount of ambition, self-seeking, self-centeredness, and self-life, and Jesus has to address this again. He has already addressed this many times before, and we have cause to allude to this as we go through. In response to the question, 'Who is the greatest in the kingdom of heaven?' He called a little child and had him stand among them. It is not a babe in arms but a child that could stand in their midst. I wonder what the age of that child may be, and some have speculated whether it is one of Peter's children because of the context that he was in Peter's home, but we do not have to let that question concern us here. As is often the case, Jesus does an object lesson. He has a child come and stand in their midst, and they are looking at this child and wondering. You would not think that Jesus would say that someone like a little child is the greatest in the kingdom. You just would not think that. When Jesus does say that, it is rather puzzling. What exactly does He mean when He says, "**Unless you change and become like little children, you will never enter the kingdom of heaven**" (v. 3b)? Jesus is making a solemn affirmation: "**Truly I tell you**" (v. 3a) and in the KJV, "**Verily I say unto you.**" This is *truth*: "unless you change." They need to change. We cannot bypass that. They are going in the wrong direction in their attitude and innermost thinking, and they must change and become like little children. Unless they change, they will never *enter* the kingdom of heaven, let alone be the *greatest* in the kingdom. Please notice how Jesus answers: He brings a child, He tells them the truth in solemn terms, calls them to be thoughtful about it, that they must change, they must become like little children, or they will not even enter the kingdom. They will not enter or begin their lives in the kingdom, let alone go on to be the greatest.

Jesus goes on and says, "**Therefore, whoever humbles himself like this child**"—and you must actively humble yourself like this little child—"**is the greatest in the kingdom of heaven**" (v. 4).[4] He addresses their question about who is the greatest, starting with the beginning and their need for change. He does it in a very dramatic way. Every time we look at little children, we are to be reminded of becoming like a little child. This is puzzling because little children do not engage in apologetics; they do not go to universities or have little children. These things happen to us in the natural course of our lives as adults. Little children do not exercise authority over others in positions of leadership. We do not elect a little child to be president of a country. Little children are hardly conscious of many things, yet we are to know the Lord, seek the Lord, and engage in many things that are specifically for adults. So what does Jesus mean when He says, "**Unless you change and become like little children**"? It certainly does not mean like a little child in *every* respect, because elsewhere the Scripture says, "In regard to evil be infants, but in your thinking be adults" (1 Cor. 14:20b). We are reminded that we are to grow up and to come to maturity, not be like children tossed back and forth by the waves.[5] It is not in every respect that we are to be like children, but in a particular respect. By saying not in every respect and just one particular respect, we are not minimizing that respect. That respect is so important that we will not enter the kingdom without it. Jesus makes a point that unless we live in that spirit at all times in the kingdom, we will not be great in the kingdom of God.

Blessed Are the Poor in Spirit: Recognizing Our Creaturely Dependence

To be like a child is a spirit that we are to have in a particular way; we do not have to look far for what that is. Our Lord spoke about this when He said, "Blessed are the poor in spirit, for theirs is the kingdom of heaven" (Matt. 5:3). We spoke about that weeks ago, and we said

---

4. NIV 1984.

5. *Ephesians 4:14.*

that the poor in spirit are those who recognize their own emptiness, that they have nothing of themselves, that they are creatures of God. We recognize our creatureliness and, as creatures, our emptiness in ourselves and our utter, full, continuous dependence on God for everything we have. We can ask, is a child like that? Is a child dependent? In some ways, does a child recognize that and perhaps live in that dependency? I believe it is in this respect that Jesus is speaking to us to become like little children. To recognize our creatureliness before God, our utter dependence on God for everything as a creature.

Jesus goes on in the Sermon on the Mount to say, "Blessed are those who mourn, for they will be comforted" (Matt. 5:4). We spoke about that as mourning concerning our sin and the redemption that comes in connection with repentance. We could tighten those two points by saying that the sin for which we are particularly in mourning is the failure to recognize our creatureliness—our creaturely dependence on God. If you think this is some small sin or that this does not make all the difference in the world, consider this: It was this sin—the first sin, the sin in the Garden—that brought woe upon all mankind. This sin is our failure to recognize our creatureliness and putting ourselves, as creatures, in the place of God to determine good and evil. As soon as we cease recognizing our creatureliness and utter dependence on God, we put ourselves in the place of God. When we do, we determine good and evil as other than what God has established it to be. There is much that comes with that—all the misery of spiritual death that comes with sin when we do not recognize our creaturely dependence on God. On the positive side, you might think this way: If we were to recognize our creaturely dependence on God, would we walk in the way of sin? Would that be sufficient to keep us from sin? It would have been enough to keep Adam from sin. We could say the same for ourselves. It is in this particular respect, then, that I believe Jesus is saying, "**unless you change and become like little children, you will never enter the kingdom of heaven**" (v. 3b).

Meaning as Significance Apart from Meaning as Intelligibility

There are many aspects of self-life; we will look at some of them as we go through the discussion. There are many aspects of the self-life and the dreadfulness of sin. We have to recognize our dependence on God, and with that dependence, our trust in God, and with that dependence and trust, we obey God and do not go our own way but walk in His way. Many fail to live in this way. Some things we can recognize are the sense of our identity, sometimes called identity politics, how we define ourselves, our self-image, how we think about ourselves, our significance, and what we think others may think about us. We often do a great deal in our lives and pursue a course in life because we want to have a sense of importance. We have turned away from our dependence on God and our creatureliness and from recognizing not only our dependence but also our dignity and significance as creatures. We try to establish some other identity for ourselves, such as how we think about ourselves and how we want others to think about us. Jesus puts it this way: "How can you believe since you accept glory from one another yet do not seek the glory that comes from the only God?" (Jn. 5:44). That is how our self-life begins to unfold and work out.

I saw a movie this week; in that movie, the mother of the hero told him that if he stayed here and did not go to war, he would have children, and they would have children, and the children would die, and soon his name would be forgotten. If he goes to war, his name would be remembered for thousands of years, but there he will die. This hero had a choice to make and he chose to go to war and fight. This hero's name is Achilles. He is now featured in this movie called *Troy*.[6] Achilles thought that the gods envy mortals because we die, and our death causes what we do now to be significant. These gods are immortals in time, not immortals outside of time, which does not have the problem of repetition in time. Achilles thought the gods envied the mortals because death puts a special significance on them. But so did another group that I was reading about—the Students for a Democratic Society in the 1960s. This group was discussed in Judge Bork's book, *Slouching Towards Gomorrah*,[7] and the effects of that time, place, and worldview on these young men. They thought this was the only life and wanted some kind of significance and achievement. They would achieve in a different way than Achilles achieved. They would bring about the ideal society by revolution. That revolutionary spirit rolled through

---

6. David Benioff, *Troy*, Directed by Wolfgang Petersen (2004, Warner Bros.).

7. Robert H. Bork, *Slouching towards Gomorrah: Modern Liberalism and American Decline* (New York: Reganbooks, 2003).

the 60s and became quiet, but it has continued in present society. It is now undermining because of its atheistic worldview that *when you're dead, you're dead.* It is undermining all the values, all the words, all the meaning of the words, what it means to be equal, and what it means to be free. It is emptying words of meaning and filling them with words that, upon analysis, lack meaning.

In the Day We Sin, We Shall Surely Die

People who try to find significance apart from God, apart from recognizing their creatureliness, end up exalting themselves in pride and bringing about destruction upon themselves and upon those around them. It is inevitable; it is necessarily true, and it cannot be avoided. It never has been and it never will be avoided. It will always be the case that in the day we sin, we shall surely die. It is the sin of the creature putting itself in the place of the Creator, as our first parents did. We have to learn to recognize death around us and not call it by some other name, and we have to recognize that this death is due to sin and learn to mourn for it. We must learn to mourn the fact that we took it upon ourselves to determine good and evil, and we drove ourselves into the ground, into death. We must take responsibility for it, humble our hearts before God, and come seeking forgiveness and cleansing from God. This happens in every sphere of life; it happens in all relationships. When we do not honor God, we relate to others in the horizontal and not first before God. We do not think of how God would have us react to a person, but we think about how we should react to what a person has done to us. We forget our creatureliness, and we wreak havoc in our lives and the lives of others and pain upon pain, day after day, because we do not recognize that we are creatures like little children depending upon God, trusting and obeying God.

I challenge each one of you here today to think about any pain and any suffering that you have gone through that is not connected with sin and death. I want you to, I ask you to, and I require you in the name of God to think right thoughts about your suffering, to call it for what it is, *the misery of death that is due to sin.* And not to excuse yourself from it or excuse others from it. Learn to fear the Lord, learn to be like that little child that Jesus put in the midst of His disciples and said, "**Unless you change and become like little children, you will never enter** the kingdom of heaven" (v. 3b). We are to change and become like that little child continually, and live a life of creaturely dependence on God, and understand what that meant from the beginning, and understand the whole worldview that goes with becoming like a child, and not understand it as some isolated piece of truth, but the whole worldview. Unless you live that way, you will not be the greatest in the kingdom; you will not be serving the Lord as you should.

Jesus spoke these words to His disciples, and He rebuked their unbelief, pride, and self-life in speaking these words. May these words remain ever with us: that we are to be like a little child in recognizing our creatureliness before God, our utter dependence upon God. Not in other respects, but in this particular respect, we are to be like a little child before God. I do not think that any of us here can make a successful qualification on that truth; that we are to recognize our creatureliness, and with our creatureliness, our dependence upon God, and with our dependence, our trust in God, and with our trust in God, obedience to God. We should not place ourselves in the position of God to determine good and evil, but we are to obey Him and seek Him. You see how big and important this one truth is, this one respect for how we are to be like little children. It will always be the case that if we do not recognize our creatureliness, we will go to self-life, and we will want to save our lives and we will end up losing it.[8] In the very particular way in which we want to save our self-life, 'our lives,' we will lose it. There are many ways in which we want to save 'our lives'—where *we* define life—and the Lord God, Creator of heaven and earth, our Creator, made us in such a way that it cannot be, and He rules in such a way to uphold His Word in the creation. The very way we seek to save our lives, in that very way, we will lose it, we will lose it utterly, we will lose it altogether.

The World's Opposition: Seduction, Taunting, and Oppression

Creatureliness and dependence are antithetical to the spirit of the world, antithetical to the flesh, and antithetical to the devil. The world, the flesh, and the devil—that is the other way of failing to recognize our creatureliness before God, and they all coordinate. We want to live our

---

8. *Matthew 16:25.*

own lives, in our own way, to do our own pleasure, to please ourselves, and the world is there to encourage us. The rock music of the 60s was the music of rebellion, the music of throwing off the restraints of any authority, doing your thing, being joyful in it, exalting in it, and that music has seeped into our souls. There is a place for rebellion; there is a place to rebel against what is not according to the Word of God. But given our self-life and the way the world is, when it plays its rock music, it is a spirit of rebellion for the sake of rebellion. It is to be your own person, to have no limits placed on the self and self-life. Be careful of this; it is in our souls. Do not think you can baptize it and make it Christian. Watch out.

The flesh is there to exalt in its autonomy and to find a special pleasure in just doing what comes naturally, not recognizing its fallenness. The world is in spiritual death; it looks down on those who would live differently. It seeks to seduce the children of God to its way. Even Satan tried to seduce in the Garden. 'Be all you can be, achieve as much as you can, be the greatest you can be, do not stop for anything short of that, do not limit yourself! Be as God knowing good and evil! You do not want to settle for less, do you?' How many times have you heard that? 'Settling for less.' The flesh hears that in a certain way. The believer can hear that in another way, but the flesh is with us, and it hears that, and it wants to reach for fullness and ends with emptiness; it ends with dust in its mouth. It shall eat dust as the serpent did. The world looks down on believers who seem to be so satisfied with so much less. Think about the painting called *American Gothic*.[9] Do you want to grow up and be like that? 'Be all you can be, leave the farm, get into the city where there is life, don't live in Kansas anymore!' It is kind of deceiving, isn't it? You go into the city, and you become an airhead, flake, flunky, loser, debased, corrupt, and perverted, and you compare that now with *American Gothic*. You look a little bit deeper and see. It is entirely possible that the souls of those in the *American Gothic* were dead; we are looking at dead souls, who died on the farm. It is just as easy to die in the city. It is perhaps easier because there are more things going on there to entice us. You have this seduction to 'be all you can be,' and you look down on the little one.

---

9. Grant Wood, *American Gothic* (The Art Institute of Chicago, 1930).

The opposition of the world may come as taunting and ridiculing. 'You benighted fundamentalist, ignorant of what has been known, discovered, and made clear by science. You don't get it, do you? You'll never get it, you and your Christianity.' We can be taunted, and many professors have taunted Christians with their unbelief. Yes, there are things in Christian lives to be ridiculed. The flesh does not discern how we come short, it does not repent, and we can stumble.

There is oppression for being a believer, seeking to honor God, not buying into the system, and not playing the game as they do: seduction, taunting, oppression. These are the ways in which the world causes the little ones who believe in Christ to stumble and sin. Jesus says, **"Woe to the world because of the things that cause people to stumble! Such things must come, but woe to the person through whom they come!"** (v. 7). There is a reality and a necessity to it—such things *must* come. The world does its work relentlessly and seductively. It does it with a certain charm, at times; it is not always just raw aggression. The world has a flair to it at times, and makes you look like you are not with it, you are not there, and it can put you down. I try to heighten the contrast between those two images, the *American Gothic* and the young man making his way in the city lights to the way of the adulterous place to live out his life.

The Seriousness of Sin

"Such things must come, but woe to the person through whom they come!" Jesus is speaking here about the seriousness of sin. The world is characterized by those who do not recognize God as the Creator and their dependence on God for everything that is good. That is one way of characterizing the world. Augustine characterized the world as those who love self more than God. But if you love the self more than God, you put the self above God. How is that different from denying God as Creator and oneself as creature and our dependence on Him? Can you be somewhat creaturely but mostly self-life? Can you mix it that way? I don't think so. Jesus said, **"If anyone causes one of these little ones—those who believe in me—to stumble, it would be better for him to have a large millstone hung around his neck and to be drowned in the depths of the sea"** (v. 6). That is a pretty dramatic description. It is not being thrown overboard, floating around, maybe staying afloat for an hour, and just finally giving up and going down. There is a deliberateness about this. A millstone is a heavy piece of equipment, and you have a millstone hung around your neck so it cannot be taken off easily, and you drop into the sea, you are not going to swim, you are going to go down. It is over. That is it. Jesus said that would be better for one who causes a little one to stumble. It is better for someone to be drowned like that than to cause someone to sin. So let us not play with this; there is a reality here about recognizing our God as the Creator, that failure to do so is sin, and recognizing the way in which the world comes against us in this. Sin is serious; it is to be taken seriously.

You will not even enter the kingdom and you will not go on to any maturity to lead unless you recognize your utter and continual dependence on God. But there is a very important point here about being the one through whom that sin comes, the woe that comes upon that person. The seriousness of sin is not only for that which is coming from outside but from within you. It is not only from the world but from the flesh. It says, **"If your hand or your foot causes you to stumble, cut it off and throw it away"** (v. 8a). Imagine yourself cutting off your hand. We have heard of that horrible story, and some of you have seen the image of this American citizen in Iraq having his head cut off. It is a pretty gruesome and horrible image, and there is something peculiarly barbaric about it. There is a gruesomeness in this idea of cutting off your hand or your foot if it causes you to sin. In the expression, **"causes you to sin,"**[10] we have to understand the word *cause* more in the sense of being an occasion.

Some of you have occasions in your life that cause you to sin. It could be the computer; it could be stuff you pick up down the road in a bottle, or in a book; it is causing you to sin. That is coming through the world, but the Lord is saying, **"cut it off."** If it has to be as dramatic as cutting off your hand or your foot—cut it off! Because you know what? There is an alternative to that, which is to perish in hell forever. Between those two, **"it is better for you to enter life maimed or crippled than to have two hands or two feet and be thrown into eternal fire"** (v. 8b). Jesus is teaching here the seriousness of sin: for the one who causes this sin from the world, that a millstone be hung around his neck, or for the one who has an occasion in his life, even their hands

---

10. NIV 1984.

and feet—he or she has to cut it off! You *cannot* indulge in sin—you have to be radical with it. You *cannot* play with it. You *cannot* make occasion for the flesh to fulfill the lust thereof. You must be radical with it. You must crucify it! There are no ifs, ands, or buts about this in the words of Jesus. No oozing and dealing with it through gradualism. Cut it out—*radically*. **"And if your eye causes you to stumble, gouge it out and throw it away"** (v. 9a). Because the alternative is so terrible, the reality of spiritual death is so terrible, you do not want to even get near it. You are playing with fire when you allow this sin to continue in your life.

Now, please, each one of us, let us take it to heart; if there is a particular sin that you are working with and you are struggling with, take it to heart, this Word of Jesus, and cut it out—dramatically. Make no provision for the flesh to fulfill its lust,[11] because if you do, this sin could lead you into the depths of hell. Do not think it cannot. Do not play with it. There is a line from Amy Carmichael, the missionary to India, in a book about her that was written by Elisabeth Elliot, *A Chance to Die*.[12] Some of you know Elisabeth Elliott, and some of you respect her; I certainly do. She wrote a line, and I think I am paraphrasing it a little bit: "Can he have followed far / Who has no wound nor scar?"[13] It is better to enter life maimed—mutilated.

We Enter and Continue in the Kingdom Through Many Hardships

Can you get far into the kingdom without bearing the cross? What is this cross? It may be some ordinary natural human joy that God has denied you. Joni Eareckson Tada was denied such a joy; she had an accident, she became quadriplegic, and she has to live. Is that a natural joy to have health, to be able to take food to your mouth? There are many other ways in which natural joys are denied us. Will we take up our cross and follow Him, and know that He is our Creator? Will we know that He is ruling in every way? Will we trust Him and submit to Him and be obedient to Him? "Can he have followed far / Who has

---

11. *Romans 13:14.*

12. Elisabeth Elliot, *A Chance to Die: The Life and Legacy of Amy Carmichael* (Grand Rapids: Revell, 1987).

13. Amy Carmichael, "Hast Thou No Scar," in *Gold Cord* (Christian Literature Crusade, 1932).

no wound nor scar?" Paul said through much suffering, through much tribulation, we enter into the kingdom.[14] Because of sin remaining in us and our attachment in that way that may pull us away from the will of God, we must bear the cross. We must take up our cross daily and follow Him.[15] No one enters into the kingdom of heaven and continues in any way without suffering and without bearing the cross—without being maimed. The maimed came to Jesus, the crippled, and they were healed. We may take from this, certainly, that God does not want us to be maimed, but there was a purpose for that. It was to reveal the connection between the physical and the spiritual, the sign and the reality. Instead of being maimed spiritually by indulging sin, it is better to be maimed circumstantially, in things that we might hold on to, and to enter into life. It is a serious matter that our Lord is speaking of here: life and death, good and evil.

Parable of the Lost Sheep: Seduced by and Recovered from Sin

Jesus warns, "See that you do not despise one of these little ones. For I tell you that their angels in heaven always see the face of my Father in heaven" (v. 10). There is a privilege and a position of a child of God who is adopted into the family. In regard to a sinner, He speaks about what is needed to recover such a one. Like a sheep going astray, the effort is made to recover such a one. In this parable, He says:

> What do you think? If a man owns a hundred sheep, and one of them wanders away, will he not leave the ninety-nine on the hills and go to look for the one that wandered off? And if he finds it, truly I tell you, he is happier about that one sheep than about the ninety-nine that did not wander off. In the same way your Father in heaven is not willing that any of these little ones should perish (vv. 12–14).

Jesus is speaking about the greatest, the attitude of dependence and creatureliness, and the dangers that come to this little one from outside, from the world, but also from the flesh and from the devil—a liar. What is his lie? His lie is that sin does not produce death: "You

---

14. *Acts 14:22.*
15. *Matthew 16:24.*

shall not surely die."[16] That is what we have to watch against. One of the ways we are taken in by this is that we do not see death as death, and therefore we do not see it as a result of sin. We have to learn to look and understand the misery and the curse (natural evil) that brings the emptiness of life and all that goes with it and trace the movements from sin into death. We *must* learn to do that so we will not be taken by surprise by the devil's lie. Behind that lie is a teaching that there is no sin; that man, the self, is the determiner. It is the lie that you can be as God determining good and evil and that it is not God as Creator who determines good and evil. In that brief statement in the Garden, Satan is a liar. He seduced our first parents. It is the very same way in which he is still trying to seduce us. He denies the connection between sin and death by emptying the word *sin* of meaning. He does that by emptying the word *God* of meaning. When he empties *sin* and *God* of meaning, then we are without meaning. We are adrift, and the death has already set in—using words without understanding and all that will come from that. Satan is a liar, and the father of it, and we have to recognize his chief lie; he has one and only one basic lie: "You will not surely die." We have to overcome that lie—whether it is the world, or the flesh, or the devil coming against those who believe in God the Creator and recognize their creatureliness as a little one, we have to overcome that lie as our Lord is instructing us here. Unless you become like little children, you will not enter the kingdom of heaven. Unless you *change* and become like little children, you will not enter the kingdom of heaven.

May God grant us to become like little children, that we may enter the kingdom of heaven, that we may remain there, and that we may not be seduced or taunted or oppressed into any kind of departure from recognizing ourselves as creatures in the image of God.

---

16. *Genesis 3:4* NIV 1984.

KINGDOM ETHICS
Forgiveness, Marriage, and Divorce

Matthew 18:15–19:12

^{18:15}"If your brother or sister sins, go and point out their fault, just between the two of you. If they listen to you, you have won them over. ¹⁶But if they will not listen, take one or two others along, so that 'every matter may be established by the testimony of two or three witnesses.' ¹⁷If they still refuse to listen, tell it to the church; and if they refuse to listen even to the church, treat them as you would a pagan or a tax collector.

¹⁸"Truly I tell you, whatever you bind on earth will be bound in heaven, and whatever you loose on earth will be loosed in heaven.

¹⁹"Again, truly I tell you that if two of you on earth agree about anything they ask for, it will be done for them by my Father in heaven. ²⁰For where two or three gather in my name, there am I with them."

²¹Then Peter came to Jesus and asked, "Lord, how many times shall I forgive my brother or sister who sins against me? Up to seven times?"

²²Jesus answered, "I tell you, not seven times, but seventy-seven times.

²³"Therefore, the kingdom of heaven is like a king who wanted to settle accounts with his servants. ²⁴As he began the settlement, a man who owed him ten thousand bags of gold was brought to him. ²⁵Since he was not able to pay, the master ordered that he and his wife and his children and all that he had be sold to repay the debt.

²⁶"At this the servant fell on his knees before him. 'Be patient with me,' he begged, 'and I will pay back everything.' ²⁷The servant's master took pity on him, canceled the debt and let him go.

²⁸"But when that servant went out, he found one of his fellow servants who owed him a hundred silver coins. He grabbed him and began to choke him. 'Pay back what you owe me!' he demanded.

²⁹"His fellow servant fell to his knees and begged him, 'Be patient with me, and I will pay it back.'

³⁰"But he refused. Instead, he went off and had the man thrown into prison until he could pay the debt. ³¹When the other servants saw what had happened, they were outraged and went and told their master everything that had happened.

³²"Then the master called the servant in. 'You wicked servant,' he said, 'I canceled all that debt of yours because you begged me to. ³³Shouldn't you have had mercy on your fellow servant just as I had on you?' ³⁴In anger his master handed him over to the jailers to be tortured, until he should pay back all he owed.

³⁵"This is how my heavenly Father will treat each of you unless you forgive your brother or sister from your heart."

¹⁹:¹When Jesus had finished saying these things, he left Galilee and went into the region of Judea to the other side of the Jordan. ²Large crowds followed him, and he healed them there.

³Some Pharisees came to him to test him. They asked, "Is it lawful for a man to divorce his wife for any and every reason?"

⁴"Haven't you read," he replied, "that at the beginning the Creator 'made them male and female,' ⁵and said, 'For this reason a man will leave his father and mother and be united to his wife, and the two will become one flesh'? ⁶So they are no longer two, but one flesh. Therefore what God has joined together, let no one separate."

⁷"Why then," they asked, "did Moses command that a man give his wife a certificate of divorce and send her away?"

⁸Jesus replied, "Moses permitted you to divorce your wives because your hearts were hard. But it was not this way from the beginning. ⁹I tell you that anyone who divorces his wife, except for sexual immorality, and marries another woman commits adultery."

¹⁰The disciples said to him, "If this is the situation between a husband and wife, it is better not to marry."

¹¹Jesus replied, "Not everyone can accept this word, but only those to whom it has been given. ¹²For there are eunuchs who were born that way, and there are eunuchs who have been made eunuchs by others—and there

are those who choose to live like eunuchs for the sake of the kingdom of heaven. The one who can accept this should accept it."

REVIEW:
Like a Little Child and Creaturely Dependence

TODAY, WE CONTINUE FROM WHERE WE LEFT off in Matthew 18. By way of review, Jesus was asked, "Who, then, is the greatest in the kingdom of heaven? He called a little child to him, and placed the child among them. And he said: 'Truly I tell you, unless you change and become like little children, you will never enter the kingdom of heaven'" (Matt. 18:3). You will not even enter the kingdom. We asked, in what respect are we to be like a little child? Not in every respect, certainly, but in this respect: we are to recognize our utter dependence on God as creatures. Recognizing our creatureliness is the beginning; this is how we enter the kingdom of God. A contrast is made between the kingdom of God on the one hand and the world on the other. The world centers upon the sin of pride, where we fail to recognize our creatureliness, take credit for ourselves that belongs to God, and live a life wholly for the self-life in every respect. There is a confrontation between the little ones of God, who recognize their creatureliness, and the world, which is opposed to the spirit of creatureliness. Sin must come because of the world remaining in the believer, but there is a warning against sin, the seriousness of sin, and there is a judgment on the one who brings it—a millstone is to be hung around his neck, and he is to be cast into the depths of the sea. There is likewise a judgment on the one who may commit sin, that it is better to enter into life maimed than, with both hands and both feet, to be cast into hell.[1] There are times when we must suffer loss of ordinary things, good things, and maybe relationships, for the sake of the kingdom of God. Sin is a serious matter. Jesus makes this very clear. It is a serious matter for one's life in the kingdom and for the kingdom of God. Recovery from sin must be sought if possible, and so the Scripture speaks about recovering a sinner. In the parable of the lost sheep, if a little one—a child of God— goes astray, we should do what we can to bring recovery of that one. There is rejoicing in the one who went astray, who is found, and who

---

1. *Matthew 18:5–8.*

is brought back, but there is also the case where the one who is going astray may not come back, and they resist coming back. That is what is taken up in this next passage about a brother who sins against you.

IF YOUR BROTHER SINS:
How Are We to Deal with Offenses?

If your brother or sister sins, go and point out their fault, just between the two of you. If they listen to you, you have won them over. But if they will not listen, take one or two others along, so that "every matter may be established by the testimony of two or three witnesses." If they still refuse to listen, tell it to the church; and if they refuse to listen even to the church, treat them as you would a pagan or a tax collector. I tell you the truth, whatever you bind on earth will be bound in heaven, and whatever you loose on earth will be loosed in heaven. Again, I tell you that if two of you on earth agree about anything you ask for, it will be done for you by my Father in heaven. For where two or three come together in my name, there am I with them (18:15–20).

This passage begins with, "If your brother sins against you,"[2] but these ones, when unrepented, end up being treated as if they are not a brother; they are to be treated as a pagan or tax collector, and they are certainly not considered brothers. There is a context in which we are looking at this passage: the little ones, the ones who recognize their creatureliness and the sin that may come, who recognize how we are to deal with sin, how we are to treat sin seriously, and make efforts to overcome it.

There are offenses in the Church. There is offense in the very state of the Church today—the Church is divided. A lot of these offenses go back to personal matters, certainly in doctrine as well, but divisions arose in a very personal way, and it has not been dealt with properly. The anticipation, the expectation here, where it says, "tell it to the church," is that there is *one* Church, not many divisions among the Church, not that if you are upset in one place, you can go off to another place

---

2. NIV 1984.

where you may do as you please. We are thinking about this now in a somewhat broken situation, but still, it can be put into practice.

We need to deal with offenses properly as against improperly. We will deal with offenses one way or another. There are divisions not only among churches but also within particular congregations. Some persons have difficulty talking with each other and being around each other, and it has been dealt with sometimes by just ignoring the other, steering clear of that person, and just leaving it there. That is not the way to deal with it, and it does not encourage brotherly relationships. We need to learn to deal with offenses in a biblical way[3] and Jesus is teaching us. Remember the context—*the little ones*. We are not to have this pride (autonomy and self-life) that causes us to commit other sins that bring offense. Paul says to be completely humble and gentle, which is part of that humility in our dealings with one another that might preserve the unity of the Spirit in the bond of peace.[4] Here again, humility is against pride, where how we view ourselves, and how we want others to think of us, is what becomes important. We are to be aware of the reality of sin in the world, the reality of sin that remains in us, and how sin works individually in us. We spoke about sin as not seeking and not understanding while pursuing something other than the knowledge of God as the good. We spoke about third-degree sin, the compounded effect of not seeking, self-deception, and self-justification, and the reality of the curse that is in the world because of sin. We begin with an awareness of ourselves as creatures, dependent on God, utterly dependent, that there is nothing to boast of in ourselves, and that we are sinful creatures. Remember, blessed are those who mourn.[5] Seeing the need to be forgiven, and having come to God for forgiveness, we are to be forgiving of each other, also.

We are going to apply this principle of offenses and forgiveness in chapter 19 as Jesus speaks about marriage and the question of divorce, sin in marriage that brings about divorce, the strains in marriage, and the need to forgive in marriage so that we do not end in that broken situation. Remember, the Lord says, **"Then Peter came to Him and said, 'Lord, how often shall my brother sin against me, and I forgive**

---

3. Gangadean, *The Westminster Confession*, 391–395.

4. *Ephesians 4:2–3.*

5. *Matthew 5:4.*

him? Up to seven times?' Jesus said to him, 'I do not say to you, up
to seven times, but up to seventy times seven'" (18:21–22 NKJV).
Anyone who has lived in marriage knows that is certainly true. But we
are not forgiving more than we have been forgiven; we are not nearly
there. If we recognize ourselves as creatures, and sinful creatures before
God, it becomes quite easy to forgive, but sin has its way of blurring
that understanding, so we have to struggle to overcome that sin, to see
clearly, and to deal with it. Sin keeps us from dealing with sin properly.
Here, the Lord is laying out how we are to deal with sin.

"If your brother sins against you" (18:15a), you may be tempted
to get mad, sit on it for a while, and wonder to yourself how a person
could possibly be like that. Then you may vent—tell somebody about
it—and get a little clique going and gossip about it. I think we recognize that we are tempted to do that. That is *not* the way. We should
not be surprised by sin; that is our first problem. We should not be
surprised that there is sin in us or in other people. One of the things
we say in our vow when we come to God is that we confess that we
are sinners before God.[6] Let's get real with ourselves. Let's get in touch
with reality. We are creatures, and we are sinful creatures, and we are
going to die. Death is a great reminder of the reality of sin. If you are
26 and you say, 'No, I'm not going to die, no way' (people at 26 say
that), well, remember you have to go to work and that is toil. By 26,
you should be out of the house on your own, your mother should not
be supporting you, you should be experiencing toil—or at least be in
graduate school, that is certainly difficult. Everyone faces toil, and you
must have some strained relationship with someone—a friend, a girlfriend, a boyfriend—and that is always painful. Or you may have no
friends, which is a form of strained relationships, isn't it? In a round-
about way—'I can't even get any friends in order to have a strained
relationship, what is going on here?' That is a reality, and if that is not
good enough, think about others who have strained relationships around
you. If that does not do anything for you, consider the ongoing war
in Iraq and Afghanistan. Think about strife and the killing involved in
war. Think about the oppression, poverty, and desolation of spirit that
exists in Cuba and other parts of the world. Certainly, toil, strife, old

---

6. Gangadean, *The Westminster Confession*, 387–388.

age, war, famine, and plague abound in the world, and we should not be surprised by the reality of sin.[7]

Matthew 18: Step One

What we should do is: "If your brother sins against you, go and show him his fault, just between the two of you" (18:15a). Notice, just between the two of you. "Go and show him his fault." I might say, if you are clear that he is at fault, then go and show him his fault and be ready to show it, as in, 'Show there must be something eternal.' Can you show that? I am getting at the idea of 'show' and the idea of 'proof'—not in a technical way, but in the spirit of seeking to recover your brother. Show him his fault, or at least bring it to his attention. Be sure that you have interpreted it right. And, it is always best to go inquiring: 'You said this, is that what you meant?' It is safe, it is easier, it is more comfortable for all concerned to go inquiring rather than judging.

Not everything that comes up needs to be brought to the attention of the other, sometimes just forbear. But if it stays with you, you should go to your brother, and it should be done in a timely way. We would say within 24 hours, before the sun goes down preferably, but let us just say within 24 hours—the rule of 24. If you bring it up *after* 24 hours, you have to ask forgiveness for the delay. That is a good and necessary consequence from the statement, "Do not let the sun go down on your wrath" (Eph. 4:26b NKJV); there is a timely way to deal with things. Do not say, 'Well, five years ago, you said that to me, and I can't forget it. I've tried and tried; I haven't forgotten it.' Suppose you have tried to forebear, and it is still there after 24 hours. In that case, you have to deal with it in this way: go to the person, "just between the two of you. If they listen to you," and there is no guarantee that he will, "If they listen to you, you have won them over" (18:15b), and you have recovered that one from something serious; you have recovered him from sin.

Matthew 18: Step Two

We have to anticipate that sometimes the person will not listen. Remember the nature of sin, the reality and the depth of it. "But if he will

---

7. Gangadean, *Philosophical Foundation*, 147–151.

not listen, take one or two others along, so that 'every matter may be established by the testimony of two or three witnesses'" (18:16). We have to do that appropriately and in the right spirit. Sometimes, it is not possible to take these steps in just this way, but you can approximate it, and you can certainly take someone else with you. We will see that there is a good reason for doing so: **"Again, I tell you that if two of you on earth agree about anything you ask for, it will be done for you by my Father in heaven"** (18:19). That is said in this context of calling someone to repentance, and regarding the discipline of the church. As human beings, we all go our own way, so we are not likely to agree. But if you can get two persons to agree on something, particularly in the matter of sin, you have a major achievement on your hands. That might even deserve the Nobel Peace Prize, because it so seldom happens. Keep in mind the witness of two or three others, and how Jesus speaks about this later on. It is important to establish things objectively, and this is done by the witness of two or three others. Notice there are one or two others, and you are the third person, making three. So there should be at least two; three is even better, but not necessary, and you establish a witness and objectivity about it. It is not just one person's word against another, it was brought out with the witness of others.

This must be done in the spirit of seeking to recover, to win your brother, not in a spirit of justifying yourself or putting down the other person. If need be, we need to pray about that before we go. Usually, what happens is that we have so much hurt with us that we are not able to go, and if we do go, we go with this hurt, we speak harshly and improperly, and we just complicate matters. We end up putting the other person on the defensive way too quickly. So we are to go in this spirit of seeking to recover a brother.

Matthew 18: Step Three

If after bringing one or two witnesses, he refuses to listen to *them*, tell it to the church. That is the third step: first, you go by yourself; second, take one or two; and third, tell it to the church. **"If they still refuse to listen, tell it to the church; and if they refuse to listen even to the church, treat them as you would a pagan or a tax collector"** (18:17). In more than 40 years as a Christian in the church, I have seldom seen this process put into practice. I have seen a lot of short-circuiting and breakdown of the process. This is the precept of Christ, and if we think about the words given to us in Scripture, we have to learn to do it; we have to ask God for grace to put it into practice and to be in the right frame of mind to put this into practice. We do need to put it into practice. And when we put it into practice, when it comes to telling it to the church, we should not have a split in the church over it. A pattern has already been established; it usually goes through the elders and is brought to the person, and after it is brought that way, if they do not listen to the church, they pretty well cut themselves off from the community. They are not in fellowship anymore. Then it may be pronounced officially, publicly, and all have to stand together in this, to treat this person as a non-believer, as a pagan or a tax collector. But not as an enemy—though if as an enemy, we are still to love our enemies. But they are to be treated as a non-believer, that is, a person who is not bearing or showing fruit in keeping with their confession of faith in Christ. When you have an entire church witnessing to one person, that becomes very powerful and it needs to be done. It may be, I hope not, but it may be in God's providence that we will be called upon to do that in this church. When the steps are taken and if this person still will not hear them, I hope that we will remember the Scripture and say, 'Yes, we will stand in this way.'

Sometimes, this happens in the case of divorce when the person will not hear, will not listen to the church, and then the church has to act. It is not incidental that these passages are side by side. If Matthew 18 is followed from step one to step three, we have the promise of Christ, that the Spirit is at work in us, and if we agree to bind something—let us say that that person is put out of the church and bound in that way—it will be bound in heaven. "**Truly I tell you, whatever you bind on earth will be bound in heaven**" (18:18a). This is the truth of God. "**And whatever you loose on earth will be loosed in heaven**" (18:18b). If the church receives persons back into the church because they have repented, confessed their sin, and humbled themselves before God, then God also receives that person. They are forgiven and received back into the kingdom of God. This is how we understand what was spoken earlier when Jesus said to Peter, "I will give you the keys of the kingdom of heaven; whatever you bind on earth will be bound in heaven, and whatever you loose on earth will be loosed in heaven" (Matt. 16:19). Jesus says, "**Again, truly I tell you that if two of you on earth agree about anything they ask for, it will be done for them by my Father in heaven. For where two or three gather in my name, there am I with them**" (18:19–20). The context here is in terms of recovering persons from sin. He does say, "**anything they ask for,**" and we may tend to take it for other things, but think about it being said in the context and condition of recovering a brother from sin. "**There am I with them.**" Christ has promised to be with the Church by His Word and His Spirit, enable us to see clearly, and enable us to carry out His will.

The Matthew 18 process is a great blessing. If we do not deal with it in this way, we will deal with it in our own way, we will have our own private excommunications. We will have two people in the same church who worship in different places in the church and do not talk to each other. That will not be pleasing to God. We have to deal with it. If people do not hear and receive a gentler discipline through the church, then they will come under God's discipline. They will come under the curse. The curse can be intensified in any number of ways by the Lord, and God is able to humble their hearts. One way or another, it will be dealt with. It is better to deal with it properly in the church and go through the process. If it is not dealt with properly in the church, as against improperly, it will be dealt with by the Lord in His discipline. It is an act of mercy to use the Matthew 18 process to reclaim an offending brother or sister. Let us ask God for grace to do this. Think about anyone with whom we may have an offense; if it is still in our thoughts and our minds, we must deal with it. First, call the person, just you and that person, then thoughtfully, prayerfully, take one or two others along, and then to the church. Do not go in the spirit of, 'Boy, this is going straight to the Supreme Court. You've had it. We're done with you. Your goose is cooked.' No, that is not the spirit of it at all. It is to recover a lost, wandering brother or sister.

HOW MANY TIMES SHALL I FORGIVE?
SEVENTY TIMES SEVEN?

Our Lord Jesus tells us how to deal with sin. We have to confess that we come short. Consider this: "**Then Peter came to Jesus and asked, 'Lord, how many times shall I forgive my brother or sister who sins**

against me? Up to seven times?'" (18:21). We have difficulty forgiving because we think that if someone repents, then they will never do
it again. That is not the reality; that is not the truth. The truth is that
people will sin and sin again and again. Just because they keep speaking harshly or they keep doing the same thing over and over, that does
not mean they are not to be forgiven. If they confess their sin, repent,
and ask forgiveness, they will be forgiven. "Jesus said to him, 'I do not
say to you, up to seven times, but up to seventy times seven'" (18:22
NKJV). I have often heard, being in the position I am, especially between husbands and wives, the exasperation that comes in. 'Well, she
keeps doing it again and again,' or 'he keeps doing it again and again.'
And there is a reluctance to forgive. Peter asked, "Up to seven times?"
We may have a fear of marriage. We may think that if we have to forgive
that many times, then maybe it is better not to marry. No, let us put
this in perspective; let us get the reality: we are creatures, we are sinful
creatures, and we have to deal with sin. The Lord is telling us how we
are to deal with sin—and He is very right on. "Jesus said to him, 'I do
not say to you, up to seven times, but up to seventy times seven.'" This
number is not an exaggeration; it is *much* closer to reality than seven
times, to put it that way. Anyone who has been married knows this.

The Parable of the Unmerciful Servant: Forgive as We Have Been Forgiven

Jesus then told a parable:

> Therefore, the kingdom of heaven is like a king who wanted to
> settle accounts with his servants. As he began the settlement, a
> man who owed him ten thousand bags of gold was brought to
> him. Since he was not able to pay, the master ordered that he and
> his wife and his children and all that he had be sold to repay the
> debt (18:23–25).

That may seem harsh, but we have to start with the assumption that
it was appropriate in the story. You and yours are sold into slavery to
pay the debt. There is a debt that is owed, and it must be paid, and this
is part of what is required by justice. In this story, the man had nothing to pay the debt. "At this the servant fell on his knees before him.
'Be patient with me,' he begged, 'and I will pay back everything'"

(18:26). Paying back everything probably was not going to happen, but the servant came with that attitude. "**The servant's master took pity on him**"—mercy—"**canceled the debt and let him go**" (18:27). Jesus is making *one* point in this parable, so let us not run with it in other areas. "**But when that servant went out, he found one of his fellow servants who owed him a hundred silver coins**" (18:28a). That is like a few dollars; keep the contrast in mind: millions of dollars compared to a few dollars. How did he respond? "**He grabbed him and began to choke him**" (18:28b). That is not the way his master dealt with him.

> "**Pay back what you owe me!**" he demanded. His fellow servant fell to his knees and begged him, "**Be patient with me, and I will pay you back.**" But he refused. Instead, he went off and had the man thrown into prison until he could pay the debt. When the other servants saw what had happened, they were greatly distressed and went and told their master everything that had happened (18:28b–31).[8]

It says the other servants who saw this were distressed; they were greatly distressed. They told their master everything that happened.

> Then the master called the servant in. "**You wicked servant,**" he said, "**I canceled all that debt of yours because you begged me to. Shouldn't you have had mercy on your fellow servant just as I had on you?**" In anger his master turned him over to the jailers to be tortured, until he should pay back all he owed (18:32–34).

The Lord said, in answer to the question, how many times should I forgive? "**This is how my heavenly Father will treat each of you unless you forgive your brother or sister from your heart**" (18:35). Notice, we must forgive, not just outwardly with words, but "**from your heart.**" And what is He saying here? He contrasts how much we owe and to whom we owe. We owe to God millions of dollars compared with the debt that another one owes to us—a few dollars. Our self-life perspective fails to see it that way. We are keenly aware, because of our pride, and we ask, 'How could you possibly treat me this way? I don't deserve this. I deserve better. I deserve a whole lot better.' Well,

---

8. NIV 1984.

we fail to see where we are compared with God. Our dignity, our majesty, and our position are very, very small in comparison to God. If someone disregards us and treats us with some measure of contempt, that is *nothing* compared to the contempt that there is against God, who is all glorious in majesty and who reveals that glory clearly! It is this proportion between the majesty of God and ours that accounts for this great debt. We owe to God millions of dollars. God has made His revelation clear, and we have disregarded His revelation.[9] This is how we are to think about debt that is owed to us, and the debt that we owe to others, specifically to God. When we pray, "Forgive us our debts, as we forgive our debtors" (Matt. 6:12 NKJV), we have to ask ourselves, do we forgive as we have been forgiven? We have been forgiven millions of dollars; should we not forgive others, and should we not forgive from our hearts? If we have any real sense of our sin against God—and if we are believers, we would have this sense—we would forgive in this way. Our not forgiving is an indication that we do not realize forgiveness. We have not really confessed our sin and seen what great a debt must be forgiven us. This comes home to us very clearly in the case of marriage.

IS IT LAWFUL TO DIVORCE FOR
ANY AND EVERY REASON?

"Some Pharisees came to him to test him. They asked, 'Is it lawful for a man to divorce his wife for any and every reason?'" (19:3). There is going to be sin, there is going to be offense, there is going to be pain and trouble, and there are many, many ways in which this manifests. This is our closest relationship and where we find sin most. The habit of people was such that they found ways and brought about ways that they might divorce their wives for just about anything. They wanted Jesus' response to this question, "Is it lawful for a man to divorce his wife for any and every reason?" As they had distorted the law in other respects, they were doing so now. When they found some sort of displeasure against their wives, they were finding reasons to put them

---

9. Gangadean, "Paper No. 102: The Clarity of General Revelation," 527–529; "Paper No. 41: What Is Clear About God," 225–229; "Paper No. 112: Why General Revelation Is Basic in the Christian Worldview," in *The Logos Papers*, 583–585.

away. Men, in their ego, had the advantage in this way at this time
in history. What is especially important to remember, in terms of our
debt to God and the debt of another toward us, is that the husband/
wife relationship is revelatory of the relationship between us and God.
Men and women are alike in the spousal position to God. If we do not
forgive our spouse, that will reflect on how we have been forgiven by
our spouse, the Lord. The whole Church stands in the feminine role
to God. We have to keep this in mind from the earlier passage: "Forgive us our debts, as we also have forgiven our debtors" (Matt. 6:12).

The Origin and Purpose of the Covenant of Marriage

Jesus gave this teaching to the people concerning divorce: He goes
back to teach the truth about male and female in the beginning and
how they were made in the image of God. He said, **"Haven't you read
. . . that at the beginning the Creator 'made them male and female'"**
(19:4). There is a difference between men and women in how we are
created, and there is a purpose for which we were created. They were
to be fruitful, multiply, and replenish the earth and subdue it and have
dominion over it.[10] All of that dominion is to be in the context of glorifying God and filling the earth with the knowledge of God. When
Jesus goes back to speak about *how* God created, we should keep in
mind *why* God created. If we lose sight of this purpose, turn aside to
something else, and expect our spouse to follow our lead, we are already in trouble—we are not leading as we should under God. We are
already in a difficult situation. Jesus also says, **"For this reason a man
will leave his father and mother and be united to his wife, and the
two will become one flesh"** (19:5). There is a further difference made:
Men *leave* their fathers and mothers, and the daughters are *given* in
marriage. This has been practiced from when God brought the woman
to the man, to see what he would name her.[11] This is archetypical of
the father giving the daughter in marriage. There is a difference between the two; we have to go back to the first part, that God **"made
them male and female."** If we do not reckon with that, we will not
understand God's way and His will. Jesus speaks about the context of

---

10. *Genesis 1:28.*

11. *Genesis 2:22–23.*

marriage when He refers back to them being made male and female, and then He says that they are to become one flesh. One flesh is constitutive of a marriage. Man was one flesh (Adam), then what was one became two (Adam and Woman)—two persons, male and female—and those two were to become one flesh. The precepts of marriage are to be in place; the goal is to be in place. The goal is to be clearly in place if we are to avoid coming to strained situations and divorce. What God is making for us is a suitable helper; Woman was made for Adam as a suitable helper. We have to think about the original purpose when we think about marriage; that a husband would be able to lead, and a wife would be a suitable helper. She is to be a helper in the context of the goal of man's chief end, which is glorifying God.

I must remind you, that if you compromise the goal a little bit, you compromise it essentially, and the marriage will be compromised. You cannot afford to get your eyes off the purpose of marriage.[12] Man taking his eyes off of the good as the knowledge of God brought about all of the misery of mankind.[13] When Adam turned away from his purpose, he listened to the voice of his wife rather than the voice of God, and he put her before God. You might try to make your relationship directly between husband and wife rather than before God, and that is the error in Adam. If we do that, we are off. If we try to find enjoyment in our spouse in this way directly, apart from the purpose in God, it will go awry. The goal must be in place. As we look for a suitable helper, we should not be looking for things that are apart from the goal. The more we have the goal in mind, the more we can see clearly whether this other person is a suitable helper. Also, in the relationship, the husband has the particular responsibility to lead, to bring the Word of God, to nurture and encourage, so as the years go by in your marriage, it becomes more and more possible, more and more doable, more and more actual—working together to serve God in this way.

---

12. Gangadean, *Philosophical Foundation*, 245–254; Gangadean, "Paper No. 138: Concerning Marriage," in *The Logos Papers*, 695–700.

13. Gangadean, *The Biblical Worldview*, 37–54, 159–176.

Further Precepts: Preparation, Time and Season, Vows and Sanctions

There is a suitability, and it is not just in terms of our fancy, but in terms of God's purpose, to work towards this end. He says, "a man will leave his father and mother." He is not a boy. There is a time when he is to leave. We might say that the time for marriage is when you come to manhood, and by the time you come to manhood, you should be prepared for marriage. Being prepared involves a measure of maturity and the ability to take on responsibility. There is a time and a season for everything and a clear time for getting married. The Scripture has a particular reference to the wife of one's youth and building a life together from an early stage. There is something natural about beginning marriage from an early stage. We are to be prepared in every way, including financially prepared, and then we take vows, and there are sanctions. Marriage occurs in terms of the family when the father gives the daughter in marriage. Marriage occurs in terms of the minister in the church, who administers the vows, assesses that people can fulfill the vows, and may give counsel. Marriage occurs before a community of people who witness those taking the vows. Marriage occurs before the state, which sanctions marriage, and makes it a requirement. If all four communities (family, friends, Church, and State) and the requirements of all are regarded properly and respected, and they are supportive, then the marriage would be stable, and you would not have to wonder if you can divorce for any and every reason. That will not come up. Church, family, friends, and the State are all involved in marriage. The more of these that agree to and support the marriage, the more stable the marriage will be, and the more lasting it will be, and there will not be questions about reasons for divorce.

What God Has Joined Together, Let Man Not Separate

Jesus then went on to say, "So they are no longer two, but one. Therefore what God has joined together, let man not separate" (19:6).[14] We tend to reverse things. We tend to join together—what man joins together is not the same as what God joins together. Sometimes, something may seem right to us, but it is not necessarily right before God.

---

14. NIV 1984.

And when God has joined together, we find reasons to separate—we just reverse the order of things. Please note, **"what God has joined together, let man not separate,"** this includes both parties so joined. Neither husband nor wife has the freedom to separate what God has joined together in marriage.

Grounds for Divorce

The question is asked, **"Why then . . . did Moses command that a man give his wife a certificate of divorce and send her away?"** (19:7). Jesus says it is because of the hardness of their hearts. **"Moses permitted you to divorce your wives because your hearts were hard. But it was not this way from the beginning"** (19:8). And He specifies that the hardness of heart is not a sufficient reason for divorce. Only marital unfaithfulness is grounds for divorce. **"I tell you that anyone who divorces his wife, except for sexual immorality, and marries another woman commits adultery"** (19:9). When one is sexually unfaithful, or when one leaves the marriage bed—a willful forsaking that cannot be remedied by the Church or by the State[15]—that becomes grounds for divorce and nothing else. The many other reasons, such as 'incompatibility,' and the multitude of such reasons that people come up with, are not grounds for divorce. That thinking has affected the Church, and people in the Church may also find other reasons for divorce besides marital unfaithfulness. This infidelity is usually at a stage far down the road; there should have been offenses being dealt with properly long before it came to that. Jesus makes clear what the grounds for divorce are.

Better Not to Marry? Marriage in God Is a Blessing

One of the responses that comes is, 'If this is the case, if this is the situation and you can't just walk out of it, it's better not to marry!' **"The disciples said to him, 'If this is the situation between a husband and wife, it is better not to marry'"** (19:10). Many people have that fear. You have to recognize that you have to forgive in marriage, and deal with offenses properly, and if you have the goal in place, a lot of ground is covered. If you have the goal in place, and you are suitably matched, according to God's purpose and the way He has made you, then a lot

---

15. Gangadean, *The Westminster Confession*, 265–273.

of this strain and trouble will not come up. But we are sinners; we do not apply these things consistently, and we have a lot of strain in our marriages. Some who are not married may be looking on and thinking, 'Well, maybe I should not get married because there are going to be difficulties, there will be trouble in the flesh.' There is a fear of marriage, particularly in light of all the divorces that are around us today. It should not be so; it is not so in God. Marriage in God is a good thing; it is a blessing.

We should recognize clearly the difference between marriage without God—or only with God nominally—and marriage in God. That is, a marriage truly, seriously, and faithfully in God. *That* would be a blessing. By the grace of God, today is 40 years since Patricia and I have been married. I thank God for that. There have been struggles, but God's grace has been there. I thank God for my life partner. It is by the grace of God that we have come to this point, and I hope that by the grace of God, it will only get better. I am able to confide in her as I can in no one else, and I can share with her. I look forward to those times when we sit together, we just talk and share, and we have gotten to know each other. It is much better at this point than it was in the beginning. Yes, there were all those *feelings* in the beginning, certainly, and that is great, but it gets better by the grace of God. This is the way it should be. I thank God for His grace in our lives and for blessing us in this way. I want to say that this grace comes to all of us—all of us— as we seek the Lord and seek to grow in Him. I think that is what has kept us together; we both have this common goal of the kingdom of God. We started way back, when we were in popular Christianity, but there was a fundamental commitment to the Word of God and to the kingdom of God, and God caused us to grow and to grow together. I remember walking out of one church and Patricia not being ready to walk out of that one, then walking out of another church and Patricia not being ready to walk out of that one, either. She had just made all her friends there. She was not ready to make decisions on the basis of doctrine, but there was a fundamental commitment to the Scriptures. We could talk, and come to agreement, and we could grow together. It was part of my responsibility to bring the Word and to communicate it, and it was the grace of God that blessed us in this so that we can come to this point in our marriage. I say that by way of thankfulness to God for His grace, and by way of encouragement, if possible, to you, that marriage in God is a blessing.

When they said to him,

> "It is better not to marry." Jesus replied, "Not everyone can accept this word, but only those to whom it has been given. For some are eunuchs because they were born that way; others were made that way by men; and others have renounced marriage because of the kingdom of heaven. The one who can accept this should accept it" (19:10b–12).[16]

One is not to renounce marriage because of a secondary concern, but because of the kingdom of God and the way God calls one to work in the kingdom. Those who are able, who can accept this, *should* accept it, but not everyone should. The Scripture warns us, "It is better to marry than to burn with passion" (1 Cor. 7:9b). We have to cultivate that relationship, understand the reality of sin, and then work through sin, biblically, by the grace of God. Brothers and sisters in Christ, may you confess the truth of God's Word concerning marriage, that it is ordained of God, it is a blessing of God, and not everyone can be single. May we put away our fears concerning being married, and be prepared to do the good and gracious work of growing together in our marriages. May the Lord bless us in this. Amen.

16. NIV 1984.

17

KINGDOM ETHICS

Sacrificial Service and Reward
in the Kingdom

Matthew 19:13–20:34

¹⁹:¹³Then people brought little children to Jesus for him to place his hands on them and pray for them. But the disciples rebuked them.

¹⁴Jesus said, "Let the little children come to me, and do not hinder them, for the kingdom of heaven belongs to such as these." ¹⁵When he had placed his hands on them, he went on from there.

¹⁶Just then a man came up to Jesus and asked, "Teacher, what good thing must I do to get eternal life?"

¹⁷"Why do you ask me about what is good?" Jesus replied. "There is only One who is good. If you want to enter life, keep the commandments."

¹⁸"Which ones?" he inquired.

Jesus replied, "'You shall not murder, you shall not commit adultery, you shall not steal, you shall not give false testimony, ¹⁹honor your father and mother,' and 'love your neighbor as yourself.'"

²⁰"All these I have kept," the young man said. "What do I still lack?"

²¹Jesus answered, "If you want to be perfect, go, sell your possessions and give to the poor, and you will have treasure in heaven. Then come, follow me."

²²When the young man heard this, he went away sad, because he had great wealth.

²³Then Jesus said to his disciples, "Truly I tell you, it is hard for someone who is rich to enter the kingdom of heaven. ²⁴Again I tell you, it is easier

for a camel to go through the eye of a needle than for someone who is rich to enter the kingdom of God."

²⁵When the disciples heard this, they were greatly astonished and asked, "Who then can be saved?"

²⁶Jesus looked at them and said, "With man this is impossible, but with God all things are possible."

²⁷Peter answered him, "We have left everything to follow you! What then will there be for us?"

²⁸Jesus said to them, "Truly I tell you, at the renewal of all things, when the Son of Man sits on his glorious throne, you who have followed me will also sit on twelve thrones, judging the twelve tribes of Israel. ²⁹And everyone who has left houses or brothers or sisters or father or mother or wife or children or fields for my sake will receive a hundred times as much and will inherit eternal life. ³⁰But many who are first will be last, and many who are last will be first.

20:1"For the kingdom of heaven is like a landowner who went out early in the morning to hire workers for his vineyard. ²He agreed to pay them a denarius for the day and sent them into his vineyard.

³"About nine in the morning he went out and saw others standing in the marketplace doing nothing. ⁴He told them, 'You also go and work in my vineyard, and I will pay you whatever is right.' ⁵So they went.

"He went out again about noon and about three in the afternoon and did the same thing. ⁶About five in the afternoon he went out and found still others standing around. He asked them, 'Why have you been standing here all day long doing nothing?'

⁷"'Because no one has hired us,' they answered.

"He said to them, 'You also go and work in my vineyard.'

⁸"When evening came, the owner of the vineyard said to his foreman, 'Call the workers and pay them their wages, beginning with the last ones hired and going on to the first.'

⁹"The workers who were hired about five in the afternoon came and each received a denarius. ¹⁰So when those came who were hired first, they expected to receive more. But each one of them also received a denarius. ¹¹When they received it, they began to grumble against the landowner. ¹²'These who were hired last worked only one hour,' they said, 'and you have made them equal to us who have borne the burden of the work and the heat of the day.'

[13]"But he answered one of them, 'I am not being unfair to you, friend. Didn't you agree to work for a denarius? [14]Take your pay and go. I want to give the one who was hired last the same as I gave you. [15]Don't I have the right to do what I want with my own money? Or are you envious because I am generous?'

[16]"So the last will be first, and the first will be last."

[17]Now Jesus was going up to Jerusalem. On the way, he took the Twelve aside and said to them, [18]"We are going up to Jerusalem, and the Son of Man will be delivered over to the chief priests and the teachers of the law. They will condemn him to death [19]and will hand him over to the Gentiles to be mocked and flogged and crucified. On the third day he will be raised to life!"

[20]Then the mother of Zebedee's sons came to Jesus with her sons and, kneeling down, asked a favor of him.

[21]"What is it you want?" he asked.

She said, "Grant that one of these two sons of mine may sit at your right and the other at your left in your kingdom."

[22]"You don't know what you are asking," Jesus said to them. "Can you drink the cup I am going to drink?"

"We can," they answered.

[23]Jesus said to them, "You will indeed drink from my cup, but to sit at my right or left is not for me to grant. These places belong to those for whom they have been prepared by my Father."

[24]When the ten heard about this, they were indignant with the two brothers. [25]Jesus called them together and said, "You know that the rulers of the Gentiles lord it over them, and their high officials exercise authority over them. [26]Not so with you. Instead, whoever wants to become great among you must be your servant, [27]and whoever wants to be first must be your slave—[28]just as the Son of Man did not come to be served, but to serve, and to give his life as a ransom for many."

[29]As Jesus and his disciples were leaving Jericho, a large crowd followed him. [30]Two blind men were sitting by the roadside, and when they heard that Jesus was going by, they shouted, "Lord, Son of David, have mercy on us!"

[31]The crowd rebuked them and told them to be quiet, but they shouted all the louder, "Lord, Son of David, have mercy on us!"

[32]Jesus stopped and called them. "What do you want me to do for you?" he asked.

³³"Lord," they answered, "we want our sight."

³⁴Jesus had compassion on them and touched their eyes. Immediately they received their sight and followed him.

INTRODUCTION:
Kingdom Ethics—The Reversal of Ordinary Expectation

W E CONTINUE NOW IN MATTHEW 19, AND we need to remember the context. The larger context that we should keep in mind is that of *kingdom ethics*. We encountered the teaching of our Lord Jesus Christ in Matthew 5, which considered how we should live in the kingdom—the Beatitudes. Now, we are looking at the time since the Transfiguration. Remember the context: He is the Christ, He must suffer before entering into His glory. That mindset, that attitude, is not there in His disciples, and He has to teach them again, and again, and again, and again. We see four instances where he must teach them again after the Transfiguration.

First, there is the healing of the epileptic boy with a demon and the disciples' lack of faith—their lack of understanding, trust, and obedience to God in dealing with this demon possession properly. Second, there is the instruction on the temple tax, who the king is, and who the children of the kingdom are—He instructs Peter concerning this. Third is the disciples' question about who is the greatest in the kingdom. Jesus brings a little child and has him stand in the midst of them, and He speaks to them about the attitude of a child in the kingdom. If you were to try and derive from one of the Ten Commandments that we should be childlike, which one would you choose? It is not so immediately apparent, but it is certainly there in the first commandment that God is our Creator; we are creatures and utterly dependent on our Creator as children. But we do not translate it in that way. We might speak about proof for the existence of God and clarity, and that is certainly needed, it is a starting point, but that is by no means the ending point. We have to translate the implication of God as Creator for ourselves and for our day-by-day, moment-by-moment relation to Him. We must set aside our attitude and tendency toward autonomy and independence, and we must trust and obey God. That is where our lives are being lived out. Jesus "called a little child to him and placed the child among them. And he said: 'truly I tell you, unless you change and become like little children, you will never enter the kingdom of heaven'" (Matt. 18:2–3). And we certainly will not progress in the kingdom unless we have that continuous attitude of God as our Creator and our Redeemer, and we are utterly dependent on Him. Therefore, we should trust in Him for everything.

I know that this is the big struggle in my life, and, I dare say, in all of our lives, the daily trust in the Lord for every circumstance and every situation that comes up in all of our trials. The Lord is pushing us and pressing us in every way through our trials, the trials of our faith, to come to know Him better and to trust in Him. Think about how you have lived out your life this past week, how you count your days, how you apply your hearts to wisdom's ways. Think about whether you have peace and joy in the Holy Spirit, whether you have a sense of the love of God with you. Consider whether you are burdened or you have a sense of gratitude and peace before God. Creaturely dependance is an area of struggle for all of us, and Jesus is teaching us. *Kingdom ethics* is radically different from the ethics of the world; it is the very opposite. Instead of recognizing the existence of God and our creatureliness and dependence on Him, we put ourselves in the place of God to determine good and evil, and all kinds of disasters fall out from that. This includes the fear and the lack of peace that is often in our lives. That is part of the death that comes and we need to recognize it as such.

Jesus is teaching the way of the kingdom to His disciples. He teaches them about who is the greatest, and then He follows with the lost sheep, the recovery of this lost one, and then connects that with forgiving and receiving each other up to seventy times seven. Again, that is very different from the way of the world. In the world, you do not forgive, you get revenge, you get even, or you just forget that person and write them off. The Lord teaches us how we are to deal with offenses. Going to the other person is part of reclaiming. The ethics of the kingdom is different from the ethics of the world, and it is different from the ethics of the self-life. We need to reckon with that and learn to live in the ethics of the kingdom. Jesus then teaches about divorce, the basis of marriage, God's purpose in marriage, and how we are to live according to that understanding. We are to understand the purpose of marriage, the goal of dominion, the knowledge of God, and the actual joy that comes from marriage in knowing God. Remember, man's chief end is to glorify God—to know His glory, to make His glory known, and to enjoy Him forever.[1] The place where we are to do this is where we are—where God has placed us in His providence. Certainly, there are other dimensions to consider. We are not just passively in this situation; we are before God and actively moving toward the goal. However, while we are moving toward the goal, we are going through all kinds of circumstances. We are learning as we go through these circumstances on our way to the goal. We are learning to be in fellowship with one another, and we are learning to forgive, to encourage, and to restore each other. We will come to the account of the little children brought to Jesus and the rich young ruler. Jesus is teaching *kingdom ethics*—a reversal of what one would ordinarily expect.

LET THE LITTLE CHILDREN COME TO ME:
False Expectations of the Kingdom

There is an interesting thing about little children and the rich young man. If we wanted to build a kingdom, we would seek out the rich young man, wouldn't we? What do little children have to give? All they do is they get, they get, they get, and they get. Our attitude about the kingdom and how it works is that we would tend to seek out the rich young ruler. There is a contrast between these two ways, and there is a context, *kingdom ethics*, and what the Lord is teaching His disciples.

Between the Transfiguration and the entry into Jerusalem, "**people brought little children to Jesus for him to place his hands on them and pray for them. But the disciples rebuked them**" (19:13). They brought children for Him to place His hands on them—to touch, to receive, to hold, to embrace, and to pray for them. They brought children to Jesus in the expectation that He would be a great king. The people may have thought, 'He touched my baby. My baby is important. This king is important, and my child is connected in this way through the sense of touch.' Isn't that right? But the disciples rebuked them. The disciples are three years into the program and do not get it! They may have thought, 'We have more important things to do, lady. Take your child away. How could you come at this time? We have important things to do!' Do you see their expectations about the kingdom? The disciples

---

1. Gangadean, *The Westminster Catechisms*, 3–4, 109–111.

rebuked those who were bringing the little children to Jesus. We must ask, is there something in our hearts about what the kingdom is, what is important, and what we expect? We tend to look for the rich young ruler because we think that he has got a lot to give. Rich rulers are the persons with whom you build a kingdom, right? But Jesus says, in the King James Version, "**Suffer little children, and forbid them not, to come unto me: for of such is the kingdom of heaven**" (19:14), and in the NIV, "**do not hinder them.**" What a perfect answer. It is just what you would expect—the way it *should* be.

We tend to build our big programs and get connected with the important people, but nothing is as important as children. We tend not to think that they are important, but they are important to the parents. Jesus recognizes this, and He is the giver of life, the giver of children, and these are to be raised up in the nurture and admonition of the Lord. So He says, "**Suffer little children, and forbid them not, to come unto me: for of such is the kingdom of heaven.**" And, "**When he had placed his hands on them, he went on from there**" (19:15). Does that tell you something about the reversal in *kingdom ethics*? Remember this reversal. Now, that does not mean there is no place for the rich young ruler; there is a place at the end of the line. Little children are first, rich young rulers are last, and we will see if the rich young ruler makes it into the line.

THE RICH YOUNG RULER:
Store Up Treasures in Heaven

"**Just then a man came up to Jesus and asked, 'Teacher, what good thing must I do to get eternal life?'**" (19:16). He was a rich young man—Luke says he was a rich ruler—and he came to Jesus and asked this question. He may be thinking, 'Wow, the Lord is working here.' Some finally started to come out of the woodwork and get with the program. He asks, "**What good thing must I do to get eternal life?**" He seems to be asking just the right question. Jesus looks at some of the assumptions and the very fact that he is asking this question. He should know the answer. The young man calls Him "**Good Teacher.**"[2] He came calling Him a good master, showing a certain amount of

---

2. NKJV.

affirmation of the honor of Jesus, and Jesus did not want him to use that term lightly. Jesus answered, **"Why do you call Me good? No one is good but One, that is, God"** (19:17a NKJV). Then He answered the question: **"If you want to enter life, keep the commandments"** (19:17b). Please notice the *kingdom ethics*; He speaks about life and the Commandments. We need to translate the Commandments beyond attitudes and into our daily actions.

For the young man, there is something amiss when Jesus says, **"Obey the commandments."**[3] That should have satisfied him as an answer, but he asks, **"Which ones?"** (19:18a). Jesus is patient and answers, **"'You shall not murder, you shall not commit adultery, you shall not steal, you shall not give false testimony, honor your father and mother,' and 'love your neighbor as yourself'"** (19:18b–19). With a measure of truth, the young ruler responds, **"All these I have kept . . . What do I still lack?"** (19:20). He was aware that something was lacking in his life. He came to Jesus, and he wanted life. Many came to Jesus, and Jesus did not turn away the rich young ruler, He did not turn away children, He did not turn away the prostitute, He did not turn away the tax collector, He did not turn away the Pharisees, the religious rulers, He did not turn away Nicodemus; He did not turn away anyone. This young man is aware of his lack: 'What do I still lack? Somehow, I've been obeying the Commandments, but I don't have this life. Something is missing here.' **"Jesus answered, 'If you want to be perfect, go, sell your possessions and give to the poor, and you will have treasure in heaven. Then come, follow me'"** (19:21). Notice the entire answer: If you want to be perfect—complete and whole—sell your possessions, give to the poor, and have treasure in heaven—all of those go together—then come, follow Me. **"When the young man heard this, he went away sad, because he had great wealth"** (19:22).

It is perhaps more proper to say his great wealth had him. He was a servant to that way of life, and wealth was the key to that kingdom—the earthy kingdom. He had one foot firmly planted in the earthly kingdom and another foot reaching out, touching, testing the waters, but not there yet. There was an excitement and an attraction to the kingdom of God, but he was still in the kingdom of the world in his thinking, so he could not give that up, and he could not give up his wealth. He

---

3. NIV 1984.

could not see a difference between the earthy treasures and the treasure in heaven in selling his wealth and giving to the poor. Monastics have used this passage to establish vows of poverty; Francis of Assisi did, as did others. We are not to simply presume that it is wrong to have wealth, but it is wrong to put our *trust* in riches, to put our dependence on riches, and to seek riches to ease our way and bring comfort; that is the problem. The attitude of this young man's heart was revealed, and he went away sad because Jesus put his finger on it.

Jesus knew what was holding the young man. Many speak about applying the law of God. Jesus does not just say, 'You shall not covet.' He did not mention that in this passage, but that was what was happening. The young man had his heart set on these earthly things and had his trust and comfort in them. 'Wouldn't it be great to have success in this world and have Jesus, too? They can be side by side.' That is basically what worship is, whether you go to the Rigveda or the Shamans in North America or wherever you go; basically, they want success, power, and pleasure: Baal worship and Ashtoreth. We desire a sense of success and blessing in this world. Jesus is teaching us again and again and again about His kingdom—this new vision, this new goal. The young man came right up against it, and Jesus put His finger on his trusting in wealth, his covetousness, and his desire to have riches before the kingdom of God. He was exposed, he had no more questions, and went away sad.

We do not know what happened; we would like to think that perhaps later on, by the grace of God, he came to repentance, but maybe he did not. We have to have our hearts set on things above, not on things below. What are the things that are above? The things above are the knowledge of God—the knowledge of the glory of God that is revealed in all of life.[4] We are not spiritualizing this and taking it away from the creation and history. The knowledge of God's glory fills the earth in every dimension of life. That is our treasure as we diligently seek Him. He is a rewarder of those who seek Him.[5] We will not get this treasure without seeking. We have to strip ourselves in the process of seeking and set aside those things that hinder us in the process of

---

4. Gangadean, *Philosophical Foundation*, 171–177, 208–211; Gangadean, *The Westminster Catechisms*, 109–111, 321–325; Gangadean, *On Natural and Revealed Theology*, 33–39, 127–139.

5. *Hebrews 11:6.*

seeking. The cares of this life often choke the Word.[6] That is some-thing that I know I have to guard against. Just something like putting away the plants, getting them all in one place so that they can be wa-tered conveniently, putting shade over the plants so they do not burn or get too hot, that becomes the care. All those things that take time. Sometimes having house plants and caring for them is a bit of a chore; when you leave, you have to have a house sitter. What are you going to do without a house sitter? The choking of the Word can come up in these little things. It seems so mundane, but we have to go through it, and hopefully, we go through it trusting in God, looking to God, and thanking God for helping us just to get more organized. One of these days, we will have a micro misting system that waters the plants automatically and has a little timer. The cares of this world can choke us, and it is not always a matter of money; it is just the ordinary things. So we do not seek the Lord diligently.

"Then Jesus said to his disciples, 'Truly I tell you, it is hard for someone who is rich to enter the kingdom of heaven'" (19:23). Why is it hard? Because we put our trust in riches. Christ illustrates this so dramatically: "Again I tell you, it is easier for a camel to go through the eye of a needle than for someone who is rich to enter the kingdom of God" (19:24). We have heard this enough to be familiar with it, but this was the response of the disciples: "When the disciples heard this, they were greatly astonished" (19:25a). This is so contrary to their expectations. The disciples had been operating with the gospel of suc-cess and power. There is a lot of that thinking in Christendom. 'You can have riches, and you can have Jesus, too.' American Christianity is largely influenced by this thinking and we do not know what it is to be without and to suffer need. A greater part of Christendom outside of the United States is in a state of need. "They were greatly astonished and asked, 'Who then can be saved?'" (19:25b). The saved, accord-ing to the disciples, are the successful and those blessed with money. They perhaps thought that success and riches were a sign of salvation. "They were greatly astonished." Jesus was repeatedly teaching them about *kingdom ethics*—there is a reversal.

"Jesus looked at them and said, 'With man this is impossible, but with God all things are possible'" (19:26). God is able to save even the

---

6. *Matthew 13:1–23.*

rich. The obstacle of trusting in riches becomes a temptation for those who have wealth. God can save us from this and bring us to see Him, trust Him, and use our riches rightly in service in the kingdom. God can save us so that our riches do not possess us, but we possess these riches for the kingdom. This is a very different view. This is *kingdom ethics*. Peter now speaks up, **"We have left everything to follow you!"** (19:27a). We should not underestimate the fact that these disciples have left a lot more than we have left, and they are expecting certain kinds of rewards. How did the Lord respond?

> **Jesus said to them, "Truly I tell you, at the renewal of all things, when the Son of Man sits on his glorious throne, you who have followed me will also sit on twelve thrones, judging the twelve tribes of Israel. And everyone who has left houses or brothers or sisters or father or mother or children or fields for my sake will receive a hundred times as much and will inherit eternal life"** (19:28–29).

Jesus is not to be outdone. Remember when they left their work of fishing? The last thing Jesus did before they left their work of fishing was to show them who was boss. "He said, 'Throw your net on the right side of the boat and you will find some.' When they did, they were unable to haul the net in because of the large number of fish" (Jn. 21:6). At the command of Jesus, there can be wealth. If He does not give wealth, it is because He wants us to learn to trust Him and obey Him. I have no doubt that God could raise up funds as it pleases Him, but this is not His ordinary way. He can provide with wealth, but we are not looking for that. We trust that God will bless us, help us by the means He has given us, and cause us to abound in grace and rejoice in Him in this way. We are to be faithful in what we have and know that God is able to supply. God is able to give a hundredfold what we may give up *and* eternal life. This is what the rich young man did not see; he sought to save his life, and he lost it.[7] The disciples, by contrast, are barely coming through. They are still not understanding, and they do not have mature faith. But, they did come, in contrast with the world, and they will have a hundredfold plus eternal life. **"But many who are first will be last, and many who are last will be first"** (19:30).

---

7. *Matthew 16:25.*

THE PARABLE OF THE WORKERS IN THE VINEYARD:
Reward and Expectation

Jesus enforces the teaching that the last will be first in the parable of the workers in the vineyard. Notice the reversal of expectation in terms of how things work in the kingdom of man and how things work in the kingdom of God. *Kingdom ethics* is radically different; it is the reversal of expectation.

> For the kingdom of heaven is like a landowner who went out early in the morning to hire workers for his vineyard. He agreed to pay them a denarius for the day and sent them into his vineyard (20:1–2).

I am reminded of the day laborers in many places around Phoenix and those who hire them. Sometimes they go out at six o'clock in the morning, hire them, and send them off to work. This landowner goes out several times during the day. I can see that there may be someone who did not get hired all day waiting out there, and they are found at the eleventh hour.

> About nine in the morning he went out and saw others standing in the marketplace doing nothing. He told them, "You also go and work in my vineyard, and I will pay you whatever is right." So they went. He went out again around noon and about three in the afternoon and did the same thing. About five in the afternoon he went out and found still others standing around. He asked them, "Why have you been standing here all day long doing nothing?" "Because no one has hired us," they answered. He said to them, "You also go and work in my vineyard" (20:3–7).

This landowner goes out early in the morning, then goes out at the third hour, which is about nine o'clock, and then goes out at the sixth and ninth hours. That is at noon and three o'clock. Imagine going out at three o'clock to find day laborers. Then, he goes out at five o'clock, which is the eleventh hour. Dramatic, isn't it? No one hired them. This day laborer example can be translated, not only to a *day* in one person's life, but it can translate to a whole *lifetime*. Some come into the kingdom late in their lives, and some come in early. Some nations come into the kingdom of God late in *history*. Think about Israel, who was early—first—and then think about the 'first and the last' teaching our Lord is bringing.

> When evening came, the owner of the vineyard said to his foreman, "Call the workers and pay them their wages, beginning with the last ones hired and going on to the first." The workers who were hired about the eleventh hour came and each received a denarius. So when those came who were hired first, they expected to receive more. But each one of them also received a denarius (20:8–10).

Notice the expectation of those who were hired first. They expected to receive more. This is the reversal; this is *kingdom ethics*. But each one of them also received a denarius.

> When they received it, they began to grumble against the land-owner. "These who were hired last worked only one hour," they said, "and you have made them equal to us who have borne the burden of the work and the heat of the day" (20:11–12).

Notice the complaint that those hired last were made "equal to us." I do not know how many of you do work and labor outside. I have worked outside, and I have asked others who labor outside how it is. I know what it is to do the burden of the work in the heat of the day— to have a long, full day's work. At the end of the day, you are glad for your wages, and if you find someone coming in late getting more, you might say, 'Boy, it'd be nice to be proportionate here!' But it was not that way. I know among us, we can have rivalries. We may say, 'Well, it just doesn't seem equal. If they work one hour and they get the same as us, it just doesn't seem equal!' We have those thoughts cross our minds. 'They came in late. Why should they be treated the same as the rest of us?' Then we may think, 'Well, maybe next time I'll come in late and get the same.' We have ways of figuring it out, or thinking we can figure it out. Jesus got to a deeper matter, and it was the same thing that was troubling the rich young ruler. "But he answered one of them, 'I am not being unfair to you, friend. Didn't you agree to work for a denarius?'" (20:13). This is contractual justice; there was an agreement. "Take your pay and go. I want to give the man who was hired last the same as I gave you" (20:14). The landowner said to the one whom he hired at the third hour, "**I will pay you whatever is right**" (20:4b). It is certainly fair when he paid them what was agreed upon. He says, "**I want to give the man who was hired last the same as I gave you. Don't I have the right to do what I want with my own money?**" (20:14b–15a). We should say yes in the context of the kingdom of God and His purpose.

"**Or are you envious because I am generous?**" (20:15b). Here is another way in which a love of money is operating. There is envy of others rather than serving the Lord. Jesus enforces the teaching regarding *kingdom ethics* as He applied it to the rich young ruler: "**So the last will be first, and the first will be last**" (20:16). God's grace is sovereign. Certainly, justice is never violated, but justice does not prevent grace from operating. If you want justice, you can have justice, but if you want justice, you will have the wages of sin, which is death.[8] We are to be thankful for the grace of God, recognize that all of us receive the grace of God, and recognize the difference between justice and grace. When it is applied to the work of the kingdom and what our reward is in the kingdom, that grace cannot be taken from us. He who works abundantly will receive abundant fruit. There are several things we need to think about and work through further regarding working hard in the kingdom and having greater reward and greater fruit. A lot of that depends on what we think our reward is, but here we are speaking about equality. The concern here is not to be envious and to understand that the first will be last and the last will be first. If we believe that our reward is in knowing Him—He is the rewarder of those who diligently seek Him[9]—we would not want that reward just for ourselves; we would want it for everyone. There is no sense of a greater reward; there is a reward in seeking Him, but it is not comparative and *greater than*. The blessing is in seeing others enjoy God. If that is the blessing in the kingdom of God, why would we compare ourselves and be envious? It is not to be that way in the kingdom.

In this context, Jesus speaks of His death:

Now as Jesus was going up to Jerusalem. On the way, he took the Twelve aside and said to them, "We are going up to Jerusalem,

---

8. *Romans 6:23.*

9. *Hebrews 11:6* KJV.

and the Son of Man will be delivered over to the chief priests and the teachers of the law. They will condemn him to death and will hand him over to the Gentiles to be mocked and flogged and crucified. On the third day he will be raised to life!" (20:17–19).

Again, He is reminding the disciples of what is to come; they are to expect His death and not a false view of the kingdom. His death is going to come by the leaders, contrary to what they may expect; He is going to be "mocked and flogged and crucified. On the third day he will be raised to life!" Jesus is preparing His disciples, yet they are not hearing. They have difficulty hearing, they do not know what to expect, and they are discombobulated. We have a hard time understanding *kingdom ethics* because we have the flesh, the self-life, and the world with us. We have a difficult time breaking away from the world. Our self-life is being reinforced and encouraged greatly by the world.

A MOTHER'S REQUEST:
Ruling with Christ—Imitating His Humility

We come to the event of a mother coming to Jesus. If I were James and John, I would be embarrassed to have my mother come and talk to Jesus about sitting at His right hand and His left hand. You know how mothers are; this is their life investment, and they want to see their children succeed. They want to see their children at Jesus' right hand and left hand. The mother and James and John do not have a clear view of the kingdom. They do not have a clear view of how it works, and they are still thinking in worldly terms about the kingdom. This event is another occasion by which we are taught *kingdom ethics*—the kingdom *ethos*, the way of feeling, and attitude, and being in the world. Let us see what the mother says.

When a mother comes, being a mother, she has a powerful argument with Jesus; how could Jesus refuse a mom? Some have made a great deal about this: 'Jesus cannot refuse His own mom, so go to Mary, and if Mary asks Jesus, you know you will get what you ask for.' We have this attitude that mothers will get what they ask for. I wonder if the mom initiated this or whether James and John did, because Jesus speaks to them as if they were there. It could be embarrassing; they could get hit upside the head by the other disciples. Once the mom gets out of the picture, the guys are going to beat them up for trying that: 'Don't ever pull that again, okay?'

> Then the mother of Zebedee's sons came to Jesus with her sons and, kneeling down, asked a favor of him. "What is it you want?" he asked. She said, "Grant that one of these two sons of mine may sit at your right and the other at your left in your kingdom" (20:20–21).

She goes for the big one; she goes for the jugular. That is where the jugular is for women, right? They want to see their children succeed. Of course, it is not a bad thing to be on the right hand and left hand of Jesus in His kingdom. How could that be bad? It depends on how you think of Jesus and His kingdom. Apparently, they are not thinking about this right. Jesus said to the mother and James and John, "'You don't know what you are asking,' Jesus said to them. 'Can you drink the cup I am going to drink?' 'We can,' they answered" (20:22). What had Jesus just told them? He is going to be "mocked and flogged and crucified. On the third day he will be raised to life!" (20:19). Now, James, the brother of John, was killed early on in the persecution. John lived to the end; he did not die by martyrdom, according to the account.

> "We can," they answered. Jesus said to them, "You will indeed drink from my cup, but to sit at my right or left is not for me to grant. These places belong to those for whom they have been prepared by my Father." When the ten heard about this, they were indignant with the two brothers (20:22b–24).

I expect the guys are going to be saying, 'You brought your mom? I can't believe you did that—mommy's boy.' Don't the brothers deserve that? That is the right response, isn't it? 'Can you believe that these guys would do a thing like that?' "They were indignant." James and John are in trouble. Jesus put it in perspective:

> Jesus called them together and said, "You know that the rulers of the Gentiles lord it over them, and their high officials exercise authority over them. Not so with you. Instead, whoever wants to become great among you must be your servant, and whoever wants to be first must be your slave—just as the Son of Man did

not come to be served, but to serve, and to give his life as a ransom for many" (20:25–28).

He had just spoken about giving His life.[10] There are other things in this passage that connect with being a servant, such as the very fact that the mother brought her sons. The arch-example of service is parents caring for their children. Do you want to be first in the kingdom? Serve as a parent does for a child—up late at night, cleaning the diapers, brushing their teeth, giving them baths, day in and day out, year after year after year for the littlest ones in the kingdom. Doesn't that seem so right? Isn't that what parents who are in authority are about? It seems so natural, and Jesus is bringing attention to service—not to rule and be served by others, but to serve. There is no greater example of service than parents caring for their little children at every moment. You know you can pay someone to do that? But this is done out of love. Little children wake you up late at night, and when you hear the child's crying, you are up and there caring for the kids. That is what work in the kingdom is like; that is how it is to be a servant. It is not far away from us; we can understand that, can't we? You pour out your life year in and year out. Even when they are 35, you are still serving; you never stop serving. Even when they leave home, you still care for and serve them.

The way parents serve is a good example, close to all of us, of how we are to serve and not get any big ideas about being served by others. Jesus comes to serve. Jesus put His hands on the little children, blessed them, and told the disciples to let them come. He is continually correcting false expectations and bringing in the law of God worked out in detail in the concrete instances of life. That is the beauty of these passages compared with the Beatitudes. The Beatitudes are being spelled out in concrete life examples—this is *kingdom ethics*.

TWO BLIND MEN RECEIVE THEIR SIGHT:
Jesus Came to Serve

The last point in this message is how Jesus comes to serve.

---

10. *Matthew 20:18–19.*

> As Jesus and his disciples were leaving Jericho, a large crowd followed him. Two blind men were sitting by the roadside, and when they heard that Jesus was going by, they shouted, "Lord, Son of David, have mercy on us!" The crowd rebuked them and told them to be quiet (20:29–31a).

The crowd says, 'Just mind your manners and keep your place. Important things are going on here. Jesus is going up to Jerusalem.' But they do not understand what the kingdom is about; He came to give sight to the blind! That is what it is about. The crowd had contrary expectations about what the kingdom is about. Notice the faith of the blind men: **"but they shouted all the louder"** (20:31). They shouted all the louder because they saw something about Jesus and His compassion.

> "Lord, Son of David, have mercy on us!" Jesus stopped and called them. "What do you want me to do for you?" he asked. "Lord," they answered, "we want our sight." Jesus had compassion on them and touched their eyes. Immediately they received their sight and followed him (20:31b–34).

Compassion is what Jesus is about, what we are to be about, and what His kingdom is about. Do you see His example and the cumulative effect of it? Do you see the reversal, the astonishment, the teaching? This is the One we serve. This is the One who is high above all else: "he humbled himself and became obedient to death—even death on a cross! Therefore God exalted him to the highest place and gave him the name that is above every name" (Phil. 2:8b–9). Jesus knows what is important, Jesus knows what the good is, He has His values clearly in focus and He lived according to them, and lived sinlessly, pleasing God. He was fully righteous and able to save us from the uttermost. Let us keep coming to Jesus. Through His Word in prayer, keep coming to Him, keep learning of Him, and keep being transformed into His image. As we come to the Lord's Table, we are to come remembering Him as He has revealed Himself to us.

———

18

JESUS' EXPECTATION
The Crisis of the World

Matthew 21

¹As they approached Jerusalem and came to Bethphage on the Mount of Olives, Jesus sent two disciples, ²saying to them, "Go to the village ahead of you, and at once you will find a donkey tied there, with her colt by her. Untie them and bring them to me. ³If anyone says anything to you, say that the Lord needs them, and he will send them right away."

⁴This took place to fulfill what was spoken through the prophet:

⁵"Say to Daughter Zion,
  'See, your king comes to you,
gentle and riding on a donkey,
    and on a colt, the foal of a donkey.'"

⁶The disciples went and did as Jesus had instructed them. ⁷They brought the donkey and the colt and placed their cloaks on them for Jesus to sit on. ⁸A very large crowd spread their cloaks on the road, while others cut branches from the trees and spread them on the road. ⁹The crowds that went ahead of him and those that followed shouted,

"Hosanna to the Son of David!"

"Blessed is he who comes in the name of the Lord!"

"Hosanna in the highest heaven!"

¹⁰When Jesus entered Jerusalem, the whole city was stirred and asked, "Who is this?"

¹¹The crowds answered, "This is Jesus, the prophet from Nazareth in Galilee."

¹²Jesus entered the temple courts and drove out all who were buying and selling there. He overturned the tables of the money changers and the benches of those selling doves. ¹³"It is written," he said to them, "'My house will be called a house of prayer,' but you are making it 'a den of robbers.'"

¹⁴The blind and the lame came to him at the temple, and he healed them. ¹⁵But when the chief priests and the teachers of the law saw the wonderful things he did and the children shouting in the temple courts, "Hosanna to the Son of David," they were indignant.

¹⁶"Do you hear what these children are saying?" they asked him.

"Yes," replied Jesus, "have you never read,

"'From the lips of children and infants
    you, Lord, have called forth your praise'?"

¹⁷And he left them and went out of the city to Bethany, where he spent the night.

¹⁸Early in the morning, as Jesus was on his way back to the city, he was hungry. ¹⁹Seeing a fig tree by the road, he went up to it but found nothing on it except leaves. Then he said to it, "May you never bear fruit again!" Immediately the tree withered.

²⁰When the disciples saw this, they were amazed. "How did the fig tree wither so quickly?" they asked.

²¹Jesus replied, "Truly I tell you, if you have faith and do not doubt, not only can you do what was done to the fig tree, but also you can say to this mountain, 'Go, throw yourself into the sea,' and it will be done. ²²If you believe, you will receive whatever you ask for in prayer."

²³Jesus entered the temple courts, and, while he was teaching, the chief priests and the elders of the people came to him. "By what authority are you doing these things?" they asked. "And who gave you this authority?"

²⁴Jesus replied, "I will also ask you one question. If you answer me, I will tell you by what authority I am doing these things. ²⁵John's baptism—where did it come from? Was it from heaven, or of human origin?"

They discussed it among themselves and said, "If we say, 'From heaven,' he will ask, 'Then why didn't you believe him?' ²⁶But if we say, 'Of human origin'—we are afraid of the people, for they all hold that John was a prophet."

²⁷So they answered Jesus, "We don't know."

Then he said, "Neither will I tell you by what authority I am doing these things.

28"What do you think? There was a man who had two sons. He went to the first and said, 'Son, go and work today in the vineyard.'

29"'I will not,' he answered, but later he changed his mind and went.

30"Then the father went to the other son and said the same thing. He answered, 'I will, sir,' but he did not go.

31"Which of the two did what his father wanted?"

"The first," they answered.

Jesus said to them, "Truly I tell you, the tax collectors and the prostitutes are entering the kingdom of God ahead of you. 32For John came to you to show you the way of righteousness, and you did not believe him, but the tax collectors and the prostitutes did. And even after you saw this, you did not repent and believe him.

33"Listen to another parable: There was a landowner who planted a vineyard. He put a wall around it, dug a winepress in it and built a watchtower. Then he rented the vineyard to some farmers and moved to another place. 34When the harvest time approached, he sent his servants to the tenants to collect his fruit.

35"The tenants seized his servants; they beat one, killed another, and stoned a third. 36Then he sent other servants to them, more than the first time, and the tenants treated them the same way. 37Last of all, he sent his son to them. 'They will respect my son,' he said.

38"But when the tenants saw the son, they said to each other, 'This is the heir. Come, let's kill him and take his inheritance.' 39So they took him and threw him out of the vineyard and killed him.

40"Therefore, when the owner of the vineyard comes, what will he do to those tenants?"

41"He will bring those wretches to a wretched end," they replied, "and he will rent the vineyard to other tenants, who will give him his share of the crop at harvest time."

42Jesus said to them, "Have you never read in the Scriptures:

"'The stone the builders rejected
  has become the cornerstone;
the Lord has done this,
  and it is marvelous in our eyes'?

43"Therefore I tell you that the kingdom of God will be taken away from you and given to a people who will produce its fruit. 44Anyone who falls on this stone will be broken to pieces; anyone on whom it falls will be crushed."

⁴⁵When the chief priests and the Pharisees heard Jesus' parables, they knew he was talking about them. ⁴⁶They looked for a way to arrest him, but they were afraid of the crowd because the people held that he was a prophet.

THE PASSION WEEK BEGINS:
The Lamb of God, the King of Zion Publicly Presented

THE FINAL WEEK OF THE THREE YEARS OF JESUS' public ministry is called the Passion Week. It begins with the Passover lamb being brought forth, so Jesus is brought forth. He comes and presents Himself publicly in Jerusalem in the temple. Jesus knows what is coming; He knows that this is now *the* crisis of the world. The prince of darkness will be cast out. He knows He is the Lamb of God who is to take away the sin of the world.[1] He knows the cruel hatred, the searing pain, the torment, and the humiliation that will come upon Him. Our Lord Jesus came to Jerusalem. We must keep in mind what He knows as He came to Jerusalem in order to understand what is before us.

As they approached Jerusalem and came to Bethphage on the Mount of Olives, Jesus sent two disciples, saying to them, "Go to the village ahead of you, and at once you will find a donkey tied there, with her colt by her. Untie them and bring them to me. If anyone says anything to you, tell him that the Lord needs them, and he will send them right away" (vv. 1–3).

Jesus has the concern to not simply take things, but to make it clear what is going on. **"This took place to fulfill what was spoken through the prophet: 'Say to the Daughter of Zion, "See, your king comes to you, gentle and riding on a donkey, on a colt, the foal of a donkey"'"** (vv. 4–5). We read in the *Call to Worship*, "Take my yoke upon you and learn from me, for I am gentle and humble in heart" (Matt. 11:29a). Jesus is coming, riding on a donkey, expressing outwardly His loneliness, meekness, humbleness, and gentleness of heart. The King of Zion, the most beautiful of all kingdoms, the kingdom that will be greater and grander than anything that anyone has ever or could ever imagine. It is presented to us as the city coming down out of heaven, shining with the light of God, like a diamond. It is vast, enormous, and greater than we

---

1. *John 1:29.*

can imagine. It is 1,400 miles long by 1,400 miles wide by 1,400 miles high.[2] Who has ever seen or conceived of a thing like that? Even right now, we cannot. He is the King of Zion—the kingdom more glorious than all the kingdoms of this world. This One comes—meek, lowly, and riding on a donkey. This is to fulfill the Scriptures.

JESUS' PRESENTATION AS KING:
Meek and Lowly

Jesus comes in His humiliation to fulfill the Word of the promise. He comes as a man, this One who is God. "And being found in appearance as a man, he humbled himself by becoming obedient to death—even death on a cross!" (Phil. 2:8). He comes in His humiliation—humble. He will come again in His glory. He comes riding upon a donkey. Then He will come with the sound of the trumpet. In all the glory of His Father, His face shining as the sun. His eyes, who can look into? They are like blazing fire.[3] He will come in His glory. Now He comes in His humility, as is fitting, as a man. "Say to the Daughter of Zion, 'See, your king comes to you, gentle and riding on a donkey, on a colt, the foal of a donkey'" (v. 5).

We are to know God, and some profess to know God as Creator, but they do not know Him as Redeemer, as Savior. Some come to know Him as Savior but do not know Him as the lowly, humble servant. We are to be conformed to His image.[4] Remember the rich, young ruler; he could not come to Jesus; he did not have the heart of a servant. He wanted to be served; he wanted to have the easy, quick way out of the curse. Jesus is going to go right into the middle of the curse, right into the very heart of darkness. Remember the disciples were asking who is the greatest in the kingdom just a few days before. Remember James and John's mother, who came asking for them to sit at His right hand and at His left, and how Jesus corrected them. Jesus comes meek and lowly, and in Matthew 5:3, Jesus began to speak about the character of the citizens of the kingdom that He came to establish. He said, "Blessed are the poor in spirit . . . Blessed are those who mourn" (Matt. 5:3a,

---

2. *Revelation 21.*
3. *Revelation 1:9–20.*
4. *Romans 8:29.*

4a)—those who recognize their creatureliness, their sinfulness, and their dependence upon God. "Blessed are those who hunger and thirst for righteousness" (Matt. 5:6a). Jesus comes meek and lowly; He does not even have His own animal to ride. Some of the judges who judged Israel rode on a white donkey, and it was their own donkey. Jesus did not have that; He did not even have a place to lay His head.[5] Yet we think of finding riches, and through riches, we look for comfort and ease. This is very much part of our very being, the fabric and fiber of our being. We need to recognize that looking to riches is not being like Jesus. We need to fix our eyes on Jesus.

If God is pleased to grant riches, we should use that to serve Him. We do not set our heart on riches or make it our desire. We should catch ourselves in that desire, because it is a way to avoid the work involved in enduring the curse. Many stumble at this point; we want to be served rather than to serve. This is so unlike what we see here in our Lord. He comes to give His life as a ransom for many.[6] That is service; that is the heart of a servant; He humbled Himself and became obedient to death.[7] Jesus presents Himself first as a suffering servant and will continue to serve. But He will serve as a king at the right hand of God, where He makes intercession for us. He is touched with the feelings of our infirmity and He is able to comfort those who have come to Him.[8] He continues to serve as priest at the right hand of God. We know the need we have for that ministry in our own lives. We need the service of our Lord Jesus Christ as our faithful high priest to succor us, uphold us, keep us, comfort us, and gently lead us. Jesus continues to serve at the right hand of God.

Jesus knew what to expect. He knew that the crowd who would greet Him enthusiastically would very soon fall silent as they watched Him carry His cross through the streets. But now, they cry out, and He comes according to the Word of Scripture, riding upon a donkey. The crowds cried out because they had seen His works. Jesus had demonstrated His life for three years. He had been presented to Israel and had shown Himself to be the Lord of righteousness, the Lord who is our

---

5. *Matthew 8:20.*
6. *Mark 10:45.*
7. *Philippians 2:8.*
8. *Hebrews 4:15, 7:24–26.*

Savior. Jesus continues to show this now. The people had remembered His work from Galilee to Jerusalem.

> The disciples went and did as Jesus had instructed them. They brought the donkey and the colt and placed their cloaks on them for Jesus to sit on. A very large crowd spread their cloaks on the road, while others cut branches from the trees and spread them on the road (vv. 6–8).

The crowd came out to meet Him, "**a very large crowd,**" the Scripture says. They spread their cloaks on the road in honor of Him. This crowd, who may have been poor in many ways, took the one last thing they had as a source of comfort and they put it before Jesus and laid it before His feet; they "**spread their cloaks on the road.**" And to celebrate the life that He brought, "**others cut branches from the trees.**" The vibrance of the leaves, the life of the branches, were brought in to make a surrounding for Him to enter. He is to be surrounded by life. I remember when a Japanese dignitary came to the University of Hawaii, many potted plants were brought out and set all around where this man would walk, to give a feeling of life. It is natural. Understandably, the crowd did this.

They "**cut branches from the trees and spread them on the road.**" Not only that, but "**the crowds that went ahead of him and those that followed shouted, 'Hosanna to the Son of David!' 'Blessed is he who comes in the name of the Lord!' 'Hosanna in the highest heaven!'**" (v. 9). We can understand this very large crowd celebrating this One who has come to them. He is their King, the King who saves, so they shout, "**Hosanna to the Son of David!**" Save—Hosanna means *save* or *salvation*, in connection with the Son of David. They had waited over a thousand years for this Son of David to come. They believe this One before them, who is coming on the colt of a donkey, is the Son of David. Indeed, He is. And they bless His name: "**Blessed is he who comes in the name of the Lord!**" Jesus knows the Son of David is righteous, and He comes according to the Word of God, speaking the truth of who God is, and doing the very works of God. The crowds know it, celebrate it, shout it, and the entire city reverberates with their shouts. The whole of Jerusalem was stirred. They confessed that this is salvation in the highest: "**Hosanna in the highest heaven!**" There is no greater salvation than this. By the grace of God, they knew this One had brought salvation, and they rejoiced in it.

"When Jesus entered Jerusalem, the whole city was stirred and asked, 'Who is this?' The crowds answered, 'This is Jesus, the prophet from Nazareth in Galilee'" (vv. 10–11). They should have known this. Jerusalem, the sophisticated city, a worldly city that knows rulers, has a long history, and has had many ways of rejoicing and being glorious. Here comes a prophet from Nazareth of whom they have heard. The leaders thought, 'What does this crowd know, this rabble that is shouting?' But this crowd knows; even as the shepherds at Bethlehem knew because they had the Word from God through the angels. This is Jesus, the prophet from Nazareth in Galilee. Let us see now what He will do as He comes to Jerusalem. He knows that Jerusalem is where He must die. He knows who it is that will bring about His death. He knows the details of what will happen. He knows the Scriptures. He knows the Scriptures will be fulfilled. What does our Lord do as He presents Himself publicly in Jerusalem?

CLEANSING THE TEMPLE:
A House of Prayer for All Nations

We should recognize a factor in the accounts of Matthew and Mark. Mark gives greater time notations about what is happening. According to Mark, "Jesus entered Jerusalem and went into the temple courts. He looked around at everything, but since it was already late, he went out to Bethany with the Twelve" (Mk. 11:11). Matthew does not give a time indicator saying that the cleansing of the temple happened immediately after the entrance into Jerusalem. We can take into account that time indication from Mark and say that Jesus came back to the temple the next day. We have to keep in mind that before this event of Jesus cleansing the temple, He had been there the night before, and He had been to the temple many times. Remember the first time He cleansed the temple was after His first miracle at Cana of Galilee.[9] This is the last time He is coming to the temple, and He is going to do the same thing He did before. There is a need to cleanse the temple of God continually. We are to remember that we, the people of God,

---

9. *John 2:12–17.*

are, in this day, the temple of God. We need to keep in mind that in the same way He was concerned that the temple would be cleansed then, He is concerned that the temple would be cleansed now, that God may dwell in His temple.

> Jesus entered the temple area and drove out all who were buying and selling there. He overturned the tables of the money changers and the benches of those selling doves. "It is written," he said to them, "'My house will be called a house of prayer,' but you are making it a 'den of robbers'" (vv. 12–13).

Jesus said, "It is written." Our Lord always came back to the Scriptures. Matthew does not add what Mark does because Matthew is writing to the Jews; Mark says, "My house will be called a house of prayer for all nations" (Mk. 11:17a). Jesus certainly said that even if Matthew does not include it here, just as Matthew spoke about the 'kingdom of heaven' rather than the 'kingdom of God' because he was addressing a Jewish audience. "My house will be called a house of prayer for all nations"—people from all nations are to go there, pray to God, seek God, and find Him, because the name of God is there. That is how the temple is described. The place of His name, where God preeminently reveals Himself. Though His name was put there, the people did not regard it. This was not the first time they disregarded the temple, but it was coming to the consummation.

Manipulation of Religion for Convenience, Comfort, and Gain

Through the centuries, we have seen how the people disregarded the revelation of God, and time and again, the temple fell into disrepair and disuse. It was made an ordinary place, closed down, and all kinds of junk was put in the temple. All kinds of behavior, conduct, and uncleanness were brought into the temple. There were carvings or paintings on the temple wall that were unclean in the days of Ezekiel when they were carried away captive to Babylon. The temple was continually defiled. The same spirit that defiled the temple in the days of Ezekiel defiled the temple in Jesus' day and defiles the temple of God today. It has to do with money in a very subtle way. It has to do with thinking godliness is a means to gain. This is the prosperity gospel that is preached in many churches. Notice that they were to bring animals for sacrifice, but instead, the people brought money to avoid the hardship of bringing the animals on the journey of so many miles. It was not altogether apart from religion, apart from needs, but it was distorted subtly by the human spirit in order to avoid the toil and the suffering that we are called to endure in the name of Christ in the cause of salvation. We have the spirit of desiring comfort and convenience; we want our religion to be convenient; we do not want our religion to be a religion of the cross. We do not want to take up our cross daily and follow Him. We might think that is extraordinary, but Jesus said, "Anyone who does not carry his cross and follow me cannot be my disciple" (Lk. 14:27).[10] Denying self and taking up the cross is the ordinary thing for all believers. *No one is exempt.* It is not that some have the personality to bear the cross and some do not. It is not that some have to strive mightily, and some strive in a limited way. All are to strive with all their might to take up their cross daily and follow the Lord. That involves effort and work, and it begins with giving attention to the Word of God, whether in reading or in listening to the preaching, and that requires effort. We may go through the motions of seeking the Lord without that effort, seeking the Lord mechanically rather than diligently. We may seek the Lord outwardly rather than with a desire to understand—that is the context of diligence here. None seek and none understand.[11] Those who seek should have understanding; we should be moved by a desire to understand.

In our desire for comfort, we transform Christianity, and we want to transform this congregation into a way and style of life that is convenient and comfortable and not a matter of discipleship and taking up the cross. I will say it again: we want to make it a matter of convenience and comfort and not a matter of discipleship and taking up the cross. We have the spirit of the world and we must be cleansed of that. Part of our comfort is just having enough money to live at ease. That is what Baal worship is: prosperity, success, and fertility. That is what has dominated—the Baals of prosperity. In every nation, Baal is worshiped in some form or other. India worships Baal as Ganesh, the elephant-headed god that overcomes obstacles and gives you success. We want success in our endeavors and prosperity and, from that,

---

10. NIV 1984.

11. *Romans 3:11.*

convenience and comfort. Let us watch ourselves against this. The Jews had taken away the heart of the message and turned it into a way of making money. They wanted ease and comfort. It was contrary to the spirit of prayer. **"He overturned the tables of the money changers and the benches of those selling doves"** (v. 12b). This is the second time He did this. In John 2:14–16, Jesus, after His first miracle in Cana of Galilee, went into the temple:

> In the temple courts he found people selling cattle, sheep and doves, and others sitting at tables exchanging money. So he made a whip out of cords, and drove all from the temple courts, both sheep and cattle; he scattered the coins of the money changers and overturned their tables. To those who sold doves he said, "Get these out of here! Stop turning my Father's house into a market!"

The second time, He did not make a whip of cords, and He said, **"'My house will be called a house of prayer,' but you are making it a 'den of robbers'"** (v. 13b). There is a way of manipulating religion for convenience and gain. The Scripture says there are some "who think that godliness is a means to financial gain" (1 Tim. 6:5b). Some people like to be in the office of pastor because it may be a soft job. You get money, and it is relatively easy. You could be kind of careless, be a hired helper, and not care much about the sheep. You could get away with not engaging in the hard work of counseling. In our self-life, we turn to money. 'Simony' is what it is called—buying offices and not being faithful in those offices and being like the hired hand that runs away.[12] Religion is continually turned into a means to gain because that is where our heart is—not in God.

Jesus cleansed His temple. Those of us who find that spirit of seeking gain in us, let us watch ourselves. Jesus is calling us away from that path. The temple should be a house of prayer, a place of discipleship, and a place of being prepared, so that all the nations of the earth may know God. The temple should be a place of doing the hard work that is necessary to come into the unity of the faith. We need to be gentle and humble. We need to learn to be strong so that we may be gentle and humble in our dealings with others. We must do the hard work necessary through discipleship and not excuse ourselves. We are not

---

12. *John 10:12.*

to go on day after day, year after year, not engaging in the work, just going about our business as is, and thanking the Lord because He helps to make our lives a bit more convenient. Jesus would have none of this religion; He said you must take up your cross daily and follow me.[13] This is for each and every Christian, not special Christians.

At the Center of Things: In Jerusalem, in the Temple, at the Passover—the Spotless Lamb of God

Jesus came, showing Himself in His holiness and righteousness, in the very center of things—publicly presented as the spotless Lamb of God. He came into Jerusalem and into the temple and stood before the priests and rulers. He did it right there, pointedly, boldly, clearly. He immediately challenged their authority, because they were allowing this kind of 'Christianity' to go on. They made religion comfortable for the people in the pew. Jesus challenged this. Take up your cross daily and seek diligently. Do the necessary work to understand and to be a faithful witness. Do not whine and complain. Enough! Do not excuse yourself; be prepared to do the work. "Take up your cross daily and follow me." The cross requires us to pay attention, get up early if need be, and read the Word. The cross requires us to labor in prayer when our mind will be distracted in a thousand different ways by the cares of this world. Cry out to God, 'Lord, help me to focus and pray.' We are not to only pray about the things that come easily, naturally, in terms of this, that, and the other need; that is the fourth request of the Lord's Prayer: "Give us this day our daily bread."[14] Our first request is, "Hallowed be your name, your kingdom come, your will be done on earth as it is in heaven" (Matt. 6:9b–10). Jesus wanted the temple to be a house of prayer, not a place of convenience.

The salvation of the Lord becomes manifest. **"The blind and the lame came to him at the temple, and he healed them"** (v. 14). When we have the Word of God, the truth of God, we will find the spiritually blind and the spiritually lame coming, and they will be healed. I assure you of that! The Word of God is effective and will bring it about. If we do that work, return to the truth of God, the old way, the path

---

13. *Luke 9:23.*
14. *Matthew 6:11* KJV.

that has already been found, and pursue that work further, it will be brought about.[15]

The Heart Is Revealed: Indignant in Opposition and Self-Justification

> The blind and the lame came to him at the temple, and he healed them. But when the chief priests and the teachers of the law saw the wonderful things he did and the children shouting in the temple area, "Hosanna to the Son of David," they were indignant (vv. 14–15).

The indignation of the chief priests and the teachers shows a kind of sincerity, but they were very wrong. They were self-deceived, and in their self-deception, they were indignant. Notice the word "**indignant.**" Indignation shows a very deep kind of righteous anger, perhaps. What we might take to be righteous anger was, in this case, altogether unrighteous; it came out of self-deception. We can be indignant at times, but not according to the righteousness of God. "**'Do you hear what these children are saying?' they asked him**" (v. 16a). They are asking Jesus, 'Are you taking glory for yourself?' Jesus had said in John 8:54, "If I glorify myself, my glory means nothing. My Father, whom you claim as your God, is the one who glorifies me." He came to do the work of His Father. He prayed on the night He was betrayed, immediately before He was betrayed, "Glorify your Son, that your Son may glorify you" (Jn. 17:1b). Before, He had said, "Except a corn of wheat fall into the ground and die, it abideth alone: but if it die, it bringeth forth much fruit" (Jn. 12:24 KJV). Jesus said this when the Greeks came to Philip and said, "Sir . . . we would like to see Jesus" (Jn. 12:21b). Jesus knew He must die in order that the Word may go out. He came to bring salvation to the earth. God loves the world, the world as a whole, the entire world—all the nations, kindreds, tribes, and tongues;[16] He loves the world. "For God so loved the world that he gave his one and only Son, that whoever believes in him shall not perish but have eternal life" (Jn. 3:16). God commissions us, His people who have come to believe in Him:

---

15. *Jeremiah 6:16.*
16. *Revelation 7:9.*

> Therefore go and make disciples of all nations, baptizing them in the name of the Father and of the Son and of the Holy Spirit, and teaching them to obey everything I have commanded you. And surely I am with you always, to the very end of the age (Matt. 28:19–20).

This is the Lord of Salvation. This is the One who comes to His temple, and He wants His temple to be cleansed so the lame and the blind may come and be healed, and men of all nations may come and pray in the Church to the God of heaven, who has created all things and who redeems men.

The crowd saw this truth in some measure. The leaders, who should have been leading the way, did not. Sin had taken a further toll in their lives, and they saw less than the people in the crowd. "**Do you hear what these children are saying?' they asked him. 'Yes,' replied Jesus, 'have you never read, "From the lips of children and infants you have ordained praise"?'"** (v. 16). When the leaders will not give praise, the Lord will raise up children who will utter the praise of God. "**Hosanna in the highest heaven!**" (v. 9b). There is no greater salvation than that which comes through Jesus Christ our Lord in *every way*. He is the One who brings the fullness of heaven to us. We have all fullness in Him. All the fullness of the Godhead dwells bodily in Him, and we are complete in Him.[17] Salvation in the highest—from the mouths of babes. "**And he left them and went out of the city to Bethany, where he spent the night**" (v. 17).

CURSING THE FIG TREE:
Cursing Outwardly What Is Revealed as Cursed—No Fruit

Then there is the account of the fig tree that withered. The order of events in time was this: He came on the first day, Palm Sunday, into Jerusalem, looked around the temple, and went out. Then, coming back in the morning, He saw the fig tree and approached it for figs. Anyone who has had a fig tree knows that if you see leaves on it, there should be fruit.

---

17. *Colossians 2:9–10.*

Early in the morning, as Jesus was on his way back to the city, he was hungry. Seeing a fig tree by the road, he went up to it but found nothing on it except leaves. Then he said to it, "May you never bear fruit again!" Immediately the tree withered (vv. 18–19).

This has been misunderstood, and some have asked if Jesus was just upset because He was hungry. Remember the temptation of Jesus. He was hungry and serving His Father in hunger, even when He was the king, and He was recognized as king shortly before, but He was still going without food. He does not doubt the love of God in His hunger; hunger does not separate Him from the love of God. This is not about hunger, rather, He is seeing what God is doing. The fig tree is a symbol of Israel, and Jesus knows how to read the signs of the times. John 5:19 says, "I tell you the truth, the Son can do nothing by himself; he can do only what he sees his Father doing, because whatever the Father does the Son also does." The night before, Jesus saw the condition of the temple. He will shortly cleanse the temple. As He sees the fig tree, He knows the failure of the chief priests and sees the lack of fruit in Israel and in Jerusalem. He knows there is a curse on the people, so they are fruitless. He sees this in the fig tree and He knows what God is doing. The people have been disobedient. The curse is upon them, according to the word spoken by Moses, and it is revealed here in the fig tree. What is already revealed about the people in the fig tree, He makes further visible—there is no fruit. "May you never bear fruit again!" And it came to pass.

When the disciples saw this, they were amazed. "How did the fig tree wither so quickly?" they asked. Jesus replied, "Truly I tell you, if you have faith and do not doubt, not only can you do what was done to the fig tree, but also you can say to this mountain, 'Go, throw yourself into the sea,' and it will be done" (vv. 20–21).

This involves seeing what God is doing. It involves understanding how to read what is going on in *reality*, and what is revealed in terms of *symbol*. The symbol is connected to the reality. Jesus is doing what He sees His Father doing; that is the context in which He speaks this: "You can say to this mountain, 'Go, throw yourself into the sea.'" If we see what God is doing, we can do what He is doing in the visible world. In this context, we are to understand that we can do what was done to the fig tree and likewise to the mountain. Some great mountain that is raised up against the Word of God shall be removed by the Word of God. Speak the Word. Any mountain of unbelief is subject to the power of the Word of God—it cannot stand. Even if it is the mountain of science today, the mountain of evolution, or the mountain of Hinduism, we can say to that mountain, by the Word of God, "**Go, throw yourself into the sea.**" We can speak the Word of God that is able to pierce—sharper than any double-edged sword.[18] The Word of God is compelling, even though it does not persuade. Unbelief cannot stand, even as Pharaoh could not stand against the Word spoken through Moses. So Jesus spoke the Word in terms of what He saw His Father doing.

BY WHAT AUTHORITY?
The Stone the Builders Rejected

Authoritarianism: Requiring Submission Without Submitting to the Authority of the Word of God

Once in Jerusalem, the chief priests confronted Jesus.

> **Jesus entered the temple courts, and, while he was teaching, the chief priests and the elders of the people came to him. "By what authority are you doing these things?" they asked. "And who gave you this authority?"** (v. 23).

This is authoritarianism. Authoritarianism is wanting to have other people submit to you without yourself being submitted to the authority of the Word of God. It is wanting people to submit to you because you are in some position, however, in that position, you are not submitted to God. There is a lot of authoritarianism in the Church today. You have confronted it, and you probably have not recognized it. They call us to submit without being themselves submitted. Naturally, the question about authority was raised, "**'By what authority are you doing these things?' they asked. 'And who gave you this authority?'**" Remember how Jesus answered the Pharisees when they said, "It is only by Beelzebul, the prince of demons, that this fellow drives out demons" (Matt.

---

18. *Hebrews 4:12.*

12:24b). Jesus very patiently endured and addressed the question and explained and applied the Word fully. He does this again.

John's Baptism: From Heaven or from Men?

> Jesus replied, "I will also ask you one question. If you answer me, I will tell you by what authority I am doing these things. John's baptism—where did it come from? Was it from heaven, or from men?" (vv. 24–25).[19]

Remember, John the Baptist was the one whom God appointed to point to Jesus: "Look, the Lamb of God, who takes away the sin of the world!" (Jn. 1:29). The application to John is *most* relevant. Jesus asks the prior question—it is presuppositional. He is asking, 'You didn't notice what happened to John, did you?' He is drawing attention to this. "John's baptism—where did it come from? Was it from heaven, or from men?" Jesus knew and understood the principle of authority, what God had done by way of authority, and He addressed it. John's authority as prophet pointed to Christ and His authority.

> They discussed it among themselves and said, "If we say, 'From heaven,' he will ask, 'Then why didn't you believe him?' But if we say, 'From men'—we are afraid of the people, for they all hold that John was a prophet" (v. 26).[20]

Avoidance: "We Don't Know"

They were caught in a dilemma. "So they answered Jesus, 'We don't know'" (v. 27a). They avoided the question. This showed their unwillingness to deal with the question, so Jesus did not give them an answer. "Then he said, 'Neither will I tell you by what authority I am doing these things'" (v. 27b).

Two Parables: On the Nature of Authority—Professed or Actual?

Now that the subject has been raised, Jesus talks further about authority.

---

19. NIV 1984.
20. NIV 1984.

> What do you think? There was a man who had two sons. He went
> to the first and said, 'Son, go and work today in the vineyard.' 'I
> will not,' he answered, but later he changed his mind and went.
> Then the father went to the other son and said the same thing.
> He answered, 'I will, sir,' but he did not go. Which of the two did
> what his father wanted? (vv. 28–31a).

Who obeyed the authority of the father? It is a pretty simple answer.
"'The first,' they answered" (v. 31). They knew the answer. They could
see. Then Jesus applied it. Jesus makes a simple connection. "**Jesus said
to them, 'Truly I tell you, the tax collectors and the prostitutes are
entering the kingdom of God ahead of you'**" (v. 31b). The worst in
our society, the scum, those you despise, those with whom you would
not associate, they "**are entering the kingdom of God ahead of you.**"
Because they said 'no' at first, disobeyed God, and then repented. 'They
repented at the preaching of John, whose authority you did not submit to! You should have seen that fruit of John's preaching, but you,
when you had seen it, did not repent.' That was part of the testimony
of John's ministry. These "**are entering the kingdom of God ahead of
you,**" and they are submitted to the authority of God.

Jesus talks further about authority.

> Listen to another parable: There was a landowner who planted a
> vineyard. He put a wall around it, dug a winepress in it and built
> a watchtower. Then he rented the vineyard to some farmers and
> moved to another place. When the harvest time approached, he sent
> his servants to the tenants to collect his fruit. The tenants seized
> his servants; they beat one, killed another, and stoned a third. Then
> he sent other servants to them, more than the first time, and the
> tenants treated them the same way. Last of all, he sent his son to
> them. "They will respect my son," he said (vv. 33–37).

We may think that this owner of the vineyard is very long-suffering and
wonder why he would send his son after they did all of these things.

> But when the tenants saw the son, they said to each other, "This
> is the heir. Come, let's kill him and take his inheritance." So they
> took him and threw him out of the vineyard and killed him. There-
> fore, when the owner of the vineyard comes, what will he do to

those tenants? "He will bring those wretches to a wretched end," they replied, "and he will rent the vineyard to other tenants, who will give him his share of the crop at harvest time" (vv. 38–41).

What a beautifully correct answer in this parable, and the Pharisees still did not see it. Jesus applied it:

> Jesus said to them, "Have you never read in the Scriptures: 'The stone the builders rejected has become the cornerstone; the Lord has done this, and it is marvelous in our eyes'?" (v. 42).

The Word of God incarnate—He is the authority; He is the capstone; all things are measured from Him and to Him, and they are questioning Him about authority. Christ is that by which authority is measured, and they are questioning His authority. How inside-out sin makes us, how twisted, how perverse. "**Have you never read?**" He said and then carried it further, "**Therefore I tell you that the kingdom of God will be taken away from you and given to a people who will produce its fruit**" (v. 43). Matthew 23 is to come, where He will specifically pronounce the woes.

This is Passion Week; remember the drama of what is going on, the deliberateness of our Lord Jesus Christ; He knows what is coming. Notice how He is presenting Himself to the people.

> When the chief priests and the Pharisees heard Jesus' parables, they knew he was talking about them. They looked for a way to arrest him, but they were afraid of the crowd because the people held that he was a prophet (vv. 45–46).

It is day two of Passion Week. What more is to come? We want to read, think about, and engage in it. We want to search the Scriptures and seek to understand.

—————

19

REDUCED TO SILENCE

The Faithful Witness of Jesus—Taking
Thoughts Captive by the Word of God

Matthew 22

¹Jesus spoke to them again in parables, saying: ²"The kingdom of heaven is like a king who prepared a wedding banquet for his son. ³He sent his servants to those who had been invited to the banquet to tell them to come, but they refused to come.

⁴"Then he sent some more servants and said, 'Tell those who have been invited that I have prepared my dinner: My oxen and fattened cattle have been butchered, and everything is ready. Come to the wedding banquet.'

⁵"But they paid no attention and went off—one to his field, another to his business. ⁶The rest seized his servants, mistreated them and killed them. ⁷The king was enraged. He sent his army and destroyed those murderers and burned their city.

⁸"Then he said to his servants, 'The wedding banquet is ready, but those I invited did not deserve to come. ⁹So go to the street corners and invite to the banquet anyone you find.' ¹⁰So the servants went out into the streets and gathered all the people they could find, the bad as well as the good, and the wedding hall was filled with guests.

¹¹"But when the king came in to see the guests, he noticed a man there who was not wearing wedding clothes. ¹²He asked, 'How did you get in here without wedding clothes, friend?' The man was speechless.

¹³"Then the king told the attendants, 'Tie him hand and foot, and throw him outside, into the darkness, where there will be weeping and gnashing of teeth.'

[14]"For many are invited, but few are chosen."

[15]Then the Pharisees went out and laid plans to trap him in his words. [16]They sent their disciples to him along with the Herodians. "Teacher," they said, "we know that you are a man of integrity and that you teach the way of God in accordance with the truth. You aren't swayed by others, because you pay no attention to who they are. [17]Tell us then, what is your opinion? Is it right to pay the imperial tax to Caesar or not?"

[18]But Jesus, knowing their evil intent, said, "You hypocrites, why are you trying to trap me? [19]Show me the coin used for paying the tax." They brought him a denarius, [20]and he asked them, "Whose image is this? And whose inscription?"

[21]"Caesar's," they replied.

Then he said to them, "So give back to Caesar what is Caesar's, and to God what is God's."

[22]When they heard this, they were amazed. So they left him and went away.

[23]That same day the Sadducees, who say there is no resurrection, came to him with a question. [24]"Teacher," they said, "Moses told us that if a man dies without having children, his brother must marry the widow and raise up offspring for him. [25]Now there were seven brothers among us. The first one married and died, and since he had no children, he left his wife to his brother. [26]The same thing happened to the second and third brother, right on down to the seventh. [27]Finally, the woman died. [28]Now then, at the resurrection, whose wife will she be of the seven, since all of them were married to her?"

[29]Jesus replied, "You are in error because you do not know the Scriptures or the power of God. [30]At the resurrection people will neither marry nor be given in marriage; they will be like the angels in heaven. [31]But about the resurrection of the dead—have you not read what God said to you, [32]'I am the God of Abraham, the God of Isaac, and the God of Jacob'? He is not the God of the dead but of the living."

[33]When the crowds heard this, they were astonished at his teaching.

[34]Hearing that Jesus had silenced the Sadducees, the Pharisees got together. [35]One of them, an expert in the law, tested him with this question: [36]"Teacher, which is the greatest commandment in the Law?"

[37]Jesus replied: "'Love the Lord your God with all your heart and with all your soul and with all your mind.' [38]This is the first and greatest commandment. [39]And the second is like it: 'Love your neighbor as yourself.' [40]All the Law and the Prophets hang on these two commandments."

⁴¹While the Pharisees were gathered together, Jesus asked them, ⁴²"What do you think about the Messiah? Whose son is he?"

"The son of David," they replied.

⁴³He said to them, "How is it then that David, speaking by the Spirit, calls him 'Lord'? For he says,

⁴⁴"'The Lord said to my Lord:
"Sit at my right hand
until I put your enemies
    under your feet."'

⁴⁵If then David calls him 'Lord,' how can he be his son?" ⁴⁶No one could say a word in reply, and from that day on no one dared to ask him any more questions.

REVIEW OF MATTHEW 21:
The Stone the Builders Rejected

W E ARE CONTINUING IN THE BOOK OF Matthew. We are in the Passion Week. This is the last week of our Lord's life before the Crucifixion. He knows what is coming, and He sets His face steadfastly to go up to Jerusalem. We saw in chapter 21 that He came into the city and was greeted by the people: 'Salvation in the highest.' We saw that He went into the temple and cleansed it. We saw that this provoked the response of the Pharisees, who asked, "By what authority are you doing these things?" (Matt. 21:23b). Jesus replied at some length; He spoke about authority, showing the futility of their thinking, and He showed that they asked the question without being serious in intent. He told the parable of the two sons and asked which did what the father wanted. He told of how the tax collectors and prostitutes repented at John's preaching and acknowledged God's authority in John, who had testified about Jesus. He told the parable of the tenants, how they seized the land for themselves, and how they even came to the point of killing the son. Jesus summed it up by saying, "The stone the builders rejected has become the cornerstone" (Matt. 21:42a). Jesus is the capstone, the cornerstone; from *Him* all things are to be measured. All things are measured from the truth that He testifies to, as Creator, as Redeemer of man, and as Lord and Savior. That truth includes the Fall, the fallen condition of man, and the reality of the curse.

Any attempt to build without squaring oneself and one's thinking with that truth, is doomed to failure and will be crushed under the weight of God's wrath as He lets us fall by the works of our own hands. "Anyone who falls on this stone will be broken to pieces, but anyone on whom it falls will be crushed" (Matt. 21:44). The one who falls upon the Rock is broken in repentance; he acknowledges the truth of God, the reality of sin and death, and that the cornerstone is Christ Jesus. He acknowledges that this is not just Jesus generally; this is Jesus as Creator, Lord, and Savior. The Church has compromised on that truth; the Church has been weakened, and the pressures from the world are crushing us. We are to acknowledge the authority that God has established, be concerned about authority, and submit our thoughts, every one, each one, to the truth that is in the Scriptures.

THE PARABLE OF THE WEDDING BANQUET:
Honoring the Son—Salvation Is by Christ Alone

Jesus continues speaking to the people and speaks to them in a way we should all understand. He speaks about a wedding. **"Jesus spoke to them again in parables, saying: 'The kingdom of heaven is like a king who prepared a wedding banquet for his son'"** (vv. 1–2). From the beginning, God spoke to us through weddings.

In Genesis 2, He established the marriage wedding of the man and the woman, and He did that because it was to be a sign of the covenant that He has established with man, by which He binds us to Himself.[1] That covenant was established in the reality of the Garden, the tree, the two ways, and the promise of life and death. It is called a covenant of works, but it is gracious. The covenant between man and woman is a sign of the covenant between God and man. Throughout Scripture, the Word of God speaks about marriage and weddings, and to the end of history, people will marry and be given in marriage. It is universal; we are all surrounded by it, so it should be easy to understand everything that is connected with weddings. Jesus is speaking to the people and the leaders about a wedding and the response to it. We all know that to be invited to a wedding is a privilege, an honor, and it is not to be

---

1. Gangadean, *The Biblical Worldview*, 147–158.

lightly regarded, but that is just what happened in this parable. The wedding day approached, and things were prepared.

> He sent his servants to those who had been invited to the banquet to tell them to come, but they refused to come. Then he sent some more servants and said, "Tell those who have been invited that I have prepared my dinner: My oxen and fattened cattle have been butchered, and everything is ready. Come to the wedding banquet" (vv. 3–4).

There is no greater celebration in the earthly realm than the wedding banquet. It is such a time of joy and anticipation, we know what that means, and we can understand it. We saw Jesus turn water into wine at the wedding in Cana, the first of His miracles, which showed His glory, anticipating the end of history, the Marriage Supper of the Lamb. The miracle at Cana was a sign of what He is going to accomplish, to bring things to consummation in the wedding spoken of in Revelation 21. After the Harlot is overthrown, the Bride comes, dressed in fine linen, white and clean, representing righteousness imputed to His people, the Church of God.

The Special Invitation and Response: Disregard and Contempt

The king prepared a wedding banquet and invited his guests, and what was the response? **"But they paid no attention and went off—one to his field, another to his business"** (v. 5). How could human beings be like that? They are privileged guests, yet they are disregarding this invitation. This is the son of the king! When you are specially invited to a wedding, who would not want to be there and to celebrate in this way? Yet, sin has done this to us. We have put our concerns about our fields and our businesses before the wedding. How should we understand this?

The things of this world—the love for these things, what our hands can supply to us, our self-sufficiency, and supplying our needs—seem to be *real*. The way in which God provides—how He provides the fields for us to till, the seed to sow, the rain and the sunshine—does not seem to be *real*. It is only what we put into it that is real. We do not see God's provision for us; we do not see God providing; we look to ourselves and what our hands can provide, and we are blind to God's way. We do not realize that every breath we draw is because of

the upholding hand of God. We take God for granted; we do not recognize the work of God; we recognize our own work only. If that is
true, it is very likely that we will ignore God. We will ignore anything
that He would provide because we believe that we are the ones who
are really providing anything that is real and worthwhile. Do you see
how that thinking can occur? When God calls us to the true banquet,
where He gives Himself to us, we do not recognize it.

We are to recognize this is a figure of speech—an analogy. In this
parable, we are the guests; in reality, we are the bride. It is one thing
for the guests to turn away, but if the bride turns away, it is a lot more
serious. That is why we have the sign and the reality. They not only
turn away but also respond with contempt. The things of God become meaningless to us, and we treat them with contempt. The way
in which God would hold us close to Him, we want to break those
bands and cast them away from us.[2] When we are called to His way,
we feel constrained, and constraint, coupled with contempt, brings
about this response. **"The rest seized his servants, mistreated them and
killed them. The king was enraged. He sent his army and destroyed
those murderers and burned their city"** (vv. 6–7). The things that we
would put our confidence in, ourselves and the works of our hands,
are destroyed because we do not recognize the work of God. We take
God for granted. That is just the first part of the parable—the invited
guests respond and they dishonor God in their response because they
dishonor God in their lives, and they fail to see the benefits and blessings that God provides for us all around. Remember, this is a parable
Jesus is speaking to the Pharisees in the Passion Week, during which
things are going to come to a head. Jesus is pressing upon them the
reality of the situation through this parable.

Those who were invited did not come, and we have to be particularly
careful about this because we are, today, in the position of the invited
guests. By God's grace, we have been brought into the Church, the
covenant people of God, and when we begin to take God for granted
and lightly esteem His blessing, then we do not see that in the things
that He gives us in this world, He is giving us Himself. What I mean
is that He is revealing Himself to us, His glory to us, and the reality is
signified in the things that He gives to us. The ring is given as a token

---

2. *Psalm 2:3.*

of love; the reality is the love, and in that love, one gives oneself to the person. We are not to become preoccupied with the gift, with the creation, except as it reveals God to us. The One who has created and sustains the creation reveals Himself to us, and He gives Himself to us. We would take the one and forget the other.

The Wider Invitation and the Guest Without Wedding Clothes: The Imputed Righteousness of Christ

No guests are coming to the wedding; that just does not seem right. This is the second part of the parable:

> Then he said to his servants, "The wedding banquet is ready, but those I invited did not deserve to come. So go to the street corners and invite to the banquet anyone you find." So the servants went out into the streets and gathered all the people they could find, the bad as well as the good, and the wedding hall was filled with guests (vv. 8–10).

This is a typical pattern in the parables: both good and bad. The net catches good and bad fish, and there are the wheat and weeds in the kingdom. Notice how sin continues even here: "**But when the king came in to see the guests, he noticed a man there who was not wearing wedding clothes. He asked, 'How did you get in here without wedding clothes, friend?' The man was speechless**" (vv. 11–12). This is also a disregard for the honor of being at the wedding. He did not come prepared for the occasion. Maybe he came just for the food— you know how that can happen—and did not really care about the persons. He was there, not prepared, and did not come to honor the persons involved, both the king and his son, on the occasion. This one, too, shows disregard and contempt for the one who has invited him by not coming with wedding clothes. To apply this, we would say that this wedding garment is nothing other than the fine linen in which the bride is clothed, representing the righteousness imputed to us—the righteousness of Christ. This is the regard for the holiness of God that can accept us into His presence only insofar as we are righteous—and we are righteous in the righteousness of Christ. It is a disregard for God.

Some people may not come to God at all, as the first group who did not even show, and others may show, but with little regard. They are in the Church, but they do not have a regard for the work of Christ and the blood of Christ; they are there without wedding clothes, and they likewise have contempt and disregard for God and His work. This one, too, comes under judgment: "**Then the king told the attendants, 'Tie him hand and foot, and throw him outside, into the darkness, where there will be weeping and gnashing of teeth**" (v. 13). He is thrown outside, away from the presence of God, into darkness, the darkness of his own mind, and he will continue there unendingly in that condition "**where there will be weeping and gnashing of teeth.**"

We see the result of sin in our response to God: either we do not come at all, or we come on our own terms to a god of our own making. There are some who are professing atheists, and some who come outwardly Christian but inwardly do not have a true conviction of sin, a true heart of repentance, and a true acceptance of the righteousness of Christ. They have no sense of the need for the righteousness of Christ, and so they come in their own righteousness. That is not a pretty sight. Our righteousness is as filthy rags.[3] How would you like to have someone come to a wedding, not just with dirty clothes from working in the dirt and grease, but filthy, like menstrual cloth? That is what it is like; such disregard, such contempt.

The invited guests do not come, and some, like the one without the wedding clothes, think they can come to God without the righteousness of Christ. They think they can come in their own righteousness—they likewise dishonor God, and they cannot enter in and have that intimate union and communion with God, that is, the marriage between the Lord and His people. This is spoken to both those in the Church, specially invited and do not come, and those who may come in from the outside on their own terms. We are warned: "**For many are invited, but few are chosen**" (v. 14). Among the people of God, among those professing belief, not everyone will be truly in the faith, and we have to examine ourselves to see if we are in the faith.

THE FINAL CHALLENGES

According to the Gospel of Matthew, the Pharisees hear this parable, and they respond in a way that they seek to trap Him. In the remainder

---

3. *Isaiah 64:6.*

of this chapter, we have the final challenges of the Pharisees to the Lord Jesus Christ and, in a sense, His challenge to them. There are four such challenges. First, there is the question concerning paying taxes to Caesar. Second, there is the question concerning marriage at the resurrection. Third, there is the question concerning the greatest law. Finally, Jesus' question to them: Whose son is the Christ? This will end in a silencing of all questions. These are the final challenges. Let us look at them and learn of our Lord Jesus Christ, how we are to be like Him, and how we are to be witnesses. Let us see how He was a faithful witness, acknowledge where we are not, repent accordingly, and ask for God's grace to be so.

THE PAYING OF TAXES TO CAESAR:
Failure to Understand Their Own Context

"**Then the Pharisees went out and laid plans to trap him in his words. They sent their disciples to him along with the Herodians**" (vv. 15–16a). The Pharisees come along with the Herodians. The Herodians are in a position of special relation with Caesar. They are ruling under the auspices of Caesar. The Pharisees bring the Herodians along to see whether Jesus can be brought to say anything that would undermine the Herodian position and bring Him into trouble. We should remember that it was this specific point that brought about His crucifixion. They said that Jesus of Nazareth, the king of the Jews, was setting Himself up as king over and against Caesar. But that is not what it was; it was not as king over and against Caesar; it was king *above* Caesar. He is King of kings; they did not go far enough.

A Trap: Hypocrisy Versus Integrity

The question about paying taxes is close to everyone's mind, quite naturally; it is very real. There are two things spoken of: death and taxes. The Sadducees speak about death, and the Pharisees speak about taxes. Imagine that. Here is the big, long windup: "'**Teacher**,' they said, 'we **know you are a man of integrity and that you teach the way of God in accordance with the truth**'" (v. 16). If they really knew that, do you think they would be trying to trap Him? We can see the absurdity of their position. They are saying these words, but they should think about what they are saying. If they had integrity, they would have meant their words truly. They show their lack of integrity because they are using words and do not mean them. They should mean the words they speak because they are professing them. If He teaches the way in accordance with the truth, are they going to be able to trap Him? Jesus is a man of integrity, in contrast with their hypocrisy, and He calls them hypocrites. They say, "**You aren't swayed by others**" (v. 16). So all of this flattery that they are giving is not going to sway Him, "**because you pay no attention to who they are**" (v. 16b). Come on, cut it out, get to the point. "**Tell us then, what is your opinion?**" 'Jesus, what is your opinion?' Jesus does not give opinions; He gives commands. His Word is law; it is ultimate. "**Tell us then, what is your opinion? Is it right to pay the imperial tax to Caesar or not?**" (v. 17). That is a question everyone can relate to. The answer, in the mind of some, is that we should not have to pay taxes to Caesar, period. It is, rather, we should not pay taxes to Caesar under certain conditions. There is a big difference, and we will have to see what is happening here.

A Loaded Question: The Dilemma

This is called the 'complex question,' or the 'loaded question.' There is also the 'complex assertion,' which is a self-referentially absurd answer. But here, the question has assumptions more than the listener is ready to assent to. It tries to put someone in a dilemma; if you answer one way, it is wrong, or another way, it is still wrong. The only way out is to get back to the assumption, which is exactly what Jesus did. He thought about the meaning of what they were saying.

Exposing the Assumption: Whose Portrait?

First, He recognized that they were hypocrites trying to trap Him, and He also thought it appropriate to speak to them on that point. "**But Jesus, knowing their evil intent, said, 'You hypocrites, why are you trying to trap me?'**" (v. 18). We should not be naive; if some persons are deceived and trying to deceive others, we should not be taken in by it. We should be aware of their deception and be on our guard. We should recognize the reality of self-deception and self-justification. He exposes their intent to trap Him first and then goes on, "**Show me the coin used for paying the tax**" (v. 19a). Notice how relevant Jesus is speaking; He is not speaking beside the point, He is not going off on a tangent, He is taking the very words that they are saying, and in a concrete way, uses the very coin that they use to pay taxes to Caesar. They could not resist that request. **"Show me the coin used for paying the tax."** Look at the coin. Get real. Look at this reality that is right in front of you. It is *clear*, if you are willing to pay attention—it is that clear. You are talking about taxes; look at the coin that is used to pay taxes. You are talking about paying taxes to Caesar; look at that coin and see what it says. **"They brought him a denarius, and he asked them, 'Whose image is this? And whose inscription?'"** (vv. 19b–20). On this coin was a portrait of Caesar and an inscription concerning Caesar.

The Coin Reveals the Captivity to Our Sin

The fact is that they are using this coin. Using coinage from a foreign power shows that they are under foreign rule. The reason the foreign power is ruling over them, according to the word of Moses, is because they have been disobedient to God. That is the reality. Because they have been disobedient to God, God has brought this power over them, as He had done many times in the past. What they need to do is humble themselves, pray, acknowledge their sin, turn to God, and repent. But, as we so often do with sin, they want to escape from the effects of sin, but not the sin itself. We are ready to not pay taxes or to do what it takes to get out of this "oppression." We want to escape the oppression of a foreign power rather than the oppression of our sin in us. **"'Whose image is this? And whose inscription?' 'Caesar's,' they replied. Then he said to them, 'So give back to Caesar what is Caesar's, and to God what is God's'"** (vv. 20–21). That coin is a testimony against them; they have sinned against God, and they are, by the power and rule of God, under the power of Caesar. They should pay the taxes to Caesar, but they should bring repentance of heart to God. Jesus saw right through what they were doing. Notice the assumptions that were appealed to by our Lord Jesus. 'You are the people of God; if you had been obedient, you would not be under the rule of another. Instead, you would be exercising the influence over the other nations'—this is clearly the word of Moses.[4]

---

4. *Deuteronomy 28.*

Acknowledging God's Sovereignty: The World's Judgment for Not Seeing What Is Clear

Jesus had this in mind, and He knew that they had this in the back of their minds, so He brought it to the fore. When God does allow foreign rule, we are to submit. Remember how they were to submit to Nebuchadnezzar? Remember how Jeremiah called them to submit repeatedly, but they did not because they were unwilling to acknowledge their sin. Psalm 80 speaks about the sin of the Church and the need for repentance; we need to reckon with sin. We need to humble ourselves before God and acknowledge that we have sinned. This is not 'their' doing, this is God's doing, because of our failure to do what He called us to do—because of our sin.

We have not been salt; we have not been light. We are scorned and held in contempt. We, corporately, the people of God, are in that position. We are using the word *we* the way Daniel used the word *we*.[5] We have sinned. Daniel was an upright man, but he recognized the corporate status of the people of God. We have sinned; we must repent. We have difficulty speaking to fellow believers about matters of doctrine. We have difficulties in overcoming divisions with those who are so close to us and even share the Bible as the Word of God. God brings the hand of foreigners upon us. They rule over us, and we must bow ourselves, not simply beneath the hand of foreigners, but beneath the hand of God. He is using foreigners as His rod. Jesus was a faithful witness; He spoke the truth and broke through that complex question by going to the assumptions in a very concrete and relevant way. We are to likewise be like Jesus and be faithful witnesses of God's truth. "When they heard this, they were amazed. So they left him and went away" (v. 22). Jesus silenced those who had come. He answered them in a relevant way, so there was no reply.

MARRIAGE AT THE RESURRECTION:
Failure to Understand the Scriptures and the Power of God

The same day, the Wednesday before Good Friday, the Pharisees left, and the Sadducees came to Jesus. "That same day the Sadducees, who say there is no resurrection, came to him with a question" (v. 23). The

---

5. *Daniel 9.*

Sadducees are like the deists; they believe in God but play down the supernatural and the resurrection. Deists believe in God; they believe in the afterlife, but they do not believe in the resurrection. Jesus responds now to the deists, or the ancient near equivalent to the deists. We have had deists in the more recent past, and I do not think we have responded to them, but we could look at how Jesus responded and learn from His response. The Sadducees say there is no resurrection, and notice their concern with meaning. The Pharisees seem to be concerned about righteousness and what is right. The Sadducees are concerned about meaning: Does it make sense? They think that it does not make sense to believe in the resurrection if you look at the Law of Moses.

> "Teacher," they said, "Moses told us that if a man dies without having children, his brother must marry the widow and raise up offspring for him. Now there were seven brothers among us. The first one married and died, and since he had no children, he left his wife to his brother. The same thing happened to the second and third brother, right on down to the seventh. Finally, the woman died. Now then, at the resurrection, whose wife will she be of the seven, since all of them were married to her?" (vv. 24–28).

They were very pleased with themselves, I'm sure. There is always a question that someone has, and they have worked at it over the months and years, and they have honed the question. There are questions like, 'How do you know that you are not a brain in a vat?' Have you ever heard that question? Well, we hone these questions, and the whole of our view comes distilled down to this one point, and now they drop it on Jesus. Jesus replied straightforwardly, **"You are in error because you do not know the Scriptures or the power of God"** (v. 29). They know neither. They do not know the Scriptures or the power of God. Notice again how Jesus appeals to assumptions. He uses good and necessary consequences. You do not get these answers immediately without thinking about the meaning of what is being said and what is assumed. The Westminster Confession of Faith 1.6 says, "The whole counsel of God concerning all things necessary for his own glory, man's salvation, faith and life, is either expressly set down in Scripture, or by good and necessary consequence may be deduced from Scripture." We have to learn to think about the meaning and draw out the implications. There are *literalists* who resist and reject drawing out implications and say, 'Unless it says it explicitly, it is not there.' That is not the sense of Scripture; God wants us to use reason and good and necessary consequences to understand the Scriptures and general revelation. Jesus uses reason and good and necessary consequences, so He is effective in giving the answer.

The Doctrine of Marriage: The Biblical Worldview Versus Fragments

First, He speaks about the doctrine of marriage: "**At the resurrection people will neither marry nor be given in marriage; they will be like the angels in heaven**" (v. 30). We do not understand the meaning of marriage; it was instituted by God for a purpose. Be fruitful and multiply, replenish the earth, subdue it, and have dominion over it.[6] The Sabbath Day says that the end of the work of dominion will occur, so marriage will end.[7] Marriage was a sign for human beings of the covenant with God, it is to be consummated in that covenant, in the Marriage Supper of the Lamb. Marriage is not forever; it will come to an end. Jesus replied, "**At the resurrection people will neither marry nor be given in marriage.**" They will have bodies, but they will not marry or be given in marriage; "**they will be like the angels in heaven.**" They will not be without bodies at the resurrection, they will have bodies, but they will not marry. Marriage serves a purpose; we need to keep that in mind; it is part of our Lord's answer. It is a very straight and simple answer. We should know that marriage is for a purpose if we pay attention to the Scriptures.

God Is the God of the Living

Jesus continues, "**But about the resurrection of the dead—have you not read what God said to you, 'I am the God of Abraham, the God of Isaac, and the God of Jacob'? He is not the God of the dead but of the living**" (vv. 31–32). We can see how He comes to this answer. The Scripture makes a difference between the living and the dead. If Abraham, Isaac, and Jacob are without bodies, they are dead; even if their souls are alive, they are dead. That is what 'dead' means; it is not

---

6. *Genesis 1:28* KJV.
7. Gangadean, *The Biblical Worldview*, 125–146.

addressing whether the soul goes on or not; it means that you are without your body, you are dead. God is the God of the living. God made us living beings in the Garden. He had the power and the goodness to do so. This is the answer to deists, too.[8] Death is not something original. If God is the God of the living, not of the dead, then they will be raised from the dead. God created the world good, without physical death; death came by God because of sin; as sin is removed, God will raise us from death. There is no problem in speaking about the power of God to create a world without death, nor the power of God to restore from the dead.

The Doctrine of Creation and the Curse

Jesus says they do not know the Scriptures. "**I am the God of Abraham, the God of Isaac, and the God of Jacob.**" You cannot say that God is the God of the dead. God is the God of the living, which means the body is restored. That is what *living* meant in the Garden, and that is what *dead* means throughout Scripture. Jesus replies to them and points out their lack of understanding how God created the world. They do not understand God's power to create the world without death, that He did so, and that He has the power to raise from the dead. They do not understand what the words *living* and *dead* mean. He affirms the resurrection of the dead in connection with understanding the power of God in creating and ruling, the reality of how God created, and the meaning of the terms *dead* and *living*. We know that God is the God of the living from the way in which He has created us since the beginning. "**When the crowds heard this, they were astonished at his teaching**" (v. 33).

Jesus answered the deists by appealing to the power of God, the Scripture, the way in which God created the world, His power to raise the dead, and that He *will* raise the dead because He is not the God of the dead, but of the living. Jesus understands what marriage is about, and He understands why death comes about—Jesus is arguing from a biblical worldview.[9] These are things that should be understood. I think without the biblical worldview, one could not get to the inferences that He is making.

---

8. Gangadean, *The Westminster Confession*, 14–18.
9. Gangadean, *The Biblical Worldview*.

WHICH IS THE GREATEST COMMANDMENT?
The Problem of Legalism and Deontology

Then a third question comes, "Hearing that Jesus had silenced the Sadducees, the Pharisees got together. One of them, an expert in the law, tested him with this question: 'Teacher, which is the greatest commandment in the Law?'" (vv. 34–36). In Matthew 5:17–19, Jesus spoke about obeying the least of these Commandments:

> Do not think that I have come to abolish the Law or the Prophets; I have not come to abolish them but to fulfill them. I tell you the truth, until heaven and earth disappear, not the smallest letter, not the least stroke of a pen, will by any means disappear from the Law until everything is accomplished. Anyone who breaks one of the least of these commandments and teaches others to do the same will be called least in the kingdom of heaven, but whoever practices and teaches these commands will be called great in the kingdom of heaven.[10]

Jesus is now speaking about the greatest commandment, but there is a problem in the way in which the Commandments were approached. They are approached in a legalistic way, without understanding them. There are Ten Commandments, and rather than seeing the unity of the Commandments, in terms of the point of the commandment, we make distinctions between greater and lesser commandments.

Let me ask you, which commandment is greater? How great is the second commandment, which speaks about the regulative principle of worship? Do some people think it is not such a great commandment? Not a big deal? How about the fourth commandment regarding eschatology and hope? Is that a great commandment, or can we be 'pan-mils'? It will all 'pan out' in the end. Have you ever heard of that? That does not sound like a great commandment, does it? We have made these distinctions and there is such a thing as fundamentalism[11]—funda-

---

10. NIV 1984.

11. Fundamentalism arose at the beginning of the 20th century in response to liberal theology. Its primary objective centered on soteriology with an emphasis on individual salvation. Fundamentalism affirmed the five fundamentals for salvation: the literal interpretation of the Bible, the inerrancy of Scripture, the Virgin Birth, resurrection, and divinity of Christ. However, these fundamentals fall short of attaining the goal of filling the earth with the

mental to what? If the goal is knowing God and loving God, can we say we can dispense with eschatology regarding the earth being filled with the knowledge of God and be 'pan-mil'? Can we dispense with the law in terms of our fallenness and our distortion of God with regard to the knowledge of God in the singing of Psalms? No, we are to glorify God and enjoy Him forever. We are to love God with our whole heart. When we do not love God with our whole heart, we begin to set one thing above another and we set up other things besides God. The deists look to the past and affirm God as Creator, but not ruler and redeemer. Otherworldly Christians look to the future and emphasize heaven. Islam looks to the future judgment. The Jews spoke about God here in this life through physical blessings. We all could take one thing over another, make that thing central, and miss the point.

'What is the greatest commandment, Jesus?' We cannot make that distinction with the Commandments. We cannot say the Commandments are essential only for some. We cannot be legalistic. We must understand the goal, the end, and the unity of the Commandments. The whole being is to respond to the whole of God. To love God partly is to love another besides God. Jesus explains what it is to love God.

> Jesus replied: 'Love the Lord your God with all your heart and with all your soul and with all your mind.' This is the first and greatest commandment. And the second is like it: 'Love your neighbor as yourself.' All the Law and the Prophets hang on these two commandments (vv. 37–40).

There is a unity; there is a point to the Commandments. If we are to love God with all our heart, we cannot say, 'Well, I love you in this way, but I won't love you in that way.' That is not loving God with all of our heart. This question has to do with the understanding of the Commandments—the basic things. Time and again, Jesus will be able to answer the questions that came to Him because He reasoned from the basic things.

---

knowledge of God through the work of dominion consistent with doxological postmillennialism.

JESUS' QUESTION:
Who Is the Christ?

Then, Jesus asked them a question, **"While the Pharisees were gathered together, Jesus asked them, 'What do you think about the Messiah? Whose son is he?'"** (vv. 41–42a). There are two questions here that sometimes get confused. Who is the Christ? Jesus of Nazareth is the Christ. *Who* is in that office? That is one question. There is another question that is prior to that; it is more basic. *What* is the office of the Christ? What is the nature of that office? The point at which Christianity differs from Judaism is on this more basic question, and Jesus brings that to the fore. **"'The son of David,' they replied"** (v. 42b). No one would doubt this answer. But their answer is in the context of the Christ conquering enemies and having a certain kind of rule. They believe in the Christ as victorious, the Christ as king, but not the Christ as the Savior and the suffering servant. Jesus' response is pointed when He uses the Word of God that is sharper than any two-edged sword:

> He said to them, **"How is it then that David, speaking by the Spirit, calls him 'Lord'? For he says, 'The Lord said to my Lord: "Sit at my right hand until I put your enemies under your feet."' If then David calls him 'Lord,' how can he be his son?"** (vv. 43–45).

"The Lord said to my Lord . . ." If David, in the Spirit, is calling Him 'Lord', **"how can he be his son?"** What kind of redemption is going to come? Will redemption come from some seed of David, who shares the sin with David and his father Adam? Can that one take away sin? Do they see the need to take away sin? Do they see the need for salvation through the Messiah? To this day, they do not. What is the office of Messiah? Is He just king, or is He Savior, too? If He is the Savior, is He just the son of David? These are the assumptions embedded in those beliefs about the son of David. Jesus brings this to the fore.

Christ is more than the son of David, a glorious king—He is the Savior. To be the Savior, He must be sinless, and to be born of David *only* is to have sin. He is the seed of a woman but not of man. No imputed unrighteousness comes to Him. He is without sin, that He might be the Savior of mankind. That is what was missing. It was there in the Scriptures, in the very verse that they may appeal to in order to say that they are looking for this glorious king. Why then is He called

'Lord' by David, if He is David's son? With this, Scripture says, "No one could say a word in reply, and from that day on no one dared to ask him any more questions" (v. 46). He had silenced the Sadducees, as it says in verse 34, "Hearing that Jesus had silenced the Sadducees, the Pharisees got together," and now the Pharisees are silenced.

SILENCING THEIR CHALLENGES:
Jesus Relies On and Shows Clarity Through the Use of Good and Necessary Consequences

The Pharisees, the Herodians, and the Sadducees—all three—asked Jesus questions, and He silenced them. Then Jesus asked them a question, and they could not respond. They had no objection to His teaching. Notice the double silence; He silenced their challenges in verses 34 and 46. And they could not silence His challenge. He did this because He used good and necessary consequences from the biblical worldview, as we have seen. He relied on clarity, and showed that clarity is available to all who seek God diligently. "And without faith it is impossible to please God, because anyone who comes to him must believe that he exists and that he rewards those who earnestly seek him" (Heb. 11:6). This is for all of us; we are to be conformed to our Lord Jesus Christ. Notice that Jesus did not bring them over, but He did silence them. A good part of our work is not necessarily going to be bringing people over directly, but we will need to silence particular leaders who would block the people, so the people may break free from the obstacles put up by the leaders.

We are called to be witnesses, but we can only witness to that which we have seen for ourselves. You have heard about clarity, but have you seen it yourself? If you have not seen it yourself, you cannot be a witness. In a court of law or a court of public opinion, if you cannot show when called upon to show or demonstrate, your testimony will fall apart, and you will avoid it. You will not be a witness. If we cannot show clarity, we will not be faithful witnesses; we will not be salt, and we will not be light. Search your hearts before the Lord. We are to be conformed to our Lord Jesus Christ. Let us give heed to these examples in the Scriptures.

20

JUDGMENT ON FALSE TEACHERS
The Seven Woes—The Cup of Iniquity Is Full

Matthew 23

¹Then Jesus said to the crowds and to his disciples: ²"The teachers of the law and the Pharisees sit in Moses' seat. ³So you must be careful to do everything they tell you. But do not do what they do, for they do not practice what they preach. ⁴They tie up heavy, cumbersome loads and put them on other people's shoulders, but they themselves are not willing to lift a finger to move them.

⁵"Everything they do is done for people to see: They make their phylacteries wide and the tassels on their garments long; ⁶they love the place of honor at banquets and the most important seats in the synagogues; ⁷they love to be greeted with respect in the marketplaces and to be called 'Rabbi' by others.

⁸"But you are not to be called 'Rabbi,' for you have one Teacher, and you are all brothers. ⁹And do not call anyone on earth 'father,' for you have one Father, and he is in heaven. ¹⁰Nor are you to be called instructors, for you have one Instructor, the Messiah. ¹¹The greatest among you will be your servant. ¹²For those who exalt themselves will be humbled, and those who humble themselves will be exalted.

¹³"Woe to you, teachers of the law and Pharisees, you hypocrites! You shut the door of the kingdom of heaven in people's faces. You yourselves do not enter, nor will you let those enter who are trying to. ¹⁴"Woe to you, scribes and Pharisees, hypocrites! For you devour widows' houses, and for a pretense make long prayers. Therefore you will receive greater condemnation"

[15]"Woe to you, teachers of the law and Pharisees, you hypocrites! You travel over land and sea to win a single convert, and when you have succeeded, you make them twice as much a child of hell as you are.

[16]"Woe to you, blind guides! You say, 'If anyone swears by the temple, it means nothing; but anyone who swears by the gold of the temple is bound by that oath.' [17]You blind fools! Which is greater: the gold, or the temple that makes the gold sacred? [18]You also say, 'If anyone swears by the altar, it means nothing; but anyone who swears by the gift on the altar is bound by that oath.' [19]You blind men! Which is greater: the gift, or the altar that makes the gift sacred? [20]Therefore, anyone who swears by the altar swears by it and by everything on it. [21]And anyone who swears by the temple swears by it and by the one who dwells in it. [22]And anyone who swears by heaven swears by God's throne and by the one who sits on it.

[23]"Woe to you, teachers of the law and Pharisees, you hypocrites! You give a tenth of your spices—mint, dill and cumin. But you have neglected the more important matters of the law—justice, mercy and faithfulness. You should have practiced the latter, without neglecting the former. [24]You blind guides! You strain out a gnat but swallow a camel.

[25]"Woe to you, teachers of the law and Pharisees, you hypocrites! You clean the outside of the cup and dish, but inside they are full of greed and self-indulgence. [26]Blind Pharisee! First clean the inside of the cup and dish, and then the outside also will be clean.

[27]"Woe to you, teachers of the law and Pharisees, you hypocrites! You are like whitewashed tombs, which look beautiful on the outside but on the inside are full of the bones of the dead and everything unclean. [28]In the same way, on the outside you appear to people as righteous but on the inside you are full of hypocrisy and wickedness.

[29]"Woe to you, teachers of the law and Pharisees, you hypocrites! You build tombs for the prophets and decorate the graves of the righteous. [30]And you say, 'If we had lived in the days of our ancestors, we would not have taken part with them in shedding the blood of the prophets.' [31]So you testify against yourselves that you are the descendants of those who murdered the prophets. [32]Go ahead, then, and complete what your ancestors started!

[33]"You snakes! You brood of vipers! How will you escape being condemned to hell? [34]Therefore I am sending you prophets and sages and teachers. Some of them you will kill and crucify; others you will flog in your synagogues and pursue from town to town. [35]And so upon you will come all the righteous blood that has been shed on earth, from the blood of righteous Abel to the blood of Zechariah son of Berekiah, whom you

murdered between the temple and the altar. ³⁶Truly I tell you, all this will come on this generation.

³⁷"Jerusalem, Jerusalem, you who kill the prophets and stone those sent to you, how often I have longed to gather your children together, as a hen gathers her chicks under her wings, and you were not willing. ³⁸Look, your house is left to you desolate. ³⁹For I tell you, you will not see me again until you say, 'Blessed is he who comes in the name of the Lord.'"

INTRODUCTION:
Prior Context and Anticipation of the Judgment to Come

WE ARE NOW COMING TO THE THIRD PART of the series in the Passion Week. Up to this point, we have seen that Jesus has presented Himself to the people and has been proclaimed King by them. He has gone into the temple and seen the condition of the people after three years. Jesus had previously cleansed the temple and saw the need for it to be cleansed again; they had not heeded, and now they must require more severe treatment. The morning after the triumphal entry, as He was coming into the city, He saw a fig tree without fruit. This was a sign of the people. Jesus cursed the fig tree, which helps us anticipate what is coming in Matthew 23. Having cursed the fig tree, He entered the temple, overturned the money tables, drove out the animals being sold, drove out the money changers, and chastised them for daring to make His Father's house a place of merchandise—a place for making money. They challenged Jesus' authority and He answered their questions. Jesus answered them in significant detail, connecting their questions with authority. Whose son is the Christ? He is not only the son of David but the Son of God, who has the power and authority, as the Son of God, to do what He is doing and to do what He is now about to do. He will carry out, in an outward way, what He did in the sign of the fig tree; He will now pronounce the curse and judgment on the people who have turned away from Him, particularly the leaders.

Moses' Seat: The Authority to Teach Ordained by God

These persons who have been asking questions are identified as the teachers of the law—those who sit in Moses' seat. Notice the reference to Moses. "Then Jesus said to the crowds and to his disciples: 'The

teachers of the law and the Pharisees sit in Moses' seat'" (vv. 1–2).
The place of authority ordained by God, and first occupied by Moses,
was to teach the law to the people, the covenant Word by which they
were to live all of life. This authority has continued, and others now
occupy this seat of authority. Jesus recognizes the original authority,
its present existence, and those who are in that position now. He calls
us to recognize the authority that He has ordained. He says, "**So you
must be careful to do everything they tell you. But do not do what
they do, for they do not practice what they preach**" (v. 3). This is a bit
problematic, because those who sit in Moses' seat will say things that
Jesus is going to denounce. So if the people were to do everything the
teachers of the law and the Pharisees tell them, without any qualification, they would be doing things contrary to God's Word. This requires
us to ask how we are to understand this command: They sit in Moses'
seat; therefore, you must do everything they tell you. The first part, that
they sit in Moses' seat, qualifies the second part, to do everything they
tell you. The teachers of the law and the Pharisees sit in Moses' seat, so
everything they say that is according to Moses' authority is to be obeyed
by the people. However, sitting in Moses' seat does not give them the
right to say what is contrary to what Moses said. The Pharisees do say
things according to Moses, but they say other things that may negate
and nullify what is according to the word of Moses. The people are to
hear and obey what the Pharisees say that is in keeping with sitting
in Moses' seat, but the Pharisees do not do these things that they say.

There are some persons in authority in our culture who tell us we
should do critical thinking. University teachers, who carry on something
of a seat of authority, say much about *reason*, and they make claims in
the name of reason. Are we to listen to everything they say? We are to
listen only to that which is consistent with that position of authority.
But do these teachers do what they say? Socrates called us to examine
our lives, but did he examine his life? Neither Socrates nor his disciple
Plato examined their assumptions about the soul and matter being
eternal.[1] Persons can be in positions of authority and say things that
are right and true, and we are to listen to them and obey, even down
to the last things they may require. So Jesus is telling us here to regard
that authority. If a ruler requires us not to preach the name of Christ

---

1. Gangadean, *Philosophical Foundation*, 129–134; Gangadean, *History of Philosophy*, 87–105.

anymore, are we, therefore, not to preach? Peter and John told the leaders, "Judge for yourselves whether it is right in God's sight to obey you rather than God" (Acts 4:19).[2] Similarly, if Nero were to command us to acknowledge him as a divine emperor, we are not to do so. Yet, Paul appealed to the seat of Caesar for justice against injustice on the part of the local authorities who were seeking to hand him over to the Jews. We are to understand that they sit in Moses' seat, so we must obey them and do everything they say that is consistent with Moses' seat.

Part of teaching is by example. The example is not being set by these leaders. The teachers of the law and the Pharisees are not consistent, so we are not to do as they do. I hope we can discern between legitimate authority, affirmed by Jesus, and persons who do wrong while holding positions of legitimate authority. Insofar as those persons who do wrong are in positions of legitimate authority and ask us to do what is legitimate, we are to obey. Their wrongdoing does not override what is more basic. This has been a problem for Christians through the centuries, but we do not have to take things out of context and get ourselves into difficulty. Jesus says, **"They tie up heavy cumbersome loads and put them on other people's shoulders, but they themselves are not willing to lift a finger to move them"** (v. 4). In the name of tradition and legalism, the Pharisees burdened the people in a way contrary to the ceremonial law. There is a God-imposed discipline structured in the ceremonial law. The people were to present the sacrifices before the priest and observe the regulations in order to be taught the way of righteousness. Remember, God imposed the curse,[3] and the priests are to teach us to recognize the curse and to deal with it properly. We are to observe, understand, take time out, and think about what the curse means. We have lost the meaning of the curse and the promise in our culture because those in authority have not taught in keeping with Moses' seat. They tie up heavy loads, we do not deny that, but Jesus said to do everything they tell you, insofar as it is consistent with Moses' seat.

2. NIV 1984.
3. Gangadean, *The Biblical Worldview*, 55–68, 275–294.

Self-Life: The Praise of Men and Honor from Another

The Pharisees act in a way that reveals the fundamental principles of the self-life. They do what they do to receive the praise of men for themselves. **"Everything they do is done for people to see: They make their phylacteries wide and the tassels on their garments long"** (v. 5). The human heart goes in that direction, left to itself. The human heart wants to exalt self more and more, and even in professing the name of God, it will exalt self. There is a desire to be seen as holy. There is something that is often troubling to me when I see someone in clerical garments in a public place. It seems to me to be giving the message of wanting to be seen as holy: **"They make their phylacteries wide."** It is drawing attention to oneself in a way that seems inconsistent. The Lord is warning us against drawing this attention to self.

They also **"love the place of honor at banquets and the most important seats in the synagogues; they love to be greeted with respect in the marketplaces and to be called 'Rabbi' by others"** (vv. 6–7). The Lord warns us about putting ourselves in a position to be called 'Rabbi' or 'Master' or 'Father.' He says,

> But you are not to be called 'Rabbi,' for you have one Teacher and you are all brothers. And do not call anyone on earth 'father,' for you have one Father, and he is in heaven. Nor are you to be called instructors, for you have one Instructor, the Messiah (vv. 8–10).

Sometimes pastors love to call others 'Pastor so-and-so,' but it seems awkward to me to be referred to in that way. I do not know if I am just missing something, or whether I am just feeling some awkwardness in connection with this, but the Lord warns us against the need to be called 'Teacher.' The point that He is making is about the self-life: we are not to bring honor to the self, but always bring the honor to God. We are inclined to exalt ourselves. We have a concern to be the greatest. This desire to excel has been perverted and put on a human level, and we desire to excel above others rather than desire to excel beyond where we are presently before God. Because of sin, the virtue in desiring to excel and be the greatest we can be becomes perverted. We desire to be greater than others rather than be the greatest we can be before God. The Lord warns us against this. If we want to be the greatest, we ought to humble ourselves and be the servant of all.[4] **"The greatest among you will be your servant. For those who exalt themselves will be humbled, and those who humble themselves will be exalted"** (vv. 11–12). If you exalt yourself, you will be humbled,[5] and it is particularly painful to see someone both exalting themselves and being humbled. We cringe inside and feel embarrassment, and we hope that we do not slip in that way.

Jesus spoke of the authority of those who sit in Moses' seat, how we should relate to them, and how and why they turn aside. He spoke about the true spirit of the Christian life. Our Lord pronounces the indictment upon those who put themselves forward and exalt themselves. We can see how all of these indictments and charges are connected with this preface, His introductory remarks, and what has happened before.

Jesus has presented Himself as King. He was received by the people and rejected by the leaders. The Pharisees told Him, "Teacher, rebuke your disciples!"[6] They wanted to stop the disciples from giving Him praise. They had made the temple into a house of merchandise. They challenged His authority with resistance and obstruction. They would not recognize the true authority of God and the One who is sent in the name of God. Remember what has been happening throughout the three years of His ministry and what has happened just in the last two days as He comes to this final week. Remember that our Lord is coming to face His death in Jerusalem; He knows exactly where this is going. He knows the end. When He pronounces the indictment, it is with all of this in mind, and we are to keep that in mind if we are to understand the indictment, the judgment, and last of all, the lament. All three are coming. Just as the prophets have spoken, our Lord Jesus speaks. He speaks to the men who occupy the position of Moses' seat as one who truly sits in the seat of Moses. He is the Word of God.

---

4. *Matthew 20:26; Mark 9:35, 10:43; Luke 22:26.*

5. *Luke 14:11, 18:14; Matthew 23:12.*

6. *Luke 19:39.*

INDICTMENTS:
The Seven Woes

The Underlying Charge of Hypocrisy

"Woe to you, teachers of the law and Pharisees, you hypocrites!" (v. 13a). Remember, Jesus said that they say and do not do. They make the outward broad, but the inward is lacking—"They make their phylacteries wide and the tassels on their garments long" (v. 5b). Hypocrisy is a violation of the third commandment.[7] It is to speak the name of God in vain. It is to lightly and thoughtlessly regard that by which God makes Himself known. This is done in the preaching, in the vows, and in everyday life because God reveals Himself in everything around us. When we regard that revelation lightly and thoughtlessly, and do not think, meditate, and seek the Lord in these things, we are breaking the third commandment. The Scriptures say, "You shall not take the name of the LORD your God in vain, for the LORD will not hold him guiltless who takes His name in vain" (Ex. 20:7). We have that Word of God in the third commandment, and this commandment is coming through here in the charge of hypocrisy. The Word comes against the teachers of the law and the Pharisees. They excel in representing the teaching of the law and the observance of the law, but it has been gutted, emptied of its meaning, and given new content. They may be very punctilious about the law but miss its meaning. This indictment comes to the teachers of the law and the Pharisees because of their hypocrisy.

First Woe: Shutting the Way to Enter the Kingdom of God

"Woe to you, teachers of the law and Pharisees, you hypocrites! You shut the kingdom of heaven in men's faces" (v. 13a).[8] This is dramatic: men are coming in, and the teachers and Pharisees shut the door in their faces. They prevent people from entering the kingdom of heaven. There are persons in authority—in the Church, in families, in the State, and in education—who would deny the kingdom of God, and hinder others from entering. They do not enter themselves and they prevent others from entering. "You yourselves do not enter, nor will

---

7. Gangadean, *Philosophical Foundation*, 199–205.

8. 1984 NIV.

you let those enter who are trying to" (v. 13b). Persons in positions of authority who do not enter the kingdom of God declare their reasons to others, and through those reasons, they shut the door and prevent others from entering. There are parents who have dissuaded young people from pursuing a life in Christ. I know of parents who have done so. There are religious teachers who have done so by calling names. There are professors who have done so.

Moses' seat was an all-encompassing authority at the beginning. His seat of authority became divided later on into prophet, priest, and king. Moses was a prophet, priest, and king at the beginning. So Moses' seat speaks about authority in general. The first indictment certainly applies to the Pharisees and the teachers of the law particularly, but it applies to more than just these particular positions. Anyone in a position of authority ordained of God who hinders others from entering the kingdom comes under this judgment: "Woe to you." This is particularly true of the Pharisees and the teachers of the law. God calls us to seek first the kingdom of God and His righteousness. Our Lord said, "For I tell you that unless your righteousness surpasses that of the Pharisees and the teachers of the law, you will certainly not enter the kingdom of heaven" (Matt. 5:20). At the very beginning of His teaching, Jesus made this point, and He is making it again. People in authority who do not enter and hinder others from doing so, particularly religious teaching offices, come under the same indictment, and we are not to be surprised.

Second Woe: Zeal Without Knowledge—Making Converts to Positive Falsehood

"Woe to you, teachers of the law and Pharisees, you hypocrites! You travel over land and sea to win a single convert, and when you have succeeded, you make them twice as much a child of hell as you are" (v. 15). This is more than the first indictment, this speaks about a certain zeal that we have for teaching our way. I heard that it costs hundreds of thousands of dollars to make one convert to Christianity. Some have programs upon programs and layers upon layers. In terms of the total number of converts and the total cost spent, $300,000 is spent for one convert. You might say that amount is worth it for one convert, but that does not seem to be the way in which God would have us go. That is just to say that sometimes a lot can be invested in making converts. We can put a lot of energy into seeking to teach our own way to others and we can put a lot of energy into seeking support for it. There are many agencies, shares, and foundation grants, and sometimes there are converts, one here and one there. But the Lord says, **"You make them twice as much a child of hell as you are"** (v. 15b). The disciple tends to take what is taught and carry it further, so we have an accumulation of evil in the following generations, and by the third and fourth generation, things get very bad. There were people teaching false things about the nature of freedom in the 1940s and 1950s. In the 1960s, it got worse. You might think that once a child of hell is enough, but the Scripture says they make them twice the child of hell. There are degrees of darkness into which a person may be brought. This is a reality. We have a zeal to promote our way and to draw the implication, and judgment comes on that false teaching.

Third Woe: Devotion to Gold (Self) Rather Than God

The third indictment concerns blind guides regarding swearing, commitments, oaths, and piety.

> Woe to you, blind guides! You say, "If anyone swears by the temple, it means nothing; but anyone who swears by the gold of the temple is bound by that oath." You blind fools! Which is greater: the gold, or the temple that makes the gold sacred? You also say, "If anyone swears by the altar, it means nothing; but anyone who swears by the gift on it is bound by that oath." You blind men! Which is greater: the gift, or the altar that makes the gift sacred? Therefore, anyone who swears by the altar swears by it and by everything on it. And anyone who swears by the temple swears by it and by the one who dwells in it. And anyone who swears by heaven swears by God's throne and by the one who sits on it (vv. 16–22).

There is a new piety being taught. Which are we to take more seriously? It says, **"If anyone swears by the temple, it means nothing; but anyone who swears by the gold of the temple is bound by that oath."** This is so backward that Jesus declares those who teach this way to be blind; they do not see. In verses 16–17, 19, and 24, He speaks of these teachers as blind to spiritual truths. They are all the more blind because they think they see and they do not see. There is a blindness where you do not see and you realize that you do not see. But you cannot get more blind than thinking you see when you do not see. Jesus says, **"You blind guides!" "You blind fools!"**[9] They are blind because they do not realize the things that are very basic. They have taken the holy things of God, the things that really mean something, and they have twisted them to fulfill the self-life.

Human beings may be devoted to self in the name of God. They have worshiped Baal and Ashtoreth in the place of God, and they continue to do this. What is being affirmed is the self-life, the life of self-indulgence, and money and greed as a means to self-indulgence. This is where they say, **"If anyone swears by the temple, it means nothing; but anyone who swears by the gold of the temple is bound by that oath."** They also say, **"If anyone swears by the altar, it means nothing."** On the contrary, it means *everything*. That is where meaning is. A vow is what true dedication to God is about. It concerns who God is and what true holiness is. But it is being reversed, and piety is twisted: instead of devotion to God, this is devotion to self and what would fulfill self. This is done with a religious veneer; it is done in the name of God, which is a further step into depravity. A new piety is being taught.

Fourth Woe: Straining at Gnats but Swallowing Camels

"Woe to you, teachers of the law and Pharisees, you hypocrites! You give a tenth of your spices—mint, dill and cumin. But you have neglected the more important matters of the law—justice, mercy and faithfulness" (v. 23a). Sometimes we can be very punctilious in the little things, and it seems that we are being careful precisely because we are concerned about the little things. But here, it is not an emphasis on the little things having done the big things, but it is an emphasis on the little things without having done the big things. It gives the *appearance* of care. The basic principles of the law—justice, mercy, and faithfulness—were not practiced; they were neglected. As a matter of fact, the tithes were being done in such a way that Jesus had to rebuke them:

> Jesus sat down opposite the place where the offerings were put and watched the crowd putting their money into the temple treasury.

---

9. *Matthew 23:24, 17.*

Many rich people threw in large amounts. But a poor widow came
and put in two very small copper coins, worth only a few cents.
Calling his disciples to him, Jesus said, "Truly I tell you, this poor
widow has put more into the treasury than all the others. They all
gave out of their wealth; but she, out of her poverty, put in everything—all she had to live on" (Mk. 12:41–44).

He is drawing attention to what true value is. Those in authority took
advantage of the widows' houses and things that should be dedicated
to the service of God. **"Woe to you, scribes and Pharisees, hypocrites!
For you devour widows' houses, and for a pretense make long prayers.
Therefore you will receive greater condemnation"** (v. 14 NKJV).
They believe that if they give large amounts of wealth to the church,
they are free from having to give service to God. In the name of the
religion, they gathered the money for themselves. The same spirit was
working in the selling of indulgences to build St. Peter's Basilica. They
have managed to monetize religion. They have omitted the weightier
matters. Jesus does not say to forget the small matters, He says, **"You
should have practiced the latter, without neglecting the former. You
blind guides! You strain out a gnat but swallow a camel"** (vv. 23b–24).
These are the teachers. Sin does that to us. It turns things inside out and
upside down. Remember that we have sin. The exact same principle
is at work in us; they had just carried it out further. In the church, we
can carry it out in our own covered-up and justified way. We are to be
careful. Jesus is speaking against sin and the death that comes with it.

Fifth Woe: Outward Cleanliness Without the Inward

> **Woe to you, teachers of the law and Pharisees, you hypocrites! You
> clean the outside of the cup and dish, but inside they are full of
> greed and self-indulgence. Blind Pharisee! First clean the inside of
> the cup and dish, and then the outside also will be clean (vv. 25–26).**

Jesus charged the Pharisees with greed and self-indulgence. Those two
are connected; it is the self-life. They indulge in all the desires of their
self-life and try to find satisfaction in that rather than knowing God,
and greed is one way to satisfy their self-indulgence. Inwardly, self-indulgence is operating, but a show is made of piety. Many in the world
have seen through that show of piety. In many churches, there is a

continual reminder to be sure that the money keeps coming in, and that is how the world sees the Church. 'Every time you turn around, they are asking for money.' The world sees through the show of piety.

Sixth Woe: Outwardly Beautiful Versus Inward Hypocrisy and Wickedness

Woe to you, teachers of the law and Pharisees, you hypocrites! You are like whitewashed tombs, which look beautiful on the outside but on the inside are full of the bones of the dead and everything unclean. In the same way, on the outside you appear to people as righteous but on the inside you are full of hypocrisy and wickedness (vv. 27–28).

Outwardly, clergy may appear righteous, having a beauty that seems appropriate. One may think there is an air about this person and this way, and it seems this place is holy. There may be that outward appearance, but inwardly, it is just the opposite, which is the nature of sin. We should not allow ourselves to be deceived. Remember, we are the first to deceive ourselves, others are not the first to deceive us. In the Garden, Adam deceived himself when he made the covering of fig leaves, and he justified himself. We are the first to deceive ourselves. Sin comes out of the heart, not from the environment. As we look at this, we are to be concerned about the sin remaining in us, by which we fall into the pit of self-deception.

Seventh Woe: The Way of Those Who Killed the Prophets

Woe to you, teachers of the law and Pharisees, you hypocrites! You build tombs for the prophets and decorate the graves of the righteous. And you say, "If we had lived in the days of our ancestors, we would not have taken part with them in shedding the blood of the prophets." So you testify against yourselves that you are the descendants of those who murdered the prophets. Go ahead, then, and complete what your ancestors started! (vv. 29–32).

We say this also—that we would not have been like them. But because of our sin, we are like them. We are like those who turn aside. Notice how this is opened up by our Lord, "So you testify against yourselves that you are the descendants of those who murdered the prophets. Fill up, then, the measure of the sin of your forefathers!"[10] They hinder those entering the kingdom, and if necessary, they hinder by killing those who would bring the message. They would kill one, they would kill all, and they would even kill the Son of God. Jesus knows that this is going to happen. This is the true nature of sin. This is the true nature of the self-life, and this is the true nature of autonomy. When we might speak about sin in the leaders, let us not forget that it is in us first. It is often because sin is in us that it is in the leaders, because God gives us the leaders that we deserve as part of His judgment upon us. But, the leaders are more responsible because they are in a position of authority. The Pharisees and teachers of the law continue to resist and kill the prophets. They resisted the Lord Jesus. They have hindered those who welcomed Jesus, those who shouted, "Hosanna to the Son of David!" "Blessed is he who comes in the name of the LORD!" "Hosanna in the highest!" (Matt. 21:9). Jesus demonstrated that salvation again and again, and they would not listen. When He cast out demons, they accused Him of casting them out in the name of the devil.

JUDGMENT PRONOUNCED:
"You Snakes! You Brood of Vipers!"

We can now understand the judgment. Notice how it is particularly focused on the summation, where all of this is heading, and it comes to a consummation. The indictments begin with resisting, stopping others from entering, deceiving oneself and deceiving others by being outwardly righteous, and if necessary, up to indictment seven, killing those who would bring the call to repentance. Jesus sees exactly the state of things. This is Jesus' holiness, this is Jesus' righteousness. He pronounces the judgment, but He does so in this way: He says, "Come to me . . . I am gentle and humble in heart, and you will find rest for your souls" (Matt. 11:28a, 29b). He pronounces the judgment, but it is accompanied by the lament. This reveals the heart of God. This reveals the heart of Jesus. Hear then, the judgment. It could not be any more pointed: "You snakes! You brood of vipers!" (v. 33a). There is not another name that is lower than "You snakes! You brood of vipers!" That

---

10. NIV 1984.

is what they are, and that is what we are. That is the nature of sin in all of us. The flesh wars against the Spirit, the Spirit against the flesh.[11]

Paul said, "What a wretched man I am! Who will rescue me from this body of death?" (Rom. 7:24).[12] It is a continual war, a savage war, an irreconcilable war, and the only way to overcome it is, by the grace of God, by the power of the Spirit, to crucify the flesh daily. If we do not take up our cross daily, it will come to this: **"You snakes! You brood of vipers! How will you escape being condemned to hell?"** (v. 33). How can those who are living in this way, who will pursue the self-life to such an extent that they would kill the prophets and kill the very One who is the Word of God incarnate, escape the judgment of hell? And so He pronounces judgment. Notice that there is not a way in which you can escape. God said in the beginning, "In the day that you eat of it you shall surely die" (Gen. 2:17b NKJV). The wages of sin is death.[13] Do not be deceived. A man reaps what he sows.[14] Those who diligently and patiently seek the Lord will come to understanding, sanctification, holiness, and joy in the Lord, but those who do not patiently and diligently seek the Lord will not. There will be emptiness, and they will try to fill the place of the Creator with the creature, which will lead to all kinds of excess. That, in itself, will be the judgment of God. The failure to see what is clear about God, in Romans 1:18–20, is to be given up to sexual impurity and to go into depravity and perversion, which is now in the land. That is the wrath of God being poured out upon men who turn away from what is clear.[15] Please keep it in your mind that the wrath of God being poured out is in connection with what is clear. We can try to disregard that, but it is in connection with clarity in Romans 1 that we are given up to sexual impurity and so on. We seek a covenant relationship with another person instead of God. Instead of finding fulfillment in God, we try to find it in another human being in the outward, physical, and visible, without understanding, and we go to sexual perversion and deeper and deeper depravity.

---

11. *Galatians 5:17–25.*

12. NIV 1984.

13. *Romans 6:23.*

14. *Galatians 6:7.*

15. *Romans 1:21–32.*

How can you escape the judgment of hell? Hell is to be understood as being given up to darkness of mind, burning without satisfaction, and the torment of the guilt of conscience. Everyone is now trying to avoid the guilt of conscience by being politically correct. Political correctness says that you must not say anything that would raise the shame or disapprobation of perverse things. But the guilt of conscience remains and continues to work in our culture and in our lives. "**How will you escape being condemned to hell?**" (v. 33b).

Jesus brings the nature of sin and the response to the witness into focus. "**Therefore I am sending you prophets and sages and teachers. Some of them you will kill and crucify; others you will flog in your synagogues and pursue from town to town**" (v. 34). This is what happens when we follow the self-life. We resist everything that would come to call us back. We will kill, and we will crucify, and we will flog, and we will pursue from town to town. That is the nature of sin. Our Lord sees it as it is. He brings things into focus as He is making the judgment. He sees the reality of a witness that has been made, from the beginning in the days of Abel, all the way down to the present day. That witness stands, cumulative, so that those who fail to hear are held responsible for every word that has been spoken. He says,

> And so upon you will come all the righteous blood that has been shed on earth, from the blood of righteous Abel to the blood of Zechariah son of Berekiah, whom you murdered between the temple and the altar. Truly I tell you, all this will come on this generation (vv. 35–36).

This generation had the culmination of the witness. The Word of God incarnate, the very Son of God, was speaking before them and engaging them before their very eyes and their faces. At this very moment, the witness of the prophets is consummated in our Lord Jesus Christ, and they have killed even that Word of God. So upon the generation that has had that consummation, this judgment will come. Judgment will come on anyone else who rejects the Word of God. We can expect that God does not change, and judgment will come. The judgment is pronounced upon them; they cannot escape it. God's judgment will come upon this generation in being condemned to hell—darkness of

mind, burning without satisfaction, and the torment of the guilt of conscience—and in the temporal judgment of the destruction of Jerusalem.

THE LAMENT:
"O Jerusalem, Jerusalem"

The indictments, the judgment, and the lament come together:

> Jerusalem, Jerusalem, you who kill the prophets and stone those
> sent to you, how often I have longed to gather your children to-
> gether, as a hen gathers her chicks under her wings, and you were
> not willing. Look, your house is left to you desolate (vv. 37–38).

There is one and only one hope. Jesus said, "**For I tell you, you will
not see me again until you say, 'Blessed is he who comes in the name
of the Lord'**" (v. 39). Until this people—any people, every people—
say, "**Blessed is he who comes in the name of the Lord**," they will not
see Him, and they will not enter the kingdom of God. Our Lord Jesus
Christ has been given the right to judge. He has put the judgment in
the words of the psalm[16] and, even more, in the very words that the
people have spoken; those words will judge them. He wants to make
it as intimate as He can. "**How often I have longed to gather your
children together.**" He knows what lies ahead: they will kill Him; they
will surely kill Him, as they have killed all the prophets. It is the same
sin that worked in Cain with Abel, down to the present time. We do
not want to have sin exposed; we will hate the light and put out the
light. This will come, yet how our Lord longs that it would not be so.
He holds out the way of repentance: "**. . . until you say, 'Blessed is he
who comes in the name of the Lord.'**"

---

16. *Psalm 118:26.*

21

THE TIME OF THE END

This Generation Shall Not Pass,
till All These Things Be Fulfilled

Matthew 24:1–35

¹Jesus left the temple and was walking away when his disciples came up to him to call his attention to its buildings. ²"Do you see all these things?" he asked. "Truly I tell you, not one stone here will be left on another; every one will be thrown down."

³As Jesus was sitting on the Mount of Olives, the disciples came to him privately. "Tell us," they said, "when will this happen, and what will be the sign of your coming and of the end of the age?"

⁴Jesus answered: "Watch out that no one deceives you. ⁵For many will come in my name, claiming, 'I am the Messiah,' and will deceive many. ⁶You will hear of wars and rumors of wars, but see to it that you are not alarmed. Such things must happen, but the end is still to come. ⁷Nation will rise against nation, and kingdom against kingdom. There will be famines and earthquakes in various places. ⁸All these are the beginning of birth pains.

⁹"Then you will be handed over to be persecuted and put to death, and you will be hated by all nations because of me. ¹⁰At that time many will turn away from the faith and will betray and hate each other, ¹¹and many false prophets will appear and deceive many people. ¹²Because of the increase of wickedness, the love of most will grow cold, ¹³but the one who stands firm to the end will be saved. ¹⁴And this gospel of the kingdom will be preached in the whole world as a testimony to all nations, and then the end will come.

[15]"So when you see standing in the holy place 'the abomination that causes desolation,' spoken of through the prophet Daniel—let the reader understand—[16]then let those who are in Judea flee to the mountains. [17]Let no one on the housetop go down to take anything out of the house. [18]Let no one in the field go back to get their cloak. [19]How dreadful it will be in those days for pregnant women and nursing mothers! [20]Pray that your flight will not take place in winter or on the Sabbath. [21]For then there will be great distress, unequaled from the beginning of the world until now—and never to be equaled again.

[22]"If those days had not been cut short, no one would survive, but for the sake of the elect those days will be shortened. [23]At that time if anyone says to you, 'Look, here is the Messiah!' or, 'There he is!' do not believe it. [24]For false messiahs and false prophets will appear and perform great signs and wonders to deceive, if possible, even the elect. [25]See, I have told you ahead of time.

[26]"So if anyone tells you, 'There he is, out in the wilderness,' do not go out; or, 'Here he is, in the inner rooms,' do not believe it. [27]For as lightning that comes from the east is visible even in the west, so will be the coming of the Son of Man. [28]Wherever there is a carcass, there the vultures will gather.

[29]"Immediately after the distress of those days

"'the sun will be darkened,
    and the moon will not give its light;
the stars will fall from the sky,
    and the heavenly bodies will be shaken.'

[30]"Then will appear the sign of the Son of Man in heaven. And then all the peoples of the earth will mourn when they see the Son of Man coming on the clouds of heaven, with power and great glory. [31]And he will send his angels with a loud trumpet call, and they will gather his elect from the four winds, from one end of the heavens to the other.

[32]"Now learn this lesson from the fig tree: As soon as its twigs get tender and its leaves come out, you know that summer is near. [33]Even so, when you see all these things, you know that it is near, right at the door. [34]Truly I tell you, this generation will certainly not pass away until all these things have happened. [35]Heaven and earth will pass away, but my words will never pass away."

INTRODUCTION AND REVIEW:
The Coming of Christ in Judgment

WE ARE ON THE FOURTH PART OF THE SERIES on the Passion Week. Let us review the preceding events. Jesus has gone up to Jerusalem, and He knows He is going to die; this must be kept in mind at all times. The Passion Week will culminate on the Passover, where He will be taken, tried, and crucified. Jesus has gone into the temple and cleansed the temple; He has questioned the leaders concerning authority; He has silenced them, and has pronounced judgment on them. We read the indictments for which they were guilty, and Jesus pronounced the judgment of woe on them for each of the seven indictments. Underlying all of these indictments was this one continual charge: hypocrisy. They were taking the name of the Lord in vain; lightly and thoughtlessly regarding that by which God makes Himself known—His Word. They were saying and not doing, and lightly thinking about what was being said. This is hypocrisy. As a result, their sin has come to the full measure, and they will be cut off and destroyed. At the end of Matthew 23, Jesus laments in connection with the judgment that will come:

> Jerusalem, Jerusalem, you who kill the prophets and stone those sent to you, how often I have longed to gather your children together, as a hen gathers her chicks under her wings, but you were not willing. Look, your house is left to you desolate. For I tell you, you will not see me again until you say, "Blessed is he who comes in the name of the Lord" (Matt. 23:37–39).

Just before this, Jesus had said,

> And so upon you will come all the righteous blood that has been shed on earth, from the blood of righteous Abel to the blood of Zechariah son of Berekiah, whom you murdered between the temple and the altar. Truly I tell you, all this will come on this generation (Matt. 23:35–36).

If we are paying attention to what Jesus is saying here, it is very clear. Yet, we find a major dispute in Christendom about the passage in Matthew 24. It should be clear to us, in Matthew 23:36, that Jesus is speaking to "this generation"—the generation that will kill Him. Yet, when that same word appears in Matthew 24:34, its meaning is said to have changed. The disciples struggled with this, and today, many believe that the teaching of Matthew 24 is yet to be fulfilled,[1] so we will have to keep that in mind as we go on. We have to realize that the disciples, even then, were not understanding a number of particular things. Jesus had just pronounced judgment on Jerusalem, where the temple is, which means that judgment will come upon the temple, also.

BECOMING SPECIFIC:
The Temple Destroyed

"Jesus left the temple and was walking away when his disciples came up to him to call his attention to its buildings" (v. 1). This was Herod's temple. Herod had built it, in part, to get on the good side of the Jews. It was a magnificent building, and the disciples admired it and drew Jesus' attention to it. What Jesus had just said did not sink into the disciples' minds, and their statement became the occasion for Jesus to make explicit what He meant by the judgment that would come on Jerusalem. They did not ask Jesus any questions after He had said, "Jerusalem, Jerusalem . . . how often I have longed to gather your children together . . . but you were not willing. Look, your house is left to you desolate." Apparently, they did not understand; they were praising the magnificent buildings of the temple and calling His attention to them. Jesus then made it as explicit as you could possibly make it. He says, "Do you see all these things? . . . Truly I tell you, not one stone here will be left on another; every one will be thrown down" (v. 2). In case they missed it, it is not just Jerusalem that will be destroyed, it is the very center of Jerusalem, what is most significant and important about Jerusalem, that will be destroyed—the temple itself. The temple that they had just pointed to, concerning which Jesus said, "not one stone here will be left on another; every one will be thrown down," will be destroyed. There will be an utter devastation of the temple.

Jesus is not speaking about a temple that will be rebuilt in Jerusalem in the future, as premillennialism would teach. He is clearly speaking

---

1. In reference to premillennialism.

about Jerusalem *then*, and the temple *there*: **"not one stone *here*. . ."**[2] Is it possible to miss that? It should not be. As things are clear from general revelation, yet we miss it because we have faulty expectations, so things are clear from special revelation, yet we miss them because we have faulty expectations. What is our expectation? Hebrews 11:6 says, "He that cometh to God must believe that he is, and that he is a rewarder of them that diligently seek him."[3] This verse speaks about expectation—the reward. The reward is the best thing we could possibly have, which is what we would want, and therefore what we expect. God is the rewarder of those who diligently seek Him.

Causes for Misunderstanding: False Hope and Expectation About the Good

Our whole conception of the meaning and purpose of life, the goal of life, the good, and eternal life is bound up in Hebrews 11:6. Some of us will believe that God exists, that Jesus is the Son of God, and that He died for our sins, but many do not believe that He is the rewarder of those who diligently seek Him. Or if we profess it, we do not believe it with understanding. As it is possible to believe in God, as in Islam,[4] without understanding, so it is possible to profess that God is the rewarder of those who diligently seek Him without understanding. How do we understand the reward? Or how do we misunderstand the reward? How does it affect our understanding of what Jesus is saying here? Why is it so difficult, even though we can point out passages specifically? Because this underlying misunderstanding continues, we do not seem to get anywhere in our discussion.

There are two basic ways in which this has been misunderstood. First, it has been misunderstood in an *otherworldly* way. Second, it has been misunderstood in a *this-worldly* way. We will align these two misunderstandings with eschatological expectations. Amillennialism expects that we will die, go to heaven, and have the fullness of the

---

2. Emphasis added.

3. KJV.

4. Gangadean, *Philosophical Foundation*, 191–192; Gangadean, *The Westminster Confession*, 21–27, 37–41, 67–69, 129–130, 236–238; Gangadean, "Paper No. 91: Christianity and Islam," in *The Logos Papers*, 479–484.

blessing there, which is an otherworldly view of the good.[5] How does that view connect with "he is a rewarder of them that diligently seek him"? Premillennials will not go that way; they believe they will die and go to heaven, too, but they expect the kingdom to come on earth. They expect Jesus to come back, to rule in Jerusalem, to conquer His enemies, and to create a great earthly kingdom of a more material sort, just as many Jews expected in Jesus' day. The premillennial view is very this-worldly and literal. There you have it; we are caught with nothing between the two. We can hardly get to the idea that He is the rewarder of those who diligently seek Him[6] and that the earth is to be filled with the knowledge of God.[7] Try explaining the meaning of these passages to either side, who have these different underlying expectations of what it is to be rewarded by God in diligently seeking, and you will not get far. You can hardly carry on a conversation for any length of time.

When we speak about Matthew 24, let us remember, presuppositionally, that there is a more basic element of the view of the good in the this-worldly and otherworldly views. The Scripture says, "He that cometh to God must believe that he is, and that he is a rewarder of them that diligently seek him." Some profess to believe that God exists, but they are not seeking Him because they do not believe that He is a rewarder of those who diligently seek Him. Some might believe that He is a rewarder of those who casually seek Him. They may think that we do not really have to read our Bible thoughtfully, prayerfully, and continually. There are a lot of Christians who do not believe what is said in Hebrews 11:6, or they believe it with misunderstanding. But you *must* believe that He is the rewarder of those who diligently seek Him if you would come to God; you absolutely must. The Scripture says that we must believe that He exists, and we must believe that He is a rewarder of those who diligently seek Him. We must believe this with understanding rather than with misunderstanding. So underlying the difficulties in this passage, we find these different views of the good.

---

5. Gangadean, *On Natural and Revealed Theology*, 9–39; Gangadean, "Paper No. 106: The Good and Heaven," 547–556; "Paper No. 116: The Knowledge of God vs. The Hope of Heaven," in *The Logos Papers*, 597–598; Gangadean, *Philosophical Foundation*, 40–41, 71–73.

6. *Hebrews 11:6* NIV 1984.

7. *Isaiah 11:9.*

TIMING BEFORE THE END OF THE TEMPLE

Suppose you were asked this question: How would you live if you knew when the end of the world would come? That is a little bit vague, isn't it? How would you act if you knew the world would end in about two years, three months, and two weeks at about six o'clock in the evening? You may react with laughter, but the day and the hour is what the disciples are asking about in this passage. The day and the hour is mentioned a number of times, and Jesus said, "But about that day or hour no one knows, not even the angels in heaven, nor the Son, but only the Father" (Matt. 24:36). A lot is speculated about the day and the hour in some eschatological circles. What if you knew the day and the hour of your death? How would you behave? How would you act? We generally know the season when most die, sometime after 70, in the winter of life, but what if you knew the day and the hour? What if you knew the day and the hour of the end of the nation? The end of the world, the end of a life, and the end of a nation are bound up in the notion of 'the end.' All of these are spoken of in this passage. The end of Jerusalem was the end of the nation, but as we see later in the passage, what Jesus speaks to becomes more particular. The term *Day of the Lord* covers a wide range of ways in which the Lord comes.[8] We will address the question about the Day of the Lord. The Day of the Lord includes the final ending of history, with the second, visible, bodily coming of the Lord from the heavens, with the sound of the trumpet, the voice of the archangel, the dead being raised, and those alive and remaining being raptured.[9] We certainly do believe in the rapture,[10] but we believe it will come at the end of history, at the time of the Second Coming.

The disciples had a concern to know when. They said to Jesus, "**Tell us, when will these things be? And what will be the sign of your coming, and of the end of the age?**" (v. 3b NKJV). Notice there are three questions put together. First, they ask, "When will these things be?" They are asking about the things He just spoke about at the end of Matthew 23, "Truly I tell you, all this will come upon this generation"

---

8. Lorraine Boettner, *The Millennium* (Phillipsburg, NJ: Presbyterian and Reformed Publishing Company, 1986), 252–262.

9. *1 Thessalonians 4:16–17.*

10. Gangadean, "Paper No. 49: Eschatology (FAQ)," in *The Logos Papers*, 271–274.

(Matt. 23:36), and about the temple, "**not one stone here will be left on another; every one will be thrown down**" (v. 2b). Jesus' response has several parts. Our Lord Jesus is always thorough.

Be Watchful: Working for the Good with True Hope

Jesus first calls them to be watchful, and He ends by calling them to be watchful. We have to keep that in mind. Jesus is specific in responding to their concern. He said, "**Watch out that no one deceives you**" (v. 4). How are we to be watchful? Generally, we are to be watchful by having the right expectation. We are to be watchful in two ways. First, we are not to be deceived and go astray. Second, we are not to cease to be active in what we should do. Both of these ways are addressed by Jesus in terms of being watchful.

We are deceived in our expectation by having false hope.[11] Imagine someone having the hope that the earth will be filled with the knowledge of God as the waters cover the sea. Imagine someone believing that the knowledge of God is the good,[12] that we will enjoy it together, that we cannot achieve it individually, and that it was meant that way from the beginning of the creation when God said, "Be fruitful and increase in number; fill the earth and subdue it" (Gen. 1:28). How would they live?[13] Imagine they know that they have one life, and when it is over, they cannot do the work. But they know others must carry on that work, and they believe it will be done. How would you live? That is your reward. That is your blessing. That is your joy. That is what makes you get up out of bed every morning. How would you live? It is not simply "duty" that makes you get out of bed; it is a duty that is most delightful. You do not feel it is something hanging over you, but it is something you are longing after. How would you live? If the good is the knowledge of God that is through diligently seeking, how would you live? What sorts of things would you engage in? How would you go about seeking? What books would you read? What issues would you engage in? Would you read just the Bible? Would you

---

11. Gangadean, *Philosophical Foundation*, 207–219.

12. Gangadean, *Philosophical Foundation*, 171–177, 208–211; Gangadean, *The Westminster Catechisms*, 109–111, 321–325; Gangadean, *On Natural and Revealed Theology*, 33–39, 127–139.

13. Gangadean, "Paper No. 115: Doxological Christianity," in *The Logos Papers*, 595–596.

read just the Book of Psalms? Or would you seek to understand how God reveals Himself in all His works of creation and history? Would you seek to get a whole sense of what God has done in history, where things are now, and where they are going? Would you actively engage in this? Do you really believe that God is a rewarder of those who diligently seek Him and that creation and history is a revelation? If I believe this, I really do not need to know the day and the hour. To know the season is sufficient.

I have a sense of season. When you are 60, you have a sense of season. You know that you are on the last stretch, and you have to make this right—all the things you have not done—you want to put it all together, get it focused, and make it happen by the grace of God. I am keenly aware of this season. We want to be able to say, with Paul, "I have fought the good fight, I have finished the race, I have kept the faith" (2 Tim. 4:7). We want to say, "I have finished the race," so that the last step across the finish line is at the point of our departure. What does that do to "the day and the hour" in terms of how we operate? It makes it secondary. When you know the season, you press on, and you know you want to finish the race.

False Christs: Understanding the Person and Work of Christ

Jesus said, **"Watch out that no one deceives you"** (v. 4). We do not watch out by looking around at something external. The deception is inward, in terms of our expectations, our goals, and our inclinations. That is how deception occurs; we are drawn away by what we desire and what we think is the good. If we have a faulty view of the good, whether this-worldliness or otherworldliness, we will pursue that view and be taken captive. **"Watch out that no one deceives you."**

The way in which deception came at that time was that the Jews were expecting the Messiah to come, but they did not accept Jesus as the Messiah. The complication is that the Christians were expecting Christ to come a second time. When they say the Messiah will come, it has two meanings. The Jewish community is waiting for the Messiah to come the first time, and the Christian community is waiting for the Messiah's Second Coming. **"Watch out that no one deceives you"** has a double, complicated, interconnected meaning. Some will come saying they are the Christ in the Jewish community, and that may catch some

Christians off guard. Some were caught that way,[14] and Jesus tells them to watch out; this will happen. He said, **"For many will come in my name, claiming, 'I am the Messiah,' and will deceive many"** (v. 5). So they are to watch out for false Christs. We will not fall for that if we understand who our Lord is and what His work is.

Wars and Rumors of Wars: The End of the Old Order Coming

Jesus said, **"You will hear of wars and rumors of wars, but see to it that you are not alarmed"** (v. 6a). We can become alarmed easily enough when we hear about wars. There is an alarm that is being raised now regarding terrorism.[15] 'What if they do break through? What if they made a major hit on an airplane and brought it down with a shoulder launched missile? What would that do? Suppose they got through with a bomb? What would that do?' There will be alarm through wars and rumors of wars. That is not the sign of Jesus' coming. Wars will happen, Jesus said, but the end is still to come. Jesus explicitly said, **"Such things must happen, but the end is still to come"** (v. 6b). We may think that when there is an alarm of war or an actual war, the end is near, but Jesus said, **"Such things must happen, but the end is still to come."** Then He said, **"Nation will rise against nation, and kingdom against kingdom. There will be famines and earthquakes in various places"** (v. 7). We have a record of some of this in the Book of Acts. But this is not the end; these things must happen. Jesus will list the things that must come first, and then He will say that the end will come. **"All these are the beginning of birth pains"** (v. 8). We have to contrast the *end* with the *beginning* of birth pains. With the beginning of birth pains, you are expecting something new and glorious. We have to apply this: The end of what? And the beginning of what? The ending of one seems to be the beginning of another. We have to understand this change.

Jesus said the kingdom would be taken from the Jews and given to another. Change is coming. The old order of things will end: Jerusalem and the temple will be destroyed. Even without this destruction, the temple will cease to have significance. The sacrifices will be no more, and

---

14. In the letters to the Thessalonians, Paul corrects faulty teaching about the return of Christ and irresponsible behavior connected with this.

15. This sermon series was given in 2004 during the War on Terror.

the priesthood will be changed. Because the Messiah has come and He has accomplished redemption, the temple ceases to have significance. But because of unbelief, and the way in which Jesus was crucified, He brings judgment on the temple.

Persecution, Hatred, and Betrayal: Let Not Your Love Grow Cold

In addition to the wars, rumors of wars, famines, and earthquakes, there is another factor. There will be persecution, hatred, and betrayal by those very close. We have to distinguish between that which comes upon believers and that which comes upon the Jews who were in unbelief. Those who are persecuted will be the Christians. **"Then you will be handed over to be persecuted and put to death, and you will be hated by all nations because of me"** (v. 9). We cannot say that the Jews were hated by all nations because of Christ; it was the Christians who were hated because of Christ.

Jesus says of the time of the persecution: **"At that time many will turn away from the faith and will betray and hate each other"** (v. 10). We can see why they would want deliverance and why they would hope for the coming of Christ. Under persecution, they will be delivered and put to death, so Jesus warns the Christians that persecution must come first. Also, **"many false prophets will appear and deceive many people"** (v. 11), and we have a record of some who came saying the resurrection had already passed. This will even be within one's own household.[16] "Brother will betray brother to death, and a father his child; children will rebel against their parents and have them put to death" (Matt. 10:21). When this kind of sin is prevailing, the response is to be disappointed, perhaps bitter, and not care. Jesus puts it this way: **"Because of the increase of wickedness, the love of most will grow cold"** (v. 12). This is a very understandable response, and it is one of the things we must watch for and guard against. Jesus, having loved His own, He loved them to the end,[17] even when one betrayed Him and others denied Him. He loved them to the very end. We are to watch that our love does not grow cold because of the abundant sin that may be in the community of believers.

---

16. *Matthew 10:36.*
17. *John 13:1.*

The Gospel Preached in All the Earth: Fulfilled by A.D. 70

Then Jesus said, "But the one who stands firm to the end will be saved. And this gospel of the kingdom will be preached in the whole world as a testimony to all nations, and then the end will come" (vv. 13–14). Before, the end was spoken of as yet to come, as the beginning of birth pains, but after the gospel is preached in the whole world as a testimony to all nations, then the end will come. Some have interpreted this to mean that when we preach the gospel to at least one person out of every nation, kindred, tribe, and tongue, then Jesus will come, so they say, 'Let us hurry and preach.' Have you heard something like that? We say, rather, that the gospel being preached in the whole world had been fulfilled in Scripture by the time the temple was destroyed. Here are the reasons:

1. Acts 17:6 says, "they dragged Jason and some other believers before the city officials, shouting: 'These men who have caused trouble all over the world have now come here.'" The message had gone into the world, and this was the response.

2. In Acts 24:5–6, when Paul was being charged during the rule of Festus, it was said, "We have found this man to be a troublemaker, stirring up riots among the Jews all over the world. He is a ringleader of the Nazarene sect and even tried to desecrate the temple; so we seized him."

3. Colossians 1:6 says, "All over the world this gospel is bearing fruit and growing."[18] And Colossians 1:23b says, "This is the gospel that you heard and that has been proclaimed to every creature under heaven."

4. 1 Timothy 3:16 says, "He appeared in the flesh, was vindicated by the Spirit, was seen by angels, was preached among the nations, was believed on in the world, was taken up in glory."

5. Acts 2:5 says, "Now there were staying in Jerusalem God-fearing Jews from every nation under heaven." Jews from every nation were converted on the Day of Pentecost, and what do you think happened after that? They went back to all their various nations and spoke the Word, in addition to Paul's work as the Apostle to the

---

18. NIV 1984.

Gentiles. We can say that the gospel being preached in the whole world, according to Scripture, has been fulfilled in Paul's day.

6. In Acts 13:46, Paul tells the Jews he will now turn to the Gentiles: "Then Paul and Barnabas answered them boldly: 'We had to speak the word of God to you first. Since you reject it and do not consider yourselves worthy of eternal life, we now turn to the Gentiles.'"

What happened particularly is that the gospel was preached to the Jews in all parts of the world, and in all parts of the world, the Jews rejected it. The Gentiles started to come in, and Jews and Gentiles in all parts of the world heard the gospel, then the end came. This is according to the usage of the term *whole world* in Scripture, that once the gospel is preached to all the world, the end will come. Today we may take "the whole world" in terms of going out to every part of the world. 'Did the gospel really go to the Philippines in Jesus' day? If it did, it certainly didn't get to Fiji.' That is not the way the term *whole world* is used in Scripture. The gospel did go out to all the world. We cannot say, 'This has not been fulfilled; therefore, the end cannot come yet.' Jesus said the gospel of the kingdom will be preached to the whole world as a testimony to all nations, and then the end will come. According to the passages above, the Scripture affirms that the gospel went into the whole world.

The Abomination of Desolation: Flee Versus Expecting Deliverance of Jerusalem

Preaching the gospel then, in all the earth, is not the same as the elect being gathered from all the nations. The elect being gathered is something still to come. Jesus said that these things will happen, and then the end will come. "So when you see standing in the holy place 'the abomination that causes desolation,' spoken of through the prophet Daniel—let the reader understand—then let those who are in Judea flee to the mountains" (vv. 15–16). At this point, they are not being told the day or the hour, but they will know that when they see the abomination, they will not have time to do anything else; all they must do is flee—immediately flee. "Let no one on the housetop go down to take anything out of the house. Let no one in the field go back to

400 THE GOSPEL OF MATTHEW

get their cloak" (vv. 17–18). Luke adds to this section: "Remember Lot's wife!" (Lk. 17:32).

Jesus is now speaking about the end of Jerusalem: "**not one stone here will be left on another**" (v. 2b). The abomination standing in the Holy Place happened when the Romans brought their symbol and put it inside the temple in Jerusalem. That was the end; the Romans had held back, and they had given the Jews a certain amount of freedom, but there was restlessness and rebelliousness on the part of the Jews, and so Jerusalem fell under Titus. That was it; when that insignia came and stood in the temple, the Romans were not going to give the Jews any more quarter. That was the end of it; the Romans were going to crush Jerusalem once and for all. Jesus says that when they see "**the abomination that causes desolation**," that symbol, that idolatrous symbol, in the temple, that is the end. Jesus is warning us.

We might have a desire to identify this nation (United States) with the kingdom of God and hope that this nation, our nation, will persevere, as the Jews hoped for Jerusalem. We may want to think that God will yet deliver us, the way they thought God would deliver Jerusalem in the days of Hezekiah.[19] So Jesus is warning, particularly Jewish believers, not to try to hold on to the old economy. And not one did; they heeded the Word of Christ, and not one believer was caught in Jerusalem when it was surrounded by the armies. They all heeded the Word of Christ, and they fled. An indication that Jewish believers fled Jerusalem is that they were selling their lands. They knew the end of the Old Testament order was coming; that is why Barnabas, Ananias, and Sapphira sold their land. The end of that order had come. So He says that when they see the abomination that causes desolation, "**let those who are in Judea flee to the mountains**"—the end has come. Do not think that God will deliver; judgment will come, and now this is the end. This event happened in A.D. 70; they were to let it go and not hold on.

---

19. *2 Kings 19.*

THE END

The Tribulation: The Seige of Jerusalem

In verses 19–22, Jesus speaks about what will happen after this signal event: it will become dreadful; it will become horrible. This is the Tribulation.

How dreadful it will be in those days for pregnant women and nursing mothers! Pray that your flight will not take place in winter or on the Sabbath. For then there will be great distress, unequaled from the beginning of the world until now—and never to be equaled again. If those days had not been cut short, no one would survive, but for the sake of the elect those days will be shortened.

Jesus is explaining to His disciples when the end will come, what will come before the end, and what the signs will be. He explains that it will happen so fast that they will not know ahead of time the day or the hour, so they cannot prepare. If they had known the hour before, they would have had enough time to go down into the house to get a cloak and then flee, but they did not know the hour. It will come instantly: "For you know very well that the day of the Lord will come like a thief in the night" (1 Thess. 5:2). The series *Left Behind* uses the reference about the thief in the night, but we will see how Scripture uses it, and it is not as it is used in that series.

Great distress will come during the siege of Jerusalem, the betrayals, the inciting, and women reduced to eating their children. Can you think of anything worse than that? Perhaps the degree to which it happened during the siege of Jerusalem was greater than ever before. There were times when that happened in some measure. Remember, the king of Israel in Samaria dealt with this; a woman called to the king for help and said, "This woman said to me, 'Give up your son so we may eat him today, and tomorrow we'll eat my son.' So we cooked my son and ate him. The next day I said to her, 'Give up your son so we may eat him,' but she had hidden him" (2 Kings 6:28–29). The king was appalled then, but the degree to which it happened during the siege in Jerusalem was greater. There had been times of suffering before, but nothing like this.

THE GOSPEL OF MATTHEW

False Hope, False Deliverance, and False Christs

In the midst of this, there will be false hope of a false Christ.

> At that time if anyone says to you, "Look, here is the Messiah!"
> or, "There he is!" do not believe it. For false messiahs and false
> prophets will appear and perform great signs and wonders to
> deceive, if possible, even the elect. See, I have told you ahead of
> time (vv. 23–25).

God allows Satan and evil spirits to have their way, and He allows
miracles to be done, not in the name of God according to His truth,
but He will allow miracles to be done that will deceive many, and if
possible, even the elect. That is the false hope in a desperate condition. They may think, "'Look, here is the Christ!' or, 'There he is!'"
but Jesus said, when He comes, it will not be like that. He tells them,

> So if anyone tells you, "There he is, out in the wilderness," do not
> go out; or, "Here he is, in the inner rooms," do not believe it. For
> as lightning that comes from the east is visible even in the west,
> so will be the coming of the Son of Man (vv. 26–27).

His glorious final coming, His Second Coming, will not be hidden;
it will be seen, and it will be known. In this context, there are Jewish
people expecting Christ (Messiah), not having received Jesus as the
Christ, and Christians alike being caught up in looking for Christ's
Second Coming. Do not go out to look for Him; that is not how the
Second Coming will occur.

The Principle of the Carcass: Disposing of Spiritual Death

The judgment coming because of spiritual death is summed up in this
verse: "Wherever there is a carcass, there the vultures will gather"
(v. 28). The birds of prey that may feed on the carcass will gather. Jerusalem is spiritually dead; it is a carcass on the earth, and God brings
the armies of Rome as vultures to dispose of the carcass, destroy it, and
scatter it. The judgment is summed up in this principle of the carcass.

THINGS AFTER THE END

The Rulers Fall, the Old Order Shaken Up

It says in verse 29, "**Immediately after the distress of those days . . .**" It does not say 2,000 years later. Is that a fair reading of "**immediately**"? Is there any question about whether this refers to the Jerusalem standing then? When He says, "**not one stone here will be left on another,**" He refers to Jerusalem. "**Immediately after the distress of those days 'the sun will be darkened, and the moon will not give its light; the stars will fall from the sky, and the heavenly bodies will be shaken'**" (v. 29). Some take this imagery literally, but it would have happened back in A.D. 70. Must this imagery be taken literally? Some think it must, but we say it is not to be taken literally. This language of the sun turning to darkness and the moon to blood has been used in Isaiah, in Joel, and in Ezekiel[20] to speak about the destruction of nations in the past. The vultures have come in, the nation is destroyed, and the lights are turned off. The rulers, who are represented as heavenly lights, are turned off: "**the sun will be darkened, and the moon will not give its light.**" This is spoken of in regard to Edom in Isaiah 34, and if this comes on Edom, the brother nation to Israel, how much more will it come on Israel? It is the same kind of language that is used. If we know the biblical language, we will not be lost in it.

The Sign of the Son of Man in Heaven: The Gathering of the Elect

Immediately after the destruction of Jerusalem, the lights will go off—the rulers will fall. That is understandable—it is gone. And now, what will happen? "**Then will appear the sign of the Son of Man in heaven**" (v. 30a). This is the sign of the Son of Man seated at the right hand of God. The sign of the Son of Man in heaven will appear. It is a sign of a reality; the sign is visible, and the reality is invisible. That is why you have a sign pointing to it. What is this sign? "**When they see the Son of Man coming on the clouds of heaven, with power and great glory**" (v. 30b). When we see those two put together—the Son of Man and

---

20. *Isaiah 13:10; Joel 2:31; Ezekiel 32:7.*

the clouds—we know that this Son of Man is a divine being. Clouds are associated with divine rule. Matthew 26:63b–64 says:

> The high priest said to him, "I charge you under oath by the living God: Tell us if you are the Messiah, the Son of God." "You have said so," Jesus replied. "But I say to all of you: From now on you will see the Son of Man sitting at the right hand of the Mighty One and coming on the clouds of heaven."

Clouds are associated with deity, and so they charged Him with blasphemy. What is this coming on the clouds **"with power and great glory"**? What is this coming that will be *seen*? The high priest will see this—in his day, it happened. The coming on the clouds, I believe, is expressed next: **"And he will send his angels with a loud trumpet call, and they will gather his elect from the four winds, from one end of the heavens to the other"** (v. 31). The sign of the Son of Man in heaven is the work that will begin. He sent His Spirit, and of the Spirit coming, it is said, "Exalted to the right hand of God, he has received from the Father the promised Holy Spirit and has poured out what you now see and hear" (Acts 2:33). What they see and hear on earth is the evidence of the Spirit sent by the Anointed One, the Messiah, who is at the right hand of God. What is seen on earth is a sign that Jesus has arrived, He is in the position of authority, and *He* can send the third person of the Godhead to come to earth, to do the work, to make disciples of all the nations—this is the gathering of the elect.

The word is translated here as *angels*, which comes from *aggelos*, which means *messengers*. Angels are not allowed to preach the gospel. An angel may tell you where you can go to find someone who will preach the gospel to you, but the work of preaching the gospel is given to those who are members of the body of Christ. Human beings will accomplish the work of preaching the gospel. Human beings are those messengers, so we need to keep that in mind in terms of calling the elect from one end of heaven to the other. Immediately after the destruction of Jerusalem, the gospel goes out into all the earth. This is when it is seen most clearly. When the Jewish believers go outside of Jerusalem and Judea, they are going to the Gentiles, and they are taking the gospel to the ends of the earth. They are leaving Jerusalem and Judea and taking the message wherever they go; they are not just fleeing for their lives. The message is going out after the destruction in Jerusalem. This is seen most clearly to those Jewish persons who remain after the great days of distress—they will see the gospel spread to the ends of the earth.

THE SEASON:
This Generation Will Not Pass away
Until the End of Jerusalem

Jesus tells them what they can expect by pointing to the fig tree. **"Now learn this lesson from the fig tree: As soon as its twigs get tender and its leaves come out, you know that summer is near"** (v. 32). If you have a fig tree, you know this; you know summer is near when you see the signs. He says, **"Even so, when you see all these things, you know that it is near, right at the door"** (v. 33). Jesus is saying to them that the time is near—it is this generation. He develops this: **"Truly I tell you, this generation . . ."** (v. 34a); it is the same generation He spoke of in Matthew 23:36: "Truly I tell you, all this will come on this generation." He is speaking of the generation that will kill Him. He said, **"Truly I tell you, this generation will certainly not pass away until all these things have happened"** (v. 34).

Those who read these references of the sun being darkened, the gospel being preached, and Christ coming in clouds of glory in a literal way, and who say that all this has not yet been fulfilled, have to address the question about **"this generation."** They try to say the word "generation" here means *race* or *nation*. They say that Israel has been a race before, and when Israel has become a nation again, then you know the end is near. Psalm 95 says, "For forty years I was angry with that generation" (Ps. 95:10a). God was not angry with that *race*, but that *generation*. The next generation, God was not displeased with. There was a 40-year term connected with "that generation." The generation with which He was angry died out.

Think about the use of the word *generation* in Matthew in the genealogies. Matthew lists 14 generations from Abraham to Moses, and 14 from Moses to David, and 14 from David to Christ. This is not speaking about 14 *races* or 14 *nations*. The Scripture speaks about another *generation* that came along that did not know Joseph.[21] The generation spoken of here is within a time frame. There are other uses, such as in Matthew 12:

> The men of Nineveh will stand up at the judgment with this gener-ation and condemn it . . . now one greater than Jonah is here. The Queen of the South will rise at the judgment with this generation and condemn it . . . now one greater than Solomon is here (Matt. 12:39–42).[22]

This passage speaks about *this* generation. It is not speaking about the whole race or the nation per se; it is one generation. So, there have been forced readings to get around the question about "**this genera-tion**" because they are taking a literalist interpretation of Matthew 24. Notice that the same literalist attitude can only see the literal, physi-cal, outward reality. They make the good into being *this-worldly.* Some react to that and make it *otherworldly.* The Two-Kingdom View[23] is a view of the good reacting against a tendency in theonomy to make the good somewhat this-worldly. It is not the earth being filled with the knowledge of God. What is your delight? What is your reward in seek-ing God? Your view of the good counts; it really does count, and you can go aside in these two ways: this-worldly and otherworldly. Watch and pray so that no one deceives you. Jesus said, "**Heaven and earth will pass away, but my words will never pass away**" (v. 35). It will be fulfilled; it will certainly be fulfilled. We will pick up with the rest of Matthew 24 in the next sermon. Amen.

---

21. *Exodus 1:8.*
22. NIV 1984.
23. David VanDrunen, *Living in God's Two Kingdoms: A Biblical Vision for Christianity and Culture* (Wheaton, IL: Crossway Books, 2010).

———

WATCH!

Living in True Expectation and
Faithful Service to Christ

Matthew 24:36–51

³⁶But about that day or hour no one knows, not even the angels in heaven, nor the Son, but only the Father. ³⁷As it was in the days of Noah, so it will be at the coming of the Son of Man. ³⁸For in the days before the flood, people were eating and drinking, marrying and giving in marriage, up to the day Noah entered the ark; ³⁹and they knew nothing about what would happen until the flood came and took them all away. That is how it will be at the coming of the Son of Man. ⁴⁰Two men will be in the field; one will be taken and the other left. ⁴¹Two women will be grinding with a hand mill; one will be taken and the other left.

⁴²Therefore keep watch, because you do not know on what day your Lord will come. ⁴³But understand this: If the owner of the house had known at what time of night the thief was coming, he would have kept watch and would not have let his house be broken into. ⁴⁴So you also must be ready, because the Son of Man will come at an hour when you do not expect him.

⁴⁵"Who then is the faithful and wise servant, whom the master has put in charge of the servants in his household to give them their food at the proper time? ⁴⁶It will be good for that servant whose master finds him doing so when he returns. ⁴⁷Truly I tell you, he will put him in charge of all his possessions. ⁴⁸But suppose that servant is wicked and says to himself, 'My master is staying away a long time,' ⁴⁹and he then begins to beat his fellow servants and to eat and drink with drunkards. ⁵⁰The master of that servant will come on a day when he does not expect him and at an

hour he is not aware of. [51]He will cut him to pieces and assign him a place with the hypocrites, where there will be weeping and gnashing of teeth."

CONTEXT AND REVIEW:
The Culmination of History and Christ's Ministry

BY WAY OF REVIEW, AS WE HAVE BEEN GOING through the Passion Week, we see that a great deal is coming to a head. This is the crisis of this world; it is the judgment of this world. All of history is coming to a culmination. All the witness that has been given through the prophets, through millennia, is coming to a head. In the life of our Lord Jesus Christ, it comes fully into display. The leaders of the people rejected that witness, our Lord pronounced seven woes of judgment upon them, and He declared to them:

> "Look, your house is left to you desolate" (Matt. 23:38). "And so upon you will come all the righteous blood that has been shed on earth, from the blood of righteous Abel to the blood of Zechariah son of Berekiah, whom you murdered between the temple and the altar. I tell you the truth, all this will come upon this generation" (Matt. 23:35–36)

The blood of all of the faithful will come upon *that* generation. The witness has been cumulative, and the Lord has completed the witness; therefore, judgment will come. Jesus declares this Word to His disciples and makes it quite specific that all of these things will come upon *this* generation, in which the witness has culminated.

As Jesus was leaving the temple, He spoke to His disciples and made it as concrete as possible, as inescapable as possible; one could not miss it: "Truly I tell you, not one stone here will be left on another; every one will be thrown down" (Matt. 24:2b). The very temple itself will be destroyed. Herod's temple was magnificent; it was greater in dimension and appearance than Solomon's. Herod built it as a way to gain favor with the Jews. Herod was from Edom, an enemy people of the Jews, from the brother of Jacob. Herod built this temple, and Jesus said of this temple, "not one stone here will be left on another; every one will be thrown down."

What if you were to hear that the United States would be no more—gone and devastated within your generation? New York, Los Angeles, Chicago, and Phoenix will be gone. In terms of the nation-state, it will be no more. It will be a desolate wasteland. There was more to it than just being a nation for the Jews; they were the people of God. But to hear that the very center of the nation will be destroyed is like saying Washington, D.C. will be destroyed. What do you think will happen to the rest of the country? If the temple is destroyed, what do you think will happen? That would shake us to our very foundation, as it did for the disciples, especially in terms of what they were expecting and *how* they were expecting the kingdom to come. They were expecting that this would be the land, the city, and the place that would be the center of all the nations, and they are being told that this would all be destroyed. How do you process that? How do you begin to hear that? How do you wrap your mind around that? This is what the disciples had to respond to. So they asked the question, "Tell us . . . when will this happen, and what will be the sign of your coming and of the end of the age?" (Matt. 24:3b). This question has sometimes been split into three questions: (1) When will Jerusalem be destroyed? (2) What will be the signs of Christ's coming? (3) What will be the signs of the end of the age? These three questions have one focus; they are the same in essence.

Some have said that these three questions apply to various times in history. A three-part interpretation is unwarranted in this passage for several reasons. First, it does not fit with what the disciples would have heard. It may fit with our *surface* hearing. When we hear "the sign of your coming," we may think of it in terms of the Second Coming rather than "the sign of your coming" in connection with this judgment that has been pronounced on the Jews and in connection with the end of the age. An age will end; there have been many ages in world history, and this will be the end of *an* age. To be the end of an age is not to be the end of the ages or the end of all history. The end of all ages will come, but Jesus is speaking here about the end of *this* age.

Second, to read this in connection with the Letter to the Hebrews is illuminating. Jesus said there would be wars and famines, betrayals and persecution, and many would abandon the faith.[1] When we read

---

1. *Matthew 24:6–13.*

the Letter to the Hebrews,[2] we see that this is the point that is being addressed. We have good reasons to believe that Paul's letter was written to the Hebrews before the temple was destroyed. The people were turning back to the old way and putting their trust in the priesthood and the ceremonial system. They did not see anything concrete developing through the sudden appearance of the kingdom of God, so they were going back to the old economy. In Hebrews 9, they are reminded that Jesus is a greater high priest, and He enters a greater temple. They were being prepared and reminded to endure like those given as examples of faith in Hebrews 11. Jesus is preparing His disciples for what is to come, and He is answering three questions that are clustered together, and we are not to split them up.

Third, we will see details of why this is not to be split up in this chapter and in parallel passages in Luke and Mark. Though we may try to split them up, we will see that they are put together in the other Gospels. This has to do with the Day of the Lord and the way in which the Day of the Lord comes.

Watch Versus Deception: False Expectation

Jesus warns us about deception, and there are several ways which He says to "watch out" in the first part of chapter 24. One of the first things to watch out for is a false christ and prophets coming who will deceive. Either the believer is thinking that Christ will come back soon, or the Jews who did not accept Christ as the Messiah were still looking for and expecting a Messiah. Believers were to be on guard against being deceived. The deception is in terms of false expectations regarding the kingdom of God.

The disciples had false expectations even after Jesus was raised from the dead and before He ascended. They were asking Him, "Lord, are you at this time going to restore the kingdom to Israel?" (Acts 1:6b). It was not until the Day of Pentecost and beyond, when the Spirit was poured out on the household of Cornelius, that it began to dawn on the Jewish believers how God was going to fulfill His promise. Acts 15, the first council of the Church, was concerning the fulfillment of

---

2. *The Epistle to the Hebrews*, Surrendra Gangadean.

the Old Testament ordinances in Christ.[3] This passage is to be read in that context. Jesus warns them in terms of their expectation. We might put it this way: we may have a false view of history, we may have a false worldview, we may have a false view of the good,[4] and we may have a false view of what the blessing is. Remember the story of the rich young ruler in Matthew 19.

> Then Jesus said to his disciples, "Truly I tell you, it is hard for someone who is rich to enter the kingdom of heaven. Again I tell you, it is easier for a camel to go through the eye of a needle than for someone who is rich to enter the kingdom of God." When the disciples heard this, they were greatly astonished and asked, "Who then can be saved?" (Matt. 19:23–25).

The disciples were equating the gospel with the prosperity gospel. That is the gospel of Baal and Ashtoreth; those gods are most prevalent in our culture, along with Moloch, the gods of prosperity and pleasure, especially sensual pleasure as embodied in Ashtoreth. These are still dominant in our culture and in the Church; in many places, we still look for deliverance from all the effects of the curse. When Jesus did miracles and delivered people from the effects of the curse, they were overjoyed. Think of it: when He raised the dead, they said, 'This is the Messiah we want!' In the Book of John, His public ministry began with the water being changed into wine at the wedding in Cana of Galilee. If we do not understand these things as signs of what Christ will do to raise us from the dead and bring in the fullness of joy in our union and communion with God, then we miss its meaning. We look for the good in an Edenic state, where there is no curse, without understanding our sin. We do not understand that God is dealing with us through the curse.

We have false expectations, and we are very vulnerable to these false expectations, such as expecting Christ to come in a certain way. Think about the premillennial view of the kingdom of God. Think about their

---

3. Gangadean, "Paper No. 16: The Historic Christian Faith," 103–114; "Paper No. 60: The Spiritual War (Part II)," in *The Logos Papers*, 329–330.

4. Gangadean, *Philosophical Foundation*, 171–177, 208–211; Gangadean, *The Westminster Catechisms*, 109–111, 321–325; Gangadean, *On Natural and Revealed Theology*, 33–39, 127–139.

view of the kingdom of Jesus reigning *visibly* from Jerusalem. Think about how widespread that is among Christians who are, in many ways, devoted to Jesus. Do not think that we can escape falling prey to false expectations. Think also about amillennialism, which has the view of the fullness of life through the beatific vision[5] at death, so that the kingdom of God does not have to overcome the kingdom of darkness on earth. These are different views of the good and different expectations which are widespread. As a matter of fact, postmillennialism is rather restricted in the world. It is highly restricted to the Reformed churches and those holding to the Westminster Confession of Faith. Some fall into a theocratic approach, expecting the kingdom to come by outwardly imposing the law of God. Others in the Reformed community are responding against the theocratic approach by appealing to the Two-Kingdom View. Both have differing expectations about the good, the coming of Christ, and the state of affairs.

The coming of Christ is not just the second, final, visible, glorious coming. As we will see, the phrase 'coming of Christ' is used in connection with the Day of the Lord. Jesus warns us against deception through false expectations. He warns us against deception of a false view of what sin and death are, in contrast to the wages of sin is death,[6] spiritual death.[7] Prior assumptions inform our eschatological views. Our assumptions involve our worldview of the curse and the promise, whether God imposed natural evil as a call back from sin and death, and whether God imposes physical death as a call back from spiritual death and the root sin of not seeking God.[8] We have seen that this judgment of God has come in the world, first in the curse,[9] certainly in the days of Noah, in the days of Babel, in the days of Egypt (when Israel came out of Egypt), in the days of Assyria, and in the days of

---

5. Gangadean, *On Natural and Revealed Theology*, 9–39; Gangadean, "Paper No. 106: The Good and Heaven," 547–556; "Paper No. 116: The Knowledge of God vs. The Hope of Heaven," in *The Logos Papers*, 597–598; Gangadean, *Philosophical Foundation*, 40–41, 71–73.

6. *Romans 6:23*.

7. Gangadean, *The Biblical Worldview*, 37–54, 197–217.

8. Gangadean, *Philosophical Foundation*, 145–161; Gangadean, *On Natural and Revealed Theology*, 141–147; Gangadean, "Paper No. 7: The Problem of Evil," in *The Logos Papers*, 33–39.

9. Gangadean, *The Biblical Worldview*, 55–68, 275–294.

Babylon. The Day of the Lord came again, notably, in the destruction of the temple in A.D. 70. The destruction of the temple was a widespread, outstanding manifestation of that Day of the Lord, the end of one era and the beginning of a new one.

We have to watch our expectations and our worldview so that we are not in a position where we can be led astray, have false expectations, and not watch as we should for God's judgment on sin. In this passage, Jesus is answering the disciples' questions, and He tells them what must come first before the Day of the Lord comes. This is what He discusses in verses 1–8; He said, "All these are the beginning of birth pains" (Matt. 24:8) and then ends verses 9–14 with, "and then the end will come" (Matt. 24:14b). The end is spoken of in connection with the temple being destroyed within that generation. He made it quite clear what is to come first. There will be wars and rumors of wars, which are the beginning of birth pains, indicating the birth of a new age. There will be persecutions that will come on the Church and the gospel will be proclaimed to all the world.[10]

When the Day of the Lord Comes

Jesus goes on to speak of the Day of the Lord. Verses 1–14 speak about before the Day of the Lord comes. In verse 15, He speaks about when the Day of the Lord has come: "So when you see standing in the holy place 'the abomination that causes desolation,' spoken of through the prophet Daniel—let the reader understand" (Matt. 24:15). When it gets to the point when they see the abomination that causes desolation, the destruction is imminent. At that time, the response is to be: "then let those who are in Judea flee to the mountains. Let no one on the housetop go down to take anything out of the house" (Matt. 24:16–17). Here, we may see one's view of the good and what one is holding onto, but He said, "Let no one in the field go back to get their cloak" (Matt. 24:18) as He spoke of how great that tribulation will be. Remember Jesus said to the women of Jerusalem, "Daughters of Jerusalem, do not weep for me; weep for yourselves and for your children" (Lk. 23:28b). The fullness of judgment will come: "For then

---

10. The proclamation of the gospel to all the world was explained in the previous sermon. It means that the gospel was shared with the known world at the time of the Apostles as attested by scriptural references.

there will be great distress, unequaled from the beginning of the world until now—and never to be equaled again" (Matt. 24:21). Jesus says, "If those days had not been cut short, no one would survive, but for the sake of the elect those days will be shortened" (Matt. 24:22). Then they are warned, "At that time if anyone says to you, 'Look, here is the Messiah!' or, 'There he is!' do not believe it. For false messiahs and false prophets will appear and perform great signs and wonders to deceive, if possible, even the elect" (Matt. 24:23–24).

Deceiving the elect is not possible, but many who outwardly joined the Church were drawn away. Remember how many came to Christ during His ministry and how many of them turned away when Christ was arrested, tried, and crucified. Those who lack understanding/faith will go back to the old way. They will think that God is going to save Jerusalem and the temple, and they will go there and put their hope in that. Many Jews were deceived. Many Jews who professed Christ out-wardly were misled: "At that time many will turn away from the faith and will betray and hate each other" (Matt. 24:10), "the love of most will grow cold" (Matt. 24:12b). Jesus is speaking here about what will happen at the time of the end. He says,

> So if anyone tells you, "There he is, out in the wilderness," do not go out; or, "Here he is, in the inner rooms," do not believe it. For as lightning that comes from the east is visible even in the west, so will be the coming of the Son of Man (vv. 26–27).

The first psalm we sang today in worship spoke about how lightning, connected with the Lord's coming, comes as judgment.[11] We may wonder whether verse 27 is the coming of the Lord in person in the Second Coming, or if it is the coming of the Lord in judgment in history. I believe the context makes it clear that it is in judgment in history, because immediately after He says, **"so it will be at the coming of the Son of Man"** (vv. 37, 39), He says, "Wherever there is a carcass, there the vultures will gather" (Matt. 24:28). Jerusalem as a body had become dead, it was a carcass and the birds of judgment were coming, and they would devour it. Jesus immediately connects the carcass and the vultures with **"so it will be at the coming of the Son of Man."** We

---

11. *97A, The Book of Psalms for Singing.*

cannot rip that out of context and put it in terms of the future and our concern about when Christ will come again in the Second Coming. It is certainly true that when Christ comes again, it will not be a secret coming; it will be bold and visible, and the whole world will know.[12] That is true, but that is not the context of what this passage is saying.

After the Day of the Lord Comes

One would have to rip open the discourse to apply these passages to sometime in the future. Jesus is speaking of what will immediately happen; He says, "Immediately after the distress of those days" (Matt. 24:29a). First, Jesus tells what is coming before, what will happen when it comes, and what will happen afterward. Two things will happen after. First, the collapse of the nations, and second, the light will go out. Notice the cosmic dimension in which He speaks: "the sun will be darkened, and the moon will not give its light; the stars will fall from the sky, and the heavenly bodies will be shaken" (Matt. 24:29b). We spoke in the prior sermon of how this verse is seen in other places of Scripture. When judgment comes, it is spoken of in a broad, widespread way: lightning connected with judgment, and the heavenly lights going out. The Lord's coming will be widespread and it will be seen. "When will this happen, and what will be the sign of your coming and of the end of the age?" (Matt. 24:3b). The questions are connected in the disciples' minds and cannot be separated the way some have tried to separate them. It is not, 'When will the destruction of Jerusalem come? And when might the Second Coming occur?' This is not how the questions occur to the disciples.

If they thought this was the Second Coming and Christ would come soon, we would have to say that the Lord is correcting them. The coming and growth of the kingdom of God will begin small and grow gradually, as described in the parables of the mustard seed and leaven. Christ will rule through the Church until all the enemies are subdued and the Great Commission is completed by discipling all the nations.[13] At the end of Matthew 24 and in 25, He speaks about the

---

12. Gangadean, "Paper No. 49: Eschatology (FAQ)," 271–274; "Paper No. 104: Eschatology (Twelve Points)," 539–544; "Paper No. 118: Eschatology (Seven Points)," 603–607; "Paper No. 119: Pauline Eschatology," in *The Logos Papers*, 609–610.

13. *1 Corinthians 15:25–26; Matthew 28:18–20.*

faithful steward, the use of talents, and how we are to watch. We cannot rip this section out of that context.

The lights will go out for the Jewish nation and the light has remained out. Some premillennialists say, 'They have been restored as a nation, and this is the beginning of the end. This is the Second Coming.' But in the context spoken here, the judgment that Christ is speaking about is *this* generation and *this* temple, in that day. The nation's collapse will follow after the distress of those days:

> Then will appear the sign of the Son of Man in heaven. And then all the peoples of the earth will mourn when they see the Son of Man coming on the clouds of heaven, with power and great glory. And he will send his angels with a loud trumpet call, and they will gather his elect from the four winds, from one end of the heavens to the other (Matt. 24:30–31).

The proclamation of the gospel will be like that trumpet call of the Old Testament calling the people to gather. The proclamation of the gospel will gather the elect. Notice it is gathering the *elect*, the people of God, and it is "from one end of the heavens to the other." This is a more universal expression that the gospel will be preached in all the world. We saw how that reference was made in the sermon last week, "this gospel of the kingdom will be preached in the whole world as a testimony to all nations" (Matt. 24:14a). This is a strong and more complete way of saying it, "from one end of the heavens to the other." The angels do not literally do this gathering; they are never given the task or the privilege of calling others to repent. The gathering of the elect and the proclamation of the gospel is through God's people. The word *angels* in this context is to be understood as *messengers*.

The gathering of the elect, the people of God, is what happened *after* the judgment in Jerusalem. The lights will go out, and there will be the birth of a new order, a new age. The birth pains coming through the suffering are the nations being prepared for the proclamation of the gospel. The curse is coming, and with it is the promise. This is the pattern throughout history.[14] This is the pattern in the Book of Revelation. The gospel is proclaimed, the promise comes, and the elect are gathered. That is what will happen after the end of Jerusalem. It is the

---

14. Gangadean, *The Biblical Worldview*, 55–68.

end of that age and the beginning of a new age. It is not the end of the ages but the beginning of a new age.

In general, Jesus focuses their attention again on expectation.

Now learn this lesson from the fig tree: As soon as its twigs get tender and its leaves come out, you know that summer is near. Even so, when you see all these things, you know that it is near, right at the door (Matt. 24:32–33).

When they see these things coming, the end is right at the door. Then He makes it as clear as He possibly can, with the greatest certainty. He says in verse 34, "I tell you the truth, this generation will certainly not pass away until all these things have happened." "This generation" is spoken of at the end of Matthew 23, and here in 24, "this generation will certainly not pass away" (Matt. 24:34). It will happen within their lifetime; a generation is about 40 years. Remember, the generation that came out of Egypt lasted 40 years in the wilderness. Within 40 years, the temple was destroyed; it was destroyed in the year A.D. 70. Jesus makes this truth still more definite: "Heaven and earth will pass away, but my words will never pass away" (Matt. 24:35).

ON WHAT DAY AND HOUR WILL THE LORD COME?

No One Knows

It is in this context that we read the statement, "**about that day or hour no one knows**" (v. 36a). This is a strong "**no one.**" It includes the angels, and it includes Himself, the Son, in His humanity: "**about that day or hour no one knows.**" But guess what? If there is one thing we want to know that even the Son does not know, we want to know that day and that hour. Isn't it strange? The Lord is making it so emphatic that not even the Son knows, yet we want to know that day and that hour. We want to know that day and that hour because we want to continue living our lives the way we have and then set the alarm clock, and when the day and the hour comes, we will seek to escape judgment. In our fallen state, people want to max out their credit cards just before the rapture. Isn't that the truth? If we can avoid having to get our B.A. degree, we will. 'What is the point of having a B.A. degree if the Lord is going to come in five years?' We want to know the day and the hour.

That attitude is very different from what our Lord says in the parable of the talents: "'Put this money to work,' he said, 'until I come back'" (Lk. 19:13b). And in the parable of the ten virgins: "Therefore keep watch, because you do not know the day or the hour" (Matt. 25:13). These parables show a very different picture about how we are to watch and how we are to be about our Master's work. **"But about that day or hour no one knows, not even the angels in heaven, nor the Son"** (v. 36a), but we still certainly want to know. Forget it, it is not going to happen; we should not deceive ourselves.

The Day of the Lord (Judgment) Is Always Unexpected

Jesus says, **"As it was in the days of Noah, so it will be at the coming of the Son of Man"** (v. 37). What is spoken of in this verse is not merely the suddenness with which the Flood came in Noah's day, it is the suddenness of judgment. Judgment has come suddenly many times in history, as it was in the days of Noah. Luke 17:26–30 says:

> Just as it was in the days of Noah, so also will it be in the days of the Son of Man. People were eating, drinking, marrying and being given in marriage up to the day Noah entered the ark. Then the flood came and destroyed them all. It was the same in the days of Lot. People were eating and drinking, buying and selling, planting and building. But the day Lot left Sodom, fire and sulfur rained down from heaven and destroyed them all. It will be just like this on the day the Son of Man is revealed.

Jesus shows the suddenness of the judgment in the days of Noah and in the days of Lot, and He says, "It will be just like this on the day the Son of Man is revealed" (Lk. 17:30). It is manifest; He comes. As it was in the days of Noah, so it will be on the day the Son of Man is revealed.

Matthew splits this into two sections; in verses 17–18, He says, "Let no one on the housetop go down to take anything out of the house. Let no one in the field go back to get their cloak." In verses 40–41, He says, **"Two men will be in the field; one will be taken and the other left. Two women will be grinding with a hand mill; one will be taken and the other left."** But Luke keeps them together:

On that day no one who is on the housetop, with his possessions inside, should go down to get them. Likewise, no one in the field should go back for anything. Remember Lot's wife! Whoever tries to keep their life will lose it, and whoever loses their life will preserve it. I tell you, on that night two people will be in one bed; one will be taken and the other left. Two women will be grinding grain together; one will be taken and the other left (Lk. 17:31–35).

We cannot say, as some say, 'The first part of Matthew applies to the first judgment, and the second part applies to His coming in the future' because they are put together in Luke. He refers to our attitudes about our goods, our things: "no one in the field should go back for anything" (Lk. 17:31b). Then, "Remember Lot's wife!" (Lk. 17:32). This is judgment. This happened not only in Noah's day but in the days of Lot. When judgment comes, it comes suddenly, and we do not know the day or the hour. We know the season; He said, "Now learn this lesson from the fig tree: As soon as its twigs get tender and its leaves come out, you know that summer is near" (Matt. 24:32). He rebuked the Pharisees in Matthew 16: "You know how to interpret the appearance of the sky, but you cannot interpret the signs of the times" (Matt. 16:3b).

We are supposed to know the season. There is a time and a season for things. We are to live in season—plant in spring, not in winter. There is a time and a place for things, and we are to know the season, but we do not know the day or the hour. The Lord does not leave us totally unprepared for times of judgment, but He says that when it does come, it comes suddenly. When others are not expecting it, we should be expecting it, even when we do not know the day or the hour. We should understand what a wicked and adulterous generation is. We should understand when the cup of iniquity is being filled, and we should know that judgment is at the door. Can we tell what has happened in our culture in the past century? Do we know how things have changed from 1968 to the present? We should know what events are happening. We should know the changes that are rapidly occurring and accumulating. We should understand the discourse that is going on in the world, in politics, in philosophy, and in every dimension of life. The Lord wants us to understand the seasons, the times, and He calls us to be awake.

In this section in Luke, after Jesus says, "Remember Lot's wife!" (Lk. 17:32), He then gives a warning. "Whoever tries to keep their life will lose it, and whoever loses their life will preserve it" (Lk. 17:33). Jesus is addressing the general view of what the good is and what it is we are seeking. Here is where there is no break in the section; "I tell you, on that night two people will be in one bed; one will be taken and the other left. Two women will be grinding grain together; one will be taken and the other left" (Lk. 17:34–35). This is to be understood in the context that one is not to go back from the field for anything. One may be taken—as Lot was spared; he was taken out. The other was left and went into captivity. One is taken and the other left, and it is because of where the heart was set. It was because Lot's wife's heart was set on this world that she looked back and was overtaken in judgment. It comes quickly. "Two women will be grinding grain together; one will be taken and the other left." There will be a separation. The disciples ask Jesus, "Where, Lord?" "He replied, 'Where there is a dead body, there the vultures will gather'" (Lk. 17:37). That refers again to the spiritual death of the nation and the judgment that will come. This is how all of these things are tied together in Luke. So we say that this coming is the destruction of Jerusalem that will end the age. The disciples did not always understand the process, but the Lord spoke to them, continued to correct them, and opened up that way to them more and more.

Some have suggested the Lord expected the kingdom to come quickly and then changed His mind when it did not. The Lord did not do that; that is a false reading of the Scripture. If we understand the parables of the kingdom, we know that this is going to be a gradual process, the process of the leaven and the mustard seed; the kingdom grows to its fullness, an expression of the process of all the nations being discipled.[15] Providence will unfold gradually, and this can be known by God's theodicy and the process of history. There is a principle of fullness in God that is manifested in providence. God permitted evil to deepen the revelation of His glory; He allows every degree and admixture of evil and unbelief to come to expression in world history so as to be taken captive by the truth.[16] That does not mean we sit back and relax and

---

15. See Sermon 10: The Parables of the Kingdom: He Who Has Ears to Hear, Let Him Hear.
16. Gangadean, "Paper No. 19: Foundation for Philosophy of History," in *The Logos Papers*, 123–125.

say, 'Well, it will be another few thousand years. We have time for coffee and a few video games.' The Lord is warning them that they do not
know the day or the hour, which will come suddenly. That is the main
emphasis there. The conclusion is, "**Therefore keep watch**" (v. 42a).

Be Awake

In Mark 13:37, Jesus says, "What I say to you, I say to everyone:
'Watch!'" All are to watch, be alert, and be awake. That is the main idea
behind watching. Does that mean we do not go to sleep? No, it means
that while you are awake physically, be awake mentally, be awake spiritually, and be aware. Have your faculties collected and focused. Do not
be in a daze or a 'spiritual coma' as in a dream. Again and again, the
Scripture says, "Be alert."[17] What is it to be watchful? We have several examples given to us, so we do not have to speculate about what it
means. The suddenness of the coming is seen in three places. (1) Isaiah
30:13: "this sin will become for you like a high wall, cracked and bulg-
ing, that collapses suddenly, in an instant." Remember the collapse of
the Twin Towers and how suddenly it happened. (2) Judgment came
suddenly on Babylon—in one night, in one hour. (3) Revelation 18
says in 4 verses, "Therefore in one day her plagues will overtake her
. . . you mighty city of Babylon! In one hour your doom has come! . . .
In one hour such great wealth has been brought to ruin! . . . In one
hour she has been brought to ruin!"[18] Babylon represented the world
system of unbelief. This system is not at one time in history only, but
at any time in history, this judgment can come. We do not know the
day or the hour, but it comes, and when it comes, it comes suddenly.

The Signs of the Times

How are we to watch? How are we to be awake? It does not mean we
do not sleep, but we do not sleep spiritually. We are focused, we understand what is going on. We spoke about the signs of the times in
Matthew 16:3. That is one way we are to be awake and alert, interpreting and understanding the times and the seasons. We are not to go
through life as if everything is continuing the same. Everything is not

---

17. *Mark 13:33.*
18. *Revelation 18:8, 10, 17, 19.*

continuing the same. There are periods; things happen from time to time, it is not the case that all is even. We are now in a different place than we were in 1968. The progress of corruption in our culture has significantly increased. The amount of bloodshed in our culture and the degree of depravity that is going on has increased considerably. It is open, bold, and flung in one's face. Things are not the same; things are gathering to a head, so be aware of this. We are to watch in the way someone may watch for a thief.

> **But understand this: If the owner of the house had known at what time of night the thief was coming, he would have kept watch and would not have let his house be broken into. So you also must be ready, because the Son of Man will come at an hour when you do not expect him** (vv. 43–44).

This hour refers to the Day of the Lord in judgment. There are many references in Scripture about the Day of the Lord coming. 2 Peter 3:10a: "But the day of the Lord will come like a thief." 1 Thessalonians 5:2: "The day of the Lord will come like a thief." In Revelation 3:3, Jesus spoke to the Church, "I will come like a thief." In this case, judgment will come suddenly on the Church.

We see there are several ways in which the Lord comes. In verses 45–51 of this chapter, I believe that Jesus is speaking about His coming to believers at death. The person He speaks of is not watching as He has told us to in the previous verses; He is speaking of the Day of the Lord coming for that one person, and that person will be cut asunder. The day of our death is unknown to us, therefore we must watch. The Lord can bring judgment on the Church or blessing on the Church. Revelation 16:15 says, "Look, I come like a thief." How we would watch for a thief in the night is how we are to watch. We are to consider that suddenness for our own lives individually and for the Church collectively. The way one would watch for a thief coming in the night is the way that we are to watch for the Day of the Lord. We can understand this by analogy.

Watch: The Faithful Servant

Watching is compared to that of a faithful and wise servant. **"Who then is the faithful and wise servant, whom the master has put in** charge of the servants in his household to give them their food at the proper time? It will be good for that servant whose master finds him doing so when he returns" (vv. 45–46). This seems to be an individual application of the Lord's coming for one servant, and the blessing that will come if he is watching: "Truly I tell you, he will put him in charge of all his possessions" (v. 47).

> But suppose that servant is wicked and says to himself, "My master is staying away a long time," and he then begins to beat his fellow servants and to eat and drink with drunkards. The master of that servant will come on a day when he does not expect him and at an hour he is not aware of (vv. 48–50).

Again, the day and the hour are not known. In many places in Scripture, it is said that the day and the hour of the coming judgment is not known. "He will cut him to pieces and assign him a place with the hypocrites, where there will be weeping and gnashing of teeth" (v. 51).

The general point is this: the Day of the Lord comes; it comes suddenly, and it comes in many ways.[19] We are to be watchful. As it was in the days of Noah, the days of Lot, the days of Babylon, or the destruction of Jerusalem, so will be the coming of the Son of Man. The Lord does come in history to judge and to bless. We are to be aware, be watchful and not let it overtake us unaware. We are to have a general attitude of watchfulness. Notice the wicked servant did not have this attitude: "'My master is staying away a long time,' and he then begins to beat his fellow servants and to eat and drink with drunkards." Among the seven deadly sins are lust, greed, avarice, and gluttony. These are the things we do when we turn away from the Lord and turn to sensual indulgence. This person is not finding pleasure in knowing God, growing in knowing God, glorifying God, and making His glory known. Because one is enjoying the creation apart from God, of which we can never get enough, we always go to excess. What is our expectation? What is our view of the good? What is our worldview? What are we looking for? It is this general attitude that leads us not to be about our Master's work and not to be watchful.

---

19. Lorraine Boettner, *The Millennium*, 252–262.

We should be looking for ways and opportunities by which we can press forward in the fight. Instead, it is like we are on a battlefield, asleep somewhere. One must have a focus and decidedness in engaging the battle. How many of us are concerned to be engaged and to take thoughts captive which are raised up against the knowledge of God?[20] I was thinking about that this week as I was engaged in writing: things that are raised up against the knowledge of God are first raised up against knowledge, and skepticism is raised up against knowledge.[21] There are many faulty views of what knowledge is that we use to excuse us from engaging in the knowledge of God. But Romans 1:20 says, "For since the creation of the world God's invisible qualities—his eternal power and divine nature—have been clearly seen, being understood from what has been made, so that men are without excuse." Yet some object to the doctrine of clarity and inexcusability. Some say, 'What clarity? What are you talking about? Oh, that's for those apologists and philosophers; it's not for everyone.'

We are not engaged intellectually in the spiritual war, the battle of ideas between belief and unbelief. Some do not even know that there is a battle: 'What battle? What are we engaged in?' What are we concerned about? If we are concerned about the knowledge of God,[22] we will be engaged with the challenges against the knowledge of God since this is one of the chief ways in which we grow. Are we asleep? Are we about our daily affairs and how to make a better living: merely eating and drinking, marrying, buying houses, and moving into them on time? You have to move in on time, but you can be absorbed in that in such a way that you lose the sense of the kingdom's work. The Lord warns us against this. The servant who is wise and engaged in his master's work when the master comes will be blessed and given greater opportunity for service. That blessing can come in *this* life. If you are faithful in little, you will be faithful in much.[23] In our day, we call it promotion; the boss promotes you, and you become the store's general manager because you have been faithful. When the boss comes back, they see

---

20. *2 Corinthians 10:4–5.*

21. Gangadean, *Philosophical Foundation*, 17–31; Gangadean, *History of Philosophy*, 10–19.

22. Gangadean, "Paper No. 102: The Clarity of General Revelation," 527–529; "Paper No. 41: What Is Clear About God," 225–229; "Paper No. 122: Contra Charismatic Distinctive," in *The Logos Papers*, 651–653.

23. *Luke 16:10.*

your faithfulness. That is the way it should be. If we are not watchful in this sense, we will invite judgment upon ourselves.

Watch: The Five Wise Virgins and the Use of Talents

We will see in the next sermon how this theme continues in the parable of the ten virgins and in the parable of the talents, both of which call us to watch. When the question is asked of the Lord by His disciples in Acts 1:6, "Lord, are you at this time going to restore the kingdom to Israel?" Our Lord said, "It is not for you to know the times or dates" (Acts 1:7a). Notice again, the day and the hour we do not know. "But you will receive power when the Holy Spirit comes on you; and you will be my witnesses in Jerusalem, and in all Judea and Samaria, and to the ends of the earth" (Acts 1:8). This is what it is to be about our Lord's business.

The application is this: Are we so overcome by our daily concerns that we are not engaged in the work of seeking first the kingdom of God? Have the worries and cares of ordinary daily concerns (the "everydayness," as Heidegger says) so taken us that we are not seeing and engaging in the work of the kingdom of God? Are we passing through life asleep? We are overcome, so that the kingdom of God is not our first priority. Our first priority is putting bread on the table. The Lord said explicitly, "But seek first his kingdom and his righteousness, and all these things will be given to you as well" (Matt. 6:33). "So do not worry, saying, 'What shall we eat?' or 'What shall we drink?' or 'What shall we wear?'" (Matt. 6:31). If we are not engaged in the work of the Master, in seeking His kingdom, and we are putting our daily lives first, we are asleep and we are not watching. We are not being a wise and faithful servant.

The Lord calls us not only to watch our general worldview, to watch against being deceived, and to watch against false expectations, but we are to give ourselves continually to the work of the Lord. We are not to be surprised by or overcome by the sin that we find in the world or be discouraged and give up loving one another. He said, "Because of the increase of wickedness, the love of most will grow cold" (Matt. 24:12). We have to know how to preserve our love. Even as Jesus said, "Love one another. As I have loved you, so you must love one another" (Jn. 13:34b). So let us watch as our Lord has called us to watch.

23

BE READY

The Coming of the Lord to Judge and Reward

Matthew 25

[1]"At that time the kingdom of heaven will be like ten virgins who took their lamps and went out to meet the bridegroom. [2]Five of them were foolish and five were wise. [3]The foolish ones took their lamps but did not take any oil with them. [4]The wise ones, however, took oil in jars along with their lamps. [5]The bridegroom was a long time in coming, and they all became drowsy and fell asleep.

[6]"At midnight the cry rang out: 'Here's the bridegroom! Come out to meet him!'

[7]"Then all the virgins woke up and trimmed their lamps. [8]The foolish ones said to the wise, 'Give us some of your oil; our lamps are going out.'

[9]"'No,' they replied, 'there may not be enough for both us and you. Instead, go to those who sell oil and buy some for yourselves.'

[10]"But while they were on their way to buy the oil, the bridegroom arrived. The virgins who were ready went in with him to the wedding banquet. And the door was shut.

[11]"Later the others also came. 'Lord, Lord,' they said, 'open the door for us!'

[12]"But he replied, 'Truly I tell you, I don't know you.'

[13]"Therefore keep watch, because you do not know the day or the hour.

[14]"Again, it will be like a man going on a journey, who called his servants and entrusted his wealth to them. [15]To one he gave five bags of gold, to

another two bags, and to another one bag, each according to his ability. Then he went on his journey. [16]The man who had received five bags of gold went at once and put his money to work and gained five bags more. [17]So also, the one with two bags of gold gained two more. [18]But the man who had received one bag went off, dug a hole in the ground and hid his master's money.

[19]"After a long time the master of those servants returned and settled accounts with them. [20]The man who had received five bags of gold brought the other five. 'Master,' he said, 'you entrusted me with five bags of gold. See, I have gained five more.'

[21]"His master replied, 'Well done, good and faithful servant! You have been faithful with a few things; I will put you in charge of many things. Come and share your master's happiness!'

[22]"The man with two bags of gold also came. 'Master,' he said, 'you entrusted me with two bags of gold; see, I have gained two more.'

[23]"His master replied, 'Well done, good and faithful servant! You have been faithful with a few things; I will put you in charge of many things. Come and share your master's happiness!'

[24]"Then the man who had received one bag of gold came. 'Master,' he said, 'I knew that you are a hard man, harvesting where you have not sown and gathering where you have not scattered seed. [25]So I was afraid and went out and hid your gold in the ground. See, here is what belongs to you.'

[26]"His master replied, 'You wicked, lazy servant! So you knew that I harvest where I have not sown and gather where I have not scattered seed? [27]Well then, you should have put my money on deposit with the bankers, so that when I returned I would have received it back with interest.'

[28]"'So take the bag of gold from him and give it to the one who has ten bags. [29]For whoever has will be given more, and they will have an abundance. Whoever does not have, even what they have will be taken from them. [30]And throw that worthless servant outside, into the darkness, where there will be weeping and gnashing of teeth.'

[31]"When the Son of Man comes in his glory, and all the angels with him, he will sit on his glorious throne. [32]All the nations will be gathered before him, and he will separate the people one from another as a shepherd separates the sheep from the goats. [33]He will put the sheep on his right and the goats on his left.

[34]"Then the King will say to those on his right, 'Come, you who are blessed by my Father; take your inheritance, the kingdom prepared for you since the creation of the world. [35]For I was hungry and you gave me something

to eat, I was thirsty and you gave me something to drink, I was a stranger and you invited me in, [36]I needed clothes and you clothed me, I was sick and you looked after me, I was in prison and you came to visit me.'

[37]"Then the righteous will answer him, 'Lord, when did we see you hungry and feed you, or thirsty and give you something to drink? [38]When did we see you a stranger and invite you in, or needing clothes and clothe you? [39]When did we see you sick or in prison and go to visit you?'

[40]"The King will reply, 'Truly I tell you, whatever you did for one of the least of these brothers and sisters of mine, you did for me.'

[41]"Then he will say to those on his left, 'Depart from me, you who are cursed, into the eternal fire prepared for the devil and his angels. [42]For I was hungry and you gave me nothing to eat, I was thirsty and you gave me nothing to drink, [43]I was a stranger and you did not invite me in, I needed clothes and you did not clothe me, I was sick and in prison and you did not look after me.'

[44]"They also will answer, 'Lord, when did we see you hungry or thirsty or a stranger or needing clothes or sick or in prison, and did not help you?'

[45]"He will reply, 'Truly I tell you, whatever you did not do for one of the least of these, you did not do for me.'

[46]"Then they will go away to eternal punishment, but the righteous to eternal life."

INTRODUCTION AND REVIEW

WE ARE ON PART SIX OF THE PASSION WEEK. This is the week in which our Lord is crucified. We have gone over the events leading up to His coming into Jerusalem, presenting Himself, being rejected, and pronouncing judgment on the religious leaders in the seven woes because of their hypocrisy. The Lord declared judgment on the temple: "not one stone here will be left on another; every one will be thrown down" (Matt. 24:2b). The disciples asked the question, "When will this happen, and what will be the sign of your coming and of the end of the age?" (Matt. 24:3b). We saw that these questions are to be taken together, not separately.

The Lord answers this question all the way through to the end of Matthew 24. At the end of 24, He spoke about the faithful and wise servant and continued the call for the disciples to watch. In Matthew 24:36 and 42, He says, "But about that day or hour no one knows, not even the angels in heaven, nor the Son, but only the Father," and "Therefore keep watch, because you do not know on what day your Lord will come." Jesus continues this theme of the day and the hour in regard to judgment. At the end of the parable of the ten virgins, He says, **"Therefore keep watch, because you do not know the day or the hour"** (v. 13). Jesus tells them to keep watch and not to be taken by surprise: "So you also must be ready, because the Son of Man will come at an hour when you do not expect him" (Matt. 24:44).

Verses 45–51 are then about the faithful and wise servant who is put in charge of his master's household, who will be commended if he is found being diligent. Here again, He says, "The master of that servant will come on a day when he does not expect him and at an hour he is not aware of" (Matt. 24:50). The theme of expectation of the Lord coming in sudden judgment on an individual, a church, or a nation continues. The day and the hour remain unknown, but the certainty that God will judge us for our unfaithfulness remains consistent.

The last section of Matthew 25, concerning the sheep and the goats, is clearly the end of the ages, when all the nations are gathered to Him. The theme of His coming in judgment remains, and the same attitude is to be in place: be watchful and ready. We are to watch, not just for His final coming but for all of the times of His coming.[1] All of the times of His coming are for judgment, rewarding the faithful, and bringing judgment upon those who are unfaithful. So, with that in mind, we remember that the coming of the Lord is for judgment in several ways, and it includes the final judgment, which involves the separation of the sheep from the goats.

As our Lord is speaking to His disciples, let us continue to hear His Word about how we are to be watchful. We need this reminder. After the immediate concerns about Jerusalem, there are four warnings: (1) The warning for the servant who is given charge of the master's household: to be diligent. (2) The warning for the ten virgins: to be wise. (3) The warning for those given charge of the talents: to bear fruit. (4) The warning for the sheep and the goats: to be obedient. All of these are woven together so that we might understand what it means to be ready and watchful. We are to be watchful so that our hearts do not turn aside from the goal and so that we are not deceived. We are to be

---

1. Lorraine Boettner, *The Millennium*, 252–262.

watchful, particularly regarding ourselves, so that we walk in the Lord steadfastly. We are not to say that the Lord is not coming and become slack in our lives, because the Lord comes in many ways. He will come at an hour and a day that we do not realize, and if we are not going about our Master's business, we can be cut off.

THE PARABLE OF THE TEN VIRGINS:
The Warning to Be Wise

We will pick up at the beginning of Matthew 25, where we read about the ten virgins. Let us see what this passage teaches us in particular.

> At that time the kingdom of heaven will be like ten virgins who took their lamps and went out to meet the bridegroom. Five of them were foolish and five were wise. The foolish ones took their lamps but did not take any oil with them. The wise ones, however, took oil in jars along with their lamps. The bridegroom was a long time in coming, and they all became drowsy and fell asleep. At midnight the cry rang out: "Here's the bridegroom! Come out to meet him!" Then all the virgins woke up and trimmed their lamps. The foolish ones said to the wise, "Give us some of your oil; our lamps are going out." "No," they replied, "there may not be enough for both us and you. Instead, go to those who sell oil and buy some for yourselves." But while they were on their way to buy the oil, the bridegroom arrived. The virgins who were ready went in with him to the wedding banquet. And the door was shut. Later the others also came. "Lord, Lord," they said, "open the door for us!" But he replied, "Truly I tell you, I don't know you." Therefore keep watch, because you do not know the day or the hour (vv. 1–13).

The kingdom of God is likened to these ten virgins who took their lamps and went out to meet the bridegroom. There is a distinction among these: five were wise, and five were foolish. This parable does not refer to mankind in general. This is a select group. These are those who profess to be the Lord's and are waiting for the Lord. Jesus is making a distinction among these people.

Five were called wise, and five were called foolish; what makes the difference? We should back up and give a little background on weddings.

In the West, we do not think about waiting for the bridegroom at an unspecified time. We usually have an hour and place when the wedding is to take place. The bridegroom comes walking in, and everyone is waiting in the church. In the East, the bridegroom usually comes riding a horse. The time is not always set; there is a day, but you do not know the exact hour. So they are waiting for the bridegroom to appear, and it is unlike our situation; we have to use a little imagination and understand that the bridegroom is coming at some unappointed time. It was understood and expected that the bridegroom would show up, though they did not know exactly when, so they would go out and wait to meet him. They would not know whether it would be during the day or at an hour of the night. So, all the virgins went out, and they all were prepared, but in varying degrees.

One group came really prepared, and one group came just somewhat prepared. Taking a lamp and oil is some degree of preparation, isn't it? We are talking about people who are close to resembling each other, but there is a difference between them. The Lord will focus on this difference and call us to be like the wise virgins. The wise ones took the lamps with oil, and in addition, they took oil in a jar. That is the extra measure of preparation. Since we do not know when the bridegroom will arrive, it could be a long time or short, we need to be ready so that we can stay all the way through. That is what is being noticed here—preparation for the long haul. We might put it this way: we want to start and finish the building. We want to not only start the race but also finish it. We want to fight the good fight and be able to complete it. Christianity is not for one year, three years, or five years. It may be 25 years, 45 years, or 65 years, but we want to be able to go all the way. We want to be ready; that is one way of speaking about readiness. Another way is to say that we have run the race,[2] which involves timing and pacing ourselves. We want to make the maximum time; we are not running against anyone else, but we are to complete the race in the best possible time in all that the Lord has given us. Think about lifetime preparation for service in the kingdom of God. Think about what that involves and how we translate this to having oil in the jar and being prepared to serve the Lord long-term. We will also see this in the parable of the talents.

---

2. *2 Timothy 4:7.*

Notice what is said: "The bridegroom was a long time in coming" (v. 5a). And again, in the next parable, it was a long time: "After a long time the master of those servants returned" (v. 19a). And before, the servant said, "My master is staying away a long time" (Matt. 24:48b). The reference occurs three times in these parables: a long time. What happens now is that all ten virgins "became drowsy and fell asleep" (v. 5b). That is not the distinguishing characteristic; they all went out to greet the bridegroom, and they all took oil and lamps, and they all fell asleep, but the one point of difference is that one group was wise; they took additional oil in a jar; they were prepared. The cry came, they all woke up and trimmed their lamps, and the foolish ones started to realize their lack. They came to the wise and said, "Give us some of your oil; our lamps are going out" (v. 8b). What did the wise ones do? Did they just say, 'Sure, we are all in this together, we will share'? That is not what the wise ones did. The wise ones were concerned to have enough oil and continued to be concerned even then. They said, "No . . . there may not be enough for both us and you" (v. 9a). In other words, we may share, but it would help neither; there will not be enough. They did not stop there; they made a suggestion. "Instead, go to those who sell oil and buy some for yourselves" (v. 9b). The foolish ones came to realize a need, but it was too late.

The Lord is commending wisdom in the Christian life, in our being ready for Him and serving Him, and we are to be prepared for the long-term. We should make choices that will serve the Lord long-term: choice of a life partner, choices with work and preparation, and choices on how we will serve Him long-term. The Lord wants us to think about how we can best be ready to serve Him and go this way long-term. Notice, "The bridegroom was a long time in coming, and they all became drowsy and fell asleep." The point being emphasized is the difference between those who came prepared and those who did not. So they went out to buy oil, and it was probably a crisis; they were scrambling. The simple, or the foolish, were not thinking ahead and are now scrambling. They apparently had some outward desire to be with Him, so if you press that point too hard, you might say, 'I think this is being too harsh. They were just about five minutes late! They just barely missed it; it just doesn't seem right.' But I think that we should not press this parable at every point.

> But while they were on their way to buy the oil, the bridegroom arrived. The virgins who were ready went in with him to the wedding banquet. And the door was shut. Later the others also came. "Lord, Lord," they said, "open the door for us!" But he replied, "Truly I tell you, I don't know you" (vv. 10–12).

On the face of it, it seems that this response is pretty rough, just for being a few minutes late. But that is the point to pay attention to. The Lord is commending the wisdom in being prepared; we do not know the day or the hour, and we are to be ready. Many go along but are not in that state of readiness. A certain heart condition is revealed here in those who are ready, wise, and prepared, and those who are not. It makes all the difference in the world when He says, "**Truly I tell you, I don't know you.**" We can have an outward connectedness with the Lord, but not be seeking the Lord prayerfully and with wisdom to be prepared to serve Him long-term, to finish the race that He has called us to run, and to keep the faith.[3] This is one way in which we are to watch.

Be wise, be prepared, and be prepared long-term. Even though there may be some similarities between the two groups of virgins, such as they both fell asleep, at least this much is clear: the wise virgins had a concern, they thought about the future, they came prepared, and their thoughtfulness and preparedness show a difference in heart commitment. We do not know the day or the hour when the Lord will come, and we should be prepared long-term. Notice the Lord could have come earlier, when the oil of the foolish virgins had not yet gone out. Had He come earlier in the night, the foolish virgins may have thought, 'We lucked out on that one. That was close.' We may think that way, but the Lord wants us to have a commitment where we are prepared for this work long-term. We do not know the day or the hour when He will come. The basic point is that the wise ones are prepared for the long-term. Do not worry about the other matters, and do not push those too hard. There is, generally, one central point in each parable, and we are to keep the focus on the central point.

---

3. *2 Timothy 4:7.*

THE PARABLE OF THE TALENTS:
The Warning to Bear Fruit

"Again, it will be like a man going on a journey, who called his servants and entrusted his wealth to them. To one he gave five talents of money, to another two talents, and to another one talent, each according to his ability" (vv. 14–15a).[4] That is an interesting dispersion of talents, a sum of money, given according to our ability and the opportunities that we have. We will see what is particularly being commended here and how we are to be watchful. Notice, they are given differing amounts of talents. The question of equality is in the diligence with which we put our talents to use, regardless of the number of talents or opportunities we have. Understandably, a householder will do this, taking a journey, giving his servants various responsibilities, and expecting them, when he comes back, to have fulfilled those responsibilities. Is this not a very natural concern to have? Perhaps we could see ourselves in a situation like this; we would want to see those responsibilities kept. From the point of view of the household, it is very natural that one would want to see the servants do their work. I think we can relate to this in this way. Let us say an employer entrusts a certain work to an employee. He is not there standing over him, watching him all the time, but he wants to have the confidence that the servant will go about doing the work and not slack off. He wants the work done, and he wants to see fruitfulness. This is very natural and easy to understand.

"The man who had received the five talents went at once and put his money to work and gained five more" (v. 16). Immediately, he puts the talents to work. He has something entrusted to him, he is keeping that trust, and he is doing the work that his master called him to do. We must think about how that applies to the work of the kingdom; we are to be involved and faithful witnesses in every situation in the world. We should be giving ourselves to this; we should not be negligent, and we should make the most of every opportunity the Lord gives us.

Then it says, "So also, the one with the two talents gained two more. But the man who had received the one talent went off, dug a hole in the ground and hid his master's money" (vv. 17–18). It is hard to imagine what was going on in this person's mind when he did this.

---

4. NIV 1984.

He dug a hole and put the money in the ground. Think about that. Did the master give him that money to deal with it that way? Is the money to just sit there? Is he to do nothing with it? The master could have given it to the bankers, or this servant could have done so. This is what the master said, **"Well then, you should have put my money on deposit with the bankers, so that when I returned I would have received it back with interest"** (v. 27). The money is given for the purpose of increase. The two servants who received five and two talents went about their work with the attitude of increase, and the third did not. **"After a long time the master of those servants returned and settled accounts with them"** (v. 19). We can expect this settling of accounts. The Lord has created us in His image, He has given us a work to do, and He will not disappear forever. He wants to see that work done. He gave that work to mankind.[5] He gives that work to Christians.[6] **"The man who had received the talents brought the other five. 'Master,' he said, 'you entrusted me with five talents. See, I have gained five more'"** (v. 20). This is commendable. **"His master replied, 'Well done, good and faithful servant! You have been faithful with a few things; I will put you in charge of many things. Come and share your master's happiness!'"** (v. 21).

There is a certain pleasure the master has in seeing this work being done. Think about our lives, what the Lord has given us, and what opportunities we have. When the Lord comes, and we are to give an account, what is your present estimate of what will happen? Do you have confidence in saying, 'Lord, here is the gain.' You may be unsure and think, 'No, I've lost it all; I dare not come before my master.' The Lord is speaking this way so that we might be prepared. We must awaken from our laziness and slothfulness and say, 'I am going to give an account before the Lord.' The Lord does want to see gain for His kingdom, and there is joy in the Master, and the servant shares in this joy. **"The man with the two talents also came. 'Master,' he said, 'you entrusted me with two talents; see, I have gained two more'"** (v. 22).

Notice the equality of these two servants, though they differ in other respects. One had five talents and one had two talents; they both went and put it to work immediately. Both had an increase, and the

---

5. *Genesis 1:26–28.*
6. *Matthew 28:18–20.*

increase was proportionate to the amount given. The one with five had produced double, and the one with two had produced double. There are similarities to show that there is an equality that the Lord looks at, and He is not necessarily expecting that the one given the two talents will get five more. The amount produced is not the point of this parable. There are other places where it speaks about how much we should produce. How much should we produce? Thirtyfold. That is not 30% more but thirtyfold, 30 times as much. "Still other seed fell on good soil, where it produced a crop—a hundred, sixty or thirty times what was sown" (Matt. 13:8). God wants us to be fruitful.

The first words that God spoke to man were: "Be fruitful."[7] The first mention has a certain prominence. Jesus says, "This is to my Father's glory, that you bear much fruit" (Jn. 15:8a), and, "I chose you . . . that you might go and bear fruit—fruit that will last" (John 15:16b). So the man who had two talents also received the same commendation:

> His master replied, "Well done, good and faithful servant! You have been faithful with a few things; I will put you in charge of many things. Come and share your master's happiness!" Then the man who had received one talent came. "Master," he said, "I knew that you are a hard man, harvesting where you have not sown and gathering where you have not scattered seed. So I was afraid and went out and hid your talent in the ground. See, here is what belongs to you." (vv. 23–25).

We have to see through the thinking of the servant who buried the talent. The master addresses his thinking; he sees his heart and says, "You wicked, lazy servant!" (v. 26a). Wicked in what way? "So you knew that I harvest where I have not sown and gather where I have not scattered seed?" (v. 26b). He knew that truth, and he did not give heed to it. Notice the servant said, "I knew that you are a hard man." The Lord says, "My yoke is easy and my burden is light" (Matt. 11:30). There is a delight in doing the work of the Lord. Why did this servant have this attitude about his master, that he was a hard man? He uses his feelings as an excuse: "I was afraid" (v. 25a). People speak that way sometimes about human leaders: 'I was afraid of you.' We should not be afraid, we should do whatever the Lord requires of us. We cannot

---

7. *Genesis 1:28.*

think that way of the Lord. If we think that in our hearts about the Lord, it shows that we do not know and understand the Lord, and we do not see the lack in ourselves. The Lord pointed out, **"You wicked, lazy servant!"** The servant's own words judged him. He says, **"Well then, you should have put my money on deposit with the bankers, so that when I returned I would have received it back with interest"** (v. 27). That is the *least* he could have done. When you put the money in the bank, you do not have to do anything with it. But at least you invested; you did not just leave it lying idle. Even the least, this servant had not brought about, so he was judged out of his own mouth and condemned. **"Take the talent from him and give it to the one who has ten talents"** (v. 28). Then the Lord says, **"For whoever has will be given more, and they will have an abundance. Whoever does not have, even what they have will be taken from them"** (v. 29). Here is the judgment: **"And throw that worthless servant outside, into the darkness, where there will be weeping and gnashing of teeth"** (v. 30).

In the parable of the ten virgins, He said, **"I don't know you"** (v. 12b). This Scripture is given to us not to further excuse ourselves by applying this judgment to us, but it is given to call us to repentance. "Today" is not the Day of Judgment. "Today" is the call to repentance according to the Sabbath.[8] If we have the thought in our heart at all that we are like that wicked, lazy servant and we stand condemned, then it is time to repent. Or if we think, as the foolish say, that we know we will end up there, then it is time to repent. We are not to continue to excuse ourselves by saying, 'Woe is me; it's all over; nothing can be done.' There is always time to repent and seek the Lord for His grace.

In this parable, we do not have much said of the suddenness of His return, but we have the watchfulness and the call to be fruitful. In the parable of the ten virgins is the call to be watchful, ready, and wise. And in the first account of the master who put His servant in charge of all His household, they were called to be diligent; these things will connect with each other. What is it to be ready and watchful against those things that will keep us from being fruitful? Be wise and diligent, and engage in the work the Lord has given us. We are not to say, 'I want to be diligent, but I don't know what to do.' The Lord has already told us clearly: be faithful witnesses, make disciples of all the nations,

---

8. Gangadean, *The Epistle to the Hebrews*, 35–49.

teach them to observe all things that I commanded,[9] be fruitful and multiply.[10]

THE PARABLE OF THE SHEEP AND THE GOATS:
The Warning to Be Obedient

In this last parable, Jesus says, "**When the Son of Man comes in his glory . . .**" (v. 31a). Again, this is about the coming of the Lord, and this is specified: "**in his glory.**" It is further specified: "**and all the angels with him, he will sit on his glorious throne. All the nations will be gathered before him, and he will separate the people one from another as a shepherd separates the sheep from the goats**" (vv. 31b–32). This is something that is very understandable in Middle Eastern terms: the animals are brought in together, and then they are separated—the sheep from the goats. "**All the nations will be gathered before him, and he will separate the people one from another.**" He is not separating nations; He is separating individuals. God will separate the people, not nations, one from another; there is no one *blessed* nation in the world. We should not think of ourselves as privileged in that way. We should think of the kingdom of God, which is scattered among all the nations of the world. In that sense, we are truly beyond nationality. We have a certain responsibility for the nation in which we live, but our responsibility and our loyalty is beyond the nation to the kingdom of God.

All the nations will be gathered, and He will separate the people from one another as a shepherd separates sheep from goats. "**He will put the sheep on his right and the goats on his left. Then the King will say to those on his right, 'Come, you who are blessed by my Father; take your inheritance'**" (vv. 33–34a). What is the inheritance? "**The kingdom prepared for you since the creation of the world**" (v. 34b). It was not prepared just lately; it was prepared from the creation of the world. It was not just prepared then and delivered here, but it was prepared since creation and is continuing and building through history. When we seek first the kingdom of God and His righteousness, we are co-neighbors with one another in Christ's kingdom. It is the work that is going on throughout history. Remember Abraham left Ur of

9. *Matthew 28:18–20.*
10. *Genesis 1:28.*

the Chaldeans seeking a city with foundations—the City of God.[11] This City of God is the People of God submitting to God in all of life and showing forth His glory. The blessing given to those on the right is the kingdom of God prepared for us since the creation of the world. I do not want you to step back because of the word 'prepared.' Many have taken the position that because it is 'prepared,' we do not have to do anything. It is prepared in the sense that it is planned for you from the creation, from the beginning. It is prepared for us, having been engaged in that work of dominion. All things are to be subdued unto Christ; the last enemy to be destroyed is death.[12] He is subduing all things to Himself, we are seated with Christ in the heavenlies, and we are reigning with Him. We share in His exercise of authority: "All authority in heaven and on earth has been given to me. Therefore go and make disciples of all nations" (Matt. 28:18–19a). We rule with Christ as we make disciples of all nations and teach them to obey the law. That rule is going on now.

Many, many, many times, I have heard, again and again, about the kingdom that will come: 'Christ is going to do this directly when He comes.' That view is missing it. It is not that we do not have to do any work because the kingdom is prepared for us. It is not that because it is Christ's work that it is not our work. "For it is God who works in you to will and to act in order to fulfill his good purpose" (Phil. 2:13). We make these dichotomies, stumble at the threshold, and we end up with one talent that we buried when the Lord returns. Let us not excuse ourselves in any way. The Lord commends the first two servants, and what He commends them for is that they served in the kingdom of God and served in ways that should be obvious. How so? **"For I was hungry and you gave me something to eat, I was thirsty and you gave me something to drink"** (v. 35a). I was hungry—I, the Lord of the kingdom, was hungry, and you gave me something to eat. I was thirsty, and you gave me something to drink. We may be inclined to think that everyone would be willing to do that. In the movie *Ben-Hur*, when Christ needed water, Ben-Hur lifted that water to Him, and he said, 'Anyone would give water to the Lord.' Well, that is not exactly true, not everyone recognized Him as the Lord of Glory. **"I was a**

---

11. *Hebrews 11:8–10.*

12. *1 Corinthians 15:26.*

stranger and you invited me in. I needed clothes and you clothed me, I was sick and you looked after me, I was in prison and you came to visit me" (vv. 35b–36).

These are some of the most obvious things, but some people try to make the ministry of the kingdom to be this and only this: visiting widows and orphans. That is only the beginning of the ministry of the kingdom. That is what it is in the most obvious sense, but it is much more than that; it is to do justice as well as mercy. It is to remove things that oppress widows and orphans, not to just pick up the broken pieces. It is to have care and concern for justice in general, but also, justice for particular ones, for the Lord Jesus Christ.

> Then the righteous will answer him, "Lord, when did we see you hungry and feed you, or thirsty and give you something to drink? When did we see you a stranger and invite you in, or needing clothes and clothe you? When did we see you sick or in prison and go to visit you?" The King will reply, "Truly I tell you, whatever you did for one of the least of these brothers and sisters of mine, you did for me" (vv. 37–40).

This is particularly addressed to those who are members of the body of Christ. It is about what they did or did not do for a brother of Christ, a sister of Christ, and the least of these. These are our brothers and sisters in Christ who are suffering. There are some who are near home, members of our body who are hurting, who need care. Some of us are not aware of this. If we were willing, looking, and inquiring about others, we would know the needs, and we would minister there. When did we see Christ hurting and we comforted Him? It is right here in this room, today, in the body of Christ. Sometimes, we think about sending our money to orphanages overseas, and that should be done, or ministering to those who are down and out in the city, and that should be done, but He is speaking particularly about the members of this body. "Whatever you did for one of the least of these brothers and sisters of mine, you did for me" (v. 40b). If charity cannot begin at home, it does not begin.

"Then he will say to those on his left, 'Depart from me'" (v. 41). So to those on the right He says, "Come, you who are blessed by my Father; take your inheritance, the kingdom prepared for you since the creation of the world" (v. 34). And to those on the left He says, "Depart from me, you who are cursed" (v. 41a). Notice, "I never knew you."[13] The doors are shut.

> Then he will say to those on his left, "Depart from me, you who are cursed, into the eternal fire prepared for the devil and his angels. For I was hungry and you gave me nothing to eat, I was thirsty and you gave me nothing to drink, I was a stranger and you did not invite me in, I needed clothes and you did not clothe me, I was sick and in prison and you did not look after me." They also will answer, "Lord, when did we see you hungry or thirsty or a stranger or needing clothes or sick or in prison, and did not help you?" He will reply, "Truly I tell you, whatever you did not do for one of the least of these, you did not do for me." Then they will go away to eternal punishment, but the righteous to eternal life (vv. 41–46).

WARNINGS TO CALL US TO REPENTANCE

The Lord will come. He comes through our history in judgment. He will come finally in the Final Judgment. He wants us to be diligent about the work that He has given us to do. He wants us to be wise; there are no excuses there. He wants us to be fruitful; there are no excuses there. He wants us to show love, concern, and compassion to our brothers and sisters sitting beside us in the church today. He wants us to be aware of the needs of our brothers and sisters. Someone may be well off in one way, but in other ways, they are hurting, and it makes all the difference. We need to learn to minister in the body of Christ.

If we do not, we could hear, "Depart from me, you who are cursed." If we do not love our brother and have concern for him, if we are not showing that love that is the work of the Holy Spirit, loving our neighbor as ourselves, if we do not have that work going on in our hearts, then the work of the ministry has not begun. We cannot say that we are believers in Christ. Remember again, do not take this message as a spirit of judgment. Take this message as a call to repentance. Do not say, 'I am that wicked and lazy servant; I know that would happen

---

13. *Matthew 7:23.*

to me.' If you use this message in that way, that is an excuse to avoid repentance. The time of judgment is not yet, but if we do not repent and give ourselves to diligence, wisdom, fruitfulness, and obedience in watching and being ready, it will certainly come upon us, and we will have no excuse. Let us turn to our Lord; His yoke is easy, and His burden is light.[14] The law of God is light when our hearts are right before Him. If we find it a burden, we should ask the Lord to change our hearts and to work in our hearts, that we might find the law a delight, because the law brings us to life in Him. It brings us to know Him and to delight in Him in every way. Amen.

---

14. *Matthew 11:30.*

———

24

THE PREPARATION
Preparing the Disciples for
What Is to Come

Matthew 26:1–46

¹When Jesus had finished saying all these things, he said to his disciples, ²"As you know, the Passover is two days away—and the Son of Man will be handed over to be crucified."

³Then the chief priests and the elders of the people assembled in the palace of the high priest, whose name was Caiaphas, ⁴and they schemed to arrest Jesus secretly and kill him. ⁵"But not during the festival," they said, "or there may be a riot among the people."

⁶While Jesus was in Bethany in the home of Simon the Leper, ⁷a woman came to him with an alabaster jar of very expensive perfume, which she poured on his head as he was reclining at the table.

⁸When the disciples saw this, they were indignant. "Why this waste?" they asked. ⁹"This perfume could have been sold at a high price and the money given to the poor."

¹⁰Aware of this, Jesus said to them, "Why are you bothering this woman? She has done a beautiful thing to me. ¹¹The poor you will always have with you, but you will not always have me. ¹²When she poured this perfume on my body, she did it to prepare me for burial. ¹³Truly I tell you, wherever this gospel is preached throughout the world, what she has done will also be told, in memory of her."

¹⁴Then one of the Twelve—the one called Judas Iscariot—went to the chief priests ¹⁵and asked, "What are you willing to give me if I deliver him over

to you?" So they counted out for him thirty pieces of silver. [16]From then on Judas watched for an opportunity to hand him over.

[17]On the first day of the Festival of Unleavened Bread, the disciples came to Jesus and asked, "Where do you want us to make preparations for you to eat the Passover?"

[18]He replied, "Go into the city to a certain man and tell him, 'The Teacher says: My appointed time is near. I am going to celebrate the Passover with my disciples at your house.'" [19]So the disciples did as Jesus had directed them and prepared the Passover.

[20]When evening came, Jesus was reclining at the table with the Twelve. [21]And while they were eating, he said, "Truly I tell you, one of you will betray me."

[22]They were very sad and began to say to him one after the other, "Surely you don't mean me, Lord?"

[23]Jesus replied, "The one who has dipped his hand into the bowl with me will betray me. [24]The Son of Man will go just as it is written about him. But woe to that man who betrays the Son of Man! It would be better for him if he had not been born."

[25]Then Judas, the one who would betray him, said, "Surely you don't mean me, Rabbi?"

Jesus answered, "You have said so."

[26]While they were eating, Jesus took bread, and when he had given thanks, he broke it and gave it to his disciples, saying, "Take and eat; this is my body."

[27]Then he took a cup, and when he had given thanks, he gave it to them, saying, "Drink from it, all of you. [28]This is my blood of the covenant, which is poured out for many for the forgiveness of sins. [29]I tell you, I will not drink from this fruit of the vine from now on until that day when I drink it new with you in my Father's kingdom."

[30]When they had sung a hymn, they went out to the Mount of Olives.

[31]Then Jesus told them, "This very night you will all fall away on account of me, for it is written:

"'I will strike the shepherd,
and the sheep of the flock will be scattered.'

[32]But after I have risen, I will go ahead of you into Galilee."

[33]Peter replied, "Even if all fall away on account of you, I never will."

34"Truly I tell you," Jesus answered, "this very night, before the rooster crows, you will disown me three times."

35But Peter declared, "Even if I have to die with you, I will never disown you." And all the other disciples said the same.

36Then Jesus went with his disciples to a place called Gethsemane, and he said to them, "Sit here while I go over there and pray." 37He took Peter and the two sons of Zebedee along with him, and he began to be sorrowful and troubled. 38Then he said to them, "My soul is overwhelmed with sorrow to the point of death. Stay here and keep watch with me."

39Going a little farther, he fell with his face to the ground and prayed, "My Father, if it is possible, may this cup be taken from me. Yet not as I will, but as you will."

40Then he returned to his disciples and found them sleeping. "Couldn't you men keep watch with me for one hour?" he asked Peter. 41"Watch and pray so that you will not fall into temptation. The spirit is willing, but the flesh is weak."

42He went away a second time and prayed, "My Father, if it is not possible for this cup to be taken away unless I drink it, may your will be done."

43When he came back, he again found them sleeping, because their eyes were heavy. 44So he left them and went away once more and prayed the third time, saying the same thing.

45Then he returned to the disciples and said to them, "Are you still sleeping and resting? Look, the hour has come, and the Son of Man is delivered into the hands of sinners. 46Rise! Let us go! Here comes my betrayer!"

INTRODUCTION AND REVIEW:
Preparation—The Time of the Passover Has Come

WE COME TO PART SEVEN OF THE PASSION WEEK, which is focused on preparation. There are several senses of preparation going on in this chapter. Certainly, as we just read, Mary poured that ointment on Jesus in preparation for His burial. But there is another sense of preparation that has been going on: Jesus is preparing His disciples for what is to come. It is so fitting that the Lord would do this, and the details spoken of in this section should be understood in terms of preparation.

By way of review and introduction, let me remind you of what has been happening this Passion Week. (1) Jesus presented Himself in

Jerusalem and was received by the people. (2) He saw what was going on in the temple, came back, and cleansed the temple. (3) The sign of the fig tree is given. (4) His authority was questioned; Jesus answered these questions and challenged them with the question: "Whose Son is Christ?"[1] They could not answer, and He silenced them. (5) Jesus pronounced judgment and the seven woes upon the religious leaders who should have prepared the way for Jesus but were blocking the way instead. (6) He pronounced judgment on the nation, on the city of Jerusalem, and on the temple. (7) Jesus taught His disciples what would happen when they asked, "When will this happen, and what will be the sign of your coming and of the end of the age?" (Matt. 24:3b). Jesus prepared His disciples, calling them to watch and be ready for what will happen in that generation. "Truly I tell you, this generation will certainly not pass away until all these things have happened" (Matt. 24:34). Jesus told them this explicitly.

Jesus not only prepared them for what is going to happen in that generation, but He prepared them for what will happen in every generation, as we saw in the parables of the faithful and wise servant, the ten virgins, the talents, and the sheep and the goats. Jesus prepares His people; He calls us to watch and to be ready. He spoke about the master going away for a long time and the servants did not know when He would return. The Lord returns to His people in several ways. I noticed this morning on the cover of Time Magazine the reference to Tim LaHaye and Jerry B. Jenkins, authors of the *Left Behind* series. It sold over 62 million copies, and there is false teaching in those books. But why is it so popular? There is a desire to know what is coming and to be prepared. It is partly because the Church has not given a clear account of eschatology that this falsehood can occur, which involves a whole worldview. There is a *need* to be prepared, and people feel that need. They will cling to what is false preparation, if need be, to get some sense of preparation. We need to take that to heart and be able to speak the Word, in particular and in general, about the preparation. Jesus wants His people prepared for what is coming. Jesus prepared them not only for that generation, and for every generation, but He prepared them for what was coming within a few days, and even within

---

1. *Matthew 22:41.*

a few hours. He wants His disciples prepared. He speaks and tells them particular things that will enable them to be prepared.

That the Scriptures May Be Fulfilled

Jesus has a number of reasons and concerns about giving this preparation. First, He wants them to see that this is according to the Scripture. According to the plan of God, things are unfolding, that the Scriptures might be fulfilled in detail. Time and again, when He tells them what is about to come, it is in the context that the Scripture might be fulfilled as it was spoken. He has a concern to establish them upon that sure Word of Scripture to see that this is not something new; this is in the plan of God from ages past. To give them a sense of the importance and significance of what is happening, God planned it down to the last detail: nothing is left to chance or law-like necessity. It is according to the plan of God that has been revealed in the Scripture, and so Jesus speaks to them in detail of what will come about. Certainly, when we get to the Gospel of John—which is not what we are covering today, but we refer to it a number of times—Jesus is preparing His disciples, especially at the time of the Passover, as He tells them of what is to come. Understanding the fulfillment of the Scriptures is the first reason why He is preparing them.

The World Must Know That I Love the Father and Do Exactly What the Father Has Commanded Me

Second, they must know that He, the Lord Jesus Christ, is going to lay down His life as Lord and as Savior. He is laying down His life; it is not something that is coming upon Him, taking Him by surprise. It is according to the Scriptures, He knows the Scriptures, and He is willingly obeying, "so that the world may learn that I love the Father and do exactly what my Father has commanded me" (Jn. 14:31). He is willingly obeying, up to His prayer at Gethsemane: "Father, if you are willing, take this cup from me; yet not my will, but yours be done" (Lk. 22:42). The world must know that Jesus is laying down His life in love, in obedience to the Father's will, and that nothing is happening apart from His knowing. There are many times and ways in which He could have set aside His obedience, even up to the point when Peter pulled a sword and struck the high priest's servant. **"Do you think I** cannot call on my Father, and he will at once put at my disposal more than twelve legions of angels?" (v. 53). Jesus is doing this in deliberate obedience to the Father. He is fulfilling what has been practiced in the Jewish nation since the time they left Egypt. He is fulfilling the Passover. The blood of bulls and goats cannot take away sin; they cannot redeem. He has come in fulfillment of the atonement they symbolize. He is fulfilling what is celebrated on the Day of Atonement. With His own blood, He will enter into the Most Holy Place, into heaven itself.[2] It was to be so from the beginning in the Garden; it was for this reason that He was incarnated.

Jesus is upholding God's holiness and love in dying on the cross. Jesus said, "Now my soul is troubled, and what shall I say? 'Father, save me from this hour'? No, it was for this very reason I came to this hour. Father, glorify your name!" (Jn. 12:27–28a). The name of God and His glory, justice, holiness, and love is being revealed. "Therefore, when Christ came into the world, He said: 'Sacrifice and offering you did not desire, but a body you prepared for me'" (Heb. 10:5). He came into the world to die. His disciples must learn this. The disciples had difficulty understanding this, because after the resurrection, He had to reprove them. He said, "O foolish ones, and slow of heart to believe in all that the prophets have spoken! Ought not the Christ to have suffered these things and to enter into His glory?" (Lk. 24:25–26 NKJV). And to this day, the nation of Israel has not seen the need for the Christ to suffer—this is no small thing. He prepares His disciples; He prepares His people. Jesus had said to them three times before that He was going to go up to Jerusalem and die, and they could not hear or receive it. So He has prepared them to see that the Scriptures must be fulfilled, that the world must know that He loves His Father, and that He does exactly what His Father has commanded Him. So we, too, should love God and obey Him.

I Told You Before So That When It Happens, You Will Believe

Third, to prepare His disciples, He said, "I have told you now before it happens, so that when it does happen you will believe" (Jn. 14:29). He prepares them that they may not stumble and go astray when these

---

2. *Hebrews 9:11–12, 24.*

things start to come about. That their hearts would not be troubled and that they would have His peace, He said, "Peace I leave with you; my peace I give you. I do not give to you as the world gives. Do not let your hearts be troubled and do not be afraid" (Jn. 14:27). Our hearts need to be prepared for what is coming, especially in times of trouble, so that we will not be led astray, not grow slack in our love, and not be faint. We should be aware that the Lord has gone before us and that the Lord is with us. We must have the peace of God, the love of God, and the joy of our Lord Jesus Christ in us, and we must persevere through whatever comes. There will be times of trouble, and the Lord wants us to know and to be prepared. He said a number of times in John that His peace would be with us, and we persevere in this.

Jesus wants the disciples to know that all that will come is according to Scripture, that this is a way of love, and that Jesus is loving His Father and obeying Him, so that their hearts would be at peace knowing this and not be troubled. Whatever trial comes upon us individually, as a group, as a people, or as a nation, we should know the peace of God and the love of God, and persevere. The psalm for this month is Psalm 46C. I want you all to make this a psalm that will be in your hearts so you can sing this when troubled: We will not therefore be afraid, though all the earth should be removed, though mountains great be hurled into the ocean's depths.[3] If there is upheaval among the nations, or in whatever form it takes, we will know that "there is a river whose streams make glad the city of God, the holy place where the Most High dwells. God is within her, she will not fall; God will help her at break of day." (Ps. 46:4–5).

God has preserved His people and will continue to preserve His people through the ages until the work He has given us is finished. He said, "Make disciples of all nations . . . teaching them to obey everything I have commanded you" (Matt. 28:19a–20a). We pray that prayer every Lord's Day: "Thy kingdom come, Thy will be done in earth, as it is in heaven" (Matt. 6:10 KJV). What are we praying? Are we praying mindlessly or thoughtfully when we pray that prayer? The will of God is not done in patches by one or two individuals in heaven; it is done *everywhere* in heaven. This is what our Lord taught us, "Thy kingdom come, Thy will be done in earth, as it is in heaven." The Lord will be

---

3. *Psalm 46:2, 46C, The Book of Psalms for Singing.*

with His people through all the troubles. He said, "Lo, I am with you always, even to the end of the age" (Matt. 28:20b NKJV). Until this work is completed, until we bring glory to the name of the Father in discipling the nations, He is with us. The Lord Jesus prepares His people.

We come now to the Word of our Lord Jesus Christ at the beginning of this chapter. Jesus prepares them for what will happen more immediately. **"When Jesus had finished saying all these things, he said to his disciples, 'As you know, the Passover is two days away—and the Son of Man will be handed over to be crucified'"** (vv. 1–2). We have to realize that they are having difficulty processing what is coming. We have to understand Judas' betrayal, Peter's denial, and the disciples' response in light of this Word; they could not process what Jesus told them, though He gave them remarkable details about what is to come. He told them these details to prepare them, so that their hearts would not be troubled. He told them so that even when they sin in the midst of this, they will remember the Word of the Lord and recover. Remember how Peter had to be recovered when Jesus asked him three times: Do you love me more than these?[4] Jesus prepares us so that instead of falling away completely, we are saved by that Word that the Lord spoke. Jesus said to Peter, **"Truly I tell you . . . this very night, before a rooster crows, you will disown me three times"** (v. 34). Peter would deny Him in a matter of a few hours. Peter vehemently said, **"I will never disown you"** (v. 35). Jesus prepared His disciples. Peter did not commit suicide the way Judas did because of the Word spoken by the Lord. You can be sure Peter felt so low that he likely could have destroyed himself, but the Lord knew him utterly. As we sang in Psalm 139A: For in my tongue no word can be, but, lo, O LORD, 'tis known to Thee.[5] There is no place we can hide from the Lord. Jesus prepares His people.

THE PLOT:
Be on Guard

We have the word concerning the plot to kill Jesus: **"Then the chief priests and the elders of the people assembled in the palace of the high**

---

4. *John 21:15.*

5. *Psalm 139:4, 139A, The Book of Psalms for Singing.*

priest, whose name was Caiaphas, and they schemed to arrest Jesus secretly and kill him" (vv. 4–5). We know from John that Caiaphas prophesied concerning Jesus, and we should understand this prophecy in the context of Matthew—the plot to kill Jesus was underway.

> Then one of them, named Caiaphas, who was high priest that year, spoke up, "You know nothing at all! You do not realize that it is better for you that one man die for the people than that the whole nation perish." He did not say this on his own, but as high priest that year he prophesied that Jesus would die for the Jewish nation (Jn. 11:49–51).

Caiaphas spoke not knowing how he was speaking. What we should notice here is that the high priests, the elders of the people, the chief priests, and the leadership of the nation had gone astray from the Word of God. Just as it is in the Church today in many sections, the leadership of the Church has gone astray in exactly the way that the leadership went astray then. The point to notice is not just that the Jewish leaders went astray, but the leadership of the Church can go astray, and it can happen to us, too. We have a greater responsibility because we have seen it happen in the past. Many segments and parts of the Church have gone astray. Not each and every one has gone astray, for God preserves the people for Himself, but this can happen in this church.[6]

Think of how deceptive that can be. While calling upon the name of Jesus and offering prayers and incense, we can go astray so as to deny the Lord. Think about what happened in the time of the Reformation, that those who would offer prayers in the name of Jesus could persecute His servants. We need to recognize the depravity in our hearts as human beings, and how, left to ourselves, even in the midst of religious paraphernalia and ritual, we can go astray. If it happens here in the church, it can happen in many other places. Even with all our piety and wit, we will still go astray. It could be Buddhist piety, Hindu piety, or Confucian piety. We go astray in the name of religion. Do not be misled. Do not be taken in. Let us fix our eyes on Jesus,[7] "for there is no other name under heaven given to mankind by which we must be saved" (Acts 4:12b). The name of Jesus upholds the justice,

---

6. Referring to Westminster Fellowship.

7. *Hebrews 12:2.*

righteousness, and holiness of God. He was willing to die on the cross to satisfy divine justice, that God may be merciful in His love and yet be righteous.

Jesus Anointed in Preparation for His Burial: Our Life Poured Out in Service to Him

A plot is afoot, and it is done slyly. It is done with the help of Judas Iscariot. We should read this reference about the anointing of Jesus in contrast to Judas. The anointing of Christ took place six days before Passover.[8] Jesus is anointed. He is anointed by Mary, and there is cross evidence elsewhere, so we can say this is the same person who anointed the Lord in John 12. John refers to her wiping His feet with her hair. Matthew refers to His head, but it does not mean His head and not His feet. We have to take it as meaning both His head and His feet. We have to see this anointing in contrast to the disciples and Judas. What Mary is doing and what Judas is doing are in contrast to each other. Judas was with our Lord for three years, and he did not see; he did not understand. And the disciples were not understanding.

Mary had a heart of devotion, and her heart of devotion enabled her to see a reality that others did not see. Her sister Martha was somewhat different; she was serving. There is a place for service, but Jesus spoke to Martha about what Mary had chosen. There is another disciple who had this heart of devotion, his name is John. He speaks of himself as the one whom Jesus loved. "This was the one who had leaned back against Jesus at the supper and had said, 'Lord, who is going to betray you?'" (Jn. 21:20b). It is that devotional spirit that the Lord wants us to have. This is why Jesus said, **"Wherever the gospel is preached throughout the world, what she has done will also be told, in memory of her"** (v. 13).

The Lord wants us to be, toward Him, as Mary and as John. He wants us to pour out our most precious gift, our very life, upon Him, in service to Him. Mary does this in thankfulness for His having raised Lazarus, her brother, from the dead—her brother whom she loved. She did this because Jesus was the Lord of life, the Creator who showed His power in raising from the dead. This miracle of raising Lazarus was the

---

8. *John 12:1–3.*

crown of all the miracles, and people came to Jesus because He had raised Lazarus from the dead. It was then that He declared, "I am the resurrection and the life" (Jn. 11:25). He is the Lord of life, and He is worthy. Mary brought her very precious ointment and poured it on His head and poured it on His feet. Jesus said, **"She has done a beautiful thing to me"** (v. 10b). This is holiness; this is devotion to the Lord.

The Lord wants us to worship Him in the beauty of holiness. Our hearts are to respond to Him in His beauty, righteousness, holiness, and love, as Mary responded. She poured her expensive perfume on His head and on His feet. She took her hair, the glory of a woman, and she wiped His feet with her hair. Mary did this to prepare Him for His burial. Six days remained until the Passover, and the fragrance remained on our Lord Jesus Christ throughout this week, and it remained with Him in Gethsemane. This devotion, this worship, and the union and communion that there is with the Lord in worship, is the joy that was set before Him—that the Lord would have an intimate relationship with His people. It was said of our Lord Jesus, "For the joy set before him he endured the cross" (Heb. 12:2). Jesus knew what was coming; it did not make it less painful or less difficult, as we shall see as we go on.

Mary worshiped Jesus in this way. The disciples did not understand; they were concerned about cost and service to the poor. They did not recognize Jesus as they should have; He had to reprove them: **"Why are you bothering this woman? She has done a beautiful thing to me. The poor you will always have with you, but you will not always have me"** (vv. 10b–11). To be able to pour that ointment on His body, on His head, on His feet, when He was physically, bodily present with us, was a special privilege. Mary worshiped Him in this way. What Mary has done will be told through all the world; it is a memorial of her, and it is for us, each one. This is our response to the Lord of glory as we see His glory. The only reason we do not worship the Lord the way Mary did is because we do not see Him in His glory. Our eyes need to be opened so that our hearts may be opened and we may worship the Lord in this way. She did it to prepare Him, His body, for burial. Mary worshiped the Lord.

Judas' response is set in contrast to Mary. Judas had his eye on some kingdom or other that he imagined, not the kingdom that Christ was to bring. He perhaps wanted to play the hand of our Lord and force His hand. Whatever the explanation, he went to the chief priests to speak to them. That was shortly after the six days before Passover when Jesus was anointed. The high priest now had this information. He knew that one would betray Jesus, and they were able to plot how it would happen two days before. Notice everyone was going to Jesus because He had done this miracle of raising Lazarus from the dead. He showed Himself to be the resurrection and the life. He displayed His glory in this way and so the people were going to Him. Two days before the Passover, with the agreement they had made with Judas, they plotted to kill Him in response to the raising of Lazarus. Mary worshiped Him, and Judas betrayed our Lord Jesus Christ.

You may wonder whether this betrayal was very great. You would want a person, after all that has been said and done, to stay with you, be with you, continue with you, and not turn against you. If you want to understand what a betrayal is, think about what happens in a marriage when one party walks out on the other. That is close to home. The proper description of that is a betrayal. You would not expect someone so close to do that to you. You expected more, expected very differently. A betrayal always hurts. The Lord was keenly aware of this betrayal.

THE LORD'S SUPPER:
Knowing What Is to Come

In this account in verses 14–16, Judas watched for an opportunity to hand Him over to the chief priests:

> Then one of the Twelve—the one called Judas Iscariot—went to the chief priests and asked, "What are you willing to give me if I deliver him over to you?" So they counted out for him thirty pieces of silver. From then on Judas watched for an opportunity to hand him over (vv. 14–16).

This passage begins with the chief priests and leaders plotting. Jesus had forced their hand by the miracle of the resurrection of Lazarus, by His presentation in the temple, and by shutting down their questions. They had no objections, so they had to do something. They could either repent or take the next step, and they did take the next step, in plotting to arrest Him, try Him, and crucify Him. It was all prepared and trumped up. In the midst of this, as we so often hear when we come to the Lord's Supper, "The Lord Jesus, on the night he was betrayed, took bread, and when he had given thanks, he broke it" (1 Cor. 11:23b–24a). Jesus had sent His disciples earlier that day to make preparations. He knew how to provide for His disciples a place to eat. He did not have a place to rest His head, but He knew and spoke that Word as Lord and sent them to a certain man in the city. They said, "**The Teacher says: My appointed time is near. I am going to celebrate the Passover with my disciples at your house**" (v. 18b). So the disciples prepared for the Passover. Jesus was with His disciples that evening at the supper, and while they were eating, He said, "**Truly I tell you, one of you will betray me**" (v. 21b). "**They were very sad and began to say to him one after the other, 'Surely you don't mean me, Lord?'**" (v. 22). Judas knew that the Lord knew.

Judas had to be there with the Lord, and Jesus did not expose Judas at that point. He could have exposed Judas and prevented the betrayal, but He knew what was to come. He did not expose Judas; the disciples were not to stumble because of Judas. The betrayal was according to Scripture, and the deliberateness with which Jesus submitted to the will of the Father is shown here. He is preparing His disciples. "**Jesus replied, 'The one who has dipped his hand into the bowl with me will betray me'**" (v. 23). John's account is: "Jesus answered, 'It is the one to whom I will give this piece of bread when I have dipped it in the dish.' Then, dipping the piece of bread, he gave it to Judas, the son of Simon Iscariot" (Jn. 13:26). This is a very intimate act. Jesus showed Judas the position he was in and the intimacy he had because of that position, yet Judas denied it, betrayed it, and turned aside. Jesus said, "**The Son of Man will go just as it is written about him**" (v. 24a), that the Scriptures might be fulfilled.

Jesus is continually bringing attention back to the Scriptures being fulfilled. "**But woe to that man who betrays the Son of Man! It would be better for him if he had not been born**" (v. 24b). Yes, it would have been better for *him*. But it is for the glory of God. Judas covered it up and said, "**Surely you don't mean me, Rabbi?**" (v. 25). He answered with the same words that the others had used; he did not want to expose himself. "**Jesus answered, 'You have said so'**" (v. 25b). Jesus knew, and Judas knew that He knew, and the other disciples came to know that Jesus knew, though He did not expose Judas. Jesus told John, who kept the confidence of the Lord. If He had said it out loud and Peter got word of it, Judas would not have made it out of that room. The disciples would have stopped Him. But Jesus showed His deliberateness, that the Scriptures might be fulfilled. Jesus is obeying the Lord, His Father.

Jesus then showed the disciples that He Himself was the fulfillment of the Passover when He said to them, **"Take and eat; this is my body"** (v. 26b). Then of the cup, He said, **"Drink from it, all of you. This is my blood of the covenant, which is poured out for many for the forgiveness of sins"** (vv. 27b–28). This is the basis on which sin is forgiven. The forgiveness of sin is not apart from the shedding of blood. Jesus identified Himself altogether as the Passover Lamb with His broken body and His shed blood. We observe the Lord's Supper to this day in place of the Passover. The Jews observed the Passover year after year through the centuries, and it all pointed to Him, the Lamb of God who takes away the sin of the world.[9] The blood of bulls, goats, and lambs could not atone for sin, so Jesus revealed Himself to be the Passover Lamb. **"When they had sung a hymn, they went out to the Mount of Olives"** (v. 30). In other portions of Scripture, in John particularly, we know much detail of what is going through the mind of our Lord Jesus. He knew all of this happened that the Scripture might be fulfilled and that God's love may be seen in His obedience.

Judas departed: "As soon as Judas had taken the bread, he went out. And it was night" (Jn. 13:30). He went his way—the way of perdition. Someone so close, so near, and yet so far. But for the rest of His disciples, Jesus continues to prepare them by quoting the Scripture: **"This very night you will all fall away on account of me, for it is written: 'I will strike the shepherd, and the sheep of the flock will be scattered.' But after I have risen, I will go ahead of you into Galilee"** (vv. 31–32). They are going to go through terrible times. They are going to be totally nonplussed, given their lack of understanding of what is happening. Even then, He is telling them enough ahead of time so that when they do forsake Him, they will remember that He knew they would forsake Him, that He is going to go ahead of them, and that He is going to recover them. He is preparing the hearts of His people. We fail, and we should know that He knows our thoughts utterly, as we sang in

---

9. *John 1:29.*

Psalm 139A.[10] "Before a word is on my tongue you, LORD, know it completely" (Psalm 139:4).

When we fall, we know that Jesus has searched us, He knows us altogether, and He has died for our sins. Our sins are under Christ's blood, and we are not to touch His blood. We cannot touch our own sin without putting our hands in the blood of Christ. When we take our sin out from where it belongs—under the blood of Christ—and beat ourselves over it, we are putting our hands in the blood of Christ. Can you atone for your guilt this way? The blood of Christ is sufficient, and the devil cannot touch it. When the devil comes condemning, point to the blood of Christ, and he will flee from you. The devil cannot touch it, nor can any other human. That sin is under the precious blood of Jesus. There is no condemnation for those who are in Christ Jesus. We ourselves must put our sin under the blood of Christ in repentance and leave it there, and it cannot be touched.

JESUS PREDICTS PETER'S DENIAL

Jesus prepares His disciples, anticipating what is to come. **"After I have risen, I will go ahead of you into Galilee"** (v. 32). Peter comes back and says, **"Even if all fall away on account of you, I never will"** (v. 33). "Therefore let him who thinks he stands take heed lest he fall" (1 Cor. 10:12 NKJV). Think about the confidence of Peter. Let us understand that we stand by God's grace and do not stand in ourselves. Peter was quite sure. The Lord had been so explicit about the details in preparing His people for what is coming. Jesus responded, **"Truly I tell you . . . this very night, before the rooster crows, you will disown me three times"** (v. 34). This is spoken for Peter, but it is spoken for all of us who, in our self-confidence, turn away and deny the Lord. God forgives that sin, and we come back and learn to trust in Him. Every time we have sinned in the Lord, we have denied the Lord. We will say, 'We will never do it again; it will never happen,' and then we do it. Every time we sin it is a denial of the Lord. Just as the disciples denied Him here. We may yield to this temptation or that temptation in the same way the disciples yielded to temptation. We will see how He prepares them and calls them, that they may not go this way. Peter hears the Word

---

10. *Psalm 139A, The Book of Psalms for Singing.*

of God and does not receive it. "**Peter declared, 'Even if I have to die with you, I will never disown you.' And all the other disciples said the same**" (v. 35). And at Peter's third denial, Scripture says, "Again Peter denied it, and at that moment a rooster began to crow" (Jn. 18:27). This reveals to Peter and those around him that the Lord knew what was coming, and the Lord is deliberately obeying His Father.

GETHSEMANE:
Watch and Pray That You Enter Not into Temptation

They come to Gethsemane, and Jesus says to his disciples,

> "Sit here while I go over there and pray." He took Peter and the two sons of Zebedee along with him, and he began to be sorrowful and troubled. Then he said to them, "My soul is overwhelmed with sorrow to the point of death. Stay here and keep watch with me" (vv. 36b–38).

Jesus knew what was going to happen. His knowing did not make it less sorrowful. Perhaps it intensified the sorrow as He anticipated sin falling upon Him. He described it as his heart being overwhelmed with sorrow. Have you gotten to that point in your life, times when you are overwhelmed with sorrow? Well, you know that your high priest has gone before you and He is touched with the feelings of our infirmity.[11] We can come to Him and find grace to help in the time of need. "**My soul is overwhelmed with sorrow to the point of death.**" He says to Peter, James, and John, "**Stay here and keep watch with me.**" Once in a while, we face dreadful situations, and we want others to just be with us, stand by us, and be near. Jesus wanted His disciples to be near Him in this hour of sorrow. How human He is. How touched with the feelings of our infirmity.

> Going a little farther, he fell with his face to the ground and prayed, "My Father, if it is possible, may this cup be taken from me. Yet not as I will, but as you will." Then he returned to his disciples and found them sleeping. "Couldn't you men keep watch with me for one hour?" (vv. 39–40).

---

11. *Hebrews 4:15* KJV.

Sometimes, that is all it takes: one hour of watching and praying with the Lord. **"Watch and pray so that you will not fall into temptation"** (v. 41a). Our Lord Jesus went before us. The Scripture says, "And being in anguish, he prayed more earnestly" (Lk. 22:44a). That is why the Scripture says, "Let us fix our eyes on Jesus, the author and perfecter of faith, who for the joy set before him endured the cross" (Heb. 12:2a).[12] Which of us has come into that kind of agony and anguish that as he prayed, "his sweat was like drops of blood falling to the ground" (Lk. 22:44b)? There is the expression 'sweating bullets.' Jesus was sweating, as it were, great drops of blood, and He was praying more earnestly. He prayed three times. He knew it was coming; He wanted to avoid it. **"My Father, if it is possible, may this cup be taken from me. Yet not as I will, but as you will"** (v. 39b). He came back to the disciples the third time and said to them, **"Are you still sleeping and resting? Look, the hour has come, and the Son of Man is delivered into the hands of sinners"** (v. 45b). He is betrayed. Time and again, that word is brought forward, **"the Son of Man is betrayed into the hands of sinners."**[13] **"Rise! Let us go! Here comes my betrayer!"** (v. 46).

Jesus has gone before us. There is no temptation that has overtaken us but such as is common to man, and our Lord has endured it and has endured it to the utmost. Let us fix our eyes on Jesus and pray more earnestly when we are in anguish, in trouble, in temptation. Let us draw near to our Lord Jesus. Let us know what it is to love our heavenly Father as our Lord Jesus loved His Father and did exactly what His Father commanded.

---

12. NIV 1984.

13. ESV.

25

BETRAYAL OF TRUST
Now Is the Crisis of the World

Matthew 26:47–27:26

²⁶:⁴⁷While he was still speaking, Judas, one of the Twelve, arrived. With him was a large crowd armed with swords and clubs, sent from the chief priests and the elders of the people. ⁴⁸Now the betrayer had arranged a signal with them: "The one I kiss is the man; arrest him." ⁴⁹Going at once to Jesus, Judas said, "Greetings, Rabbi!" and kissed him.

⁵⁰Jesus replied, "Do what you came for, friend."

Then the men stepped forward, seized Jesus and arrested him. ⁵¹With that, one of Jesus' companions reached for his sword, drew it out and struck the servant of the high priest, cutting off his ear.

⁵²"Put your sword back in its place," Jesus said to him, "for all who draw the sword will die by the sword. ⁵³Do you think I cannot call on my Father, and he will at once put at my disposal more than twelve legions of angels? ⁵⁴But how then would the Scriptures be fulfilled that say it must happen in this way?"

⁵⁵In that hour Jesus said to the crowd, "Am I leading a rebellion, that you have come out with swords and clubs to capture me? Every day I sat in the temple courts teaching, and you did not arrest me. ⁵⁶But this has all taken place that the writings of the prophets might be fulfilled." Then all the disciples deserted him and fled.

⁵⁷Those who had arrested Jesus took him to Caiaphas the high priest, where the teachers of the law and the elders had assembled. ⁵⁸But Peter followed him at a distance, right up to the courtyard of the high priest. He entered and sat down with the guards to see the outcome.

[59]The chief priests and the whole Sanhedrin were looking for false evidence against Jesus so that they could put him to death. [60]But they did not find any, though many false witnesses came forward.

Finally two came forward [61]and declared, "This fellow said, 'I am able to destroy the temple of God and rebuild it in three days.'"

[62]Then the high priest stood up and said to Jesus, "Are you not going to answer? What is this testimony that these men are bringing against you?" [63]But Jesus remained silent.

The high priest said to him, "I charge you under oath by the living God: Tell us if you are the Messiah, the Son of God."

[64]"You have said so," Jesus replied. "But I say to all of you: From now on you will see the Son of Man sitting at the right hand of the Mighty One and coming on the clouds of heaven."

[65]Then the high priest tore his clothes and said, "He has spoken blasphemy! Why do we need any more witnesses? Look, now you have heard the blasphemy. [66]What do you think?"

"He is worthy of death," they answered.

[67]Then they spit in his face and struck him with their fists. Others slapped him [68]and said, "Prophesy to us, Messiah. Who hit you?"

[69]Now Peter was sitting out in the courtyard, and a servant girl came to him. "You also were with Jesus of Galilee," she said.

[70]But he denied it before them all. "I don't know what you're talking about," he said.

[71]Then he went out to the gateway, where another servant girl saw him and said to the people there, "This fellow was with Jesus of Nazareth."

[72]He denied it again, with an oath: "I don't know the man!"

[73]After a little while, those standing there went up to Peter and said, "Surely you are one of them; your accent gives you away."

[74]Then he began to call down curses, and he swore to them, "I don't know the man!"

Immediately a rooster crowed. [75]Then Peter remembered the word Jesus had spoken: "Before the rooster crows, you will disown me three times." And he went outside and wept bitterly.

[27:1]Early in the morning, all the chief priests and the elders of the people made their plans how to have Jesus executed. [2]So they bound him, led him away and handed him over to Pilate the governor.

³When Judas, who had betrayed him, saw that Jesus was condemned, he was seized with remorse and returned the thirty pieces of silver to the chief priests and the elders. ⁴"I have sinned," he said, "for I have betrayed innocent blood."

"What is that to us?" they replied. "That's your responsibility."

⁵So Judas threw the money into the temple and left. Then he went away and hanged himself.

⁶The chief priests picked up the coins and said, "It is against the law to put this into the treasury, since it is blood money." ⁷So they decided to use the money to buy the potter's field as a burial place for foreigners. ⁸That is why it has been called the Field of Blood to this day. ⁹Then what was spoken by Jeremiah the prophet was fulfilled: "They took the thirty pieces of silver, the price set on him by the people of Israel, ¹⁰and they used them to buy the potter's field, as the Lord commanded me."

¹¹Meanwhile Jesus stood before the governor, and the governor asked him, "Are you the king of the Jews?"

"You have said so," Jesus replied.

¹²When he was accused by the chief priests and the elders, he gave no answer. ¹³Then Pilate asked him, "Don't you hear the testimony they are bringing against you?" ¹⁴But Jesus made no reply, not even to a single charge—to the great amazement of the governor.

¹⁵Now it was the governor's custom at the festival to release a prisoner chosen by the crowd. ¹⁶At that time they had a notorious prisoner, called Barabbas. ¹⁷So when the crowd had gathered, Pilate asked them, 'Which one do you want me to release to you: Barabbas, or Jesus who is called Christ?' ¹⁸For he knew it was out of self-interest that they had handed Jesus over to him.

¹⁹While Pilate was sitting on the judge's seat, his wife sent him this message: "Don't have anything to do with that innocent man, for I have suffered a great deal today in a dream because of him."

²⁰But the chief priests and the elders persuaded the crowd to ask for Barabbas and to have Jesus executed.

²¹"Which of the two do you want me to release to you?" asked the governor.

"Barabbas," they answered.

²²"What shall I do, then, with Jesus who is called the Messiah?" Pilate asked.

They all answered, "Crucify him!"

²³"Why? What crime has he committed?" asked Pilate.

But they shouted all the louder, "Crucify him!"

²⁴When Pilate saw that he was getting nowhere, but that instead an uproar was starting, he took water and washed his hands in front of the crowd. "I am innocent of this man's blood," he said. "It is your responsibility!"

²⁵All the people answered, "His blood is on us and on our children!"

²⁶Then he released Barabbas to them. But he had Jesus flogged, and handed him over to be crucified.

INTRODUCTION AND REVIEW:
The Stage Is Set

THIS IS THE EIGHTH MESSAGE ON THE PASSION Week, leading up to Jesus' arrest, trial, and crucifixion. Everything comes to a head at this point. In John 12:31, Jesus said, "Now is the judgment of this world" (KJV). The literal term in Greek for the word *judgment* in this verse is *krisis*—everything comes to a head. Jesus ministered to the people for three years in the northern part of Israel and in Jerusalem. During His last week, He had come into the temple *again*, and He cleansed the temple *again*; it was a rebuke to those who were to watch for the holiness of God's ways, His ordinances, and His name. They had failed. In cleansing the temple, Jesus exercised the authority of the One sent by God, the Son of God, to make things whole and make things right. He said, "It is written . . . 'My house will be called a house of prayer,' but you are making it 'a den of robbers'" (Matt. 21:13). This precipitated fierce questioning by the rulers: "'By what authority are you doing these things?' they asked. 'And who gave You this authority?'" (Matt. 21:23b). He answered their questions and silenced them. The last question He asked them was: Whose Son is the Christ?

> While the Pharisees were gathered together, Jesus asked them, saying, "What do you think about the Christ? Whose Son is He?" They said to Him, "The Son of David." He said to them, "How then does David in the Spirit call Him 'Lord,' saying: 'The Lord said to my Lord, "Sit at My right hand, Till I make Your enemies Your footstool"'? If David then calls Him 'Lord,' how is He his Son?"

And no one was able to answer Him a word, nor from that day on did anyone dare question Him anymore (Matt. 22:41–46 NKJV).

If He is the son of David merely, how is it that His father, David, is calling Him "my Lord"? A father does not refer to His son as "my Lord."

In the last sermon, we also saw how Jesus continued explaining to His disciples when the judgment would come, and He continued to prepare them. They were being prepared for what is to come both within their generation—30 or 40 years—and within any generation. They are to watch as the wise virgins and as the wise steward. They are to watch what is to come in a matter of days—two days, and then hours, and then minutes. At Gethsemane, Jesus was praying and preparing Himself for the trial that was to come. "And being in anguish, he prayed more earnestly, and his sweat was like drops of blood falling to the ground" (Lk. 22:44). He said to His disciples, "What! Could you not watch with Me one hour?" (Matt. 26:40b NKJV). They were called to be watchful in prayer, that they may be prepared for what was to come. Then Jesus said at the end of that time of praying, "Rise! Let us go! Here comes my betrayer!" (Matt. 26:46). So Jesus knows exactly what is happening. He lets His disciples know that He knows, so that when it comes to pass, they may believe. He is preparing them in that way. He sees that the Scripture is going to be fulfilled; He shows His love for the Father by doing exactly what the Father has commanded, and He shows that He is willingly obedient. Jesus knows what is coming, and He is still proceeding. It is not that events have overtaken Him; He laid down His life. No one took it from Him. He was willingly an offering for sin according to the will of the Father. The disciples were prepared as far as they could be prepared so that they would not utterly despair when the trials overwhelm them—when the great waves go over them.[1] At the end of the section that we closed with last time, Jesus spoke explicitly about the one who would betray Him. Jesus "returned to the disciples and said to them, 'Are you still sleeping and resting? Look, the hour has come, and the Son of Man is delivered into the hands of sinners. Rise! Let us go! Here comes my betrayer!'" (Matt. 26:45–46).

---

1. *Psalm 42:7.*

I struggled with choosing the title of this message. I wanted to connect the four main items under one heading. There is Judas, there is Caiaphas, there is Peter, and there is Pilate, and Jesus will come before all of them. I wanted to use the word "betrayal" merely, but "betrayal" could seem too narrow, so I titled it "Betrayal of Trust," which is on a larger scale. When someone is in an official position and has been entrusted with carrying out an office appropriately, and they fail, then they betray that trust. This is a common element in this section, the *betrayal of trust*, and we have to consider how betrayal works. There are many ways we may encounter betrayal around us. We must consider how it can exist and does exist within us, so that we might repent.

The players are all in position. All of their lives now come together in a crisis. In a play, a climactic event brings everything to a head, and afterward, the *denouement*: the unfolding of the revelation of what is in the hearts of men. Well, now, we have come to the crisis. It is not just the crisis of that time, but it is the crisis of the entire world, the history of the world, from the beginning, from the foundation of the world. In the plan of God, everything is coming to a head. When this crisis comes about, things will never be the same afterward. They will either turn for the worse or for the better, but the turning point in the history of the world is now occurring.

JUDAS:
The Most Heinous Form of Betrayal

The players are all in position, and the crisis begins.

> While he was still speaking, Judas, one of the Twelve, arrived. With him was a large crowd armed with swords and clubs, sent from the chief priests and the elders of the people. Now the betrayer had arranged a signal with them: "The one I kiss is the man; arrest him." Going at once to Jesus, Judas said, "Greetings, Rabbi!" and kissed him (26:47–49).

This is an obvious sense of betrayal. Judas is perhaps a paradigm, a classic case: the one who betrays. Betrayal is certainly this, and it is more than this in principle, but Judas is an exceptional instance of betrayal in every way. Judas comes at night. Jesus said, "Every day I was with you in the temple courts, and you did not lay a hand on me. But this is your hour—when darkness reigns" (Lk. 22:53). This is the hour that the wickedness of this world will have its way. Judas comes with a crowd, swords, and clubs, as if against some common criminal. Jesus explicitly confronts this. Judas approaches Jesus and kisses Him. Judas had access to Jesus, and trust was open to him and extended to him, and he used that very trust as the way to betray Jesus. In that respect, it is the most heinous form of betrayal. In Luke 22:48, Jesus asked explicitly, "Judas, are you betraying the Son of Man with a kiss?" Jesus saw through it. He saw the intent, He saw clearly the deceptiveness, and He saw how using a kiss to betray is particularly against everything that is decent, everything that is right.

I know someone whose husband left her for another woman. I have seen the woman respond, and the way she expresses her feelings toward her husband. That is certainly a betrayal in a very intimate way. One has an access into the innermost life of a person, and they turn away from that person. But there is an intent, a deliberateness here on the part of Judas, at least to some degree. Some may fall away because they are drawn away by lust, but there is still a betrayal. We encounter betrayals in the world in many ways, and we will see other ways as we go through the message. Upon the kissing of Jesus, they seized Jesus. For the first time, men laid their hands upon Him, upon His very body. Time and again, they had tried to approach Him, but it said that no one touched Him, and no one laid a hand on Him.[2] Jesus knew what was coming, He prepared His disciples. He allowed the crowd to seize Him, literally, physically, with their hands, and arrest Him. This, the disciples had not seen before. They had seen how the Lord had often overcome in this situation, and we can understand something of Peter's response. He was nonplussed; he was taken aback. Jesus did not do what He ordinarily did: walk through the midst of them.[3]

Peter's Response: The Sword

John tells us about when the soldiers came to arrest Him: "Jesus, knowing all that was going to happen to him, went out and asked them,

---

2. *John 7:30, 44.*

3. *Luke 4:30.*

'Who is it you want?' 'Jesus of Nazareth,' they replied. 'I am he,' Jesus said. (And Judas the traitor was standing there with them.) When Jesus said, 'I am he,' they drew back and fell to the ground" (Jn. 18:4b–6). At this very moment, Jesus had that power. But when they seized Him and laid their hands on Him, a line was crossed, and in Peter's mind, this was the time to act. He **"reached for his sword, drew it out and struck the servant of the high priest, cutting off his ear."** (26:51b). We know from the Gospel of Luke that "Jesus answered, 'No more of this!' And he touched the man's ear and healed him" (Lk. 22:51). Jesus rebuked Peter: **"Put your sword back in its place . . . for all who draw the sword will die by the sword"** (26:52). We are often quick to resort to force to resolve problems. But this is Jesus' first response: **"Put your sword back in its place,"** and the explanation is, **"for all who draw the sword will die by the sword."** Jesus calls us here to engage in the spiritual war as He was engaging. We are to be like Him and not take the use of the sword as our first response.

Because of sin in the world, because of criminal activity and war crimes, it is necessary that there is a government, and the primary function of that government is to use the power of the sword to restrain evil externally when it comes to criminal activity, including war crimes. There is a place for that power of the sword to restrain, but that is because there has been a failure to engage in the war spiritually. I do not say that across the board, because clearly, our Lord Jesus Christ was faithful in His witness. He came to this hour to die, to bring redemption. He made this point: **"Do you think I cannot call on my Father, and he will at once put at my disposal more than twelve legions of angels?"** (26:53). One angel would be enough—one angel struck down 185,000 of Sennacherib's men when they came against Jerusalem. Twelve legions of angels were at His disposal. But our Lord Jesus, who had this power at His disposal, declined to use it in order that the Scripture may be fulfilled. We often think about people desiring power to be able to exercise that power. We think of *The Lord of the Rings* and the way that ring was used occasionally to escape difficulty by placing it on one's finger. Jesus had 12 legions of angels at His disposal at once and did not use any of that power. He was going to go to the cross.

Jesus Willingly Obeyed

Men have often fought to maintain physical power over others. Jesus showed His obedience to the Father by not using His power. He could have used that power to command the stones to be made into bread, but Jesus submitted to His Father after 40 days of fasting—unlike the temptation in the Garden when they were surrounded by food. Let us fix our eyes upon our Lord Jesus. Let us see Him in the glory of His strength and His trust in His Father. Let us follow Him. Jesus showed in this that the Scriptures are to be fulfilled. He said this twice: in verse 54, **"But how then would the Scriptures be fulfilled that say it must happen in this way?"** and in verse 56, **"But this has all taken place that the writings of the prophets might be fulfilled."** Jesus saw what was written of Him and He obeyed. He had already prayed, "My Father, if it is possible, may this cup be taken from me. Yet not as I will, but as you will" (Matt. 26:39b). He prayed this in the greatest of agony. The Scripture says, "And being in anguish, he prayed more earnestly" (Lk. 22:44a).

How many of us have been tempted anywhere close to how Jesus had been tempted? Yet the Scripture says He is tempted in all points as we are: "For we do not have a high priest who is unable to empathize with our weaknesses, but we have one who has been tempted in every way, just as we are—yet he did not sin" (Heb. 4:15). "No temptation has overtaken you except what is common to mankind. And God is faithful; he will not let you be tempted beyond what you can bear. But when you are tempted, he will also provide a way out so that you can endure it" (1 Cor. 10:13). Think of the many ways we face trials daily and think of our Lord Jesus. Think of how He prayed; think of how He submitted. We are called to know our Lord Jesus Christ in obeying as He obeyed.

Jesus put a question to the crowd, **"Am I leading a rebellion, that you have come out with swords and clubs to capture me? Every day I sat in the temple courts teaching, and you did not arrest me"** (26:55). Jesus was not leading a rebellion, He was teaching. Rebellion is when you take up arms to oppose the existing order. Jesus took up the sword of the Spirit to oppose the existing order, and it is in that way that the response must come, but they came against Him as if He were a leader of some rebellious group. Jesus is not fighting for a kingdom of this world in an outward, physical way. It is a kingdom that rules from within, from the heart. He will conquer more deeply; our very inmost being will be willing servants of His in every area of life.

Response to Teaching: NARD and the Use of Force

Jesus came teaching in the temple. This teaching is avoided by personal attack. All kinds of recriminations and evil things were said of Him, as it is said of us. People often use name-calling of one sort or another to avoid addressing what is said. People often misrepresent another's position, or use threats, or appeal to love and say, 'Can't we all just get along? Doctrine divides. Do you have to keep bringing up doctrine?' There is an appeal in war when the other side is not fighting cleanly, and we can be tempted to fight as they fight. Sometimes, people appeal to authority illegitimately. The Jews appealed to the authority of the rulers, the Roman authority, but it was not relevant. In all of these, we neglect, avoid, resist, and deny the light that God has put in us. We shut our eyes to avoid seeing what is clear and to avoid engaging and responding. This avoidance happens with family members. Sometimes, those of your own house are the ones who most oppose you. The avoidance of engaging and responding to a position happens in politics. It is certainly happening in the cultural wars that are being fought in this country. The culture war is the most manifest part of the spiritual war. It happens with fellow believers—literalists and fideists. It happens in Reformed circles. It happened between Catholics and Protestants in Church history. It happens with Marxists. It happens with terrorists and their ideology. Instead of engaging the fundamental questions and responding to teaching, as Jesus came teaching, it is avoided in various ways. Fundamental questions are not addressed. Religion is marginalized. Those in authority avoid dealing with questions by saying, 'Well, that is religious.' Those of you who read Phillip Johnson's book know that is how it begins.[4] Discussions of evolution and the reasons for and against it are avoided by saying, 'Well, that is religious, and we don't bring religion into this matter; this is science.'

Jesus brought teaching and the people did not respond to His teaching; now they are responding by using force. From the beginning, we

---

4. Phillip E. Johnson, *Darwin on Trial* (Downers Grove, IL: Intervarsity Press, 1991).

were told about asymmetrical warfare: "He will crush your head, and you will strike his heel" (Gen. 3:15b). From the beginning, in the Garden of Eden, we are told that Satan will be crushed spiritually and be destroyed, but he will strike back physically. Time and again, Satan resorts to worldly powers and those who wield power in this world and strikes back at believers. Here, Satan is using the Jewish authority and the Roman authority to strike at Jesus. When he is bested in the spiritual war, he comes back and strikes physically, and we are not to go there. We are to trust in God, submit to our Lord's will, and obey Him. For ourselves individually, we are not to take up the sword to oppose. That is the place of the government.[5] We may become agents of the government in the army, but the government's role is to carry out justice by the physical sword. Believers are not expected to take up the sword and strike back. We are to be faithful and fight spiritually. We are not to make any excuse for ourselves by resorting to the physical use of force. We know what to expect. The world clings to power and will not give it up, and Jesus shows that He does not cling to power. He shows the difference between self-life—preserving self through the use of raw power—and the spiritual life there is in God.

We Should Know What to Expect

Jesus told His disciples again what to expect. The Enlightenment philosophers in the 18th and 19th centuries who denied the Fall failed to recognize the nature of evil, and often, toward the end of their lives, they railed against mankind because of the evil they saw. Mark Twain, who seemed to have been the most sympathetic of men in the earlier part of his life, became so cynical that he described mankind as a 'mass of maggots.' Enlightenment philosophers who do not understand evil cannot go the long run in the fight against evil; they cannot fight spiritually. Jean-Paul Sartre went this way, and we could name many more. As they get older, they see their hopes about mankind fall apart. But we do not have to go that way. We understand spiritual death—sin and death. We understand physical death. We understand something about the depths of evil because we understand physical death as a call back,

---

5. Gangadean, *The Westminster Confession*, 253–262.

imposed by God from the Garden. It was imposed as a call back from sin, not as punishment; the punishment is spiritual death.

CAIAPHAS THE HIGH PRIEST:
Condemning the True High Priest

Jesus is brought before Caiaphas. Judas played his part, having agreed with the chief priests and elders to betray Jesus, and now Jesus is brought before the high priest. There is no indication that Jesus had any particular contact with Caiaphas before. Caiaphas was in the background, but now Jesus stands before him. The high priest is an office appointed by God to bring men to God. And because of sin in human beings, the high priest himself is affected by sin, and now he is standing in the way, preventing men from coming to God. Of all peoples on the face of the earth who should be bringing men to God, it should be the high priest! But here, the one who most resists is the high priest. That is the nature of sin. Jesus stands before Caiaphas.

The Word of God Versus Authoritarianism

Jesus is kissed by Judas and betrayed. Caiaphas has been raised to this position to bring men to God, and God the Son incarnate stands before Caiaphas, and Caiaphas is about to condemn Him. Is that a betrayal? Is that a betrayal of trust, having been called to the office of high priest? I think we must say so. How does it unfold? **"Those who had arrested Jesus took him to Caiaphas the high priest, where the teachers of the law and the elders had assembled"** (26:57). This is a gathering of all those in authority in this particular culture; they have gone awry because they have not sought God and submitted to the Word of God. Those in authority are to lead us to the truth. Instead, we see how they neglected, avoided, resisted, and denied the truth. They exercised "truth" by mere personal will. They had become authoritarians. Time and again, people are accused of not submitting to the current authority. The authority is always, ultimately, the Word of God, and those in positions of authority are to be submitted to the Word of God. Luther said at the Diet of Worms,

Unless I am convinced by the testimony of the Scriptures and by clear reason (for I do not trust in the pope or councils alone, since it is well known that they have often erred and contradicted themselves), I am bound by the Scriptures I have quoted. My conscience is captive to the Word of God. I cannot and I will not retract anything, since it is neither safe nor right to go against conscience. Here I stand. I cannot do otherwise. God help me. Amen.[6]

Those in positions of authority had not exercised authority by the Word of God. This happens time and again.

Looking for False Evidence: Keeping the Appearance of Legitimacy

Notice the attitude of the people at the trial of Jesus. They were looking for false evidence. It says so explicitly in the Scriptures. In verse 59, "The chief priests and the whole Sanhedrin were looking for false evidence against Jesus so that they could put him to death." If they had a shred of genuine evidence, they would have brought it forward. But they already agreed this is what they wanted to do to save their own positions. When one reads everything or listens to everything a person says, they may be looking to catch that person in their words. This is an attitude in which people may come. They want to find something that they can lay on a person in order to throw them out. That is not the way in which we are supposed to engage in truth or search for truth; we are not to look for false evidence. We should try to understand what the person is really saying, and we will see an example of this explicitly mentioned shortly. They want to keep up the appearance of legitimacy. They must make it appear that they did go through the process—procedural justice—but without an ounce of substance. Sometimes, people will try to catch you on that basis. There are many church courts that are good at procedural justice. Sometimes criminals get off on procedural justice. Procedure is not the same as substance, but they go through the process to make it appear legitimate. They could have just said, 'Kill him, get him out of here.' But they go through an *appearance* of a trial. There is some remnant of common grace in the

---

world that requires them to keep up an appearance. So they were looking for false evidence. They had to keep up appearances. Many false
witnesses came—*many*—but no genuine evidence was found.

Jesus Remained Silent

"But they did not find any, though many false witnesses came forward. Finally two came forward and declared, 'This fellow said, "I
am able to destroy the temple of God and rebuild it in three days"'"
(26:60–61). They were referring to what Jesus said in John 2:18–19,
"The Jews then responded to him, 'What sign can you show us to prove
your authority to do all this?' Jesus answered them, 'Destroy this temple,
and I will raise it again in three days.'" He was referring to the temple
of His body, but His words were twisted. To bring this statement on its
own is not a concern for truth. They did not ask what Jesus meant by
it. No benefit of the doubt was given at all. The trial was a charade of
justice—mere procedure. "Then the high priest stood up and said to
Jesus, 'Are you not going to answer? What is this testimony that these
men are bringing against you?' But Jesus remained silent" (26:62–63a).
It was as if somehow the sheer number of witnesses, without solid evidence, was grounds for accusing Him. Jesus said not a word. There are
times when we must say not a word and let it be.

"I Charge You Under Oath by the Living God: Tell Us If You Are the Christ, the Son of God"

Jesus' silence forced the high priest's hand, and now he required Jesus
to testify against Himself. He placed Jesus under oath and required
Him to answer a question. "The high priest said to him, 'I charge you
under oath by the living God: Tell us if you are the Christ, the Son
of God'" (26:63b).[7] The very question assumes that the Christ is the
Son of God, but it is also known that the Christ is the son of David.
So He is the Son of Man, and He *is* the Son of God. This question is
put to Jesus and an answer is required under oath when Jesus would
say nothing. He was forced to testify against Himself, contrary to what
should be. We know of the Fifth Amendment; we can say, 'I plead the
Fifth,' and do not have to answer to incriminate ourselves. In legal

---

7. NIV 1984.

procedure, that is done, but here, Jesus is put under oath and required to answer. "**'Yes, it is as you say,' Jesus replied**" (26:64a).[8] Jesus did not merely answer in light of this trial; He was speaking in light of all He has been doing, including raising Lazarus from the dead. Jesus was the One sent by God. He said, "Even though you do not believe me, believe the works" (Jn. 10:38a). He is speaking about His works in the past, but He also speaks about the future in a particular way. He said, "**But I say to all of you: In the future you will see the Son of Man sitting at the right hand of the Mighty One and coming on the clouds of heaven**" (26:64b).[9] He is a man, and He is in a position of authority at the right hand of God. He is telling them when they will see Him, and how they will see Him: "**In the future you will see . . .**" We believe that this happened when Jesus ascended into heaven and sent the Holy Spirit that enabled the Church to be witnesses to Him in the world. That generation would see this happen. The gospel was going into the world as it had not for 1,800 years, since God called Abraham. The evidence of the spread of the gospel into the world is evidence of the working of the Holy Spirit. The Holy Spirit is accompanying people who are coming to God and calling upon Him. The gospel going into the world means that the Holy Spirit is *sent* to enable the Church to be effective witnesses. Only the Son, who has redeemed man, can be in the position to send the Holy Spirit. He is called the Christ, the Anointed One, the One who sends the Spirit to enable His people to do their work. That is what Jesus was referring to when He said, "**In the future you will see . . .**"

Jesus Is Charged with Blasphemy: "He Is Worthy of Death"

The high priest is beside himself because of what he just heard. "**Then the high priest tore his clothes and said, 'He has spoken blasphemy! Why do we need any more witnesses? Look, now you have heard the blasphemy. What do you think?'**" (26:65–66a). He calls it blasphemy that Jesus is saying He is the Christ, the Son of God. Yet his question assumed that the Christ is the Son of God. We must wonder what is going on in the mind of the person who is asking that question. Does

---

8. NIV 1984.
9. NIV 1984.

he hear himself? What does he mean by that question? Is the Christ both the Son of God and the Son of Man? The answer is yes. So, when someone who is a man says that He is also the Son of God and will be seated at the right hand of the Most High, affirming deity for Himself, is that blasphemy? The declaration of the Jews is: "You, a mere man, claim to be God" (Jn. 10:33). Any other human claiming to be God would be guilty of blasphemy, and, according to the practice in the Jewish economy, worthy of death. But Jesus is not just any other man. Jesus is the Son of Man, the seed of the woman, the promised Savior, the Son of God incarnate. He and only He can make the claim that He is the Son of God. But they count it as blasphemy, and all pronounced that Jesus is worthy of death, and they expressed their utter contempt for Him—they spit in His face. "**'He is worthy of death,' they answered. Then they spit in his face**" (26:66b–67a). It is one thing to spit at someone's feet, or to spit when speaking a curse, but to spit in the face of someone is an expression of utter contempt. Then they "**struck him with their fists. Others slapped him and said, 'Prophesy to us, Messiah. Who hit you?'**" (26:67b–68). They struck Him, slapped Him, mocked Him, and blindfolded Him. He was in their power, and they exercised the power as ungodly, sinful men.

PETER DISOWNS JESUS:
Take Heed Lest You Fall

The scene shifts to Peter. Peter was warned that he would deny the Lord, and he protested strongly, but now it comes upon him. He disowns Jesus. The disciples had all fled, but now Peter is in the courtyard, warming himself at the fire. Perhaps he wants to see this thing through to the end to see what happens.

> **Now Peter was sitting out in the courtyard, and a servant girl came to him. "You also were with Jesus of Galilee," she said. But he denied it before them all. "I don't know what you're talking about," he said. Then he went out to the gateway, where another servant girl saw him and said to the people there, "This fellow was with Jesus of Nazareth." He denied it again, with an oath: "I don't know the man!" After a little while, those standing there went up to Peter and said, "Surely you are one of them; your accent gives you**

away." Then he began to call down curses, and he swore to them, "I don't know the man!" Immediately a rooster crowed (26:69–74).

In Luke, we are told, "The Lord turned and looked straight at Peter" (Lk. 22:61). What was in that look? Jesus knew, and Peter knew. In light of all that He had said, Jesus was in absolute control; He knew exactly what was happening, and Peter knew that Jesus knew. He was the Lord. Time and again, the Lord comes to us in this way, and we know it is the Lord. When God brings His chastening hand upon the people, He is saying, 'You know that I am the Sovereign Lord. You know that I am the Lord.' Peter knew that Jesus was the Lord; he knew how utterly he had come short and that he was betraying his Master by denying his Master. And he went out and wept bitterly. **"Then Peter remembered the word Jesus had spoken: 'Before the rooster crows, you will disown me three times.' And he went outside and wept bitterly"** (26:75). Think about the thoughts in Peter's heart. Think about whether we are capable of denying the Lord. Think about whether we may have disowned the Lord and not recognized it by not confessing Him before men. It is so easy to turn away, because if we confess Him before men, we will suffer some loss. Paul says in 1 Corinthians, "Therefore let him who thinks he stands take heed lest he fall" (1 Cor. 10:12 NKJV) and again in Galatians, "You who live by the Spirit should restore that person gently. But watch yourselves, or you also may be tempted" (Gal. 6:1b). And Jesus did restore Peter after His resurrection.

JUDAS AND THE SANHEDRIN:
Blood Money

When Judas saw that Jesus was condemned, **"he was seized with remorse and returned the thirty pieces of silver to the chief priests and the elders. 'I have sinned,' he said, 'for I have betrayed innocent blood.' 'What is that to us?' they replied. 'That's your responsibility'"** (27:3b–4). They speak about responsibility, and Pilate is going to speak about responsibility, too. They gave the money to him, so is it now merely 'his' responsibility? That is a total copout. But men are made in the image of God, and they are aware of responsibility. They have to deal with guilt, which is one of the things that will torment us forever. Guilt is a worm that dieth not.[10] That is why we are forever trying to excuse ourselves and justify ourselves. God has made us in His image with a conscience; it cannot be obliterated. "**So Judas threw the money into the temple and left. Then he went away and hanged himself**" (27:5).

This is the crisis of this world, and the thoughts of the hearts of men are being revealed. Wanting to live according to the law, the chief priests bought a field with the money that they could not put in the offering.

> The chief priests picked up the coins and said, "It is against the law to put this into the treasury, since it is blood money." So they decided to use the money to buy the potter's field as a burial place for foreigners. That is why it has been called the Field of Blood to this day (27:6–8).

The money paid to Judas was blood money. Even in the very field that they bought, they recognized it was blood money, and that they had made a decision that made it a matter of blood. "**Then what was spoken by Jeremiah the prophet was fulfilled: 'They took the thirty pieces of silver, the price set on him by the people of Israel, and they used them to buy the potter's field, as the Lord commanded me'**" (27:9–10). Jesus is not the one who is controlling and maneuvering to bring about the fulfillment of Scripture. He is obeying and doing His part, but it is the Sovereign Lord who is working and bringing it about, through the desires and thoughts of men, so that men are responsible. What was spoken by Jeremiah was fulfilled; it was so that the Scripture might be fulfilled.

PILATE THE GOVERNOR:
The Blood of Jesus Is Upon Us All

> Meanwhile Jesus stood before the governor, and the governor asked him, "Are you the king of the Jews?" "You have said so," Jesus replied. When he was accused by the chief priests and the elders, he gave no answer. Then Pilate asked him, "Don't you hear the testimony they are bringing against you?" But Jesus made no reply, not even to a single charge—to the great amazement of the governor (27:11–14).

---

10. *Mark 9:44* KJV.

Pilate is going through the process, and now there is a choice before Pilate.

> Now it was the governor's custom at the Feast to release a prisoner chosen by the crowd. At that time they had a notorious prisoner, called Barabbas. So when the crowd had gathered, Pilate asked them, "Which one do you want me to release to you: Barabbas, or Jesus who is called Christ?" For he knew it was out of envy that they had handed Jesus over to him (27:15–18).

Pilate knew that it was out of envy that they delivered Jesus to him. He asked who they would have him release: Barabbas, one taken for leading a rebellion, or Jesus. At this time, Pilate's wife sent a message to him and said, "Don't have anything to do with that innocent man, for I have suffered a great deal today in a dream because of him" (27:19b). Pilate is a governor; in his hands is the power of life and death. He is in a position, called by God, to fulfill that office. Will Pilate fulfill the office entrusted to him, or will he shrug his shoulders and betray a trust? The crowd is persuaded by the leaders to choose Barabbas. Pilate then asked them about Jesus. "'What shall I do, then, with Jesus who is called the Messiah?' Pilate asked. They all answered, 'Crucify him!'" (27:22). They kept shouting, "Crucify him!" And they kept shouting. When Pilate saw that an uproar was starting, he tried to free himself from this by washing his hands. "When Pilate saw that he was getting nowhere, but that instead an uproar was starting, he took water and washed his hands in front of the crowd. 'I am innocent of this man's blood,' he said. 'It is your responsibility!'" (27:24).

Pilate thought he could wash his hands forever, but he can never rid himself of the guilt of his share of the responsibility for delivering Jesus over to be crucified. He may wring his hands forever in hell, but he will never escape that guilt. We are called by God and we are placed by God in certain positions of trust. And before God, we must give an answer. Pilate tried to escape the guilt. He said, "I am innocent of this man's blood." He knew Jesus was innocent. So why did he not keep the course, even if he had to lose his position as governor, and protect Jesus? He said, "It is your responsibility!" And the people uttered that most fateful word: "His blood is on us and on our children!" (27:25b). Then Jesus is handed over to be crucified. Some have taken this and have had hard thoughts and words for the Jews. But Jesus prayed, "Father, forgive them; for they know not what they do" (Lk. 23:34a KJV). That should be our attitude. Our attitude should be that His blood is upon all of us because He bore the sins of all of us. God, in His own way, will deal with those who immediately handed Jesus over to the high priest, in terms of the measure of light they had—but we are all responsible. Pilate said, **"It is your responsibility!"** It is all of our responsibility. Everyone who has sin drove Jesus to the cross, for there He bore the sins of all. Let us acknowledge our responsibility in this and not pass it off. Jesus is now handed over to be crucified. From this point on, we follow the very passion of the Lord in His crucifixion. God, grant us to keep our eyes on our Lord Jesus and see His faithful witness even unto death, that we might honor Him with our lives. Amen.

———

26

THE HUMILIATION OF THE CHRIST

Christ's Love for the Father and the Human Heart Revealed

Matthew 27:27–66

²⁷Then the governor's soldiers took Jesus into the Praetorium and gathered the whole company of soldiers around him. ²⁸They stripped him and put a scarlet robe on him, ²⁹and then twisted together a crown of thorns and set it on his head. They put a staff in his right hand. Then they knelt in front of him and mocked him. "Hail, king of the Jews!" they said. ³⁰They spit on him, and took the staff and struck him on the head again and again. ³¹After they had mocked him, they took off the robe and put his own clothes on him. Then they led him away to crucify him.

³²As they were going out, they met a man from Cyrene, named Simon, and they forced him to carry the cross. ³³They came to a place called Golgotha (which means "the place of the skull"). ³⁴There they offered Jesus wine to drink, mixed with gall; but after tasting it, he refused to drink it. ³⁵When they had crucified him, they divided up his clothes by casting lots. ³⁶And sitting down, they kept watch over him there. ³⁷Above his head they placed the written charge against him: THIS IS JESUS, THE KING OF THE JEWS.

³⁸Two rebels were crucified with him, one on his right and one on his left. ³⁹Those who passed by hurled insults at him, shaking their heads ⁴⁰and saying, "You who are going to destroy the temple and build it in three days, save yourself! Come down from the cross, if you are the Son of God!" ⁴¹In the same way the chief priests, the teachers of the law and

the elders mocked him. [42]"He saved others," they said, "but he can't save himself! He's the king of Israel! Let him come down now from the cross, and we will believe in him. [43]He trusts in God. Let God rescue him now if he wants him, for he said, 'I am the Son of God.'" [44]In the same way the rebels who were crucified with him also heaped insults on him.

[45]From noon until three in the afternoon darkness came over all the land. [46]About three in the afternoon Jesus cried out in a loud voice, "Eli, Eli, lema sabachthani?" (which means "My God, my God, why have you forsaken me?").

[47]When some of those standing there heard this, they said, "He's calling Elijah."

[48]Immediately one of them ran and got a sponge. He filled it with wine vinegar, put it on a staff, and offered it to Jesus to drink. [49]The rest said, "Now leave him alone. Let's see if Elijah comes to save him."

[50]And when Jesus had cried out again in a loud voice, he gave up his spirit.

[51]At that moment the curtain of the temple was torn in two from top to bottom. The earth shook, the rocks split [52]and the tombs broke open. The bodies of many holy people who had died were raised to life. [53]They came out of the tombs after Jesus' resurrection and went into the holy city and appeared to many people.

[54]When the centurion and those with him who were guarding Jesus saw the earthquake and all that had happened, they were terrified, and exclaimed, "Surely he was the Son of God!"

[55]Many women were there, watching from a distance. They had followed Jesus from Galilee to care for his needs. [56]Among them were Mary Magdalene, Mary the mother of James and Joseph, and the mother of Zebedee's sons.

[57]As evening approached, there came a rich man from Arimathea, named Joseph, who had himself become a disciple of Jesus. [58]Going to Pilate, he asked for Jesus' body, and Pilate ordered that it be given to him. [59]Joseph took the body, wrapped it in a clean linen cloth, [60]and placed it in his own new tomb that he had cut out of the rock. He rolled a big stone in front of the entrance to the tomb and went away. [61]Mary Magdalene and the other Mary were sitting there opposite the tomb.

[62]The next day, the one after Preparation Day, the chief priests and the Pharisees went to Pilate. [63]"Sir," they said, "we remember that while he was still alive that deceiver said, 'After three days I will rise again.' [64]So give the order for the tomb to be made secure until the third day. Otherwise,

his disciples may come and steal the body and tell the people that he has been raised from the dead. This last deception will be worse than the first."

65"Take a guard," Pilate answered. "Go, make the tomb as secure as you know how." 66So they went and made the tomb secure by putting a seal on the stone and posting the guard.

INTRODUCTION:
The Passion

W E HAVE BEEN CONTINUING THROUGH THE Passion Week. Our Lord has set His face toward Jerusalem; He knows He is going to go to Jerusalem, and there, be crucified. He has prepared His disciples for this, and He has prepared His heart. He has submitted to the hands of sinners; He has been taken and tried. He has been condemned. After being flogged, Jesus is handed over to the soldiers to be crucified. We come now to the Passion itself, the suffering of our Lord Jesus Christ. We want to look at the events up until His death and His burial. We will try to reflect on it in light of what Isaiah said, and try to make sense of and understand what has occurred here.

FIRST GROUP:
The Soldiers Mock Him

Jesus is handed over to the soldiers to be crucified. These soldiers take Jesus into the praetorium and gather the whole company of soldiers around Him.

> Then the governor's soldiers took Jesus into the Praetorium and gathered the whole company of soldiers around him. They stripped him and put a scarlet robe on him, and then twisted together a crown of thorns and set it on his head. They put a staff in his right hand. Then they knelt in front of him and mocked him. "Hail, king of the Jews!" they said. They spit on him, and took the staff and struck him on the head again and again. After they had mocked him, they took off the robe and put his own clothes on him. Then they led him away to crucify him (vv. 27–31).

We should think about soldiers and what they are called to do, what manner of persons they are, their attitude, and their virtue and vice. We should consider the occasion that Jesus handed to them and how Jesus, by His very being and presence, causes the human heart to be revealed. So, the hearts of these soldiers are likewise revealed. They are human beings, like us, men from our midst, not so foreign, and not so far away from us. Yet we see how the soldiers came short. They came short in ways that are typical characteristics of soldiers. We have been hearing of abuses in the prison in Iraq, and we have heard of abuses elsewhere—what soldiers have done in this war and that war. Soldiers are supposed to protect human life and uphold the dignity of human beings. Here, the soldiers failed to do this. Instead, having Jesus in their hands, they stripped Him. They stripped Him of His clothes, and there He was, standing before them, stripped, and very likely, we think, naked. They put a scarlet robe on Him. Scarlet signifies royalty, and Jesus is delivered to them under the accusation that He is the King of the Jews. He is going to be crucified for this, which is considered by the rulers to be a false claim, egregiously false, and deserving of death. Being delivered to them for this, they deal with Him according to their heart's desire.

You should know that this is not something they were required to do; this is something they did by their own will and desire. They stripped Him of His clothes and put a scarlet robe on Him, then twisted together a crown of thorns and set it on His head. You can imagine it is not just gently set upon His head; it is a crown of thorns. Then they put a staff in His right hand, signifying His authority and power, and they put Him before them as king in a mock show of royalty. Then they knelt in front of Him, mocked Him, and said, **"Hail, king of the Jews!"** (v. 29b). To show that they were, of course, mocking Him, they not only put this crown on Him and pushed it into His head, but they spit on Him. Earlier, they had spit on Him; the rulers had spat upon Him as someone accursed—a lawbreaker, a miscreant, someone who is guilty of heinous sin and deserves to be condemned and cast out from among men. They spit on Him, and then they took the staff and struck Him on the head again and again.

This is what the soldiers did to the Lord Jesus. They mocked Him. They humiliated Him. They scorned Him. They despised Him. They treated Him despicably. All this time, Jesus was standing there, and with one word, Jesus could have utterly destroyed them. All He had to do was speak one word, and they would be reduced to nothing. We must keep this in mind. As the soldiers treated Jesus in this way, He had the power to do so. He certainly had the power to call upon His Father for legions of angels, but He has faced that trial before, during the temptation and arrest. He prayed, "My Father, if it is possible, may this cup be taken from me. Yet not as I will, but as you will" (Matt. 26:39b). Jesus is showing His love for His Father by perfectly obeying—standing still, quiet, without opening His mouth—under this further humiliation. When it was in His power to command stones to be made bread to satisfy His hunger, He refused to do so. He would obey His Father in everything—a voluntarily imposed restraint under the will of God.

They spit upon Him as they uttered these words, **"Hail, king of the Jews!"** and they struck Him with the rod again and again, as the crown of thorns was pressing into His brow, into His head, causing pain with every moment, every move. Jesus bowed before His Father. Without His love for His Father and His love for us, for you and me, we would not be saved from our sin. Without His humiliation, without His crucifixion, we would not be saved. This shows the love of our Lord Jesus as He suffered in our place. What He endured is what we deserve. We are the ones who put ourselves in the place of God—wrongfully. We are the ones who want to be the king of our lives and the king of the world around us. We want to do our own will and have others do our will. We deserve to be cast out. Jesus stands in our place and receives what we deserve.

The soldiers mocked Him, as He was mocked before by the chief priests and elders and teachers of the law. Mockery is something that we seek to avoid; we want to be approved and accepted by men. We want the praise of men, which often leads us not to regard the Word of God. We do many things to avoid being humiliated, shamed, scorned, spit upon, despised, and rejected. But Jesus voluntarily undergoes this in our place; He is suffering what we deserve. The soldiers mocked Jesus when they should have carried out the execution. Cruel and unjust as it was (though they did not think it was unjust), they should have carried out the execution and maintained the dignity of the person. Instead, they despised Him and mocked Him. Having mocked Him, they took off the scarlet robe, put His own clothes on, and led Him away to crucify

Him. That is stage one, being in the hands of the soldiers. Soldiers have the temptation to take things into their own hands, as human beings, and use their force brutally. Jesus knew what it was to face that kind of evil and use of raw power. He knows the brutality of the soldiers. He was not protected from this raw force that came against Him—that comes against us. Often enough, in history, believers have had to endure raw force. Jesus went before us in this. Jesus has experienced a kind of brutalizing of Himself. Consider how Jesus was treated, and think of how He suffered in all ways as we do, yet without sin.

THE CRUCIFIXION:
For All to See

Jesus was led out to be crucified. **"As they were going out, they met a man from Cyrene, named Simon, and they forced him to carry the cross"** (v. 32). Jesus was carrying the cross and probably was stumbling from the previous, brutal treatment. He probably was stumbling, not only under the brutal treatment, but under the weight of the sin of the world. He was struggling to carry the cross. Think about that: as He was falling under its weight, He had to exercise every nerve in His being to get up and take that cross and carry it. It should be a daily act for us to take up our cross and follow Him.[1] There are times when we have to exert every ounce of strength that we have, under extreme pain, to take the next step, and the next step, and the next step. There are times when we are called upon to say 'No' to our own lives and our self-life, as it is raging within us. Our Lord calls us to obey Him. Scripture says we have not resisted unto the point of blood in our struggle against sin.[2] Jesus certainly had been to that point. He had been in prayer, sweating, as it were, great drops of blood.[3] He was being bloodied from the crown of thorns and being struck again and again with that rod—bruised and beaten. Why? Keep in mind that He was in our place, bearing our sin, the penalty of our sin.

Simon of Cyrene is forced to carry the cross. It is said that Simon, in heaven, is rejoicing that he had the opportunity to carry the cross

---

1. *Matthew 16:24.*

2. *Hebrews 12:4.*

3. *Luke 22:44.*

for Jesus. It was hard for Simon. He was forced to carry it, but if we are forced to carry it, and we do, then the cross is for our Lord, as Jesus had said, "Whatever you did for one of the least of these brothers and sisters of mine, you did for me" (Matt. 25:40b). If we carry that cross for another, to help another, we are learning what it is to be like Jesus. So they came to a place called Golgotha, which means 'the place of the skull.' There were probably gruesome memories and associations connected with that place. As they prepared to crucify Jesus, it seemed that they would show some measure of compassion, but even that measure of compassion was not pure. They gave Him wine to drink, a particularly strong drink, but it was mixed with gall, the bitterest substance. Scripture says, **"They came to a place called Golgotha (which means 'the place of the skull'). There they offered Jesus wine to drink, mixed with gall; but after tasting it, he refused to drink it"** (vv. 33–34). While strong drink may have an effect on dulling the suffering, as Solomon says, "Give strong drink unto him who is perishing" (Prov. 31:6a NKJV), probably in that sense, they gave Him wine, but it was not allowed to be an act of compassion—it was mixed with gall. Jesus did not turn His face away from shame and being spit upon; He did not turn Himself away from the agony of the cross; He did not try to dull the suffering in this way. He refused to drink it.

The soldiers nailed Him to the cross. They nailed His hands and His feet, and they raised the cross, dropped it into the ground, and He was left there, hanging on the cross. Cursed is anyone who hangs on the tree,[4] the Scripture says, and Jesus was hung on the tree of the cross. In their indifference to the Lord while He was still alive, they started to divide His clothes among them by casting lots. All of this happened according to the Scriptures. Psalm 22 says, "They pierce my hands and my feet" and "They divide My garments among them, and for My clothing they cast lots" (Ps. 22:16, 18).[5] All of this occurs in the most ordinary way, yet the eternal purpose and plan of God is being fulfilled, being realized, in what is coming to pass, and all freely. These people are desiring to have His clothes, they are desiring to be cruel to Him. They desire to have their own way, so their hearts are expressed in these activities, which are coming to pass according to the

---

4. *Deuteronomy 21:23* NKJV.

5. NKJV.

Scriptures. Having done so, they sat down, and **"they kept watch over him there"** (v. 36b).

The soldiers nailed over His head the charge that was against Him so that all who came by could read, and see, and understand, and perhaps learn and be afraid. **"Above his head they placed the written charge against him: THIS IS JESUS, THE KING OF THE JEWS"** (v. 37). John tells us that the charge read: Jesus of Nazareth, the King of the Jews. That was the charge for which He was crucified. He was not crucified for being the Son of God, although this is why He was delivered over to the Romans. In Roman law, He was crucified for claiming to be king and, in that sense, trying to usurp authority and lead a rebellion. Yet Jesus is, indeed, the King of the Jews. He is crucified for the truth of who He is. The charge is placed above His head. Jesus is hanging on the cross, soldiers are sitting and keeping watch, and others are walking by and seeing the spectacle.

SECOND GROUP:
The Robbers and Those Who Pass by Hurl Insults

Jesus is crucified between two thieves, and they are going to respond. They are going to respond in the way that others are responding. His disciples are far off, and the women who ministered to His needs are there standing, watching, grieving, and Jesus is hanging on the cross.

> **Two rebels were crucified with him, one on his right and one on his left. Those who passed by hurled insults at him, shaking their heads and saying, "You who are going to destroy the temple and build it in three days, save yourself! Come down from the cross, if you are the Son of God!"** (vv. 38–40).

"If you are the Son of God . . ." That statement was to go beyond "the King of the Jews." They remember His words, and now they taunt Him with His very words that they misunderstood. They taunt Him with the truth—understood in a false way. They taunt Him with the misunderstanding of what it is to be saved. This expression comes up again and again: 'Save yourself. Do something.' It seems most natural to man, left to himself, to want to save himself. Why is it that Jesus would not do this most natural, and therefore seemingly reasonable, of all things? Why would He not save Himself, especially if He saved others? Could Jesus have saved Himself? Could Jesus have come down from the cross? Yes, He could have come down. But Jesus hung on the cross; He submitted under His Father's hand. This was the will of God for Him. But imagine how the taunts and mockery were received when they came. Psalm 69:20 says, "Reproach has broken my heart, and I am full of heaviness; I looked for someone to take pity, but there was none; and for comforters, but I found none." Those that passed by mocked Him. "**Those who passed by hurled insults at him, shaking their heads and saying, 'You who are going to destroy the temple and build it in three days, save yourself! Come down from the cross, if you are the Son of God!'**"

They mocked Him with the truth, twisted. They mocked Him because of their misunderstanding. 'Save yourself. Come down if you are the Son of God. Command these stones to be made bread if you are the Son of God.' Jesus had faced that temptation to exercise His power on His own behalf early on. But He came as a man, and He came for one reason: a body you have prepared for me, to die.[6] He did not come to bring a new message; the prophets brought the message—the message was already given. He did not come to teach a new way, although His being here showed more fully the way of God. Jesus was born to die. He became man, that He might represent man, stand in the place of man, and take the penalty that is due to man. They say, "**Come down from the cross, if you are the Son of God!**"(v. 40b), but He is hanging there as the Son of Man, for man, for those very ones who are insulting Him, for the very ones who spit upon Him, and struck Him, and charged Him with blasphemy. Jesus prayed for them: "Father, forgive them; for they know not what they do" (Lk. 23:34a KJV). Some would say people will do these things deliberately in sin, knowingly doing evil.[7] Instead, Christ points out how their culpable ignorance led them to do this, and that they are without excuse for their ignorance. Jesus prayed, "Father, forgive them; for they know not what they do."

---

6. *Hebrews 10:5.*

7. Gangadean, "Paper No. 120: Contra Voluntarism," in *The Logos Papers*, 611–647.

THIRD GROUP:
The Chief Priests, Teachers of the Law, and Elders Mock Him

The third group comes to mock Jesus for the second time; they are the chief priests, the teachers of the law, and the elders. This insistent pattern is occurring: the soldiers mocked Him, those passing by mocked and insulted Him, and the chief priests and teachers of the law mocked Him. All mocked Him, despised Him, spat upon Him, and hurled insults at Him. In our sin, we are equal. We all respond to Jesus in the same way. Whether we are soldiers carrying out His crucifixion, passersby, or those who accused and brought about His execution—all respond in the very same way. They mocked Him.

Think of the contempt that is in a person when they begin to mock. Think of what it is like to try to mock someone. How utterly ridiculous and contemptible it seems. It is more than wrong. What word can we use to describe how wrong a person is that would lead Him to be mocked in this way? The attitude of the heart expresses itself in mockery. We must acknowledge that this is exactly what is in our hearts. We will see that these things are in our hearts. Sin is the same in all, at its root. Sin is a disregard for God, where we have no obligation, no regard for God, and we owe nothing to God. We turn our backs on the Word of God, and we treat His Word lightly, thoughtlessly, and contemptibly. That Word, who becomes incarnate, will also be treated contemptibly. We will find ways of justifying our contempt in our minds.

"**In the same way the chief priests, the teachers of the law and the elders mocked him. 'He saved others,' they said, 'but he can't save himself! He's the king of Israel!'**" (vv. 41–42a). That is what man is concerned with. 'Save yourself, do something!' It seems to be the most legitimate, basic concern that we could have. 'Save yourself!' It seems to be great to be king and ruler and have this power and to exercise that power. "**Let him come down now from the cross, and we will believe in him**" (v. 42b). Then perhaps the insult that hurt most of all is thrown in His face. "**He trusts in God. Let God rescue him now if he wants him, for he said, 'I am the Son of God'**" (v. 43). Perhaps no other insult penetrated so deeply. A person trusts in God, but it seems as if God is far away and that God has abandoned them. He is supposed to be loved by God, and yet He is in utter destitution, utter forsakenness. How do you hold on to the truth, to the reality, that you are not forsaken by God, when you are in the midst of your pain, torment, and distress? What faith, what understanding does that require? Our Lord Himself struggled with this as He hung on the cross. Perhaps something came upon the Lord that He had not realized, but it wrung out of Him a cry that has been heard through the centuries, through the ages. Wherever there is sin, and God leaves us in our sin, and we experience the consequence of our sin, we hear this cry. It will be realized fully by those who are truly forsaken by God forever in the judgment.

Notice in verse 44, "**In the same way the rebels who were crucified with him also heaped insults on him**" (v. 44). We know that one of the robbers turned back and confessed his faith in Him: "He said, 'Jesus, remember me when you come into your kingdom.' Jesus answered him, 'Truly I tell you, today you will be with me in paradise'" (Lk. 23:42–43). But both of the robbers started out this way: they "**heaped insults on him.**" So those who are soldiers, those who are passersby, those who are chief priests and rulers, and those who are robbers—all insulted Him.

THE DEATH OF JESUS

"**From noon until three in the afternoon darkness came over all the land**" (v. 45). Darkness came over the land. There is a record of an eclipse, a darkness that came over the land in that part of the world. It was known and wondered about. We must see this as a sign from God. God covered over His crucifixion, covered over the sun so that light would not shine upon Him. As He came into the world, there was light—He is the One who would bring light—so as He goes out of the world, in this way, it seems appropriate that there is darkness. We may consider whether it is the Father veiling the Son in some way from this cruel, more than cruel, most heinous of all sins. God covered that scene with darkness for three hours. No one had known for there to be darkness at noon. Surely it would have caused them to stop and wonder.

After hanging on the cross for at least three hours, and possibly longer, "**Jesus cried out in a loud voice, 'Eli, Eli, lema sabachthani?' (which means 'My God, my God, why have you forsaken me?')**" (v. 46). Jesus, who knew the intimate fellowship with the Father, now experiences a forsaking of the Father. Is Jesus merely uttering a cry that the psalmist had recorded, or is the psalmist recording a cry that Jesus will utter? We believe it is the latter. Jesus is undergoing an experience that is unfathomable, and this is the height of His crucifixion. It is not just the pain of the cross, the nails in His hands, and the agonizing way in which He must draw each breath. It is not just the insults that are heaped upon Him, though those are enough to break His heart, but it is something more. This is what men can do to the body, but here, in His innermost being, in His very soul, He experienced the act of God, the hand of God, the striking of God—He experienced the forsaking of His Father. He, who knew no sin, became sin for us, that we might be made the righteousness of God in Him.[8]

God, who is holy, cannot look upon sin. He cannot tolerate it. He must judge it, He must condemn it, He must forsake it. This is what became of Jesus as He bore the sin of the world; He experienced the forsaking of the Father. Nothing else pained so much, and it wrung out of Him that cry: **"My God, my God, why have you forsaken me?"** This is what our sin deserves. In our sin, we forsake God; we turn our backs on God and go our own way. I think we can say, without any hesitation, that what our sin deserves is that we would be given up by God to go our own way, to be forsaken by God. Jesus experienced that forsaking. He experienced that in *our* place—He experienced that in *your* place, and He experienced that in *my* place. When we look at our Lord Jesus hanging on the cross, this, above all else, we must keep in mind: we deserve to be utterly forsaken by God, and Jesus stood in our place.

> **When some of those standing there heard this, they said, "He's calling Elijah." Immediately one of them ran and got a sponge. He filled it with wine vinegar, put it on a staff, and offered it to Jesus to drink. The rest said, "Now leave him alone. Let's see if Elijah comes to save him"** (vv. 47–49).

The people would have loved to see a spectacle. Would Elijah come down from the heavens in some chariot of fire and save Him? This was going through their minds and their imagination. They thought maybe something great would happen, maybe something miraculous; maybe the skies would rend apart! Instead, the skies were covered in darkness, and the rending occurred in His inmost soul as He experienced the

---

8. *2 Corinthians 5:21.*

forsaking of the Father. What happens instead is: **"When Jesus had cried out again in a loud voice, he gave up his spirit"** (v. 50).

In Luke, we are told that "Jesus called out with a loud voice, 'Father, into your hands I commit my spirit.' When he had said this, he breathed his last" (Lk. 23:46). He gathered His strength to speak that word in a loud voice. Normally, someone who is crucified is hanging in such a way that it becomes extremely difficult to utter a sound, because they cannot catch their breath. After hours of hanging in this way, it gets worse and worse. Jesus would have had to gather His strength to cry out in a loud voice and commit Himself into the hands of His Father. He said, **"Why have you forsaken me?"** Nevertheless, He also knows, understands, and believes that God is His Father, and He commits Himself into the hands of God. John tells us, "So when Jesus had received the sour wine, He said, 'It is finished!' And bowing His head, He gave up His spirit" (Jn. 19:30 NKJV). What He came to do in His work on the cross was finished. He endured it to the end, and He accomplished redemption.

THE MEANING:
The Effect of Atonement from Adam On

What happened at that moment, at the death of Jesus? **"At that moment the curtain of the temple was torn in two from top to bottom"** (v. 51a). This is recorded by Matthew, with a particular reference to the Jewish way of worshiping. The curtain torn in two signifies that the way to the Most Holy Place is open. The curtain separated the Most Holy Place, where the presence of God was, from the rest of the temple, because of human sin. Once a year only, the high priest could go in with the blood of an animal and sprinkle it on the mercy seat. At the death of Jesus, that veil, which was a thick, heavy veil that could not be rent by human hands ordinarily, would be rent from the top to the bottom, signifying a supernatural occurrence. God Himself, at the death of Jesus, declared thereby that this old economy was over.[9] What was anticipated in the act of animal sacrifice year after year through the centuries, Jesus had now fulfilled. When Jesus uttered the word, "It is finished," that whole Old Testament waiting was finished. He

---

9. *The Epistle to the Hebrews*, Surrendra Gangadean.

had accomplished what was supplied. The veil of the temple was rent in two, from the top to the bottom.

Accompanying the curtain being rent in two, not only were the heavens darkened earlier for three hours, but now the earth shook, and the rocks split apart. This was not a mere display of power; miracles are more than this; they are signs pointing to a reality. **"The earth shook, the rocks split and the tombs broke open. The bodies of many holy people who had died were raised to life"** (vv. 51b–52). The holy people who had died were waiting for that work of redemption to be completed, and when Jesus said, "It is finished," the work was completed. **"They came out of the tombs after Jesus' resurrection and went into the holy city and appeared to many people"** (v. 53). We are to note that the resurrection of many holy people came about in connection with the death of Jesus and His accomplishment of redemption. Jesus had paid the penalty. He had accomplished redemption, it was being applied, and the mark of that is the resurrection of the dead and the removal of all effects of sin and the curse. This is the firstfruit of what is to come. All of us will be raised; even the unrighteous will be raised and judged in their bodies for the deeds done. But all of us will be raised because Jesus has accomplished redemption.

Think about these two things: the rending of the veil from top to bottom; the finishing of that old way because Jesus has died and has accomplished redemption, and the benefit of that seen in the resurrection—the raising from the dead.

> **When the centurion and those with him who were guarding Jesus saw the earthquake and all that had happened, they were terrified, and exclaimed, "Surely he was the Son of God!" Many women were there, watching from a distance. They had followed Jesus from Galilee to care for his needs. Among them were Mary Magdalene, Mary the mother of James and Joseph, and the mother of Zebedee's sons** (vv. 54–56).

The women were there and watching, and the account will pick up, after the burial, with the women watching and coming to Jesus' tomb.

> **As evening approached, there came a rich man from Arimathea, named Joseph, who had himself become a disciple of Jesus. Going to Pilate, he asked for Jesus' body, and Pilate ordered that it be**

given to him. Joseph took the body, wrapped it in a clean linen cloth, and placed it in his own new tomb that he had cut out of the rock. He rolled a big stone in front of the entrance to the tomb and went away (vv. 57–60).

We know from John that Nicodemus was there with Joseph: "And Nicodemus, who at first came to Jesus by night, also came, bringing a mixture of myrrh and aloes, about a hundred pounds. Then they took the body of Jesus, and bound it in strips of linen with the spices, as the custom of the Jews is to bury" (Jn. 19:39–40 NKJV). He was laid in Joseph's own tomb. Joseph was a rich man. This is in fulfillment of the Scripture, "He was assigned a grave with the wicked, and with the rich in his death" (Is. 53:9a). "He rolled a big stone in front of the entrance to the tomb and went away" (v. 60b). And the women were there; the women were watching. "Mary Magdalene and the other Mary were sitting there opposite the tomb" (v. 61).

The next day, the one after Preparation Day, the chief priests and the Pharisees went to Pilate. "Sir," they said, "we remember that while he was still alive that deceiver said, 'After three days I will rise again.' So give the order for the tomb to be made secure until the third day. Otherwise, his disciples may come and steal the body and tell the people that he has been raised from the dead. This last deception will be worse than the first" (vv. 62–64).

Matthew says, "This story has been widely circulated among the Jews to this very day" (Matt. 28:15b). This is how they will explain away the Resurrection. They will say that the disciples stole the body. So Pilate gave them 16 soldiers to guard the tomb: "'Take a guard,' Pilate answered. 'Go, make the tomb as secure as you know how.' So they went and made the tomb secure by putting a seal on the stone and posting the guard" (vv. 65–66). Not only was a stone rolled in front, but it was secured by putting a seal on the stone and posting the guard.

THE REPRESENTATIVE IN PLACE OF ADAM— VICARIOUS ATONEMENT

Jesus is the chief cornerstone. The way human beings respond to Him reveals what is in their hearts. Anyone who rejects the chief cornerstone, is to be rejected. That is an obvious truth. He is the chief cornerstone. The rejection of Him shows that they are not legitimately in a place of rule, and they have to be removed from that position of authority. He is a rock of offense and a stone of stumbling.[10] We are to come to our Lord Jesus, acknowledging our sin, and acknowledging that He has died in our place. We have sin; this is what our sin deserves, and we must repent of our sin. Jesus bore the sins of many. He was smitten by God. God Himself was pleased to crush Him. God made His soul a guilt offering, an offering for sin. It says of Him in Isaiah, "He poured out his life unto death and was numbered with the transgressors. For he bore the sin of many, and made intercession for the transgressors" (Is. 53:12b). Let us then come to the Lord Jesus Christ. Let us acknowledge Him as the Lamb of God who takes away the sin of the world,[11] the One who takes away our sin.

---

10. *1 Peter 2:8* NKJV.

11. *John 1:29.*

———

27

THE RESURRECTION OF CHRIST

Declared with Power to
Be the Son of God

Matthew 28

¹After the Sabbath, at dawn on the first day of the week, Mary Magdalene and the other Mary went to look at the tomb.

²There was a violent earthquake, for an angel of the Lord came down from heaven and, going to the tomb, rolled back the stone and sat on it. ³His appearance was like lightning, and his clothes were white as snow. ⁴The guards were so afraid of him that they shook and became like dead men.

⁵The angel said to the women, "Do not be afraid, for I know that you are looking for Jesus, who was crucified. ⁶He is not here; he has risen, just as he said. Come and see the place where he lay. ⁷Then go quickly and tell his disciples: 'He has risen from the dead and is going ahead of you into Galilee. There you will see him.' Now I have told you."

⁸So the women hurried away from the tomb, afraid yet filled with joy, and ran to tell his disciples. ⁹Suddenly Jesus met them. "Greetings," he said. They came to him, clasped his feet and worshiped him. ¹⁰Then Jesus said to them, "Do not be afraid. Go and tell my brothers to go to Galilee; there they will see me."

¹¹While the women were on their way, some of the guards went into the city and reported to the chief priests everything that had happened. ¹²When the chief priests had met with the elders and devised a plan, they gave the soldiers a large sum of money, ¹³telling them, "You are to say, 'His disciples came during the night and stole him away while we were asleep.' ¹⁴If this report gets to the governor, we will satisfy him and keep you out of

trouble." 15So the soldiers took the money and did as they were instructed. And this story has been widely circulated among the Jews to this very day.

16Then the eleven disciples went to Galilee, to the mountain where Jesus had told them to go. 17When they saw him, they worshiped him; but some doubted. 18Then Jesus came to them and said, "All authority in heaven and on earth has been given to me. 19Therefore go and make disciples of all nations, baptizing them in the name of the Father and of the Son and of the Holy Spirit, 20and teaching them to obey everything I have commanded you. And surely I am with you always, to the very end of the age."

INTRODUCTION

W E COME TO THE END OF THE GOSPEL OF Matthew at the end of the series on the Passion Week: the resurrection of our Lord and Savior Jesus Christ. In this section, we want to observe some notable and obvious things, and think about the meaning of these things in light of the rest of Scripture. We want to make several points regarding Matthew 28: (1) The deity of Christ in relation to the resurrection. (2) The authority of Christ. The closing words of the gospel are, "**All authority in heaven and on earth has been given to me**" (v. 18b). We are looking at the relation between the authority of Christ and the resurrection. (3) Throughout Scripture, there is much about the hope of the resurrection and how our hope is connected with the resurrection. (4) The witness to the resurrection by six categories of witnesses. (5) There is an apologetic to the resurrection from general and special revelation. We want to see and consider how we might give an apology for the resurrection to the Jews and to all men as part of our witness to which Christ, our risen Lord, calls us: "You will be my witnesses in Jerusalem, and in all Judea and Samaria, and to the ends of the earth" (Acts 1:8b).

In the last sermon, we ended with Christ's burial. The guard was posted at the tomb, and the women were watching at a distance. Matthew tells us that "Mary Magdalene and the other Mary were sitting there opposite the tomb" (Matt. 27:61). The women were there watching out of devotion to Christ and out of grief of heart. They cannot turn away; they want to be there, and they want to be with Him in every possible and tangible way. They were present, and they were watching.

The Lord uses that devotion and that condition of heart to open things up in this account and in this new age in history.

Out of devotion, the women came to the tomb the next morning. Luke says they brought spices for His body, and Mark says they wondered who would roll the stone away. The accounts say they came at dawn after the Sabbath, on the first day of the week. A new day is dawning, a new day for all of us in the history of the world and for the Church. This is the end of the old order and the beginning of the new, the beginning of the Christian Sabbath, which begins on the first day of the week. Why is that? The principle is kept: In creation, God worked and ended His work and observed the Sabbath.[1] Sin entered through the first parents, God worked again, and He completed the work of accomplishing redemption with the Resurrection. Christ entered His rest by accomplishing redemption; now, the application of redemption is to follow. The principle of work and rest continues, but the application changes because of the change in circumstances. The principle of work and rest remains the same. Christ is raised to life after the Sabbath, at dawn, on the first day of the week. Christians celebrate that first day of the week as the Sabbath for the rest of their days on earth, until God ushers in that complete final Sabbath when the work is done. So, the women came out of devotion, yet without being aware of the principle of work and rest and its application in this context.

THE WITNESSES TO THE RESURRECTION

"After the Sabbath, at dawn on the first day of the week, Mary Magdalene and the other Mary went to look at the tomb" (v. 1). Notice how devotion works. We want to be near our loved one in any and every possible way. People still show this devotion by going to the place of burial of their loved ones. They place flowers, and they sometimes go there to talk to their departed loved ones. The women went to the tomb. "There was a violent earthquake, for an angel of the Lord came down from heaven and, going to the tomb, rolled back the stone and sat on it" (v. 2). I like that the angel sat on the stone; it is a nice place to sit. Angels are spirits, but they can manifest themselves with bodies, and here, one does so, and he sits in heavenly disdain on this

---

1. *Genesis 2:1–3.*

rock that they would attempt to put in the way of the life of God, the reality of God. He sat on it in the sight of all the guards. Here are the guards that the authorities placed in front of the tomb, and the angel just rolls back the stone, sits on it, and he says, 'Alright, what are you going to do about it?'—so to speak. They could do nothing about it.

"His appearance was like lightning, and his clothes were white as snow" (v. 3). The glory of this other world shines through. It certainly did for our Lord at the Transfiguration, and supremely, when He is described in the Book of Revelation: "The hair on his head was white like wool, as white as snow, and his eyes were like blazing fire" (Rev. 1:14). The angels are in the presence of God. They manifest this glory in visible ways. It is interesting to note that "the guards were so afraid of him that they shook and became like dead men" (v. 4). The women presumably saw the same thing, but they did not shake and become "like dead men." These brave Roman soldiers shook and became like dead men. The women were afraid, but their hearts were in the right place. They were devoted to the Lord in righteousness. The guards were trying to do the wrong thing. It is as if the angel declared his allegiance to Christ by opening the way, and the guards knew who they were facing. This is important because the guards are going to be witnesses of this event.

"The angel said to the women, 'Do not be afraid'" (v. 5a). They were not like dead men, but they were afraid. "For I know that you are looking for Jesus, who was crucified. He is not here; he has risen, just as he said" (vv. 5b–6a). Notice the words of the angel; they are always first showing care and concern for the person they are speaking to. This is the subjective factor. If we speak to someone who is in fear, we need to reckon with that and bring comfort and peace. This is the way of God: to always bring comfort and peace to a troubled heart. The angel's first words are, "Do not be afraid." We have to have that word repeatedly spoken to us because many things cause us to be afraid. Some circumstances trouble us, and we are so frail and easily troubled. "Do not be afraid." We need to encourage each other with these words, spoken in truth, not just idly. He said, "For I know that you are looking for Jesus." They are here for Jesus, and he made immediate contact with the women about this concern: "I know that you are looking for Jesus."

The guards are there, and so are the women, and I wonder if the guards saw the women and said, 'There are those women again. They were here on Passover night, and now they are here again.' The angel is speaking to the women, and the guards are shaking and they become like dead men. **"I know that you are looking for Jesus, who was crucified"** (v. 5b). The angel makes a total connection: emotionally and intellectually, in terms of their needs and concerns, and to the point. We should speak this way always—relevantly. Now, the angel communicates his message: **"He is not here; he has risen"** (v. 6a). Notice, he connects with them again when he says, **"Just as he said."** The angel does not leave it there, he says, **"Come and see the place where he lay"** (v. 6b). He has a concern about the heart, to give the evidence, and he connects so many things appropriately and right to the point. The angel is there for a mission, and he tells them, **"Then go quickly and tell his disciples"** (v. 7a). There is something urgent about this. He tells the women to tell the ones whom Jesus had called and who had been with Him as His disciples; these are the ones to tell. **"'He has risen from the dead and is going ahead of you into Galilee. There you will see him.' Now I have told you"** (v. 7b). The angel completes the message.

How much has been put together appropriately in that short message to the women? The angel is a witness to the resurrection of Jesus. He witnesses to the women and intends it, beyond that, for the disciples. The angels announced Christ's birth, and the shepherds in the field went and spread the word.[2] The angel announced, to human beings, that Christ had risen, and they were the ones to tell other human beings. Angels bring the message to our attention, but it is to human beings that the work is given to be witnesses on the earth; the angels do not witness. **"Tell his disciples: 'He has risen from the dead and is going ahead of you into Galilee. There you will see him.'"**

"So the women hurried away from the tomb, afraid yet filled with joy, and ran to tell his disciples" (v. 8). How do you put "afraid" and "filled with joy" together? Have you ever had that admixture? Would you be joyful if you saw the place where Jesus laid? They came, thinking He was dead, and this one comes announcing He is risen. They saw the very appearance of the angel, the rock had been rolled away, the guards were like dead men, they looked into the tomb, they heard the

---

2. *Luke 2:8–20.*

message, and the particulars of the message—all of it fits so well. They were convinced. They were obedient. They were hurrying, afraid from what they had seen—a special kind of fear in the presence of the holy. They were filled with joy, and they were running. They were **"filled with joy, and ran to tell his disciples."** They might have been anticipating how the disciples would hear the news. From the other accounts, we know how they responded: Peter and John ran back and saw the tomb.

So, the women ran to tell the disciples, and as they were going, Jesus, our Lord Himself, who was raised from the dead, greeted them. In John, Jesus spoke to Mary Magdalene and asked her, "Woman, why are you crying?" (Jn. 20:13b). But here in Matthew, it is said, **"Suddenly Jesus met them. 'Greetings,' he said"** (v. 9a). It was more than a mere greeting when He uttered those words. Other translations say, **"Rejoice!"** **"They came to him, clasped his feet and worshiped him. Then Jesus said to them, 'Do not be afraid. Go and tell my brothers to go to Galilee; there they will see me'"** (vv. 9b–10). That is the appropriate response, the right response, the required response. They responded so appropriately. They came to Him, clasped His feet, and worshiped Him. Jesus is the Son of God, declared by the resurrection from the dead. They worshiped Him in response to the resurrection of our Lord Jesus Christ from the dead. Those who knew Him believed that He is the Christ, believed that He is the Son of God, and they worshiped Him. Twice in this passage, in connection with the resurrection, we have this act of worship by the women and the disciples.

THE DEITY OF CHRIST

In Revelation 5:12, the song is sung in heaven: "Worthy is the Lamb, who was slain, to receive power and wealth and wisdom and strength and honor and glory and praise!" Notice who is involved in worshiping this One. If there is any question that anyone has in mind about the deity of Christ, one should read this, and if Jehovah's Witnesses come to your door, bring this passage to them to show that He is worshiped, He is God. Revelation says,

> The four living creatures and the twenty-four elders fell down before the Lamb. . . . because you were slain, and with your blood you purchased men for God from every tribe and language and people

and nation. . . . Then I looked and heard the voice of many angels, numbering thousands upon thousands, and ten thousand times ten thousand. They encircled the throne and the living creatures and the elders. In a loud voice they sang: "Worthy is the Lamb, who was slain . . ." Then I heard every creature in heaven and on earth and under the earth and on the sea, and all that is in them, singing: "To him who sits on the throne and to the Lamb be praise and honor and glory and power, for ever and ever!" The four living creatures said, "Amen," and the elders fell down and worshiped.[3]

They worshiped the Father and the Son. The theology of the Trinity is most clearly revealed in the worship of the people of God, in the Lord's Supper, and in baptism. They worshiped the Father and the Son, all the creatures in heaven and earth. Jesus is declared to be the Son of God by the resurrection of the dead.

This point is explicitly made in Romans 1:1–4. We must pause and consider its meaning:

Paul, a servant of Christ Jesus, called to be an apostle and set apart for the gospel of God—the gospel he promised beforehand through his prophets in the Holy Scriptures regarding his Son, who as to his human nature was a descendant of David, and who through the Spirit of holiness was declared with power to be the Son of God by his resurrection from the dead: Jesus Christ our Lord.[4]

"Declared with power to be the Son of God." The Resurrection affirms, declares, and confirms that Jesus is the Son of God, and the Church expresses this in worship. It is the appropriate response of the creature to God the Father and God the Son.

Romans 4:25 says that he was raised again for our justification: "He was delivered over to death for our sins and was raised to life for our justification." He could not have been raised to life if He had not satisfied the demand of the Holy God with respect to sin. To satisfy the justice of God, He must be sinless. That means He is sinless in everything He says, including the claim for which He was delivered up to be crucified: that He is the Son of God. He was sinless in this. God

---

3. *Revelation 5:8–14* NIV 1984.
4. NIV 1984.

attested to His sinlessness in raising Him from the dead. The rest of mankind stayed under the power of death and saw decay. Jesus was raised for our justification, showing that He was truthful in what He said, and God testified to Him in this. It was impossible for death to hold Him, as said in Acts 2:24, "But God raised him from the dead, freeing him from the agony of death, because it was impossible for death to keep its hold on him." This is Christ victorious. Hebrews 2:14 says, "He too shared in their humanity so that by his death he might destroy him who holds the power of death."[5] Revelation 1:18 says, "I am the Living One; I was dead, and behold I am alive for ever and ever! And I hold the keys of death and Hades."[6] Christ is exalted to the right hand of God through the resurrection, raised to be seated according to His sinlessness, His truthfulness, and His completing the work that has been given to Him to atone for sin. "He was delivered over to death for our sins and was raised to life for our justification" (Rom. 4:25). Had Christ not satisfied the justice of God, He would not have been raised, and He is raised to the right hand of God in the place of power.

In Psalm 2:7, we have a passage that is often quoted: "The LORD has said to Me, 'You are My Son, Today I have begotten You'" (Ps. 2:7b NKJV). This is parallel to: "declared with power to be the Son of God" (Rom. 1:4).[7] Jesus is speaking in this psalm:

> I will proclaim the decree of the LORD: He said to me, "You are my Son; today I have become your Father. Ask of me, and I will make the nations your inheritance, the ends of the earth your possession. You will rule them with an iron scepter; you will dash them to pieces like pottery." Therefore, you kings, be wise; be warned, you rulers of the earth (Ps. 2:7–10).[8]

When God says, "You are my Son; today I have become your Father," it is spoken in connection with the resurrection of the dead. He was, He is, He will ever be the Son of God; He is the eternal Son of God. It is one thing to *be* the Son of God; it is another to be *declared* to be the Son of God. This is how this passage is to be understood: 'This day I

---

5. NIV 1984.
6. NIV 1984.
7. NIV 1984.
8. NIV 1984.

have brought you forth by the power of being raised from the dead to declare that you are the Son of God.' In Acts 13:33, Paul is preaching and refers to this passage, "As it is written in the second Psalm: 'You are my Son; today I have become your Father.'" Hebrews 1:5 says, "For to which of the angels did God ever say, 'You are my Son; today I have become your Father'" and Hebrews 5:5 says, "But God said to him, 'You are my Son; today I have become your Father.'" This passage is quoted three times in the New Testament. The day that He is brought from the dead, He is declared by the resurrection to be the Son of God. He did not *become* the Son of God; He is *declared* to be the Son of God by being brought forth from the dead. In every way, the resurrection of our Lord Jesus Christ declares Him to be the eternal Son of God, whom He claimed to be. He became incarnate for us that He might bear our sins and take them away.

THE AUTHORITY OF CHRIST

The authority of Christ is revealed in the resurrection. Matthew 28:18 says, **"Then Jesus came to them and said, 'All authority in heaven and on earth has been given to me.'"** You cannot have more authority than all authority in heaven and on earth. This is as complete as it can be. He is the One who is worshiped, the Lamb of God, who, because He died, is "worthy to take the scroll and to open its seals" (Rev. 5:9a). This is signifying the ruling in history and causing history to unfold according to the plan of God. Because He has laid down His life unto death, because He redeemed man, because He is in the place of Adam, given that position of rule, and more than that, as the Son of God, all authority has been given unto Him in heaven and on earth. Revelation 5:9, which was just referenced, "You are worthy to take the scroll and to open its seals," is signifying again His authority to rule. This is further signified in Numbers 16 and 17, where the resurrection is connected with authority. There was an uprising against Moses and Aaron, and it was said, "You have gone too far! The whole community is holy, every one of them, and the LORD is with them. Why then do you set yourselves above the LORD's assembly?" (Num. 16:3b). The plague came down, and some of the rebels died, but the murmuring continued. In order to silence that murmuring, God asked the leader of every tribe to bring the staff representing that tribe with the names on them, and these staffs were laid up before God. The next day, Moses brought up the staffs. The rod of Aaron, signifying the house of Levi and Aaron, and the position of the priesthood, had budded and blossomed and bore fruit. This dead stick had come to life. The resurrection life, the resurrection power, was seen in that stick as a sign to the people, showing that the One whom God raises from the dead is the One whom God has appointed to rule. This rod of Aaron was laid up in the Most Holy Place as a permanent testimony before the people. It is the One whom God raises from the dead who is given the authority to rule. In Matthew 26:63–64, Jesus speaks to the high priest:

> The high priest said to him, "I charge you under oath by the living God: Tell us if you are the Messiah, the Son of God." "You have said so," Jesus replied. "But I say to all of you: From now on you will see the Son of Man sitting at the right hand of the Mighty One and coming on the clouds of heaven."

Christ will sit in the position of rule, and He will exercise that rule. His coming on the clouds of heaven was seen as He sent forth His Spirit. The Spirit enabled the Church to be witnesses in the world, and people from every nation were gathered, beginning on the Day of Pentecost. Christ has been given authority, all authority in heaven and earth, and He is exercising that authority, and He spoke this truth to the leaders. His resurrection testifies to the truth of His identity as the Son of God. The resurrection is also demonstrated before them in the spread of the kingdom by the message of the gospel going out to the ends of the earth. Christ is in that position of authority and is exercising that authority in connection with the resurrection. Psalm 110:1 says, "The LORD says to my lord: 'Sit at my right hand until I make your enemies a footstool for your feet.'" Jesus is appointed to rule in connection with the resurrection. In Revelation 19:11, we see Christ exercising that rule along with His people, the Church: "I saw heaven standing open and there before me was a white horse, whose rider is called Faithful and True. With justice he judges and wages war." Christ is ruling through the spiritual war, subduing the hearts of people to Himself.

The authority of Christ is given in connection with His being raised from the dead. His deity is declared, His authority is given, and in this passage, relevantly, it comes to a head by this commission that the Lord gave to His disciples, saying,

> All authority in heaven and on earth has been given to me. Therefore go and make disciples of all nations, baptizing them in the name of the Father and of the Son and of the Holy Spirit, and teaching them to obey everything I have commanded you. And surely I am with you always, to the very end of the age (vv. 18b–20).

Jesus continues that work even now as His disciples engage in that spiritual war to subdue hearts through preaching God's Word. Both the deity of Christ and the authority of Christ are declared in the details of this passage in connection with His resurrection.

THE HOPE OF THE RESURRECTION

The hope of the resurrection is seen in the response of the disciples. There is a conviction, a commitment, on the part of the disciples, to our Lord, in connection with His defeating death Himself—personally. He had done all sorts of miracles: multiplied loaves and fish, changed water into wine, calmed the storm, cast out demons, healed the sick, and raised the dead. And now He had gone through that valley, He had died on the cross, He was buried, He Himself was raised from the dead, and all joy broke out in the creation and in the hearts of God's people. He is raised from the dead. In connection with that joy, we can understand all the hope of everything that has been expected is connected with the resurrection of the Lord Jesus Christ. *Surely*, now, He will most certainly accomplish His purpose. Having been raised from the dead and ascended to the right hand of God, He sent forth the Spirit, enabling His disciples to be witnesses. There is hope in connection with the Lord Jesus: His resurrection from the dead.

Sin has been atoned for; there is a change in the order of things, and we no longer go to the temple and make sacrifices; that is completed, and the message of the gospel is intended for the ends of the earth, and it will be, and the disciples gave themselves to this work. They gave themselves to this in hope, and in joy, connected with the resurrection. Paul spoke of this in Acts 23:6, when he said, "I stand on trial because of the hope of the resurrection of the dead." Paul summed up all that he was concerned about with Christ's resurrection and what it signifies: the renewal of all things and the completion of all things, including our own resurrection at the consummation. "I stand on trial because of the hope of the resurrection of the dead." Notice how he puts it: the *hope* of the resurrection—all the future, which believers have waited for, will come to pass. It is a confirmation and a *seal* that the resurrection of the dead will indeed happen. Who of us can doubt that if Christ has been raised from the dead, has ascended, is seated at His right hand with all authority, and will be with us until the end of the age—who can doubt that the promise will be fulfilled to the uttermost? Christ will fill everything in every way.[9]

Our hope is grounded in the resurrection. Paul speaks of this in 1 Corinthians 15:19: "If only for this life we have hope in Christ, we are of all people most to be pitied." We have hope in the life to come, and in the future ages that will come, that the work will be completed. When the work is completed, our own resurrection will occur. Paul speaks of this in 1 Corinthians 15:21–26:

> For since death came through a man, the resurrection of the dead comes also through a man. For as in Adam all die, so in Christ all will be made alive. But each in his own turn: Christ, the firstfruits; then, when he comes, those who belong to him. Then the end will come, when he hands over the kingdom to God the Father after he has destroyed all dominion, authority and power. For he must reign until he has put all his enemies under his feet. The last enemy to be destroyed is death.

We have hope that the work will be completed and consummated with the resurrection of the dead. Because Christ has been raised from the dead, we have hope that this will indeed occur.

We have hope in the resurrection. In Ephesians 1:18–19, the connection between hope and the resurrection is also made. Paul is praying for the disciples in Ephesus:

> I pray also that the eyes of your heart may be enlightened in order that you may know the hope to which he has called you, the riches

---

9. *Ephesians 1:23.*

of his glorious inheritance in his holy people, and his incomparably great power for us who believe.

To have *hope* in a certain goal, there must be power. He wants us to know the greatness of that hope and the greatness of that power. He specifies where that power is demonstrated. He continues,

> That power is the same as the mighty strength, he exerted when he raised Christ from the dead and seated him at his right hand in the heavenly realms, far above all rule and authority, power and dominion, and every name that is invoked, not only in the present age but also in the one to come. And God placed all things under his feet (Eph. 1:19b–22a).

Notice the power of God in raising Christ and seating Him at His right hand and the hope that we have that it will be fulfilled. What will come about? God placed all things under His feet, as he did with Adam, but more with Christ, and "appointed him to be head over everything for the Church, which is his body, the fullness of him who fills everything in every way" (Eph. 1:22b–23). This fullness will come about; our hearts long for that fullness. We cannot articulate it sometimes, but that is what we long for—fullness. This includes overcoming all divisions among mankind. We desire fullness, and this is guaranteed to us by the resurrection of Christ, because the mighty power of God is shown in the resurrection. So we have the deity of Christ displayed, the authority of Christ displayed, and the hope of the resurrection displayed.

THE WITNESSES TO THE RESURRECTION CONTINUED

Let us look briefly at the witnesses in Matthew's passage and then, last of all, we will look at the apologetics in this passage. First, we spoke about the angel being a witness to the women, and he was certainly a witness to the guards. Then the women at the tomb saw the place where He lay; they saw Jesus Christ, clasped His feet, worshiped Him, and touched Him. The women went to the disciples and witnessed to them—the second witness. Third, the guards also witnessed: **"While the women were on their way, some of the guards went into the city and** reported to the chief priests everything that had happened" (v. 11). That is certainly a witness. It was not the intent of the guards that they would be a witness, but nevertheless, they did witness. The guards were there; they saw it. God intended them to see it and to make witness to the high priest. Of all persons to make witness, the most believable for the high priest would be the guards, because they were set to seal and protect the tomb—16 soldiers.

"When the chief priests had met with the elders and devised a plan, they gave the soldiers a large sum of money, telling them, 'You are to say, "His disciples came during the night and stole him away while we were asleep"'" (vv. 12–13). Matthew is particularly concerned about this story, because he is writing to the Jews. This was one of the ways in which the Jewish leaders tried to maintain their hold—by spreading this falsehood. That same falsehood has been spoken in the history of the Church as the Swoon Theory. It states that in the tomb, Christ was brought back from His swoon, or He was given something to drink, He went into an unconscious state, then after the crucifixion and burial, the disciples got the body and revived Him. There was a witness to be made to the Jews by the Roman soldiers concerning the resurrection of Christ, and the leaders dismissed it and tried to explain it away. This tells us something about the hardening of their hearts. Think about Pharaoh and the witness that came to Pharaoh and how he failed to see what was clear in special revelation—he hardened his heart. That is true for general and special revelation; people can harden their hearts. We must be mindful of that condition. We must be watchful of it in ourselves and mindful of it in others.

"'If this report gets to the governor, we will satisfy him and keep you out of trouble.' So the soldiers took the money and did as they were instructed. And this story has been widely circulated among the Jews to this very day" (vv. 14–15). So, fourth, there is a false witness, not only of the guards, but also of the leaders in the hardening of their hearts and in their continuing to resist.

Fifth, this message is given to the disciples in the Great Commission: "Therefore go and make disciples of all nations" (v. 19a). The disciples are to proclaim the gospel, which certainly includes Christ's death for sin, His resurrection from the dead, that He is seated at the right hand of God, and His coming again. The disciples, too, become witnesses to this, and we are heirs of their witness. The witness has gone down through the centuries; not only the witness of human beings, but accompanying that witness, the testimony of the Holy Spirit, bearing witness by and with the Word of God that this is indeed the truth.

The last group of witnesses is ourselves. We are the sixth group of witnesses. We are to be witnesses of the resurrection. We have experienced the resurrection power when Christ came into our lives and brought us from spiritual death to life. Jesus said in John, "I am the resurrection and the life" (Jn. 11:25a). He is the resurrection, both from spiritual and from physical death. We know that Christ is raised from the dead in terms of the witnesses that have come down, but there is a more general sense in which we can and should know and be able to witness to the resurrection. I would like us to give attention to these points. When we witness to the resurrection of the dead, we have to keep these things in mind.

AN APOLOGY FOR THE RESURRECTION

1. *Original creation and the goodness of creation:* If we start with God the Creator, *ex nihilo,* who reveals Himself in creation and has infinite power, then we can know that creation was good, and that there was no death. A direct inference of infinite power and goodness is that original creation was good.[10]

2. *The Fall and covenant representation:* If creation was good, then there was a Fall,[11] because it is not good now. And if there is a Fall, there is representation.[12] We are born into a world in which there is death, which came through the act of one man. We can know this from general revelation. Original creation was good. Sin came in by one man, so there is representation.

---

10. Gangadean, *The Biblical Worldview,* xxi–xxii, xxvi, 91–108; Gangadean, *The Westminster Confession,* 75–79.

11. Gangadean, *The Biblical Worldview,* 159–239; Gangadean, *The Westminster Confession,* 99–110; Gangadean, *The Westminster Catechisms,* 141–152; Gangadean, "Paper No. 145–147: The Biblical Worldview," in *The Logos Papers,* 733–757.

12. Gangadean, *The Biblical Worldview,* 147–176; Gangadean, *The Westminster Confession,* 111–120.

3. *The curse and the promise:*[13] We can know from the reality and meaning of physical death that there is a curse that has been imposed, not as punishment, but as a merciful call back from sin. With that curse, now we have reason to expect Scripture, special revelation, and how the promise will come. The promise was given in the beginning, so when we talk to others, some of these basic things must be in place. We can know and believe in the resurrection on the basis of the curse as a call back. God created us, we are fallen, and God imposed the curse as a call back. That means we can hope there is redemption in that call back, and part of redemption will include restoring us to the original goodness—the removal of death. On that basis, we have every reason to believe in the resurrection of the dead.

4. *The Messiah is the new representative and the Messiah must suffer:* With the promise, we have representation. Just as there was representation in the Fall, there is representation in the promise—the seed of the woman. We know that Adam and Eve were clothed with coats of skin—this is special revelation, we can know this only from Scripture: that through the death of another, we are covered. Adam wore skin garments day in and day out. In light of their nakedness before, the meaning of this is that through the death of another, we are covered.[14] So we have the promise in this representative One to come, the seed of the woman, the One who becomes Messiah. In speaking to the Jews, we can say that the Messiah is promised, and the Jews, if they hold to Scripture at all, must say that is true. The Jews also hold to the teaching of atonement; they have to say there is a need for atonement. Now we can ask the question, can atonement occur by the blood of animals, or must it be through the Messiah, as a representative man? These are good and necessary consequences. The Confession addresses understanding the redemptive content of Scripture when it says, "The whole counsel of God concerning all things necessary . . . is either expressly set down in Scripture, or by good and necessary consequence may be deduced from Scripture" (WCF. 1.6). This is not apart from general revelation. So we

---

13. Gangadean, *The Biblical Worldview*, 55–68, 236–239, 283–294.

14. Gangadean, *The Biblical Worldview*, 295–309; Gangadean, *The Westminster Confession*, 149–156; Gangadean, *The Westminster Catechisms*, 193–198.

can know these things as we approach the Scriptures.[15] We can and should know that He is a representative and He must suffer.

5. *The resurrection in general (redemption in light of God's goodness) and the Messiah that suffered must be raised from the dead:* Sin cannot have rule over Him; it is impossible for Him to remain in the grave. If He is going to redeem us, He must be raised from the dead. As well as raise us all! If we have that in mind as a witness to Jews and other people, it becomes a very small step to say that He is raised.

6. *He has been raised—The Holy Spirit given to disciple the nations, and the nations are being discipled (the cloud of witnesses):* The evidence that Christ was raised from the dead, for us today, is the existence of the Church. Christ, being raised, sent forth the Spirit, which we now see and hear, working in the hearts of men, causing that witness to go into all the world, and without the working of the Spirit, no one who is spiritually dead will come to Christ. We can know that Christ is at the right hand of God, seated, and sends His Spirit. He is carrying on His work, and that is where He is. This is what Jesus appealed to when He spoke to the high priest: "You will see the Son of Man sitting at the right hand of the Mighty One and coming on the clouds of heaven" (Matt. 26:64b). Revelation says, "'Look, he is coming with the clouds,' and 'every eye will see him, even those who pierced him'; and all the peoples of the earth 'will mourn because of him.' So shall it be! Amen" (Rev. 1:7). "And he will send his angels with a loud trumpet call, and they will gather his elect from the four winds, from one end of the heavens to the other" (Matt. 24:31). That is the evidence: that Christ was not only raised from the dead but that He is seated at the right hand of God and accomplishing the work.

We are to be witnesses of the resurrection. Believers believed in the resurrection long before it actually occurred. Believers believed in the Messiah long before He actually came. Believers believed in the atonement, that the Messiah would atone, long before He actually came—and we should have. And if believers did not, then we are slow to believe all that the Scriptures have said, and we deserve the rebuke of our Lord:

---

15. Gangadean, *The Westminster Confession*, 14–18; Gangadean, *The Biblical Worldview*, xvii–xix.

"How foolish you are, and how slow of heart to believe all that the prophets have spoken! Did not the Messiah have to suffer these things and then enter his glory?" And beginning with Moses and all the Prophets, he explained to them what was said in all the Scriptures concerning himself (Lk. 24:25–27).

These words of Christ caused their hearts to burn. "Were not our hearts burning within us while he talked with us on the road and opened the Scriptures to us?" (Lk. 24:32). That is the way it should be. Our hearts should *burn* when the Word of Truth comes to us. So Christ has been raised, and we are witnesses of His resurrection. Praise be to God! Hallelujah! Christ is risen *indeed*, and we are witnesses of these things. With those who have gone before us, let us continue to be faithful witnesses to God in all of His truth concerning the resurrection of Christ and all that that means. Amen.

INDEX

Aaron, 132, 170, 246, 507-508
Abel, 370, 384-385, 389, 408
Acts 15, 230, 410
Adam
  and Eve, 514
Ahab, 45, 203
allegorical(ism), 42
Ananias, 400
antinomianism, 78-79, 97, 110
apologetic(s), 280, 500, 511
Apostles' Creed, xxxiii
Arianism, xvii
Arminian(ism), 110
atonement (*see also* vicarious
  atonement), 111, 252, 254, 450,
  495, 497, 514-515
  vicarious, 254, 497
Augustine, St., 24, 26, 286
autonomy, 255, 285, 295, 314, 382

Babel, 9-10, 412
beatific vision, 412
biblical worldview (*see also* creation–
  fall–redemption), 363
born again, 63, 225

Caiaphas, 445, 453, 463, 468, 474
Calvin, John, xxvii, 24, 82
charismatic, 424
chastening, 229, 479
Christianity, 82, 93, 184
City of God, the, 451
clarity, x, 89, 367, 424
  of general revelation, 89
concept(s), xvii, xxv, 149, 163
conscience, 57, 202, 384-385, 475,
  480
contextual, x-xi

interpretation, xi
covenant
  children, xxx
  of grace, 110, 195
  of marriage, 304
  of works, 352
  relationship, 383
  representation, 513
creation
  and providence, xxvi-xxviii
  doctrine of, 44, 363
  ex nihilo, 513
  is revelation, xix, 113
  original, 513
  special, 270
culpable ignorance, 54, 491

death
  physical, 473
  spiritual, xxii, 412
decree(s), 16, 18, 506
deontology, 86, 364
diligence, 338, 435, 443
divine justice, 454
division(s), 52, 101, 109-110, 113,
  150, 294-295, 360, 511
doctrine, xi, 44, 62
dominion, 114, 192, 304, 362
  mandate, 41
  work of, 6, 9, 11, 114, 191-192,
    223, 362, 365, 440
doxological
  focus, x
  postmillennialism, 192, 365

elect, the, 145, 388, 399, 401-404,
  414, 416
Elisha, 264-265

ABOUT THE AUTHOR

DR. SURRENDRA GANGADEAN (1943–2022) was professor of Philosophy at Phoenix College and at Paradise Valley Community College for forty-five years. He regularly taught courses in Introduction to Philosophy, Logic, Ethics, Philosophy of Religion, History of World Religions, and Introduction to Christianity. For ten years, he taught courses in the History of Eastern Civilizations and in Interdisciplinary Humanities. In addition, he taught courses in the Philosophy of Art, Philosophy of Literature, Philosophy of History, and Theology. He led seminar discussions for faculty, students, and the public in the Great Books Reading and Discussion Program. He received an M.A. degree in Literature from Arizona State University, an M.A. degree in Philosophy from the University of Arizona, and a Ph.D. in Natural Theology from Reformed International Theological Seminary. He presented academic papers and public lectures on the topics of Natural Theology and the Moral Law.

www.ingramcontent.com/pod-product-compliance
Lightning Source LLC
Chambersburg PA
CBHW020427130626
46549CB00001B/16